Orderic Vitalis
Life, Works and Interpretations

Orderic Vitalis
Life, Works and Interpretations

Edited by
Charles C. Rozier,
Daniel Roach,
Giles E. M. Gasper &
Elisabeth van Houts

THE BOYDELL PRESS

© Contributors 2016

All Rights Reserved. Except as permitted under current legislation no part of this work may be photocopied, stored in a retrieval system, published, performed in public, adapted, broadcast, transmitted, recorded or reproduced in any form or by any means, without the prior permission of the copyright owner

First published 2016
The Boydell Press, Woodbridge
Paperback edition 2019

ISBN 978 1 78327 125 2 hardback
ISBN 978 1 78327 402 4 paperback

The Boydell Press is an imprint of Boydell & Brewer Ltd
PO Box 9, Woodbridge, Suffolk IP12 3DF, UK
and of Boydell & Brewer Inc.
668 Mt Hope Avenue, Rochester, NY 14620–2731, USA
website: www.boydellandbrewer.com

A catalogue record for this book is available from the British Library

The publisher has no responsibility for the continued existence or accuracy of URLs for external or third-party internet websites referred to in this book, and does not guarantee that any content on such websites is, or will remain, accurate or appropriate

Designed and typeset in Adobe Jenson Pro by
David Roberts, Pershore, Worcestershire

In memory of Marjorie Chibnall, 1915–2012

Contents

List of Illustrations	viii
Acknowledgements	ix
List of Abbreviations	xi
Chronology of the Lives of Odelerius and his Son Orderic Vitalis	xii
Composition of the *Historia ecclesiastica*	xiv

Introduction: Interpreting Orderic Vitalis
   Daniel Roach and Charles C. Rozier — 1

Orderic and his Father, Odelerius
   Elisabeth van Houts — 17

Following the Master's Lead: The Script of Orderic Vitalis and the Discovery of a New Manuscript (Rouen, BM, 540)
   Jenny Weston — 37

Orderic Vitalis as Librarian and Cantor of Saint-Évroul
   Charles C. Rozier — 61

Saint-Évroul and Southern Italy in Orderic's *Historia ecclesiastica*
   Daniel Roach — 78

Orderic and English
   Mark Faulkner — 100

Inscriptions in Orderic's *Historia ecclesiastica*: A Writing Technique between History and Poetry
   Vincent Debiais and Estelle Ingrand-Varenne — 127

Reading Orderic with Charters in Mind
   Thomas Roche — 145

Orderic Vitalis and the Cult of Saints
   Véronique Gazeau — 172

Orderic's Secular Rulers and Representations of Personality and Power in the *Historia ecclesiastica*
   William M. Aird — 189

Worldly Woe and Heavenly Joy: The Tone of the *Historia ecclesiastica*
   Emily Albu — 217

Orderic Vitalis, Historical Writing and a Theology of Reckoning
   Giles E. M. Gasper — 247

Jesus Christ, a Protagonist of Anglo-Norman History? History and
    Theology in Orderic Vitalis's *Historia ecclesiastica*
        Elisabeth Mégier   260

'Studiosi abdita investigant': Orderic Vitalis and the Mystical Morals
    of History
        Sigbjørn Olsen Sønnesyn   284

Meanders, Loops, and Dead Ends: Literary Form and the Common
    Life in Orderic's *Historia ecclesiastica*
        Thomas O'Donnell   298

Orderic and the Tironensians
        Kathleen Thompson   324

'One single letter remained in excess of all his sins ...': Orderic Vitalis
    and Cultural Memory
        Benjamin Pohl   333

The Reception of Orderic Vitalis in the Later Middle Ages
        James G. Clark   352

Appendix 1: Archaeological Investigations at the Abbey of
    Saint-Évroult-Notre-Dame-des-Bois
        Anne-Sophie Vigot   375

Appendix 2: Descriptive Catalogue of Manuscripts Featuring the
    Hand of Orderic Vitalis
        Jenny Weston and Charles C. Rozier   385

Select Bibliography   399

List of Manuscripts Cited   405

General Index   407

Illustrations

Jenny Weston
Following the Master's Lead: The Script of Orderic
Vitalis and the Discovery of a New Manuscript

Fig. 1	Rouen, BM, 540, fol. 1r	39
Fig. 2	Rouen, BM, 540, fol. 54r	40
Fig. 3	Rouen, BM 540, fol. 54v	41
Fig. 4	Rouen, BM, 1174, fol. 11r	46
Fig. 5	Rouen, BM, 540, fol. 54v	55
Fig. 6	Rouen, BM, 31, fol. 15v	56
Fig. 7	Rouen, BM, 1174, fol. 3r	57
Fig. 8	Rouen, BM, 1174, fol. 3v	58

Figs. 1–8 by kind permission of Collections de la Bibliothèque municipale de Rouen.

Charles C. Rozier
Orderic Vitalis as Librarian and Cantor of Saint-Évroul

Fig. 1	Paris, BnF, Lat. 10062, fol. 80v	64

By kind permission of the Bibliothèque nationale de France.

Anne-Sophie Vigot
Appendix 1: Archaeological Investigations at the
Abbey of Saint-Évroult-Nôtre-Dame-des-Bois

Fig. 1	Aerial view of the monastic church of Saint-Évroul, showing the excavations from 2014 on the site of the chapter-house	377

The editors, contributors and publishers are grateful to all the institutions and persons listed for permission to reproduce the materials in which they hold copyright. Every effort has been made to trace the copyright holders; apologies are offered for any omission, and the publishers will be pleased to add any necessary acknowledgement in subsequent editions.

Acknowledgements

THE editors would, above all, like to thank the contributing authors for their excellent scholarship and eager assistance throughout the editorial process. Their continued enthusiasm for the project is a testament to the vitality and breadth of current Orderic Vitalis studies.

This volume traces its origins back to the establishment of two reading groups in 2010 at the University of East Anglia and the University of York, led by Professor Stephen Church and Professor Elisabeth Tyler, respectively. While the initial aim of these groups was to read the whole of Orderic's *Historia ecclesiastica* from start to finish and reflect on its contents, the range of discussions which they stimulated encouraged the present editors to undertake a more detailed exploration of Orderic's life and works. Following a two-day workshop hosted at Durham University's Hatfield College in 2011, a much larger conference, titled 'Orderic Vitalis: New Perspectives on the Historian and his World', took place on 9–11 April 2013 in the pleasant surroundings of St John's College, Durham. Much of the material published here was first shared at that conference, and we offer our thanks to the Durham University Institute of Medieval and Early Modern Studies (then the Institute of Medieval and Renaissance Studies) and the Royal Historical Society for their generous sponsorship. Our thanks also go to the staff at St John's College and to the small army of colleagues and postgraduate students who kindly volunteered to lend their valuable assistance during the conference. In addition, we gratefully acknowledge the generous financial contribution to the publication of this volume by the Master and Fellows of Emmanuel College, Cambridge, and by the Institute of Medieval and Early Modern Studies, Durham University.

The editors would like to thank our publishers, Boydell & Brewer Limited, for agreeing to publish what we hope will provide a worthy and long-standing contribution to the established canon of Orderic scholarship. In particular, we would like to thank Caroline Palmer for fostering the project from the outset, and for her continued patience and encouragement as the volume has taken shape. It has been a great pleasure to work with her and the rest of the team at Boydell & Brewer. Elisabeth van Houts and Giles Gasper would like to thank Charlie Rozier and Daniel Roach for their sterling efforts in bringing the volume together, and for their energy and persistence in guiding this project to fruition through the reading groups, the conference, and on to completion in written form. In turn, Charlie and Daniel would like to thank Elisabeth and Giles for assisting their development as editors and for being on hand to offer advice and support whenever required.

This volume is offered in honour of Marjorie Chibnall, who devoted much of her working life to the study of Orderic and his world. In considering her influence both on the field in general and on this volume in particular, the editors echo the sentiments of David Bates, who declared that the name of Marjorie Chibnall, alongside those of other major Norman historians such Charles Homer Haskins, David Douglas and John Le Patourel,

> must head any list of acknowledgements since it is on their devoted attention to the history of eleventh-century Normandy that this book tries to build. Where disagreement on general interpretation or on a point of detail has to be registered, it is done with a profound awareness that any history of the duchy which neglected or belittled their endeavours would be a miserable thing.[1]

It was with great sadness that we learned of Marjorie Chibnall's passing shortly before the Durham conference, at which many of the contributing speakers expressed their heartfelt gratitude for her enthusiasm for future studies on Orderic Vitalis. This volume is dedicated to her memory.

---

[1] D. Bates, *Normandy before 1066* (London and New York, 1982), p. vi.

Abbreviations

Albu, *Normans in their Histories*	E. Albu, *The Normans in their Histories: Propaganda, Myth, and Subversion* (Woodbridge, 2001)
ANS	*Anglo-Norman Studies*
BL	London, British Library
BM	Bibliothèque municipale
BnF	Paris, Bibliothèque nationale de France
Chibnall, 'General Introduction'	*HE*, I, pp. 1–128
Chibnall, *World*	M. Chibnall, *The World of Orderic Vitalis: Norman Monks and Norman Knights* (Woodbridge, 1984)
Delisle, 'Matériaux'	L. Delisle, 'Notes sur les manuscrits autographes d'Orderic Vital', part 1 of 'Matériaux pour l'édition de Guillaume de Jumièges, préparée par Jules Lair, avec une préface et des notes par Léopold Delisle', *Bibliothèque de l'école des chartes* 71 (1910), 481–526
Delisle, 'Notice'	L. Delisle, 'Notice sur Orderic Vital', in *Orderici Vitalis ecclesiasticae historiae libri tredecim*, ed. and trans. A. Le Prévost, 5 vols. (Paris, 1838–5), V, pp. i–cvi
Escudier, 'Orderic et le scriptorium'	D. Escudier, 'Orderic Vital et le scriptorium de Saint-Évroult', in *Manuscrits et enluminures dans le monde Normand (X^e–XVe siècles)*, ed. Pierre Bouet and Monique Dosdat (Caen, 1999), pp. 17–28
GND	*The Gesta Normannorum Ducum of William of Jumièges, Orderic Vitalis, and Robert of Torigni*, ed. and trans. Elisabeth van Houts, 2 vols. (Oxford, 1992–5)
HE	*The Ecclesiastical History of Orderic Vitalis*, ed. and trans. M. Chibnall, 6 vols. (Oxford, 1969–80)
Hingst, *Written World*	A. J. Hingst, *The Written World: Past and Place in the Work of Orderic Vitalis* (Notre Dame, IN, 2009)
HSJ	*Haskins Society Journal: Studies in Medieval History*
Nortier, *Les Bibliothèques médiévales*	Geneviève Nortier, *Les bibliothèques médiévales des abbayes bénédictines de Normandie* (Paris, 1971)
PL	*Patrologia Latina*
Shopkow, *History and Community*	L. Shopkow, *History and Community: Norman Historical Writing in the Eleventh and Twelfth Centuries* (Washington, DC, 1997)

Chronology of the Lives of Odelerius and his Son Orderic Vitalis

c. 1000	Birth of Constantius (of Orléans?), father of Odelerius
1034	Birth of Odelerius, at Orléans?
1040×1050s	Odelerius schooled, at Orléans?
1050×1060s	Odelerius becomes a priest?
1060s	Odelerius becomes clerk to Roger of Montgomery (d. 1094)
1067 or later	Odelerius becomes Earl Roger's priest at Shrewsbury
1070s (early)	Odelerius meets the English woman who is to be the mother of his sons
1075, 16 Feb.	Birth of Orderic Vitalis
1077	Murder of Earl Roger's wife, Mabel
1070s (late)	Earl Roger marries Adelaide of Le Puiset
1078	Birth of Orderic's brother Benedict
c. 1080×1081	Birth of Everard, son of Earl Roger and Adelaide Birth of Orderic's brother Everard Death of Odelerius's 'wife'? Orderic sent to the household of Siward the noble priest
1082 (spring–summer)	Odelerius's penitent pilgrimage to Rome While at St Peter's, Rome, Odelerius promises to found a monastery Orderic's oblation at Saint-Évroul arranged for 30 marks
1083, 25 Feb.	Foundation ceremony of St Peter's, Shrewsbury Benedict's oblation arranged at St Peter's Odelerius promises his lands to St Peter's, with his son Everard as tenant Odelerius's own promise to become a monk at St Peter's
1085 (summer)	Orderic departs for Normandy
1085, 21 Sept.	Orderic becomes Vitalis, tonsure at Saint-Évroul
1091, 15 March	Orderic becomes sub-dean
1093, 26 March	Orderic becomes dean
1094	Earl Roger dies and is buried at St Peter's, Shrewsbury

Chronology of the Lives of Odelerius and Orderic Vitalis

1094 or later	Odelerius becomes a monk, making a gift of £200 to St Peter's
1102	Odelerius dies aged 66/7
1108, 21 Dec.	Orderic becomes a priest
c. 1125	Orderic mentions Odelerius, Godebald and Herbert in *HE*, bk IV
c.1127	Orderic gives a brief outline of his life story at the start of *HE*, bk V Orderic tells his oblation story from Odelerius's perspective, in *HE*, Bk V
1141, Sept.	Orderic tells his oblation story from his own perspective in *HE*, Bk XIII epilogue
c.1142, 13 Jul?	Orderic dies

Composition of the *Historia ecclesiastica*

Book no.	Dates composed	Contents	Volume & pages (HE, ed. Chibnall)
I	1136–1136×1138	Christ's Life and excerpts	I, pp. 130–63 (extracts)
II	1137–1139×1140	Deeds of Apostles, Evangelists, Popes and excerpts	I, pp. 164–200 (extracts)
III (I)	1114–1123/4	Foundation of Saint-Évroul; events of 1066	II, pp. 2–188
IV (II)	c. 1125	Events of 1067–75; history of Crowland (pp. 262–3 note Odelerius as clerk)	II, pp. 190–360
V (III)	c. 1127	Events of 1075; benefactions to Saint-Évroul (pp. 6–7: brief version of Orderic's life story) (pp. 142–51: Odelerius's story)	III, pp. 4–210
VI (IV)	c. 1130–1133×1137	Benefactions to Saint-Évroul; *Life* of St Évroul	III, pp. 212–360
VII (V?)	c. 1130×1133 [lost start]	Events of 1075–87	IV, pp. 6–108*
VIII (VI?)	1133×1135	Events of 1087–95	IV, pp. 110–340*
IX	1135–9	Events of First Crusade, 1095–8	V, pp. 4–190
X	1133–5	Events of 1098–early 1100s	V, pp. 192–380
XI	1136–June 1137	Events of 1104–13	VI, pp. 8–182
XII	c. 1137	Events of 1118–1130s†	VI, pp. 183–392
XIII	c. 1137–1137×1141	Events of 1130–7	VI, pp. 394–556
Epilogue	Sept. 1141	Orderic's life story	VI, pp. 550–6

* There is no autograph manuscript of Books VII and VIII.
† There is a gap in the narrative between 1113 and 1118, which Chibnall identified.

Interpreting Orderic Vitalis

Daniel Roach and Charles C. Rozier

ORDERIC Vitalis (1075–c. 1142) is predominantly known to modern readers as the author of narrative texts relating to the history of Normandy and the deeds of Norman secular and ecclesiastical personalities at home and abroad, during the period c. 1050–1142. Orderic's two principal works are his interpolated copy of William of Jumièges' *Gesta Normannorum ducum*, completed c. 1113, and his own much larger and more ambitious thirteen-book *Historia ecclesiastica*, completed c. 1141. Together, they provide a wealth of contemporary commentary on some of the most important social, political and ecclesiastical affairs of Orderic's lifetime, as witnessed and interpreted from his home at the monastery of Saint-Évroul in southern Normandy.

The last decades of the eleventh century and the first half of the twelfth witnessed an upsurge of historical writing at a number of intellectual centres throughout England and Normandy.[1] Orderic's historical works should be viewed in the context of this new wave of historiographical enquiry, in which a range of authors sought to rediscover the events of the past and to preserve the memory of their own times for future generations, especially future generations of the communities within which and for which they wrote. Writing in the 1120s, the English author William of Malmesbury reflected on this renewed desire to write history by lamenting the paucity of sources for English history after Bede, and declaring his intention to 'mend the broken chain of our history'.[2] Across the English Channel in Normandy, Orderic also recognised the need for new historical narratives. Writing in the 1130s, he introduced the first book of the

---

[1] General overviews of this historiographical revival are available in: R. W. Southern, 'Aspects of the European Tradition of Historical Writing, 4: The Sense of the Past', *Transactions of the Royal Historical Society* 5th series 23 (1973), 243–63; Antonia Gransden, *Historical Writing in England*, 2 vols. (London, 1974–82), I, pp. 136–218; Elisabeth van Houts, 'Historical Writing', in *A Companion to the Anglo-Norman World*, ed. Christopher Harper-Bill and Elisabeth van Houts (Woodbridge, 2002), pp. 103–21; G. Martin and R. M. Thomson, 'History and History Books', *Cambridge History of the Book in Britain*, vol. 2: *1100–1400*, ed. R. M. Thomson and N. J. Morgan (Cambridge, 2007), pp. 397–415.

[2] William of Malmesbury, *Gesta regum Anglorum: The History of the English Kings*, ed. and trans. R. A. B. Mynors, completed by R. M. Thomson and M. Winterbottom, Oxford Medieval Texts, 2 vols. (Oxford, 1998–9), I, pp. 14–15: 'interruptam temporum seriem sarcire'.

Historia ecclesiastica by stating his ambitions to bring a new energy to the creation and preservation of historical texts:

> I set about composing an account of the events which we witness and endure. It is fitting that, since new events take place every day in this world, they should be systematically committed to writing to the glory of God, so that just as past deeds have been handed down by our forebears present happenings should be recorded now and passed on by the men of today for future generations.[3]

Orderic and William of Malmesbury, alongside other historians including Eadmer of Canterbury, John of Worcester, Henry of Huntingdon and Robert of Torigni, and many additional scribes and authors whose names are not known, compiled new works within the genres of the annal, chronicle and narrative history, while also copying popular examples within these genres by well-known authors including Josephus, Eusebius of Caesarea, and Bede.[4] Although precise figures for England and Normandy as a whole cannot be known, Gameson has estimated that books containing historical texts amounted to around one in every eighteen produced or acquired in England during the late eleventh century, increasing to as many as one book in ten by the 1130s.[5]

This marked rise of interest in historical writing has been the focus of considerable modern scholarly activity. Southern observed a 'historical revival' in late twelfth-century England, and van Houts described an 'outpouring' of historical writing in the period c. 1090–1140.[6] The productions of the period have been identified as significant not merely in their own context and culture, but also more generally, in the longer development of historical reflection in the European and British traditions. Thus Damian-Grint portrayed eleventh- and twelfth-century authors writing in England as 'some of the most important of all

---

[3] *HE*, I, pp. 130–1: 'nunc dictare de his quæ uidimus seu toleramus. Decet utique ut sicut nouæ res mundo cotidie accidue, sic ad laudem Dei assidue scripto tradantur, et sicut ab anterioribus preterita gesta usque ad nos transmissa sunt; sic etiam presentia nunc a presentibus futuræ posteritati litterarum notamine transmittantur.' A detailed discussion of this theme in Orderic's writing features below: Benjamin Pohl, '"One single letter remained in excess of all his sins …": Orderic Vitalis and Cultural Memory'.

[4] For Orderic's work in copying historical texts, see below, Appendix 2, items 9, 15 and 16.

[5] R. G. Gameson, 'English Book Collections in the Late Eleventh and Early Twelfth Centuries: Symeon's Durham and its Context', in *Symeon: Historian of Durham and the North*, ed. D. W. Rollason (Stamford, 1998), pp. 230–53; R. G. Gameson, *The Manuscripts of Early Norman England, 1066–c. 1130* (Oxford, 1999), pp. 23–5, 36–8.

[6] Southern, 'The Sense of the Past', p. 246; van Houts, 'Historical Writing', pp. 120–1.

medieval historians', while Martin and Thomson have suggested that this same period marked the beginning of what they describe as 'one of the greatest epochs in the long tradition of historical writing in Britain, both qualitatively and quantitatively'.[7]

The place of Orderic's *Gesta Normannorum ducum* and *Historia ecclesiastica* within the Anglo-Norman revival of interest in historiography, and the importance of these works as sources for modern enquiry, have been widely acknowledged. As early as 1855, Léopold Delisle highlighted the value of Orderic's *Historia* not only as a historical source, but also as a landmark in the development of historical writing in French regions.[8] On completing her edition of the text in 1980, Marjorie Chibnall declared that the *Historia* was 'fundamental to our understanding of feudal society, social custom and monastic culture', and later stated that 'it is daunting to think of what we would not know about the twelfth-century Anglo-Norman world if he [Orderic] had never written his *Ecclesiastical History*'.[9]

These observations are borne out by the regularity with which modern scholars have used Orderic's historical works across a wide range of interests and subjects. Themes explored to date include the monks and patrons of Saint-Évroul,[10] the Grandmesnil and Giroie families,[11] Norman episcopal power,[12] violence against women,[13] Christ

---

[7] P. Damian-Grint, *The New Historians of the Twelfth-Century Renaissance: Inventing Vernacular Authority* (Woodbridge, 1999), pp. 43–8, at p. 44; Martin and Thomson, 'History and History Books', p. 397.

[8] Delisle, 'Notice', p. i.

[9] Chibnall, 'General Introduction', p. 1; Chibnall, 'World', p. 220.

[10] Marjorie Chibnall, 'Les Moines et les patrons de Saint-Évroult dans l'Italie du Sud au XIe siècle', in *Les Normands en Méditerranée: Dans le sillage des Tancrède*, ed. P. Bouet and F. Neveux (Caen, 1994), pp. 161–70.

[11] Joseph Decaëns, 'Le Patrimoine des Grentemesnil en Normandie, en Italie et en Angleterre aux XIe et XIIe siècles', in *Les Normands en Méditerranée: dans le sillage des Tancrède*, ed. Pierre Bouet and François Neveux (Caen, 1994), pp. 123–40; M. Hagger, 'Kinship and Identity in Eleventh-Century Normandy: The Case of Hugh de Grandmesnil, c. 1040–1098', *Journal of Medieval History* 32 (2006), 212–30. P. Bauduin, 'Une Famille châtelaine sur les confins normanno-manceaux: Les Géré (X^e–XIIIe s.)', *Archéologie médiévale* 22 (1992), 309–56; Jean-Marie Maillefer, 'Une Famille aristocratique aux confins de la Normandie: Les Géré au XIe siècle', in *Autour du pouvoir ducal Normand X^e–XIIe siècles*, ed. Lucien Musset, Jean-Michel Bouvris and Jean-Marie Maillefer, Cahier des Annales de Normandie 17 (Caen, 1985), pp. 175–206.

[12] Pierre Bouet, 'L'Image des évêques normands dans l'œuvre d'Orderic Vital', in *Les évêques normands du XIe siècle*, ed. Pierre Bouet and François Neveux (Caen, 1995), pp. 253–75.

[13] Jean Blacker, 'Women, Power, and Violence in Orderic Vitalis's *Historia Ecclesiastica*', in *Violence Against Women in Medieval Texts*, ed. Anna Roberts (Gainesville, FL, 1998), pp. 44–55.

and Scripture,[14] hair and identity,[15] vengeance,[16] emotions and power,[17] physical objects and historical memory,[18] and the First Crusade.[19] Yet while Orderic's writing may be well known, closer examination of his life, the process of his historical writing and his various activities away from the writing of the past have remained topics comparatively untouched. Until relatively recently, a prevailing tendency was to approach Orderic's *Gesta Normannorum ducum* and *Historia ecclesiastica* in a manner that Southern described in the 1970s, when he commented that modern readers too often regarded medieval works of history as little more than 'quarries of facts that require to be sifted and purified in order to make them useable for our purposes'.[20] This is shown by the criticisms of Orderic's apparent lack of linear narrative and organisational structure articulated in a number of studies produced, in the main, before the completion of Chibnall's critical edition in 1980. In the nineteenth century, Delisle claimed that Orderic presented his information in 'disorder' and

---

[14] Elisabeth Mégier, '*Cotidie operatur*. Christus und die Geschichte in der *Historia ecclesiastica* des Ordericus Vitalis', *Revue mabillon* 71 (1999), 169–204; Elisabeth Mégier, '*Divina pagina* and the Narration of History in Orderic Vitalis' *Historia Ecclesiastica*', *Revue bénédictine* 110:1–2 (2000), 106–23.

[15] Pauline Stafford, 'The Meanings of Hair in the Anglo-Norman World: Masculinity, Reform, and National Identity', in *Saints, Scholars, and Politicians: Gender as a Tool in Medieval Studies. Festschrift in Honour of Anneke Mulder-Bakker on the Occasion of her Sixty-Fifth Birthday*, ed. Mathilde van Dijk and Renée Nip (Turnhout, 2005), pp. 153–71.

[16] Thomas Roche, 'The Way Vengeance Comes: Rancorous Deeds and Words in the World of Orderic Vitalis', in *Vengeance in the Middle Ages: Emotion, Religion and Feud*, ed. Susanna A. Throop and Paul R. Hyams (Aldershot, 2010), pp. 115–36.

[17] Richard E. Barton, 'Emotions and Power in Orderic Vitalis', *ANS* 33 (2011), 41–59.

[18] Daniel Roach, 'The Material and the Visual: Objects and Memories in the *Historia ecclesiastica* of Orderic Vitalis', *HSJ* 24 (2013), 63–78.

[19] Daniel Roach, 'Orderic Vitalis and the First Crusade', *Journal of Medieval History* 42:2 (2016), 177–201.

[20] R. W. Southern, 'Aspects of the European Tradition of Historical Writing, 1: The Classical Tradition, from Einhard to Geoffrey of Monmouth', *Transactions of the Royal Historical Society* 5th series 20 (1970), 173–96, at pp. 173–4. This use of medieval sources is also described in: R. D. Ray, 'Medieval Historiography through the Twentieth Century: Problems and Progress of Research', *Viator* 5 (1974), 33–59; W. A. Goffart, *The Narrators of Barbarian History, A.D. 550–800: Jordanes, Gregory of Tours, Bede, and Paul the Deacon* (Princeton, 1988), p. 15; G. Constable, 'Past and Present in the Eleventh and Twelfth Centuries: Perceptions of Time and Change', in his *Culture and Spirituality in Medieval Europe* (Aldershot, 1996), pp. 135–70, at p. 136.

surmised that, 'Occupied only by [a desire] to increase the mass of his inquiries, Orderic did not have the time to coordinate them into a regular and methodical plan.'[21] In the 1970s, Gransden criticised Orderic's writing style and the complex structure of his *Historia* by arguing that:

> He did not learn from the English writers how to arrange his material according to subject-matter or chronological order. Rather he let his interests pursue their bent. He interrupts subjects, repeats himself and digresses [...] The result is a very long book, full of vivid detail and unique information but hard to use for reference.[22]

Gransden's observations can be said to typify modern reactions to the narrative structure of the *Historia*, which continued even after Chibnall had provided a detailed commentary on the text and its development.[23] Chibnall's edition of the text, and in particular her extensive study of the author's original manuscripts, detailed the development of an organic work which, though influenced by numerous past and contemporary sources, was, at the same time, quite unlike any other work of the period. The attentions and ambitions of its author altered and expanded considerably during the course of its near thirty-year composition. One of the most important legacies of Chibnall's edition is that scholars now have a far greater understanding of how historical texts developed during Orderic's lifetime, and of the particular individual interests and ambitions of Orderic himself as an author of history. Chibnall's seminal contribution to Orderic Vitalis studies sprang from her profound knowledge of his *Historia*, which enabled her to publish on a wide range of themes arising from the text.[24]

---

[21] Delisle, 'Notice', p. xliv: 'Uniquement occupé d'augmenter la masse de ses renseignements, Orderic n'a point eu le loisir de les coordonner entre eux et de les disposer d'après un plan régulier et méthodique.'

[22] Gransden, *Historical Writing in England*, I, p. 161.

[23] N. F. Partner, 'The New Cornificius: Medieval History and the Artifice of Words', in *Classical Rhetoric and Medieval Historiography*, ed. E. Breisach (Kalamazoo, MI, 1985), pp. 5–59, at p. 15; Jean Blacker, *The Faces of Time: Portrayal of the Past in Old French and Latin Historical Narrative of the Anglo-Norman Regnum* (Austin, TX, 1994), pp. 10–11. For more positive perspectives, see Daniel Roach, 'Narrative Strategy in the *Historia ecclesiastica* of Orderic Vitalis' (unpublished PhD thesis, University of Exeter, 2014), and below, T. O'Donnell, 'Meanders, Loops, and Dead Ends: Literary Form and the Common Life in Orderic's *Historia ecclesiastica*'.

[24] Chibnall, 'General Introduction'; Chibnall, *World*. A full list of Chibnall's publications on these themes is presented in the bibliography at the end of this book. Some notable examples include: Marjorie Chibnall, 'Orderic Vitalis and Robert of Torigni', *Millénaire monastique du Mont Saint-Michel* 2 (1966), 133–9; Chibnall, 'The Merovingian Monastery of St Evroul in the Light of Conflicting Traditions', *Studies in Church History* 8 (1971),

Following the appearance of Chibnall's edition, the number of publications related to Orderic and, in particular, the study of the *Historia ecclesiastica* has continued to grow at a steady pace.[25] This research has established many of the details of Orderic's life, his various travels away from Saint-Évroul, the dates and development of his writings, and his additional interests and activities as a scribe, an avid participant in the study and debate of theology and moral philosophy and as a skilled exponent of Latin poetry and music.

The sheer variety of material provided in Orderic's own works and in the manuscript evidence ensures that there remains great potential for further study in this area. In recent years, the development of new approaches to the reading of medieval works of history and the re-examination of manuscript evidence has taken the analysis of Orderic's life and writing in new directions and given fresh impetus to the discussion of long-established suppositions. By applying anthropological theories of space and place, Hingst has shed light on a variety of topics not previously considered, most notably on the prominence of the past in the daily life at Saint-Évroul, and on Orderic's interaction with monuments in the landscape.[26] Recent evaluation of material objects in the narrative of Orderic's *Historia ecclesiastica* has suggested some of the ways in which he interacted with the past through physical evidence.[27] Such studies highlight the value of applying new interdisciplinary approaches within the study of Orderic Vitalis and his works. As is noted throughout this book, Orderic himself was competent in many fields of learning: in his histories, written in persuasive Latin prose and verse, he applied his knowledge of language, moral philosophy, theology and exegesis in order to study and evaluate human action through time. Without continued exploration of these and other related themes within his writings, it will

---

31–40; Chibnall, 'Charter and Chronicle: The Use of Archive Sources by Norman Historians', in *Church and Government in the Middle Ages: Essays Presented to C. R. Cheney on his 70th Birthday*, ed. C. N. L. Brooke, D. E. Luscombe et al. (Cambridge, 1976), pp. 1–17; Chibnall, 'Women in Orderic Vitalis', *HSJ* 2 (1990), 105–21. Many of her articles have been republished in Chibnall, *Piety, Power and History in Medieval England and Normandy* (Aldershot, 2000).

[25] L. Musset, 'L'Horizon géographique, moral et intellectuel d'Orderic Vital, historien anglo-normand', in *La Chronique et l'histoire au Moyen Âge*, ed. D. Poirion (Paris, 1984), pp. 101–22; N. Lettinck, 'Comment les historiens de la première moitié du XIIe siècle jugaient-ils leur temps?', *Journal des savants* 1–2 (1985), 51–77; Denis Escudier, 'L'œuvre entre les lignes d'Orderic Vital', in *Le Livre au Moyen Age*, ed. Jean Glenisson (Turnhout, 1988), pp. 193–5; Mégier, '*Cotidie operatur*'; Mégier, '*Divina pagina*'; Albu, *Normans in their Histories*; Escudier, 'Orderic et le scriptorium'.

[26] Hingst, *Written World*.

[27] Roach, 'The Material and the Visual'.

be impossible fully to understand the range of purposes and audiences for which he wrote.

Orderic and the *Historia ecclesiastica*

A DETAILED discussion of Orderic's life, family background and the chronology of his historical writing is provided by van Houts in the first chapter of this book.[28] Knowledge of Orderic the man is derived from the pages of his *Historia*, in particular the autobiographical summaries featured at the beginning of Book V and the end of Book XIII.[29] Orderic was born in 1075 at Atcham, on the River Severn outside Shrewsbury. He was the eldest son of Odelerius of Orléans, a priest in the service of Earl Roger of Montgomery, and an unknown mother who is assumed to have been English.[30] Between the ages of five and ten, Orderic was taught Latin by a tutor in Shrewsbury named Siward, and he may also have learned to write at this time.[31] In September 1085 he was given over to serve as a child oblate at the monastery of Saint-Évroul, where, upon arrival, he was immediately given the new name 'Vitalis', because his English name 'sounded harsh to the Normans'.[32] Orderic provided few details on his early adult life, but did note that he was ordained sub-deacon at sixteen, deacon at eighteen and priest aged thirty-three, on 21 December 1108.[33] He described himself as a student ('discipulus') of master John of Rheims, and noted John's skill in poetry, the Latin classics and biblical exegesis, suggesting that he was given instruction in these subjects under John's tutelage.[34] Orderic's autobiographical epilogue in Book XIII of the *Historia* records that he was ordained as sub-deacon by Gilbert, bishop of Lisieux, deacon by Serlo, bishop of Séez, and priest by William, archbishop of Rouen.[35]

Orderic probably began writing history towards the end of the 1090s. Chibnall and van Houts have identified his contributions to a collection of Easter-table annals and his copying and expansion of the *Gesta Normannorum ducum* as his first forays to historical writing, dating each to the last years of the 1090s.[36] Chibnall claimed that Orderic first made

---

[28] See below, Elisabeth van Houts, 'Orderic and his Father, Odelerius'.

[29] *HE*, III, pp. 6–9, and *HE*, VI, pp. 552–3.

[30] See below, van Houts, 'Orderic and his Father, Odelerius'.

[31] For a detailed review of how much English Orderic may have learned to speak and write during his early years, see the contribution below by Mark Faulkner, 'Orderic and English'.

[32] *HE*, VI, pp. 554–5.

[33] Ibid.

[34] *HE*, III, pp. 168–71.

[35] *HE*, VI, pp. 554–5.

[36] Chibnall, 'General Introduction', p. 24 n. 1 and p. 29; *GND*, I, p. lxvii.

additions to the annals (now BnF, MS Lat. 10062, fols. 138v–160r) from 1095, but it is in fact very difficult to know the precise point at which he began this work.[37] He worked backwards to add notices on events occurring several centuries before his own lifetime, and the first of his more detailed, near-contemporary entries records events in 1084, when he was still living in England as a child. However, although we do not know precisely when he made the additions, we can at least say that Orderic was the principal author of the entries recording events between 1084 and 1139.[38]

Orderic's additions to the *Gesta Normannorum ducum* can be dated with more accuracy. Van Houts has shown that he had completed the major part of his redaction by 1109, continuing to add material and revisions to the text down to c. 1113.[39] Orderic copied and revised William of Jumièges' base text, interpolating new material and expanding the text's scope with his own independent knowledge of historical events from book six onwards. Van Houts has stated that this work must have taken Orderic several years to complete, and as such has suggested that he probably began working on his *Gesta Normannorum* from c. 1095.[40] Almost all of Orderic's text survives in his autograph copy, now Rouen, BM, MS 1174 (Y14), fols. 116r–139v, though the text is incomplete, following the loss of two quires at the end in the middle of the seventh and last book.[41]

It is likely that Orderic began his *Historia ecclesiastica* shortly after ceasing work on the *Gesta Normannorum ducum*. Chibnall noted that the earliest sections of the *Historia* resemble a cartulary-chronicle concerning the refoundation and development of the community at Saint-Évroul from 1050, and proposed that the visit of King Henry I in 1113 to confirm the rights and properties of the community acted as a catalyst for the production of such a text.[42] Reading from Book III (the first to be written), the work begins as an account of the foundation and development of Orderic's home community at Saint-Évroul, before evolving gradually into a much wider narrative of English, Norman and crusade history during the eleventh and twelfth centuries. The *Historia* occupied the greater part of Orderic's working life from this point onwards, resulting in a total of thirteen books that combine to narrate the story of Saint-Évroul and

---

[37] Chibnall, 'General Introduction', p. 29.

[38] Fols. 153v–154r. For discussion of Orderic's work in these annals, see below, Charles Rozier, 'Orderic Vitalis as Librarian and Cantor of Saint-Évroul'; and Alison Alexander, 'Annalistic Writing in Normandy, c. 1050–1225' (unpublished PhD thesis, University of Cambridge, 2011), pp. 133–40, 209–11.

[39] *GND*, I, pp. lxviii–lxix.

[40] Ibid., p. lxviii.

[41] Ibid., pp. ciii–civ.

[42] Chibnall, 'General Introduction', pp. 31–2.

its environs, as well as recording donations from various benefactors and recounting many of the deeds of its patron families. More than this, though, the *Historia* explains the role of this monastic community within a much wider secular and ecclesiastical history of Normandy and the various lands with which Norman families and institutions came to be connected. In this way Orderic produced a lengthy, and at times seemingly meandering, narrative, which at various points describes the origins of the Norman people and their culture, their conquests in England, their settlement in southern Italy (Books III to VII) and, based on the account of Baldric of Bourgueil, their deeds in the Holy Land on the First Crusade (Book IX). Having already completed a great deal of work on near-contemporary events by the mid-1130s, Orderic added two books on the early history of the Christian church and deeds of the apostles; these he inserted as new Books I and II, renumbering the remaining books accordingly. Orderic's autobiographical epilogue to the *Historia* states that he brought his work to a close in his sixty-seventh year of life and fifty-sixth year as a monk of Saint-Évroul, giving a date of 1141/2.[43] The work concludes with the line, 'Here ends the life of Vitalis, who wrote this book', suggesting that Orderic died not long after its completion.[44] The later twelfth-century necrology of Saint-Évroul (now Paris, BnF, 10062, fol. 19v) contains a note that records the death of an 'Orderic' on 13 July, and this almost certainly provides the death date of Orderic Vitalis in 1142.

The final version of Orderic's *Historia ecclesiastica* survives in a near-complete copy written in Orderic's own hand, now contained in three volumes listed as BnF, MS Lat. 5506 vols. I and II, and MS Lat. 10913.[45] Although the autograph of Books VII and VIII is now lost, these books are preserved in Rome, Vatican Reginensis Latina MS 703B (formerly 703A), a mid-twelfth-century manuscript which Chibnall showed to have been copied at St Stephen's, Caen.[46] Delisle's suggestion that the Paris manuscripts represent Orderic's autograph has facilitated the identification of a further fifteen manuscripts which feature his characteristic script.[47] Together, these works witness Orderic's work as

---

[43] *HE*, VI, pp. 550–1.

[44] Ibid., pp. 556–7.

[45] For a detailed description of these manuscripts, see Chibnall, 'General Introduction', pp. 118–21; and Delisle, 'Matériaux', pp. 7–9.

[46] Chibnall, 'General Introduction', p. 121. The item was published in facsimile in *Orderici Vitalis historiae ecclesiasticae libri VII at VIII e codice vaticano reg. 703 A* (Paris, 1902). See also Shopkow, *History and Community*, pp. 218–19.

[47] Delisle, 'Matériaux', pp. 487–9. For an overview, see below, Appendix 2, and Jenny Weston, 'Following the Master's Lead: The Script of Orderic Vitalis and the Discovery of a New Manuscript (Rouen, BM, 540)'. See also Escudier, 'Orderic et le scriptorium'.

scribe, annotator and corrector across a range of disciplines including history, poetry, theology, and biblical exegesis.

Although Orderic's reputation among modern readers is almost exclusively based on his work as a historian, a considerable body of additional evidence shows he was active in several other areas of study. His editorial work on existing texts reveals an interest in saints' lives and miracles,[48] an interest which is also apparent in the *Historia*. There we find accounts on the lives, translations and miracles of a number of saints, including Judoc, William of Gellone, Guthlac and Nicholas of Myra.[49] Orderic's knowledge of Latin poetry is shown by his frequent borrowings in the *Historia* from well-known classical Latin poets, including Virgil, Lucan and Ovid.[50] He also copied three short poems or hymns into Alençon, BM, MS 1, which may represent original compositions: the first is on the transient nature of worldly glory, the second is a penitential piece and the third a litany.[51] Orderic also transcribed funerary poems into his *Historia* and composed several original epitaphs for tombs at Saint-Évroul.[52] Based on the appearance of *neumes* within several of his manuscripts, it has been proposed that he also knew and wrote music.[53] On a scribal level, Orderic engaged with several works of theology and exegesis,[54] while his addition of a Life of Christ, a history of the early Church and regular pronouncements on the relative vices and virtues of his protagonists within the *Historia ecclesiastica* together demonstrate his ability to combine historical, eschatological and didactic readings of human history.[55]

Even allowing for the notable variety of his skills and interests, Orderic emerges from both his original compositions and his work as a copyist as a voracious reader and student of the past. In addition to his own works,

---

[48] Below, Appendix 2, items 2, 3, 12, 16, 17 and 18.

[49] *HE*, II, pp. 156–67 and 322–39; III, pp. 322–38; IV, pp. 54–8, respectively. See also Chibnall, 'General Introduction', pp. 61–2.

[50] For an overview of Orderic's borrowings, see Chibnall's 'Index of Quotations and Allusions', *HE*, I, pp. 217–21.

[51] Below, Appendix 2, item 1.

[52] See below, Vincent Debiais and Estelle Ingrand-Varenne, 'Inscriptions in Orderic's *Historia ecclesiastica*: A Writing Technique between History and Poetry'.

[53] D. Escudier, 'L'œuvre entre les lignes', pp. 193–5.

[54] Below, Appendix 2, items 4, 11, 14, 15 and 16.

[55] See below, William M. Aird, 'Orderic's Secular Rulers and Representations of Personality and Power in the *Historia ecclesiastica*'; Elisabeth Mégier, 'Jesus Christ, A Protagonist of Anglo-Norman History? History and Theology in Orderic Vitalis's *Historia ecclesiastica*'; and Giles E. M. Gasper, 'Orderic Vitalis, Historical Writing and a Theology of Reckoning'.

he copied the whole of Bede's *Historia ecclesiastica gentis Anglorum*,[56] and transcribed entire texts and numerous extracts into the pages of his *Historia ecclesiastica*; these include Baldric of Bourgueil's *Historia Ierosolimitana*, William of Poitiers' *Gesta Guillelmi ducis*, Paul the Deacon's *Historia Langobardorum* and a *Liber pontificalis*.[57] Orderic noted that he had read historical texts at Worcester, Cambrai and Crowland, and at Crowland he was invited to compose new works on the history of the monastery, which he later abridged and added to his *Historia*.[58] When he came to compose the introductory preface to the restructured *Historia* in the second half of the 1130s, he placed his work within an established canon of historical writing, citing predecessors such as Dares Phrygius, Pompeius Trogus, Eusebius, Orosius, Bede, and Paul the Deacon:

> Our predecessors in their wisdom have studied all the ages of the erring world from the earliest times, have recorded the good and evil fortunes of mortal men as a warning to others, and, in their constant eagerness to profit future generations, have added their own writings to those of the past [...] this we find in Dares Phrygius and Pompeius Trogus and other historians of the gentiles, this too we see in Eusebius and the *De Ormesta mundi* of Orosius and Bede the Englishman and Paul of Monte Cassino and other ecclesiastical writers. I study their narratives with delight, I praise and admire the elegance and value of their treatises, I exhort the learned men of our own time to imitate their remarkable erudition.[59]

Following its completion in 1141/2, Orderic's *Historia* was used by a number of later medieval authors. During the 1160s and 1170s sections of Books VII and VIII were used by Wace, the Jersey-born canon of St Stephen's, Caen, when writing his verse chronicle the *Roman de Rou*.[60]

---

[56] Now Rouen, Bibliothèque municipale, MS 1343 (U. 43), fols. 34r–129v. See below, Appendix 2, item 16.

[57] For a detailed overview of Orderic's sources for the *Historia*, see Chibnall, 'General Introduction', pp. 48–77.

[58] *HE*, II, pp. 322–51.

[59] *HE*, I, pp. 130–1: 'Anteriores nostri ab antiquis temporibus labentis seculi excursus prudenter inspexerunt, et bona seu mala mortalibus contingentia pro cautela hominum notauerunt, et futuris semper prodesse uolentes scripta scriptis accumulauerunt [...] hoc in Darete Phrigio et Pompeio Trogo comperimus aliisque gentilium historiographis, hoc etiam aduertimus in Eusebio et Orosio de Ormesta mundi anglicoque Beda et Paulo cassiniensi aliisque scriptoribus æcclesiasticis. Horum allegationes delectabiliter intueor, elegantiam et utilitatem sintagmatum laudo et admiror, nostrique temporis sapientes eorum notabile sedimen sequi cohortor.'

[60] Wace, *Roman de Rou*, ed. and trans. Glyn S. Burgess and Anthony J. Holden (St Helier, 2002).

It is likely that Wace borrowed from the Vatican manuscript which was copied at St Stephen's in the mid-twelfth century. As a result, Wace's work shares a many similarities with the *Historia ecclesiastica*, which have been summarised by Chibnall.[61] In their recent edition of the *Warenne Chronicle*, van Houts and Love have noted that the text shares a large number of structural similarities with Orderic's *Historia*, and agrees with it against other sources.[62] They suggest that the Warenne chronicler is likely to have had direct access to Orderic's autograph at Saint-Évroul.[63] Chibnall has suggested that Robert of Torigni's own extension of William of Jumièges' *Gesta Normannorum ducum* may have borrowed from Orderic's *Historia*, and, owing to a lack of verbatim quotations, proposed that Robert had read Orderic's text on a visit to Saint-Évroul.[64] In his study of Earl Waltheof's cult at Crowland Abbey, Watkins suggested that a large proportion of the early thirteenth-century *Vita et Passio Waldeui Comitis* derived from Orderic's account of Waltheof, which, as Orderic writes, was written as part of his separate history of Crowland and later added to the pages of the *Historia ecclesiastica*.[65] Edoardo D'Angelo has recently identified similarities between Orderic's *Historia* and the *Liber de regno Sicilie* and the *Epistola ad Petrum Panormitane Ecclesie thesaurarium*, both written by the so-called Pseudo-Hugh Falcandus, thereby suggesting that Orderic's influence reached south into Italy.[66] In the present volume, Clark presents convincing evidence to suggest that information derived from Orderic's *Historia* was added to a compilation commissioned by Abbot Guillaume of St Stephen's, Caen in the first quarter of the fifteenth century, and proposes that through this Orderic's work became a 'potent weapon in the struggle for royal dominion' during the Hundred Years' War.[67]

---

[61] *HE*, IV, pp. xxi–xxii.

[62] *The Warenne (Hyde) Chronicle*, ed. and trans. Elisabeth van Houts and Rosalind C. Love (Oxford, 2013), pp. xix–xxvi.

[63] Ibid., pp.xliii–xlvi.

[64] Chibnall, 'General Introduction', p. 114. See also: Chibnall, 'Orderic Vitalis and Robert of Torigni'. For discussion of Robert and his redaction of the *Gesta Normannorum*, see *GND*, I, pp. lxxvii–xci.

[65] Carl Watkins, 'The Cult of Earl Waltheof at Crowland', *Hagiographica* 3 (1996), 95–111, at pp. 96–7. Orderic's history of Crowland appears in *HE*, II, pp. 310–50.

[66] Edoardo D'Angelo, 'The Pseudo-Hugh Falcandus in his own Texts', *ANS* 35 (2013), 141–61, at p. 152. We are grateful to the author for providing details of these references. *La historia; o, Liber de Regno Sicilie e la Epistola ad Petrum panormitane ecclesie thesaurarium*, ed. G. B. Siragusa (Rome, 1897).

[67] See below, James G. Clark, 'The Reception of Orderic Vitalis in the Later Middle Ages'.

Editions of the *Historia ecclesiastica*

BETWEEN 1503 and 1536, Dom William Vallin, a monk at Saint-Évroul, copied Books I to VI and IX to XIII of Orderic's *Historia ecclesiastica* from the surviving three autograph codices which, he claimed, could not be read by those unused to Orderic's twelfth-century script.[68] Several other copies were also made during the sixteenth century. The first complete edition of the *Historia* was published by André Duchesne in his five-volume *Historiae Normannorum scriptores antiqui* (Paris, 1619), which remained the basic printed text from which all subsequent extracts were derived until the nineteenth century. In five volumes published between 1838 and 1855, Auguste Le Prévost and Léopold Delisle produced an edition of the *Historia*, complete with an extensive introduction, entitled *Orderici Vitalis Ecclesiasticae Historiae libri tredecim*, and this remains the only complete edition of the entire text from Books I to XIII.[69] A four-volume French translation was completed by Francois Guizot between 1825 and 1827, based on Duchesne's edition,[70] while Le Prévost's edition was used as the basis for the four-volume English translation of the *Historia* produced by Thomas Forester between 1853 and 1856.[71] Marjorie Chibnall's critical edition, with an English translation and an extensive introductory commentary, appeared in six volumes published between 1968 and 1980.[72] While this remains the standard edition, Chibnall nevertheless chose not to produce the full text of Books I and II, instead reproducing only brief summaries and extracts from these books and those sections in which Orderic commented on the nature of his work.[73] She explained that this decision was taken based on the fact that these books were predominantly derived from other sources already in print.[74]

---

[68] What follows summarises Chibnall, 'General Introduction', pp. 115–17. See also, Delisle, 'Notice', pp. xcix–ci. Nortier, *Les Bibliothèques médiévales*, pp. 111–12 and n. 81, notes that Dom William Vallin's copy survives as BnF, MS Lat. 12.713.

[69] *Orderici Vitalis ecclesiasticae historiae libri tredecim*, ed. and trans. A. Le Prévost, 5 vols. (Paris, 1838–5).

[70] *Histoire de Normandie*, trans. F. Guizot, 4 vols. (Paris, 1825–7).

[71] *The Ecclesiastical History of England and Normandy*, trans. T. Forester, 4 vols. (London, 1853–6). Delisle's introductory commentary features in the fifth volume, pp. i–cvi.

[72] *HE*. For the introductory commentary, see I, pp. 1–125, referenced throughout the present volume as Chibnall, 'General Introduction'.

[73] *HE*, I, pp. 130–200.

[74] Ibid., pp. 127–8.

New Perspectives on Orderic and his Works

THIS book represents the first complete volume of essays entirely devoted to the study of Orderic Vitalis. The discussions it features aim to disseminate important new research related to a range of well-established topics within the field (such as the chronology of Orderic's life and historical writings, the manuscripts copied by him and the later reception of his works) while also opening up new directions for future analysis and debate. The chapters draw on the range of existing themes noted above, while applying new interpretations from across the disciplines of medieval manuscript studies, English language studies, archaeology, theology and cultural memory studies, and revisiting previously established readings within the study of medieval history, literature and manuscript studies. Despite this diversity, Orderic's status as historian provides a constant unifying theme. Largely thanks to his writing history in a style which vividly reflected his own personal interests, skills and experiences, today we are able to examine Orderic both as a historian and as a personality; this has given his works an immediacy which is practically unrivalled by any of those composed by his contemporaries, and which has fuelled much of the research and analysis which follows here.

Discussion begins with studies of Orderic's life. Here, Elisabeth van Houts reviews Orderic's family background and childhood, analysing evidence for the life of his father, Odelerius, his unknown mother and little-known siblings, and assessing the ways in which memories of these early years influenced Orderic's historical writing in later life. Following this, Jenny Weston provides a comprehensive description of Orderic's handwriting, builds a case for identifying a previously unknown manuscript witness to Orderic's work, and, using this evidence, explores Orderic's role as a teacher and supervisor of other, more junior, scribes at Saint-Évroul. Charles Rozier follows this by revisiting the evidence for Orderic's status as librarian of Saint-Évroul, and suggests that he acted as librarian as part of his duties as monastic cantor within the community. Daniel Roach explores Orderic's narration of events in southern Italy within the *Historia ecclesiastica* in order to examine the position of Saint-Évroul within an evolving matrix of secular and ecclesiastical affairs that stretched far beyond the borders of the duchy. Following this is Mark Faulkner's analysis of Orderic's knowledge and use of English within his historical works, providing much material for the study of Orderic's early life and education and his sense of English identity, as well as making a broader contribution to the study of the English language in the eleventh and twelfth centuries.

The next five chapters explore themes related to Orderic's use of evidence and selection of subject matter within his historical writing. Vincent Debiais and Estelle Ingrand-Varenne consider his use of funerary inscriptions and poems in his writing, before Thomas Roche continues by examining his multifaceted use and presentation of charter evidence. Véronique Gazeau examines the extensive descriptions of saints featured in the *Historia ecclesiastica*, identifying the various types of saint described and commenting on Orderic's presentation of each sub-type. Following this, William Aird analyses the ways in which Orderic described the acts of secular rulers in his own time, before Emily Albu explores the tone of his historical writing both in his additions to the *Gesta Normannorum* and in the *Historia*. Together, these two studies provide commentary on Orderic's tendency to moralise on recent history, and identify how he judged the events of his own time. All five chapters in this section make important new contributions to the study of how Orderic used the sources he found around him within the monastery of Saint-Évroul, as well as adding to our understanding of related institutions which he is known to have visited and his methods and aims in writing history.

The next five chapters focus attention on Orderic as an active participant in the monastic devotional life and the pursuit of theological study. Giles Gasper explores Orderic's status as a monastic theologian who developed a particularly strong sense of his own place in a wider, theologically informed, historical landscape. Elisabeth Mégier expands her previous analysis of history and theology in Orderic's *Historia* by reviewing the presence and significance of Christ in the wider narrative, and Sigbjørn Sønnesyn examines the multiple levels of reading and meaning available to Orderic's presumed monastic readership. Tom O'Donnell explores Orderic's *Historia* as a tool for the establishment and consolidation of monastic communal identity at Saint-Évroul, and, in so doing, seeks to explain the multiple and often challenging directions taken by Orderic's narrative structure. Kathleen Thompson continues discussions on Orderic's perceptions of the monastic life, by considering his account of the community founded at Tiron in the first years of the twelfth century.

The final two chapters provide a much-needed reinterpretation of the reception of Orderic's historical works by near-contemporary and later medieval audiences. Benjamin Pohl writes on Orderic and cultural memory, exploring some of the ways in which the author conceived of his work as a guarantee against the loss of cumulative social memory and historical awareness. This theme is tested by James Clark, who examines the legacy of Orderic's *Historia ecclesiastica* in later medieval works and discusses some possible examples of recourse to Orderic's narrative during the later Middle Ages.

Two appendices supplement the discussions featured in the main chapters. In the first, Anne-Sophie Vigot presents the preliminary findings of archaeological explorations within the ruins of Orderic's home foundation at Saint-Évroult in Normandy, carried out in 2013 and 2014. In doing so she discusses the various stages of occupation from the early seventh-century foundation of Saint-Évroul down to the present day. The second appendix provides a detailed descriptive catalogue of Orderic's additions within surviving manuscripts, compiled by Jenny Weston and Charlie Rozier. This aims to assist the development of scholarship on Orderic's activities as a scribe, copyist and author.

The story of Orderic's life, works and the later reception and interpretation of his writings over the nearly nine centuries since his death continues to be revised and expanded as his works are studied by new generations of students. As a consequence, it is hoped that further details will be added to this picture in future, and that the discussions presented in this volume will help light the way for scholars for many years to come.

Orderic and his Father, Odelerius

Elisabeth van Houts

MUCH has been written about autobiographical writing or, to use the phrase coined in the 1970s by Michel Foucault, 'self-writing'.[1] In the Middle Ages the two were not the same. We have to distinguish between an author writing about himself from the start, focusing on his own life and thoughts (*'autobiographie'*), and an author on occasion inserting details about himself in any kind of narrative (self-writing). The medieval period is framed by two famous autobiographies: St Augustine's *Confessiones*, written c. 397×400, and Petrarch's *Letters* and *Secretum*, composed c. 1347×1153.[2] In the time of Orderic Vitalis the autobiographies of two Benedictine monks, Guibert of Nogent (c. 1055–c. 1125) and Peter Abelard (1072–1142), stand out as full-scale narratives about the self. Guibert wrote his *De vita sua* towards the end of his life, in 1114–15, a decade or so into his abbacy at Nogent-sous-Coucy.[3] Peter Abelard's *Historia calamitatum* was composed in the early 1130s about fifteen years after the most traumatic incident of his life – his castration by Fulbert, the uncle-canon of his lover, Heloise, in Paris.[4] These autobiographies represent the trend for the rediscovery of the individual in the twelfth-century renaissance, when self-examination came to form part of the penitential process of the individual monk. There were various ways in which the medieval monk, as part of a closed-off community, engaged with his inner thoughts. However, such preoccupation with interiority was not concerned, as it would now be, with understanding one's character and psychology, but with coming closer to God.[5] The rise of the autobiography is at the same time linked with the

---

[1] M. Foucault, 'Self-Writing', in *The Essential Works*, vol. 1: *Ethics: Subjectivity and Truth*, ed. P. Rabinow, trans. R. Hurley *et al.* (New York, 1993), pp. 207–22.

[2] G. Zak, 'Modes of Self-Writing from Antiquity to the Later Middle Ages', in *The Oxford Handbook of Medieval Latin Literature*, ed. R. J. Hexter and D. Townsend (Oxford, 2012), pp. 485–505.

[3] *Guibert de Nogent, Autobiographie*, ed. and trans. E-E. Labande, Les classiques de l'histoire de France au Moyen Âge (Paris, 1981); *Self and Society: The Memoirs of Abbot Guibert of Nogent*, trans. J. F. Benton, Medieval Academy Reprints for Teaching 15 (Toronto, 1984).

[4] *The Letter Collection of Peter Abelard and Heloise*, Letter 1, ed. D. Luscombe, trans. B. Radice (Oxford, 2013), pp. 2–121.

[5] I. van 't Spijker, *Fictions of the Inner Life: Religious Literature and Formation of the Self in the Eleventh and Twelfth Centuries*, Disputatio 4 (Turnhout, 2004), pp. 1–16.

flourishing of historical writing in which historians included themselves as actors in their narratives. Yet, the focus on well-known authors should not blind us to the fact that throughout the Middle Ages many historians, whether they were modest annalists, chroniclers, hagiographers or authors of substantial histories, inserted information about themselves into their books. While most did so anonymously, a few included details about their own lives. It is as one of the latter category that I will discuss Orderic Vitalis (1075–c. 1142).[6]

Orderic does not become visible until a decade into the authorship of the *Historia ecclesiastica*, begun c. 1114, even though about five years earlier, while still a young apprentice historian, he had revised the *Gesta Normannorum ducum*.[7] His revision can be dated to the years c. 1109×1113, when he simplified William of Jumièges' Latin prose style and interpolated extra material into books VI and VII of the *Gesta Normannorum ducum*, on dukes Robert the Magnificent (1027–35) and William of Normandy (1035–87). He never extended the narrative beyond c. 1070, but regularly inserted accounts of events up to his own time, such as Anselm of Bec's accession as archbishop of Canterbury, the abbacies of several monks of Saint-Évroul and so forth.[8] Throughout, he identified himself with William of Jumièges as (collective) author of the *Gesta Normannorum ducum*, which is written in the genre of the serial *gesta* (deeds) that made interpolation and updating so attractive. What is important to stress in the present context is that Orderic was the first person to do this silently and anonymously, even going so far as to keep intact the letter of dedication by William of Jumièges to William the Conqueror with which the *Gesta Normannorum ducum* opens. Orderic took on William of Jumièges' *persona* as author, adopting William's authorial voice as his own and never revealing his own identity. This contrasts with William of Jumièges' approach in the dedicatory letter to William the Conqueror.[9] There he explained how he had abbreviated and continued Dudo of Saint-Quentin's history of the dukes of Normandy.[10] The main difference was, of course, that Orderic's revisions to William's work were interpolations, not continuations of the kind William had added to Dudo, and Robert

---

[6] In what follows I shall concentrate on Orderic's own early story before he became a monk, especially his relationship with his father. I believe that we can come closer to understanding him despite Marjorie Chibnall's advice to see Orderic 'in the context of his age, and that we should do well not to attempt too psychological a study, for he has left no analysis of his personal feeling' (Chibnall, 'General Introduction', p. 39).

[7] GND, I, pp. lxvi–lxxvii.

[8] Ibid., pp. 162–3 (the death of Abbot Mainer in Robert Curthose's reign (on 6 March 1089), and the appointment of Abbot Serlo as bishop of Séez in 1091).

[9] Ibid., Epistola, I, pp. 4–5.

[10] Ibid., Epistola, I, pp. 4–7.

of Torigni would add to Orderic's own version of the text. What remains interesting, though, is that for all Orderic's silence about himself, his autograph copy provides the well-known illuminated initial 'P' (for 'Pio' – 'pious') of the *Gesta Normannorum*'s dedicatory letter, in which a kneeling monk (William) offers a book (the *Gesta Normannorum*) to an enthroned king (William the Conqueror). Taking the notion of collective authorship to its logical conclusion, the image might also be interpreted as representing Orderic, who may have offered his version of the text to King Henry I, perhaps when the king visited Saint-Évroul in 1113.[11]

Before we delve deeper into the detail of the autobiographical sections in the *Historia ecclesiastica* it is crucial to point out when Orderic wrote his own life stories. He refers to his father in three places. The first is in Book IV (composed in 1125), when Orderic, then aged fifty, briefly mentions Odelerius as one of the three clerks of Earl Roger in Shropshire, but without identifying him as his father.[12] The second instance was composed a couple of years later (1127), when Orderic started Book V; this book, as he explains, concerns events in the year of his birth (1075).[13] In his account of that year he gave a brief outline of his own early life, before setting out the history of the early benefactions to his monastery. In Book V, c. 14, having recorded the gifts of his father's employer, Earl Roger of Montgomery, he embarked on a lengthy history of the foundation of St Peter at Shrewsbury, back in 1083.[14] This, the second and most substantial section of autobiographical material, is then repeated at the end of Orderic's life, when, in the autumn of 1141, aged sixty-seven, he added an autobiographical epilogue (Book XIII, c. 45) modelled on that in Bede's *Historia ecclesiastica*.[15] I will set out the bare bones of the father and

---

[11] For Henry I's visit in early February 1113 to Saint-Évroul, see *HE*, VI, pp. 174–7, and Chibnall, 'General Introduction', p. 32.

[12] *HE*, II, pp. 262–3. Roger of Montgomery came to England for the first time in November 1067, see J. F. A. Mason, 'Roger of Montgomery', in *The Oxford Dictionary of National Biography* (Oxford, 2004); Roger probably received Shropshire in 1068 when he was created earl, see Chris Lewis, 'The Early Earls of Norman England', *ANS* 13 (1990), 207–23, at p. 219. For Roger of Montgomery's clerical entourage, see J. F. A. Mason, 'The Officers and Clerks of the Norman Earls of Shropshire', *Transactions of the Shropshire Archaeological Society* 56 (1957–60), 244–57, at pp. 252–6.

[13] *HE*, III, pp. 6–7: 'a prefato nempe anno [1075] placet inchoare presens opusculum, quo in hanc lucem xiiii kal. Martii [16 February] matris ex utero profusus sum.'

[14] Ibid., pp. 142–51.

[15] *HE*, VI, pp. 550–7. For Orderic and Bede, see Chibnall, 'General Introduction', p. 56, and *HE*, II, p. xvii. Orderic's copy of Bede's *Ecclesiastical History* survives in Rouen, BM, MS 1343; for Orderic's writing, see Denis Escudier, 'Orderic et le scriptorium', and the contribution by

son story first, and then analyse the significance of these autobiographical sections.

Orderic's father, Odelerius of Orléans (c. 1034–1103), a priest, emerges from the historical record with two other clerks: Godebald (d. after 1086), and Herbert the Grammarian. They appear in the service of Earl Roger of Montgomery (d. 1094), in post-conquest England, in the border province of Shropshire. Odelerius held the church of St Peter at Shrewsbury from Earl Roger, making him the poorest of the three clerks. Like Godebald, Odelerius began a sexual relationship, perhaps a marriage, with an unknown English woman. Both men had sons, Godebald one (Robert) and Odelerius three.[16] Orderic, the eldest of Odelerius's sons, was born and baptised by the priest Orderic at Atcham in 1075. The second son, Benedict, was baptised in 1078, and the youngest son, Everard, followed a couple of years later. In 1080, aged five, Orderic was sent to Shrewsbury to live with a priest, the noble Siward, to learn letters and psalms. Two years later, in 1083, having been to Rome in the previous year (1082), Odelerius persuaded Earl Roger of Montgomery to build a monastery in Shrewsbury on the site of the church of St Peter, which Roger had given him. On this occasion Odelerius promised to give his second son, Benedict, and himself as monks to the new foundation, together with his house and furnishings and land; he also offered his third son, Everard, as the monks' tenant. Around the same time he also arranged for his son Orderic to become an oblate at Saint-Évroul in Normandy. In 1085, aged ten, the boy left home, crossed the sea and came to Normandy; he never saw his father again. Finally, after the death of Earl Roger of Montgomery in July 1094, Odelerius, aged sixty, left the world and entered the monastery of St Peter at Shrewsbury, giving the foundation his lands, house and cash. He died eight years later, in 1103.

Having set out the skeleton of the story, I will now turn to the detail that Orderic provided about his father. Odelerius of Orléans was the son of Constantius.[17] His life would have started under a cloud if his birth did indeed take place in that city, because only two years before, in 1032, Orléans had been attacked by Duke Robert the Magnificent and his Norman army.[18] Odelerius was apparently learned man, described by his

Jenny Weston below, 'Following the Master's Lead: The Script of Orderic Vitalis and the Discovery of a New Manuscript (Rouen, BM, 540)'.

[16] For Godebald's son, Robert, see Mason, 'The Officers', p. 253.

[17] HE, III, pp. 142–3. Note that it is not until the end of the chapter (pp. 150–1) that Orderic reveals that he is the son of Odelerius. For evidence that Constantius was a common name, see Hans Wolter, *Orderic Vitalis: Ein Beitrag zur kluniazensischen Geschichtsschreibung* (Wiesbaden, 1955), p. 48.

[18] HE, IV, pp. xxxii, 74–6, and *Recueil des actes des ducs de Normandie de 911 à 1066*, ed. M. Fauroux, Mémoires de la Société des Antiquaires de Normandie 36 (Caen, 1961), no. 91, pp. 239–42. For its authenticity, see

son as 'a man of remarkable intelligence, eloquence and learning [...] [with a] passionate love of justice [...] a wise counsellor of the earl'.[19] Although Orderic never mentions him in this capacity, as a member of the secular clergy and a priest Odelerius may have had an excellent education in Latin, law and rhetoric, all of which were on offer in the schools of Orléans in the 1040s and 1050s.[20] He may have been schooled privately in the household of a priest, as was Orderic himself, or, less likely, in a monastic school.[21] If

---

O. Guillot, *Le Comté d'Anjou et son entourage au XIe siècle*, 2 vols. (Paris, 1972), II, pp. 49–50. Note that Orderic does not connect the story of the Norman attack on Orléans with the birth of his father. Conceivably, the information comes from the now lost section of William of Poitiers' biography of William the Conqueror. Orderic remained interested in Orléans. His copy of King Charles III the Simple's charter dated to 900 (Alençon, BM, MS 14, fols. 38r–v) concerns a royal gift to the early canons of Saint-Évroul. It carries a postscript in which Orderic explains that Abbot Robert of Grandmesnil (1059–61) had found the charter at Orléans and had it copied by the monk Goscelin (*Recueil des actes de Charles III le Simple, roi de France*, ed. P. Lauer (Paris, 1949), pp. 74–6; and *HE*, III, pp. xvi–xvii and 322–3).

[19] Ibid., pp. 142–3: 'uir ingenio et facundia et eruditio litterarum [...] amator æquitatis feruidus; utilisque iam dicti comitis erat auricularius'.

[20] Odelerius (*Oilerius*) is called a priest ('sacerdos' and 'presbyter') in documentation for Shrewsbury Abbey, see *Cartulary of Shrewsbury Abbey*, ed. Una Rees, 2 vols. (Aberystwyth, 1975), I, pp. 30, 33, 41, II, pp. 255, 256. For education in eleventh-century Orléans, see E. Lesne, *Les Écoles de la fin de VIIIe siècle à la fin du XIIe*, Histoire de la propriété ecclésiastique en France 5 (Lille, 1940), p. 189; P. Riché, *Écoles et enseignement dans le haut Moyen Âge (fin du Ve–milieu du XIe siècles)* (Paris, 1979), pp. 184 and 338; for what has survived of the manuscript collection of the cathedral of Sainte Croix and the nearby monastic houses, see *Catalogue des manuscrits en écriture latine portant des indications de date, de lieu ou de copiste*, vol. 7: *Ouest de la France et Pays de Loire*, ed. M-C. Garand, G. Garand and D. Muzerelle (Paris, 1984), pp. xxxvi–vii.

[21] Chibnall, 'General Introduction', p. 4; Wolter, *Orderic Vitalis*, p. 48, suggests that he was educated in or near Orléans as a guest pupil (*Gastschüler*) in a monastic school on the grounds of the following quote: 'I have been for a long time from my youth up an adviser of monks and have come to know their way of life from close observance.' (For education in Norman monastic schools, see V. Gazeau, *Normannia monastica*, vol. 1: *Princes normands et abbés bénédictins (X^e–XIe siècle)* (Caen, 2007), pp. 245–54; for education of the young in priests' households as a first step on the path to becoming a priest, see Julia Barrow, 'Grades of Ordination and Clerical Careers, c. 900–c. 1200', *ANS* 30 (2007), 41–61; good introductions to central medieval education can be found in M. Münster-Swendsen, 'Regimens of Schooling', in *The Oxford Handbook of Medieval Latin Literature*, ed. R.J. Hexter and D. Townsend (Oxford, 2012), pp. 403–22; and G. Lobrichon, 'The Early Schools, c. 900–1100', in *The*

Odelerius had been educated in a monastery as a child, his son would not have written that he had been an adviser and observer of monks from his youth ('a iuuentute'), that is, from his mid-teens.[22]

At some stage, probably in the 1060s, Odelerius came into contact with Roger of Montgomery. Chibnall, acknowledging our lack of information on this matter, leaned towards the possibility that Odelerius might have been Norman,[23] schooled in Orléans but then living as a youth in Normandy, possibly in one of the monastic houses associated with the Montgomery family; this might explain how Roger came to know him.[24] An alternative, which is perhaps more likely, is that Odelerius, like his father, Constantius, grew up in the Orléannais and moved to Normandy from there (perhaps alongside his colleagues Godebald and Herbert the Grammarian) in search of work, as did many other clergy, monks and knights.[25] A French, not Norman, ancestry would explain Orderic's self-presentation as a stranger and foreigner in Normandy.[26] Whatever the route he took, Odelerius and his fellow clerks eventually made their way into the service of Earl Roger in post-conquest Shropshire, where all three acted on his behalf.[27]

From there, Odelerius's story becomes entwined with that of his sons, and in particular that of his eldest, Orderic, who, in 1080, aged five, was sent to Siward the noble priest at Shrewsbury. There he was taught the letters of the alphabet, psalms and hymns.[28] While at Siward's house Orderic and his brothers became part of his father's plan for their future, and Orderic's story turns into a narrative of how one family collectively paid for the sins of the father by entering monastic life. The crucial questions are: why did Odelerius become so passionate about collective

---

New Cambridge History of the Bible, vol. 2: *From 600–1450*, ed. R. Marsden and E. A. Matter (Cambridge, 2012), pp. 536–54. See also, S. C. Jaeger, *The Envy of Angels: Cathedral Schools and Social Ideals in Medieval Europe, 950–1200* (Philadelphia, 1994), pp. 54–62 (on the type of school Odelerius may have attended), and pp. 76–118 (on the humanist education he may have received).

[22] *HE*, III, pp. 144–5: 'A secretis monachorum a iuuentute mea diutius extiti; et mores eorum familiariter rimatus edidici.'

[23] Chibnall, 'General Introduction', pp. 4–5.

[24] Ibid.; Chibnall, *World*, p. 8.

[25] For monks, clergy and secular French or foreigners flocking to Normandy, see David Bates, *Normandy before 1066* (Harlow, 1982), p. 100; Gazeau, *Normannia monastica: Princes normands*, pp. 194–220 (abbots from outside Normandy).

[26] *HE*, III, pp. 6–7.

[27] *HE*, II, pp. 262–3.

[28] *HE*, VI, pp. 552–3. This is very similar to what Walther of Speyer tells us, more poetically, in his autobiography, *Der 'Libellus scholasticus' des Walther von Speyer*, ed. and trans. [German] P. Vossen (Berlin, 1962), lines 9–11.

penance, and why did he feel that his penance needed to be shared by his sons? The reason, as others have suggested before me, is that he felt he had sinned deeply. Understanding one's sinful nature, and doing penance for one's sins in order to attain salvation after death, was what the Christian religion was all about. Monasticism was the ultimate form of penance, as men and women would sacrifice worldly existence by dedicating themselves to God for the rest of their lives.

The purest offering to God was the child oblate, as the gift of a child was the greatest gesture a parent could make.[29] Christianity was certainly not the only religion that sacrificed children; there is a long and widespread tradition of offering to a divine power what humankind holds most dear.[30] In the early Middle Ages, up to c. 1150, child oblates were given to monasteries on the grounds that parents sacrificed to the Almighty their most precious treasure.[31] Families would select one child to be given as oblate, though in due course more members of the same family might also enter the cloister.

Odelerius was unusual in that he sacrificed not only himself but also two of his sons: Orderic and Benedict. What is even more unusual is that he sent Orderic to so distant a monastery as Saint-Évroul. In Orderic's 1127 account, centred on the foundation of St Peter's monastery in Shrewsbury, Orderic reported how in 1083 his father had promised fifteen pounds in silver to make a start with the building of the monastery, plus at a later stage himself and his second son, Benedict, still aged five, along with half his goods.[32] The other half of his possessions would go to the monks indirectly, as the youngest son, Everard, would hold them from St Peter's.[33] Orderic here also reported his father as saying that he had already arranged for his eldest son to be educated by a priest, and had paid the monks of Saint-Évroul in Normandy thirty marks from his own *porismas* for Orderic's oblation.[34] Negotiations with Saint-Évroul may have been conducted through intermediaries, or by Odelerius himself. Odelerius could have made the arrangements either *en route* to Rome in 1082 (a journey I will return to) or earlier still, in May 1081, at Winchester (if, as

---

[29] M. de Jong, *In Samuel's Image: Child Oblation in the Early Medieval West* (Leiden, 1996), esp. chapter 8, pp. 267–89.

[30] For example, the Inca and Aztec funeral practices evidenced by the mummified children found on mountain tops, who were offered as gifts to the gods.

[31] Giles E. M. Gasper, 'Contemplating Money and Wealth in Monastic Writing, c. 1060–c. 1160', in *Money and the Church in Medieval Europe, 1000–1200: Practice, Morality and Thought*, ed. Giles E. M. Gasper and Svein H. Gullbekk (Aldershot, 2015), pp. 39–76, at p. 53.

[32] *HE*, III, pp. 146–7.

[33] Ibid.

[34] Ibid. Note the use of the word 'porismas' as the source for Odelerius's wealth. Chibnall translates this as 'substance'.

Earl Roger's clerk, he had attended the king's court at which Abbot Mainer of Saint-Évroul had sought confirmation of his monastery's endowments from William the Conqueror).[35] In 1127, when he reported the situation of 1083, Orderic quotes his father's (reconstructed) words explaining the motivation for his actions:

> So out of love for my Redeemer I renounce my first born son and destine him for exile amongst strangers; free from every tie of kinship and fatal affection he may devote himself utterly to the observance of the monastic rule and the worship of God. All these things I have long hoped for through God's holy inspiration, and I have chosen that my children and I shall devote ourselves to such occupations so that aided by God's grace I and they together may deserve to be numbered with the elect in the Last Judgment.[36]

As reported by his son, Odelerius gave up that which was dearest to him, his eldest son, by sending him so far away that contact with home, family and friends was nearly impossible. This sacrifice was deemed much greater than the sacrifice of Benedict's oblation, or the giving of his lands to St Peter's, Shrewsbury, to be held by his youngest son, Everard, who remained in the world. Odelerius clearly hoped that by becoming monks he and his two sons, plus Everard, would be guaranteed a place in heaven.

Having told the story of his own oblation through the eyes of his father, Orderic briefly apologised to his readers for having given them 'a memorial of my father', because 'I never saw him again after he sent me into exile for love of his Creator as if I had been a rejected stepson.'[37] In this way the reader of the 1127 account is left under no illusion that Orderic felt deeply distressed about having been given away by his father, albeit for the noblest

---

[35] *Regesta Regum Anglo-Normannorum: The Acta of William I (1066–1087)*, ed. David Bates (Oxford, 1998), no. 255, pp. 770–3; and *HE*, III, pp. 232–40. It is conceivable that on this occasion Abbot Mainer brought back the original manuscript with the St Æthelwold dossier that Orderic copied later, in what is now Alençon, BM, MS 14, see: *Wulfstan of Winchester, The Life of St Æthelwold*, ed. and trans. M. Lapidge and M. Winterbottom (Oxford, 1991), pp. clvii–clviii; *HE*, I, p. 202. For Orderic's use of this material, see *HE*, VI, pp. 150–3.

[36] *HE*, III, pp. 146–7: 'Sic pro redemptoris amore primogenitum michi filium abdico et trans pontum in exilium destino, ut ultroneus exul inter externos regi militet æthero, ubi liber ab omni parentum cura et affectu lætifero, eximie uigeat in obseruatione monastica et cultu dominico. Hæc inspirante Deo iam dudum desideraui, ac ad talia me progeniemque meam applicare studia peroptaui; ut merear opitulante gratia Dei; cum prole mea inter electos in ultimo examine computari.'

[37] Ibid., pp. 150–1: 'Parce queso bone lector, nec molestum tibi sit precor; si de patre meo aliquid memoriæ tradiderim litterarum, quem non uidi ex quo me uelut exosum sibi priuignum, et pro amore creatoris pepulit in exilium.'

of reasons. His use of the vocabulary of exile and of unwanted family (the 'stepson') is a telling sign of the rejection, an emotion which, he tells us, remained with him for the rest of his life:

> Forty-two years have passed since then and during that time many changes have taken place throughout the world. These things are often in my mind and I record a few in these pages as I deliberately fight against sloth, busying myself with composing.[38]

Keeping his mind busy was the medicine for his mental wound. It prevented Orderic from dwelling on the one momentous event of his life, when his father not only gave him away as an oblate, but did so in a drastic manner by sending him overseas. The implicit contrast drawn with the fate of his brothers, who were allowed to stay home (or at least nearby), is poignant.

At the end of his life, in the autumn of 1141, when he was sixty-seven, Orderic repeated most of his autobiographical detail, though this time, instead of speaking through his father, he spoke himself, elaborating the story with fresh information. He tells us of his early education from the age of five by the noble priest Siward, who taught him 'letters, psalms, hymns and other necessary knowledge', before returning to the moment of his departure in 1085.[39] He wrote movingly of how it was God's will that he could not serve at home, where the ties of kin and family might hinder his exclusive service to God. Do we read here an implicit reproach that, by staying together in Shrewsbury, Odelerius, Benedict and Everard had been a potential distraction to each other? Whether this is the case or not, it seems to me significant that Orderic continued his account by stressing that his oblation had been his father's decision, albeit one inspired by God:

> O glorious God [...] you did inspire my father Odelerius to renounce me utterly and to submit me in all things to your governance. Weeping, he gave me, a weeping child, into the care of Reginald and sent me away in exile for the love of you and never saw me again. [...] So I left behind my homeland and parents and every relative and intimates and friends. And they weeping and wishing me well, commended me with kind prayers to you, almighty God.[40]

Not only Orderic's father but also his kinsfolk and friends tearfully said

---

[38] Ibid.: 'Iam xlii anni sunt; in quibus multæ mutationes rerum late per orbem factæ sunt. Dum sepe de his cogito, et quædam cartis insero; caute resistens ocio, sic dictans me exerceo.'

[39] HE, VI, pp. 552–3: 'Illic Siguardus insignis presbiter per quinque annos Carmentis Nichoastratæ litteras docuit me, ac psalmis et hymnis aliisque necessariis instructionibus mancipauit me.'

[40] Ibid.: 'Icciro gloriose Deus qui Abraham de terra patrisque domo et cognatione egredi iussisti, Odelerium patrem meum apirasti ut me sibi penitus abdicaret, et tibi omnimodis subiugaret. Rainaldo igitur monacho

their farewells. And with some of the most moving words in medieval writing Orderic ended his work with the following words:

> And so, a boy of ten, I crossed the English Channel and came into Normandy as an exile, unknown to all, knowing no one. Like Joseph in Egypt, I heard a language which I did not understand. But you [God] did allow me to suffer through your grace to find nothing but kindness and friendship amongst strangers.[41]

Although we now read these words at a distance of more than 800 years we cannot help but be moved deeply by the emotional world which Orderic conjures up for us.

What is particularly striking about these autobiographical sections is that Orderic told the story of his exile at two very important junctures in his life. In 1127, when he penned the story of his childhood and forced departure from home, Orderic was in his early fifties – a similar age to his father in 1085, when he sent his son away to Normandy. Telling the story from his father's perspective, in his father's own (reconstructed) words, and at a similar age allowed Orderic to mentally absorb what that decision must have meant for Odelerius. I would suggest that Orderic literally put himself in his father's shoes in an attempt to understand how a father could have made a decision which he, as a son, albeit a devout Christian monk, so obviously found distressing. Through the persona of his father, Orderic constructed the narrative of his own oblation in a conventional monastic way, as determined by God's will and as a sacrifice and a penitential necessity.

Fourteen years later, in 1142, well into his sixties, Orderic went through the whole episode again in Book XIII of the *Historia*. This time the account is given primarily from his own perspective, stressing the emotional turmoil of abandonment and grief, which spills over in tears not only for himself but also for his father, family and friends. Gone is the wish to rationalise the price of penance, for at the end of his life the time had come to remember, without reservation, the tears and desolation which he had felt during that moment of the final farewell. It is not mere coincidence that Orderic wrote the epilogue aged sixty-seven, exactly the same age as his father had been at his death in 1103. On both occasions, in 1127 and in 1142, Orderic was thus at an age that was significant in his father's life; and on both occasions he went to great lengths to express the extent to which he identified with that father, whom he had loved, but also, one suspects, must sometimes have hated for sending him so far away. By

plorans plorantem me tradidit, et pro amore tuo in exilium destinauit, nec me unquam postea uidit.'

[41] Ibid., pp. 554–5: 'Decennis itaque Britannicum mare transfretaui, exul in Normanniam ueni, cunctis ignotus neminem cognoui. Linguam ut Ioseph in Ægipto quam non noueram audiui. Suffragante tamen gratia tua inter exteros omnem mansuetudinem in familiaritatem repperi.'

putting his own story on paper in his own words, Orderic finally found peace of mind.

Let me return now to the father. What exactly caused Odelerius's personal crisis, which necessitated in his view the heavy toll he imposed upon himself and his sons? What did Odelerius consider so sinful that it could not have been settled by him alone but had to be shared by the next generation as well? Biblical admonition was ambiguous: there are certainly passages that stress how a person's actions will have repercussions across the generations, from father to sons, grandsons and great-grandsons; yet in other places the Bible states that sons should not be held to account for their father's sins.[42] Paying the price for someone's sin across generations was a concept ingrained in the monastic world through oblation, with children sharing parental penance.[43] In Odelerius's case there are two possible explanations, and they are inextricably linked. The first is a deeply personal one, as it concerns Odelerius's status as a married priest, while the second is related to his involvement in the Norman Conquest of England, not least as a beneficiary of its massive spoils. I will begin with the issue of clerical marriage.

The gaping hole in Orderic's narrative – the elephant in the room, so to speak – is the absence of the English woman who was Orderic's mother, the wife or partner of Odelerius.[44] Orderic refers to her indirectly by describing himself as 'Angligena' ('born from an English mother') and saying that he was born from his mother's womb.[45] Some historians have argued that the reason for Orderic's silence was shame. According to Wolter, Orderic's mother might have been a serf, causing Orderic not mention her out of shame for her social status.[46] In contrast, Chibnall – more plausibly – observed that because Odelerius was a priest, his

---

[42] Exodus 20:5, 34:7; Numbers 14:8; Deuteronomy 5:7 (three or four generations). Ezekiel 18:19–20 (sons do not pay for fathers' sins).

[43] Cf. *HE*, VI, pp. 212–13: 'Innocens itaque infantia parentum nefas, proh dolor, miserabiliter luit' ('Innocent childhood, alas, paid miserably for the sin of the father'). This is Orderic's comment on Henry I's barbaric treatment of his own granddaughters (by his illegitimate daughter Juliana and her husband, Eustace) when their parents rebelled against him.

[44] Whether Orderic's mother was also the mother of Benedict and Evrard is unknown. Without evidence to the contrary I am assuming she was. What is interesting is that Orderic bore an English name (after the priest at Atcham who baptised him *HE*, III, pp. 6–7) but his younger brothers had French names. Note that the youngest one bore the same name as Earl Roger's son by Adelaide of Le Puisset.

[45] *HE*, III, pp. 6–7. Here too the vocabulary for birth refers to his mother: 'matris ex utero profusum sum' ('I was born from my mother's womb', Chibnall translates 'I was born'); *HE*, VI, pp. 552–3.

[46] Wolter, *Orderic Vitalis*, pp. 50–1. I am sure 'ancilla' here is a reference to the Church.

marriage was the most likely reason for shame on his and Orderic's part. By the time Orderic wrote the account c. 1127, priestly marriages were forbidden in Normandy and England as a result of the first Lateran council. Convened at Rome in 1123, this had forbidden clerical marriages in the Christian world, though there had been no such prohibition at the time of Orderic's parents' partnership, back in the 1070s.[47] Still, Chibnall suggested that Orderic's silence represented a 'negative attitude to his mother' due to his parents' marriage.[48] There is much to be commended in her argument. Writing in 1127, the very year in which he recounted Odelerius's involvement in the foundation of St Peter's, Shrewsbury, Orderic did not mince his words when he related Pope Leo IX's rule on clerical celibacy at Reims in 1049. In the context of the early benefactors of Saint-Évroul who, having been married priests, paid penance and entered the monastery, he wrote:

> At that time he [Leo IX] held a general council there and amongst other decrees [...] he utterly prohibited priests from bearing arms or taking wives. From that time the fatal custom began to wither away little by little. The priests were ready enough to give up their arms but even now they are loath to part with their mistresses or to live chaste lives.[49]

While not denying that Orderic the fifty-year-old monk disapproved of clerical marriage (which, incidentally, he thought had been imported to Normandy by Rollo and his Viking men),[50] it should be doubted whether Orderic the young boy had thought about his parents' relationship in such legalistic terms.[51] Rather than expressing his own shame over his parents' marriage at the time of his exile, it seems more likely that the 1127 account expresses his father's sense of guilt, or reconstructs what he thought was his father's sense of guilt, about the marriage and the sexual acts in which he had engaged.

Orderic had almost certainly been present at Earl Roger's foundation ceremony for St Peter's, Shrewsbury, in February 1083.[52] The monastery incorporated the church held by the noble priest Siward, with whom

---

[47] Ibid., p. 51; Chibnall, 'General Introduction', pp. 2–3; and Chibnall, *World*, pp. 8–9.

[48] Ibid., p. 9.

[49] *HE*, III, pp. 120–3: 'Tunc ibidem generale concilium tenuit, et inter reliqua æcclesiæ commoda quæ constituit; presbiteris arma ferre et coniuges habere omnino prohibuit. Exinda letalis consuetudo paulatim exinanire cœpit. Arma quidem ferre presbiteri iam gratanter desiere; sed a pelicibus adhuc nolunt abstinere, nec pudiciæ inherere.'

[50] Ibid., pp. 120–1.

[51] Ibid.

[52] Ibid., pp. 146–7.

Orderic lived at that time, so it seems natural to assume that all those in Siward's household would have attended the occasion.[53] Another Siward, son of Æthelgar, whose property the church had been before Earl Roger had given it to Odelerius (who had in turn installed Siward the noble priest there), exchanged the site for land elsewhere.[54] Orderic's detailed information about Odelerius's promise of money and land highlights a common feature of such ceremonies at which family members would be present to give their consent: the 'laudatio parentis'.[55] Children would accompany their fathers so that in due course they could pass on knowledge of the event. Across Europe, boys from the age of seven were required to attend important occasions of gifts of lands, when sometimes they would be slapped or otherwise 'mistreated' as mnemonic devices to ensure that they would remember the events. As adults, they could then act as witnesses in case of disputes arising from the transactions.[56] Seen in this light, Odelerius would have sought to impress the significance of the event upon his eldest son, not least as an opportunity to announce his plans for Orderic's future as an oblate in Normandy. In such a context we might imagine the little boy asking for reasons for his father's decision, and the father replying in terms understandable to a small boy. He would have stressed the notion of sin and penance, possibly even going some way to explaining that, as a priest, he was not supposed to have had a sexual relationship with a woman and that his need for penance would necessarily involve his children too. If his parents had lived in sin it would make sense that the children they begat would be the very embodiment of their error, and must therefore be involved in the penitential act.

There is, I suggest, a very obvious reason why Orderic did not give more information about his mother, in that she had probably died when he was still relatively young. There are good reasons to assume that she died not long after the birth of her third and youngest son, Everard, which can be tentatively dated around 1080 or 1081.[57] This would explain why Orderic, then five years old, would have been placed with Siward

---

[53] Ibid., p. 146 n. 4.

[54] See below, n. 62.

[55] Stephen D. White, *Custom, Kinship and Gifts to Saints: The Laudatio parentum in Western France, 1050–1150* (Chapel Hill, NC, 1988), stresses the preponderance of males, especially benefactors' sons and uncles, among witnesses (p. 97), but specifies that uncles seldom act with sons (p. 107).

[56] E. van Houts, 'Gender and Authority of Oral Witnesses in Europe (800–1300)', *Transactions of the Royal Historical Society* 6th series 9 (1999), 201–20, at pp. 206–7.

[57] The children's dates of birth are as follows: Orderic in February 1075, Benedict in 1078, and Everard between that date and 1083 at the latest. Note that Everard must have been born around the same time as Everard the son of Roger of Montgomery and his second wife, Adelaide of Le Puiset, who married around c. 1080 (Mason, 'Roger of Montgomery').

in Shrewsbury, who educated him until he left for Normandy. It was quite common for boys destined for the church to be given to a priest to be educated at an early age, normally between five and ten, which puts Orderic in the earliest age group. His younger brothers perhaps stayed at home, where their mother's kin (about whom nothing is known) may have looked after them. Such was the (hypothetical) arrangement when Odelerius travelled to Rome in 1082. In his 1127 account of the foundation ceremony of St Peter's, the occasion of Odelerius's decision about his own and his sons' monastic destiny, Orderic makes no mention of a wife (or mother), and this is a significant omission. If she had still been alive, Odelerius would have needed her permission to become a monk in due course, and no such agreement is mentioned. I suggest that it was not necessary because she had died.[58] An early death, during or shortly after the birth of the third son c. 1080/1, would also explain why she was not among the tearful farewell party on the occasion of Orderic's departure for Normandy in 1085. It is difficult to believe that Orderic would not have mentioned his mother if she had still been alive at that time. I am therefore inclined to interpret the silence about his mother as the result of loss and grief rather than, as others have suggested, of shame.

In this context it is worth pointing out a suggestion made by Delisle and Wolter, who believe that a Latin *sequens* ('Summe pater, coeli rector') preserved in a Saint-Évroul manuscript might be Orderic's work (the manuscript is now Alençon, BM, MS 1, fols. 30–32; see Appendix 2, item 1).[59] The *sequens* occurs as the second of three early twelfth-century poems added on some blank pages in a book otherwise filled with texts from the Prophets. The poem represents the prayer of a penitent monk whose sinfulness revealed itself even when he was a child, when he kept his parents from sleeping for two years due to the soreness of his mother's breasts caused by feeding him as a baby.[60] The poems were

---

[58] Orderic is scrupulous to record such permissions of spouses whenever he mentions marriages being broken up for reasons of monastic entry by husband or wife.

[59] L. Delisle, 'Vers attribués à Orderic Vital', *Annuaire-bulletin de la Société de l'Histoire de France* 1:2 (1863), 1–13, at pp. 7–9. Wolter (*Orderic Vitalis*, p. 51 nn. 79–80) quoted some lines of the poem, but failed to identify the manuscript, and referred to the wrong Delisle publication. Misled by Wolter, whose reference she copied (*HE*, I, pp. 1–2), Chibnall never saw the whole poem and dismissed the idea of Orderic's authorship on the grounds that the poem 'follows too closely themes taken from the confessions of St Augustine'. The poem, *Summe pater, coeli rector, qui es sine tempore*, is not listed in H. Walther, *Initia carminum ac versuum Medii Aevi posterioris Latinorum: Ergänzungen und Berichtigungen zur 1. Auflage von 1959* (Göttingen, 1969), either the original or the later updates.

[60] Delisle, 'Vers attribués à Orderic Vital', pp. 7–8, lines 13–18: 'Post nouem menses materna nudus liqui uiscera;/ et duobus annis infans suxi matris

almost certainly written by a Saint-Évroul monk in Orderic's lifetime, but whether they can be attributed to Orderic himself is a question that at present cannot be answered.[61]

A second explanation as to why Odelerius, according to Orderic, felt the burden of sin is related to his benefitting from the spoils of the Norman Conquest, which made him a very rich man. How did Odelerius raise the colossal sum of £200 of silver that he contributed to St Peter's, Shrewsbury, on the occasion of his entry as monk in 1102? Orderic tells us that his father held the church of St Peter just outside the east gate of Shrewsbury, which was founded by the noble Siward, son of Æthelgar, a relative of King Edward the Confessor.[62] The church, probably a minster church, was one of six in Shrewsbury, an exceptional number revealing the status and wealth of the city as an important centre in the West Midlands.[63] According to Domesday Book, the church held two hides of land in 1066 (at Boreton and Lowe), each with an income of 5s., as well as the tithes of Upton Magna, whose lands were valued at £10.[64] The church of St Peter also held one hide in Wrockwardine, which has been identified as the one hide at Charlston given by Odelerius to St Peter's abbey in 1102;

---

ubera. Heu in quibus plura Deus peregi facinora./ Janque patris uultum spui caris in amplexibus;/ Matris genas laceravi paruis meis unguibus/ et persepe somnum eis ademi vagatibus'.

[61] John of Reims wrote several 'carmina' on the Virgin Mary and is perhaps the more likely author of these verses, given that the third poem is indeed about the Virgin Mary (*HE*, III, pp. 170–1).

[62] Ibid., pp. 142–3. In Book IV (*HE*, II, pp. 194–5) Orderic refers to him as one of two brothers, Siward and Ealdred, the sons of Æthelgar, grandsons of King Edward ('pronepotes Eduardi regis'), in a list of names of high-ranking English noblemen (who c. 1070 made peace with King William) embedded in William of Poitiers' biography of William the Conqueror (*HE*, II, p. 194 n. 1). The identity of King Edward is puzzling because neither Edward I the Martyr (975–8) nor Edward the Confessor (1042–66) had offspring. More likely, 'pronepos' here means grandson of the person's [i.e. the king's] sibling, and thus a cousin twice removed. According to Domesday Book (Great Domesday Book [hereafter GDB], fol. 259v), Siward, son of Æthelgar, held Cheney Longville in Wrockwardine Hundred in 1066; by 1086 he held it from Earl Roger, according to the *Cartulary of Shrewsbury Abbey* (I, no. 35, pp. 31–40), in exchange for the site of St Peter's (cf. *HE*, III, 142 n. 2).

[63] S. Bassett, 'Anglo-Saxon Shrewsbury and its Churches', *Midland History* 16 (1991), 1–23.

[64] *Prosopography of Anglo-Saxon England* (http://www.pase.ac.uk) [hereafter PASE], see locations under 'Boreton', 'Lowe', 'Upton Magna'. The tithe information comes from *Cartulary of Shrewsbury Abbey*, I, p. 33. For a discussion, see Bassett, 'Anglo-Saxon Shrewsbury', pp. 13–14.

its income was also 5*s*.[65] The total annual income in 1066 for the priest of St Peter's church was thus 15*s*., the most meagre of the incomes of the three clerks of Earl Roger of Montgomery.[66] This sum comes nowhere near those we have seen Odelerius spent: thirty marks for Orderic, £15 for the building of the church and to secure his own entry and that of Benedict, and £200 bestowed on St Peter's at the time of his entrance. Either the latter sum represented the total value of St Peter's three hides (rather than its annual income), or it comprised much more, including cash.

The most likely source of Odelerius' wealth upon his death must surely have been the spoils of conquest in Shrewsbury and Shropshire generally, where Earl Roger's income was an annual £750.[67] Odelerius must have shared in the gifts the earl is said in Domesday Book to have given to his clergy and chaplains, many of which came at the expense of the six Shrewsbury churches.[68] Moreover, the marriages of Orderic and Godebald

---

[65] GDB, fol. 253r; for an edition, see *Domesday Book: A Complete Translation*, ed. and trans. A. William and G. H. Martin, Alecto Historical Editions (London, 2002), p. 692. See also PASE, locations under 'Wrockwardine'; *Cartulary of Shrewsbury Abbey*, I, no. 35, p. 33, charter of Henry I in 1121 ('Oilerius sacerdos unam hidam in Cerleton'). On p. 39 Rees hypothesises that because Charlton was part of Earl Roger's manor of Wrockwardine, it was the church of Wrockwardine's hide mentioned in 1086 (GDB, fol. 253r) that was given by Odelerius to St Peter's abbey in 1102. For further confirmations of Odelerius's gift, see *Cartulary of Shrewsbury Abbey* I, no. 36, p. 41, charter of Henry II in 1155 ('de dono Oilerii presbiteri unam hidam in Cherletona'), and II, no. 279, p. 256, charter of Stephen embedded in charter of Edward I ('Oilerius sacerdos dedit hidam unam in Cherletona').

[66] That this was a colossal amount for a priest is commented upon by Judith Green, *The Aristocracy of Norman England* (Cambridge, 1997), p. 400.

[67] GDB, fol. 252r. According to Mason's calculations, the Earl Roger's English wealth amounted to £2,078 *per annum*, of which £1,031 was from his demesne. This made him the second-wealthiest tenant-in-chief (the wealthiest being Bishop Odo of Bayeux): see Mason, 'Roger of Montgomery', and J. F. A. Mason, 'Roger de Montgomery and his Sons', *Transactions of the Royal Historical Society* 5th series 13 (1963), 1–28, at p. 5.

[68] For example, GDB, fol. 252v: Stoke St Milborough taken away from St Milburgh in Shrewsbury and given to the earls' chaplains. GDB, fol. 253r, reveals the many estates originally held outright by St Alkmund, Shrewsbury, but in 1086 held by Godebald, Odelerius's companion, as the main tenant, who presumably took most of the lands' income. GDB, fol. 253r, tells a similar story for the minster at Morville, which originally held eight hides, three of which were given to the earl's chaplains. For these and other examples of post-conquest despoliation, see Mason, 'The Officers', pp. 253–4; and J. Blair, *The Church in Anglo-Saxon Society* (Oxford, 2005), pp. 264–5.

raise the question to what extent their wealth might constitute (part of) their English in-laws' possessions. If St Peter's church (and its three hides) came to Odelerius via his wife's family, a transmission sanctioned by Earl Roger, the implication is that she must have been related to St Peter's founder, Siward, son of Æthelgar, the relative of King Edward.[69] Though such a relationship seems unlikely, as we might have expected Orderic to have been more explicit about a noble maternal background, Chibnall raised the possibility of maternal kinship with the priest Orderic, who baptised him in 1075 at Atcham, or the noble priest Siward, who taught him.[70] We simply do not know. In the case of the clerk Godebald, we know that his son, Robert, succeeded to his lands.[71] In Anglo-Saxon England clerical positions of priests and canons were often held across generations in priests' dynasties, in the male and female lines.[72] After the Norman Conquest intermarriage helped to legitimise the holding of land or office by the conquerors by right of their wives' families.[73] We may therefore conclude that, based on the evidence provided by his son, Odelerius was almost certainly burdened by a sense of guilt based on the twinned sins of clerical marriage and the despoiling of English churches. It seems that his journey to Rome may well have been prompted by a combination of the two, as well as a desire to follow the penitential guidance provided in the so-called 'Penitential Ordo' of Bishop Eremfrid of Syon, which was issued for the Norman bishops in 1067.[74] Two clauses in particular are relevant: one providing an indication of the penance required for 'those who committed adulteries or rapes or fornications' (clause 10), and the other 'Similarly concerning the violation of churches' (clause 11).[75]

We only know about Odelerius's pilgrimage from Orderic's relatively laconic reference in the 1127 account of the foundation ceremony of St Peter's, Shrewsbury, in 1083. There he set out that the foundation of St Peter's was the result of a promise made by Odelerius on the altar of St Peter at Rome the year before (i.e. in 1082). The conventional

---

[69] Chibnall, *World*, p. 10.

[70] Ibid.

[71] Mason, 'The Officers', p. 253.

[72] Blair, *The Church*, pp. 361, 493, 520–1.

[73] E. van Houts, 'Intermarriage in Eleventh-Century England', in *Normandy and its Neighbours: Essays for David Bates, 900–1250*, ed. D. Crouch and K. Thompson (Turnhout, 2011), pp. 237–70.

[74] *Councils and Synods with other Documents relating to the English Church, vol. i: A.D. 871–1204*, ed. Dorothy Whitelock, Martin Brett and Christopher N. L. Brooke, 2 parts (Oxford, 1981), pt II, no. 88, pp. 581–4; trans. in R. A. Brown, *The Norman Conquest*, Documents of Medieval History 5 (London, 1984), no. 187, pp. 156–7.

[75] *Councils and Synods*, I:II, p. 584: 'De adulteriis et raptis et fornicationibus quibuscumque acsi in patria sua pecassent penitent' (clause 10); 'De violatione ecclesiarum similiter' (clause 11).

explanation is that Odelerius went to Rome on a pilgrimage, probably a penitential pilgrimage.[76] On the face of it this plausible, given that Odelerius himself, according to his son, linked a promise in Rome at the altar of St Peter to the founding of a monastery of St Peter in Shrewsbury. Clearly anyone travelling to Rome might be expected to pay a visit to St Peter's and make whatever promise about his/her future seemed opportune at the time of the visit. Promises to do penance for a grave sin were common, but far more so in England than on the Continent.[77] Perhaps Odelerius was inspired to go by what happened to his English wife.[78] Although in England priestly marriages were condemned but not forbidden, in Normandy and other parts of France they were actually prohibited, as a result of local councils. It is perhaps no surprise that Odelerius's decision came shortly after one such local council, that of Lillebonne (1080), where clerical celibacy for priests, deacons and sub-deacons was upheld.[79]

The timing of the Rome visit was a risky affair. In 1082 the city was besieged three times by the Holy Roman Emperor, Henry IV: first during the whole of Lent (9 March – 17 April) by the emperor himself, then by Wibert of Ravenna on Henry's behalf during the rest of the summer, while the emperor was in Tuscany, and for the third time in December.[80]

---

[76] Wolter, *Orderic Vitalis*, pp. 49–50, makes the link between the journey ('Reisen') and Odelerius's marriage.

[77] Robin Ann Aronstam, 'Penitential Pilgrimages to Rome in the Early Middle Ages', *Archivum Historiae Pontificae* 13 (1975), 65–83; penitential pilgrimages were particularly common in Anglo-Saxon England, see Francesca Tinti, 'England and the Papacy', in *England and the Continent in the Tenth Century: Studies in honour of Wilhelm Levison (1876–1947)*, ed. David Rollason, Conrad Leyser and Hannah Williams (Turnhout, 2010), pp. 163–84, at pp. 182–3. An Englishman who accidentally killed his son received seven years' penance from the pope.

[78] Given the year, 1082, the journey to Rome – by my reckoning – must have followed the death of his wife (perhaps in childbirth). I suggest Odelerius believed her death to be a sure sign of God's wrath about their forbidden sexual relationship.

[79] J. D. Thibodeaux, 'The Defence of Clerical Marriage: Religious Identity and Masculinity in the Writings of Anglo-Norman Clerics', in *Religious Men and Masculine Identity in the Middle Ages*, ed. P. H. Cullum and K. J. Lewis (Woodbridge, 2013), pp. 46–63; and E. van Houts, 'The Fate of Priests' Sons in Normandy, with Special Reference to Serlo of Bayeux', *HSJ* 25 (2013), 57–105, at pp. 59–63 and appendix 1, pp. 79–80.

[80] I. S. Robinson, *Henry IV of Germany, 1056–1106* (Cambridge, 1999), pp. 216–22. However, Orderic himself places Henry IV's siege of Rome in 1084, in a telescoped narrative that has survived in a section of his chronicle that is not his autograph (*HE*, IV, pp. 6–8). Orderic's erroneous dating explains why neither Orderic himself, nor his editor, Chibnall, mentions Odelerius's journey to Rome in this context.

Assuming that most journeys to Rome would have been made in the spring or early summer, Odelerius would have encountered armed forces of diverse sorts *en route* to Rome. He would not have travelled alone but would have joined other groups of travellers for mutual safety.[81] If, however, the reason for Odelerius's journey was business rather than pilgrimage, it is harder to establish a reason. It may have been connected with Earl Roger of Montgomery's refoundation of Much Wenlock (formerly a college of secular canons) c. 1079×1082, which was populated with monks for Charité-sur-Loire.[82] He may have visited this daughter house of Cluny, half-way between Orléans and Cluny, on his way to Rome.[83] Either way, it seems strange that Orderic was so reticent in regard to his father's having travelled to Rome, and never explained why he went. He does not raise the subject in his narrative of Emperor Henry IV's siege of Rome, where the siege is misdated to 1084.[84] On balance, given the context of Odelerius's actions, a penitential journey seems the most likely scenario.

The final question for consideration in this present study relates to Odelerius's preference for Saint-Évroul as the new home for his son. The monastery had been founded by members of the Giroie and Grandmesnil families, who invited monks from the abbey of Jumièges c. 1050.[85] Orderic arrived in 1085, towards the end of the abbacy of the fourth abbot Mainer (1066–89), during whose time in office some ninety monks had made

---

[81] D. Birch, *Pilgrimage to Rome in the Middle Ages: Continuity and Change* (Woodbridge, 1998), pp. 43–6, for the various routes taken from Northern France; for penitential pilgrimages, see Robin Ann Aronstam, 'Penitential Pilgrimages to Rome in the Early Middle Ages', *Archivum historiae pontificae* 13 (1975), 65–83. Note that Abbot John of Fécamp complained about robbery in Rome during his visit there c. 1050 (ed. Migne, PL 143, cols. 798–9). See also G. A. Loud, *The Age of Robert Guiscard: Southern Italy and the Norman Conquest* (Harlow, 2000), p. 115; V. Gazeau, *Normannia monastica*, vol. 2: *Prosopographie des abbés bénédictins (X^e–XIIe siècle)* (Caen, 2007), p. 107.

[82] Mason, 'Roger of Montgomery'.

[83] That is, if he went to Rome – it is possible that he never went to Rome, but that he stopped at Cluny, which had become a substitute for Rome from the mid-eleventh century as argued by Dominique Iogna-Prat, *Order and Exclusion: Cluny and Christendom Face Heresy, Judaism and Islam (1000–1150)*, trans. Graham Robert Edwards (Ithaca, NY, and London, 2002), pp. 78–84. If that is the case, 'sicut anno transacto ante aram sancti Petri principis apostolorum Romae uotum feci' does not mean 'as I vowed to do a year ago before the altar of St Peter the chief of the apostles, at Rome' (*HE*, III, pp. 146–7), but 'as I vowed to do a year ago before the altar of St Peter of Rome, the chief of the apostles.'

[84] *HE*, IV, pp. 10–11.

[85] *HE*, II, pp. 16–21. For the first abbot, Thierry de Mathonville, monk of Jumièges, see Gazeau, *Normannia monastica: Prosopographie*, pp. 273–5.

their profession.[86] According to Chibnall, the monastery was well known in Shropshire, and so may have been recommended to Odelerius.[87] Another possibility might be that Odelerius knew it through his contacts back home in Orléans. One of the most prominent monks in the time of Abbot Mainer was Geoffrey (d. 1124), prior from sometime in the 1090s to 1109, when he became abbot of Crowland in England.[88] Orderic, who knew Geoffrey well and stayed with him at Crowland in 1114,[89] described him as a Frenchman from Orléans who from boyhood had studied the liberal arts there and was deeply learned in letters. He had been attracted to Saint-Évroul 'because it was richer in holiness than in worldly wealth'.[90] Most importantly, Earl Roger of Montgomery himself was a benefactor of Saint-Évroul. In the very year that Orderic arrived (1085), and perhaps not unconnected to his arrival, the earl confirmed the possessions of the abbey. Orderic provides the text of the charter immediately following his *encomium* of the earl, his second wife, Adelaide (not named), and their son, Everard, earned because the earl had realised his own wrongdoings and those of his first wife, Mabel of Bellême, who had been murdered in her bed.[91] The conjunction of the just death of Mabel, the 1085 charter and Orderic's apology on behalf of the earl in the very year of his own arrival (although not mentioned by Orderic) suggests that the earl might have leant on his priest, Odelerius, to hand over his eldest son to Abbot Mainer as an additional sign of atonement by the extended *familia* of Montgomery.

At the end of his life, Orderic composed the final pages of his history by providing, as has been seen, his life story in his own words. Gone is the reference to any abbot, gone is the notion of obedience to his father. Here, at last, Orderic, old and tired, was his own man writing his own history as he had experienced it and lived through it emotionally. He wrote it down as he personally felt it. In the same way as his father had shed tears when he said farewell to his weeping son, so Orderic aged sixty-seven was in tears when he laid down his pen and commended himself to God. It is fair to conclude that, even as a devout monk, Orderic never shook off the sense of his father's rejection, however well it was meant.

---

[86] Chibnall, *World*, p. 17.

[87] Ibid., p. 14.

[88] Geoffrey had been prior since at least 1098, when he went to England to collect the body of Hugh of Grandmesnil for burial at Saint-Évroul (*HE*, II, pp. 336–7). Mainer made him prior fifteen years after his profession, which, counting back from 1098, makes 1083 the latest date for his profession.

[89] *HE*, II, p. xxvi.

[90] Ibid., pp. 346–9: 'Ibi nimirum quia locus idem magis religione quam diuitiis sæcularibus abundat.'

[91] Ibid., pp. 136–43, with the charter printed on pp. 138–43; and Mason, 'Roger de Montgomery and his Sons', p. 10.

Following the Master's Lead: The Script of Orderic Vitalis and the Discovery of a New Manuscript (Rouen, BM, 540)

Jenny Weston

ORDERIC Vitalis is arguably one of the most famous scribes of the twelfth century. His distinct and somewhat unusual handwriting was first identified by Léopold Delisle and has been traced in seventeen surviving manuscripts.[1] This discussion introduces an eighteenth manuscript to the corpus of books copied by Orderic – Rouen, Bibliothèque municipale 540 (*olim* U. 148) – recently discovered at the municipal library of Rouen.[2] The manuscript contains two texts by

---

I would like to thank the NWO-funded VIDI-project 'Turning Over a New Leaf: Manuscript Innovation in the Twelfth-Century Renaissance', and its principal investigator Dr Erik Kwakkel (Leiden University), for funding the research for this present chapter. I would also like to thank the Bibliothèque municipale de Rouen for authorising the publication of photos from their collection.

---

[1] Delisle first mentions the possibility that BnF, lat. 5506, I and II, and BnF, lat. 10913, are autograph copies of the *Historia ecclesiastica* in his 'Notice', p. xcv. He later confirms this view in his 'Notes sur les manuscrits autographes d'Orderic Vital', part 1 of 'Matériaux pour l'édition de Guillaume de Jumièges, préparée par Jules Lair, avec une préface et des notes par Léopold Delisle', *Bibliothèque de l'école des chartes* 71 (1910), pp. 481–526, at p. 488. Delisle also discusses autograph copies of Orderic's works in his letter to Jules Lair: 'Lettre à Mr Jules sur un exemplaire de Guillaume de Jumièges, copié par Orderic Vital', *Bibliothèque de l'école des chartes* 34 (1873), pp. 267–82. Although Delisle was the first to describe the handwriting of Orderic in relation to the autograph copies of the *Historia ecclesiastica*, Denis Escudier notes that Orderic's handwriting was originally identified in the three autographed volumes by Julien Bellaise, who created a catalogue of Saint-Évroul manuscripts in 1682. See Escudier, 'Orderic et le scriptorium', pp. 19–20. François Avril, in his catalogue of Norman manuscripts, also includes a number of books copied by Orderic, such as Rouen, BM, 1389. See F. Avril, *Manuscrits normands, XIe–XIIe siècles* (Rouen, 1975). For a comprehensive list of manuscripts containing the handwriting of Orderic see Appendix 2 in this volume, compiled by Charles Rozier and myself.

[2] The current shelfmark is Rouen, BM, 540; the ancient shelfmark is U. 148.

Anselm of Canterbury, *De libero arbitrio* and *De casu diaboli*, as well a hagiographical text on the Carolingian saint Opportuna. As this chapter will show, Rouen, BM, 540 was partly copied, rubricated, and corrected by Orderic Vitalis, probably between the years 1100 and 1142.[3] The identification of a previously unclassified manuscript featuring the handwriting of Orderic presents an opportunity to re-evaluate the scribal activities of this famous author and scribe, as well as the books he helped to copy at the abbey of Saint-Évroul in the early twelfth century. As such, the discussion of Orderic's additions to Rouen, BM, 540 will be placed within a wider review of his additions to other surviving manuscripts, and of trends within his various roles in the production and care of books at the monastery of Saint-Évroul.

This discussion begins with a brief description of the new manuscript find, Rouen, BM, 540, including an overview of the manuscript's contents, codicological profile, and the points at which Orderic's handwriting can be found. Using this newly identified manuscript as a primary example, this chapter also examines some of the distinctive qualities of his handwriting by means of a brief palaeographical overview. Despite the unique aspect of his handwriting, there are few resources currently available that specifically address his work as a copyist in the scriptorium of Saint-Évroul. To offset this gap in the current scholarship, this chapter offers a nuanced look at various letter-forms, ligatures, and abbreviations frequently used by Orderic, each accompanied by a visual example. Equipped with a better understanding of his handwriting, the final section considers the often cursory, yet prominent, nature of Orderic's scribal contributions in the books he helped to copy. While most scholars agree that Orderic spent the majority of his life at the abbey of Saint-Évroul writing and copying books, this discussion uses surviving manuscript evidence to suggest a more prominent role for Orderic in the scriptorium: the position of master scribe.

The Discovery of Rouen, BM, 540

PERHAPS the most striking characteristic of Rouen, BM, 540 is the extensive damage that affects the opening of the volume: the top half of each of the first twenty-two folios is almost entirely destroyed, and the edges of the remaining parchment are crisp and brittle to the touch.[4] At first glance, it would seem that the manuscript briefly caught fire, but upon closer inspection it seems more likely that the damage was caused by a particularly aggressive case of mould. It is believed that some of the books

---

[3] G. Nortier, *Les Bibliothèques médiévales*, p. 29.

[4] Fortunately by fol. 23v the damage fades and the remainder of the volume is fully legible.

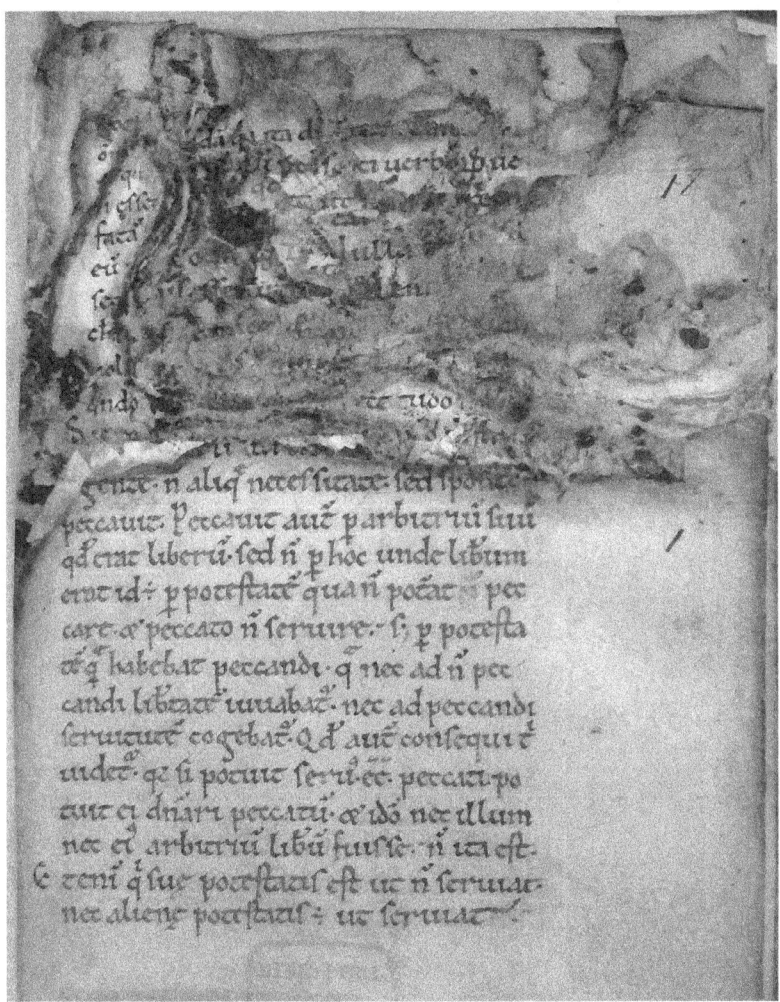

Fig. 1 Rouen, BM, 540, fol. 1r

from the Rouen library collection were stored in a cave during the French Revolution, which resulted in a number of volumes being damaged by water.[5] It is very possible that Rouen, BM, 540 was among this collection and suffered similarly. Whatever the source of injury, the opening pages of the manuscript are now very fragile and require the utmost care in handling (Fig. 1).

Beyond its disfigured opening, Rouen, BM, 540 appears to be a fairly typical early twelfth-century manuscript. It measures 165×110 mm and

[5] Betty Branch, 'The Development of Script in the Eleventh- and Twelfth-Century Manuscripts of the Norman Abbey of Fécamp' (unpublished PhD dissertation, Duke University, 1974), p. 105.

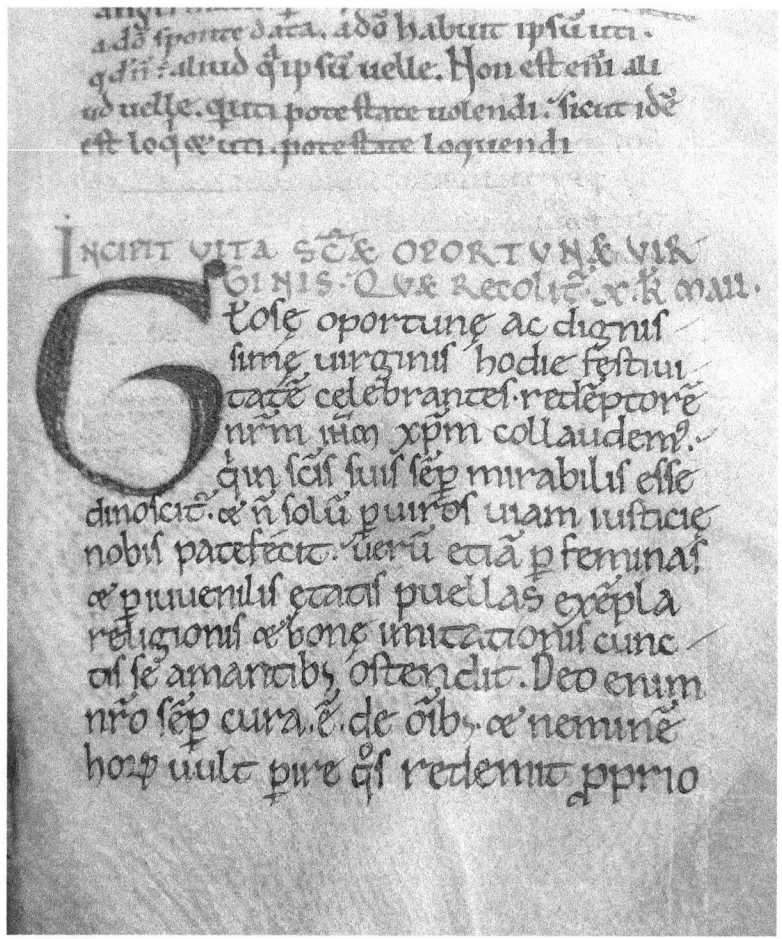

Fig. 2 Rouen, BM, 540, fol. 54r

contains three texts in sixty-seven bifolia. The first text is an incomplete copy of Anselm of Canterbury's *De libero arbitrio* (fols. 1r–14v); the second text is Anselm's *De casu diaboli* (fols. 15r–54r); and the third is a hagiographical text titled *Vitae sanctae Oportunae virginis* (fols. 54r–67v). All three texts are presented in single columns with no illumination or decoration. Certain sections have been rubricated and initials and chapter numbers have been added in various places (primarily in the first part of the book).

Rouen, BM, 540 was copied by at least three scribes. The first scribe is currently unidentified and is responsible for copying the first two texts, Anselm's *De libero arbitrio* and *De casu diaboli* (fols. 1r–54r collectively). On fol. 54r (Fig. 2), at the opening of the *Vitae sanctae Oportunae virginis*, Orderic briefly takes over and begins to copy the main text block. On this page he adds the large initial **G** (for *Gloriosae*), the rubricated *incipit*

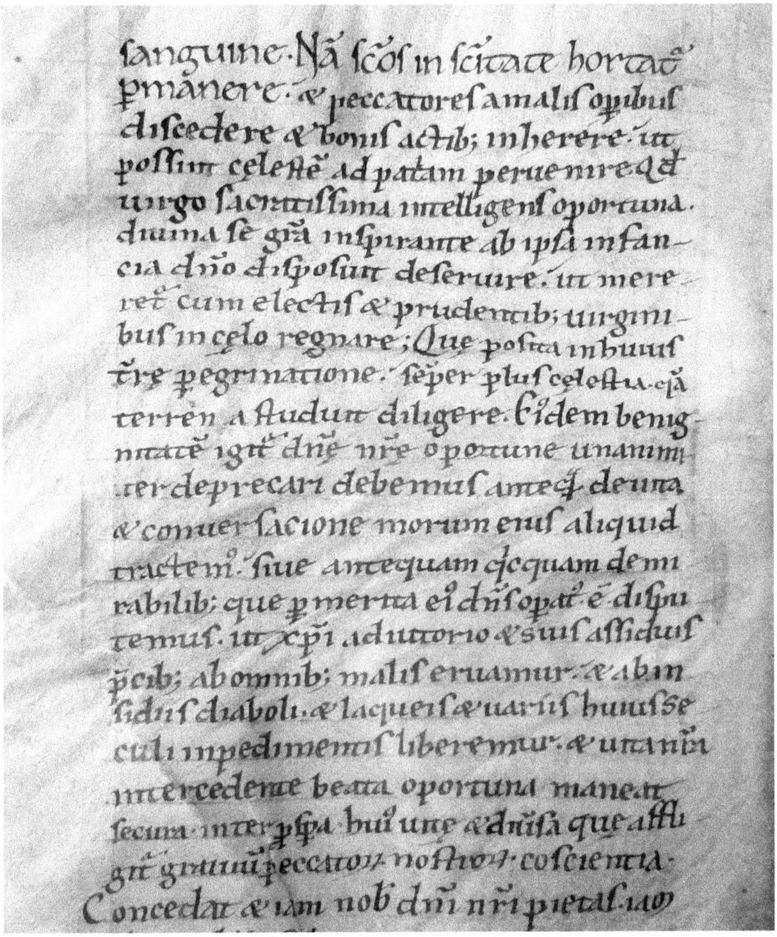

Fig. 3 Rouen, BM 540, fol. 54v

heading (two lines) and the first thirteen and a half lines of the text – twelve lines on fol. 54r and one and a half lines on fol. 54v. At the top of the verso (fol. 54v, Fig. 3) Orderic stops copying after the word 'permanere', at which point a different scribe takes over. Orderic then returns to add the rubricated *explicit* for the prologue and the following initial **S**, on fol. 55v.

In addition to the opening lines of the *Vitae sanctae Oportunae* on fols. 54r–v, and the *explicit* on fol. 55v, Orderic makes various other additions and corrections to the manuscript.[6] In the last section of Anselm's *De casu diaboli*, immediately preceding the opening of the *Vitae sanctae Oportunae* (fol. 54r), for example, Orderic copies one and a

---

[6] For more details on Orderic's contribution to Rouen, BM, 540, see Appendix 2, item 14.

half lines of text: 'd[eu]s sponte dat, s[ed] etia[m] quod iniuste rapit deo'. Early in the volume, he also adds corrections to Anselm's *De casu diaboli*: on fol. 26r, for example, it is possible that Orderic supplies an in-text correction over an erasure, adding the word 'alitate' and then, one line lower, the word 'sed'. On fol. 46v Orderic corrects the text by supplying a portion of missing text in the margin, which had been accidentally skipped by the original scribe. Slightly less certain are Orderic's potential additions to fol. 65r, where he may have added three lines of text (fourteen lines from the top), beginning with 'tanto maiora' and ending with 's[an]c[t]a int[er]cessione', as well as a possible marginal correction found on fol. 67v, presented in the abbreviated word 'templum'. A third unidentified scribe is responsible for copying the main text for the final folios of the manuscript (fols. 54v–67v).

Currently, the suggested origin of Rouen, BM, 540 is the scriptorium of l'Abbaye de la Trinité de Fécamp, a Benedictine house located on the coast of Normandy. This Fécamp provenance was first proposed by the French palaeographer Geneviève Nortier and later affirmed by Betty Branch, though it is unclear if Branch makes her judgment independently of Nortier.[7] In her 1974 study of Fécamp manuscripts, Branch provides very limited information about Rouen, BM, 540, only noting that it originated from the abbey of Fécamp, which suggests that she may not have actually examined the manuscript *in situ*.[8] The presence of Orderic's handwriting in the volume, however, suggests a more likely origin in the scriptorium at the abbey of Saint-Évroul.

It is currently unknown how the manuscript came to be listed as a product of Fécamp, though there are a number of possibilities to account for its current classification. For example, the manuscript may have been copied at Saint-Évroul, then later lent or donated to the nearby abbey of Fécamp. It is well known that an extensive network of book lending and borrowing existed between Benedictine abbeys in Normandy during the eleventh and twelfth centuries, witnessed through surviving letter collections (many of which feature abbots and monks requesting books from neighbouring houses to make copies).[9] It is also possible, though somewhat less likely, that Orderic travelled to the abbey of Fécamp and copied the manuscript there. This is less probable, however, given the fact that most monks were prohibited from leaving their home-monastery unless on essential business. That said, Orderic was granted permission

---

[7] Nortier, *Les Bibliothèques médiévales*, pp. 26–30; Betty Branch, 'Inventories of the Library of Fécamp from the Eleventh and Twelfth Century', *Manuscripta* 23 (1979), 159–72, at p. 165; Branch, 'The Development of Script', p. 159.

[8] Ibid.

[9] See, for example, Anselm of Canterbury's surviving correspondence, *The Letters of Saint Anselm of Canterbury*, trans. Walter Frölich (Kalamazoo, MI, 1990), esp. at pp. 95–7, 119.

from his superiors to make a number of short trips during his career as a monk. For example, Delisle and Chibnall observe that he travelled to France in 1105, and to the abbey of Croiland [Crowland] in England in 1115; he was potentially a participant at the council of Reims in 1119; and he attended a religious reunion at the basilica of Cluny in 1132.[10] However, there is no evidence to suggest that Orderic spent any time at the abbey of Fécamp, or that he made any special trips to copy manuscripts for the benefit of neighbouring communities. Despite the fact that Orderic travelled on occasion, it seems more likely that the manuscript was copied at Saint-Évroul and later given or lent to the community at Fécamp.

Nortier dated the production of Rouen, BM, 540 to a broad period of c. 1100–1200.[11] Branch provides a slightly narrower date range of 1075–1150, which spans the collective abbacies of three Fécamp leaders: John of Ravenna (1028–78), Roger of Argences (1108–39), and Henry of Sully (1139–87).[12] This date range, however, is somewhat dependent on the assumption that the manuscript was produced at the abbey of Fécamp during a period of high-intensity manuscript production.[13] Based on palaeographical grounds, as well as the presence of Orderic's handwriting throughout the manuscript (providing a *terminus ad quem* of 1142), it is most likely that Rouen, BM, 540 was produced sometime between 1100 and 1142.

Until now, Orderic's contribution to Rouen, BM, 540 has been consistently overlooked by scholars working in the field of Orderic manuscript studies. Currently, Rouen, BM, 540 is not listed in any of the books related to his scribal work, among them Léopold Delisle's original list of manuscripts, Marjorie Chibnall's expanded list of manuscripts copied or annotated by Orderic (presented as an appendix to her edition of the *Historia ecclesiastica*), the articles devoted to Orderic's life and work at Saint-Évroul by Denis Escudier, and the catalogue of Norman manuscripts prepared by François Avril (where he specifically addresses Orderic's hand in various other manuscript examples).[14]

It is possible that Rouen, BM, 540's exclusion from the corpus of Orderic manuscripts stems from its current classification as a product of the abbey of Fécamp, as opposed to the abbey of Saint-Évroul. Given the fact that all of the other currently identified Orderic manuscripts are attributed a Saint-Évroul provenance, previous scholars may not have felt

---

[10] Delisle, 'Notice', p. xxxvi; Chibnall, 'General Introduction', pp. 25–7.

[11] Nortier, *Les Bibliothèques médiévales*, p. 29.

[12] Branch, 'The Development of Script', p. 159.

[13] See Branch, 'Inventories of the Library of Fécamp', p. 165.

[14] Chibnall, 'General Introduction', pp. 1–112, and the appendix 'Manuscripts Copied or Annotated by Orderic', in *HE*, I, pp. 201–3; Delisle, 'Matériaux', pp. 486–7; Escudier, 'Orderic et le scriptorium', pp. 17–28; Avril, *Manuscrits normands*.

the need to expand their search for books to other Benedictine collections. Indeed, the discovery of Rouen, BM, 540 in the collection of Fécamp was largely the result of a chance encounter. The original purpose of the research was to document the presence of navigational reading aids in the manuscripts produced at Fécamp in the twelfth century, and it was only by happenstance that I noticed the presence of Orderic's handwriting on fol. 54r.

It is also possible that previous scholars may have examined Rouen, BM, 540 *in situ* but simply did not recognise the handwriting of Orderic. Had they seen it themselves, there is no doubt that Chibnall, Delisle, Escudier, Avril and others who have spent time working with manuscripts copied by Orderic would have easily identified his work in Rouen, BM, 540. Other scholars, such as Nortier and Branch, may not have been familiar with Orderic's handwriting, and may have simply missed his contribution to the volume. It is important to note that the ability to identify Orderic's handwriting is not just useful for those studying his scribal activities, but can also be important for those examining his role as historian, author and monk. Pin-pointing Orderic's contributions to particular volumes and texts, for instance, may reveal further evidence of his various intellectual and literary pursuits. As demonstrated by Rozier in this present volume, Orderic's substantial scribal contributions to the Saint-Évroul annals (BnF, Lat. 10062) may help to confirm his scholarly interest in the history of the abbey and its community – an argument that derives from the ability to identify Orderic's handwriting in the surviving manuscript evidence.[15] Therefore, in order to facilitate further study of Orderic's work as a copyist, the following section presents an introductory palaeographical overview of his handwriting, including images of select letter-forms, ligatures and abbreviations for easy reference.[16]

---

[15] See Charles Rozier's chapter in this present volume.

[16] All visual samples created by J. Weston. Each visual example is traced directly from digital photographs taken of previously identified examples of Orderic's work.

The Script and Handwriting of Orderic Vitalis

Like most early twelfth-century scribes in Western Europe, Orderic's script might best be described as 'pre-gothic' or 'proto-gothic'.[17] This form of script is based primarily on Caroline minuscule, the dominant script used in Western Europe from the late eighth century to the late eleventh century. It also features a growing number of 'new features' that are now recognised as emerging elements of the later 'gothic script', the most popular form of bookhand used in Western Europe by the early thirteenth century.[18]

In the most basic terms, pre-gothic script tends to be slightly more angular than its earlier Caroline counterpart, with the feet at minims often flicking out to the right, frequent abbreviations, and the gradual merging of certain letter-forms, such as **pp** and **de**. To be clear, it is not actually Orderic's *script* that makes him stand out from other scribes of the period – he follows many conventions of the pre-gothic form – but rather his individual presentation of the standard letter-forms, ligatures, and abbreviations. Essentially speaking, it is Orderic's *handwriting* that is different: the subtle, personalised elements that he adds to each stroke of his pen.

Perhaps the best place to begin is with the general appearance (or *aspect*) of Orderic's handwriting as a whole. Ever since Delisle first suggested that the three surviving volumes of the *Historia ecclesiastica* are, in fact, autograph copies, scholars have attempted to capture the general essence of Orderic's style.[19] While such descriptions tend to be rather vague, they nonetheless provide a good place to start. In a published letter to Jules Lair, Delisle presents a brief description of Orderic's handwriting as presented in the interpolated copy of William of Jumièges' *Gesta Normannorum ducum* now contained in Rouen, BM, 1174 (Y. 14). Here Delisle notes that Orderic's letters are firm and clear ('ferme et nette'), with a special quality that make Orderic's work stand out from other scribes of the same period.[20] He also observes a slight inconsistency in Orderic's writing, which distinguishes him from other scribes who

---

[17] This form of script has been described in various different ways, including 'Late Caroline' and 'Primitive Gothic'. See Albert Derolez, *The Palaeography of Gothic Manuscript Books: From the Twelfth to the Early Sixteenth Century* (Cambridge, 2003), p. 57.

[18] Derolez, *The Palaeography of Gothic Manuscript Books*, pp. 56–71; Erik Kwakkel, 'Biting, Kissing and the Treatment of Feet: The Transitional Script of the Long Twelfth Century', in *Turning Over a New Leaf: Change and Development in the Medieval Book*, ed. E. Kwakkel, R. McKitterick and R. Thomson (Leiden, 2012), pp. 79–125.

[19] Delisle, 'Matériaux', pp. 487–9.

[20] Delisle, 'Lettre à M. Jules Lair', p. 270; Escudier, 'Orderic et le scriptorium', p. 20.

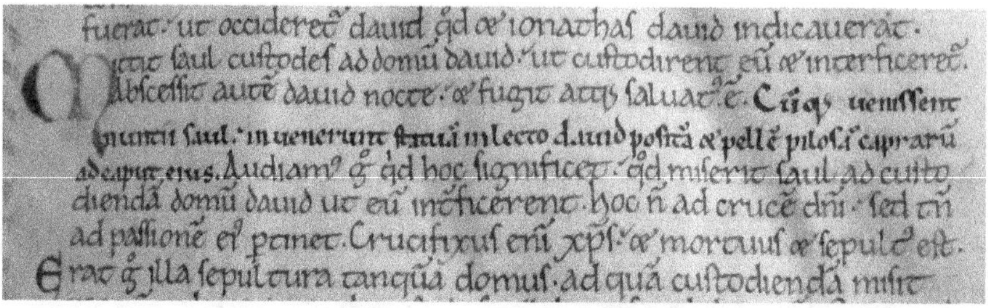

Fig. 4 Rouen, BM, 1174, fol. 11r

somehow managed to copy books comparable to printed versions.[21] In a separate article Delisle also notes an English quality (or 'Saxon' character) to Orderic's letter-forms, which may reflect his training in England as a boy.[22] Writing somewhat later, Denis Escudier provides another general overview, noting the lack of linearity in Orderic's letters (due to a seeming reluctance to observe formal ruling), the fineness of certain strokes, and the often cluttered feel of the text – the result of ascenders getting tangled with descenders dropping down from the line above.[23]

This distinctive 'tangle-effect' is often brought on by the large size of Orderic's letter-forms. Unlike other Norman scribes in this period, who tend to compress their letters, Orderic's letters are tall, wide, and round. This over-sized and extra-round quality creates a style of writing that stands out in comparison to the rather sober work of other contemporary scribes. In manuscripts that feature Orderic working in collaboration with other scribes, the generous height and width of his letters are particularly noticeable. For example, on fol. 11r of Rouen, BM, 1174 (Fig. 4) one can easily see the contrast between Orderic's hand, presented in light brown ink, and that of another scribe, presented in black ink. The second scribe's handwriting is clearly compressed in comparison to Orderic's, leaving a stark white space above the line of text.

The wide aspect of Orderic's writing also tends to limit the number of words he can fit onto a line. For example, in Rouen, BM, 31, fol. 41v, he tends to fit approximately nine or ten words onto a single line. In the middle of the folio a different scribe temporarily takes over, writing in a far smaller and more compressed style. This scribe is able to fit approximately fifteen words onto the line, ruled at the same length.

While it is important to acknowledge that Orderic's letters are firm, clear, fine, tall, wide, and round, such descriptions can be difficult to visualise. What might look 'clear' to Delisle, for example, might look tangled to another. To really become familiar with the nuances of Orderic's

---

[21] Delisle, 'Lettre à M. Jules Lair', p. 270; Escudier, 'Orderic et le scriptorium', p. 20.

[22] Delisle refers to Alençon, BM, 14 in 'Matériaux', p. 503.

[23] Escudier, 'Orderic et le scriptorium', p. 21.

handwriting, it is best to examine the specific letter-forms, ligatures and abbreviations that contribute to the overall appearance of his work. These features can often be described in far more tangible and objective terms, and once learned they can be easily recognised in surviving manuscript examples.

The following section presents a representative selection of Orderic's letter-forms, ligatures, abbreviations and symbols that I believe are most distinctive and recognisable. This overview is not meant to serve as a conclusive or comprehensive survey of Orderic's handwriting, but instead aims to present a general introduction to some common characteristics of his work.[24] As Delisle noted above, Orderic's writing tends to be firm and clear, but not adverse to variation. For this reason, when trying to identify Orderic's handwriting it is important to examine more than one letter-form or abbreviation, as it is often the collected ensemble of features that makes his work stand out so dramatically, and which ultimately points to Orderic as the scribe.

There are also a number of manuscripts (BnF, Lat. 10062, Rouen, BM, 456 and Rouen, BM, 461, for example) that feature a hand very similar to that of Orderic, and that may have been copied by a scribe trained by Orderic himself.[25] In some cases it can be a challenge to discern the difference between Orderic and this otherwise unknown 'copy-cat' scribe. The striking similarity even made Chibnall doubt the copy-cat's existence: she posits that the slight differences may simply be the result of Orderic changing pens or suffering from hand-cramps. Whether the mysterious Orderic protégé exists or not, it is important to pay attention not only to the general form and style of individual letters, ligatures and abbreviations, but also to the precise way in which they are executed.

---

[24] This present overview excludes Orderic's use of majuscule and capital letter-forms. However, Orderic often used these forms for *incipit* and *explicit* headings and for rubricating the texts he helped to copy. For examples, see BnF, lat. 10913, fol. 457r–v; and BnF, lat. 12131, fols. 1r–82v (Appendix 2, below, items 8 and 11).

[25] For example, Chibnall notes that BnF, lat. 5506, II (Appendix 2, item 7), may have been partially copied by a scribe trained by Orderic, but also notes that the change in aspect may be the result of Orderic changing pens. See Chibnall, 'General Introduction', pp. xxxix–xl, 118 n. 2.

Description of Orderic's Hand: Letter-Forms and Ligatures

Letter a

Orderic primarily uses an uncial form of the letter **a**. The letter features a single compartment that appears oval and slightly compacted; the top of the compartment is often thinner in duct than the lower portion of the compartment. The shaft of the letter is nearly upright, but it can also lean to the left slightly. In some cases the head of the shaft curves to the left in an arch (1), and in other cases it ends just above the compartment (sometimes with a small vertical stub), making the shaft almost appear as a minim (2).[26]

a a
(1) (2)

Letter d

Orderic uses two forms of the letter **d** interchangeably: a straight form (half-uncial) and an uncial form.[27] The straight form features a vertical ascender with a fork or club at the top, as well as a curved bowl for the round compartment, which begins slightly adjacent to the vertical stroke. This gap is closed with a short horizontal stroke, creating a noticeable flat top on the compartment of the letter (1).

The uncial form of the letter **d** appears rounder, and comprises a single stroke forming the minim and the compartment in one movement. Occasionally the ascender of the minim leans over to the left, though this is not always the case (2). Orderic sometimes uses both forms in a single word.[28]

d δ
(1) (2)

Letter g; Ligature -ga

Orderic uses a form of the letter **g** that features a single rounded compartment and a curved descender with a small hook or club at the end (1). There is also a long horizontal flag extending from the right of the compartment, which often forms a ligature with the following letter (especially if the following letter features a rounded compartment, such

---

[26] For further details about the formation of the letter **a** in pregothic script, see Derolez, *The Palaeography of Gothic Manuscript Books*, p. 60.

[27] Orderic's use of two forms of the letter **d** is also noted in Escudier, 'Orderic et le scriptorium', p. 21.

[28] See, for example, the name 'David' in Rouen, BM, 1174, fol. 111r.

as an **a**, **e** or **o** (2). Perhaps the most distinctive feature of the **g** – and a key identifying feature – is that the descender is nearly horizontal before it curves and extends below the line.

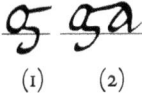

(1) (2)

Letter m

Orderic favours a form of the letter **m** that consists of three minims, all with very sharp and angular feet flicking upwards to the right. There is often a small club or flag at the top of the first minim. His connecting strokes between the minims are curved and smooth.

Letter p

Orderic uses two forms of the letter **p**. The first form features a long descender with a club at the top and a small foot on the minim, often presented at a slight angle. The compartment of the letter features a sharp upwards angle at the top and the compartment itself is slightly squashed (1). The second form of the letter **p** features a long descender with a club at the top, but no foot on the minim. The sharp angle of the compartment is still visible in this form (2).

(1) (2)

Letter q

Orderic uses a form for the letter **q** that features a single compartment with a horizontal top. The compartment is formed in two strokes: first Orderic creates the rounded bowl, in the shape of the letter **u**, and then he fills in the space with a horizontal stroke, creating a flat top to the compartment. On occasion Orderic adds a small foot or club to the descender.

Letter r; Ligature -ra

Orderic's style of the letter **r** features a short vertical stroke with a small club at the top of the minim and a small foot at the bottom flicked upwards. The second stroke is very angular and features an extended flag, flicked upwards to the right (1). Depending on the subsequent letter, this flag can extend directly into a ligature (most typically the ligatures -ra and -re) (2).

r̂ ra
(1) (2)

Letter s; Ligature -st

Orderic uses both a long-form (half-uncial) letter s, and an uncial version.²⁹ The long-form s consists of a tall minim stroke with a flag at the mid-point on the left-hand side. There is also a small curved stroke at the top of the minim and a small foot at the bottom flicking upwards (1). In most texts Orderic chooses to use this long form for the letter s, especially at the beginning and in the middle of words. On occasion he uses the uncial s, almost always as the last letter of a word (2). Orderic's -st ligature features a tall curving stroke connecting the ascender of the long s and the ascender of the minuscule t (3). All forms of Orderic's letter s tend to stand on the line, a feature typical of pre-gothic script.³⁰

ſ s ſt
(1) (2) (3)

Letter t; Ligature -ta

Orderic favours a style of the letter t that features a single curved stroke to form the shaft of the letter, and a crossing horizontal stroke. The top of the shaft is often visible sticking up just above the horizontal stroke (1). The horizontal stroke can also be extended to form a ligature with the next letter (especially if the following letter is an a, o or i) (2).

t ta
(1) (2)

Letter x

Orderic uses a form for the letter x that consists of two curved strokes. The first stroke extends far below the line and features a small flag or club. The second stroke is more steeply curved and stays well above the line. The top portion of this second stroke is noticeably thick while the lower portion is much finer.

---

[29] Orderic's use of two forms of the letter s is also noted in Escudier, 'Orderic et le scriptorium', p. 21.

[30] Derolez, *The Palaeography of Gothic Manuscript Books*, p. 61.

Ligature -et (ampersand)

Unlike some twelfth-century scribes, Orderic continues to use the ampersand as the ligature for 'et', as opposed to a tironian note. Orderic uses two distinct forms of the ampersand. The first version features two compartments with a short stroke extending downwards from the lower compartment. At the mid-point of this descending stroke, a longer ascending stroke emerges with a small fork at the top. There is a noticeable space between the double compartments and the beginning of the ascending stroke (1). The second version also features two compartments, though they lean slightly to the right, and the ascending stroke emerges at the mid-point of the two compartments, and not at the mid-point of the descending stroke. In this second version there is no space between the double compartment and the beginning of the ascending stroke (2).

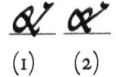

(1) (2)

Orderic uses these two forms of the ampersand interchangeably in the manuscripts he copies.[31] For example, in the autograph *Historia ecclesiastica* now contained in BnF, Lat. 5506, I (Prologue and Books I–II), he uses the second version (2). In the second volume of the *Historia ecclesiastica*, BnF, Lat. 5506, II (Books III–VI), he uses the first version (1) (see Appendix 2, items 6 and 7). In Rouen, BM, 1343, he uses both versions (Appendix 2, item 16).[32]

Description of Orderic's Hand: Abbreviations and Symbols

General Abbreviation

Orderic uses a general abbreviation symbol to signify that a word has been altered in some way (usually signifying a missing letter **m** or a contraction of some kind). He places this abbreviation symbol above the section of the word affected. It consists of a single angular stroke with a small curved bowl in the centre and a slight fork or club on the top right.

---

[31] Manuscripts featuring the first version of the ampersand include: Rouen, BM, 1174, and Rouen, BM, 31; Manuscripts featuring the second version of the ampersand include: BnF, lat. 5506, I; Rouen, BM, 1376; Alençon, BM, 6; and Alençon, BM, 26.

[32] For fols. 1–129v, Orderic uses the first version of the ampersand (with a clear space). However, towards the end of the manuscript, particularly in the section containing the works of Severus Sulpicius, he tends to use the second version (without a space). See, for example, fol. 130v.

Abbreviation -orum

Orderic uses a rather elaborate abbreviation for the Latin ending '-orum' (typically found on plural second-declension nouns in the genitive form).[33] This abbreviation consists of three parts: the first is the letter **o**, attached to the letter **r**, which connects to two compartments and a long descender with an angular foot on the minim.

Abbreviation -us

For the abbreviated Latin ending '-us', typically found on second- and fourth-declension nouns in the nominative (and sometimes accusative) form, Orderic attaches a small swirl to the last letter of the word. The placement of the swirl depends on the specific letter, but it usually begins at the top right of the preceding letter. In cases where the letter **l** precedes the abbreviation, the swirl is directly attached to the minim of the letter. The image presented here shows the '-us' abbreviation on the letter **p**.

Abbreviation -ibus

For the Latin ending '-ibus', typically found on third- and fourth-declension dative/ablative plural nouns, Orderic presents a long stroke tracing an ogee curve at the mid-point following the letters **i** and **b** (presented in their regular form). The final stroke typically extends slightly below the bottom line. This abbreviation presents similar features to the '-ibus' abbreviation commonly used in Italy during this period, which often took the form of a 'narrow letter s'.[34]

---

[33] This abbreviation is also briefly discussed in Escudier, 'Orderic et le scriptorium', p. 21, and Delisle, 'Lettre à M. Jules Lair', p. 270.

[34] Derolez, *The Palaeography of Gothic Manuscript Books*, p. 68.

Abbreviation -ue

Orderic uses an abbreviation for the letters '-ue' that is very similar to his abbreviation for the Latin ending '-ibus'. This abbreviation also features a long ogee curve, but the mark is positioned higher on the line, and typically does not extend below the line. The preceding letter is almost always the letter q, to make the common Latin ending '-que'.

Abbreviation -ur

For the Latin ending '-ur', common for third person, passive and deponent verbs, Orderic uses a symbol that is very similar to his general abbreviation mark. To distinguish the '-ur' ending, however, he adds a small curl to the bottom of the stroke, and it is very often found above the letter t.

Paragraph Mark

One of the most distinct and recognisable features of Orderic's script is his presentation of the paragraph mark. There are various different styles of paragraph mark used by Western European scribes in the early twelfth century, though most derive from a simple presentation of two strokes: a vertical stroke and a horizontal stroke meeting at the axis point. In many of the manuscripts Orderic copies this simple stroke has been embellished into what looks like modern bubble lettering, where Orderic adds additional strokes and bobbles.[35] In some cases he begins with the simple presentation of the paragraph mark (simple vertical and horizontal lines attached), and then later, when rubricating the manuscript, he adds in the additional embellishment strokes.

---

[35] For examples of Orderic's paragraph mark, see BnF, lat. 5506, I, fols. 12v, 47r (Appendix 2, item 6); BnF, lat. 5506, II, fols. 36r, 43r (Appendix 2, item 7); Rouen, BM, 1343, fols. 44r, 51r, 120r (Appendix 2, item 16); Rouen, BM, 1376, fol. 43v (Appendix 2, item 17); and BnF, lat. 10913, fols. 42v, 102v, 327r, and 483r (Appendix 2, item 8).

Orderic as Master Scribe

THERE is little doubt that Orderic spent a great part of his life working in the scriptorium at the abbey of Saint-Évroul. The fact that he copied so many books, composed one of the most well-known histories of the church (the *Historia ecclesiastica*) and provided a redacted edition of William of Jumièges' *Gesta Normannorum ducum* has led some to believe that Orderic may have worked as master of the Saint-Évroul scriptorium.[36] While it is clear that he was, indeed, a prolific copyist and a talented author, these activities in themselves do not necessarily prove that he also performed the role of scriptorium master – instructing novice scribes, reviewing copies of books, making corrections, ordering new volumes, and overseeing book-production. To better determine whether or not Orderic served as master scribe at Saint-Évroul, we can turn our attention back to the manuscript evidence, with a particular focus on the 'new' manuscript discovery, Rouen, BM, 540.

As noted above, in this new example Orderic begins copying the opening lines of the *Vita Sanctae Oportunae virginis* on fol. 54r. On this folio, he copies the large initial **G**, the rubricated *incipit*, and twelve lines of main text. At the top of the following verso, fol. 54v, he adds another one and a half lines, at which point another scribe takes over. This second scribe copies the remainder of the *Vita* text, though Orderic returns to add the rubricated *explicit* on fol. 55v. The brevity of Orderic's contribution is notable, yet based on other manuscript examples, not particularly unusual. In various manuscripts that feature Orderic working in collaboration with other scribes, he often copies the opening folios, and after only a few pages, or even a few lines in some cases, another scribe takes over to fill in the bulk of the text. In Rouen, BM, 31, for example, Orderic only copies the opening pages of the *Liber pontificalis*, fols. 9r–15v, before handing the work over to a second scribe. He then returns to the manuscript to copy the opening lines of Ambrose's *Expositio de psalmo* (fol. 41r), but ends mid-sentence (fol. 41v), at which point a different hand takes over (Appendix 2, item 13). Similarly in Rouen, BM, 1174, between fols. 1r and 110v Orderic copies only short sections, most often beginning at the opening of a new text, directly after the large initial (Appendix 2, item 15); in Alençon, BM, 6, Orderic begins the verse *Life* of St Launomar on fol. 143v, but hands over the page to other scribes by fol. 145v. Like in Rouen, BM, 31, he then returns to the manuscript and copies the opening section of the *Passion* of Saints Neureus and Achilles (fols. 150r–151v): he copies the whole first page, as well as the *incipit*, but again a different scribe soon takes over (fol. 151v) and finishes the remainder of the text (Appendix 2, item 2).

---

[36] Chibnall, *World*, pp. 33–4; Escudier, 'Orderic et le scriptorium', p. 24. See also discussions by Rozier in the present volume.

Fig. 5 Rouen, BM, 540, fol. 54v

Such examples seem to show Orderic prompting the text, perhaps offering layout and script samples for others to imitate, and ensuring that the opening of the new text was started properly, before handing over the responsibility to other, perhaps less-experienced, scribes.[37] The idea that Orderic deliberately copied the opening sections of texts to serve as a model is strengthened by the fact that he often starts and stops copying at very visible places in the manuscript. When other medieval scribes worked together to copy a manuscript, it was common for them to try to mask their collaboration by switching hands as discretely as possible – often at the end of a text or at the bottom of a folio.[38] In contrast, when Orderic works with other scribes he makes certain that his handwriting is easily visible to the subsequent copyist by stopping at the top of the folio or in the middle of a sentence.

In the new manuscript discovery (Rouen, BM, 540), for example, Orderic does not stop copying the *Vita* text at the bottom of fol. 54r, allowing the subsequent scribe to discreetly pick up at the top of the next page, but instead he carries on to the verso, copying another line and a half (Fig. 5). By choosing to end his contribution at the top of the verso in the middle of the line, as opposed to the bottom of the preceding page, Orderic ensures that his handwriting is in view for the remainder of the page.

As it turns out, this very conspicuous end-point in Rouen, BM, 540 is not unique in the manuscripts that Orderic helped to copy. In Rouen, BM, 31, for example, he copies the opening folios of the *Liber pontificalis*, fols. 9r–15v, as mentioned above. He then abruptly ends his contribution at the top of fol. 15v ('patenam auream', Fig. 6), after copying hardly more than a line of text – presenting an almost identical scenario to Rouen, BM, 540.

---

[37] This scenario is also briefly mentioned by Chibnall in the introduction to her appendix. See *HE*, I, p. 201.

[38] For an example, see Avranches, BM, 225, fol. 49v. In this twelfth-century manuscript the first scribe finishes copying at the end of a text, and the second scribe begins his copying stint at the opening of the following text.

Fig. 6 Rouen, BM, 31, fol. 15v

If one was to look at either Rouen, BM, 540 or Rouen, BM, 31 independently, one might not notice anything out of the ordinary; perhaps one would assume that Orderic's unusual end-point in the middle of a sentence was an error or one-time phenomenon. With the newly discovered Rouen, BM, 540 placed next to Rouen, BM, 31, however, we quickly see evidence of an intentional scribal technique. It seems that Orderic consciously chose to copy only a few opening lines of text, ending on the verso of the folio, at which point he hands the page over to another scribe.

Naturally, Orderic's decision to stop copying at such a visible place on the page still requires explanation. One possibility is that he wished to provide an easily-referenced script sample for the following scribes to emulate. By carrying the text over to the verso of the folio, Orderic makes sure that his handwriting is easily visible; the second scribe does not have to awkwardly flip back and forth between the recto and verso in order to see the master's style of script and handwriting. It is important to note, however, that in both Rouen, BM, 540 and Rouen, BM, 31 the scribe that follows Orderic has a style of handwriting noticeably different from that of the alleged master. In Rouen, BM, 540, for example, the subsequent hand displays letter-forms that are smaller and more compressed; in Rouen, BM, 31 several hands follow Orderic's contribution, none of which feature overtly similar characteristics to the master's hand. If Orderic intended to leave a script sample at the top of the page, it seems that the novices under his charge were not paying very close attention. It is also possible that the subsequent scribes were not novices at all, but experienced copyists already trained to shape their letter-forms independently from the master's unique style. Even if Orderic was the master of the Saint-Évroul scriptorium, it is not beyond the realm of possibility that he chose to collaborate with mature scribes for the official copying of library books, as opposed to using these books as an opportunity to develop a beginner's skill with the pen.

It is also possible that Orderic felt that the top of the verso was an easier place to transition from one scribe to another, as it may have limited the possibility of accidentally skipping words or phrases during the switch. This potential for 'eye-skip' was particularly an issue for scribes making the transition between the recto and verso of the folio, where words can easily get lost as the page is turned. By stopping at the top of the verso, either mid-line or mid-sentence, Orderic would have better enabled the subsequent scribe to pick up the text seamlessly where he left

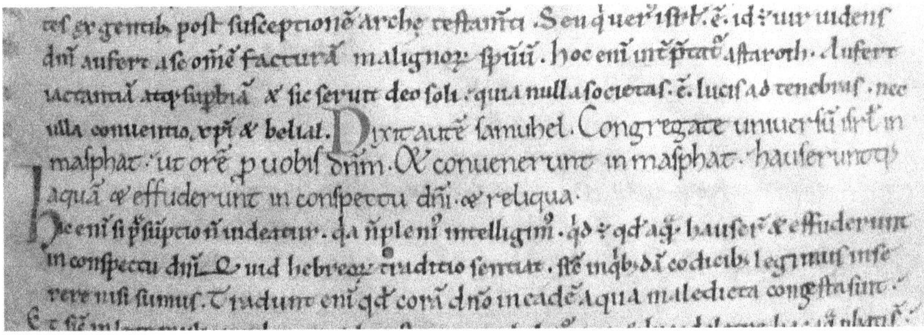

Fig. 7 Rouen, BM, 1174, fol. 3r

off, lessening the potential for eye-skip during the transition. Orderic's cautious approach to scribal transition, and the fact that he was regularly responsible for copying the opening pages of new texts, suggest a significant degree of leadership and point to Orderic as the master of the Saint-Évroul scriptorium.

Just as he clearly expressed an interest in making sure that the text was properly initiated, there is further evidence to suggest that Orderic did not stray very far while another scribe worked on the manuscript. As noted above, in Rouen, BM, 540, Orderic copies the first thirteen and a half lines of the prologue, after which a different scribe takes over. Orderic returns, however, on fol. 55v to supply the rubricated *explicit* for the prologue. A similar example can be found in Rouen, BM, 31, fol. 15v, where Orderic handed over the text to be finished by another scribe. He returns, however, to copy the opening pages of the following text, Ambrose's *Expositio de psalmo*, fol. 41r–v, ending mid-sentence on fol. 41v. He briefly returns again to copy fols. 44r–45r, at which point he stops, again mid-line, and allows another to finish the text. He also copies short sections intermittently throughout the first hundred folios of Rouen, BM, 1174 (fols. 1r–100v). Examples of these various exchanges can be found on fols. 3r–v (Fig. 7), 4r, 8r–9v, 11r–12v, 14r, and 19r–20r.[39]

This back and forth between Orderic and other scribes – evident in Rouen, BM, 31, Rouen, BM, 540, and Rouen, BM, 1174 – suggests that when collaborating with other scribes, Orderic does not simply give the book to another to finish, but instead remains involved in the copying process, returning on occasion to supply various lines. The recurrence of Orderic's hand in the manuscripts he copies, even once another scribe has taken over, gives the strong impression of a watchful master, looking over the shoulder of his fellow scribes as they write, and even intervening on occasion.

In many books that Orderic helped to copy, he can also be found supplying in-text and marginal corrections. These further support the

---

[39] Another example is Rouen, BM, 1174, fol. 8v, where Orderic interjects four times over the course of a single folio (Appendix 2, item 15).

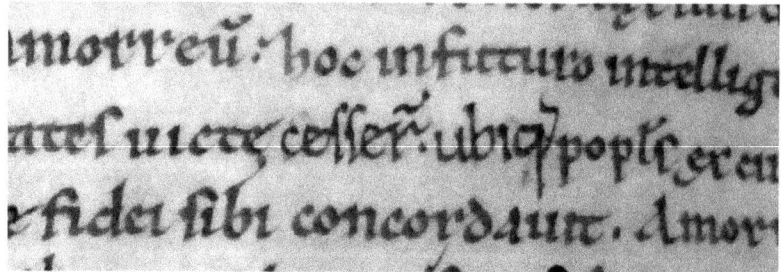

Fig. 8 Rouen, BM, 1174, fol. 3v

claim that he functioned as scriptorium master.[40] Out of the eighteen currently known manuscripts that feature Orderic's handwriting, eleven books witness Orderic working as a corrector in some capacity.[41] It is often easy to overlook his corrections, particularly in cases where he only supplies a single word over an erasure.[42] With a closer look, however, the unique aspect of Orderic's handwriting inevitably betrays his presence. An example of this can be seen in Fig. 8, where Orderic has added a correction over an erasure ('cesser[um] ubiq[ue]').

In other examples Orderic's corrections are more noticeable, such as those instances where he supplies additions and portions of missing text in the margins of the page. In Rouen, BM, 540, for example, he supplies a missing section of text in the margin of Anselm's *De casu diaboli*, fol. 46v ('M. At tanto iustior erat quanto magis volebat stare').[43] In Rouen, BM, 1343, he corrects large sections of Remigius of Auxerre's *Expositio missae* and the *Gesta saluatoris*, with most of his additions presented in the margins.[44] In some cases, he highlights the marginal addition with a small decorative border, such as in Rouen, BM, 1174, fols. 94v and 96r.[45]

---

[40] Chibnall has similarly noted that it is not unusual to find Orderic providing marginal notations in the various books that he helped to copy. See *HE*, I, pp. 201–3. Delisle also notes that in BnF, lat. 5506, II, fol. 64v, Orderic forgot to copy a line of text, which he later added in the form of a marginal notation (Delisle, 'Matériaux', p. 489).

[41] These books are: Alençon, BM, 1; Alençon, BM, 6; Alençon, BM, 14; Alençon, BM, 26; Rouen, BM, 31; Rouen, BM, 540; Rouen, BM, 1174; Rouen, BM, 1343; Rouen, BM, 1376; BnF, lat. 5506, I; and BnF, lat. 12131.

[42] See, for example, Rouen, BM, 1376, fol. 54v: Orderic may have supplied the word 'hystoria'.

[43] For an edition of the text [*De casu diaboli*], see *S. Anselmi Cantuariensis Archepiscopi oper omnia*, ed. F. S. Schmitt (Edinburgh, 1946), I, pp. 231–76.

[44] See, for examples, fols. 8v, 9r, 10r, 18r, 25v, 29v, and 32v.

[45] For an edition of the text found in Rouen, BM, 1174 (around fol. 94v), see *S. Agobardi, Lugdunensis Episcopi, Eginhardi Abbatis opera omnia*, ed. J. P. Migne, Traditio Catholica, Saeculum IX. Annus 840 (Paris, 1864), p. 801.

The frequency of corrections provided by Orderic in the books he helped to copy further proves that he served as master of book-production in the Saint-Évroul scriptorium. As a corrector of manuscripts, Orderic would have read through each line of text carefully, comparing the newly created copy with the exemplar to check for errors. This activity implies an authoritative role, as other scribes appear to have turned to him for the final review of their work.

In addition to prompting the text material, ensuring smooth transitions between scribes, staying close at hand to interject when necessary, and providing corrections, Orderic can also be found adding the final touches to the manuscripts in the form of rubrication and *incipit* and *explicit* headings. In many of the books he helped to copy, Orderic provides the rubricated headings, often in a combination of uncial, majuscule or capital letter-forms. In Rouen, BM, 540, for example, Orderic provides the opening rubricated *incipit* for the *Vita sanctae Oportunae viriginis*, on fol. 54r, as well as the *explicit* for the prologue, on fol. 55v. He can also be found adding rubrication and the *incipit* or *explicit* headings in Alençon, BM, 6; Alençon, BM, 14; Alençon, BM, 26; Rouen, BM, 31; Rouen, BM, 1174; Rouen, BM, 1343; BnF, Lat. 5506, I and II; BnF, Lat. 10508; BnF, Lat. 12131; and BnF, Lat. 6503.[46] In BnF, Lat. 10508 (a gradual containing Gui d'Arezzo's *Micrologus sive de arte musica*), Orderic copies none of the main text, but was probably responsible for rubricating the gradual and supplying the *incipit* headings, coloured initials, and the coloured lines for the musical notation.

The addition of rubrication, often in the form of *incipit* and *explicit* titles, initials, and other headings in the text, was often the final stage of manuscript production in the Middle Ages. This is suggested by the fact that many surviving manuscripts from this period feature blank spaces in the text where coloured initials, headings, or other details were meant to be filled in later by a rubricator, but, for whatever reason, the task was not completed. For example, in BnF, Lat. 12131 – a manuscript entirely rubricated by Orderic – some of these blank spaces were slightly too short for the intended rubric, compelling Orderic to force the headings into place.[47] The fact that it was Orderic who was responsible for adding the 'final touches' to the page further indicates his role as supervisor and director of book production in the Saint-Évroul scriptorium.

Some may question the impact of a new Orderic manuscript discovery, such as the recent find of Rouen, BM, 540 in the municipal archives of Rouen. After all, much of Orderic's renown in the field of medieval studies has been linked to the already high number of manuscripts that can be attributed to him. What difference can one more manuscript make? Why should we continue to search for new manuscripts, especially

---

[46] See Appendix 2 for descriptions of each manuscript.

[47] See, for example, fols. 25v and 75v (Appendix 2, item 11).

if such efforts require lessons in twelfth-century palaeography? While we have been lucky to have had seventeen manuscripts featuring Orderic's handwriting available to work with until now, this chapter has shown that the addition of a new manuscript to the corpus has the potential to open new avenues of research in terms of Orderic's life and work. Rouen, BM, 540 is not a deluxe manuscript, and Orderic's contributions to its pages are undeniably brief, amounting to little over thirteen and a half lines of text and a few corrections. Despite this, Rouen, BM, 540 serves as an important witness to Orderic's rather unusual scribal techniques, providing a valuable example of his prompting the text, ensuring smooth transitions between scribes, making corrections, and supplying rubrication – activities that strongly point to him being the master of the Saint-Évroul scriptorium. Indeed, Orderic's unusual tendency to stop copying at the top of a verso, often mid-line, may not have been recognised as a pattern until Rouen, BM, 540 was placed alongside other known examples of his work, such as Rouen, BM, 31 and Rouen, BM, 1174.

The fact that Rouen, BM, 540 is currently classified as a product of the neighbouring Fécamp scriptorium also opens up a potential, and currently unexplored, connection between the abbeys of Saint-Évroul and Fécamp. Although to date it is still unclear how Rouen, BM, 540 came to be counted as a product of Fécamp, the mystery will hopefully prompt scholars to investigate the lending and borrowing practices between these two Benedictine abbeys further. Although it takes time to learn the nuances and idiosyncratic tendencies of Orderic's handwriting, and it is notably quite rare to come across a previously unidentified Orderic manuscript, it is to be hoped that this discussion, and the discovery of Rouen, BM, 540, motivates others to join in the search for more manuscripts, and thus help to expand the legacy of Saint-Évroul's most famous master scribe.

Orderic Vitalis as Librarian and Cantor of Saint-Évroul

Charles C. Rozier

AN established consensus included in almost every recent study of Orderic Vitalis's life and works suggests that he acted as librarian of Saint-Évroul.[1] His well-documented role in helping to compile the twelfth-century Saint-Évroul book-list, and his identified activities in reviewing and correcting manuscripts completed by other, perhaps more junior, scribes, have encouraged several notable, if brief, statements on the topic.[2] Chibnall argued that in adding to the book-list and the calendar of Saint-Évroul's 'chapter-book', Orderic was 'perhaps acting as librarian', and elsewhere suggested that he had worked as an *armarius*.[3] Similarly, Nortier cited Orderic's role in the book-list in the course of her proposition that the list was compiled, and perhaps even ordered, by Orderic's authority.[4] Van Houts suggested that Orderic's corrections to several manuscripts highlight his possible roles 'in charge of the scriptorium at Saint-Évroul and perhaps librarian and archivist as well'.[5] More recent are Escudier's

---

I would like to thank those who have read or informed early versions of this chapter, including Jenny Weston, Sigbjørn Sønnesyn, Giles Gasper and Dan Roach.

---

[1] Palaeographical analysis featured within this chapter draws on research carried out in collaboration with Jenny Weston towards the accompanying Appendix 2 of the present volume, and towards the authoritative description of Orderic's hand featured in her contribution, 'Following the Master's Lead: The Script of Orderic Vitalis and the Discovery of a New Manuscript (Rouen, BM, 540)'. Manuscript research presented in this chapter was carried out with the help of a Royal Historical Society Postgraduate Research Grant (2013).

[2] Chibnall, 'General Introduction', p. 24; Nortier, *Les Bibliothèques médiévales*, p. 108; Elisabeth van Houts, 'Introduction' in *GND*, I, p. lxvii; Escudier, 'Orderic et le scriptorium', p. 24. For discussion of Orderic's manuscript additions, see Delisle, 'Matériaux', pp. 481–526; F. Avril, *Manuscrits normands, XIe–XIIe siècles* (Rouen, 1975); *HE*, I, pp. 201–3; Escudier, 'Orderic et le scriptorium'; Weston, 'Following the Master's Lead', and below, Appendix 2.

[3] Chibnall, 'General Introduction', p. 24; Chibnall, *World*, pp. 33–4.

[4] Nortier, *Les Bibliothèques médiévales*, p. 108: 'il est bien certain que ce travail fut exécuté sous son inspiration, peut-être sous sa direction.'

[5] *GND*, I, p. lxvii.

remarks that Orderic worked as librarian for the last thirty years of his life.[6]

Despite the frequency of this claim that Orderic was librarian at Saint-Évroul, the precise circumstances in which he was given charge of books within the community, and the exact duties associated with the role, remain surprisingly little explored given their potential significance within the study of Orderic's life and works. The discussion which follows attempts a detailed analysis of Orderic as librarian at Saint-Évroul, drawing on evidence from within the *Historia ecclesiastica*, alongside a fresh examination of his additions to the surviving corpus of Saint-Évroul manuscripts, in order to understand the nature of his role more accurately and comprehensively.

As Chibnall noted, a monastic librarian active in Normandy during the eleventh and twelfth centuries was likely to have been an appointed official known as an *armarius*.[7] While descriptions of this role are found in a number of contemporary guides to the organisation of communal religious life, the position is also sometimes referred to as that of *precentor*, or the more common form of *cantor*.[8] For example, a mid-eleventh-century Cluniac text known as the *Liber tramitis* uses both *cantor* and *armarius*, while Ulrich of Zell's near-contemporary *Consuetudines antiquiares Cluniacenses* uses *precentor* and *armarius*.[9] Another near-contemporary text linked to the Cluniac tradition, Archbishop Lanfranc of Canterbury's

---

[6] Escudier, 'Orderic et le scriptorium', p. 24.

[7] Chibnall, *World*, p. 33.

[8] For an overview of scholarship on the role, see F. Wormald, 'The Monastic Library', in *The English Library before 1700*, ed. F. Wormald and C. E. Wright (London, 1958), pp. 15–31; M. E. Fassler, 'The Office of the Cantor in Early Western Monastic Rules and Customaries: A Preliminary Investigation', *Early Music History* 5 (1985), 29–51; D. Hiley, 'Thurstan of Caen and Plainchant at Glastonbury: Musicological Reflections on the Norman Conquest', *Proceedings of the British Academy* 72 (1986), 57–90; J. Grier, 'Roger de Chabannes (d. 1025), Cantor of St Martial, Limoges', *Early Music History* 14 (1995), 53–119; N. Hunt, *Cluny under Saint Hugh, 1049–1109* (London, 1967), pp. 62–5; J. Grier, *The Musical World of a Medieval Monk: Adémar de Chabannes in Eleventh-Century Aquitaine* (Cambridge, 2006), esp. chapter 6; A. Bagnall Yardley, *Performing Piety: Musical Culture in Medieval English Nunneries* (New York, 2006), and essays in *Medieval Cantors and their Craft: Music, Liturgy and the Shaping of History, 800–1500*, ed. K. A.-M. Bugyis, A. B. Kraebel and M. E. Fassler (York, forthcoming).

[9] *Liber tramitis aevi Odilonis abbatis*, ed. P. Dinter, Corpus Consuetudinum Monasticum (Siegburg, 1980), pp. 238–9; Ulrich of Zell, *Consuetudines antiquiares Cluniacenses*, PL 149, cols. 643–779, at cols. 749A–750A.

Decreta, uses only the term *cantor*,[10] while the twelfth-century *Liber ordinis* of Saint-Victor uses only the term *armarius*.[11] By the third quarter of the thirteenth century, a joint customary of Saint Augustine's in Canterbury and Saint-Peter's in Westminster applied all three terms interchangeably.[12] Although the names applied to each role clearly varied depending on the text and precise circumstances in the community in which it was written, it is clear from each description that the three roles involved similar responsibilities for the care of books and the supervision of the liturgy. As such, this present discussion refers to the role at Saint-Évroul as that of the *cantor*, even if it is equally likely that this official may have been known as the *precentor* or *armarius* during Orderic's lifetime.

The cantor was an authoritative figure whose experience, skills and interests allowed him to supervise the delivery of liturgical services to the appropriate standard and in line with the liturgical calendar. As argued by Fassler, the role became increasingly associated with the care of books from the eighth century onwards, particularly as liturgical practices became increasingly normalised and more commonly recorded and disseminated in liturgical books throughout the Frankish realm.[13] By Orderic's lifetime the circulation of commentaries and guides to religious life, such as those noted above, suggests standardisation and an increasingly prescriptive approach to the organisation of religious communities.[14] These sources provide the first detailed descriptions of the cantor's role, and, with it, important information on the typical duties which might be expected of a monastic librarian.

The *Liber tramitis*, Lanfranc's *Decreta* and the *Liber ordinis* all stipulate that the ideal cantor assumed responsibility for the care and production of books.[15] The *Liber ordinis* opens with the instruction that 'The armarius has in his care all of the books of the church', and stipulates that the incumbent should protect the books against threats such as damp and

---

[10] *The Monastic Constitutions of Lanfranc*, ed. and trans. David Knowles and Christopher N. L. Brooke (Oxford, 2002), pp. 118–23. On its links with Cluniac customaries, see pp. xxxix–xlii.

[11] *Liber ordinis Sancti Victoris Parisiensis*, ed. L. Jocqué and L. Milis, Corpus Christianorum: Continuatio Medievalis 61 (Turnhout, 1984), pp. 78–86.

[12] *Customary of the Benedictine Monasteries of Saint Augustine, Canterbury, and Saint Peter, Winchester*, ed. E. M. Thompson, 2 vols. (London, 1904), I, pp. 82 and 90–7, and II, pp. 28–36.

[13] Fassler, 'Office of the Cantor', pp. 31–3.

[14] I. Cochelin, 'Évolution des coutumieres monastiques dessinée à partir de l'étude de Bernard', in *From Dead of Night to End of Day: The Medieval Customs of Cluny*, ed. S. Boynton and I. Cochelin (Turnhout, 2005), pp. 29–66; G. Melville, 'Action, Text, and Validity: On Re-examining Cluny's *Consuetudines* and Statutes', ibid., pp. 67–84.

[15] *Liber tramitis*, pp. 238–9; *Monastic Constitutions of Lanfranc*, pp. 122–3; *Liber ordinis*, pp. 78–81.

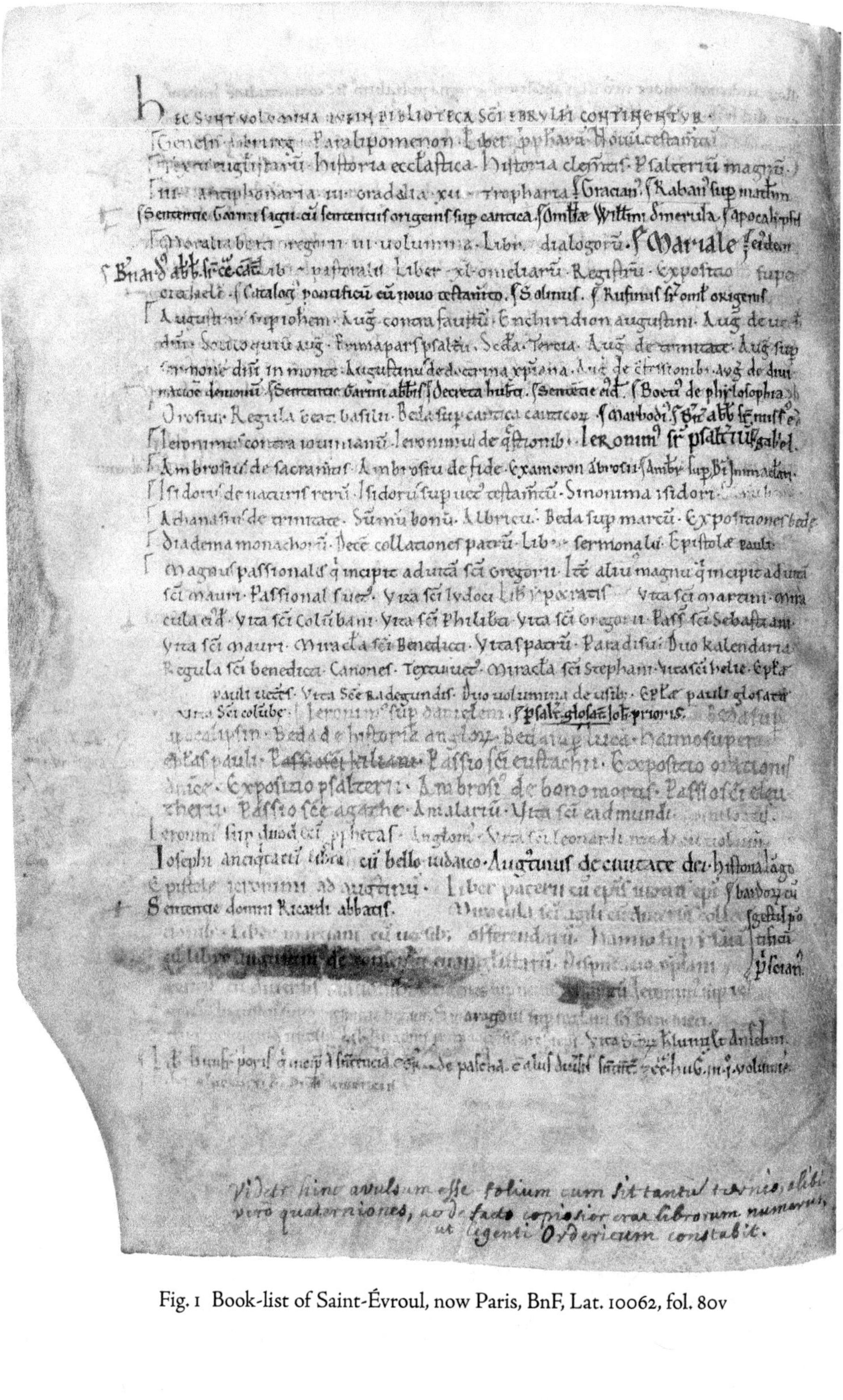

Fig. 1 Book-list of Saint-Évroul, now Paris, BnF, Lat. 10062, fol. 80v

mould, and maintain up-to-date records relating to the contents of the book-collection.[16] The text instructs further that the armarius should have total authority over all writing within the community. No writing was ever to be done without the permission and supervision of the armarius, from whom all writing materials were to be obtained at all times.[17] The section pertaining to these duties ends with the prescription that the armarius should know the location of all books, whether borrowed by members of the community, or kept in daily use.[18]

Close study of Orderic's additions within the surviving corpus of Saint-Évroul manuscripts suggests that he was working towards all of these goals. As previously noted, Orderic has been regarded traditionally as one of the principal contributors to the twelfth-century book-list featured on fol. 80v of Paris, BnF, MS, Lat. 10062, which Chibnall knew as the Saint-Évroul chapter-book (Fig. 1). However, previous discussions of Orderic's likely additions to this list are vague and imprecise.[19] Research carried out in preparation for the catalogue of manuscripts featuring Orderic's hand within the present volume (Appendix 2) sheds some light on this key issue. The first three lines of text down to the penultimate entry on line three, which records 'Historia Clementis', all appear to have been added in Orderic's hand. These lines display all of the characteristic letter-forms identified by Weston, most notably his 'horizontal-descender g', and are presented in Orderic's typically large hand. Thereafter, the majority of contemporary entries, which form lines 4–18 and perhaps down to line 23, are written in a hand which closely resembles Orderic's in letter-forms, but is smaller and slightly neater than his usual writing (in particular, leaving ample space between lines of text) and lacks the typical form for the letter g which so regularly distinguishes Orderic's work from that of his contemporaries. If Orderic began the list, as is suggested here, it provides evidence of his involvement in the process of monitoring the contents of the library at Saint-Évroul.

Orderic's role in beginning the first three lines of the book-list before apparently handing over to others supports Weston's suggestion that he mentored the work of other scribes.[20] Weston has shown that Orderic regularly began copying texts before handing over to other scribes, for example in sections of Rouen, BM, MSS 31 and 1174.[21] In a similar

---

[16] *Liber ordinis*, p. 78: 'Armarius omnes ecclesiae libros in custodia sue habet, quos omnes nominibus propriis sigillatim annotatos habere debet at per singulos annos ad minus bis aut.'

[17] Ibid., pp. 79–80.

[18] Ibid., pp. 81–2.

[19] Delisle, 'Matériaux', p. 13; Nortier, *Les Bibliothèques médiévales*, pp. 106–8; Escudier, 'Orderic et le scriptorium', p. 24.

[20] Weston, 'Following the Master's Lead'.

[21] See below, Appendix 2, items 13 and 15.

manner, Alençon, BM, MS 6 shows Orderic beginning the verse *Life* of St Launomar at fol. 143v before ceasing to write on fol. 145v and allowing others to continue the work; he likewise started to copy the *Passion* of saints Nereus and Achilles on fols. 150r–151v, but stopped on fol. 151v.[22] Weston's analysis of Orderic's role in Rouen, BM, MSS 540 and 1174 presents firmer evidence that he provided particularly close supervision to certain scribes, perhaps in a master–student dynamic. Weston sees Orderic as 'prompting the text, perhaps offering layout and script samples for others to imitate [...] before handing over the responsibility to other, perhaps less experienced, scribes'.[23]

A number of manuscripts show that, in addition to these supervisory duties, Orderic also corrected the books produced under his supervision, and several others besides. Of the thirty-one surviving manuscripts known from Saint-Évroul in Orderic's lifetime, Weston cites eleven in which Orderic worked as corrector.[24] With over 130 items which are recorded in the book-list now lost, Orderic may have corrected many more manuscripts than the eleven identified to date. The precise nature of his corrections to the surviving material varies. For example, he appears to have added a number of small corrections over erasures within the text of the *Rule of St Benedict* now contained on fols. 98r–123r of the chapter-book, mentioned above.[25] On fol. 100v he erased the text on col. 2, line 19, and wrote 'redditur[us] est. Et ne causetur', and similarly added 'scamnis legant[u]r uicissi[m] a fr[atr]ib[us]' on the third line of fol. 109r. All display a change in general aspect, with Orderic writing in a slightly larger script, and with a thinner pen, than the main scribe, and using his characteristic letter-forms and abbreviations. Weston points to other instances in which Orderic added more substantial corrections and additions, for instance adding missing sections of text to Rouen, BM, MS 540, and several larger marginal additions to Rouen, BM, MS 1343.[26] Study of Orderic's manuscript additions shows his probable involvement in recording the contents of Saint-Évroul's book-collection, training and mentoring more junior scribes, and ensuring the quality of the text within books already produced. This evidence confirms that Orderic contributed to the duties of a monastic librarian as described in contemporary customaries, indicating that he held a position of authority within the community.

[22] Ibid., item 2.

[23] *HE*, I, p. 201; Weston, 'Following the Master's Lead'.

[24] Weston, 'Following the Master's Lead', n. 41. These are: Alençon, BM, MSS 1, 6, 14, 26; Rouen, BM, MSS 31, 540, 1174, 1343, 1376; Paris, BnF, MSS Lat. 5506, I, and 12131. See also descriptions of Orderic's work in Appendix 2, below.

[25] Paris, BnF, MS Lat. 10062: fols. 99v, col. 2; 100v, col. 2, line 19; 105r, col. 2, line 3; 106v, col. 2, line 29; 107v, col. 1, lines 5–6; 108v, col. 2, line 18; and 110v, col. 2, lines 11–13.

[26] Weston, 'Following the Master's Lead'.

Further study of several additional trends within Orderic's activities suggests that he was probably also carrying out some of the essential duties required of a monastic cantor. The remainder of this discussion considers that evidence, which sheds light on the nature of Orderic's work as librarian. More significantly, it also has the potential to influence our reading of his wider works, and to inform our understanding of his vision in writing the *Historia ecclesiastica*.

Although responsibilities within the library and scriptorium provide a constant thread within the cantor's remit, the surviving customaries leave little doubt that a cantor was primarily concerned with singing, and, in particular, with ensuring the accuracy of chanted liturgy. The *Liber tramitis*, Lanfranc's *Decreta* and the *Liber ordinis* all stipulate that cantors were charged with coordinating and monitoring the delivery of the daily offices. This could involve anything from choosing readers and arranging rehearsal, to instant interjection in the event of an error during the offices. Lanfranc summarised his vision of the role as follows:

> Whenever anyone is to read or chant anything in the church the cantor shall, if need be, hear him go over his task before he performs it in public. It is the cantor's business to watch carefully at all times, so that no negligence occurs in any service in the monastery. If through forgetfulness someone fails to begin a responsory or antiphon or suchlike when he should, or if, having begun it correctly, he goes astray in any way, the cantor should be quite ready to begin without delay what should have been begun, or to lead back into the right road one who has strayed.[27]

Evidence from within Orderic's *Historia ecclesiastica* and the corpus of manuscripts containing his hand provides a number of clues towards the assessment of Orderic's ability to fulfil these duties. Several sections of the *Historia* highlight his apparently keen interest in, and detailed knowledge of, liturgical and musical traditions within the community at Saint-Évroul. In narrating the foundation and early development of the monastery after 1050, Orderic singled out the contributions of an individual named Guitmund, with whose work he appears to have been particularly familiar. Having arrived in the community during the 1060s, Guitmund is likely to

---

[27] *Monastic Constitutions of Lanfranc*, pp. 118–21: 'Quicunque lecturus aut cantaturus est aliquid in monasterio, si necesse habet, ab eo priusquam incipiat debet auscultare. Ipsius est omni hora sollicite prouidere, ne eueniat neglegentia in quocunque obsequio quod fit in monasterio. Si quis obliuiosus non inceperit, cum incipere debet, responsorium, aut antiphonam, uel aliud huiusmodi, siue in eodem iam bene incepto aliquo modo deuiauerit, ipse debet esse prouisus atque paratus, ut sine mora, quod incipiendum erat, incipiat, uel eum, qui fallendo deuiauerat, in uiam reducat.'

have been known to Orderic during early adulthood.[28] Orderic noted that Guitmund had composed several chants for the monks of Saint-Évroul, with a hint of personal interest visible in his suggestion that Guitmund's work had provided 'some of the sweetest melodies in our troper and antiphonary'.[29] Orderic demonstrated a deep knowledge of Guitmund's additions to the musical liturgy of Saint-Évroul, writing that:

> He [Guitmund] gave the final form to the office of our holy father, St Évroul, by adding nine antiphons and responsories.[30] He composed four antiphons for the psalms at Vespers and added the last three antiphons for the second nocturn at Matins, as well as the fourth, eighth, and twelfth responsories and the antiphon for the canticles; he also composed the most beautiful antiphon for the magnificat at second Vespers.[31]

Orderic's narration of Abbot Roger's journey to southern Italy and the establishment of several linked monastic communities in the region displays a similar sense of pride in the musical compositions of Saint-Évroul monks. Orderic praised Berengar, a former monk and oblate of Saint-Évroul and later abbot at Vensa, as one who 'excelled in reading and chanting'.[32] Concluding with a reflection on the achievements of these Italian exiles, Orderic proudly declared that 'the liturgy of St Évroul' had been successfully transferred to new climes, thereby suggesting that although they were now distant from their Norman confraters, the inhabitants of these new communities were united nevertheless, by observing a shared liturgy.[33]

A body of manuscript evidence suggests that Orderic may have been able to read and musical notation and even compose, using both *neumes* and alphabetical indicators. Escudier identified notation marks in sections of text copied by Orderic across six separate manuscripts. These include a sacramentary, a tropary, two miscellaneous collections of saints' *lives* and *passions*, a volume containing three poems, and one volume of Orderic's

---

[28] *HE*, II, pp. 108–9.

[29] Ibid.: 'Plures enim dulcisonos cantus in trophario et antiphonario edidit.'

[30] Orderic refers to this text as a 'historia', which Chibnall translated as 'office'.

[31] *HE*, II, pp. 108–9: 'Hic hystoriam sancti patris Ebrulfi additis ix antiphonis et tribus responsoriis perfecit. Nam ad uesperas super psalmos quatuor antiphonas condidit, et in secundo nocturno tres ultimas adiecit; quartum etiam responsorium et octauum et duodecimum et antiphonam ad cantica et ad secundas uesperas ad canticum de Euangelio pulcherrimam antiphonam edidit.'

[32] Ibid., pp. 100–3: 'peritiaque legendi et canendi'.

[33] Ibid.

Historia ecclesiastica.³⁴ Observing Orderic's role in copying or authoring all of these texts, Escudier suggested that it was Orderic himself who added these indications of pitch and metre, and as such, argued that Orderic might be known as a musician.³⁵ For the most part, it is difficult to ratify Escudier's suggestions. The majority of the marks consist of simple upward strokes, with few defining features which might allow comparison with the remainder of Orderic's work. However, those present on fol. 36v of Rouen, BM, MS 273 do include a mark similar to Orderic's 'general abbreviation' as identified by Weston.³⁶ Furthermore, the more detailed system of alphabetical notation used on fol. 43v of Rouen, BM, MS 1376 displays several key features of Orderic's hand, especially the 'horizontal-descender g', and 'sharp-feet m'.³⁷ The notes on fol. 26r of Paris, BnF, MS Lat. 5506, II, may be linked to Orderic's reference to an antiphon, 'Peccata mea Domine', within the *Historia ecclesiastica*.³⁸ Although it is impossible to know whether Orderic himself made these notes while writing the *Historia*, this small section of text provides further suggestive evidence of his ability to transcribe what was sung into a form of written notation.

Several of Orderic's additions within the Saint-Évroul chapter-book offer further evidence of his engagement with, and possible supervision of, liturgical observances. The manuscript contains a series of confraternity records on fols. 78r–81v. Numerous hands of varying dates added to these lists over time, reflecting the cumulative growth of contacts between Saint-Évroul and its partners in prayer. Orderic made one addition, providing the last line of the main body text on fol. 78r.³⁹ Interestingly, his note records an agreement with the monastery of Holy Trinity in Venosa ('P[ro] def[uncto] mo[nacho] cenobii s[an]ct[e] trinitatis venusie'), further highlighting his apparent drive to commemorate contacts between his home foundation and its associated houses in southern Italy.⁴⁰ While Orderic may have made this single addition to the list simply because he was a competent scribe, perhaps following an order to do so, the agreement

---

³⁴ D. Escudier, 'L'œuvre entre les lignes d'Orderic Vital', in *Le livre au Moyen Age*, ed. Jean Glenisson (Turnhout, 1988), pp. 193–5. The manuscripts in question are: Alençon, BM, MS 1; Paris, BnF, MSS Lat. 5506 II, 6503, and 10508; Rouen, BM, MSS 273 and 1376.

³⁵ Escudier, 'L'œuvre entre les lignes', p. 195; Escudier, 'Orderic et le scriptorium', p. 27.

³⁶ Weston, 'Following the Master's Lead'.

³⁷ Ibid.

³⁸ This is reproduced in Escudier, 'Orderic et le scriptorium', p. 27, fig. 10; *HE*, II, pp. 90–1.

³⁹ Appendix 2, item 9.

⁴⁰ For further discussion of Orderic and southern Italy, see the contribution of D. Roach in this volume: 'Saint-Évroul and Southern Italy in Orderic's *Historia ecclesiastica*'.

with Venosa may also have been written as part of his possible duties as cantor. Lanfranc's *Decreta* stipulates that it was the cantor's duty to 'supervise the letters sent out to ask for prayers for the dead brethren'.[41] Orderic's role in adding to these lists suggests that he may have supervised prayer agreements at Saint-Évroul in just this way. Judging by the number of agreements completed before his addition, there was already a well-developed programme of prayer union within the community before his assumption of these responsibilities.

Elsewhere in the manuscript, six liturgical ordnances were added to the second column of fol. 123r, on a previously blank folio at the end of a *Rule of St Benedict*. The first four of these appear in a single hand, before Orderic appears to have added the fifth, which fills lines 23–32.[42] Beginning on line 13, the previous ordnance records the refoundation of the Saint-Évroul community in 1050. Orderic's addition commemorates the dedication of the new abbey church, which occurred in 1099, and also notes the succession of Pope Paschal and the capture of Jerusalem in the same year.[43] Although brief, Orderic's addition of this short note indicates a role in recording the development of liturgical traditions within the community at Saint-Évroul, for which cantorship provides a logical explanation.

The final area of cantor's activities to which Orderic can be shown to have contributed is that of computistical studies. The *Liber ordinis* and Lanfranc's *Decreta* both instructed cantors to keep the date and to announce any important anniversaries in advance.[44] As Lanfranc put it, the cantor's duty was to 'to keep count of the week's and month's mind'.[45] In order to fulfil such a requirement, it was necessary for a cantor to have sufficient knowledge of computus, so as to be able to organise the liturgical calendar. Commenting on Orderic's 'chronological system', Chibnall

---

[41] *Monastic Constitutions of Lanfranc*, pp. 122–3: 'Cura breuium, qui foras mitti solent pro defunctis fratribus [...] eum pertinet.'

[42] Appendix 2, item 9.

[43] The dedication of the new abbey church at Saint-Évroul is recounted in *HE*, III, pp. 94–5, 130–1, and *HE*, V, pp. 264–7. The text of Orderic's ordnance reads: 'Prefate eccl[esi]e dedicatio anno ab incarnatione d[omi]ni millesimo XCIX t[empor]e rogeri abbatis facta est (idus novembris die dominico). Giselbert[us] Luxoniensis ep[iscopu]s et Giselbertus Eboracensis atq[ue] Serlo sagiensis predicte dedicationi int[er] fueritus. Eode[m] anno, vi kalends augusti Urban[us] papa defunct[us] e[st] et Paschalis xvi die post ei[us] obitu[m] ei subrogate[us] e[sse]. Paulo ante id[us] mense iulio Ierusalem gentilib[us] auxiliante deo subtracta e[st] et [Christ]ianis qui de Normannia de Gallia uel Anglia siue calabria p[er] amore dei p[er]egre p[er]rexant reddita e[st].'

[44] *Monastic Constitutions of Lanfranc*, pp. 122–3; *Liber Ordinis*, pp. 84–5.

[45] *Monastic Constitutions of Lanfranc*, pp. 122–3: 'et cura numerandi tricenaria, et septenaria, ad eum pertinet'.

suggested that, though he primarily preferred to copy the dating systems found in his sources verbatim, his ability to date events according to the year of indiction suggests some engagement with Bede's *De temporum ratione*.[46] However, though Chibnall claimed that Orderic's hand 'predominates' in the extracts from Bede's *De temporum* on fols. 130r–137v of the chapter-book, the evidence presented in Appendix 2, below, shows that he actually had no involvement in this section of the manuscript.[47]

Orderic's addition of numerous marginal annals within the Easter-tables featured in the next section of the manuscript (fols. 138v–160r) provides some more positive evidence of his ability to negotiate computistical theory. Reading the annals in chronological order, Orderic's hand at first makes sporadic additions, supplementing the main outline of papal, regnal and imperial succession. For example, on fol. 148r Orderic noted the death of King Cædwalla of Wessex in Rome (689), the death of Archbishop Theodore of Canterbury (690), Pope Sergius's ordination of St Willebrord as bishop of the Frisians (695), and Theodosius succeeding Anastasius as Byzantine Emperor (715). Orderic's supplementary additions continue until fol. 152r, on which he made a lengthy additions recording the struggle for Byzantine imperial succession between Constantine VII, his guardian Romanus, and Stephen son of Romanus, which Orderic records for the year 954. Orderic added almost all of the annals from the entry for 1084 on fol. 153v, down to 1139 on fol. 154v. Previous scholars have characterised his work in these annals as a valuable element in his development as a historian.[48] However, the manuscript context – immediately adjacent to the extracts from Bede's *De temporum* and numerous additional diagrams and schematic tables – suggests that Orderic may also have been engaging with a level of *computus* theory which would have been compatible as much with the duties of a cantor as with a historian.[49]

So far, this discussion has presented a variety of evidence to support the hypothesis that Orderic worked as librarian at Saint-Évroul because

---

[46] Chibnall, 'General Instruction', pp. 110–12.

[47] Appendix 2, item 9.

[48] Chibnall, 'General Introduction', pp. 29–31; *GND*, I, pp. lxviii–lxix.

[49] On links between *computus* and the writing of historical annals, see R. Poole, *Chronicles and Annals: A Brief Outline of their Origin and Growth* (Oxford, 1926); M. McCormick, *Les Annales du haut Moyen Âge occidental*, Typologie des sources du Moyen Âge 14 (Turnhout, 1976); K. H. Krüger, *Die Universalchroniken*, Typologie des sources du Moyen Âge 16 (Turnhout, 1976); Paul Antony Hayward, *The Winchcombe and Coventry Chronicles: Hitherto Unnoticed Witnesses to the Work of John of Worcester*, 2 vols. (Tempe, AZ, 2010), I, pp. 11–61; C.C. Rozier, 'Contextualizing the Past at Durham Cathedral Priory, c. 1090–1130: Uses of History in the Annals of Durham, Dean and Chapter Library, MS Hunter 100' *HSJ* 25 (2013), 107–23.

of his appointment as cantor to the community. A considerable range of manuscript evidence reveals Orderic to have been active in monitoring the contents of the library collection, ensuring the accuracy of texts contained within it by working as editor and training the next generation of scribes, whose future endeavours would continue this work. Orderic's *Historia* shows the author's interest in the development of music and liturgy at Saint-Évroul and its associated houses, and Escudier's theory that Orderic was able to read and write early forms of musical notation lends further weight to the suggestion that he was actively engaged in furthering these traditions, as do his additions to the lists of confraternity agreements and notes of liturgical ordinance within the Saint-Évroul chapter-book. With Orderic's additions to the Easter-table annals completing the evidence, it may be concluded that he was active in every area of a cantor's most significant duties, according to descriptions of the role featured in contemporary monastic customaries.

It should, however, be noted that Orderic did not refer to himself as cantor at any point within his own works. While the autobiographical epilogue of the *Historia* notes his promotion to sub-deacon, deacon and priest, the office of cantor is absent from this list.[50] Yet further study reveals the omission of this title to have been relatively common among contemporary cantor-authors. Therefore, while Eadmer of Canterbury was described as a cantor by the later twelfth-century author Gervase, Eadmer did not mention this within his own extensive semi-autobiographical histories.[51] Symeon of Durham, another contemporary cantor-historian, is also known only to have been cantor as a result of certain rubrics within later twelfth-century manuscripts of his works.[52] Likewise, William of Malmesbury, whose status as cantor is recorded in Robert of Cricklade's *De connubio patriarche Iacob*, chose to refer to himself not as cantor but as 'bibliotecarius' in the prologue to his *Historia novella*.[53] The fact that

---

[50] *HE*, VI, pp. 554–7.

[51] *The Historical Works of Gervase of Canterbury*, ed. William Stubbs, 2 vols. (London, 1879–80), I, p. 7, II, p. 374. For analysis, see R. W. Southern, *Anselm and his Biographer: A Study of Monastic Life and Thought, 1059–c. 1130* (Cambridge, 1963), p. 237; R. W. Southern, *Saint Anselm: A Portrait in a Landscape* (Cambridge, 1990), pp. 418–21; Eadmer of Canterbury, *Lives and Miracles of Saints Oda, Dunstan and Oswald*, ed. Andrew Turner and Bernard Muir (Oxford, 2006), p. xxvi.

[52] Symeon of Durham, *Libellus de exordio atque procursu istius hoc est Dunhelmensis, ecclesie*, ed. and trans. D. W. Rollason (Oxford, 2000), pp. xlii–xliv; and Charles C. Rozier, 'Symeon of Durham as Cantor and Historian at Durham Cathedral Priory, c. 1090–1129', in *Medieval Cantors and their Craft: Music, Liturgy and the Shaping of History*, ed. K. A.-M. Bugyis, A. B. Kraebel and M. E. Fassler (York, 2016, forthcoming).

[53] Oxford, Bodleian Library, MS Laud. Misc. 725, fol. 129v: 'Guillelmi Meldunensis ecclesie monachi et cantoris'. For discussion, see R. W.

Orderic did not name himself as cantor within his works need provide no barrier to the suggestion that he occupied the office during his time at Saint-Évroul.

Evidence from the *Historia ecclesiastica* highlights Orderic's familiarity with the cantor's role. In total, Orderic includes references to eight cantors within the *Historia*: seven described as cantor, and one as precentor, and records the names of two Saint-Évroul cantors.[54] Reconstructing the apparent succession of cantors of Saint-Évroul suggests that the office would have become vacant when Orderic was about forty years old. His account of the community in its early years as featured in Book III of the *Historia* named two cantors: the first called Hugh, and the second William Gregory. Orderic wrote that, on the foundation of Saint-Évroul in 1050, Abbot Thierry brought with him from Jumièges certain individuals, who together 'established regular life' and 'well-ordered liturgy'.[55] Among these was an individual named as 'Hugonem cantorem', who, Orderic later added, was responsible for copying several volumes for the first library of Saint-Évroul, one of which featured a text described in the twelfth-century book-list as a 'cantica Hugonis'.[56] From this brief description it seems likely that Hugh was the first cantor of Saint-Évroul at the foundation of the community in the early 1050s. As cantor, Hugh seems to have held responsibilities similar to those described in the contemporary customaries; namely, in supervising liturgy and contributing to manuscript production, including his own book of canticles.

The second probable cantor at Saint-Évroul was named by Orderic as William Gregory. Orderic's third book records that William arrived within the community as a child oblate aged nine, and that this William was still alive at the time of Orderic's writing.[57] Chibnall dated this passage to not later than 1114 or 1115, and in doing so proposed that William had been one of the first oblate entrants to the new community, arriving at some point

---

Hunt, 'English Learning in the Late Twelfth Century', *Transactions of the Royal Historical Society* 4th series 19 (1936), 19–42, at pp. 31–2; William of Malmesbury, *Historia novella: The Contemporary History*, ed. Edmund King, trans. K. R. Potter (Oxford, 1998), pp. 2–3. For discussion, see R. M. Thomson, *William of Malmesbury* (Woodbridge, 2003), p. 74.

[54] These can be found in: HE, II, pp. 18–19, 86–9, 96–7, 108–9, 292–5; HE, III, pp. 20–1, 22–5, and HE, IV, pp. 70–1. Chibnall translated Orderic's term 'cantor' as 'precentor' in all cases.

[55] HE, II, pp. 18–19: 'Cum quibus et per quos regularem obseruantiam et modestum rigorem aptamque serium in diuino cultu feruenter erexit.'

[56] Ibid., pp. 48–9; H. Omont, *Catalogue général des manuscrits des bibliothèques publiques de France, Départements*, vol. 2: *Rouen (suite et fin): Dieppe, Eu, Fécamp, Elbeuf, Gournay-en-Bray, Le Havre, Neufchâtel-en-Bray, Bernay, Conches, Gisors, Louviers, Verneuil, Evreux, Alençon, Montivilliers* (Paris, 1888), p. 469, item 151.

[57] HE, II, pp. 86–7.

before 1061.[58] While Chibnall's translation does not suggest that William was the cantor, but merely a singer, there are grounds to suggest that Orderic's term 'cantor' should in fact be understood as denoting the office rather than the skill of singing. Orderic's description of William's talents recognises that William was involved in the production of books, and that these books were to be used for reading and singing ('ad legendum et canendum'). Orderic's account suggests that William was active in several areas related to a likely cantor's remit, including reading, singing and scribal work, as follows:

> He was an able reader and chanter, and a distinguished scribe and illuminator of books. The works executed by his own hands for reading and singing are still models which encourage us to put away idleness and follow his example.[59]

The date of William's arrival within the community increases the likelihood of his cantorship. Having been nine years old c. 1050–61, William was therefore a generation younger than the first cantor, Hugh. This, added to his particular skills in reading and singing, would have made him a prime candidate to succeed Hugh as the second cantor of Saint-Évroul, and to have remained in office until at least 1114 or 1115, when Orderic composed his description.

It is not possible to know whether Orderic's great teacher, John of Rheims, ever took over as cantor after William. Orderic's obituary of John in the fifth book of his *Historia* notes only that John had served as sub-prior, and that he was skilled at composing works of verse, which may have been intended for public readings.[60] John's hand has not been identified within the Saint-Évroul manuscript corpus. Therefore, as it stands, it is impossible to reconstruct a more precise outline of his activities within the community.

If Orderic's description of cantor William was composed in 1114–15, as suggested by Chibnall and van Houts, William is likely to have been aged between fifty-three and sixty-four at the time of writing (depending on whether he began his oblation closer to 1050 or 1061).[61] While Orderic does not record William's death, he is unlikely to have lived much later than the mid-1120s. At this point, Orderic would have been in his early to mid-thirties, with significant scribal training behind him, and clear

---

[58] Ibid. The possible date of William's arrival is discussed on p. 87 n. 2.

[59] Ibid.: 'Nam peritus lector fuit et cantor; praecipuusque scriptor et librorum illuminator. Opera manum eius ad legendum et canendum nobis adhuc ualde prosunt, et per similis exercitii probitatem nos a nobis ociositatem depellere erudiunt.'

[60] Orderic's obituary features in *HE*, III, pp. 168–71, and mentions John's skills in poetry twice.

[61] *HE*, II, p. 87 n. 2; Cf. 'Composition of the *Historia ecclesiastica*' (p. xiv above).

intellectual and bibliographical talents and interests. It is therefore plausible to suggest that Orderic might have assumed the cantor's duties in the period following William's death.

The evidence that Orderic may have acted as cantor of Saint-Évroul lends weight to the argument that he may have been librarian. This, in turn, casts further light on the particular circumstances in which he made an inventory of books, edited them, supervised the production of new texts, and trained more junior scribes at Saint-Évroul, even if this brings an element of circularity to the discussion. More remains to be done to explore Orderic's apparent role as a scribal tutor, especially given the close similarities between his own writing style and several other, apparently contemporary, hands within the Saint-Évroul manuscript corpus. For particular consideration is the matter of whether Orderic's supervisory role and use of a distinctive script led to the development of an idiosyncratic house style at Saint-Évroul, as his juniors attempted to copy and emulate the script of their tutor, or whether Orderic's characteristic handwriting bears similarities to other hands precisely because he was the one working hard to emulate a particular house style following his arrival from England in 1085.

A role as cantor would also explain some of Orderic's additions within the surviving manuscript corpus, most notably those he made to the confraternity records, liturgical ordnances and the Easter-table annals. Such additions bear striking similarity to Symeon of Durham's work in a comparable collection from Durham that contains the essential organisational texts from Durham Cathedral Priory, among them a martyrology, Lanfranc's *Decreta*, and a Gospel lectionary.[62] Like Orderic, Symeon wrote history in an attempt to define and enshrine the identity and influence of his particular monastic community.[63] By composing a directly comparable, albeit more substantial, record of his own community at Saint-Évroul, Orderic, arguably, sought to achieve similar goals. The role of cantor and the writing of history were mutually supportive. In considering the impact of Orderic's possible role as cantor upon the theory and practice of his historical writing, it might therefore be stressed that almost all of his work was channelled towards the same ultimate goal of maintaining the identity and influence of the monastic community at Saint-Évroul.

Orderic manifests an acute awareness of the story of his community as witnessed in its music, liturgy and books, an awareness that found its fulfilment in his composition of the *Historia ecclesiastica*. This work

---

[62] For this item, see A. J. Piper, 'The Durham Cantor's Book (Durham, Dean and Chapter Library, MS B.IV.24)' in *Anglo-Norman Durham, 1093–1193*, ed. David Rollason, Margaret Harvey and Michael Prestwich (Woodbridge, 1994), pp. 79–92; Rozier, 'Symeon of Durham as Cantor and Historian'.

[63] Ibid.

would provide an additional, complementary, element in the creation and maintenance of a historically informed identity within the community of Saint-Évroul. In the middle of his fifth book, Orderic observed that his *Historia* would:

> give a brief account of the properties of the church of Saint-Évroul, so that alms given in faith may be brought to the knowledge of the novices, and when they make use of them they may know when and by whom they were given, or sold at a price.[64]

Returning to this theme in the middle of the sixth book, Orderic later wrote:

> I commemorate our benefactors. For I wish to commit to writing an account of our founders and those who so generously helped them, for the lasting remembrance of future generations, so that the sons of the church may commemorate in the presence of God and his angels those by whose gifts they are supported in this mortal life and enabled to serve the maker of all things.[65]

By recounting the deeds of Saint-Évroul's monks and their lay patrons, Orderic's *Historia* provided an extended supplement to the types of liturgical remembrance for which he might also have been responsible as cantor within the community. His account informed contemporaries and successors of the lives and deeds of those whose names they were remembering, and in doing so fused liturgy, history and patronage into a single vision of community, which appealed to his intended local audience on multiple levels.

As a lifelong member of the community, guardian of its books, enthusiast of the past and possible coordinator of its monastic liturgy during the second half of his adult life, Orderic gained a wide-ranging insight into the history of his home foundation and the actions of those whose gifts and works had supported its development. This knowledge found its ultimate expression in the genesis, evolution and completion of his *Historia ecclesiastica*. Orderic's long and complex work merged

---

[64] HE, III, pp. 122–3: 'Possessiones Vticensis ecclesiae uolo hic breuiter adnotare. Ut eleemosinae fideliter datae pateant novitiorum notitiae, ut utentes eis sciant a quibus vel quo tempore datae sint uel pretio comparatae.'

[65] Ibid., pp. 260–1: 'Huc usque de rebus S. Ebrulfi diutius locutus sum, quae nostrum magna ex parte implent libellum. Inde mihi queso non indignentur lectores, si, beneficii accepti memor, recolo nostros benefactores. Opto equidem fundatores et beneuelos cooperatores eorum scripto commendare tenaci memoriae posterorum, ut filii ecclesiae coram Deo in conspectu angelorum memores sint eorum, quorum beneficiis in hac mortali uita sustentantur, ad peragendam seruitutem conditoris uniuersorum.'

many elements of his experience as a monk, at various junctures drawing on his knowledge of biblical exegesis and theology, hagiography and sacred biography, and liturgy, music and poetry. In doing so it appealed to the diverse but interconnected sensibilities of the participants in, and supporters of, monastic life at Saint-Évroul.

Saint-Évroul and Southern Italy in Orderic's *Historia ecclesiastica*

Daniel Roach

THIS chapter explores the ties that bound the abbey and monks of Saint-Évroul with the peninsula of southern Italy, focusing on the ways in which Orderic repeatedly linked the two regions in Books III to VII of his *Historia ecclesiastica*. Beginning in Book III of the *Historia*, the material on southern Italy constitutes the first major outward movement of the narrative beyond the borders of the Normandy. The discussion that follows considers why and how Orderic wrote about this region. It suggests that the close links between Saint-Évroul and southern Italy were established and maintained by the movement of many monks, patrons and founders of the monastery to and from the peninsula, and of various relics and other physical objects that came into the possession of the extended network of houses associated with Saint-Évroul, both in southern Italy and in Normandy. These movements of people and material, and the memorial culture in which they were understood, encouraged Orderic to narrate the activity of Norman families and church men in southern Italy and enabled him to do so in such a way as to link this material to the remainder of the work. While the works of authors such as William of Apulia, Geoffrey Malaterra and Amatus of Montecassino can be used to corroborate and occasionally enhance our understanding of individuals related to Saint-Évroul, it appears that these medieval chroniclers were unaware of the majority of these links. Only in Orderic's *Historia* are such connections stressed.

Orderic had already written on events in southern Italy while copying and expanding William of Jumièges' *Gesta Normannorum ducum*, between c. 1109 and c. 1113.[1] There Orderic chronicled the exile of Robert of Grandmesnil, one of the co-founders of Saint-Évroul and also its second abbot, and the foundation of the abbey of St Euphemia in Calabria.[2] Such episodes meant that the story of Saint-Évroul overlapped with that of the

---

[1] *GND*, I, pp. xxi, lxvi–lxxvii. On the relationship between Orderic's interpolations into the *Gesta Normannorum* and his *Historia*, see Chibnall, *World*, pp. 176–7. For a brief overview of Orderic's information on southern Italy in the *Gesta Normannorum*, see Olivier Guyotjeannin, 'L'Italie méridionale vue du royaume de France', *Il Mezzogiorno normanno-svevo visto dall'Europa e dal mondo mediteranneo* (Bari, 1999), pp. 143–75, at pp. 148–9.

[2] *GND*, II, vii.29–30, pp. 152–8.

Norman conquest of southern Italy by Robert Guiscard and his brothers in the second half of the eleventh century. Each of these episodes was later used by Orderic in Book III of the *Historia*, along with other information not found in the *Gesta Normannorum ducum*. Orderic's material on southern Italy focuses on events in the eleventh century. It is dispersed across the narrative of Books III to VII, and can be grouped under four broad headings: the death of William Giroie and the theft of gifts for Saint-Évroul;[3] the exile of Robert of Grandmesnil and the establishment of daughter houses in southern Italy;[4] Robert Guiscard's campaigns in the Byzantine Balkans;[5] and the translation of the relics of St Nicholas of Myra.[6] At issue here is how such passages were constructed by Orderic, and the significance of this presentation for scholarly understanding of his work as a whole.[7] It will be seen that Orderic's descriptions of the activities of the monks and patrons of Saint-Évroul, in stories that often involve relics, physical objects and other items of material culture, suggest much about the nature and sources of his information on southern Italy, furthering our understanding of why he wrote about it so much.

Orderic's material on southern Italy has long been of interest to historians. Jamison observed that Orderic was 'incomparably the greatest' of those chroniclers who wrote about Norman Italy in the first half of the twelfth century; she argued that Orderic's account provided 'a picture clear-cut and vivid of the day-to-day process of the Norman migration to the south', adding that 'he came to paint it because the actors were men and women he had known [...] It is all real to him, and through him to us'.[8] Such views were heavily criticised by R. H. C. Davis, who argued that Orderic's perspective was both 'eloquent' and 'idiosyncratic'.[9] Davis stated that 'Orderic's picture of these family and monastic connections is so vivid that there is a great temptation to assume that it was typical, and to generalise from it, but there are strong reasons for thinking that his experience was exceptional.'[10] Though analysis of the connection between Saint-Évroul and southern Italy in the pages of the *Historia* has been

---

[3] *HE*, II, pp. 56–64.

[4] Ibid., pp. 64–74, 94–104.

[5] *HE*, IV, pp. 10–38.

[6] Ibid., pp. 54–74.

[7] In this it pays heed to Olivier Guyotjeannin's observation that Orderic's passages on southern Italy ought to be examined and discussed in the context within which they appear. Guyotjeannin 'L'Italie méridionale', p. 147.

[8] Evelyn Jamison, 'The Sicilian Norman Kingdom in the Mind of Anglo-Norman Contemporaries', *Proceedings of the British Academy* 24 (1938), 237–85, at pp. 242–3.

[9] R. H. C. Davis, *The Normans and their Myth* (London, 1976), pp. 13–15.

[10] Ibid., p. 64.

provided by a range of scholars,[11] the bulk of research on the Normans in the south has drawn almost exclusively on the works of Amatus of Montecassino, William of Apulia and Geoffrey Malaterra.[12]

In Book III of the *Historia*, Orderic moves quickly from the prologue to the story of the foundation of Saint-Évroul in 1050.[13] While this material is well known and its inclusion at the beginning of a house history is to be expected, his decision to relate not long after in Book III how William Giroie left the duchy in order to visit Apulia, never to return, is somewhat more surprising. Orderic claimed that William left not as the result of exile or for selfish gain, but 'in the interests of the church of Ouche' ('pro utilitatibus Vticensis aecclesiae').[14] This phrase presages the expansion of the narrative of the *Historia* in a new geographical direction: towards southern Italy. Orderic introduced his material on the activities of the founders, benefactors and monks of Saint-Évroul in the Italian peninsula

---

[11] Jamison, 'Sicilian Norman Kingdom', p. 242–7; Davis, *The Normans and their Myth*, pp. 63–4; Barbara MacDonald Walker, 'The Grandmesnils: A Study in Norman Baronial Enterprise' (unpublished PhD thesis, University of California Santa Barbara, 1968), pp. 116–56; Joseph Decaëns, 'Le Patrimoine des Grentemesnil en Normandie, en Italie et en Angleterre aux XIe et XIIe siècles', in *Les Normands en Méditerranée: Dans le sillage des Tancrède*, ed. Pierre Bouet and François Neveux (Caen, 1994), pp. 123–40, at pp. 135–7; Marjorie Chibnall, 'Les Moines et les patrons de Saint-Évroult dans l'Italie du Sud au XIe siècle', ibid., pp. 161–70; Marjorie Chibnall, 'The Translation of the Relics of St Nicholas and Norman Historical Tradition', in *Le relazioni religiose e chiesastico-giurisdizionali. Atti del IIo Congresso Internazionale sulle Relazioni fra le due Sponde Adriatiche* (Rome, 1979), pp. 33–41; Graham A. Loud, *The Latin Church in Norman Italy* (Cambridge, 2007), pp. 84–91; Graham A. Loud, 'Churches and Churchmen in an Age of Conquest: Southern Italy, 1030–1130', *HSJ* 4 (1992), 37–53, at pp. 42–3, 45; Graham A. Loud, 'The Kingdom of Sicily and the Kingdom of England, 1066–1266', *History* 88:4 (2003), 540–67, at pp. 546–8.

[12] Kenneth Baxter Wolf, *Making History: The Normans and their Historians in Eleventh-Century Italy* (Philadelphia, 1995); Albu, *Normans in their Histories*, pp. 106–44; on the Norman campaigns in the Balkans, see William B. McQueen, 'Relations between the Normans and Byzantium, 1071–1112', *Byzantion* 56 (1986), 427–76; R. Upsher Smith Jr., 'Nobilissimus and Warleader: The Opportunity and the Necessity Behind Robert Guiscard's Balkan Expeditions', *Byzantion* 70:2 (2000), 507–26; Michael Angold, 'Knowledge of Byzantine History in the West: The Norman Historians (Eleventh and Twelfth Centuries)', *ANS* 25 (2003), 19–33, at pp. 29–31; Georgios Theotokis, *The Norman Campaigns in the Balkans, 1081–1108* (Woodbridge, 2014).

[13] For the dating of Book III, see *HE*, II, pp. xv, 8–14.

[14] Ibid., p. 52. William Giroie's journey to southern Italy and death there conclude Orderic's account of the foundation of Saint-Évroul in the *Gesta Normannorum ducum*, *GND*, II, vii.23, p. 142.

by summarising what little he knew about the arrival of the Normans there.¹⁵ While he began with the exile of a certain Osmund Drengot from Normandy to Apulia,¹⁶ the rest of this passage is spent describing how a Norman named Drogo, who was returning home from a pilgrimage to Jerusalem along with a hundred of his knights, came to the aid of Duke Gaimar of Salerno when his lands were attacked by 20,000 Saracens who demanded tribute from him and his people. According to Orderic, the return of Drogo's company to Normandy along with a great deal of treasure in reward for their services inspired many other Normans to travel to Italy in the hopes of making a similar fortune for themselves. Once there, they quickly began to carve out lands for themselves, 'which', Orderic observed, 'are in the possession of their heirs to this day' ('quae usque hodie heredes eorum possident').¹⁷ Orderic, however, was not nearly as interested in this overarching story of the arrival in southern Italy of Norman people in general as he was in the local story, that the sons of the patrons of his monastery were numbered among those who left Normandy and migrated to southern Italy in the mid-eleventh century.¹⁸ The reality of this becomes apparent when Orderic states that William of Montreuil, the son of William Giroie (another of Saint-Évroul's founders), and Arnold of Grandmesnil, son of Robert of Grandmesnil, are listed alongside Robert Guiscard and the other six sons of Tancred of

---

[15] The classic study by Ferdinand Chalandon, *Histoire de la domination normande en Italie et en Sicile*, 2 vols. (Paris, 1907), remains the most thorough examination of this subject. See also Graham A. Loud, *The Age of Robert Guiscard: Southern Italy and the Norman Conquest* (Harlow, 2000); Graham A. Loud, 'How "Norman" was the Norman Conquest of Southern Italy?', *Nottingham Medieval Studies* 25 (1981), 13–34; Einar Joranson, 'The Inception of the Career of the Normans in Italy – Legend and History', *Speculum* 23:3 (1948), 353–96; Hartmut Hoffmann, 'Die Anfänge der Normannen in Süditalien', *Quellen und Forschungen aus Italienischen Archiven und Bibliotheken* 49 (1969), 95–144; John France, 'The Occasion of the Coming of the Normans to Italy', *Journal of Medieval History* 17:3 (1991), 185–205.

[16] On the nature and importance of exile to southern Italy, see Ewan Johnson, 'The Process of Norman Exile into Southern Italy', in *Exile in the Middle Ages*, ed. Laura Napran and Elisabeth van Houts (Turnhout, 2004), pp. 29–38.

[17] *HE*, II, pp. 56–8. For more on the significance of the term *usque hodie* in the *Historia ecclesiastica*, see Daniel Roach, 'The Material and the Visual: Objects and Memories in the *Historia ecclesiastica* of Orderic Vitalis', *HSJ* 24 (2013), 63–78, at pp. 69–72.

[18] The most detailed prosopographical study of this remains Léon-Robert Ménager, 'Inventaire des familles normandes et franques emigrées en Italie méridionale et en Sicile (XIᵉ–XIIᵉ siècles)', in *Roberto il Guiscardo e il suo tempo: Relazioni e comunicazioni nelle prime giornate Normanno-sveve (Bari, Maggio 1973)* (Rome, 1975), 259–390.

Hauteville[19] whose names are now considered to be synonymous with the conquest of southern Italy.[20] All of this, however, is merely a preamble to the major episodes in Orderic's account of the links between Saint-Évroul and southern Italy.[21]

As has already been noted, Orderic sought to highlight the role of the benefactors of Saint-Évroul and their kinsmen in his brief account of the Norman migration into southern Italy, for this was one of his main priorities in writing the *Historia* for the monks of Saint-Évroul. Having done so, he then moved on to relate how, in spite of his activities in southern Italy,[22] William of Montreuil remained closely connected to his family's monastic foundation in the pays d'Ouche.[23] It was this relationship between William of Montreuil and Saint-Évroul which caused his elderly father, William Giroie, to visit him in southern Italy some time before 1056.[24] William Giroie travelled across the Alps to Rome and then to Apulia where he was reunited with his son 'and other friends and relatives and kinsfolk' ('aliosque amicos et affines ac parentes'). There he faithfully performed his duties in the service of the monastery and was given 'many great gifts' ('multa et magna munera') to take back to the needy monks at Saint-Évroul. Desiring to get some of these gifts home as soon as possible, he sent one of his companions from Saint-Évroul, the monk Gunfrid, back 'with great wealth' ('magno censu'). Gunfrid was fatally poisoned while wintering in Rome and the riches meant for Saint-Évroul were stolen. More dramatic than this, though, and of greater importance to the history of Saint-Évroul, was the fact that William Giroie also died while on his return journey to the pays d'Ouche, of natural causes brought on by old age.[25] William's continued remembrance at Saint-Évroul, as one of the four co-founders of the house, explains the detailed attention given

---

[19] *HE*, II, p. 58; for more on Arnold of Grandmesnil, see Decaëns, 'Le Patrimoine des Grentemesnil', p. 135.

[20] See, for example, *Les Normands en Méditerranée: Dans le sillage des Tancrède*, ed. Pierre Bouet and François Neveux (Caen, 1994); Loud, *The Age of Robert Guiscard*.

[21] A point also noted by Chibnall, *HE*, II, p. 58 n. 3.

[22] The fullest account of these is provided by Amatus of Montecassino. See Aimé du Mont-Cassin, *Ystoire de li normant: Édition du manuscrit BnF fr. 688*, ed. Michèle Guéret-Laferté (Paris, 2011), IV.25, p. 366; VI.1–4, 6–8, 10–12, pp. 415–19, 420–3, 424–6. For an English translation, see *The History of the Normans by Amatus of Montecassino*, trans. Prescott N. Dunbar and Graham A. Loud (Woodbridge, 2004), IV.27, pp. 119–20; VI.1–7, 11–12, pp. 148–52, 154–5.

[23] *HE*, II, p. 58.

[24] Ibid., p. 59 n. 4; for more on connections between the Giroie family and southern Italy, see Chibnall, 'Les Moines et les patrons', pp. 161–2.

[25] *HE*, II, p. 60.

to the circumstances surrounding his death in Book III of the *Historia*. Orderic tells us that:

> The monks, meanwhile, having heard about the death of the founder of their church, were greatly saddened, and faithfully offered prayers and masses and other benefits for his soul to God [...] which their successors work fervently to observe to this day.[26]

The move from the past to the present tense in this passage, coupled with the use of *usque hodie*, is, as I have argued elsewhere, a significant and widespread feature of Orderic's writing in the *Historia*.[27] Here it is used to stress the continuous link between the early history of Saint-Évroul in the mid-1050s and the 'present' of the 1110s and 1120s, when the first books of the *Historia* were being written. Moreover, as Chibnall noted, the Necrology of Saint-Évroul celebrated the obit of William Giroie on 5 February.[28] Here in Book III of the *Historia*, Orderic sought, therefore, to stress that he and the other monks of Saint-Évroul had fulfilled their promise to pray for the soul of their dead founder. In doing so, they not only remembered his life and the vital contribution he had made to the growth of the monastery that he had founded, but also recalled the theft of further valuable gifts for Saint-Évroul, which he had entrusted to one of his companions as he lay dying at Gaeta.

Orderic writes that as William lay dying he called to his bedside his two remaining companions, Anquetil of Noyer and Theodelin of Tanaisie, and charged them with the safe return of these gifts to Saint-Évroul. Thereafter, Anquetil visited the monastery in order to inform the monks of William's death in southern Italy, but said nothing of the objects entrusted to him.[29] This treachery was later exposed by Theodelin, and Anquetil was forced to return to the monks of Saint-Évroul a 'silver chalice, two chasubles, an elephant's tooth and a griffin's claw along with certain other things'.[30] Further objects are also mentioned in this passage. Yet, having confessed his guilt and begged for pardon, Anquetil was forgiven by Abbot Thierry and the other monks of Saint-Évroul. In compensation for his actions, he pledged a third of the town of Ouche to the monks and also donated 'a silk cloak which was made into a cantor's cope' ('unam pallam

---

[26] Ibid., p. 62: 'Coenobitae autem audita morte fundatoris aecclesiae suae nimium contristati sunt, precesque et missas et alia beneficia pro anima eius Deo [...] fideliter obtulerunt, quae successores eorum usque hodie feruenter obseruare satagunt.'

[27] Roach, 'The Material and the Visual', pp. 69–72.

[28] *HE*, II, p. 61 n. 3. For the Necrology, see 'Ex Necrologio Uticensi', in *Recueil des Historiens des Gaules et de la France* 23, ed. Martin Bouquet (Paris, 1894), pp. 484–91, at p. 484.

[29] *HE*, II, pp. 60–2.

[30] Ibid., p. 62: 'Calicem solummodo argenteum et duas casulas dentemque elephantis et ungulam griphis cum aliis quibusdam rebus difficulter exegit.'

ex serico unde cappa cantoris facta est').[31] This story performs the same role in the *Historia* as a charter, documenting the monks' acquisition of landed wealth and other valuable objects. Orderic recorded Anquetil's theft because the events were associated with the death and posthumous remembrance of William Giroie. While the recovery of these gifts and their safe return to Saint-Évroul brought both stories to an end, it is clear from the text itself that their memory lived on long in the mind of the monks of the pays d'Ouche. It is likely that the silver chalice, the two chasubles, the elephant's tooth and the griffin's claw were still in existence in or around Saint-Évroul at the time of Orderic's writing, as so many other objects seem to have been.[32] Of particular interest in this regard is the silk cloak which Anquetil donated to Saint-Évroul. Orderic's statement that this was made into a cantor's cope is significant. In recording this detail, he provided his readers with a small piece of information about the 'afterlife' of the cloak, an item which, though initially used by an individual whose actions threatened to limit the prosperity of the monastery, eventually came to be used by the monks of Saint-Évroul for much more profitable ends.[33] Such details mattered to Orderic as he sought to narrate the changing fortunes of his community for current and future generations of monks.

The second narrative sequence linking Saint-Évroul and southern Italy in the *Historia* relates the exile of Robert of Grandmesnil and the establishment of daughter houses of Saint-Évroul in southern Italy. Robert was elected as the second abbot in June 1059.[34] His exile in 1061, as a result of wider troubles in Normandy,[35] provided Orderic with another opportunity to extend his narrative into southern Italy. This he had previously done while interpolating Book VII of the *Gesta Normannorum ducum*, which begins with Duke William's exile of Hugh of Grandmesnil, Arnold of Échauffour and Robert of Grandmesnil before then moving on to relate how the latter was given the foundation of St Euphemia in Calabria by Robert Guiscard.[36] In this way, the historical troubles of Saint-Évroul were also narrative opportunities, which could and were used to great effect by Orderic in his historical writing. In the *Historia* he related how, having been exiled, Robert of Grandmesnil went first to Pope Nicholas II (1059–61) in Rome to plead his case, before then visiting his kinsmen in Apulia. Although the exiled abbot was unable to secure his

---

[31] Ibid., pp. 62–4.

[32] Roach, 'The Material and the Visual'.

[33] For a further example concerning cantor's copes, see *HE*, III, pp. 160–2.

[34] For a prosopographical overview of his life, see Véronique Gazeau, *Normannia monastica*, vol. 2: *Prosopographie des abbés bénédictins (X^e–XIIe siècle)* (Caen, 2007), pp. 275–6.

[35] For this, see *HE*, II, pp. 74–90.

[36] *GND*, II, vii.29–30, pp. 152–8.

own reinstatement at Saint-Évroul,[37] his command to the monks that they abandon Osbern, his successor, and follow him to southern Italy met with far greater success. Orderic wrote:

> Who can relate the many tribulations by which the church of Ouche was shaking, both inside and out? Behold, Robert, the founder and ruler of the same house, had been unjustly forced from his seat, was forced to roam among foreign households, and a stranger to his house was promoted in his place by the secular power, who though he was skilled and religious, and fervent in the order, was nevertheless distrusted and fearful, not entirely trusting in the indigenous brothers [...] Almost all wished to leave; but the young and infirm, who were kept under close watch, remained unwillingly. Others, however, who were stronger, voluntarily followed their father into exile.[38]

A significant number of the monks departed from Saint-Évroul at this time, with Orderic listing nine at this point in the narrative: Herbert and Hubert of Montreuil, Berengar, son of Arnold, Reginald the Great, Thomas of Anjou, Robert Gamaliel, Thurstan, Reginald Chamois and Walter the Small.[39] Two further names should be added to this list: the monks Fulk and Ursus, who had departed with Robert of Grandmesnil at the time of his exile.[40] In all, then, eleven monks migrated to southern Italy. The fact that so many monks from Saint-Évroul acted in this way can only have increased the interest of Orderic's readers in southern Italy.

Orderic stated that once in Italy Robert sought aid from Robert Guiscard, duke of Calabria.[41] There follows an important passage in Book III that stresses the links between Guiscard and Robert of Grandmesnil, as the duke entrusted the exiled abbot with not one but three monasteries in southern Italy: St Euphemia, Holy Trinity, Venosa, and St Michael

---

[37] *HE*, II, p. 94.

[38] Ibid., pp. 94–6: 'Quis referre potest quot tribulationibus Vticensis aecclesia intus et exterius tunc quatiebatur? En Rodbertus eiusdem fundator et rector de sede sua iniuste fugatus, cogebatur uagari per externas domus, et eiusdem in loco saeculari potestate successit uir extraneus, qui licet sollers esset ac religiosus et in ordine feruidus, suspectus tamen et meticulosus non satis credebat indigenis fratribus [...] Pene omnes discedere uoluerunt; sed infantes et infirmiores qui artiori custodia constringebantur inuiti remanserunt. Alii uero qui fortiores erant, et maiorem licentiam usurpabant, patrem suum secuti sponte exularunt.'

[39] Ibid., p. 96.

[40] Ibid., p. 90.

[41] For a further account of this, see Chibnall, 'Les Moines et les patrons', pp. 162–4.

the Archangel at Mileto.[42] For Orderic, Guiscard's patronage of Robert of Grandmesnil was crucial. Guiscard is highly spoken of at this point in the *Historia* and praised for his military victories against the Byzantine emperor, Alexius Comnenus. While the reality concerning the duke's campaigns in the Balkans in 1081–4 was far less triumphant, ultimately ending in failure, in the context of Orderic's account of the establishment of the daughter houses of Saint-Évroul in southern Italy this did not matter. What mattered was the link between Guiscard, the renowned Norman conqueror in southern Italy, and the monastic network of Saint-Évroul. The fact that one of the co-founders and abbots of Saint-Évroul had engaged directly with the duke is likely to have made for a memorable story that was transmitted orally and lingered long in the memory of the monks of the pays d'Ouche. The passage not only summarises memories of Saint-Évroul's influence in southern Italy, but may also have acted to crystallise them, constituting a satisfying, coherent and much simplified story which would have been easy to both remember and repeat to the monks at Saint-Évroul.

The link with Guiscard in Book III enlivened Orderic's narrative and underscored the prominent associations of his house from the time of its foundation to the present day. He noted not only that the duke was a keen supporter of Abbot Robert, granting him care of three monasteries, but that he and his magnates were also faithful patrons of the first foundation, St Euphemia in Calabria, where his mother, Fredesenda, was buried.[43]

---

[42] *HE*, II, pp. 100–2. The existing scholarship on St Euphemia is of limited value, but see Ernesto Pontieri, 'L'Abbazia benedettina di Sant'Eufemia in Calabria e l'abate Roberto di Grantmesnil', *Archivio storico per la Sicilia* 22 (1926), 92–115; Giuseppe Occhiato, 'Rapporti culturali e rispondenze architettoniche tra Calabria e Francia in eta Romanica: l'Abbaziale Normanna di Sant'Eufemia', *Mélanges de l'école Française de Rome: Moyen Âge; temps modernes* 93:2 (1981), 565–603; Giuseppe Occhiato, 'Robert de Grandmesnil: Un abate "architetto" operante in Calabria nell'XI secolo', *Studi medievali* 28:2 (1987), 609–66. Venosa has been well served by Hubert Houben, *Die Abtei Venosa und das Mönchtum im normannisch-staufischen Süditalien* (Tübingen, 1995). For more on Mileto, see Léon-Robert Ménager, 'L'Abbaye bénédictine de la Trinité de Mileto, en Calabre, à l'époque normande', *Bullettino dell' 'Archivio paleografico italiano'* 4–5 (1958–9), 9–94. More generally, see Léon-Robert Ménager, 'Les Fondations monastiques de Robert Guiscard', *Quellen und Forschungen aus italienischen Archiven und Bibliotheken* 39 (1958), 1–116.

[43] Guiscard's brothers and two of his close companions were also buried at Venosa. See Geoffrey Malaterra, *De rebus gestis Rogerii Calabriae et Siciliae comitis et Roberti Guiscardi ducis fratris eius*, ed. Ernesto Pontieri, Rerum Italicarum Scriptorum 5 (Bologna, 1927–8), II.XXXVII, p. 47; for an English translation, see Geoffrey Malaterra, *The Deeds of Count Roger of Calabria and Sicily and of his Brother Duke Robert Guiscard*, trans. Kenneth Baxter Wolf (Michigan, 2005), 2.37, p. 115; William of Apulia, *La geste de*

Guiscard was himself later buried at Venosa, the second of the daughter houses in southern Italy, as is related in a passage we shall return to in due course.[44] The placing of all three of these foundation stories together in this way suggests that this may be all that was remembered about the subject at Saint-Évroul by the time of Orderic's writing. The differing circumstances surrounding Robert of Grandmesnil's appropriation of St Euphemia, Venosa and Mileto have been melded into one story, as though they all took place at the same time and were all granted to the abbot by Guiscard c. 1061–2.

Orderic makes no reference to the charters of these houses and it is unlikely that he had any access to them. Had he done so he would surely have used them to inform his account of their foundation, as is so often the case with his narrative of the establishment of Saint-Évroul.[45] Although problematic,[46] the charter record for St Euphemia, Venosa and Mileto confirms the essential narrative provided by Orderic about the establishment of these houses,[47] while also adding valuable nuance and detail to the picture presented in the *Historia*.[48] The charters indicate that these houses were closely associated with Duke Robert Guiscard and his brother, Count Roger of Sicily. Their growth in the second half of the eleventh century was almost certainly the result of the numerous and often extensive benefactions which these documents record.

Viewed in light of the charter collections of these houses, the brief and greatly compressed nature of Orderic's account of their establishment in Book III of the *Historia* becomes quickly apparent. St Euphemia was given to Robert of Grandmesnil in the early 1060s, Venosa to Berengar c. 1068–9, and Mileto to William son of Ingran in 1080. These details, which can be

Robert Guiscard, ed. Marguerite Mathieu (Palermo, 1961), II, lines 364–80, p. 152.

[44] *HE*, IV, p. 38.

[45] *HE*, I, pp. 63–77; *HE*, III, pp. xxxxiv; for more on this subject, see the contribution of Thomas Roche to this volume, 'Reading Orderic with Charters in Mind'. See also Marjorie Chibnall, 'Charter and Chronicle: The Use of Archive Sources by Norman Historians', in *Church and Government in the Middle Ages: Essays Presented to C. R. Cheney on his 70th Birthday*, ed. C. N. L. Brooke, D. E. Luscombe et al. (Cambridge, 1976), pp. 1–17.

[46] Loud, *Latin Church*, p. 91.

[47] Chibnall, 'Les Moines et les patrons', p. 165.

[48] For the foundation charter for St Euphemia, see *Recueil des actes des Ducs normands d'Italie (1046–1127), vol. 1: Les Premiers Ducs (1046–1087)*, ed. Léon-Robert Ménager (Bari, 1980), pp. 38–47, no. 11. The many charters that survive from the abbey of Holy Trinity, Venosa, have been edited by Hubert Houben in his thorough study of the abbey, *Die Abtei Venosa*, pp. 230–423. The charters of St Michael the Archangel, Mileto, have been edited by Ménager, 'L'Abbaye bénédictine de la Trinité de Mileto'.

teased out of the charters, are absent from the narrative of the *Historia*. What the reader is provided with in Book III is a schematic account of the establishment of these three houses in southern Italy, which was probably substantially derived from the way in which these important events were remembered at Saint-Évroul over half a century after Abbot Robert of Grandmesnil's exile. The key ingredients were all present: Guiscard's vital support for Robert; his entrusting of St Euphemia to the abbot and his monks and subsequent patronage of the house; the growth of Venosa during Berenger's abbacy; and, finally, the appointment of William as Abbot of Mileto. Above all, what Orderic emphasised throughout this brief passage was the continued strong links between these houses and Saint-Évroul. All three of the houses were given to one of Saint-Évroul's co-founders, and monks who had begun their careers at the mother house were installed as abbots at each. This emphasis is continued in Orderic's final observation that the liturgical chant of Saint-Évroul 'is chanted' ('canitur') there, and the monastic rule 'is observed' ('obseruatur') there 'to this day' ('usque hodie').[49] Although the exile of Robert of Grandmesnil to southern Italy had taken place during a difficult period for the monastery in the pays d'Ouche, Orderic sought to show that, through the providence of God, these circumstances had been turned to good account, allowing the influence of Saint-Évroul to be felt even in southern Italy. This was a story from their history which the novices at Saint-Évroul would have found both informative and edifying.

Orderic's material on Robert Guiscard's invasion of the Byzantine Balkans appears near the beginning of Book VII of the *Historia*. These two campaigns, lasting 1081–3 and 1084–5, centred on the strategically important port city of Durazzo (now Durrës in modern Albania).[50] Orderic's narrative of these events is prefaced by an account of the many political changes which took place in the Byzantine world in the preceding years, including Nicephorus III Botaneiates's coup in 1078 and Alexius Comnenus's subsequent seizure of power in 1081. Having provided this context, Orderic launched into his account of Guiscard's attack on Durazzo in that same year, noting that 'William of Grandmesnil [...] took part in this expedition'.[51] William was the second son of Hugh of Grandmesnil, one of the four co-founders of Saint-Évroul, and some of the details of his eventful life are summarised alongside those of Hugh's four other sons at the very end of Book VIII of the

---

[49] *HE*, II, p. 102; for more on this, see Chibnall, 'Les Moines et les patrons', pp. 166–7. On Orderic's interest in music and his possible role as cantor at Saint-Évroul, see the contribution of Charles C. Rozier to this volume, 'Orderic Vitalis as Librarian and Cantor of Saint-Évroul'.

[50] For a helpful overview, see Paul Stephenson, *Byzantium's Balkan Frontier: A Political Study of the Northern Balkans, 900–1204* (Cambridge, 2000), pp. 156–73.

[51] *HE*, IV, p. 16: 'Guillelmus de Grentemaisnilo [...] huic expeditioni aderant.'

Historia.[52] The significance of the Grandmesnil family and the prominence of their long-standing association with their foundation would almost certainly have meant that the very mention of the family name within the cloister of Saint-Évroul could trigger a range of thoughts, feelings, and even conversations among the monks there.[53] These would have related not only to the Grandmesnils' generous benefaction of the church at the time of its refoundation in 1050, but also to their activities thereafter. Among these memories are likely to have been such notable events as Robert of Grandmesnil's time as prior and then abbot at Saint-Évroul and his exile to southern Italy thereafter, Hugh of Grandmesnil's participation in the Norman Conquest of England, the involvement of Arnold of Grandmesnil, son of Robert, in the migration of Normans to southern Italy, and the flight of Hugh's three sons, William, Ivo and Aubrey of Grandmesnil, from the walls of Antioch during the First Crusade.[54]

In all of this, it is notable that Orderic made no mention of William of Grandmesnil's rebellion against Duke Roger Borsa between 1093 and 1094, which was discussed over two chapters in Book IV of Geoffrey of Malaterra's *De rebus gestis*, where greed is repeatedly given as the prime motivation for William's actions.[55] While it would be tempting to suggest that this was a deliberate omission on Orderic's part, designed to spare the Grandmesnils and their monastery from shame, it is important at this point to remember that Orderic had no access to Malaterra's work and knew little of the affairs of the monks and patrons of Saint-Évroul in southern Italy from the final decade of the eleventh century onwards.[56] Though one of Orderic's contemporaries at Saint-Évroul, the monk Arnold of Tilleul, apparently visited St Euphemia around this time, the latest episode concerning such individuals for which Orderic provided

---

[52] Ibid., p. 338; for more on William of Grandmesnil, see Evelyn Jamison, 'Some Notes on the *Anonymi gesta Francorum*, with Special Reference to the Norman Contingent from South Italy and Sicily in the First Crusade', in *Studies in French Language and Mediaeval Literature Presented to Professor Mildred K. Pope by Pupils, Colleagues and Friends* (Manchester, 1939), pp. 183–208, at pp. 199–200; Walker, 'The Grandmesnils', pp. 133–42; Decaëns, 'Le Patrimoine des Grentemesnil', pp. 136–7.

[53] On the role of tombs and grave stones in the memorialising process, see Hingst, *The Written World*, pp. 102–9.

[54] On this see Daniel Roach, 'Orderic Vitalis and the First Crusade', *Journal of Medieval History* 42:2 (2016), 177–201.

[55] Geoffrey Malaterra, *De rebus gestis*, ed. Pontieri, IV.XXI–XXII, pp. 99–101; in English, *The Deeds of Count Roger*, trans. Wolf, IV.21–2, pp. 199–202; see also Walker, 'The Grandmesnils', pp. 138–40.

[56] HE, II, pp. xxii–xxiii; Loud, 'The Kingdom of Sicily and the Kingdom of England', p. 546 n. 24, p. 548. For the earlier argument that Orderic did make use of Geoffrey Malaterra, see Jamison, 'Sicilian Norman Kingdom', p. 245; Davis, *Normans and their Myth*, p. 92.

a date is William Pantulf's return from Apulia in 1092. He knew much about Guiscard's campaigns in the Byzantine Balkans and the translation of the relics of St Nicholas, as will be seen below, but these events took place in the first and second half of the 1080s. Malaterra's account of William of Grandmesnil's rebellion provides scholars with a valuable episode about which they would otherwise be unaware. The mere mention of William of Grandmesnil's name, embedded as it is in the midst of Book VII of the *Historia*, would have both stimulated and perpetuated the remembrance of further details concerning this notable son of one of the co-founders of Saint-Évroul.

The passage which follows exhibits an even stronger textual link between Durazzo and Saint-Évroul. It recounts a battle between a small foraging party led by Guiscard's son, Bohemond, and a much larger Byzantine force, in which the Normans emerged victorious. Crucially, Orderic stated that:

> At that time they lost the bronze cross which the Emperor Constantine, having seen a cross in the sky, had made to fight against Maxentius [...] the Greeks, having lost their Lord's cross, felt grave sorrow and despair; they laboured greatly to redeem it with the greatest sum of gold. However, Guiscard considered it an indignity to conduct such a trade because he valued the bronze in the cross more precious because of Christ's virtues than all gold [...] since his death the monastery of Holy Trinity Venosa has reverently preserved it to this day [*usque hodie*], and honoured it along with the other relics of the saints.[57]

This passage functions as an explanation of how the monks of Holy Trinity Venosa came to be the custodians of this sacred cross. The final sentence is the most important of all, governing everything which precedes it. As is so often the case in Orderic's *Historia*, the text moves from the past to the present in order to stress that the cross which purportedly belonged first to Constantine, then to Alexius Comnenus, then to Robert Guiscard, continued to be 'preserved' and 'honoured' at Venosa 'to this day' ('usque hodie').

Objects and their previous owners are a regular feature in Orderic's narrative structure. In Book III of the *Historia*, Orderic, relating Robert of Grandmesnil's acquisition of 'a great psalter' ('magnum psalterium')

---

[57] *HE*, IV, p. 18: 'Tunc aeream crucem perdiderunt; quam Constantinus imperator pugnaturus contra Maxentium uisa cruce in coelo fecerat [...] Pelasgi autem grauissimum dolorem et diffidentiam pro amissa cruce Domini habuerunt; quam maximo auri talento redimere multum laborauerunt. Verum Wiscardus talem mercatum agere indignum duxit; quia aes in cruce pro uirtute Christi preciosius omni auro estimauit [...] quam post mortem eius cenobium sanctae Trinitatis Venusiae reuerenter usque hodie custodit, et cum aliis sanctorum pignoribus excolit.'

for Saint-Évroul, listed each of its previous owners in order to stress the object's illustrious history.[58] But in Book VII the history of the object is presented to the reader not in the form of a list of names, but as a narrative account. The lines written here by Orderic are the principal layers of the story as it was remembered and retold, first at Venosa, and then later at Saint-Évroul. What mattered most to Orderic was what happened to the cross after Guiscard's death. Here, once more, the reader is provided with a glimpse of the close association between Guiscard and Venosa, and therefore also, by extension, with Saint-Évroul. Of final significance is the fact that the cross was 'honoured' ('excolit') by the monks of Venosa 'with the other relics of the saints' preserved there. This clearly suggests that there were a number of relics in the possession of the monks at the abbey of Holy Trinity. While not necessarily a remarkable thing in and of itself, it will be seen that Orderic substantiated this claim later in Book VII by providing further relic stories, this time linking the relics of St Nicholas of Myra with Venosa. The prominence of such relic stories throughout Orderic's material on southern Italy reveals that the construction of these portions of the *Historia*'s narrative depended upon the survival of physical objects and other relics within the network of monastic houses associated with Saint-Évroul.

Orderic's version of events in the Balkans is highly misleading, presenting Guiscard's forces as having won important victories against the Byzantine empire. According to the *Historia*, the Normans were not defeated by the Byzantines; rather their campaign was undermined by Guiscard's second wife, Sichelgaita of Salerno.[59] Orderic's portrayal of events says nothing of the much more widely acknowledged reasons for the Norman defeat at the hands of the Byzantine emperor.[60] The final scene of his account of the Norman campaigns in the Byzantine world moves the action from the city of Durazzo to the death-bed of Robert

---

[58] HE, II, p. 42; for further discussion of this passage, see Roach, 'The Material and the Visual', pp. 67–9; Elisabeth van Houts, *Memory and Gender in Medieval Europe, 900–1200* (Basingstoke, 1999), pp. 114–15; see also Philippe Buc, 'Conversion of Objects: Suger of Saint-Denis and Meinwerk of Paderborn' *Viator* 28 (1997) 99–144, at p. 101.

[59] HE, IV, pp. 28–32. For more on Sichelgaita, see Patricia Skinner, '"Halt! Be Men!" Sikelgaita of Salerno, Gender and the Norman Conquest of Southern Italy', *Gender and History* 12:3 (2000), 622–41.

[60] For these see McQueen, 'The Normans and Byzantium', p. 447; Stephenson, *Byzantium's Balkan Frontier*, pp. 168–73. For more on attitudes towards the Byzantine empire before and after the First Crusade, see John France, 'Byzantium in Western Chronicles before the First Crusade', in *Knighthoods of Christ: Essays on the History of the Crusades and the Knights Templar, Presented to Malcolm Barber*, ed. Norman Housley (Aldershot, 2007), pp. 3–16; Angold, 'Knowledge of Byzantine History in the West', pp. 29–32.

Guiscard. He relates how the dying duke called his key nobles and kinsmen to hear his final words, noting that William of Grandmesnil was among them.[61] Orderic then concluded his account by relating how, after his death, Guiscard's body was taken back to southern Italy:

> those returning to Apulia carried the body of the duke to Venosa, and buried it there in the monastery of Holy Trinity with great sorrow. The venerable abbot Berengar, the son of Arnold son of Heugon, was in charge of the same monastery, whom the pious abbot Thierry had educated at Ouche, and then Abbot Robert had brought to Calabria with him. Thereafter he was consecrated as abbot for the monastery of Venosa; and he was also promoted, after several years, because of his meritorious life and wise doctrine, to the bishopric of the aforesaid city by Pope Urban.[62]

Although this passage begins as an account of what happened to Guiscard's body after his death, the second half of the text is dominated by the abbey of Holy Trinity, Venosa, as Orderic once more anchored the story of the duke's siege of Durazzo in the wider story of Saint-Évroul and its monks and daughter houses in southern Italy. The significance of this point should not be overlooked, coming as it does at the end of Orderic's material on the Norman invasion of the Byzantine world. While a number of other writers noted that Guiscard had been buried at Venosa,[63] Orderic used this as an opportunity to remind his monastic readers once again of the links between the monks of Venosa and their own house, Saint-Évroul. To him it was these associations which added most lustre to the name of Venosa, and not the associations with the house of Hauteville, and it was for this reason that the story was included in the pages of the *Historia*.

Elsewhere, two other references provide further glimpses of links between Saint-Évroul and Durazzo: in Book V, Orderic noted that Ansold of Maule, one of the patrons of Saint-Évroul's dependency at

---

[61] *HE*, IV, p. 32. For a later reference to William of Grandmesnil, see p. 168.

[62] Ibid., p. 38: 'Remeantes autem in Apuliam corpus ducis Venusiae detulerunt; ibique in coenobio Sanctae Trinitatis cum luctu magno sepelierunt. Venerabilis Berengarius abbas filius Ernaldi filii Helgonis eidem monasterio praeerat; quem Teodericus archimandrita pius apud Vticum educauerat, et inde Robertus abbas secum in Calabriam adduxerat. Deinde ab Alexandro papa Venusiensi monasterio abbas consecratus est; atque post aliquot annos pro merito uitae et sapientiae doctrina ad pontificatum praefatae urbis a papa Vrbano promotus est.'

[63] William of Malmesbury, *Gesta regum Anglorum: The History of the English Kings*, ed. and trans. R. A. B. Mynors, completed by R. M. Thomson and M. Winterbottom, Oxford Medieval Texts, 2 vols. (Oxford, 1998–9), III.262, pp. 482–4; Geoffrey Malaterra, *De rebus gestis*, ed. Pontieri, III. XLI, p. 82; in English, *The Deeds of Count Roger*, trans. Wolf, 3.41, p. 171; William of Apulia, *La geste*, ed. Mathieu, V, lines 391–409, pp. 256–8.

Maule, took part in the siege;[64] in Book VII, he related how Robert of Grandmesnil was fatally poisoned by St Euphemia's Saracen baker after returning from the battle of Durazzo.[65] Such textual links meant that Orderic's account of Guiscard's campaigns in the Byzantine Balkans, recounted in Book VII of the *Historia*, remained firmly rooted in the monastic landscape and story of Saint-Évroul. When examined together, these passages reveal remarkable similarities and demonstrate that memories of the Byzantine world were probably drawn from individuals and objects which had previously been there, and thus that they were presumably well remembered first at Venosa and finally at Saint-Évroul.

The translation of the relics of St Nicholas of Myra to Bari in 1087 was, as Chibnall observed, 'an event of significance for the whole Mediterranean world'. An account of the translation written by John, archdeacon of Bari, by 1089[66] quickly circulated in Normandy, with copies made at Jumièges and Bec before the end of the eleventh century. A miracle collection was also produced at Bec, and copies of it were made for Lyre and Saint-Évroul.[67] Orderic incorporated his own account of the translation of St Nicholas's relics mid-way through Book VII of the *Historia*.[68] While this was based on John of Bari's *Translatio*,[69] it was carefully edited and abridged, and contained three further episodes added by Orderic. Orderic hinted at his reason for making these additions in the following passage, stating that 'neither [John] nor another was able to note all the cures and other reliefs that followed, which almighty God has mercifully shown to this day to his servants faithfully entreating him, by the merits of the most holy bishop Nicholas'.[70] Gransden attributed Orderic's material on the translation of St Nicholas to the general 'encyclopaedic quality' of the

---

[64] *HE*, III, p. 180.

[65] Ibid., IV, pp. 22–4. While this detail is unique to Orderic, Amatus recorded an example of the abbot performing a military role in guarding Vicalvi for Count Roger of Sicily, his brother-in-law, with all of his knights: Amatus of Montecassino, *Ystoire*, ed. Guéret-Laferté, VII.11, p. 450; in English, *The History of the Normans*, trans. Dunbar and Loud, VII.11, p. 170.

[66] *HE*, IV, pp. 353–4; for this text and others, see Francesco Nitti Di Vito, 'La traslazione delle reliquie di San Nicola', *Japigia* 8 (1937), 295–411.

[67] Chibnall, 'Translation of the Relics', pp. 34–6. Nortier, *Les Bibliothèques médiévales*, p. 231.

[68] *HE*, IV, pp. 54–68.

[69] For the text of John of Bari's *Translatio*, see Di Vito, 'La traslazione', pp. 357–66.

[70] *HE*, IV, p. 68: 'sed nec ipse nec alius omnes sanitates et alia subsidia posteris notificare potuit, quae Deus omnipotens pro meritis sanctissimi pontificis Nicholai seruis suis fideliter petentibus usque hodie clementer exhibuit.'

Historia,⁷¹ but this passage indicates that Orderic's purposes may have been more specific. On closer inspection, the additions all seem intended to show readers how the translation of the relics of St Nicholas was closely connected to the monastic network of Saint-Évroul.

Orderic stated that some of the 'holy relics' ('sanctis reliquiis') had been obtained by 'other peoples' ('aliae gentes') outside southern Italy. This phrase indicates that in writing about the relics in the *Historia* Orderic's real focus centred upon the monastery of Saint-Évroul and its network of associated houses. This suggestion is reinforced by a passage located at the very end of his material on the relics of St Nicholas:

> Thus we have truthfully inserted this account of the translation of the body of St Nicholas into our work, and we faithfully implore the same worker of miracles that, mindful of our remembrance of him, he might have pity and intercede with God on our behalf without ceasing.⁷²

This passage suggests that Orderic incorporated material on St Nicholas into Book VII because of the close associations between the monastic network of Saint-Évroul and the cult of St Nicholas. For just as the monks of Saint-Évroul sought to commemorate the saint and remember him in all they did, so too there was an expectation that St Nicholas himself would remember the monks in his prayers. The relationship was mutually beneficial. Orderic's concern with the relics of St Nicholas in the *Historia* was thus merely an extension of this process of prayerful remembrance, this time achieved by means of the written rather than the spoken word.

Orderic's additions to John's account consist of three anecdotes on the theft and acquisition of some of these relics from Bari, each time emphasising how the relics thereafter came into the possession of the monks of Holy Trinity at Venosa and the priory of Noron in Normandy. While Chibnall noted the presence of these stories in the *Historia*,⁷³ their significance has been little studied by scholars. From the moment that the bones of St Nicholas were taken from Myra, further attempts were made to steal them by the thieves themselves.⁷⁴ Orderic followed John of Bari in recounting how the progress of the sailors back from Myra to Bari had been halted at Makry by a strong northerly wind, recounting how

---

⁷¹ Antonia Gransden, *Historical Writing in England*, vol. I: *c. 550–c. 1307* (London, [1974] 1998), p. 162.

⁷² *HE*, IV, pp. 72–4: 'Haec itaque de translatione corporis sancti Nicholai ueraciter operi nostro inseruimus, ipsumque mirabilium opificem fideliter deposcimus; ut suorum memorum memor nostri misereatur, et pro nobis Deum indesinentur deprecetur.'

⁷³ Chibnall, 'Translation of the Relics', p. 36; Chibnall, 'Les Moines et les patrons', p. 168.

⁷⁴ For more on the theft of relics see Patrick J. Geary, *Furta sacra: Thefts of Relics in the Central Middle Ages* (Princeton, 1978).

favourable winds had only returned after many of the men had returned the relic fragments which they had stolen.[75] This set the tone for what was to follow in the first of the stories told by Orderic, where a certain Christopher who took part in the translation of St Nicholas 'retained a rib for himself in his sleeve' ('unam costam in manica sua sibi retinuit'). After taking refuge at Venosa to recover from a sudden illness which had gripped him, he became a monk there and 'presented the rib of St Nicholas, with himself, to Holy Trinity and recovered from the sickness'.[76] Like so many other stories in the *Historia* which concern southern Italy, the episode takes place at the abbey of Holy Trinity, Venosa. As Orderic had earlier written, God himself had permitted the diffusion of the relics ('permittente Deo') so that the monks of Saint-Évroul and its extended network of houses could also be blessed by them.[77]

The second story concerning the relics of St Nicholas describes another relic which entered into the possession of the monks of Holy Trinity, Venosa. Orderic explained how Stephen, the former cantor at the monastery of St Nicholas in Anger, became a cleric at Bari:

> Finally, having perceived the opportunity, he secretly seized the arm of St Nicholas, which had been suitably covered with silver and kept outside the tomb as a sign to the people, and endeavoured to flee to France and to enrich his country and his monastery with this great treasure.

In an attempt to avoid capture, Stephen, like the sailor Christopher before him, took refuge at Holy Trinity, Venosa. Short of money, he separated the silver from the relic in order to buy food. Orderic wrote that 'rumour of this resounded in the monastic community' ('in conuentu monastico rumor huiusmodi perstreperet'). As a result, a monk named Erembert confronted Stephen and obtained the arm of St Nicholas for the monks of Holy Trinity:

> He received it with great joy and then carried it to the monastery of Holy Trinity, praising God with the monks and all the citizens, and there St Nicholas, to this day, through his relics, miraculously helps those faithfully asking in their many needs.[78]

The passage ends with a short description of Erembert's life and background. The way in which the story is related permits three principal

---

[75] *HE*, IV, pp. 64–6.

[76] Ibid., pp. 68–70: 'secumque costam sancti Nicholai sanctae Trinitati presentauit, et de morbo conualuit'.

[77] Ibid., p. 68.

[78] Ibid., pp. 70–2: 'Quod ille cum ingenti gaudio recipit et mox ad cenobium sanctae Trinitatis monachis et cunctis ciuibus Deum laudantibus deuehit; ibique sanctus Nicholaus usque hodie pignora sua fideliter poscentibus in multis necessitatibus mirifice succurrit.'

conclusions regarding, respectively, the relic collection at Venosa, the usage (once again) of the phrase *usque hodie*, and the description of the monk Erembert.

These two stories, concerning a rib and an arm of St Nicholas, explain Orderic's usage of the plural, 'pignora sua', when he describes the saint's relics. Combined with the bronze cross from Durazzo, this means that, in all, Book VII of the *Historia* contains three relic stories relating to the abbey of Holy Trinity at Venosa. While Chibnall noted the long-term nature of links between Saint-Évroul and Venosa,[79] these stories allow the argument to be taken further. The frequency of such stories concerning Venosa may explain the relative prominence of this house in the narrative of the *Historia* when compared with either of the other two monasteries with which Saint-Évroul was connected (St Euphemia and Mileto). The survival of such important relics and other physical objects at Venosa resulted in the circulation of stories explaining their acquisition by the abbey. According to Orderic, these objects still attracted pilgrims to the site in the late 1080s and 1090s, and St Nicholas continued to heal the faithful at Venosa at the time of the writing of Book VII, thought to have been between 1130 and 1133.[80] Of final interest in this passage is the attention given to the monk Erembert. Orderic speaks highly of him, describing his noble life both before and after conversion. The inclusion of these details about Erembert's life in the pages of the *Historia* was doubtless because of his crucial role in procuring a second relic of St Nicholas for the monks of Holy Trinity, Venosa. In so doing, he not only enriched that house, but, by extension, the history of Saint-Évroul as recorded in Orderic's work.

The third and final story which Orderic told regarding the relics of St Nicholas concerned William Pantulf, the benefactor of Saint-Évroul and founder of Noron, about whom he had previously written in Book V of the *Historia*.[81] On this occasion, the story concerns a tooth and two fragments of the tomb of St Nicholas, and relates not to Venosa but to William's foundation at Noron:

> because he greatly esteemed St Nicholas, [William] searched a great deal for his relics; and because his aim was pleasing to God, he obtained a tooth and two bits from the marble tomb from the translators of the relics [...] And so in the year of the incarnation of our Lord 1092, the fifteenth indiction, the tooth of the cherished confessor, Nicholas, was brought from Apulia with other relics of the saints by William Pantulf, and was received with honour in the church of Noron that had been established, at a previous time, in honour of St Peter. Roger, abbot of Ouche, and Ralph, at that time

---

[79] Chibnall, 'Les Moines et les patrons', pp. 167–8.

[80] *HE*, IV, p. xix.

[81] *HE*, III, pp. 154–64.

the then abbot of Séez but afterwards archbishop of Canterbury [...] received the holy relic [...] and carefully fitted it into a silver casket generously provided by the above-mentioned knight. The often-mentioned relics were frequently sought out by many with fevers and other sicknesses, and, by the merits of the cherished Bishop Nicholas, those asking in faith regained the health they desired.[82]

The relics which William Pantulf brought back from southern Italy increase in significance as the story develops. While the sick went to Noron to be healed, stories concerning the precious objects travelled outwards from St Peter's to the surrounding foundations and to the monastery of Saint-Évroul, of which it was a dependency. William's close association with Saint-Évroul may perhaps explain why Orderic says little about the circumstances surrounding the acquisition of the relics, other than that they were obtained from some of the sailors who had originally taken part in the translation of the relics of St Nicholas from Myra to Bari. The action of inserting the relics into the reliquary transformed their meaning and the nature of the memories associated with them.[83] In noting this, Orderic showed that a strong mnemonic connection had been made between William Pantulf and the relics of St Nicholas, one which overrode past associations.

It is important to highlight that evidence of Saint-Évroul's connections with the Italian peninsula are not confined to the *Historia ecclesiastica*. They survive in a number of the other manuscripts produced by the monks of the pays d'Ouche, many of which were written, either wholly or in

---

[82] HE, IV, p. 72: 'quia sanctum Nicholaum ualde diligebat de reliquiis eius multum quesiuit; Deoque iuuante procurationem eius a reliquiarum translatoribus unum dentem et duo frusta de marmoreo tumulo optinuit [...] Dentem itaque tanti baronis nactus in Normanniam rediit; et ad proprium predium quod Noron dicitur plures personas ut congrue reliquias susciperent denunciato die accersiit. Anno itaque dominicae incarnationis MºXCºIIº indictione xv dens almi confessoris Nicholai cum aliis sanctorum reliquiis a Guillelmo Pantulfo de Apulia delatus est; et in basilica Noronensi in honore sancti Petri prisco tempore condita honorifice susceptus. Ad hanc utique susceptionem Rogerius Vticensis abbas et Radulfus tunc temporibus Sagiensis abbas sed postmodum Cantuarensis archiepiscopus accersiti sunt [...] sanctas reliquias [...] susceperunt, et in argentea pixide a supradicto milite liberaliter parata diligenter coaptauerunt. Frequenter a multis febricitantibus et ab aliis egrotantibus sepedicta pignora requisita sunt; meritisque almi presulis Nicholai pie postulantes optatam sanitatem adepti sunt.'

[83] For a stimulating discussion of the relationship between reliquaries and memory, see Amy G. Remensnyder, 'Legendary Treasure at Conques: Reliquaries and Imaginative Memory', *Speculum* 71:4 (1996), 884–906.

part, by Orderic himself.[84] Therefore, alongside the names of individuals such as William Giroie, William Pantulf and Robert of Grandmesnil, the necrology of Saint-Évroul also contained those of Berengar, the first abbot of Venosa and later bishop of that city ('Berengarius, abbas et episcopus'), and Abbot William of St Euphemia ('Willelmus, abbas Sanctae Eufemiae'), whose obits were commemorated on the 25 and 27 December respectively.[85] Similarly, the annals of Saint-Évroul, which were maintained by Orderic until his death,[86] record the journey of Abbot Thierry to Cyprus in 1058, Abbot Robert of Grandmesnil's journey to Rome in 1060 and his replacement by Osbern of Cormeilles, and, finally, the translation of the body of St Nicholas from Myra to Bari, celebrated on 9 May 1087.[87] The *liber memorialis* also displays a further aspect of the relationship between Saint-Évroul and southern Italy, namely that prayers were said for the deceased monks of the abbey of Holy Trinity, Venosa, listed there along with the words 'we must do so as we do for ourselves' ('agendum est nobis sicut pro nobis ipsis').[88] Finally, among the roll of earliest charters that survive from Saint-Évroul there is a charter which records the donation of a certain Guitmund *de Maisnil* and his son, Robert, of ten carucates of land to the monks.[89] While no date is given for this donation, the scribe nevertheless noted the striking detail that it took place 'in the year in which Arnold our monk returned from Apulia' ('anno quo Ernaldus monachus noster reversus est de Apulia').[90] This is a clear reference to Arnold of Tilleul, a long-serving monk and contemporary of Orderic at Saint-Évroul and a close kinsman of the Grandmesnil family. More details concerning his journey to Apulia are provided in Book VIII

---

[84] Escudier, 'Orderic et le scriptorium'.

[85] 'Ex Necrologio Uticensi', pp. 484, 486, 490–1.

[86] For more on Orderic's career as an annalistic writer, see Alison Alexander, 'Annalistic Writing in Normandy, c. 1050–1225' (unpublished DPhil thesis, University of Cambridge, 2011), pp. 133–40, 209–11. See also this volume, Rozier, 'Orderic as Librarian and Cantor', and Appendix 2, item 9.

[87] *Orderici Vitalis ecclesiasticae historiae libri tredecim*, ed. and trans. A. Le Prévost, 5 vols. (Paris, 1838–5), V, pp. 139–72, at pp. 157–8.

[88] For the *liber memorialis*, see Jean Laporte, 'Tableau des services obituaires assures par les abbayes de Saint-Evroul et de Jumièges', *Revue Mabillon* 46 (1956), 141–88, at p. 173. See also Rozier, 'Orderic as Librarian and Cantor', where it is suggested that Orderic added a confraternity agreement with Venosa to the manuscript.

[89] I have been unable to identify who these donors were. For more on the charters of Saint-Évroul see Roche, 'Reading Orderic with Charters in Mind.'

[90] For this charter, see *Orderici Vitalis ecclesiasticae historiae libri tredecim*, ed. and trans. A. Le Prévost, 5 vols. (Paris, 1838–5), V, p. 185 (charter no. 6).

of the chronicle.⁹¹ There Orderic wrote that Arnold travelled to southern Italy, staying at St Euphemia with his brother William, the then abbot, and also with his cousin, William of Grandmesnil, for the express purpose of obtaining valuable goods from his kinsmen which could then be taken back to Normandy and used to benefit Saint-Évroul.⁹²

While the existing scholarship has emphasised the oral nature of Orderic's information on southern Italy, with Chibnall in particular arguing that his knowledge was derived either 'directly or indirectly' from the patrons of Saint-Évroul,⁹³ it is important to stress that Orderic never once acknowledged his sources for the southern Italian material in the *Historia*. I have argued elsewhere that relics and other physical objects mattered a great deal to Orderic, as evidenced by their prominence throughout the *Historia*.⁹⁴ Such textual descriptions point to the continued existence of these objects in the possession of Saint-Évroul and its extended network of associated houses. In this chapter it has been argued that the same can be said of many of Orderic's passages on southern Italy. As has been seen, these objects included a bronze Byzantine cross and the rib, arm, and two teeth of St Nicholas of Myra, all of which found their way into the collections of houses closely connected to Saint-Évroul. The movement of such relics was enabled by the already well-established links between Saint-Évroul and southern Italy, links which the relics also served to maintain. That descriptions of these objects are always accompanied by an account of the circumstances surrounding their acquisition suggests that much of Orderic's information regarding connections between his own house and southern Italy was derived from material objects which remained in these monasteries long after human contact between the two houses had reduced to a mere trickle. Thus it was not just the stories told by the monks and patrons of Saint-Évroul which enabled Orderic to construct this part of the *Historia*'s narrative, but also the objects which those people carried. The material on southern Italy dispersed across Books III to VII of the *Historia* is not peripheral to the work but is, rather, an important and carefully integrated part of the much larger whole. Its inclusion within the *Historia*, as with so many other subjects treated within the narrative, was rooted in the history of the monastery of Saint-Évroul. In reading it, the monks there could not have failed to be reminded of their rich communal past.

---

[91] This journey is likely to have taken place in the 1090s: Walker, 'The Grandmesnils', p. 133.

[92] *HE*, IV, p. 142. Arnold of Tilleul reappears in a number of places throughout the pages of the *Historia*, performing similar duties for the monastery: Roach, 'The Material and the Visual', pp. 74–5.

[93] Loud, 'The Kingdom of Sicily', p. 548; *HE*, II, p. xxii.

[94] Roach, 'The Material and the Visual'.

Orderic and English

Mark Faulkner

NARRATING Henry I's attempts to recapture Robert of Bellême in 1102 in Book XI of his *Historia*, Orderic describes the surrender of Bridgnorth and Henry's subsequent journey with his 60,000 troops north-west to Shrewsbury via the road across Wenlock Edge, widening the cutting as they went.[1] This cutting was a bare ten miles south-east of Orderic's birthplace in Atcham, and it is therefore no surprise that he is well informed about the troops' movements. It is also no surprise that Orderic knew the English name of this pass – 'Huvel hegen' – glossing this as 'malum callem vel vicum' (translated by Chibnall as 'evil path' or 'road'). Orderic's inclusion of the English road name raises questions about not only how much knowledge of English he retained in later life, but also his reasons for including this detail in an account of a conflict over English territory between two primarily French-speaking adversaries, written for a Francophone monastic audience within his home monastery of Saint-Évroul.

Chibnall reconstructs the road name given by Orderic as Middle English *uvel hege*, 'evil hedge or undergrowth', but given that Orderic describes it as 'a deep cutting [...] overshadowed on both sides by a thick wood', it would be preferable to connect the second element with *ege*, 'ridge'.[2] There is, moreover, reason to believe that *hegen* should be construed as a plural, so that the road name should in fact be 'evil edges'.[3]

I am grateful to my colleagues at the University of Sheffield, Graham Williams and Robyn Orfitelli, for their comments on a draft of this chapter.

---

[1] HE, VI, pp. 28–31.

[2] Ibid., p. 29 n 4. For *ege* in the sense 'crest (of a hill), ridge', see *Middle English Dictionary*, **egge** (n. (2)), 3(c), and compare *Dictionary of Old English*, **ecg** 3: *Middle English Dictionary*, ed. Hans Kurath, Sherman M. Kuhn and Robert E. Lewis (2001), online at <http://quod.lib.umich.edu/m/med/>; *Dictionary of Old English: A to G online*, ed. Angus F. Cameron, Ashley Crandell Amos and Antonette diPaolo Healey (2007), online at <http://tapor.library.utoronto.ca/doe/dict/index.html> [both accessed 19 December 2014].

[3] As it stands, the concord of 'huvel hegen' cannot be reconciled with Old English norms. The lack of inflection on 'huvel' suggests the road name should be understood as grammatically nominative. Since *ecg* is a light jō-stem, we would expect **yfelu ecg*, with *–u* rather than *–ø* on the adjective and *–ø* rather than <-en> on the noun. In transitional English, <-en>

Orderic's translation of this name is thus doubly wrong: first in that renders *hege* with *callis* or *vicus*, both of which essentially mean 'road', thus missing the topographical significance of the name; second, in that he translates as singular a noun that is plural, implying a somewhat shaky recollection of his childhood language. But, as his very inclusion of this phrase suggests, writing in English, and getting it right, seem to have remained important to Orderic. This is apparent from his hypercorrection here. Francophones like Orderic would have been unused to pronouncing [h] at the beginning of words; thus, if they tried to speak English, they would have struggled to pronounce words beginning with [h].[4] Consequently, Francophones may have written <h> where they would not have pronounced it: this is the most economical explanation for the inorganic <h> at the beginning of both 'huvel' and 'hegen' in Orderic's text.[5] Orderic's determination to get the English right here, even at a cost of getting it wrong, thus provides evidence for the importance he attached to the English he retained in the mid-1130s, some forty years after he had left England.[6]

This chapter offers a thorough account of Orderic's knowledge of English, analysing whether he was taught to read and write the language as a child, and how much of it he recalled as an adult.[7] Historians have long been interested in how Orderic's biography shaped his writing of history – a biography briefly comprising his birth in the 'remote parts of Mercia' as the offspring of a putatively mixed marriage between an immigrant from central France and an English woman; his entry into Saint-Évroul as a ten-year-old oblate, where he found the other monks spoke a language he did not know; and, with a developing reputation as a historian, his sojourn

---

is more likely to be a reflex of historical <-V(n)> (i.e. any bare vowel or any vowel followed by <n>) than –ø. For this reason, Orderic's <-en> is more likely to reflect the plural *yfele ecga*, probably via analogy with the *an*-declension, which in any case better suits the topography.

[4] Word-initial [h] had been lost in Late Latin, creating considerable difficulties for speakers of Late Latin when writing the language. The sound was used in Old French only in a handful of words borrowed from Germanic. See further M. K. Pope, *From Latin to Modern French* (Manchester, 1934), §28.

[5] If my interpretation of *hegen* as a plural is correct, then this would constitute a third instance of hypercorrection, whereby Orderic tried to counter the tendency towards denasalisation in transitional English by mistakenly restoring <-n> where it was not required.

[6] For 1135×1137 as the date of Book XI, see Chibnall, 'General Introduction', p. 47.

[7] Previous comments have been much briefer, for example those of R. M. Thomson on William of Malmesbury's use of, and therefore ability to read, texts in Old English: see R. M. Thomson, *William of Malmesbury*, rev. edn. (Woodbridge, 2003), p. 46.

in Crowland to write the history of the abbey there.[8] Key to this biography is that Orderic grew up speaking English, but wrote a Latin history in a Francophone monastery. Ascertaining how much of his childhood English he retained in his later years is thus a necessary first step in assessing his use of English in the *Historia*, and may also help decide whether it is likely he used vernacular sources for some of his English material. Furthermore, since Anglo-Saxon England was the one territory in early medieval Europe where the vernacular had a role in state formation and nation building, establishing Orderic's knowledge of English may ultimately enable us to better understand his attitude to England, Englishness and the Anglo-Saxon state.[9] Given this, it is disappointing how little evidence of English the *Historia* contains: one sentence in English (and that quoted at second hand);[10] the English terms for *carrucate* and *feast*;[11] and Latin etymologies

---

[8] Thus Amanda Jane Hingst draws several connections between Orderic's English upbringing and his historical writing in Hingst, *Written World*, especially pp. xiii, 50, 65. For Chibnall, Orderic's early years in England meant 'he could not fail to know at first hand the grievances of the English' (Chibnall, 'General Introduction', p. 79), while his oblation at Saint-Évroul 'undoubtedly enabled [him] to become one of the greatest of Norman historians' (ibid., p. 5). For Shopkow (*History and Community*, p. 100), Orderic writes as 'an Englishman defending his people' against the 'negative insinuations' of William of Jumièges and William of Poitiers. For Jean Blacker (*The Faces of Time: The Portrayal of the Past in Old French and Latin Historical Narrative of the Anglo-Norman Regnum* (Austin, TX, 1994), p. 15), the fact that Orderic 'always thought of himself as an Englishman in exile' meant 'he approached his task' of writing a history for the Normans 'with a touch of irony'. See also the comments of Robert M. Stein, *Reality Fictions: Romance, History and Governmental Authority, 1025–1180* (Notre Dame, IN, 2006), pp. 97–100.

[9] For Anglo-Saxon England as the exception to the rule that in the early Middle Ages 'language simply did not appear among the various strategies used for the mobilisation of unity', see Patrick J. Geary, *Language and Power in the Early Middle Ages*, The Menahem Stern Jerusalem Lectures (Waltham, MA, 2013), p. 73.

[10] 'That wat min lauert Godel mihtin that ic sege soth' (*HE*, III, p. 350). This is included in a *miraculum* of St Æthelthryth that Warin des Essarts, later abbot of Saint-Évroul, wrote up for Hervey, bishop of Ely, in epistolary form, and which Orderic quotes in its entirety in Book VI. A narrative of the same events is included in the *Liber Eliensis* (ed. E. O. Blake, Camden Society 3rd series 92 (London, 1962), pp. 266–9). For discussion, see most recently Helmut Gneuss, 'More Old English From Manuscripts', in *Intertexts: Studies in Anglo-Saxon Culture Presented to Paul E. Szarmach*, ed. Virginia Blanton and Helen Scheck (Tempe, AZ, 2008), pp. 411–21, at pp. 413–15.

[11] *HE*, II, p. 230: 'Conuiuiis prouincialium quæ uulgo firmam appellant' ('the feasts of the country people which are colloquially known as "feorms"'); *HE*, IV, p. 172: 'carrucatas quas Anglice hidas uocant' ('the ploughlands

of seven English names, several again at second hand.¹² Fortunately, the text contains large numbers of English place and personal names, and these provide valuable, if difficult, evidence for Orderic's knowledge of English.

1 Names as Evidence

USING name forms as linguistic evidence is far from new. For example, Alistair Campbell's *Old English Grammar* accepts 'the names contained in the early manuscripts of Bede's *Historia ecclesiastica*' as, alongside manuscript texts and inscriptions, 'a further source for Northumbrian'.¹³ However, as Campbell and subsequent scholars have acknowledged, names are a vexed source of linguistic evidence.¹⁴ One problem is what exactly they offer evidence of. Though it is cognate with

---

which in English are called hides'). The reference to *feorms* is very possibly taken from the lost conclusion of the *Gesta Guillelmi* of William of Poitiers (see *HE*, II, p. xviii, for Orderic's use of this source).

[12] Place Names: 'Crulandia enim crudam id est cenosam terram significat' ('Crowland means rough or boggy land', *HE*, II, p. 339), a hybrid French–English etymology (compare *Anglo-Norman Dictionary*, **cru**, 3 ('(of earth) untilled, uncultivated') [*Anglo-Norman Dictionary*, ed. William Rothwell, Louise Stone and T. B. W. Reid (2007), online at <http://www.anglo-norman.net/gate/> accessed 19 December 2014]; compare also the etymology given by V. E. Watts, *The Cambridge Dictionary of English Place-Names* (Cambridge, 2004) [henceforth *CDEPN*]: < **crūw* + **land**, 'the land in a bend'); 'Torneia quippe spinarum insula nuncupatur Anglice' ('Thorney is the English name for "island of thorns"', *HE*, VI, p. 151).

Tribe Names: 'North enim anglice aquilo, man uero dicitur homo. Normannus igitur aquilionalis homo interpretatur' ('in the English language "aquilo" means "north" and "homo", "man"; Norman therefore means "man of the North"', *HE*, V, p. 24).

Personal Names: 'Guthlacus, id est belli munus' ('Guthlac, meaning "Gift of War"', *HE*, II, p. 324), following Felix's *vita* (ed. Bertram Colgrave (Cambridge, 1956), p. 79).

Bynames: 'Edmundi Irneside id est Ferrei Lateris' ('Edmund called Ironside', *HE*, II, p. 180); 'Edricus quoque [...] cognomento Streonæ id est siluaticus' ('Edric known as the wild', *HE*, II, p. 194); 'Edrici [...] cogomento Streonæ id est adquisitoris' ('Edric called Streona, or "the rapacious"', *HE*, II, p. 194). All three explanations may ultimately be indebted to William of Poitiers.

In addition to these, note also 'Hugoni Dirganæ id est grosso' ('Hugh "Digri", that is "the stout"', *HE*, V, p. 224), where the etymon is Old Norse *dyggr*.

[13] A. Campbell, *Old English Grammar* (Oxford, 1959), §7.

[14] See, most recently, Carole Hough, 'Evidence from Sources Prior to 1500', in *The Oxford Handbook of the History of English*, ed. Terttu Nevalainen and Elizabeth Closs Traugott (Oxford, 2012), pp. 37–49, esp. §4 ('Names').

the noun *cniht*, 'boy', the Old English name **Cniht** is not itself a lexical word.[15] There are sound changes that affect only names.[16] This means that evidence from names is not necessarily applicable to the language more broadly.[17] Another problem is that not all name data is equally helpful. The spelling of particularly common names (for example **Alfred**) was liable to fossilise into a standard form that ceased to replicate sound changes affecting the lexical words.[18] Thus the first element of King Alfred's name is spelled *Ælfred* in the Parker Chronicle, retaining the Mercian spelling *Ælf-* in preference to the **Ielf-* that we might predict were it a lexical word.[19]

Despite these difficulties, when used with care names can offer valuable linguistic evidence. One large project that makes exclusive use of onomastic material is Gillis Kristensson's *Survey of Middle English Dialects, 1290–1350*, completed in 2001.[20] Kristensson's delineation of dialect boundaries is based on evidence from the Lay Subsidy Rolls. Though written in Latin, these Rolls contain numerous place and personal names, given in – Kristensson argues – what is likely to be a faithful transcription of the preliminary local return, and therefore ultimately an accurate reflection of local pronunciation.[21] While Kristensson's work has

---

[15] On the linguistic status of names, see Fran Colman, *The Grammar of Names in Anglo-Saxon England: The Linguistics and Culture of the Old English Onomasticon* (Oxford, 2014), pp. 21–95.

[16] One example is the development of **Æthel-** to **Ægel-** in the tenth and eleventh centuries, discussed by Fran Colman, 'The Name Element *Æðel-* and Related Problems', *Notes and Queries*, n. s. 28 (1981), 295–301.

[17] Thus Cecily Clark talks of 'onomastic sound change', and Carole Hough notes that onomastic isoglosses can differ from lexical isoglosses: Cecily Clark, 'Towards a Reassessment of "Anglo-Norman Influence on Place-Names"', in *Language Contact in the British Isles: Proceedings of the Eighth International Symposium on Language Contact in Europe, Douglas, Isle of Man, 1988*, ed. P. Sture Ureland and George Broderick (Tübingen, 1991), pp. 275–95, reprinted in *Words, Names and History: Selected Writings of Cecily Clark*, ed. Peter Jackson (Cambridge, 1995), pp. 144–67, esp. pp. 150–2; Carole Hough, 'The Role of Onomastics in Historical Linguistics', *The Journal of Scottish Names Studies* 3 (2009), 29–46, esp. pp. 33–4.

[18] For fossilisation, see especially Fran Colman, *Money Talks: Reconstructing Old English* (Berlin, 1992), p. 15.

[19] Example from Colman, *Grammar of Names in Anglo-Saxon England*, p. 23. For the putative development to **Ielf-* (via breaking and i-umlaut), see Richard M. Hogg, *A Grammar of Old English*, vol. 1: *Phonology* (Oxford, 1992), §5.74 n. 3.

[20] Gillis Kristensson, *A Survey of Middle English Dialects, 1290–1350*, 4 vols. in 5 (Lund, 1967–2001).

[21] For Kristensson's methodology, see particularly his 'Another Approach to Middle English Dialectology', *English Studies* 46 (1965), 138–56, along with

been somewhat overshadowed by the contemporary *Linguistic Atlas of Late Middle English*, and doubts must remain over whether the place and personal names in the Rolls do invariably represent local pronunciations, reviewers have generally received it and its methodology favourably.[22]

The methodology of this essay differs from Kristensson's, and from that of other studies that use names as a source of linguistic evidence, in several ways. One of the major questions about the *Survey* has been 'how much the names that Kristensson used for his data might have been altered for the copyists and perhaps not representative of local forms'.[23] Since we have access to Orderic's autograph text of the majority of his *Historia*, we need not worry about whether later scribes altered his spelling. Instead, we are confronted with a different, but related, problem, for while we can be confident that the informants behind the Lay Subsidy Rolls were people from the relevant localities, we do not always know who Orderic's informants were, and some of those informants were texts which (as will emerge below) used a variety of different orthographical systems. However, with care, it is possible to make sense of the surface variety of forms Orderic uses.

2 Methodology

THIS assessment of Orderic's knowledge of English is primarily based upon all the English place and personal names found in Books III–VI and IX–XIII, that is, all those parts of the *Historia* to survive in autograph that are printed in full by Chibnall. This data was collected by reading through Chibnall's text and in total consists of 167 place names, collectively occurring over 400 times, and 121 personal names, collectively found over 300 times. In establishing Orderic's usage, I have relied more heavily on place names than personal names; this is because place names, by virtue of their greater variety, are less susceptible to fossilisation than personal names. Personal names are primarily used to confirm or query patterns detected in the place name evidence.

Two further considerations inform my handling of this evidence. First, in order to control for the possibility that a particular place-name form

---

the 'General Remarks' that open *A Survey of Middle English Dialects, 1290–1350: The West Midland Counties* (Lund, 1987), pp. ix–xiii.

[22] Richard Dance observes the volume 'follows the same tried and tested format as its predecessors', in his '[Review of] Gillis Kristensson, *A Survey of Middle English Dialects 1290–1350: The Southern Counties, Part I, Vowels (Except Diphthongs)* (Lund, 2001)', *Notes and Queries*, n. s. 49 (2002), 398–9, at p. 398.

[23] Keith Williamson, 'Middle English: Dialects', in *English Historical Linguistics: An International Handbook*, ed. Alexander Bergs and Laurel J. Brinton (Berlin, 2012), I, pp. 480–505, at p. 482.

may reflect a fossilised spelling rather than Orderic's idiolectal usage, I have compared his spellings of place names with the autograph forms of two near-contemporary historians: Eadmer of Canterbury (c. 1060 – in or after 1126) and William of Malmesbury (c. 1090 – in or after 1142).[24] A second factor that needs to be controlled is the possibility that Orderic took the spelling of a particular place name from a written source, and that its orthography in the *Historia* is that of the source, not Orderic. For example, as I show below (§3.1.1), Orderic generally writes the reflex of Old English /y(:)/ as <u>, but his transcription of William the Conqueror's pancarte for Saint-Évroul includes three <e> spellings. To control for this possibility, I have relied on Chibnall's account of Orderic's sources, as presented in the introductions to the relevant volumes of her edition and aggregated in the introductory volume which completed it.[25]

Finally, a brief account of how historical linguists interpret spellings is in order. Spellings ultimately represent spoken linguistic forms, but there is seldom a simple relationship between orthographical representation and the phonology of the underlying language. No one writes as he speaks. To interpret spellings we therefore need to bring a range of evidence to bear, including an awareness of the different orthographical systems available (here principally Latin, 'Standard' Old English, and French, in so far as this had a stable orthography in the second half of the eleventh century), and knowledge of the phonology of both Old English and West Midlands Middle English.[26] While we can never be entirely sure what a

---

[24] For Eadmer, I have collected relevant forms from the indexes of *Eadmeri Historia novorum in Anglia*, ed. M. Rule, Rolls Series 81 (London, 1884) [hereafter *HN*], and to ensure full coverage of this text, *Eadmer's History of Recent Events in England: Historia Novorum in Anglia*, trans. Geoffrey Bosanquet (London, 1964); *The Life of St Anselm, Archbishop of Canterbury, by Eadmer*, ed. R. W. Southern (Oxford, 1962) [hereafter *VA*]; *Vita Sancti Wilfridi Auctore Edmero: The Life of Saint Wilfred by Edmer*, ed. Bernard J. Muir and Andrew J. Turner (Exeter, 1998) [hereafter *VW*]; and *Eadmer of Canterbury: Lives and Miracles of Saints Oda, Dunstan, and Oswald*, ed. Andrew J. Turner and Bernard J. Muir (Oxford, 2006) [hereafter *SL*]. All these texts are based upon Eadmer's autograph manuscript, MS Cambridge, Corpus Christi College, 371 (described in R. W. Southern, *Saint Anselm and his Biographer* (Cambridge, 1966), pp. 367–74). For William, I have used his *Gesta Pontificum Anglorum: The History of the English Bishops*, ed. M. Winterbottom and R. M. Thomson, 2 vols. (Oxford, 2007) [hereafter *GP*], an edition based on his autograph, MS Oxford, Magdalen College, Lat. 172.

[25] Chibnall, 'General Introduction', pp. 48–77; *HE*, II, pp. xvi–xxix; III, pp. xv–xxviii; IV, pp. xix–xxv; V, pp. xiii–xix; VI, pp. xvii–xxi.

[26] For an excellent introductory example of phonological reconstruction, see Roger Lass, 'Phonology and Morphology', in *The Cambridge History of the English Language*, vol. 2: *1066–1476*, ed. Norman Blake (Cambridge, 1992), pp. 23–155, at pp. 27–30. For 'Standard' Old English, see §3.2 below.

given spelling might represent, it is possible to know within certain bounds, and thereby to extrapolate from Orderic's use of place and personal names some sense of how he spoke, and to identify aspects of his mapping of sounds to graphs (in other words, of his spelling system) that are idiosyncratic for the first half of the twelfth century.

3 Results

IN this section, I demonstrate that Orderic retained a Shropshire pronunciation of English late into his life, but that his proficiency in English diminished as he grew older. I argue that he was not taught to read or write English before he departed for Normandy. Using the English language was probably not a part of his self-identity as *Angligena*.

3.1 Orderic as a Speaker of Shropshire English

There is good evidence that Orderic retained a South-West Midlands pronunciation of English, consistent with his early upbringing in Shropshire, throughout his life. This is suggested by three particular features of his orthography: his preference for representing the reflex of OE /y(:)/ as <u>, the presence of forms that seem to show Second Fronting, and the occurrence of several forms with <o> for OE [ā].

3.1.1 <u> for OE /y(:)/

The reflex of Old English /y(:)/ has usually been taken as one of the most dialectally diagnostic features of Middle English texts, with /e/ found in Kent, Sussex, Surrey and the South-East Midlands, especially Essex and Suffolk, /i/ in the North-East Midlands and the North, and /y/ (spelled <u>) in the West Midlands, Gloucestershire, Devon, Wiltshire and Hampshire.[27] Orderic has <u>, <e> and <i> for historic /y(:)/, with <u> in:

> For Shropshire Middle English, the most important evidence is 'AB', the language of the Katherine Group and *Ancrene Wisse*, on which see most recently Richard Dance, 'The AB Language: The Recluse, the Gossip and the Language Historian', in *A Companion to Ancrene Wisse*, ed. Yoko Wada (Cambridge, 2003), pp. 57–82. The most thorough grammar of AB remains *Þe Liflade ant te Passiun of Seinte Iuliene*, ed. S. R. T. O. D'Ardenne, Early English Text Society o. s. 248 (London, 1961 for 1960), pp. 177–250.

[27] Richard Jordan, *Handbook of Middle English Grammar: Phonology*, trans. Eugene E. Crook, Janua Linguarum Series Practica 218 (The Hauge, 1974), §§39–42. Kristensson (*A Survey of Middle English Dialects 1290–1350: The West Midland Counties* (Lund, 1987), maps 8, 9) confirms that Shropshire was consistent /y(:)/ country, and in AB the reflex of OE /y(:)/ is likewise regularly /y/, spelled <u> (*Seinte Iuliene*, ed. D'Ardenne, p. 193).

Bridgnorth, Shrops. (< OE brcyg [later + ME north], 'bridge'): Brugiam [V, p. 224; VI, p. 24]; Brugiæ [VI, p. 28]

Brinsop, Herefords. (< *Brynes* + *hop*, 'Bryni's enclosed valley'): Bruneshopa [III, p. 248]

Cambridge(shire), Cambs. (< *Granta* + brycg, 'bridge over the Granta'): Grontebrugæ [II, p. 218]; Grantesbrugescira [III, p. 140]; Grantesbrugæscira [III, p. 234 (twice)]

Eynesbury, Cambs. (< *Eanwulfes* (reanalysed as Continental Germanic *Einulfes*) + byrig, 'Eanwulf's fortified place'): Enolfesburiæ [II, p. 342]

Malmesbury, Wilts. (< *Maildub* + byrig, 'Maildub's fortified place'): Malmesburiensi [V, p. 298]

Tewkesbury, Glos. (< **Teodeces* + byrig, 'Teodec's fortified place'): Teochesburiæ [III, p. 228]

Tonbridge, Kent (< tun + brycg, 'bridge by the town'): Tonnebrugiam [V, p. 208]

Tutbury, Staffs. (< *Tuttan / Stutes* + byrig, 'Tutta's / Stut's fortified place'): Stotesburia [VI, p. 518]; Stutesburiæ [II, p. 264]

Shrewsbury, Shrops. (< **scrobbes* + byrig, 'the fortified place of the scrubland'): Scrobesburiæ [II, p. 224; V, p. 222; VI, p. 520]; Scrobesburiam [II, p. 228; VI, pp. 24, 28, 552]; Scrobesburiensis [II, p. 286; VI, p. 318]

But <e> in:

Brickhill, Bucks. (< Proto Welsh *brig + OE hyll, 'hill called Brick'): Brichella [III, p. 238]

Burghill, Herefords. (< OE burh + OE hyll, 'fort hill'): Burchella [III, p. 248]

East Shilton, Leics. (< OE scylf + tun, 'shelf settlement'): Sceltonæ [III, p. 234]

And <i> in:

Bristol (< brycg + stow, 'assembly place by the bridge'): Bristou [VI, p. 518]

The spelling <u> thus predominates, and, on closer inspection, the minority <e> and <i> forms can be dismissed: *Bristou* appears to be a fossilised spelling (cp. William of Malmesbury, GP, §154); *Brichella* and *Sceltonæ* occur only in Orderic's transcription of William the Conqueror's pancarte for Saint-Évroul; and *Burchella* is found in Orderic's summary of a grant made by Bernard, son of Geoffrey of Neufmarché, to the canons of Auffay.

Orderic's use of <u> in these contexts is idiosyncratic: William of Malmesbury almost always has <-berie> for place names in -byrig;

Eadmer's two relevant forms, 'Westberi' and 'Westberiam' [SL 244, 248], both for Westbury-on-Trym (Gloucs.), likewise have <e>.[28] Additional forms support the conclusion that both usually spelled the reflex of OE /y(:)/ as <e>.[29] Orderic's use of <u> in these words cannot therefore be dismissed as a conventionalised Latinisation of historic English /y(:)/. Nor can Orderic's spellings derive from passively reporting the spellings of local documents, since he has <u> for places in /e(:)/ territory, for example Tonbridge in Kent. This suggests that Orderic pronounced these place names with /u(:)/, as we might predict from what we know of the Shropshire dialect of Middle English. This conclusion is corroborated by his spelling of OE *yfel* as 'huvel' when he gives the name of the road across Wenlock Edge in Book XI. The most economical explanation is therefore that Orderic writes <u> in these words because he retained the accent he grew up speaking in Shropshire late into his adult life. This suggestion is corroborated by two further features of his spelling.

3.1.2 Second Fronting

As a result of the sound change known as Second Fronting, pre-Conquest Mercian texts, particularly the Vespasian Psalter gloss, have <e> where other dialects have <æ>, thus *deg*, 'day', rather than *dæg*.[30] The 'AB' texts from around 1200 have <e> in similar contexts, though in Kristensson's material from a hundred or so years later, spellings with <a> predominate.[31]

---

[28] *Ambresberiae, Ambresberiense* [GP 87.1] for Amesbury, Wilts. (< **Ambres** + **byrig**, 'Ambre's fortified place'); 'Meldunense, quod nunc corruptior aetas Malmesberiam nuncupat' [GP 197.2] for Malmesbury, Wilts. (< *Maildub* + **byrig**, 'Maildub's fortified place'; cf. *Maldelmesburuh* [GP 252.3] where William is copying S796); *Ramesberia(m)* [GP 14.1, 75.1, 80.4, 83.6] for Ramsbury, Wilts (< **hræfnes** + **byrig**, 'raven's fort'); *Scrobbesberia* etc. [GP 144.1, 171.1] for Shrewsbury, Shrops. (< ***scrobbes** + **byrig**, 'the fortified place of the scrubland'); *Theokesburia* etc. [GP 157] for Tewkesbury, Gloucs. (< ***Teodeces** + **byrig**, 'Teodec's fortified place'); and *Westberiam* [GP 150.ß3] for Westbury-on-Trym, Gloucs. (< **west** + **byrig**, 'west fortified place').

[29] William of Malmesbury has *Wellis* etc. [GP 75.1, 90.1, 130.1] for Wells, Somerset (< **wyllum**, '(at) the springs'); and *Warewelle, Warewellense* [GP 78.7, 87.1] for Wherwell, Hants. (< **hwer** + **wyllum**, 'cauldron streams'). Eadmer has *Petteham* [HN p. 75] for Petham, Kent (< **pytt** + **hamm**, 'pit valley').

[30] Hogg, *Old English Grammar*, §§5.87–5.92. The phonemic interpretation of the <e> spelling is controversial.

[31] *Seinte Iuliene*, ed. D'Ardenne, p. 181; Kristensson, *The West Midland Counties*, pp. 30–42. See also Jordan, *Handbook*, §32.

While Orderic usually has <a> in relevant contexts, it is striking that he has <e> in a number of place names where it is otherwise rare.[32] He spells the opening syllable of Glastonbury (< *Glæstinga* + **byrig**, 'the fortified place of the Glæstingas') once as *Glast-* [II, p. 242] but four times as *Glest-* [II, pp. 242, 270 (twice), 344]. William of Malmesbury and Eadmer almost invariably have *Glast-*.[33] Moreover, in a passage describing the rebellions of 1069, Orderic has *Dorseta* [II, p. 228] for Dorset (< *Dorn* + **sæte**, 'the Dorn people') and *Summerseta* [II, p. 228] for Somerset (< *Sumortun* + **sæte**, 'the people dependent on Somerton').[34] While these forms are all found in Book IV, and may therefore come from William of Poitiers, three of them occur after Orderic by his own declaration had ceased to use the *Gesta Guillelmi*. These forms therefore suggest Orderic grew up speaking a dialect that had undergone Second Fronting, and retained some pronunciations involving Second Fronting later in his life. This conclusion might be corroborated by his reference to his baptism at *Etingesham* (Atcham, Shrops.), though the derivation of the first element

---

[32] Thus Orderic has <a> in the following place names: *Habundoniam* [HE, V, p. 298] and *Abundoniam* [HE, II, p. 242] for Abingdon (< **Æbban** + **dun**, 'Æbba's hill'; cp. William of Malmesbury's *Ab(b)endonia* [GP 75.37, 86.6, 88.1], and Eadmer's *Abendonia* [HN p. 293; SL p. 192]); *Badense* [HE, V, p. 204] and *Bada* [HE, VI, p. 16] for Bath (< OE **bæth**, '(hot) bath'; cp. Eadmer's *Bathoniensem* [SL p. 84]); *Traditon* [HE, III, p. 162] for Drayton, Shrops. (< **dræg** + **tun**, 'place where loads have to be dragged'), summarising a bequest to Saint-Évroul; *Clenefeld* [HE, III, p. 236] for Glenfield, Leics. (< OE **clæne** + **feld**, 'clear open ground'), quoting the Conqueror's pancarte; *Hastingas* [HE, II, pp. 168, 170, 221] for Hastings (< *Hæsta* + **ingas**, 'people called after Hæsta'; cp. William of Malmesbury's *Hastingensis* [GP 23.5], and Eadmer's *Hastinges* [HN, p. 47]); *Estaford-* [HE, II, pp. 228, 237, 324 (twice)] and *Staphord-* [HE, III, p. 140] for Stafford, Staffs. (< **stæth** + **ford**, 'the landing-place ford'; cp. William of Malmesbury's *Statfordensi* [GP 172.1]); *Guaris* [HE, III, pp. 234, 236] for Ware, Herts. (< **wæras**, 'the wiers'), both times in William I's pancarte; and *Guareuico* [HE, V, p. 18] and *Guareuichæ-* [HE, II, p. 234] for Warwick, Warks. (< **wæring** + **wic**, 'the dwellings by the wick'; cp. William of Malmesbury's *Warwicensem* [GP 153.1]). He also has *that* (OE *þæt*) twice in the English sentence he quotes at second hand in Book VI [HE, III, p. 350].

[33] William of Malmesbury (all GP): *Glastonia* [91.1], *Glastoniam* [83.4], *Glastoniae* [19.6, 83.5], *Glastoniense* [209.2], *Glastoniensi* [75.35], *Glastoniensem* [90.6], *Glastoniensibus* [228.1], but also *Glestonia* [91.1]; Eadmer (all SL): *Glastoniensis* [p. 20], *Glastoniae* [p. 50], *Glastoniam* [pp. 66, 80]. Unfortunately the Somerset volume of the English Place Name Society remains unpublished, and the majority of the forms cited in CDEPN come from late-medieval copies of Anglo-Saxon charters.

[34] William of Malmesbury, by contrast, predominantly has *-a-*: *Dorsatensem* [GP 79.1, 217.2], *Dorsatensi* [GP 84.1, 217.6], and *Dorsatensis* [GP 14.1, 80.3], but *Dorseta* [GP 95.5].

of this place name is sufficiently uncertain for this to be only very slight supporting evidence.[35]

3.1.3 <o> for OE [ā]

Before a nasal, Old English texts represent the low back vowel [a] as either <o> or <a>, with <o> generally characteristic of Anglian texts, and <a> of non-Anglian texts, including those written in 'Standard' Old English.[36] In Middle English, only West Midland texts preserve <o>, probably representing [ɔ].[37] There is some very slender evidence that Orderic grew up with [ɔ] here and retained it. While he has <a> in most relevant place-name elements (for instance, **-hamm**, **hramsa-**, **-land** and **langa-**, and **sand-**),[38] when naming the River Granta and Cambridge,

---

[35] *CDEPN*, pp. 25–6, offers three suggestions: (1) *Ætti*; (2) *Eata*; (3) ***ætting** or ***etting**, 'eating or grazing place'. A first element beginning *æ*- best explains Orderic's variation between *Etingesham* [*HE*, III, p. 6] and *Attingesham* [*HE*, VI, p. 552].

[36] Hogg, *Grammar of OE*, §§5.3–5.6.

[37] Jordan, *Handbook of ME Grammar*, §30.

[38] **-hamm** (all *HE*): *Buchingeham* [II, p. 264], *Buccingeham-* [III, p. 238], *Buc(c)ingehamensis* [V, p. 214], *Bucchingeham* [VI, p. 36] for Buckingham, Bucks. (< *Bucc* + **ingas** + **hamm**, 'river bend land of the Buccingas'); *Suthhamtonæ pagum* [V, p. 285] for Hampshire (< **sūth** + **hamm** + **tūn**, 'southern Hampton (= estate in a river bend)'; cp. William of Malmesbury's *Amptunensem* [*GP* 79.1]); *Northamtoniæ* [II, pp. 262, 312], *Northamtoniensis* [II, p. 344], *Northamtonæ-* [III, p. 238] for Northampton, Northants. (< **north** + **hamm** + **tūn**, 'northern Hampton (= estate in a river bend)'). I have excluded *Etingesham* [III, p. 6], *Attingesham* [VI, p. 552] for Atcham, Shrops. from consideration since *CDEPN* does not commit on whether the second element is **hamm** or **hām**.

hramsa- (all *HE*): *Ramesiæ* [II, p. 242], *Ramesiensi* [III, p. 350] for Ramsey, Cambs. (< **hramsa** + **ēg**, 'wild garlic island', cp. William of Malmesbury's consistent *Ram-* [*GP* 74.2, 180.1, 181.1 etc.]).

-land (all *HE*): *Bocalanda* [VI, p. 16] for Buckland, Oxon. (< **bōc** + **land**, 'estate granted by royal charter'); *Croland-* [II, pp. 230, 336] or *Cruland-* [II, pp. 322 (twice), 324, 326, 338] for Crowland, Lincs. (< **crūw** + **land**, 'the land in the bend'; cp. William of Malmesbury's consistent *Croland* [*GP*, 180.1, 182.1, 182.4]).

langa-: *Langhetonæ* [*HE*, III, p. 234] for Church Langton, Leics. (< **langa** + **tūn**, 'the long village'), where Orderic is quoting the Conqueror's pancarte for Saint-Évroul.

sand-: *Sanguicum* [*HE*, II, p. 226] for Sandwich, Kent (< **sand** + **wīc**, 'trading place on/at the sand'; cp. William of Malmesbury's *Sandwic* [*GP*, 100.18], and Eadmer's *Sandicum* [*VW*, 29]).

Note that, for the purposes of this discussion, it does not matter whether so-called 'Homorganic Cluster Lengthening' (Hogg, *Grammar of OE*, §§5.202–4) had occurred in the elements **-land**, **langa-**, and **sand-**, since the output in the West Midlands would have been [ɔ:], spelled <o>.

the fenland city that takes its name from the river, Orderic twice writes *Gronta(-)* for OE *Grante(-)*.³⁹ His reference to the River Granta in Book IV as the *Gronta* [II, p. 326] may perhaps owe its spelling to the manuscript of Felix's *Life of Guthlac* that he was abridging at this point, but his inclusion of *Grontebrugæ* among the three castles William the Conqueror constructed in late 1068 [II, p. 218] does not seem to derive from a surviving source, and, even if it does come from a text no longer extant (like the lost conclusion to William of Poitiers' *Gesta Guillelmi*), that text is very unlikely to have had an <o> spelling.⁴⁰ Given that many of Orderic's <a> forms occur in place names with fossilised Latin spellings (for example, Crowland and Ramsey), or where he was following a documentary source (for example, Church Langton), this solitary <o> form might, in conjunction with the much stronger evidence that he had a West Midlands pronunciation for the reflex of Old English [y(ː)], suggest he also retained West Midlands [ɔ], albeit barely.⁴¹

3.2 Was Orderic Taught to Read and Write English?

Describing his upbringing in Book V of the *Historia*, Orderic tells us that he was sent, aged five, 'to learn his letters' ('literis erudiendus') with Siward, a priest at the church of St Peter in Shrewsbury.⁴² He studied with Siward for five years, mastering the 'first rudiments' ('prima rudimenta') of learning, which, according to Book XIII, comprised the alphabet, psalms, hymns and other necessary knowledge ('necessariis instructionibus').⁴³ Orderic does not give any further details about what he learned with Siward, but it has been suggested that eleventh-century students would have first learned the alphabet, then begun to pronounce texts out loud – initially the Lord's Prayer and then the Psalms – and only then moved on to Latin grammar.⁴⁴

Research on present-day languages suggests that learning to read (that is, to produce a word aloud on the basis of seeing it in writing) also develops the skills required to spell. However, 'more information is needed

---

³⁹ Cf. also *Grantesbrugescira* [HE, III, p. 140] and *Grantesbrugæscira* [HE, III, p. 234 (twice)], though all three occur where Orderic is following Saint-Évroul charters.

⁴⁰ Among the many forms cited for Cambridgeshire, Cambridge and the River Granta by P. H. Reaney, *The Place Names of Cambridgeshire and the Isle of Ely*, English Place Name Society 19 (Cambridge, 1943), pp. 1, 6, 36–7, only those from Felix and Orderic have <o>.

⁴¹ Orderic's spelling shows no sign of another twelfth-century South-West Midland feature: the voicing of initial fricatives (Jordan, *Handbook of ME Grammar*, §159).

⁴² HE, III, pp. 6–8. *Siward* is of course Old English Sigeweard.

⁴³ HE, VI, pp. 552–3.

⁴⁴ Nicholas Orme, *Medieval Schools: From Roman Britain to Renaissance England* (New Haven, 2006), pp. 40–6.

to produce a correct spelling than a correct reading'.[45] Even if Orderic did not learn to write in England – and palaeographers remain divided on the issue – it is therefore likely that he did at least begin to learn to spell in Latin.[46] My interest in this section is in whether Orderic also learned to spell English with Siward. On the basis of manuscript alphabets that include the insular letter forms *wynn, eth, thorn* and *aesc* after Latin characters, Nicholas Orme has suggested that pupils generally learned to pronounce English texts as well as Latin in Anglo-Saxon schools.[47] Yet Orderic never uses *wynn, eth* or *thorn* in the *Historia*, and little significance can be attached to his use of <æ> since this remained a legitimate, if minority, graph in Latin.[48] Indeed, I conclude that Orderic encountered very little written English during his early education in Shrewsbury in the early 1080s.

The principal system for writing the vernacular in the eleventh century was 'Standard' Old English, developed in the 970s as part of the Benedictine Reform and written, or at least copied, with more or less consistency, until the first or second decade of the twelfth century.[49] This variety was still being written in Worcester during the episcopacy of St Wulfstan (1062–95).[50] While it is conceivable that Orderic learned to

[45] Linnea C. Ehri, 'Learning to Read and Learning to Spell are One and the Same, Almost', in *Learning to Spell: Research, Theory, and Practice Across Languages*, ed. Charles A. Perfetti, Laurence Rieben and Michael Fayol (Mahwah, NJ, 1997), pp. 237–69, at p. 247.

[46] See especially Léopold Delisle, 'Matériaux', and the chapter by Jenny Weston in this volume. I am grateful to her for discussing Orderic's script with me.

[47] Orme, *Medieval Schools*, p. 40.

[48] For Orderic's occasional use of <ð> in his reworking of Wulfstan Cantor's *Life of St Æthelwold*, see HE, I, p. 202 (and note also Chibnall's comment (HE, I, p. 5 n. 1) that this character 'slipped naturally from his pen in copying English manuscripts').

[49] Key here are Helmut Gneuss, 'The Origin of Standard Old English and Æthelwold's School at Winchester', *Anglo-Saxon England* 1 (1972), 63–83 [reprinted with important addenda as the first article in his *Language and History in Early England* (Aldershot, 1996)]; Mechthild Gretsch, 'Winchester Vocabulary and Standard Old English: The Use of the Vernacular in Late Anglo-Saxon England', *Bulletin of the John Rylands University Library of Manchester* 83 (2001), 41–87; and Mechthild Gretsch, 'In Search of Standard Old English', in *Bookmarks from the Past: Studies in Early English Language and Literature in Honour of Helmut Gneuss*, ed. Lucia Kornexl and Ursula Lenker (Frankfurt-am-Main, 2003), pp. 33–67.

[50] See, for example, the comments of J. C. Pope, *Homilies of Ælfric: A Supplementary Collection*, Early English Text Society o. s. 259 (London, 1967), p. 77, concerning the language of MSS Oxford, Bodleian Library, Junius 121 + Hatton 113, 114, a homiliary produced at Worcester in the third quarter of the eleventh century.

read and write English using an entirely different set of conventions, as noted above, no vernacular texts or manuscripts written in Shropshire survive from which these conventions could be known, and the moneyers' names on coins produced by the Shrewsbury mint during the reign of Edward the Confessor do not, in any case, suggest a radical departure from the established norms for writing the vernacular.[51] The next section therefore focuses on assessing whether Orderic had learned 'Standard' Old English spelling. To eliminate the possibility that he arrived at 'Standard' spellings by chance (on the basis of invention or analogy from Latin or French orthographies), the discussion examines two phonetic environments where the 'Standard' spelling had become artificial as a result of sound change, so that any ongoing use of these spellings would be explicable only through early training in the 'Standard'.

3.2.1 <VfV> for [VvV]

By the time of the earliest Old English texts, Old English /f/ had voiced between voiced segments, hence Present Day English pairs like *wolf* ~ *wolves*.[52] In 'Standard' Old English, however, this sound was always represented <f>, thus Old English *wulf* ~ *wulfas*. Instead of 'Standard' <f> in these contexts, Orderic varies between <f>, <u> and <ph>. Thus, with <u>:[53]

> Byfield, Northants. (< **bī** + **feld**, '[the settlement] beside the open land'): Biuella [III, p. 238]

and with <ph> or <f>:

> Graffham, W. Sussex (< **grāf** + **hām**, 'the grove homestead'): Grafan [III, p. 140]; Graphan [III, p. 334]
>
> Stafford(shire), Staffs. (< **stæth** + **ford**, 'the landing-place ford'): Estafort [II, pp. 228, 237]; Staphordscira [III, p. 140]; Estafordæscira [III, p. 234 (twice)]

In each of these cases, however, Orderic was probably following the spelling of his sources: the Conqueror's pancarte for Saint-Évroul ('Biuella', 'Graphan', 'Estafordæscira'), Roger of Montgomery's charter for the same monastery from the mid-1080s ('Grafan', 'Staphordscira'), and the lost conclusion to William of Poitiers' *Gesta Guillelmi* ('Estafort', twice). A particularly neat illustration of Orderic's debt to William of Poitiers is his spelling *Peneusellum* [II, pp. 168, 170, 196] for Pevensey, East Sussex. The first element here can be established, on the basis of spellings in other texts,

---

[51] A range of these spellings are handily collected by Colman, *Money Talks*, pp. 313–16.

[52] Hogg, *Grammar of OE*, §§7.54–8.

[53] Also perhaps relevant is *Noueslai* [HE, III, p. 236] for Noseley, Leics. (< **Nōthewulfes** + **lēah**, 'Nothwulf's wood or clearing').

as the genitive singular of the OE personal name *Pefen*; Orderic's form, lifted from William of Poitiers, must therefore show the double confusion of <n> and <u> in bookhand (i.e. *Peneus-* for *Peuens-*).[54] Strikingly, when Orderic refers again to Pevensey in Book X when narrating the rebellion against William Rufus in 1089, an account reliant 'in the main on oral sources, he again writes *Peneusellum* [V, p. 208].[55] This illustrates forcibly how ready Orderic was to be guided by his sources as regards English spelling, suggesting he did not himself have strong convictions about how the language should be spelled.

3.2.2 <hC-> for [C-]

'Standard' Old English included a number of word-initial <hC-> clusters: <hn-> (for example *hnacod*, 'naked'), <hl-> (for example *hlūd*, 'loud'), <hr-> (for example *hræfn*, 'raven') and <hw-> (for example *hwæt*, 'lo!'). With the partial exception of words which historically had <hw->, these initial <hC-> clusters disappeared in early Middle English, suggesting that whatever sound the <h-> represented, it was lost within a century or two of the Conquest.[56] While what this <h-> indicated remains controversial, it has recently been persuasively argued that 'it was lost in late Old English and survived in eleventh-century writings largely because of the spread of a standard form of the vernacular in eleventh-century England'.[57]

Orderic eschews <hC-> clusters in all relevant place names. His relevant forms are:

Ramsey, Cambs. (< **hramsa** + **ēg**, 'wild garlic island'): *Ramesiæ* [II, p. 242]; *Ramesiensi* [III, p. 350]

Repton, Derbs. (< *Hrypa* + **dūn**, 'Hill of the people called *Hrype*'): *Ripadum* [II, p. 324]

---

[54] See especially *HE*, II, p. 170, taken from the *Gesta Guillelmi of William of Poitiers*, ed. and trans. R. H. C. Davis and Marjorie Chibnall (Oxford, 1998), ii, 38.

[55] On the sources of Book X, see *HE*, V, p. xii.

[56] Hogg, *Grammar of OE*, §7.48.

[57] Donald Scragg, 'Sin and Laughter in Late Anglo-Saxon England: The Case of Old English *(H)leahtor*', in *Saints and Scholars: New Perspectives on Anglo-Saxon Literature and Culture in Honour of Hugh Magennis*, ed. Stuart McWilliams (Cambridge, 2012), pp. 213–23, at p. 213. Hogg suggests interpreting these clusters as [xl, xn, xr, xw], while Campbell states that <h-> 'is used as a diacritic to indicate a voiceless consonant in *hl, hr, hn, hw*': Richard M. Hogg, 'Phonology and Morphology', in *The Cambridge History of the English Language*, vol. 1: *The Beginnings to 1066*, ed. Hogg (Cambridge, 1992), pp. 67–167, at p. 94; Campbell, *OE Grammar*, §61. The best account remains Karl Luick, *Historische Grammatik der englischen Sprache*, rept. edn (Oxford, 1964), §704.

Since identical spellings are found in William of Malmesbury's *Gesta pontificum*, these h-less forms may well be fossilised Latinisations. Nevertheless, the conclusion that Orderic did not know the 'Standard' <hC-> spellings is supported by relevant personal names:

> Hlothere, king of Kent (d. 685): Lotheris [II, p. 264]; Lothere [VI, p. 320]
>
> Hwætred, subject of a miracle by St Guthlac: Wehtredus [II, p. 330][58]

Orderic's references to Hlothere come in a rhetorical passage on Odo of Bayeux's control of Kent in Book IV, and a lament for the accession of a canon rather than a monk, William of Corbeil, to the archbishopric of Canterbury in Book XII. Whether or not Orderic used a written source for the information about early Kentish history given in these passages, he evidently did not see fit to write these names with initial <h->.

Thus, in neither of the consonant segments discussed in §3.2.1 and §3.2.2 does Orderic consistently use the 'Standard' Old English spelling. Though he does have two <-f-> spellings, these seem likely to derive from his practice of reproducing the spelling of his sources. Since we do not have complete access to those sources, it is difficult to state definitively that a particular form is Orderic's own spelling, but his heavy use of <u> for the reflex of Old English /y(:)/ (§3.1.1), contrasted with his non-use of <-f-> or <hC->, strongly suggests he did not have firm ideas about how English should be written beyond that it should reflect his pronunciation. This implies that he was not taught to read and write English by Siward, corroborating Chibnall's suggestion that Latin was Orderic's 'first written language'.[59] However, this is not to say that Orderic was entirely unfamiliar with written English. For example, his apparent use of <-en> as a plural inflection in *hegen* seems to indicate his awareness that orthographic <-n> could correspond to what was for him phonetically zero.[60]

3.3 The Attrition of Orderic's English

Language attrition is the process by which a speaker's competence in a particular variety declines over time.[61] A common type of attriter is someone who grew up speaking one language, then moved to a second

---

[58] Compare *Felix's Life of St Guthlac: Texts, Translation, Notes*, ed. Bertram Colgrave (Cambridge, 1985), p. 127, where the name is printed as *Hwætred*.

[59] Chibnall, *World*, p. 11.

[60] For example, King Eadred's appearance as *Ædredus* in Orderic's history of monasticism in Book IV [*HE*, II, p. 242], if not copied verbatim from his 'notes taken from earlier annals', may indicate his familiarity with the orthographical interchange of <æ> and <ea> in late Old English.

[61] For a recent introduction, see Monika S. Schmid, *Language Attrition*, Key Topics in Sociolinguistics (Cambridge, 2011).

country where one or more different languages were used. That person may lack the opportunity to use his or her original language, leading to a decline in his or her fluency in speaking it. Research on attrition has therefore very often focused on European migrants, for example Germans, to the United States; by virtue of his move from England to France, Orderic also fits this mould well.

Work on attrition has established that vocabulary, phonology, morphology and syntax can all be attrited once a speaker ceases to be exposed to a language. Assessing whether Orderic's knowledge of English attrited is challenging. For one thing, most studies of attrition have worked with live subjects, whose linguistic knowledge can be experimentally tested. However, there have been several papers which have used written texts, specifically collections of letters sent home by particular migrants, to trace the attrition of lexis, morphology and syntax over time.[62] Unfortunately, the nature of the evidence for Orderic's English — principally place and personal names — makes it impossible to assess anything except phonology, for which written texts, by their very nature, offer only indirect evidence. A second challenge is that we have no evidence for how much English Orderic knew when he left England, no information which would provide a baseline against which we could measure his subsequent knowledge. One recent study has found that migrants who leave their home country before the age of twelve (as Orderic did) can suffer rapid or even total attrition of their first language.[63] Moreover, studies have suggested that, regardless of age at migration, attrition is rapid for the first ten or fifteen years, and then slows considerably.[64] Since the earliest evidence we have for Orderic's English is Book III, begun according to Chibnall in 1114, twenty years after Orderic arrived in Normandy, it is not clear whether we could expect to see any significant decline in his English through the *Historia*. Despite these problems, I argue that it is possible to observe the attrition of Orderic's knowledge of at least one English phone in the text.

---

[62] Koen Jaespart and Sjaak Kroon, 'From the Typewriter of A. L.: A Case Study in Language Loss', in *Maintenance and Loss of Minority Languages*, ed. Willem Fase, Koen Jaspaert and Sjaak Kroon (Amsterdam, 1992), pp. 137–47; Matthias Hutz, 'Is There a Natural Process of Decay? A Longitudinal Study of Language Attrition', *First Language Attrition: Interdisciplinary Perspectives on Methodological Issues*, ed. Monika S. Schmid et al. (Amsterdam, 2004), pp. 189–206.

[63] Emanuel Bylund Spångberg, 'Maturational Constraints and First Language Attrition', *Language Learning* 59 (2009), 687–715.

[64] For example Hutz, 'Is There a Natural Process of Decay?', p. 203.

3.3.1 Despirantisation

One phonological feature that distinguishes Old English from Latin and Old French is the frequency with which it used the unvoiced and voiced dental fricatives, [θ~ð]. Except in a few Greek loanwords, Latin did not have any dental fricatives, and while early Old French did develop dental fricatives intervocalically and finally, these were lost in the course of the twelfth century.[65] There is, moreover, some evidence that as early as the second half of the tenth century French speakers struggled to pronounce these sounds in other languages.[66]

In English texts, these sounds were represented by the insular characters <ð> and <þ>. While some Latin texts did use these characters, the majority represent these sounds with the digraph <th> or <d> (rarely also <t>). While <th> unquestionably denotes a fricative, <d> is ambiguous. In early manuscripts, for example the eighth-century Leningrad Bede and ninth-century Durham *Liber vitae*, it is clear that it represents [θ~ð].[67] Yet this spelling is also found in early Middle English manuscripts, where it may sometimes be the product of two genuine sound changes, dubbed by Lass and Laing 'Later Dental Hardening' and 'Theta Hardening'.[68] It is thus difficult to be sure whether Orderic's <d> spellings represent [d] or [θ~ð]. Orderic, however, has far more <d> and <t> spellings than either Eadmer or William of Malmesbury (Table 1). This disparity could, of course, simply reflect differing orthographical convention. However, because it is clear that <th> was part of Orderic's active repertoire, and that he therefore had the option of writing it where he retained a fricative pronunciation, it can tentatively be suggested that his heavier use of <d> reflects, at least in part, his pronunciation of this segment as a stop rather than a fricative.[69]

With the possible phonetic significance of Orderic's <d> spellings established, we can look at Orderic's representation of historic [θ~ð]

---

[65] Pope, *From Latin to Modern French*, §§333, 335, 346.

[66] Thus Abbo of Fleury comments in his *Quaestiones grammaticales* (ed. A. Gurreau-Jalabert (Paris, 1982), §28) that 'you English can distinguish aspirations well, who for θ frequently write and pronounce þ' ('sed aspirationes bene uos, Angli, peruidere potestis qui pro θ frequentius þ scribitis et effertis'). For discussion, see Roger Wright, *Late Latin and Early Romance in Spain and Carolingian France* (Liverpool, 1982), p. 138.

[67] Hogg, *Grammar of OE*, §2.59 and n. 1.

[68] Roger Lass and Margaret Laing, 'Databases, Dictionaries and Dialectology: Dental Instability in Early Middle English: A Case Study', in *Studies in English and European Historical Dialectology*, ed. Marina Dossena and Roger Lass (Frankfurt-am-Main, 2009), pp. 91–131.

[69] We know this because Orderic uses <th> in passages where he seems not to have had a written source, for example in his reference to the construction of the New Forest around 'Suthamtonæ pagum' ('the shire around Southampton' [*HE*, V, p. 285]).

Table 1 Tokens with <d, t> for historic [θ~ð] in place names

Author	Total	Number with <d, t>	Percentage with <d, t>
Orderic	37	25	68%
William of Malmesbury	32	13	41%
Eadmer	17	7	41%

Table 2 Spelling of [θ~ð] in the *Historia*

Book	Number of occurrences			Percentage of total	
	<th>	not <th>	Total	<th>	not <th>
3	4	9	13	31%	69%
4	13	33	46	28%	72%
5	1	3	4	25%	75%
6	3	19	22	14%	86%
9	0	1	1	0%	100%
10	2	3	5	40%	60%
11	1	8	9	11%	89%
12	1	5	6	17%	83%
13	1	1	2	50%	50%
All	26	82	108	24%	76%

as evidence for phonological attrition, whereby the absence of dental fricatives in spoken French, and their extreme scarcity in Latin, led the dental stops and dental fricatives to converge in Orderic's phonological system, such that he did not distinguish them in pronunciation or in writing.[70]

My corpus of place and personal names from the autograph books of Orderic's *Historia* includes 108 instances of historic [θ~ð].[71] Dividing these usages by book, there seems a general decline in the frequency of <th> spellings in the later books, which were completed last (Table 2). However, the paucity of the data in certain books (for example Books IX and XIII) considerably obscures this pattern. Grouping the books by when they were written (before 1130 in the case of Books III–V; after 1130

---

[70] For phonological convergence as a result of attrition, see Schmid, *Language Attrition*, pp. 52–3. One might compare certain varieties of Hiberno-English, where the dental fricatives have fortified to stops: see Raymond Hickey, *Irish English: History and Present-Day Forms* (Cambridge, 2007), pp. 318–19.

[71] Notice that I have not attempted to subdivide this data by phonetic environment (for example intervocalic *vs* word-initial). This is because there are not enough data points for such a fine-grained analysis.

Table 3 Spelling of [θ~ð] in the *Historia*, grouped by date of writing

Books	Number of occurrences			Percentage of total	
	\<th\>	not \<th\>	Total	\<th\>	not \<th\>
3–5	18	45	63	29%	71%
6, 9–13	8	37	45	18%	82%

in the case of Books IX–XIII)[72] yields clearer results (Table 3). Tables 2 and 3 show that there is indeed tentative evidence that Orderic's ability to recall which words in English were pronounced with a dental fricative declined when he was in his late fifties and sixties. The data is not robust enough to argue this point conclusively ($\chi^2 = 1.673$, $p = 0.2$), but given the small sample size, the generally limited effect on phonology found by previous studies of attrition, and the possibility that Orderic's knowledge of English had already attrited significantly by the time he began writing the *Historia*, I suggest that it should be taken seriously. Other occasional forms, for example, 'Esledas' for Leeds in Kent in Book XIII, also suggest that interaction with French speakers influenced Orderic's pronunciation of English.[73]

3.4 Orderic's Spelling and his Identity

Spelling is a social practice, in which spellers can convey different social meanings by choosing from among the range of spellings available to them for a particular word or sound.[74] One example of this is the graffito <OKUPACÍON> (that is, *ocupacíon*, 'occupation'), transcribed by Sebba from a wall in Ripoll, Catalonia.[75] In Spanish, the phoneme /k/ is usually

---

[72] See van Houts's chapter in this volume, and 'Composition of the *Historia ecclesiastica*' (p. xiv above).

[73] *HE*, VI, p. 520. *CDEPN* suggests three possible etymologies: (1) OE **hleda, hlyda**, 'a seat, shelf'; (2) OE **hild**, 'a door, a gate, an opening'; (3) the stream name, **Hlyde*, 'the loud one'. Of these (1) or (3) seems preferable, since these are compatible with Orderic's *Ludas* (which would then show OE /y(:)/ > /u(:)/, established above as Orderic's pronunciation). None of these, however, explain the on-glide which the spelling here strongly suggests (see Pope, *From Latin to Modern French*, §§361, 603). Earlier in the work, Orderic has relevant forms both with and without spellings indicative of an on-glide (for example *Estentona* for Stainton, Lincs. (< **steinn + tun**, 'stone village, farm') and *Stotonæ* for Stoughton, Leics. (< **stoc + tun**, 'outlying farm with enclosure')), but the occurrence of a spelling of this sort in a book for which Orderic's sources were largely oral is suggestive.

[74] For a general introduction to spelling as a social practice, see Mark Sebba, *Spelling and Society* (Cambridge, 2007).

[75] Sebba, *Spelling and Society*, pp. 3–4, 48–50.

represented by <c>, occasionally <qu>, but as <k> in loanwords only. The scarcity of <k> has made it iconic in Spanish, 'the favourite letter of *okupas* ['occupations'], war resisters, *bakaleros* [adherents of a type of techno music, also associated (in stereotype at least) with recreational drugs], *ákratas* ['anarchists', university students and high-school teenagers who are anti-establishment] and gay movements'.[76]

The majority of work on spelling as a social practice has focused on modern, standard languages, most of which permit some limited variation (for example, *-ise* vs *-ize* in Standard English).[77] Without such variation, there would be no scope for choice, and thereby no scope for conveying social meaning through choice. It has been argued that there is no scope for such expression in unstandardised languages, since the pool of variants from which to choose is potentially infinite. Yet twelfth-century English spelling, though it permitted diverse practices, was not lawless.[78] It is the purpose of this section to explore what Orderic's spelling of place and personal names can tell us about his sense of identity.

Attempting to make this connection is, however, a very delicate process. In the most straightforward of the two segments analysed below, Orderic's 'choice' (if choice it was, given the growing picture of his general deference to the orthographic forms of his exemplars) was between an English representation, on the one hand, and a French or Franco-Latin representation on the other; for example, between <sc> and <s> to represent [ʃ]. However, even in this case, Orderic's choice might have been restricted by a limited awareness of the conventions of 'Standard' Old English (§3.2 above) and, if he was choosing between this and a French or Franco-Latin orthography, his choice may not have been driven by purely orthographical considerations. Phonological issues may also have been a factor, since [ʃ] was not present in the phonemic inventory of twelfth-century French, and his time in Normandy might have caused Orderic to pronounce this sound as [s]. Despite these difficulties, it is argued below

---

[76] A. Castilla, 'La Letra "malkerida": 'Okupas", "Bakaleros", "Vallekanos" y "Ábraktas" Revindican la "k"', *El País*, 16 February 1997, translated in Sebba, *Spelling and Society*, pp. 3–4.

[77] Though some of Cecily Clark's work on twelfth-century spelling could definitely be framed in these terms: see particularly her 'L'Angleterre Anglo-Normande et des ambivalences socio-culturelles: Un coup d'oeil de philologue', *Les Mutations socio-culturelles au tournant des XIe–XIIe siècles: Actes du colloque international du Centre national de la recherche scientifique – Études anselmiennes (IVe session)*, ed. Raymonde Foreville (Paris, 1984), pp. 99–110.

[78] A point most forcefully apparent from the work of Roger Lass and Meg Laing, who show how even superficially prodigal orthographies are rule bound. See especially their 'Shape-Shifting, Sound-Change and the Genesis of Prodigal Writing Systems', *English Language and Linguistics* 13 (2009), 1–31.

that Orderic's handling of place and personal names suggests he felt no connection between English spelling, and, more broadly, the English language, and his self-identity as *Angligena*.

3.4.1 [ʃ]

In 'Standard' Old English, the unvoiced post-alveolar fricative /ʃ/ was spelled <sc>. The sound [ʃ] did not develop in French until the thirteenth century, and it is not uncommon to find the sound represented by <s> in post-Conquest Latin records dealing with English place and personal names.[79] Orderic's text shows variation in the spelling of this sound. Thus he has non-'Standard' <s> in:

Butler's Marston, Warks. (< **mersc** + **tun**, 'marsh settlement'): Merestonam [III, p. 234]; Mersitonæ [III, p. 236]

Marston, Staffs. (< **mersc** + **tun**, 'marsh settlement'): Mersitonam [III, p. 140]; Mersitonæ [III, p. 234]

Marston St Lawrence, Northants. (< **mersc** + **tun**, 'marsh settlement'): Merestona [III, p. 238]

Oxhill, Warks. (< *Ohta* + **scylf**, 'Ohta's shelf'): Ostesiluæ [III, p. 236]

Shingay, Cambs. (< *Scene* + **inga** + **eg**, 'the low lying land of the people of Scene'):[80] Senegai [III, p. 234]

Shenley, Bucks. (< **sciene** + **leah**, 'bright clearing'): Sanleia [III, p. 238]

but 'Standard' <sc> consistently in shire names like *Northamtonæscira* [III, p. 238], as well as in the following place names:

East Shilton, Leics. (< **scylf** + **tun**, 'shelf-settlement'): Sceltonæ [III, p. 234]

Shrewsbury, Shrops. (< ***scrobbes** + **byrig**, 'the fortified place of the scrubland'): Scrobesburiæ [V, p. 222; VI, p. 520], Scrobesburiæ [II, p. 224]; Scrobesburiensis [II, p. 286; VI, p. 318]; Scrobesburiam [VI, pp. 24, 28]; Scrobesburiam [II, p. 228; VI, p. 552]

Shropshire: Scrobesburiæ [III, p. 148; VI, p. 144]; Scrobesburiensem [II, p. 210]

Unfortunately, the vast majority of these place and county names, whether spelled <sc> or <s>, occur only in the section of Book VI where Orderic is making heavy use of Saint-Évroul documents. The only forms that might indicate his active usage are thus those for Shrewsbury and Shropshire, both of which had more or less fossilised Latin spellings in the

---

[79] Pope, *From Latin to Modern French*, §194.
[80] Not in *CDEPN*; etymology from Reaney, *Place Names of Cambridgeshire*, p. 65.

twelfth century.[81] But while Orderic's active usage must remain undecided, it is clear he could passively produce both native <sc> and non-native <s>. That he did not programmatically insist on <sc> suggests spelling English names with English orthography was not a priority for him.

3.4.2 [w]

Orderic's orthography for [w] varies between <gu> and <u, uu, w>. The former is a distinctively Franco-Latin spelling, not found in the work of Eadmer or William of Malmesbury.[82] Orderic almost never uses the spelling <gu> medially, hence Æthelwulf is 'Adeluulfi' [II, p. 340].[83] In initial position, however, there is considerable variation: in the section of Book V devoted to the history of Crowland, Waltheof is 'Walleuus' [for example II, p. 314] and 'Gualleuus' [for example, II, p. 320] interchangeably. Across the *Historia*, <gu-> is Orderic's most frequent spelling, but he uses <u-, uu-, w-> in a greater range of words (Table 4). This distribution seems to suggest that <u-, uu-, w-> was Orderic's instinctive orthography, but that he used <gu-> in a small range of names that he had seen written in that way, in Continental historical texts such as the *Gesta Guillelmi* of William of Poitiers. This conclusion is corroborated by Orderic's describing having seen a copy of Sigebert of Gembloux's chronicle at 'Wigornæ' and not 'Guigornæ' in an autobiographical passage for which he can hardly have had a textual source [II, p. 188].

Table 4 A type-token analysis of Orderic's spelling for [w-]

	Types	Tokens
<gu->	0.380	0.639
<u-, uu-, w->	0.620	0.361

The distribution of Orderic's various of spellings for [w] suggests that he did not regard English orthography as an inherent part of English names. Thus, he is quite happy to follow William of Poitiers in giving Eadric the Wild's byname as 'Guilda' [II, p. 228]. Preserving English spelling conventions and avoiding orthographies characteristic of Franco-Latin was not important to Orderic, and thus not likely to have been part

---

[81] *Scrobbesberia* [GP 144.1]; and *Scrobbesberiam, Scrobbesburiense* [GP 171.1]. More generally, see the forms listed by Margaret Gelling, *The Place-Names of Shropshire*, part 1: *The Major Names of Shropshire*, English Place Name Society 62–3 (Nottingham, 1990), pp. 267–71.

[82] For the phonological developments implied by <gu>, see Pope, *From Latin to Modern French*, §636.

[83] The exceptions are the spellings like *Northguici* [HE, II, p. 226] beside *Nortwicensis* [HE, II, p. 310] for Norwich (< **north** + **wīc**, 'the north hamlet'), and *Sanguicum* [HE, II, p. 226] for Sandwich, Kent (< **sand** + **wīc**, 'trading place on or at the sand').

of his sense of identity as an *Angligena*. This challenges recent work that has asserted a connection between language choice and identity in twelfth-century England.[84]

4 Conclusion

As a named author with a known biography and educational history, Orderic provides singularly valuable evidence for the English language and its cultural status in the immediate post-Conquest period. Orderic wrote his *Historia* during the linguistic transition from Old to Middle English, described in one recent history as 'the most dramatic change in the English language', which saw (among other changes) the loss, or at least dramatic reduction, of grammatical categories like gender and case, diminishing flexibility in word order, and the collapse of the highly focused conventions of 'Standard' Old English.[85] Moreover, Orderic grew up in Shropshire, a county for which almost the only pre-Conquest linguistic evidence comes from moneyers' names on coins, yet which a hundred years later produced, in 'AB', one of the most important literary varieties of early Middle English.

While no one could pretend that it is simple to extract meaningful data about English from place and personal names in a Latin history written by an author who had left England aged twelve and whose history was in part based on written sources, a better understanding of the linguistic history of the twelfth century requires the use of as wide a range of evidence as possible.[86] Historical linguistic analyses of the transition to Middle English have typically based their findings on a small number of long texts. Thus, the Helsinki Corpus includes no English texts composed in the second quarter of the twelfth century, when Orderic completed his

---

[84] Elaine Treharne, *Living through Conquest: The Politics of Early English, 1020–1220* (Oxford, 2012), *passim* (and, for some comments on the arguments advanced there, my review in *Review of English Studies* 65 (2014), 922–3). For earlier work that questions the connection between language and identity, see, for example, Tim William Machan, *English in the Middle Ages* (Oxford, 2003), p. 71; Hugh M. Thomas, *The English and the Normans: Ethnic Hostility, Assimilation and Identity, 1066–c. 1220* (Oxford, 2003), esp. pp. 377–90; and Laura Ashe, *Fiction and History in England, 1066–1200* (Cambridge, 2007), esp. pp. 1–19.

[85] The quotation is from Elly van Gelderen, *A History of the English Language* (Amsterdam, 2006), p. 91.

[86] For further discussion of this point, and an illustration of how one neglected type of evidence (readers' annotations) can contribute to revising these histories, see Mark Faulkner, 'Archaism, Belatedness and Modernisation: "Old" English in the Twelfth Century', *Review of English Studies* 63 (2012), 179–203.

Historia. Similarly, there is only one text from this period in the Penn-Helsinki Parsed Corpus of Middle English: the first continuation of the Peterborough Chronicle, which was maintained in the years between 1122 and 1131.[87] Furthermore, besides increasing our awareness of language change, a more nuanced grasp of linguistic history would also contribute to the recent reappraisal of the literary history of this pivotal period.[88]

The findings of this chapter contribute to this reappraisal in several ways. First, it has established that idiosyncratic aspects of the orthography of native place and personal names in a Latin history (for example <-buri> for -*bury*) can reveal features of the author's local dialect; in doing so it has demonstrated the feasibility of using onomastic evidence to flesh out the evidentiary base of existing studies. Second, in showing that Orderic did not learn to read or write English with Siward when he was taught Latin, it provides invaluable indirect evidence for late eleventh-century educational practices, in particular by showing that instruction in 'Standard' Old English does not seem to have been available with a secular priest in Shropshire, though major Benedictine houses of the time do appear to have offered such tuition. Finally, in its suggestion that Orderic did not use English to reinforce his self-identity as *Angligena*, this chapter challenges Treharne's recent attempt to explain twelfth-century vernacular writing through reference to English resistance to Norman oppression.

I should like to end where I began, however, with Orderic's inclusion of the name of the road between Bridgnorth and Shrewsbury in his account of Henry I's conflict with Robert of Bellême. Orderic's transcription of the road name as 'huvel hegen', and his translation of it as 'malum callem vel

---

[87] For Helsinki, see Merja Kytö, *Manual to the Diachronic Part of the Helsinki Corpus of English Texts*, 3rd edn (Helsinki, 1996) [available from http://clu.uni.no/icame/manuals/HC/INDEX.HTM]; for PPCME and its sister YPCOE, see Ann Taylor, 'The York-Toronto-Helsinki Parsed Corpus of Old English Prose', in *Creating and Digitising Language Corpora*, vol. 2: *Diachronic Databases*, ed. Joan C. Beal, Karen P. Corrigan and Hermann L. Moisl (Basingstoke, 2007), pp. 196–227.

[88] For the resurgence of interest in twelfth-century literary history, see the bibliography in Faulkner, 'Rewriting English Literary History'. More recent work includes A. N. Doane and William P. Stoneman, *Purloined Letters: The Twelfth-Century Reception of the Anglo-Saxon Illustrated Hexateuch (British Library, Cotton Claudius B. iv)* (Tempe, AZ, 2011); Sara Harris, 'Twelfth-Century Perceptions of the History of Britain's Vernacular Languages' (unpublished PhD thesis, University of Cambridge, 2013), esp. ch. 2; Bruce O'Brien, *Reversing Babel: Translation among the English during an Age of Conquests, c. 800 to c. 1200* (Newark, DE, 2011); Stephen Pelle, 'Source Studies in the Lambeth Homilies', *The Journal of English and Germanic Philology* 113 (2014), 34–72, plus other papers by the same author; Treharne, *Living through Conquest*; and George Younge, 'The Canterbury Anthology: An Old English Manuscript and its Anglo-Norman Context' (unpublished PhD thesis, University of Cambridge, 2012).

vicum', expose his attrited knowledge of English orthography, morphology and semantics. He includes the original English despite the probability that his Norman audience would have had no understanding of the vernacular name, and despite, as I have argued, the relative insignificance of the English language in his identity as *Angligena*. Why include it then? To answer that we might turn to the track 'USA' from I-Wolf and Burdy's 2004 album *Meet the Babylonians*. Half-way through this track the rapper RQM, whose parents 'snatched [his] ass up' from Poland when he was seven and took him to New York, confides that he's 'never, ever rhymed in Polish before', but switches into that language anyway.[89] To highlight in English a shift into Polish on a French-language track about an English-speaking country on a multilingual album released on an Austrian record label can only be understood as an assertion of the irrelevance of linguistic difference in the globalised world. Orderic's inclusion of the road-name might similarly be understood as an assertion of the irrelevance of linguistic difference, but of the irrelevance of linguistic difference in a pan-European Norman imperium under a Christian God, who understood, and oversaw the creation of, all languages.

---

[89] 2Sheep4Coke, 'RQM: An Emcee without Border', *Jeckyll et Hyde*, 27 May 2010 <http://jekyllethyde.fr/2010/05/rqm-english-interview/> [accessed 19 December 2014]. While this comparison might be thought sensationalist or trivalising, I include it to reinforce my point above that we cannot project post-Enlightenment equations of language choice and identity back on to the Middle Ages. Orderic and RQM have similar biographies, but very different ways of handling the multilingual repertoires to which their transnational upbringings gave them access. The uniformitarian principle does not hold for sociolinguistics.

Inscriptions in Orderic's *Historia ecclesiastica*: A Writing Technique between History and Poetry

Vincent Debiais and Estelle Ingrand-Varenne

ORDERIC Vitalis's composition of his *Historia ecclesiastica* is characterised by his insertion of 'exogenous' documents throughout his narrative. Over 100 sources appear in this way, including theological, literary and historical works from the abbey library, and legislative and diplomatic texts. One of the most common types of source used in this way is epigraphic texts. Thirty-eight epitaphs commemorating Anglo-Norman lay or clerical aristocrats are dotted throughout the *Historia ecclesiastica*, from Book IV onwards (the first three books do not contain any).[1] Unevenly distributed throughout the different books, the epitaphs appear only in sections depicting events contemporary to Orderic, concerning the north of France or England, or tracing the history of Norman monasteries, their founders or benefactors. The inscription is, therefore, just one kind of writing among many others within the *Historia ecclesiastica*, but one that Orderic appears to have known well and particularly liked deploying, in a variety of contexts and for a variety of purposes.

The eleventh and twelfth centuries mark the peak of the popularity of the epitaph as a poetic genre among Latin authors of the Middle Ages. Baldric of Bourgueil, Hildebert of Lavardin, Foulcoie of Beauvais and, to a lesser extent, Marbodius of Rennes wrote several dozen of these metric compositions.[2] Mortuary rolls, which flourish during the same period, show another way to express funeral poetry.[3] The epitaph itself can be

---

[1] For an overview of these epitaphs, see Sabrine Mouktafi, 'Textes épigraphiques et manuscrits: La Place des inscriptions dans l'*Histoire ecclésiastique* d'Orderic Vital (1114–1141): Mémoire et biographie' (unpublisher Master's thesis, University of Poitiers, 2003).

[2] A comprehensive study of these texts has not yet been carried out due to the large number of literary epitaphs. For an overview of these texts, especially those of Baldric of Bourgueil and Hildebert of Lavardin, see volumes 23–5 of the *Corpus des inscriptions de la France médiévale*, gen. ed. Edmond-René Labande (Paris, 1974–) (hereafter *CIFM*).

[3] See Véronique Gazeau, 'La Mort des moines: Sources textuelles et méthodologie (XIe–XIIe siècles)', in *Inhumations et édifices religieux au Moyen Âge entre Loire et Seine*, ed. A. Alduc-Le Bagousse (Caen, 2004), pp. 13–21; Jean Dufour, *Recueil des rouleaux des morts (VIIIe siècle–vers*

considered the monumental version of the eulogy and *planctus*, stripped back to its basics. Individual examples vary greatly in the tone of the eulogy, the length of the text, and the themes emphasised. There are, however, a number of rules which seem to have been observed, and which need to be taken into account. The poems always contain both a death notice (sometimes with a precise date) and information about the tomb (for example, a reference to the funeral monument or the context of the burial). They almost always end with a prayer request to the reader and/or a pious wish that the soul of the deceased might be saved.

The literary epitaph has a number of similarities with the funerary inscription in verse, which had existed in the form of epigraphic texts since classical antiquity, but enjoyed a revival in the Middle Ages.[4] Literary epitaphs can be analysed using the formulas or common themes that create intertextuality, to reveal their place in the wider series of works authored by the poet.[5] In the most ancient written tradition they are presented as pieces of verse, unrelated to one another and copied into codices which contain various texts, in prose or in verse. With the exception of Foulcoie of Beauvais, who composed what amounted to a collection of literary epitaphs,[6] these funerary poems make up a series, or a homogeneous part of an author's work, only at a later date, and do not seem to be part of a defined project or an epigraphic programme (except, perhaps, for some texts written by Baldric of Bourgueil and destined for a single deceased person).[7]

1536), 5 vols. (Paris, 2005–13); and Pascale Bourgain, 'La Mémoire des défunts dans les rouleaux des morts', in *Écritures latines de la mémoire* (Paris, 2010), pp. 107–29.

[4] On funerary inscriptions of the High Middle Ages, see Cécile Treffort, 'Les Inscriptions funéraires des XIIe–XIIIe siècles en France', in *Las inscripciones góticas: Actas del segundo congreso internacional de epigrafía medieval*, ed. M. E. Martín López and V. García Lobo (León, 2010), pp. 161–84.

[5] Vincent Debiais, 'L'Écrit sur la tombe: Entre nécessité pratique, souci pour le salut et élaboration doctrinale: À travers la documentation épigraphique de la Normandie médiévale', *Tabularia* 7 (2007), pp. 179–202; Debiais, 'Épitaphes, inscriptions et textes funéraires pour la famille ducale de Normandie (de Rollon à Mathilde): Une Nécropole sans corps', *Fécamp et les ducs de Normandie: Actes du colloque de Fécamp (2009)* (forthcoming).

[6] The bibliography on Foulcoie of Beauvais is unfortunately rather sparse, see *Dictionnaire des lettres françaises: Le Moyen Âge* (Paris, 1992), pp. 461–2; Henri Omont, 'Épitaphes métriques en l'honneur de différents personnages du XIe siècle composées par Foulcoie de Beauvais, archidiacre de Meaux', in *Mélanges Julien Havet: Recueil de travaux d'érudition dédiés à la mémoire de Julien Havet (1853–1893)* (Paris, 1895), pp. 211–36.

[7] Otto Schumann, 'Baudri von Bourgueil als Dichter', in *Studien zur lateinische Dichtung des Mittelalters: Ehrengabe für Karl Strecker zum 4 September 1931* (Darmstadt, 1969), pp. 330–42; Jean-Yves Tilliette, 'Culture

The funerary inscriptions Orderic composed or referred to in the *Historia ecclesiastica* are part of the epitaph genre, and should be identified as such within the long-neglected original corpus of medieval Latin poetry. Their integral part in the storyline of this historical text gives the inscriptions a specific place in the wider corpus, though their structure, content and function is yet to be defined. A full study of these compositions within the *Historia ecclesiastica* is still to be conducted, but a detailed case-study can be offered within the limited framework of the present discussion. The analysis here concentrates on Orderic's Book V and its inscriptions, which have been selected for three key reasons. First of all, quantity: this book, along with Book VIII, contains the highest number of inscriptions (eight). Book V focuses on events occurring from 1075 to 1087, a period of prosperity for the monastery whose community Orderic joined in 1085, and contains epitaphs which commemorate Hugh of Eu, John of Avranches, Rollo, William I Longsword, Mabel of Bellême, John of Rheims, Peter of Maule and Ansold of Maule. The second reason is the quality of the particular texts: in Book V, Orderic copied inscriptions from their original engravings, texts composed at the death of important figures, and included a poem he wrote himself at the death of John of Rheims, a monk of Saint-Évroul. The third reason is documentary in nature: Book V is preserved as a manuscript written in its entirety by Orderic himself, which allows not only the texts themselves, but also the textual layout and mise-en-page, to be studied as constructed by the author.[8]

The inscriptions copied by Orderic in Book V provide opportunities to catch a glimpse of the writer at work, to discover some of his literary and political ambitions. To understand them, it is necessary to consider the function of funeral texts in historical writing and in the general structure of the work, alongside the aesthetic implications of including such inscriptions in the *Historia ecclesiastica*.

---

classique et humanisme monastique: Les Poèmes de Baudri de Bourgueil', in *La Littérature angevine médiévale: Actes du colloque de samedi 22 mars 1980* (Angers, 1981), pp. 77–88; *Dictionnaire de biographie française* (Paris, 1951), V, pp. 903–4; *Dictionnaire des lettres française*, pp. 132–4.

[8] The importance of Book V lies in the fact that it shows the change of plan in the architecture and design of the *Historia* as a whole. It is, in fact, mostly dedicated to the history of the monastery of Saint-Évroul. Book V occupies fols. 101–157v of BnF MS Lat. 5506, vol. II.

Funerary Inscriptions as Historical Evidence

THE main role played by the inscriptions is to attest the veracity of the events recounted by Orderic.[9] They back up what he says, as irrefutable proof for the case to which they refer. They show the historian at work, gathering documents from different places, always taking care to quote his evidence *verbatim* and in its entirety. The texts never seem abridged, and Orderic never alludes to an inscription without presenting the text to be read. However, it is important to remember that Orderic is almost always the only surviving source of the epitaphs, which have not been preserved elsewhere and do not appear in contemporary accounts. There is, therefore, no way of verifying or corroborating what he says. As with charters or acts of council, Orderic adds the epitaphs to his texts as arguments, mentioning the original author whenever he can.[10] These authors are: Archbishop Maurilius of Rouen for Rollo and William I Longsword,[11] Odon of Montreuil for Ansold of Maule,[12] John of Rheims for Peter of Maule,[13] and the monks of Troarn for Mabel of Bellême.[14] When the epitaph for John of Rheims is presented, which Orderic composed himself, he does not use the first person but rather writes: 'Vitalis angligena discipulus ejus super illo versificavit.' [15] This

---

[9] Bernard Guénée, *Histoire et culture historique dans l'Occident médiéval* (Paris, 1980), p. 87: 'Tous les historiens, les uns plus sporadiquement, les autres plus systématiquement, ont cherché les sépultures et relevé les épitaphes gravées sur elles ou auprès d'elles pour en nourrir leur histoire.'

[10] For further discussion of Orderic's use of charters, see the contribution of Thomas Roche in the present volume, 'Reading Orderic with Charters in Mind'.

[11] The first funerary inscription that appears in the *Ecclesiastical History*, in Book IV, is for this exact figure, who died in 1067. It opens the series of thirty epitaphs that come after.

[12] *HE*, III, p. 198: 'His utique exequiis Odo Monasterolensis interfuit, ibique sacerdotale officium peregit brevique loco nomen et officium diemque obitus ejus et magnam pro eo precem sic comprehendit.'

[13] Ibid., p. 178: 'et in claustro monachorum secus australem basilicae maceriam sepultus requiescit. Epitaphium autem hujusmodi Iohannes Remensis super illum edidit.'

[14] Ibid., p. 136; *CIFM* 22, 57, pp. 102–3: 'Denique Troarnensis conventus (cui Durandus abbas praerat) cadaver frustratim dilaceratum nonas decembris sepelivit, et non prerogativam meritorum, sed pro favore amicorum super tumulum has nenias edidit.'

[15] Ibid., p. 168–70: 'Et quia multos ipse versus edidit, Vitalis angligena discipulus ejus super illo versificavit, et inter lacrimas in die dormitionis ejus tumulatione peracta carmen hujusmodi composuit.' Orderic is the author of ten of the thirty-eight funerary inscriptions written in the *Historia ecclesiastica*. A cursory reading of the *Historia* reveals the ease with

epitaph is presented as a tribute from the disciple to his master, who also wrote poems himself. The fact that Orderic names the authors of the epigraphs he incorporates into his narrative (including naming himself) is particularly important, as the authors did not name themselves within the inscriptions they produced. Indeed, funerary inscriptions seldom mention their author, who generally remains anonymous.[16] When a voice is expressed, it is generally the deceased person speaking from the tomb or beyond. By providing the epitaph and naming an author in this way, Orderic gives the texts more authority, while his authorial ascriptions must be drawn directly from his own knowledge or experience. Each poem becomes an *instrumentum*, a proof of the historical validity of recounted events or of descriptions of the characters.

Besides the author, Orderic also refers to the physical 'authority' of the funerary monument itself, describing precisely the nature of the tomb, the form of the inscription and the surroundings of the grave. For example, in the cases of Rollo and William I Longsword, whose bodies were transferred to the Cathedral of Rouen when it was consecrated in 1065 after renovation and extension work, Orderic points out that their epitaphs (*titulus*) were written in gold letters:

> Corpora vero ducum Rollonis et Guilelmi reverenter in sacram edem transtulit, et Rollonem prope hostium australe et Guilelmus secus hostium aquilonae tumulavit, et epitaphia eorum super illos litteris aureis annotavit.[17]

> [He had the bodies of Duke Rollo and Duke William reverently transferred to the same building, and buried Rollo near to the south door, and William beside the north door, inscribing their epitaphs on their tombs in letters of gold.]

Because these examples were among the first princely graves on the Continent to be placed in a cathedral instead of an abbey, Orderic wished to provide accounts of their precise locations and to describe them in detail.[18] The funerary monument of Hugh of Eu is also described as being

---

which Orderic uses the first person in other contexts, never hesitating to share his feelings and reactions, or to add details about his own life, of which there are plenty of examples in Book V.

[16] On the question of the author of the inscription, see Robert Favreau, *Épigraphie médiévale* (Turnhout, 1995), pp. 113–40; Robert Favreau, 'Commanditaire, auteur, artiste dans les inscriptions médiévales', in *Auctor et auctoritas: Invention et conformisme dans l'écriture médiévale* (Paris, 2001), pp. 37–59. See also Vicente García Lobo and Encarnación Martín López, *Epigrafía medieva: Introducción y álbum* (León, 1995).

[17] *HE*, III, p. 90.

[18] On these questions, see *Fasti ecclesiae gallicanae: Répertoire prosopographique des évêques, dignitaires et chanoines*, vol. 2: *Diocèse de Rouen*, ed. V. Tabbagh

made up of different components, including the tomb, a stone plaque, and a copper strip on which an inscription was engraved as follows: 'Mausoleo tanti presulis congruus lapis appositus est; et epitaphium adonico metro quod dactilo spondeoque constat editum est in lamminis cupri litteris aureis sic exaratum est.'[19] White marble covered John of Avranches' tomb, which was placed in the baptistery of his cathedral (it is possible that this was alabaster; the Latin vocabulary pays more attention to the colour of the stone rather than the precise kind of material: 'monumentum ejus ex albo lapide factum est').[20] Peter of Maule's tomb and inscription were in the cloister along the southern wall.[21] Apart from the long funeral eulogy composed by Orderic for John of Rheims, all the epitaphs are preceded by palaeographical or topographical information precise enough to establish the material reality of the original inscription. The author provides the reader not only with a piece of verse, but with the entire funerary monument, defined by size, material, location and, sometimes, aesthetic qualities.

Orderic's contextualisation of the funerary monuments can be seen in a number of examples. The *planctus* for John of Rheims is included after the description of the place and conditions of the monk's burial. It is part of the creation of the funerary monument in the medieval sense, that is to say, the collection of all commemorative displays associated with one figure: grave, tombstone, inscriptions, poetic compositions, texts about death, liturgical celebrations, pious foundations, alms, and monumental decorations.[22] While conserving their function as evidence for Orderic's narrative, the inscriptions and their monumental or material context give the story tangibility. The brief descriptions given by introductory sentences before the epitaph open the reader's eyes to the epigraphic texts. Orderic describes how the text is actually written, its layout, such as for Ansold: 'brevique loco nomen et officium diemque obitus ejus et magnam pro eo precem sic comprehendit [he compressed into his short epitaph

(Turnhout, 1998).

[19] *HE*, III, p. 18. Translation: 'A fitting stone was set up on the tomb of this great bishop; and an epitaph composed in the adonic metre, which consists of a dactyl followedby a spondee, was engraved in gold-leaf letters on a copper plate.'

[20] Ibid., p. 22.

[21] Ibid., p. 178: 'et in claustro monachorum secus australem basilicae maceriam sepultus requiescit. Epitaphium autem hujusmodi Iohannes Remensis super illum edidit.'

[22] On the notion of funerary monuments, see Cécile Treffort, 'La Mémoire d'un duc dans un écrin de pierre: Le Tombeau de Guy Geoffroy à Saint-Jean-de-Montierneuf de Poitiers', *Cahiers de civilisation médiévale* 47 (2004), 249–70.

his name and station, the day of his death, and a hearfelt prayer on his behalf]'.[23]

Peter of Maule's epitaph, written by John of Rheims upon Peter's death in 1101 or 1102, is copied in the last section of Book V and is dedicated to the benefactors of the monastery of Saint-Évroul.[24] It consists of eleven hexameters, all Leonine apart from line 4, and sometimes in identical rhyme (lines 3, 5, 6, 7, 9, 11). The text reads as follows:

> Post annos agni centum cum mille superni
> Flos procerum Petrus prope iani decidit idus
> Dapsilis et letus multum fuit atque facetus
> Plus epulis quam militiae studiosus agoni
> Summus apud proceres et nobilium fuit haeres
> Vixit honoratus terra qua pausat humatus
> Et dedit hanc sedem Christi genetricis ad aedem
> Bis senus iani sol nubilus extitit illi
> Sed sol justiciae prece fulgidus esto Mariae
> Plangit Parisius, pangat super hunc paradisus
> Per sanctos sedem quibus hanc concessit et aedem.[25]

Over half of the poem is dedicated to the obituary report (lines 1–2) and a very well-developed sequence beseeching prayer (lines 8–11). Lines 3–7 consist of an original description of the deceased, in which John of Rheims wishes to commend the generosity and the cheerful, simple and warm character of Peter of Maule. Orderic mentions these two exact qualities in the accompanying prose portrait, which he presents before the epitaph. It is possible to see a number of echoes between the two parts of the description, and although the tone is different, particularly as Orderic does not hesitate to criticise Peter of Maule's overzealous attitude, the prose prepares the reader for the content of the epitaph. By this point in Orderic's narrative the two adjectives at the beginning of line 3 ('dapsilis et letus') have already appeared, albeit the other way round, in a passage which recounts Peter's agreement to give two churches from the village of Maule to the monks of Saint-Évroul. The first term makes another appearance a few lines before the epitaph, to describe the patronage

---

[23] *HE*, III, p. 198.

[24] Ibid., p. 178.

[25] Translation: 'After the birth of Christ a thousand years/ And then a hundred more had passed, when Peter,/ Most noble lord, died near the Ides of January./ Generous and light of heart he was, and merry,/ And more intent on feasting than on wars;/ Heir to a noble race, first of his peers,/ Honoured in life here, where he buried lies;/ He gave this church in honour of Christ's mother./ The misty new year's sun had risen twelve times;/ Now, Sun of Justice, shine through Mary's prayers./ Mourn, Paris; open, Paradise, for him,/ By the saints' prayers for whom he gave the dwelling.'

of Peter ('dapsilis patroni'). By insisting on Peter of Maule's generous and spirited nature, the contrast with his son's character is made more obvious – Ansold was a virtuous and sober knight. In a continuous reading of the *Historia ecclesiastica*, not taking into account the fact that the text by John of Rheims was written earlier, the narrative seems to influence the content of the epitaph. The effect produced by the double presentation of the information is more than a repetition, but rather that of an assertion or a confirmation, demonstrating that the contents of the historical work are true.

The epitaph Orderic copied for John of Avranches, archbishop of Rouen, who died in 1079, has a different status.[26] Made up of six elegiac couplets and placed at the beginning of the fourth chapter of Book V, it is not incorporated into the biography of the prelate. It is the longest description of the deceased given by Orderic, and there is no obvious repetition of the prose in the verse. Orderic does refer to John of Avranches' character and reports some anecdotes from his life several times over the preceding chapters; we learn that he was *ferox* and *turgidus*, and that he had lost the use of his voice following an accident. However, the reforming works of the archbishop are hardly mentioned, although they are known to have been important. The epitaph then gives details of the actions which were supposed to restore order among the Norman clergy:

> Metropolita tuus jacet hic urbs Rotomagensis,
> Culmine de summo quo moriente ruis.
> Aecclesiae minuuntur opes, sacer ordo tepescit,
> Provida religio quem sua constituit.
> Haec neglecta diu canonum decreta reformans,
> Instituit caste vivere presbyteros.
> Dona Dei sub eo venalia nulla fuere,
> Hinc et opes largas contulit aecclesiae.
> Lingua diserta, genus, sapientia, sobria vita,
> Huic fuit, exiguus quem tegit ipse lapis.
> Nona dies Septembris erat cum carne Johannes
> Expoliatus abit, sibi vera quies. Amen.[27]

This epitaph uses a classical vocabulary and formulae, such as directly addressing the mourning city of Rouen, of which John was archbishop, in the first couplet, and noting his moral qualities in the fifth. Indeed, it is

---

[26] *HE*, III, p. 22.

[27] Translation: 'Rouen, now mourn, plunged in the abyss of death/ From your high pinnacle; here your bishop lies./ So is the Church made poor; the priestly order,/ Shaped by his pious foresight, now grows lax./ He re-established old, neglected laws,/ Prescribing chastity of life for priests,/ Forbidding sale of spiritual gifts,/ And giving bountifully to his church./ Eloquence, lineage, wisdom, sober life/ Were his; this little stone now covers all./ Put off this flesh; may lasting peace be his. Amen.'

tempting to read the funerary poem text merely as a description of a good episcopal government at the time of the Gregorian reform.[28] In fact, using the page layout, Orderic adds the epitaph in such as way as to highlight the actions of the deceased. The verse stands in for prose description. Orderic chooses to speak about the archbishop's reforming policy by means of an epitaph, as poetic writing has particular qualities of truth and the absolute in the search of history. Making clear that he did not write the epitaph himself, he describes at the beginning of the fourth chapter its geographical and physical situation.[29] Orderic can dispense with narrating the prelate's activities, on the grounds that they are certified and recorded in an ancient document which he produces as proof (as he would do with a charter), a proof, moreover, that took the form of an inscription on white marble, which at the time of Book V's composition had been visible for half a century in the baptistery of the cathedral of Rouen.

The verse funerary inscriptions in Orderic's *Historia ecclesiastica* have a specific and recognisable structure, which is used in very different cases without losing any of its diplomatic or historical use. The verse texts are mingled with Orderic's prose descriptions of particular figures, and highlight one aspect or another of the individual's personality or actions. The *Historia ecclesiastica* is devised for the reader, in this sense, as a gallery of shining examples in which each epitaph exalts the qualities of a deceased person. Reading it is a path of discovery, and Orderic constructs a poetic necropolis as he writes.

The Role of Inscriptions in the Narrative and Argumentative Material

ORDERIC does not, however, quote epitaphs for all the figures mentioned in the prose of his *Historia ecclesiastica*. The necessarily 'shaped time' of history-writing opposes the linearity of history as experienced. The choice of inserting or not inserting an inscription shows Orderic's interpretation of events, and his decisions in highlighting particular figures. Those to whom he dedicates a eulogy (often the funerary inscription) are enshrined as the subject of a poem that exists for all time (and, depending on the function of the inscription, for universal and durable publicity). Although the inscriptions are

---

[28] On the use of these formulae in funerary inscriptions, see the expressions collected by Bernadette Mora, 'Le Portrait du défunt dans les épitaphes (750–1300): Formulaires et stéréotypes', *Le Moyen Âge* 97 (1991), 339–53. For the Carolingian period, see the synthesis of Aurelio Gonzales Ovies, *Poesía funeraria latina: Renacimiento carolingio* (Oviedo, 1995).

[29] HE, III, p. 22: 'In baptisterio basilicae ad aquilonem tumulatus est. Monumentum ejus ex alto lapide factum est in quo hujusmodi epitaphium solerter insertum est.'

exogenous, they are not thrust into the *Historia* without thought. Their use is carefully considered, and each one brings something to the author's arguments.

Hugh of Eu's epitaph shows this clearly.[30] It appears at the end of the section in which Orderic reports the final hours of the bishop of Lisieux, who, knowing he was ill and being taken to his church on his demand, died on the journey, on 17 July 1077. A quarrel then broke out between the canons at Lisieux and the sisters at Nôtre-Dame, where Hugh had died. They argued about where to bury the bishop, and the matter was brought, eventually, to the king's court in Rouen. The king sided with the sisters and put John the bishop in charge of the funeral ceremony. Unwilling to comply with the king's orders, the latter suddenly developed aphasia, and in the end it was Gilbert, bishop of Lisieux, who, along with the sisters, buried Hugh. The epitaph seems to reward the sisters' success, as they keep and celebrate the memory of the prelate. The textual context Orderic provides for the epitaph is also instructive: the chapter in which it is quoted is replete with vocabulary of light and brilliance. It begins, in fact, with the story of the basilica of Lisieux being struck by lightning ('ingens choruscatio') during a service. The church catches fire ('scintillans ignis') and panic takes over, resulting in the death of ten people. Images of light and glowing are used again in the description of the bishop. In the epitaph, engraved in gold letters ('litteris aureis') on a strip of copper ('in lamminis cupri'), the deceased's qualities are resplendent, as the adjective 'clarus' (line 3) highlights; the idea is picked up again, indirectly, in the evocative expression 'stemmate morum' (line 8), which brings to mind adornment.[31] Even the date of Hugh's death is conveyed using light and the sun: 'Luce sequenti/ Phebus iniuit/ Signa leonis' (lines 16–18).[32] The poetic style of the pre-existing epitaph thus shaped Orderic's prose account of Hugh of Eu and his death. He adopted the theme of light in both obituaries, the first in verse ('Sol erat in Cancro radians splendore chorusco/ Sparsis pontificem velat radiis morientem'),[33] the second in prose ('In tanta claritate et loci amenitate nobilis antistes Hugo collocatus jacuit').[34]

Orderic also included in Book V the inscription commemorating Mabel of Bellême, wife of Earl Roger of Montgomery, to whom he had

---

[30] Ibid., p. 18; *CIFM* 22, 30, pp. 68–9.

[31] 'Clarus honore/ Pontificatus.'

[32] Translation: 'While the sun's chariot/ Waited to enter/ The sign of the Lion.'

[33] Translation: 'High is the south the sun, in dazzling splendour/ With radiant brightness clothed the dying bishop.'

[34] Translation: 'So in clear sunlight in this sweet spot the noble prelate Hugh was laid down.'

already dedicated several pages in Book III.³⁵ In the two paragraphs which precede the transcription of the epitaph written on her tomb in the abbey of Troarn, Orderic describes Mabel's cruelty towards the foundation's benefactors: she despoiled the abbey, confronted the monks, and nurtured a blind hatred against the Giroie, the founders of the monastery. Her murder is described in detail by Orderic as a legitimate act of revenge, which liberated the monastery from the domination of the countess, and pleased many ('multi de ruina ejus exultavere'). Having reiterated her crimes and her bad behaviour, Orderic reports her epitaph in a strange way, reminding us of the circumstances under which it was written: the monks of Troarn buried her and wrote the text, not for her own worth, but as an acknowledgement to her friends.³⁶ The funeral text is at odds with Orderic's previous description of her actions. It restores an image which complies with the norm for lay aristocracy, emphasising birth, reputation, worth, intelligence, dynamism, eloquence, advice, generosity and protection – all of which are mentioned in the first ten lines. Her murder is even described as treachery:³⁷

> Alta clarentum de stirpe create parentum
> Hac tegitur tumba maxima Mabilia.
> Haec inter celebres famosa magis mulieres
> Claruit in lato orbe sui merito,
> Acrior ingenio, sensu vigil, impigra facto,
> Utilis eloquio, provida consilio,
> Exilis forma sed grandis prorsus honestas,
> Dapsilis in sumptu, culta satis habitu,
> Haec scutum patriae fuit, haec munitio marchae.
> Vicinisque suis gratia vel horribilis.
> Sed quia mortales non omnia possumus omnes.
> Ha periit gladio nocte perempta dolo.
> Et quia nunc opus est defunctae ferre juvamen.
> Quisquis amicus adest subveniendo probet.³⁸

---

³⁵ *HE*, III, p. 136; *CIFM* 22, 57, pp. 102–3.

³⁶ *HE*, III, p. 136: 'Et non prerogativam meritorum, sed pro favore amicorum super tumulum has nenias edidit.'

³⁷ *CIFM* 22, 57, p. 102, v. 12: 'Ha periit gladio nocte perempta dolo.'

³⁸ Translation: 'From the high stock of noble parents sprung,/ Mabel, great lady, lies beneath this tomb./ She among famous women showed most worth,/ Known for her merits over all the earth./ In mind most keen, alert, tireless in deed,/ She spoke with purpose, counselled well in need./ In stature slight, but great in probity,/ Lavish in spending, dressed with dignity;/ The shield of her inheritance, a tower/ Guarding the frontier; to some neighbours dear,/ To others terrible; she died by the sword,/ By night, by stealth, for we are mortals all./ And since in death she sorely wants our aid/ Pray for her: prove your friendship in her need.'

The epitaph is that of a lord, metaphorically named 'shield of the land' and 'bulwark of the border' (line 9).[39] There is, then, a strange discrepancy between Mabel of Bellême's behaviour and the virtuous model described in the epitaph. Nonetheless, the verse does echo Orderic's report of the crime, which notes that the countess was relaxing in bed after a bath ('in lecto post balneum deliciantem') when she was beheaded ('sui ense detruncavit'). By introducing the funerary inscription, Orderic alerts the reader to the fact that when reading and interpreting memorial texts one should keep in mind that their aim was to glorify the deceased, even if that meant presenting a sanitised version of the truth. Orderic shows that he can take a step back from sources like these. The imperative in line 13, stating that it is now important to assist the deceased, is meant truthfully: without a doubt, Mabel needed the monks of Troarn to pray for her. Beyond the tragic irony which results from the contrast between the criticism of the prose and the eulogy in the epitaph, how should Orderic's choice to place the poem here be interpreted? Is it not counterproductive to juxtapose two such contradictory texts as these?

To answer this question, it is necessary to read the next section of Book V, in which Orderic reveals that Earl Roger remarried after the murder. His new wife, Adelais, was different from Mabel in every way: her kindness and devotion were remarkable, and she constantly advised her husband to assist the monks and protect the poor.[40] The end of the thirteenth chapter deals with a charter in which Earl Roger confirmed that Saint-Évroul was among his possessions, and granted it several properties. This part of the chapter is, therefore, the counter to what is presented before Mabel's epitaph. The epitaph therefore acts as a pivot and a structural brace in the account, a way to bridge the gap between the disorder of the despoliation and murder, and the subsequent balance of spiritual and temporal powers. The metric epitaph, as a literary genre, is positive by definition, and merges with the eulogy in its descriptive contents. Orderic's including this kind of text in the *Historia ecclesiastica* only makes sense as an effort to glorify the figures he describes. The life and death of the countess Mabel of Bellême, enemy of the monks, become an opportunity for Earl Roger to improve his lifestyle, and for harmony to be re-established in the history of the monastery of Saint-Évroul, which is the central subject of the *Historia ecclesiastica*. It is fundamentally important to distinguish between the event and its historical record, and

---

[39] See Martin Aurell, 'Les Femmes guerrières (XIe et XIIe siècles)', in *Famille, violence et christianisation au Moyen Âge: Mélanges offerts à Michel Rouche*, ed. Martin Aurell and Thomas Deswarte (Paris, 2005), pp. 319–30.

[40] 'Sequens a priori matrona dispar moribus extitit. Nam maturitate et religione viguit, virumque suum ad amorem monachorum et defensionem pauperum frequenter incitavit.' *HE*, III, p. 138.

the epitaph is one of the ways in which Orderic Vitalis manœuvres from one to the other.[41]

Orderic generally uses the epitaph as a means to conclude sections dealing with the life and actions of a particular figure. It is placed at the end, as if to bring together all the different elements, allowing Orderic to close the passage in a complete and natural way. Importantly, it is never followed by further details, or a return to something which has already been mentioned. In effect, it provides the 'final word', a 'last breath'. For example, after giving the date of John of Avranches' death in 1079, and his funerary inscription, Orderic moves on to the election of his successor, William, abbot of Caen.[42] In the end, the funerary inscription is less of a break than a useful link which Orderic uses to move from his relation of one figure to another. He does not use the information given in the inscriptions for his narrative. They are only a part of the report, but they are not merely illustrative.

These texts stand out particularly from the page layout of the manuscript. As noted above, Book V is preserved in Orderic's autograph, and this allows a study of the author's own page layout for the eight funerary poems.[43] He consistently leaves one or two blank lines before and after each inscription, which makes them instantly visible; they cannot escape the attention of the reader. Orderic also starts a new line for each line of the poem, providing greater clarity, which is also helped by the staggered disposition of the lines, more or less pronounced in form, from one epitaph to another. The first word of each line has a capital letter. The only other capitals are for the names of the dead, which are also written in larger letters than the rest. These palaeographical details visually isolate the epigraphic texts from the rest of the writing. They have a special status as copies of the originals, and hold a central place in the progression of the narrative.

The epitaphs are completely integrated into the structure, rhythm and ambition of the text. Orderic provides organised and well-argued matter, in their case as well as in the case of diplomatic insertions. The transitions between the prose and verse are kept for particular points at which the author decides to introduce the epitaph. He then announces that a text is about to be shown, and comments on a piece of biographical information or some other detail which it gives. In the dynamic movement of the text, the epitaph is considered as a narrative lever, allowing the

---

[41] On the notion of events, see Alain Bourreau, *L'Événement sans fin: Récit et christianisme au Moyen Âge* (Paris, 1993). The murder of Mabel of Bellême was also retold by Orderic in Book IX of the *Historia*, on which see Daniel Roach, 'Orderic Vitalis and the First Crusade', *Journal of Medieval History* 42 (2016), 177–201.

[42] *HE*, III, p. 22.

[43] BnF, MS Lat. 5506, vol. II, entirely from Orderic's hand between 1127 and 1130. See Appendix 2, item 7.

narration to move on to another subject. Transition from prose to verse provides a definitive break, halting to the sound and cadence of Orderic's often rhyming and rhythmic prose. Moreover, this action is graphically represented in the page layout of the manuscript. However, such a break does not alter the fluidity of the narrative, a metaphor of the continuity of history itself, and introducing epitaphs at irregular intervals allows the author to highlight joints, accidents, accelerations and breaks, in accordance with the medieval vision of time and history: linear, but not smooth. Orderic is selective about how he handles inscriptions, choosing whether or not to mention a text according to the figures involved, deciding upon the nature of the introductory sentences, and selecting the text's location in the narrative and position in the manuscript. The epitaph, the target of much attention from the historian at work, has a function in the storyline. But though it is not only an *ornamentum* of the writing, its insertion always carries an aesthetic aspect.

The Aesthetics and Pleasure of the *varietas*

THE inscriptions included in Orderic's *Historia* are not used only as historical evidence and a narrative tool. They also have stylistic value and add variety. Inserting an inscription into the narrative is a writing procedure that attempts to please the reader, to avoid boredom and to create surprise and interest. Inserting them creates a triple break. The first is in the rhythm. Inscriptions are in essence short texts, with brief sentences that provide an alternative rhythm to the narrative.[44] Although they vary from five to fifty lines in length, the average epitaph contains around fifteen lines. The second break is formal, between prose and verse. The narratives are composed as prose and only the inscriptions in verse, albeit they are not the only versified elements in the text. (When Orderic gives a list of the forty-six bishops of Rouen, he copies the poem written by the clergy of the cathedral in order to educate future generations, in which each incumbent is recorded in a heroic couplet (*heroicum disticon*, or two hexameters).[45] He does not provide the entire poem in one motion, but presents a fragment each time he speaks of one of the bishops.) What is more, these funerary poems are almost like chants (although they were never really sung), as the author likes to point out by using the term *nenia*,

---

[44] Estelle Ingrand-Varenne, 'La Brièveté des inscriptions médiévales: D'une contrainte à une esthétique', *Medievalia* 16 (2013), pp. 213–34; Vincent Debiais and Estelle Ingrand-Varenne, 'The Medieval Inscriptions: A Codified Discourse', in *Voprosy èpigrafiki, vyp. VII: Materialy I Meždunarodnoj konferencii "Voprosy èpigrafiki"*, ed. A. G. Avdeev (Moscow, 2013), II, pp. 26–51.

[45] *HE*, III, pp. 94–6.

for instance in introducing Mabel of Bellême's or William I Longsword's inscriptions.[46] This term refers to a funerary chant in classical vocabulary. The last break is on another level, relating to voices living and those from beyond the grave. Orderic makes his characters speak, so there is much direct speech to be read and heard (a process used by historians since Thucydides). This living, direct, spontaneous and evanescent (although fixed by writing) voice is juxtaposed with the voice from beyond the grave represented by the epitaph (even if the deceased does not actually 'speak' within it), which has a durable or even permanent nature. There is a true polyphony within the pages of the *Historia ecclesiastica*, and this layering of different voices adds undoubtedly to the melodic effect of the narrative.

Orderic's desire to create this variation is obvious, even between the various epitaphs in the text.[47] These epitaphs concern very different figures, including clerics (bishop, archbishop and monk) and laymen (duke, count, countess, lord). The author presents a wide array of funerary inscriptions, though the genre could have provided very repetitive examples. Types of verse, length of the text and rhymes are just a few elements of this variation. Hugh of Eu's epitaph is in Adonic verse, or twenty lines (not counting the final 'amen') each made up of a dactyl and a spondee.[48] Orderic explains this himself, thereby highlighting how uncommon it was at the time, and further emphasising his appreciation of aesthetics.[49] This very short form of verse breaks with the usual metres (hexameter and pentameter) not only because it is made up of half or a third of the number of feet, but also because its structure is fixed, whereas other types of verse are more flexible.[50] John of Avranches was honoured with a text consisting of six elegiac couplets;[51] Rollo with an epitaph of ten Leonine elegiac couplets, often with identical rhymes;[52] William I Longsword with a funerary poem of seven Leonine elegiac couplets with identical rhymes;[53] the text for Mabel consists of seven elegiac couplets, mostly in

---

[46] The same word is used in Book VI in the phrase preceding Gauthier d'Auffay's epitaph.

[47] On the place of the verse writing in Orderic Vitalis's work, see Léopold Delisle, 'Vers et écriture d'Orderic Vital', *Journal des savants* n. s. 1 (1903) 428–40.

[48] *HE*, III, p. 18.

[49] Ibid.: 'Et epitaphium adonico metro quod dactilo spondeoque constat editum est.'

[50] The first four feet of a hexameter can consist of a dactyl and a spondee. For the last foot the trochee can be replaced by a spondee, but the dactyl of the fifth foot is fixed.

[51] *HE*, III, p. 22.

[52] Ibid., p. 90; *CIFM* 22 187, pp. 277–9.

[53] *HE*, III, p. 90; *CIFM* 22, 188, pp. 280–2.

general rhyme;[54] that of John of Rheims comprises fifty hexameters;[55] that of Peter of Maule, eleven;[56] Ansold of Maule's epitaph is made up of five hexameters, the last of which contains three rhymes ending in *-ies/-is* and in *-ei*, with caesuras on the third and the fifth foot (trihemimers and penthemimers).[57] In showing such variety of poetic form, Orderic appears as a multi-talented author, even though he did not write all these texts himself. He fits perfectly into the tone, the taste or the trend of the period, during which funerary texts attracted much interest; as stated earlier, in the eleventh and twelfth centuries inscriptions in verse were a real literary genre. They even formed the basis of literary contests. Orderic relates that at the death of William the Conqueror in 1087, Thomas, the archbishop of York, won all the votes for his verse, owing to his archiepiscopal dignity.[58] Orderic shows himself not only as the historian who wrote the *Historia ecclesiastica*, but also as a poet and connoisseur of the genre, by a sort of game of mirrors and duplication.

The funerary poem for John of Rheims is part of a series of epitaphs Orderic wrote himself.[59] It is a particularly long text, containing fifty lines, while the other poems are short. Orderic even points out that brevity in one instance, by using the expression *brevi loco* for the poem of Ansold of Maule. This contrast draws attention to his own poem and his gift for versification.[60] However, unlike other epitaphs, it is doubtful whether Orderic's epitaph ever made its way onto the actual tomb of the deceased. Orderic, who wrote this poem while mourning the loss of his master, offers us a eulogy which, if it does portray the image of an ideal religious life with all the virtues of his order, gives us a precise description of the

---

[54] *HE*, III, p. 136; *CIFM* 22, 57, pp. 102–3.

[55] *HE*, III, pp. 168–70.

[56] Ibid., p. 178.

[57] Ibid., p. 198.

[58] *HE*, IV, p. 110: 'Sed solius Thome archiepiscopi Ebroachensis versus hujus modi, pro dignitate metropolitana, ex auro inserti sunt.'

[59] Orderic is the author of nine funerary inscriptions inserted into his work: besides the one for John of Rheims, there is one for Count Geoffroi of Watheolf, who died in 1124 (Book IV); one each for Avice and her husband, Gauthier of Auffay (Book VI); one for Thierry, abbot of Saint-Évroul in 1058 (Book VI); one for Robert of Rhuddlan, who died around 1093 (Book VIII); one for Hugh of Grandmesnil (d. 1098) (Book VIII); one for Roger, bishop of Sées and abbot of Saint-Évroul (d. 1126) (Book XII); and, lastly, one for Warin of Essarts, abbot of Saint-Évroul (d. 1137) (Book XIII).

[60] *HE*, III, p. 198: 'His utique exequiis Odo Monasterolensis interfuit, ibique sacerdotale officium peregit brevique loco nomen et officium diemque obitus ejus et magnam pro eo precem sic comprehendit.' Translation: 'Odo of Montreuil was present at these obsequies and there performed the priest's functions; and he compressed into this short epitaph his name and station, the day of his death, and a heartfelt prayer on his behalf.'

actions of the dead man. In line 29 we learn that he wrote a life story, in metrics, of St Évroul for his archbishop ('Versifice sancti vitam descripsit Ebrulfi'); the names of his parents appear in line 4 ('Ilbertusque pater fuit illi Poncia mater'); how he joined the monastery is told in the second quarter of the poem.

The personalisation of texts using anecdotes (in the literary sense: a historical detail the telling of which can explain the meaning of events and the psychology of men) is one of the main characteristics of the epitaphs written by Orderic and included in his *Historia ecclesiastica*. They describe the actions not merely of a model character, but a particular character, described morally, sometimes physically, along with that person's genealogy and life path, from childhood to death. Where Baldric of Bourgueil and Foulcoie of Beauvais often created rather neutral epitaphs, in which only the name, appearing in a turn of a phrase, precisely identifies the deceased, in commemorating John of Rheims Orderic chose to use the epitaph or funerary poem as a veritable personal description.[61] The two epitaphs he copied for the priory of Maule particularly stand out from the texts he himself composed for persons of the same rank or function. In the former there is no precise information about the dead person concerned; the texts are more like a version of their obituaries in verse, with a few laudatory formulae.

The epigraphic function of John of Rheims's commemoration can also be doubted, not so much because of the length of the poem, but because there is no information about the tomb, unlike the text of Robert of Rhuddlan, which begins with the following couplet: 'Hoc in mausoleo Robertus de Rodelento conditur humano more soli gremio.'[62] If the text was not destined for epigraphic materiality by being engraved or painted, what is its status within the *Historia ecclesiastica*? The date at which Book V was written makes it possible that John died during its creation – unlike the other poems, the eulogy for the monk of Saint-Évroul could have been especially written for the *Historia ecclesiastica*; certainly, the dynamic of the writing is similar to the prose in the section immediately before.[63] The epitaph for John of Rheims does not have the status of a historical source or document within the great memorial project carried out by Orderic, but rather appears because it forms a spontaneous testimony from the pupil to his master, and in this way it is anecdotal. The variety of writing devices used is often linked to the variety of feelings and emotions presented to the reader. Chibnall pointed out that Orderic inserts passages in verse

---

[61] For example, the series of poems for Alexandre written by Baldric of Bourgueil (*CIFM* 25, 105–8, pp. 126–9).

[62] *HE*, IV, pp. 144–6; *CIFM* 22, 134, pp. 210–13.

[63] On the composition of Book V, see 'Composition of the *Historia ecclesiastica*' (p. xiv above).

when the narrative of his *Historia* brings out 'deep sentiments' in him.[64] Without a doubt, this is also the case for the inscriptions he was ordered to write at a person's death, and more so for the ones that he created spontaneously. Citing real epitaphs, such as those for Rollo and William I Longsword in Book V, does not respond to the same literary ambition, in that they are neither a way to connect with the reader on an emotional level, nor the sign of any particular affection on the part of the author.

Through their variation in form, and the diversity of feelings they present, the inscriptions mentioned or written by Orderic Vitalis in Book V offer a panorama of the literary genre of the verse epitaph in the High Middle Ages. The historian and poet converse using changes in metre and rhyme, offering a rhythmic, colourful and ever-changing story from Normandy. Orderic's deployment of literary strategies demonstrates a desire to match his writing style to the movements of history.

Conclusions

THE study of the funerary inscriptions in Book V grants insight into how Orderic used them to construct his *Historia ecclesiastica*. In his work the funerary inscriptions were not part of a competitive poetry game popular amongst scholars at the time. Nor were they forced into the *Historia* as an afterthought, like an appendix to his history. They are fully integrated into the weft and weave of the narrative, and more generally into the whole structure of Orderic's work. They allow a pause in the course of time, both in history and, because they require a specific layout, in writing. Thanks to this layout, the epitaph is easily legible and, thanks to its poetic form, it is also memorable. While the precise status of each epitaph in Book V varies, they are not mere embellishments, but instead were used as historical evidence, arguments, narrative turning points or poetic emphasis. Providing a counterpoint to the prose, poems help narrate the revelation of truth and the story of the world. In the overall course of the narrative the funerary poems offer a distinctive writing style. The hybridisation of various literary genres, between *historia* and *poesis*, together with the prosimetric form, played an important role in the construction of a totality. In Orderic's case, that totality was the salvation history which he was attempting to write. Finally, behind the portraits of the deceased painted by the epitaphs, there was another figure: that of the author and copier. The inscriptions allowed Orderic to show himself not only as a true historian, but also as a great narrator and a talented poet.

---

[64] Chibnall, 'General Introduction', p. 29.

Reading Orderic with Charters in Mind

Thomas Roche

Drops of holy water on an altar, whereupon a nobleman laid down his gift ...[1]

A SMALL detail, set in a few words, but specific enough to turn the description of a gift by William of Breteuil, on the very day of the abbatial church's dedication, into a narrative that escapes the usual dryness of a diplomatic text – and to support, to the historian's eye, not only the credibility, but also the value that Orderic Vitalis added to this kind of source. Indeed, as his editors, whether Auguste Le Prevost assisted by Léopold Delisle,[2] or the late Marjorie Chibnall,[3] have pointed out, Orderic made frequent use in the *Historia ecclesiastica* of diplomatic sources, often when reporting either the story behind the refoundation of Saint-Évroul (in Book III) or its acquisitions (mainly in Book V).[4] This has strengthened the idea, expressed casually by some historians, that there is little distance between Orderic and themselves, that he is one of *us*, a medievalist, because he used *sources*, and among them *records* and *charters*, as 'real' historians do.[5] The fact that Orderic is known to have included in his narrative stories told by witnesses, often old monks at Saint-Évroul, or scenes he himself witnessed, means that he is usually regarded as a good *informant*[6] regarding subjects such as noble mentality, feuding, and the sense of the supernatural, and also, in all likelihood, on literacy.[7]

---

[1] *HE*, III, p. 130: 'donationem super altare adhuc sacrosancta consecratione madidum deposuit'; and Chibnall's comment, ibid., p. xxiii.

[2] A. Le Prevost, *Orderici Vitali Historiæ ecclesiasica libri tredecim* (Paris, 1838).

[3] *HE*.

[4] The focus will be here on the *Historia*, as Orderic's only use of charter material in his interpolations to the *Gesta Normannorum ducum* seems to be Saint-Évroul's foundation charter; see, however, below, nn. 32 and 82. William of Jumièges did not make extensive use of diplomatic sources.

[5] See for example Hingst, *The Written World*, p. xx; Shopkow, *History and Community*, p. ix, quoting Richard Southern.

[6] That is the reasoning behind Chibnall, *World*.

[7] See for instance G. Duby, 'Dans la France du Nord-Ouest au XIIe siècle: Les 'Jeunes' dans la société aristocratique', *Annales: Économies, sociétés, civilisations* 19 (1964), 835–46; M. Bennett, 'Violence in 11th-Century Normandy', in *Violence and Society in the Early Medieval West*, ed. G. Halsall (Woodbridge, 1998), pp. 126–40; T. Roche, 'The Way Vengeance Comes: Rancorous Deeds and Words in the World of Orderic Vitalis', in

'Reading Orderic with charters in mind' could simply mean that the historian tracks down all Orderic's references to diplomatic texts within the pages of the *Historia*, first of all to consider how he used them as *sources* for his own work, and second to gather facts on his contemporaries' uses of the written word – in our case of charters, what might be termed their *diplomatic* literacy. The first trail has already been followed by Chibnall in the introductions to her magisterial edition of the *Historia*, both the general introduction and those of specific volumes (especially volumes II and III). While the second aspect of the task has not yet been conducted systematically, the *Historia* has already been used as a seam of examples mined by historians of monastic culture. This present study seeks to follow a different path. My concern is to try to look at the charters used by Orderic, whether implicitly or explicitly, not as 'sources' of information, but as 'textual material' to which he applied literary devices – not only because of his aims as a writer, but also, above all, because he was a monk; as such he shared a common framework with his fellow monks, whether charter-drafters or liturgical technicians, for whom the text was nothing but a processed fabric covering community-wide projects.

A Source for Diplomatic Literacy?

THE huge amount of information on monastic life and culture reported by Orderic has indeed turned the *Historia ecclesiastica* into a *passage obligé* in the discussion of medieval literacy.[8] Quotations from or allusions to a large range of classical and even contemporary texts, whether historiographical or hagiographical, echo the catalogue of Saint-Évroul's library and complement it.[9] They also offer glimpses of Orderic's reading, selecting and writing habits, as he occasionally alluded to events he had read about *in chartis* but chosen not to include in the *Historia* on account of their having already been reported elsewhere, or because the precise details were uncertain, or because he was hurrying to copy onto wax tablets a book loaned from a fellow monk visiting from across the Channel.[10] Furthermore, he dwelt at length on the

---

Vengeance in the Middle Ages: Emotion, Religion and Feud, ed. S. Throop and P. Hyams (Farnham, 2010), pp. 115–36; C. S. Watkins, *History and the Supernatural in Medieval England* (Cambridge, 2007).

[8] B. Stock, *The Implications of Literacy: Written Language and Models of Interpretation in the Eleventh and Twelfth Centuries* (Princeton, 1983).

[9] Nortier, *Les Bibliothèques médiévales*.

[10] See, for example, *HE*, V, p. 358: Orderic did not dare commit to writing the number of knights fallen at the battle of Ramlah, for fear of making a mistake; ibid., p. 218.

manuscripts which had either been copied at Saint-Évroul or given to the community.[11]

Orderic was a first-hand witness to the evolving monastic attention to literacy. For him and his fellows, a good monk was one who knew how to write, not in the sense of providing literary contributions of his own, but in the most basic sense of beautifully composing letters. The case in point is the model provided by Abbot Thierry, or by Orderic's own master, John of Reims.[12] Regardless of whether Orderic was Saint-Évroul's cantor, as Rozier suggests in this volume,[13] he nevertheless stressed, in parallel with writing, another means of sharing a text: by singing it. It is striking that ability as a singer usually figured alongside ability as a copyist in Orderic's praises of important monastic figures.[14]

Among all the information on literate practice reported by Orderic, it is not surprising to find several occurrences of diplomatic documents or letters contained within the pages of the *Historia*. Letters were sent to and from Rome at the time of Abbot Robert's flight; when a council was convened, they brought the excuses for the bishop of Evreux, for instance, and they were also used when a queen of France allegedly plotted to kill her stepson.[15] Charters were being written, confirmed, read, put in the archives, and used in discussions. Before turning to those uses, it should be noted that letters are usually clearly distinguished from charters in the *Historia*, not least by the terms Orderic used. Letters are *epistola*, *litteris*, and most often *apices*, and are almost systemically characterised as sealed ('sigillatos').[16] This reflected the practice of closing letters with wax that had to be broken before reading,[17] which provided, in Orderic's mind, a sense of security. This heightened the scandal of King Philip's letter to Henry I, actually written by Queen Bertrade, in which the king plotted to have Louis of France murdered.[18] As will be discussed below, 'charter'

---

[11] For example, *HE*, II, p. 48 (books copied at the time of Abbot Thierry); ibid., p. 42 (gift of a psalter); *HE*, III, p. 128 (gift by William of Breteuil); ibid., p. 231 (gift by Roger of Warenne).

[12] Abbot Thierry: ibid., p. 336 (his epitaph); see also Abbot Warin (ibid., p. 346); John of Reims: ibid., pp. 6–8.

[13] See his contribution above, 'Orderic Vitalis as Librarian and Cantor of Saint-Évroul'.

[14] *HE*, III, p. 346, evoking the metrical songs composed by Abbot Warin; or ibid., p. 24, about William Bonne-Âme.

[15] *HE*, II, p. 108; VI, pp. 202, 50.

[16] *HE*, II, p. 338 (*epistola*, *litteris*); VI, p. 50 (*apices*); p. 378 (William Clito's letter to Henry I); p. 322 (Saint-Évroul to Henry I); on sealing, p. 50, p. 378.

[17] See the contemporary description by Eadmer in the case of a letter from Thomas of York to Anselm: *Historia novorum in Anglia*, ed. M. Rule (London, 1884), p. 210.

[18] This story was probably made up by Orderic himself. *HE*, VI, p. 50.

('charta') conveys a wider meaning than the strict diplomatic category of a subjective text bearing a legal value, of which the finest category is the solemn *diploma*. Orderic also used the terms *testamentum* or *chirographum*, which had the generic meaning of 'authentic document', not necessarily a bipartite charter.[19] Yet when one considers the scope and the size of the *Historia ecclesiastica*, compared to shorter texts by authors such as William of Malmesbury or Eadmer of Canterbury, such references to charters are comparatively few in number.[20] Fewer than thirty of them are explicitly mentioned or used by Orderic.

In turning to consider what Orderic wrote about charters, only a handful of cases put the charters on centre stage and thus provide explicit information on diplomatic practice. Orderic shows us charters being written, often under dictation, and proclaimed, but there are only four such occurrences in the pages of the *Historia*. Fulcher of Chartres is said to have elegantly dictated the terms of his donation charter to a Robert Andreas, labelled as a 'famous scribe' ('scriptor egregius').[21] A noble layman, William of Roumare, also personally dictated his confirmation charter to Saint-Évroul. No further indication is provided on the scribe.[22] The diplomatic author of a text was not always its real composer. John of Reims wrote the text of Hugh Pain's donation under the dictation of Hugh Fresnel, another monk at Saint-Évroul.[23] The charter bearing the benediction of the bishop of Lisieux to the new abbot-elect of Saint-Évroul was dictated by Radulf, abbot of Sées, written by Robert, a monk

---

[19] *HE*, III, p. 286 (this wording may derive from a previous source); and *HE*, V, p. 260.

[20] For instance, though Eadmer quoted only one letter in his *Vita Sancti Anselmi* (ed. R. Southern (London, 1962)), he included in his *Historia novorum in Anglia*), the full text of forty-five letters exchanged mostly between Anselm, the pope and the king of England. According to Julia Barrow, William of Malmesbury quoted fifty-one documents in his *Gesta Regum* and sixty-three in his *Gesta Pontificum*: J. Barrow, 'William of Malmesbury's Use of Charters', in *Narrative and History in the Early Medieval West*, ed. E. Tyler and R. Balzaretti (Turnhout, 1999), pp. 67–89. Both authors used letters more often than charters, but William seemed also to demonstrate a wide range of uses for charters, closer to Orderic's, in the (yet interpolated) *De antiquitate Glastoniensis ecclesiae*: J. Scott, *The Early History of Glastonbury: An Edition, Translation and Study of William of Malmesbury's 'De antiquitate Glastonie ecclesie'* (Woodbridge, 1981). William's use of charters would deserves a proper investigation, in addition to the observations already made by Richard Southern, 'Aspects of the European Tradition of Historical Writing, 4: The Sense of the Past', *Transactions of the Royal Historical Society* 5th series 23 (1973), 243–63; by Rodney Thomson, *William of Malmesbury* (Woodbridge, 1987); and by Julia Barrow.

[21] *HE*, III, p. 150.

[22] *HE*, VI, p. 380.

[23] *HE*, III, p. 210; on Hugh Fresnel, see p. 174.

of the same house, and finally proclaimed by the bishop's chaplain to a careful audience.[24] Thus it was not only the oral proclamation but also the associated performance of the spoken word's being committed to writing and the solemn reading which brought authority to the action. It should be noticed that the vocabulary used echoed the case of a non-diplomatic text, the canons of the Reims council, which Orderic quoted in the *Historia* after indicating that they were dictated by John, bishop of Cremona, noted by John, a monk from Saint-Ouen of Rouen, and then 'clearly and distinctively' ('distincte et aperte') proclaimed by Chrysogonus, a Roman deacon.[25]

Twice, charters are described as constituting part of the abbey's archives. In the reconstructed story of the former house of Saint-Évroul, charters were part of the treasury that was split up between Frankish barons in the tenth century.[26] More precisely, Abbot Mainier was said to have put the confirmation of Saint-Évroul's English possessions by King William in the abbey's *archivis* – here one should picture a chest, probably located in the chapter house – as soon as he came back.[27] Generally speaking, Orderic did not show much interest in the provenance of the written diplomatic sources he used.

The contents of a charter could also be discussed. At the council of Reims, the debate on Cluny's privileges was fuelled by the examination of its foundation charter, the terms of which, particularly the fact that the abbey was originally erected *in alodio*, were picked to serve a legal argument.[28] Reporting Richard of Leicester's election as abbot, Orderic took the opportunity to stress the normative framework provided to the community of Saint-Évroul by four reference points: the *Rule of St Benedict*, the legal privileges of the Church, monastic custom and William's confirmation charter. The fact that William had marked the charter by the sign of his authority, as well as those of his prelates and magnates, is a point especially underlined by Orderic.[29] The letter which Abbot Osbern sent to the pope justifying his legitimacy as head of the community at Saint-Évroul[30] also held a specific place in the monastery's network of (written and unwritten) reference points. Not only did Orderic quote this letter extensively in his narrative, he also reported that Osbern

---

[24] *HE*, V, p. 260.

[25] *HE*, VI, p. 274.

[26] *HE*, III, p. 322.

[27] Ibid., p. 240; see, more generally, S. Barret, 'L'Institutionnalisation de la mémoire: Les Archives ecclésiastiques', in *Pensiero e sperimentazioni istituzionali nelle 'Societas Christiana' (1046–1250): Atti della sedicesima Settimana internazionela di studio, 2004* (Milan: 2007), pp. 463–85.

[28] *HE*, VI, p. 270.

[29] Ibid., p. 488.

[30] *HE*, II, p. 108.

had it read at his bedside just before his death.[31] The reference to the re-enactment of the abbot's words, whose argument had been accepted by the pope, is aimed at definitively validating the community at Saint-Évroul, and straightening out the sinuous path of its early history.

While the information which Orderic provides highlights the specific processes of writing, drafting and confirming charters, it provides little information that could not be gleaned from other sources, especially from charters themselves. For example, Orderic often reported the ceremony of validation, as the duke (or the king) confirmed a charter by inscribing the sign of the cross and handing it to his bishops, who in turn ratified it while pronouncing formulas of excommunication against any future violators.[32] This kind of scene constituted only a dramatisation of the validation formulas and, as confirmation and corroboration left physical traces on a document (crosses, *signa*, seals), is something that could have been deduced from the *critique externe* (the analysis of external elements) of the original charter – or even of a copy, if joined by sufficient description. Such narratives therefore do not provide proof that Orderic had specific sources relating what happened on the day a charter was confirmed. He may simply have reconstructed events from a close reading of the text, the description of the *signa* or the seals themselves. This should not come as a surprise. As Chibnall pointed out, charter materials from the period have a strong narrative nature.[33] They are not bound by a strict formulary and so are not altogether different from what a chronicler could write. Orderic, working on this textual material while producing his own text, did not draw firm lines between what he took from the particular source, what he knew from other sources, and what he reconstructed.

Charter Material in Orderic's Time

BEFORE turning to the literary devices Orderic used to deal with diplomatic texts, it is important first to consider what the charter material Orderic had at hand looked like.[34] Traditionally, early medieval diplomatic texts are divided into *charters* and *notices*, based on the

---

[31] Ibid., p. 132.

[32] The best case is provided by the foundation charter, ibid., pp. 16, 38; See also GND, II, p. 140.

[33] HE, III, pp. xxi–xxii.

[34] On Anglo-Norman diplomatics and documentary evolutions, see especially D. Bates, *Re-ordering the Past and Negotiating the Present in Stenton's 'First Century'* (Reading, 2000); D. Bates, 'La "mutation documentaire" et le royaume anglo-normand (seconde moitié du XIe siècle–début du XIIe siècle)', in *Les Actes comme expression du pouvoir au haut Moyen Âge: Actes de la table ronde de Nancy, 26–27 novembre 1999*, ed. B.-M. Tock and M.-J. Gasse-Grandjean (Turnhout, 2003), pp. 33–49.

style – either subjective or objective – and the legal meaning of the act – either a deed or a mere report of a transaction. Charters are written in the first person and record the will of the self-announced author, expressed as the legal action in question becomes effective. Notices, by contrast, record past transactions, in the third person.[35] Even in Normandy there was obvious continuity with the Carolingian era in the way charters were drafted, in terms of both formulas and layout. Solemn charters, diplomas, were usually written with an elegant calligraphy, and elongated letters on the first line or in the subscriptions. They carried signs of validation, though seldom monograms, which are typical in royal acts, but rather crosses, often allograph.[36] In Normandy, nonetheless, as in western France, there was a noticeable trend for confirmation by autograph crosses (or, at least, crosses traced so as to appear autograph) in the eleventh century, before the appearance and diffusion of the seal in the twelfth century.[37] The development of the notice style also characterises eleventh-century diplomatics, especially in western France, where it often used to be seen as a symptom of the crisis of public authority and legal culture. However, this trend should rather be understood as a creative evolution in the manner in which monks used the written word to fit their needs in asserting themselves to the outside world.[38] There were, nevertheless, no clear-cut distinctions between charters, which could include narrative features, and notices, which could also bear signs of validation. The recourse to notices declined during the twelfth century. Another developing practice in Norman diplomatics, recourse to the chirograph to record agreements, dates from the mid-eleventh century. Whether it had been drafted as a subjective charter, or, as was more common, as a notice introducing itself as a *conventio*, the same text was copied twice onto a single sheet of parchment, with the copies separated by a *divisio* (usually the simple term

---

[35] O. Guyotjeannin, J. Pycke and B.-M. Tock, *Diplomatique médiévale*, L'atelier du médiéviste 2 (Turnhout, 1995).

[36] C. Potts, 'The Early Norman Charters: A New Perspective on an Old Debate', in *England in the Eleventh Century: Proceedings of the 1990 Harlaxton Symposium*, ed. C. Hicks (Stamford, 1992), pp. 25–40.

[37] M. Parisse, 'Croix autographes de souscription dans l'ouest de la France au XIe siècle', in *Graphische Symbole in mitteralterlichen Urkunden: Beiträge zur diplomatischen Semiotik* (Sigmaringen, 1996), pp. 143–55; B.-M. Tock, *Scribes, souscripteurs et témoins dans les actes privés en France (VIIe–début du XIIe siècle)* (Turnhout, 2005).

[38] O. Guyotjeannin, '"Penuria scriptorum": Le Mythe de l'anarchie documentaire dans la France du Nord (X^e–première moitié du XIe siècle)', *Bibliothèque de l'École des chartes* 155 (1997), 11–44; D. Barthélemy, 'Une Crise de l'écrit? Observations sur des actes de Saint-Aubin d'Angers (XIe siècle)', *Bibliothèque de l'École des chartes* 155 (1997), 95–117; T. Roche, 'Les Notices de conflit dans la Normandie ducale (milieu du XIe–milieu du XIIe siècle environ)', *Tabularia* 7 (2007), 51–73.

cyrographum). This was then cut, so both parties could retain their part of the document.[39]

A further way of viewing these documents is by considering them as processes. For charters were part of a legal and social process by which relative statuses and relationships were negotiated and asserted, a process of which they are the only surviving trace available to the historian. The recourse to the written word cannot be studied without taking into account the agglomerate of oaths and gestures into which it fits.[40] The *liturgy* of a diplomatic document varied with context: that for a ducal charter, which would become the central object in a ceremony of validation by the prince, and which could also turn into a true anathema liturgy led by the bishops who added their authority to its confirmation, necessarily differed from that of a simple notice written by a monk witnessing or remembering a transaction taking place in his chapter room. Writing in itself was a process. Charters were not simply written down and validated instantly. Their drafting, authenticating, copying and keeping took time. An act could well refer to its own use in the ceremony accompanying the transaction it witnessed. Does this mean that it was written beforehand, or is this just an illusion created by the style of the charter? Witnesses often traced their crosses on the sheet of parchment to corroborate the transaction recorded. Some cases reveal that the crosses were drawn before the writing down of the main text, but the opposite practice can also be detected, in carefully prepared charters with spaces left for crosses to be drawn. Moreover, *signa* could be added to a previous charter long after it had been produced, as if to record successive authorities on it or re-enact its value.[41] A transaction, of any sort, did not imply the drafting of a diplomatic document. Moreover, the choice between the different kinds of diplomatic text evades all obvious explanation. The nature of the authority involved and the solemnity invested in the charter are surely to be taken into account, but are not enough to explain all cases.[42] Orderic is not so

---

[39] M. Parisse, 'Remarques sur les chirographes et les chartes-parties antérieurs à 1120 et conservées en France', *Archiv für Diplomatik* 32 (1986), 546–67; O. Guyotjeannin and L. Morelle, 'Tradition et réception de l'acte médiéval: Jalons pour un bilan des recherches', *Archiv für Diplomatik* 53 (2007), 367–403; T. Roche, 'Des conventions infiniment variées': Normes et coutumes dans les concordes des moines de Saint-Wandrille (XIe–XIIe siècles)', in *Coutumes, doctrines et droit savant*, ed. J.-M. Augustin and V. Gazeau (Poitiers, 2007), pp. 13–42.

[40] B.-M. Tock, 'La mise en scène des actes en France au haut Moyen Âge', *Frühmittelalterliche Studien* 38 (2004), 287–96.

[41] See, for example, *Recueil des actes des ducs de Normandie de 911 à 1066*, ed. M. Fauroux (Caen, 1961), nos. 55, 68, the latter a Carolingian diploma signed by Duke Robert a century and a half after it was written.

[42] L. Morelle, 'Instrumentation et travail de l'acte: Quelques réflexions sur l'écrit diplomatique en milieu monastique au XIe siècle', *Médiévales* 56

much a source on these written documents as himself a participant, albeit an unusual one, in their production.

This brief overview of diplomatic practices would not be complete if it did not also stress the development of archival practices, which are not always easy to isolate from specific uses of the written word. Summaries of charters or notices were compiled, not only to facilitate their preservation, but, above all, in order for the transactions to be confirmed by an authority, usually in Normandy the duke or the king. The drafting of these pancartes was already a recomposition of diplomatic texts.[43] Notices could also be copied or, more likely, be written directly onto a roll of parchment. This practice is well attested at Saint-Évroul, for which a late eleventh-century roll has been preserved. In the case of pancartes as well as rolls, it is very probable that some transactions were first put into writing at the time of compilation. In other words, they were transactions with no 'original' sources.[44] This point is worth bearing in mind before one turns to consider Orderic's attitude towards written transactions or, as the case may sometimes have been, merely the common memory of them. A further step, both in terms of information preservation and ease of retrieval, and in terms of setting a community's identity within the commemoration of past benefactions, was the compilation of charters in a single manuscript codex, the cartulary.[45] The earliest Norman cartularies date back to the end of the eleventh and the first half of the twelfth centuries, though some are now lost, as in the case of Fécamp.

All these reuses, this 'afterlife', of charters placed them in a meta-narrative. While some notices and charters already contained internal narrative elements, the mere accumulation of simple documents in a pancarte, sometimes implying a direct causal relationship with the first of them, usually the foundation charter or its ducal confirmation, also created a larger narrative of a successful wave of benefactions to a monastery. In some cartularies the meta-narrative came not from the simple compilation they provided, but from the wider project they embodied. For example, the cartulary of Mont-Saint-Michel began with hagiographical texts, to place the community within a longer history. Another issue at stake was the complex treatment of the canons present at Mont-Saint-Michel

(2009), 41–74.

[43] M. Parisse, 'Écriture et réécriture des chartes: Les Pancartes aux XIe et XIIe siècles', *Bibliothèque de l'École des chartes* 155 (1997), 247–65; D. Bates, 'Les Chartes de confirmation et les pancartes normandes du règne de Guillaume le Conquérant', *Pancartes monastiques des XIe–XIIe siècles*, ed. M. Parisse (Turnhout, 1998), pp. 97–109.

[44] A point made, in the case of Caen, by L. Musset, *Les Actes de Guillaume le Conquérant et de la reine Mathilde pour les abbayes caennaises* (Caen, 1967).

[45] *Les Cartulaires: Actes de la table ronde organisée par l'École nationale des chartes et le GDR 121 du CNRS*, ed. O. Guyotjeannin, L. Morelle and M. Parisse, Mémoires et documents de l'École des chartes 39 (Paris, 1993).

before its refoundation.[46] The way in which charters were compiled also affected the cartulary's implicit narrative line. The monk transcribing the document could add elements of context undetectably, marginally or at greater length. One of the most difficult, and less documented, parts of his job was the selection of which documents to include. The contents of the resulting cartulary might therefore vary according to his community's project, or simply due to the care or carelessness of the compiler.[47] In this respect, there is no hard line between a project centred on the compilation of charters, and another taking shape as a historical narrative which drew on charters as sources, such as the specific use of the Glastonbury material by William of Malmesbury.[48] Moreover, the pragmatic or legal nature of the cartulary is more difficult to grasp than one might think, as we have little understanding of their legal use once they were compiled.

Although eleventh- and even twelfth-century records are scarce in the case of Saint-Évroul, with only a few charters surviving (as originals, as thirteenth-century copies, and in the late eleventh-century roll edited by Léopold Delisle), it can be seen that the monastery's documentary practices in the century following its refoundation reflect the characteristics and dynamics of Norman monastic production. A comparison with other Norman houses, in particular Jumièges, from which Saint-Évroul's first abbot originated, and Lyre, whose first abbots came from Saint-Évroul, is revealing in this regard.[49]

As mentioned above, the roll of Saint-Évroul is the best extant witness for the recording of notices in a single 'object'. Though Orderic did mention the composition of a commemoration roll, he was actually

---

[46] *The Cartulary of the Abbey of Mont-Saint-Michel*, ed. K. S. B. Keats-Rohan (Stamford, 2006); *Chroniques latines du Mont-Saint-Michel (IXe–XIIe siècle)*, ed. P. Bouet and O. Desbordes, Manuscrits du Mont Saint-Michel: Textes fondateurs 1 (Caen, 2009).

[47] L. Morelle, 'The Metamorphosis of Three Monastic Charter Collections in the Eleventh Century (Saint-Amand, Saint-Riquier, Montier-en-Der)', in *Charters and the Use of the Written Word in Medieval Society*, ed. K. Heidecker, Utrecht Studies in Medieval Literacy 5 (Turnhout, 2000), pp. 171–204.

[48] Scott, *The Early History of Glastonbury*, pp. 13–18.

[49] On Jumièges: see brief remarks in Bates, 'La "mutation documentaire"; and D. Bates, 'Charters and Historians of Britain and Ireland: Problems and Possibilities', in *Charters and Charter Scholarship in Britain and Ireland*, ed. M. T. Flanagan and J. A. Green (Basingstoke, 2005), pp. 1–14; I intend to publish further research on this abbey's documentary production. For now, see T. Roche, 'Les Moines de Jumièges et les moulins de Montataire', in *Saint-Leu d'Esserent et l'implantation monastique dans la basse vallée de l'Oise*, ed. D. Hanquiez and A. Petit, Histoire médiévale et archéologie 25 (Amiens, 2012), pp. 37–58. There is no recent work on Lyre, for which see C. Guéry, *Histoire de l'abbaye de Lyre* (Évreux, 1917).

pointing to another use of the roll form, to record names of the abbey's deceased patrons and donors in order that the monks might pray for them.[50] Nevertheless, the spiritual and commemorative aspects of land or rights transactions recorded in the charter roll should not be played down. Orderic elaborated on the gifts of Robert of Rhuddlan, reported by a notice from this roll, but he might have got the information from a now lost charter.[51] He does not seem to have used other notices from the partially damaged roll. However, as will be seen below, Orderic did use and recompose notices from other origins within the text of the *Historia*.

A composite manuscript to which Orderic contributed included the records of spiritual associations of the monastic community with other religious houses.[52] The structure of some of these documents fits the same pattern as notices of more earthly agreements: for instance, both kinds of document use the *Hec est conventio* incipit. These spiritual records might therefore be regarded as diplomatic-like documents inserted into a liturgical and hagiographical compendium, a practice not uncommon at the time,[53] for example at Mont-Saint-Michel. The Saint-Évroul monks also kept working on the recomposition of their accumulated benefactions as pancarte and confirmation charters. Beyond the charter of foundation, which Orderic mentioned three times (in his interpolations to the *Gesta Normannorum ducum* as well as in the *Historia*) and of which the thirteenth-century cartulary kept two other versions,[54] this practice is witnessed by the coexistence of two texts of King William's confirmation for English lands.[55] Another possible witness is the 1127 confirmation by King Henry, though Orderic wrote nothing of this and there appear to be grounds for suspicion regarding its authenticity, as far as one can tell from the poor textual tradition.[56] This work of compiling, recomposing, and somehow interpolating general confirmation charters was common at the

---

[50] *HE*, II, p. 114.

[51] *Rotulus*, nos. 9 and 11 (BnF, MS N. Acq. Lat. 2527); an edited text by Leopold Deslisle is included in *Orderici Vitalis ecclesiasticae historiae libri tredecim*, ed. and trans. A. Le Prévost, 5 vols. (Paris, 1838–5), V, pp. 182–95; see also *HE*, IV, pp. 136–8.

[52] BnF, MS Lat. 10062, fols. 77–81. For discussion of Orderic's additions, see below, Appendix 2, item 9.

[53] J.-L. Lemaître, 'Les Actes transcrits dans les livres liturgiques', in *Les Cartulaires: Actes de la table ronde organisée par l'École nationale des chartes et le GDR 121 du CNRS*, ed. O. Guyotjeannin, L. Morelle and M. Parisse, Mémoires et documents de l'École des Chartes 39 (Paris, 1993).

[54] *Recueil*, ed. Fauroux, no. 122; M. Chibnall, 'Le Privilège de libre élection dans les chartes de Saint-Évroult', *Annales de Normandie* 28 (1978), 341–2.

[55] *Regesta regum Anglo-Normannorum: The Acta of William I (1066-1087)*, ed. D. Bates (Oxford, 1998), no. 255.

[56] D. P. Henri and D. J. Taschereau, *Gallia Christiana in provincias ecclesiasticas distributa*, XI (Paris, 1759), instr. 204.

time. The monks of Lyre, for instance, kept working on their foundation pancarte, of which three versions are still extant, which fuelled other confirmation documents, such as the great charter of Henry II. Moreover, they also regularly and systematically sought episcopal confirmation for their many English possessions.[57]

By the stress he put on validation marks, drawing, as mentioned above, from elements present in the charters themselves, Orderic also witnessed the production at Saint-Évroul of charters in all likelihood bearing crosses. Though, generally speaking, the association of charter and validation by crosses not only from the duke but also from his family and his entourage was a distinctly Norman custom, practice varied from one scriptorium to another. Thus, while the monks of Saint-Ouen of Rouen took great care over the graphic solemnity of their charters, they scarcely used crosses as a mark of validation, and even when they did it was often only the allograph cross of the duke himself. In contrast, the Jumièges charters are simpler in their formulas and layout, but emphasise crosses, autograph or apparently so. This recourse to crosses faded out by the end of the eleventh century, as the use of chirograph increased, but Orderic never alluded to this peculiar charter form.

Using the Charters' Text

Now that the Norman documentary background has been set, we shall consider charters as texts, with which Orderic dealt as a writer. Which literary devices did he use to incorporate them into his own project? This kind of study has been made regarding his literary sources, such as William of Poitiers,[58] but not for his use of charters.[59] However, the use of charters by other monastic writers has been investigated, by authors such as Laurent Morelle.[60] Chibnall pointed out only two different stances in Orderic's work:

---

[57] See M. G. Cheney et al., *English Episcopal Acta: Worcester, 1062–1185*, English Episcopal Acta 33 (Oxford, 2007), p. 94; T. Roche, 'Henry of Blois and Normandy', in *Henry of Blois and the Twelfth-Century Renaissance*, ed. John Munns and W. Kynan-Wilson (forthcoming).

[58] P. Bouet, 'Orderic Vital, lecteur critique de Guillaume de Poitiers', in *Mediaevalia Christiana, XIe–XIIIe siècles: Hommage à Raymonde Foreville de ses amis, ses collègues, et ses anciens élèves*, ed. C. E. Viola (Paris, 1989), pp. 25–50.

[59] See however Chibnall's remarks on the foundation charter in her introduction to Books V and VI of the *HE*, pp. xxii–xxiii.

[60] L. Morelle, 'La Mise en "œuvre" des actes diplomatiques: L'"auctoritas" des chartes chez quelques historiographes monastiques (IXe–XIe siècles)', in *'Auctor' et 'auctoritas': Invention et conformisme dans l'écriture médiévale*,

From his material Orderic selected and amplified. Sometimes he gave the texts as they stood; sometimes he tried to make a story of them, recreating the scenes and supplying the narrative of events that seem to lie behind them. The second method, though more lively and readable, sometimes added extra confusion to records that were already diplomatically very confused.[61]

The most basic use of a charter occurred when Orderic described its physical aspect. He rarely provided much detail in this regard, but instead focused particularly on the presence of seals as he dramatised a validation ceremony (on which more will be said below). His treatment of Crowland's forgeries is especially interesting. King Æthelbald's and King Edgar's charters are described as sealed.[62] However, their texts provide no clue pointing to the existence of a seal. Either Orderic had access to the original forged document, which could have been fraudulently sealed, or his description of a sealed document might be a literary embellishment, suggesting that he could not describe a royal charter without stressing the physical trace of its validation, and above all its sealing. When Orderic did mention that he had consulted a charter, he said nothing of its archival aspects. He mentioned neither the location of charters he was using, though this was implicit in the case of the charters at Crowland, nor their tradition. His focus on validation marks points to the examination of original charters, but, as noted, clues are present in whatever way the text was transmitted. Orderic never expressed any doubt about their content, even if he used plainly forged charters. This indicates that he was, in all likelihood, not aware of their status.

Another straightforward use of a charter may be its transcription in Orderic's *Historia*. There are several examples of fully quoted texts within the work, for instance council canons. These are introduced to the reader as such, with the use of textual markers such as the phrase 'Hec est textus', but quotations were not provided with specific layouts in the autograph manuscripts.[63]

The clearest example of a quoted charter is the inclusion of the full text of the gift by Foucher de Chartres, for which the original

---

actes du colloque de Saint-Quentin-en-Yvelines (14–16 juin 1999), ed. M. Zimmermann (Paris, 2001), pp. 73–96.

[61] HE, III, p. xxii.

[62] S 82, purportedly dated 706, and S 741, purportedly dated 966; respectively HE, II, pp. 338 and 342.

[63] See for example the last autograph volume of the *Historia*, covering Books X–XIII. The letter of Abbot Roger to Henry I and the royal writ (*HE*, VI, pp. 322–4) are not given any special treatment, nor are they headed by any rubric: BnF, MS Lat. 10913, pp. 388–9. This is in contrast to epigraphic documents included in verse, as pointed out in this volume by Vincent Debiais and Estelle Ingrand-Varenne, pp. 127–9.

survives.[64] Orderic's transcription is accurate, which is usually taken to mean that the other charters he quoted, for which the originals have been lost, were copied just as faithfully.[65] There are several other cases of possibly quoted charters (not including letters),[66] yet we cannot make assumptions as to the accuracy with which they were transcribed. King William's confirmation for English lands is enlightening in this regard. It is, indeed, the only other case of a quoted charter in which a version independent of Orderic is extant, the foundation charter excepted. Although a thirteenth-century cartulary copy, and not an original as in Foucher's case, the elements it provides are enough to let its most recent editor adjudge that those two texts are witnesses to two different lines of tradition, which he interprets as reflecting probably two different versions of the original charter.[67] Neither is more accurate than the other, but their coexistence proves that, at some point, reinterpretation and rewording of the original charter gave birth to two different versions. Moreover, this point of textual divergence may well have been the original itself, meaning that two versions of the charter could have been drafted simultaneously. This would not be an extraordinary case in Norman diplomatics.[68] In any case, such a complex situation may raise suspicion regarding other instances in which we have an even weaker grasp of the variety of textual traditions represented.

In two cases Orderic's transcription raises no suspicion. Henry I's confirmation of the abbey's possessions by the time of Abbot Warin's election is a writ, a kind of document both short and formulaic, of which the text given by Orderic does not sound at all anomalous.[69] The benediction charter granted by the bishop of Lisieux also seems plausible.[70] Orderic provided no full transcription of a charter elsewhere in the *Historia*, preferring instead to quote the main part of a given document. He probably omitted the final validation formulas because converting the charter into the third-person helped him to create a narrative from the document and dramatise the scene, a point to which we shall return below. This appears to be the case with the attribution of a rent for the lights of Saint-Évroul's church by Roger of Montgomery, the text of which seems to have been quoted extensively. In this instance the list of witnesses is not

---

[64] *HE*, III, p. 150.

[65] Ibid., p. xxiv.

[66] See Osbern's letter (*HE*, II, p. 108); Roger's letter to Henry I (*HE*, VI, p. 322); see also the transcriptions of council canons such as Reims (*HE*, VI, pp. 274–6).

[67] *Acta of William I*, no. 255.

[68] See for instance ibid., no. 266, and the comment in Bates's introduction, pp. 39–40.

[69] *HE*, VI, p. 322.

[70] *HE*, V, p. 260.

treated as such, but rather integrated into Orderic's report of the charter corroboration in Alençon.[71] Orderic handled William of Breteuil's gift of an annual rent in a similar manner.[72] In this last case, the quoted text of William's charter was preceded by a summary of its main disposition. Here we see how, rather than quoting a document, Orderic could perhaps have used not only the information it gave, but also its structure and its vocabulary, and turned the original's dispositive sentences, as a first-person text, into an objective style, eventually reducing it to its core elements.

In the report of the dispute with Roger de Witot, witnesses of the sale of the land to Saint-Évroul are given 'as written in the charter' ('in carta notatis'), with no other indication.[73] The existence of a charter can only be inferred, as Marie Fauroux did when she included Orderic's text in her edition of the *acta* of the Norman dukes as a now lost document.[74] It may also be likely that the core of the charter had been calendared by Orderic. He did not dwell long on William Rufus's confirmation for Saint-Évroul, which is treated similarly as a brief summary.[75] Other such instances are William of Roumare's establishment of seven monks in Neufmarché[76] and Hugh Payen's gift of the *vicaria* of Villegats.[77] The use of the calendar by Orderic could sometimes be ambiguous. In most examples given here, he actually referred to the fact that a charter was drawn up, at least by mentioning the charter as his source, and often by adding more details on its drafting[78] or validation. Elsewhere, however, it is harder to tell a calendared charter from an inserted notice. Orderic also reported the main clause of a *pactum* between William of Breteuil and Raoul of Tosny.[79] Such an agreement between magnates was not unheard of in late eleventh- or twelfth-century Normandy.[80] We cannot assume,

---

[71] *HE*, III, p. 138.

[72] Ibid., p. 128.

[73] *HE*, II, p. 120.

[74] *Recueil*, ed. Fauroux, no. 155.

[75] *HE*, IV, p. 254.

[76] *HE*, VI, p. 380. No charter is extant, but there is a confirmation by Archbishop Hugh of Rouen in the Saint-Évroul cartulary. However, there seems to be no connection between Orderic's text and the charter's, which would probably have summarised considerably the text of the original document.

[77] *HE*, III, p. 206

[78] Roumare's and Payen's cases are instances where information is given on the dictation and the calligraphy of the charters, see above.

[79] *HE*, IV, p. 216; see also *HE*, VI, p. 548, a *foedus* between Robert of Leicester and Rotrou of Perche.

[80] V. Bourrienne, *Antiquus cartularius ecclesiæ Baiocensis (livre noir)* (Rouen, 1902), no. 76; see also the agreements between Henry I and Robert of Flanders: *Regesta regum Anglo-Normannorum, 1066–1154*, vol. 2: *Regesta*

however, that a *conventio* was then actually written down. Even if it had been, would Orderic have known it from the text, or only from the report of eyewitnesses or his community's memories? Whatever the case, calendar as literary device paved the way for a more elaborate reordering of the text of a charter: dramatisation or narrativisation.

Dramatisation is the use of a charter's elements to build up a scene. Orderic especially focused, as already mentioned, on the depiction of the validation process as traced in the document or reconstructed from its marks. He never introduced parts of a first-person charter as speech in their author's mouth. Orderic introduced King William's English charter by stressing that the gifts listed therein were confirmed by his 'royal speech' ('regali auctoritate'), but never disguised the fact that he was using a written document, which he then went on to quote.[81] Only in the case of Saint-Évroul's charters did Orderic actually turn charter clauses into a royal speech. Having recapped the initial wave of donations to the abbey, which William Giroie and Robert of Grandmesnil commanded to be written down in order for these transactions to be presented to the duke, Orderic reported William's consent and used the final clauses of the charter to set the stage for the corroboration of the document. First, he introduced as William's own words the validation clause, including the ducal subscription formula and the excommunication of any future malefactor. Then he reported that the duke drew his autograph cross, followed by the prelates and magnates attending his court.[82] Chibnall rightly stressed that Orderic's presentation made it appear as though the gifts and their ducal confirmation were closely connected events, whereas the endowment of a new abbey was actually a much slower process. Orderic's focus on dramatisation of *signa* even led him to present all signatories to a charter as actual witnesses to the confirmation it recorded, despite the fact that they were not all alive at the same time, and some of them added their marks afterwards.[83]

The dramatisation process could also lead Orderic to elaborate longer

---

Henrici primi, 1100–1135, ed. Charles Johnson and H. A. Cronne (Oxford, 1956), pp. 515, 941. See also the views on such *conventiones* in E. King, 'Dispute Settlement in Anglo-Norman England', *ANS* 14 (1991), 115–30; and D. Crouch, 'A Norman "conventio" and Bonds of Lordship in the Middle Ages', in *Law and Government in Medieval England and Normandy*, ed. G. Garnett and J. Hudson (Cambridge, 1994), pp. 299–324.

[81] *HE*, III, p. 232.

[82] *HE*, II, p. 38; this is also the main element Orderic reported of the charter in *GND*, II, pp. 140–1. In the *Historia* as well as in the *Gesta*, Orderic included a developed date clause, but in the latter he added elements (the years of pontificate of Pope Leo and of reign of Emperor Henry) that did not come from the charter, but rather from the *Annals* of Saint-Évroul (Le Prévost, V, pp. 156–7).

[83] *HE*, III, p. 150; and Chibnall's remark at p. xxiii.

stories, thus contextualising a charter. Does this mean that Orderic knew more than the charter said, or was his narrative a free interpretation of the document? A good case study here is Ralph of Tosny's charter. We can trace Orderic's reordering and rewording of this charter thanks to the preservation of the document in Saint-Évroul's cartulary.[84] Were it not for this, we would probably have interpreted Orderic's text as a simple calendar of the lost original. Of course, we cannot exclude the fact that, as in the case of the English royal confirmation charter, Orderic might have used another version of the original. Nevertheless, this scenario appears to be quite unlikely. Even if the cartulary text is not entirely accurate, we should also suspect Orderic of a large amount of rewriting, for he reported Ralph's donations in three stages, whereas the charter took them as a whole. Ralph made his first visit to Saint-Évroul's chapter house because he wished to reconcile with the monks after his support for Arnold Giroie's ruthless expedition to the abbey at the time of Abbot Robert of Grandmesnil's exile. He placed a token on the altar and promised 'a lot' ('multa promisit').[85] Sometime later – according to Orderic, after his return from Spain – he returned to Saint-Évroul to give many gifts to the monks, including a vineyard at Tosny. Several years thereafter, he added further gifts from his new English possessions. The charter itself lists all the gifts mentioned in the *Historia*, but passes over their chronology. Orderic not only altered the order of the elements present in the charter's text in order to stress the three stages of Raoul's gifts, but also inserted information on one of his companions, his doctor, Goisbert, who decided to become a monk at Saint-Évroul. Indeed, Goisbert may have been Orderic's source for this story, but the close similarities between the two texts show that it is more likely that Orderic actually picked elements from the enumeration of Raoul's gifts to form the backbone of his narrative. Orderic even mentioned the men listed as witnesses in Raoul's charter as attending King William's confirmation of this gift. This royal confirmation, unnoticed in Raoul's charter, may well have been in only the 1081 English confirmation charter. Later in the *Historia* a further trace of these donations can be found, as they are reported, with some amplification, alongside the wave of donations following the dedication of the church of Saint-Évroul. They were probably inserted in a pancarte drafted at that time, if Orderic's text was not in itself the only compilation of these post-dedication updates to previous gifts.

In order to report William of Breteuil's gifts to Saint-Évroul, Orderic first recalled his donation of an ornate book, then proceeded with the calendar of William's charter donating an annual rent. As Roger of Le Sap, who would become abbot in 1091, transmitted the book, this first gift must have come before. We may conjecture that it was used as a token,

---

[84] Ibid., pp. 124–6; Le Prevost, V, pp. 180–1.
[85] *HE*, III, p. 126.

positioned on the altar, for the later gift, but the two gifts may also have been separated by a few years. Orderic continued by quoting the charter for the gift of an annual rent, excluding the validation clause, which he turned into indirect speech. He followed up with the report, a couple of years later, of the increase of that gift on the occasion of the dedication of the church of Saint-Évroul, and concluded with the fact that William's final gift had been confirmed by King Henry's seal. The latter gift probably caused a new charter to be written. Though the possibility cannot be entirely excluded that it would have been presented, after William's death and Henry's victory, to the new duke of Normandy, this scenario seems unlikely. It is more probable that Orderic drew elements from that hypothetical second charter, or from a pancarte composed after the dedication, elements such as the precise date clause, the dramatisation of William's gesture in placing his token on the altar, the detail of the drops of water on the freshly blessed altar and the fact that his gift figured in King Henry's charter of confirmation (1113), the context of which Orderic staged a couple of books later. The text of the 1113 charter may have itself been based on an eventual dedication pancarte.

In the case of the 1113 confirmation charter, a contrast can be drawn between Orderic's report and the version of the charter preserved by later copies, and especially in the thirteenth-century cartulary.[86] What appears there lacks the contextualisation added by Orderic, who kept from the charter only the list of witnesses and a clause on future pleas that were to be judged by the king's court, which he put into the royal mouth. As in the case of the foundation charter, the royal speech, here in indirect speech, is presented by Orderic as coming at the time of the validation, whereas the charter had already been drafted, a point made clear by Orderic's narrative. We may try to reconcile the charter evidence and Orderic's view by stressing that the proclamation of a written charter, and eventually the voicing of its main clause by its diplomatic author, may have been the final step in the validation process.

The richest use of diplomatic material within the pages of the *Historia* happens when Orderic intertwines, implicitly, texts from *notices* into his own narrative, composing hybrid texts. Here one must bear in mind the very thin line that existed between calendaring a charter and inserting a notice into another text. As Chibnall pointed out, to track this feature is not an easy task, and it is made all the more complex by the fact that Orderic did not always mention that he had consulted a written document.[87] Yet there are many contextual clues that should be examined: the occasion (when an individual is on his deathbed, or becomes a monk), the place (at the chapter), the audience (witnesses are named), the action and its objects (the person puts a token on the altar,

---

[86] *HE*, VI, p. 174; Le Prevost, V, pp. 196–9.
[87] *HE*, III, p. xxiii.

often a book, or receives from the monks money or a gift out of *caritas*), the issues at stake (gift, quitclaim, entering the *societas* of the monks). Even if there is no stable formulary in notices, a common scenario, sharing a common vocabulary, draws itself (suggesting that the charter roll is indeed a chapter roll). In this regard, there is no distinction to make between notices reporting gifts or transactions, as present in the roll, and notices of spiritual service, such as the ones copied in Saint-Évroul's liturgical manuscript.[88] Orderic obviously used both kinds of notice. As narrative texts, they could easily be inserted into his own writing, whereas charters, because of their subjective style, either had to be quoted, or to have their parts recombined or dramatised in order to fit into the narrative of the *Historia*.

The comparison between a sample notice from the roll and some extracts from the *Historia* is striking, to the extent that it becomes difficult to tell which was written by Orderic:

> Before his death, Girard Trove quit the claim he had on a land we hold at Moulins. One of our monks came to him, as he was lying in his sickness, and gave him the monastic cloak; he, as we have said, quit all his claims on that land, and so did his wife, to whom it had come as heritage, and his brother, Ernald Trove. Warin fitz Osmund, who was with the monk, witnessed all this. On the day of the funeral, Girard's wife and Ernand came to the chapter-house to receive our association. They confirmed all that Girard conceded when alive, and placed it on the altar. The witnesses were, etc.[89]

> When [Fulk] became a monk he gave to Saint-Évroul the church of Guernanville with the land belonging to it, and also another piece of land which Hugh of Bayeux had given him in the same village, and which he had held for a long time from William fitz Osbern, the same bishop's nephew. Furthermore, William, Fulk's son and heir, granted this publicly in the chapter-house, and together with his father placed the gift on the altar of St Peter the Apostle, in recognition of which he received an ounce of gold as a free gift from the monks. William of Breteuil and

---

[88] BnF, MS Lat. 10062, fols. 78r–81v.

[89] *Rotulus*, no. 4: 'Calumpniam quam Girardus Troue habebat super terram quam apud Molins habemus, antequam obiret, dimisit. Quidam enim monachus noster venit ad eum, illo adhuc in infirmitate iacente, deditque ei habitum monachicum, et tunc, sicut diximus, omnem calumpniam de ipsa terra dimisit, et uxor illius de cuius hereditate erat ipsa terra, et frater eius Ernaldus Trove. Testis est de hoc Uuarinus filius Osmundi, qui cum monacho erat. In die vero quo eum sepeliuimus, venit uxor ipsius Girardi et Ernaldus frater eius in capitulum, et acceperunt beneficium huius loci, et concessionem quam fecerant Girardo adhuc uiuente confirmauerunt et super altare posuerunt. Testes […]'.

Gilbert Crispin, with two sons of theirs, also confirmed these gifts.[90]

No textual clue marks the insertion of this last notice into the *Historia*. Its nature is demonstrated only by the similarity of structure and vocabulary between it and the roll. Another clue which is sometimes provided is stylistic rupture. To take a simple example, when Orderic resumed his narrative after having inserted a notice, he usually referred to its protagonist as *heros*. This word he sometimes used as a term for 'leader' or 'lord', sometimes as a moral qualification, and sometimes, what concerns us here, as a way to resume a narrative centred on a character. A common occurrence was to follow up on a lord's gifts to Saint-Évroul with the inclusion of textual and factual elements from a notice after a genealogical or topographic digression.

The case of Auffay provides such an example. Orderic's text weaves together the story of the Auffay family with the repeated donations to Saint-Évroul. However, Orderic explicitly mentioned his quoting of a charter. The word *heros*, which though unusual in a charter was common in Orderic's vocabulary,[91] is used to refer to Gilbert d'Auffay in the main body of the charter text, therefore pointing to Orderic's intervention. This may have been a minor alteration of the original text, of which we have no evidence today. We cannot, however, exclude the idea that Orderic might also have actually composed a document which he claimed to have quoted. The last explanation would be that Orderic himself had been behind the original charter, or at least, the royal confirmation charter. However, as Orderic has never been elsewhere associated with the drafting of charters, such an occurrence would be exceptional. This case stresses that the amount of rewriting Orderic performed inside the text of notices should not be underestimated. The account of Robert of Rhuddlan's gifts to Saint-Évroul is another significant example, as Orderic's text can be compared to a notice copied in the roll.[92] Orderic undoubtedly drew elements from that notice, just as he did with Raoul of Tosny's charter,

---

[90] *HE*, III, p. 122: 'Hic dum monachus factus est, æcclesiam de Guarleinuilla et terram ad eam pertinentem sencto Ebrulfo dedit, aliamque terram similiter dedit quam in eadem uilla Hugo Baiocensis episcopus ei dederat, quamque idem diu a Guillelmo Osberni filio nepote prefati presulis tenuerat. Guillelmus autem Fulconis filius et heres hæc in capitulo palam concessit, et cum patre suo donationem super altare sancti Petri apostolic posuit, et ince pro recognitione tunc unciam auri ex karitate monachorum recepit. Hæc etiam Guillelmus de Britolio et Gislebertus Crispinus cum duobus filiis suis concesserunt'.

[91] So unusual it could not be found in current charters databases ARTEM (http://www.cn-telma.fr/originaux/index/) or CBMA (http://www.cbma-project.eu); DEEDS records it once, but in a thirteenth-century Austrian document (http://deeds.library.utoronto.ca).

[92] *HE*, IV, pp. 136–8.

but reordered them and included them in the wider story of Robert's achievements. Orderic's narrative ends up with Robert's burial at Saint-Évroul, detailing the role then played by his brother, Arnold of Tilleul, a monk there. It is interesting to contrast this life-centred narrative to the roll, which included after the notice of Robert's gifts the report of their confirmation by his son. Orderic apologised for his long digression on Robert's donations, but his words are also a reminder of his original purpose as a monastic writer, which was dissimilar from the aims of his fellow monks who took care of the ordinary business of charter-drafting and notice-copying.

So, far more than simply copying notices, Orderic was reconstituting them and, as a result, turned mere reports, whether written or oral, and even memories, into elaborate texts. He may even appear to have been composing a hybrid text, containing long notices devoted to places given to his abbey by a family of lords on whom he temporarily focused his attention by stressing genealogical and liturgical connections. This is not far from the odd familial 'commemorative' notice identified by Chantal Senséby in the cartulary of Saint-Julien de Tours.[93] Such an attitude is particularly prevalent in Books V and VI of the *Historia*, which contain many instances of such topographical and genealogical insertions constructed from different parts of liturgical and diplomatic *notitiae*.

Orderic catalogued consecutive gifts by Ralph of Montpinçon and his successors to build a broader development.[94] The report of a gift by William of Moulins, which sounds like a notice, opens with a genealogical summary of his familial connections, then returns to the benefactions of his heirs.[95] The account of the church of Noron, likewise, follows the story of William Pantulf and his familial and seigneurial connections. It even includes a miracle story: the victorious ordeal passed by William after having been unjustly accused of taking part in Mabel of Bellême's murder.[96] Similarly, the case of Lommoie mixed a miracle story with the text of a more traditional notice of a gift by the parents of the unfortunate Ralph of Cravent.[97] An extreme example of such commemorative notices is the long passage on the priory of Maule, centred on the figures of Peter of Maule and his son Ansold, which not only reuses notices, but also quotes parts of charters.[98] The issue here is not from where Orderic received his information, which was often Chibnall's interest, but rather

---

[93] C. Senséby, 'Entre gesta, chronique et nécrologe: Une *notitia memorialis* de Saint-Julien de Tours (début XIIe siècle)', *Journal des savants* 2 (2006), 197–251.
[94] *HE*, III, p. 164.
[95] Ibid., p. 134.
[96] Ibid., pp. 154–64.
[97] Ibid., p. 244.
[98] Ibid., pp. 172–206.

the significance of his interweaving of narrative, genealogical, legal and supernatural elements, which points to his adherence to a monastic framework shared by his contemporaries. Ultimately it was Orderic's combination of these elements, each present in the community's shared memories, which he committed to writing in the *Historia*.

Orderic's Monastic Framework

EVENTS involving both local and national figures, their identity within their family, their gifts and their prayers crystallised in certain texts: a notice in the charter roll, maybe, or a notice in the local *Liber Vitae*. These events were recalled and discussed, for each time the monks spoke of this land, of that book that was given or was used as token to be put on the altar, each time they sat near that tomb in the cloister or the chapter room, gave an opportunity for memory and gossip, in addition to the technical, liturgical commemoration that was due. That is why the notion of a 'source' is questionable, because it imposes on documents the traditional notion that *a* fixed text pre-existed, where in reality these events were discussed and remembered in many different ways. Each event could justify the writing and rewriting of a different text that still would not have captured all the details. Orderic's *Historia* is not a final point in their trajectory, but rather a part of an ongoing process of writing and rewriting that was necessary in order to deal with polyvalent events which were legal acts as well as spiritual ones.

Commemoration is at the heart of this monastic framework, where the written word is a means for conveying complex issues. Its object, memory, is often, technically, a liturgical *memoria*. Charitable gifts also needed to be remembered because these acts of piety were what justified the possessions of the abbey. The written word provided a means for saving memories, by storing them on record. Orderic demonstrated this as he apologised when lack of time and space prevented him from preserving *in chartis* famous deeds of great figures, implying that the written record was the favoured way of retaining such memories, at least to his mind. But the written record was an aid to commemoration not only in its status as a text, but also as an object – an object with the potential to invoke floating memories and to crystallise them. This is a function written texts share with other objects.[99] Some were used as tokens of gifts, as recorded by donation charters or notices; such a use of knives, for instance, is well attested in the Anglo-Norman documentation, from charters reporting jokes made by William I to the famous example studied by Michael

---

[99] For more on this subject see Daniel Roach, 'The Material and the Visual: Objects and Memories in the *Historia ecclesiastica* of Orderic Vitalis', *HSJ* 24 (2013), 63–78.

Clanchy.[100] But books – bibles and liturgical books above all – could also be used as tokens. Several examples figure in Saint-Évroul's charter roll.[101] The term *donatio*, also used alone, may have referred to the donation charter itself. Was it written in advance to commemorate a gift that had yet to occur, or was it left blank? In the latter case, was it already conveying the value that would eventually be enshrined in the text it would contain? How do we reconcile this view with the fact that these transactions are now known by notices copied on a roll, but not on actual charters? The cases reported by Orderic often referred to the object placed as token on the altar as a *donum*, which could possibly mean a written document.[102]

Moreover, objects involved in a transaction could also reveal themselves as memorial containers. Monks gave horses or knightly equipment 'out of charity' to the brother or the son of their benefactor. It was an act remembered, obviously because it was written down, but also, and perhaps above all, as it involved the recipient's memory, not only of having received a gift, but also of having been present, and by this having consented to the exchange. This story of consent became associated with its token, which could possess a history of its own. As their son died, Engenulf of Laigle and his wife begged for monastic fellowship with Saint-Évroul, giving the community the young man's splendid horse. It was claimed by his relative, Arnold Giroie, in exchange for the land of Bocquencé and the service of its tenant, Baudry, to the monks.[103] The horse simultaneously represented the spiritual service required to commemorate the dead man, and the restored lordly status of the abbey on the land of Bocquencé, and, still, the special link between the monks and the founders' extended family. It is not unlikely that a notice traced this exchange. For most of the monks recalling the story, perhaps including those from whom Orderic may have actually received it, it was the horse, when invoked, that revived the duty of commemoration and the memory of lordship. The memory of the confirmation and endowment of the church of Neufmarché by William of Roumare was similarly mediated through the charter he personally dictated, but perhaps even more through the physical trace he left by renovating the church's chancel, an act preserved in many memories, especially those of the monks.[104]

[100] M. Clanchy, 'Medieval Mentalities and Primitive Legal Practice', in *Law, Laity and Solidarities: Essays in Honour of Susan Reynolds*, ed. P. Stafford, J. L. Nelson, and J. Martindale (Manchester, 2001), pp. 83–94; see also M. Clanchy, *From Memory to Written Record: England 1066–1307* (Oxford, 1992).

[101] *Rotulus*, nos. 11, 32, 38, 43, 47 (*per librum*), 33 (*per textum paratum evangeliorum*), 45 (*per textum*).

[102] *HE*, III, p. 202 (a book); see however on this issue Morelle, 'Instrumentation et travail de l'acte', p. 46.

[103] *HE*, II, p. 82.

[104] *HE*, VI, p. 380.

The drops of water on Saint-Évroul's altar, mentioned at the outset of this study, lived on in the shared memory of the monastic community and probably also of its extended network of associated fellows. In a way, they tagged the scene and helped the monks to remember the whole event. But this peculiar fact could only trigger a memory such as this in a community that had also retained strong memories of the Breteuil family connection to the abbey, of the lands given and the consent witnessed. Orderic and his fellow monks did remember and commemorate. As mentioned above, if he relied on the text of charters, he never dwelt on their physical aspect, beyond their marks of validation. In his case, at least, the diplomatic document acted as a medium for commemoration only in its status as a text, not as an object – except, that is, for the seal or the ink dried in the shape of a cross.

The second key element in Orderic's monastic framework was the issue of authority. I have mentioned above the dramatisation which he brought to his use of charters, especially royal charters, which was probably a convenient literary device for working parts of a subjective charter into a narrative, while also stressing the signs of validation, described as gestures or traces in the diplomatic document. Nonetheless, the issue of dramatisation extends far beyond a simple literary technique, for it created an active memory of the genesis of the charter. When describing the crosses and the seals, by putting the emphasis on the ducal or royal will that was inscribed on the document and also made bishops leave their marks, written and proclaimed (excommunication), Orderic was actually re-creating these actions, reviving the weight of authority which these actors had put into the document.

What Orderic did through writing and dramatising, monks could also do through reading the texts, or even displaying them. Charters are not here acting as written proof, but rather as living witnesses of past authority. Unsurprisingly, confirming charters, adding one's own authority to that of one's ancestors, was part of good lordship or kingship, as William's words on his deathbed demonstrated:

> By my royal authority I freely confirmed the charters preserving these gifts ('cartas largitionum') against all who might covet or attack them.[105]

The vocabulary here is interesting. The verb used with these dramatised charters is *confirmare*. Elsewhere in the *Historia* the verbs *firmare* or *confirmare* are mainly used only of one other situation, when Orderic wrote of someone's faith strengthening by living like a saint or witnessing a miracle.

The third aspect that shapes the monastic framework shared by Orderic was the need for the collective appreciation of custom. The

---

[105] *HE*, IV, p. 92: 'cartas largitonum contra omnes emulos et infestatores principali auctoritate gratis confirmaui'.

occasions of charters are public ceremonies – narratives stressed this point. Even when a charter reported a gift or a spiritual association as linking a layman and a saint, it also involved much wider groups. The collective dimension is obvious, as most transactions involving monks took place in the church or in the chapter room, therefore implying the community's presence. Spiritual or more earthly transactions, staged authority, needed an audience – not only because they required witnesses to be remembered, but also because their 'public' dimension was part of their effectiveness. The public and collective 'occasion' constituted a forum where customs were appreciated, discussed and reshaped. They were gatherings where agreement on common norms was sought, as a preliminary to deeper concords. The appeal to these collective, common, customary rules was also meaningful spiritually, as the stress on the use of a common liturgy or on customary rules regarding funerary arrangements demonstrated.

Final Thoughts

ORDERIC quoted, dramatised and recomposed diplomatic material in his *Historia*. Some of the passages within the work, especially the commemorative genealogical and topographical notices he constructed, themselves tend to sound like diplomatic texts. Orderic's first aim was to record the history of his community, and he later apologised for feeling the need to include in his much broader narrative the references to benefactions made to his monastery. In other words, he was apologising for using diplomatic material that diverted him from the general, political narrative of the *Historia*. His initial project was not only commemorative. He comments that, in hindsight, he also had in mind its legal aspect (if by this term we understand the customary, collective acknowledgement of statute), as he regretted, for example, that properties were lost as a result of unclear information at the time of Abbot Osbern.[106] The topographical, genealogical and legal notices provided a sense of identity for his community, including its spiritual associates, who were at the same time its benefactors. They constituted a compendium of Saint-Évroul's possessions, in a similar, if more narrativised, way to the cartularies.

Does this make Orderic a 'cartulary-chronicler'? As mentioned above, notices, and charters contained some narrative elements by nature. Simply compiling them already composed a greater narrative of the accumulation of possessions by the addition of graces. More complex projects, such as the compilation of a cartulary, or a document's inclusion in a manuscript whose texts were carefully selected, could also give charters a larger meaning, transforming them into identity markers for the community they involved. In this regard, in his attitude to charters Orderic was closer to

---

[106] *HE* II, p. 96.

the author of the *Historia ecclesie Abbedonensis*,[107] or even to William of Malmesbury in the *De antiquitate Glastonie ecclesie*,[108] at least when he endorsed the role of chronicler of his community. Indeed, his recourse to diplomatic material became rarer as he turned to general history, where he barely ever used it as proof, as *pièces justificatives*, contrasting with Eadmer of Canterbury or William of Malmesbury in the *Gesta regum Anglorum*, who both widely inserted extracts of letters or charters to support their report of Anselm's troubles or of the institutional ecclesiastical history of the Anglo-Norman realm.

The co-production of 'diplomatic' material by Orderic may seem a technical, even a secondary, issue. Historiographically, among the students of Orderic's works and beyond, lies the idea that his narrative complements, and even outweighs, diplomatic documents as a historical source. Historians usually read charters with Orderic in mind, rather than reading Orderic with charters in mind. For example, the genealogical and chronological information his *Historia* conveys can be of high value in dating (mostly undated) Anglo-Norman charters.[109]

Orderic provides independent pieces of information on what known charters report. Yet he does so in the same way as multiple variant texts – a chirograph and a notice or instance – may provide different views on a single transaction. But the contrast, and relative value, of Orderic's text and diplomatic material is not only a matter of precision or depth of knowledge. It is, above all, an issue of perspective. This is striking even in Orderic's own pages, where two lines of narrative became intertwined. On the one hand, the *Historia ecclesiastica* may appear merely as a stereotypical, cyclical story of charitable gifts to Saint-Évroul. Mainly in Book V, but also elsewhere, the impression is given of regular waves of donations, by lords alternately promoting the monks, then doubting them, then repenting, generation after generation. It is also a linear story of capitalised faith, of gifts and authority, that had to be re-enacted. It thus has a timeless quality, though not without its own evolutions. On the other hand, Orderic reported the dynamic story of war and peace, with the same individuals as actors. The pious lords of Maule, in Book V, were, at the same time, protagonists in the turmoil of Anglo–French conflicts. This kind of tale, political and military, is attractive because it conveys not only a chronology but also a sense of causality as one tries to make sense of the flood of events reported by Orderic and other chroniclers. Histories of Normandy are indeed being written with this political framework in mind, putting the duke or the king centre stage, and perhaps affecting the way we read other historical material.

---

[107] *Historia ecclesie Abbendonensis: The History of the Church of Abingdon*, ed. J. Hudson, Oxford Medieval Texts (Oxford, 2002).

[108] Scott, *History of Glastonbury*.

[109] M. Gervers, *Dating Undated Medieval Charters* (Woodbridge, 2000).

Orderic's political narrative may incidentally show institutions at work, but his project was a *Historia ecclesiastica*, not a history of institutions. The presence of legal terms in his text, coming from the text of charters or notices, need not mean that he mastered these notions and played by the same rules when he used them. Charters are similarly often used by historians merely as mines for legal facts, terms, and ideas. However, their writers drafted them with extra-legal notions in mind, just as Orderic did, in his own way. They staged authority and collective action, as they were willing to remember more than legal facts. This weakens the foundations of works such as Haskins's *Norman Institutions*, as it makes cross-checking sources more difficult than we thought. Orderic Vitalis is a seductive chronicler, and charters have their charms too. Historians should remain humble when crossing texts, not cutting, scratching and pasting them, but respecting their logic and, in pointing out the parts which do not easily fit together, recognising that it is not always necessary for them so to do.

Orderic Vitalis and the Cult of Saints

Véronique Gazeau

OVER the past few years, various historians have focused on the *Historia ecclesiastica* of Orderic Vitalis, of which Chibnall produced such a wonderful edition over thirty years ago. They have discussed in particular the work's intended audience and the author's methods, but none of their studies discuss to any great degree the treatment of the cult of saints by the historian of Saint-Évroul. Thus, the article Mégier published in 2000 (offering an explanation for the work's limited audience) refers to the work's historical content, but does not explicitly mention the cult of saints.[1] Other historians have focused their attention on the historian *angligena* of the pays d'Ouche, most notably Albu and Hingst, and Bickford-Smith has acknowledged the theological and biblical aspects of the *Historia ecclesiastica*, but none of these studies pays any particular attention to the way in which Orderic deals with the cult of saints.[2] In fact, the only person who may have shown an interest in the question of the cult of saints is Ray. His thesis, defended in the late 1960s, remains unpublished, but from it came an article that attempts to demonstrate that Orderic's work, conceived in a monastic context, was destined to be used liturgically by the monks of the abbey.[3]

In *The World of Orderic Vitalis*, Chibnall offers a brief survey of some of the saints mentioned in the *Historia ecclesiastica*, focusing in particular on saints Évroul, Nicholas, Judoc, Guthlac and Waltheof.[4] For each of these individuals, Chibnall cites hagiographical texts as well as the miracles and relics mentioned in Orderic's work. There are, however, more than 100 saints mentioned at least once in the *Historia ecclesiastica*. Simply to compile list of these saints would not reveal Orderic's criteria for choosing to mention them, whereas asking about the extent of his knowledge for each one, and what he records about them, would provide enough material to fill a thesis. This discussion, therefore, will examine a number of case

---

[1] E. Mégier, '*Divina pagina* and the Narration of History in Orderic Vitalis' Historia ecclesiastica', *Revue bénédictine* 110:1–2 (2000), 106–23.

[2] Abu, *The Normans in their Histories*; Hingst, *Written World*. J. Bickford-Smith, *Orderic Vitalis and Norman Society, c. 1035–1087* (unpublished DPhil thesis, University of Oxford, 2006). I am very grateful to the author and to Richard Allen for securing for me a copy of Bickford-Smith's work, and for help in the translation of this paper.

[3] Roger D. Ray, 'Orderic Vitalis and his Readers', *Studia monastica* 14 (1972), 17–33.

[4] Chibnall, *World*, pp. 99–109.

studies that seem to characterise Orderic's methods and interests. The first section concerns those saints honoured in the time of the Franks (that is to say, before the accession of the Normans in the duchy) and the Anglo-Saxons, the second will deal with the warrior saints, and the final section will reconsider the case of St Nicholas.

Excluding the archbishops of Rouen, around a dozen saints of the early Church and of the Frankish period, predominantly bishops and monks, are honoured with a place in Orderic's work on account of their holy status. Orderic's method is to group saints together, or mention them through association: thus at Jumièges we find Philibert, Hugh and Achard. The same Philibert is found also in a list of contemporaries, along with the abbots Eustace of Luxeuil, Agilus of Rebais, Faron of Meaux and Omer of Boulogne, who are characterised as *excellentissimae religionis*.[5] In these instances Orderic deals with founder saints, whose holiness, along with that of other bishops and abbots, 'was proclaimed by heaven-sent miracles' (though Orderic says nothing more about the miracles themselves).[6] He also groups together, on two occasions, the saints of the abbey of Fontenelle, namely Wandrille, Ansbert and Wulfram.[7] Though he seems unsure as to where they were buried, he refers to these three individuals as 'confessor saints'.[8] While speaking of the first monastic foundations under the Merovingians, Orderic mentions St Ouen, 'beatus presul',[9] as well as St Wandrille, who 'brought together a great army of monks at Fontenelle',[10] and St Philibert, who 'won fame as the gallant standard-bearer of a famous spiritual legion at Jumièges'.[11] Orderic records the exodus of relics following the arrival of the Normans,[12] and also speaks of their return.[13] St Ouen, again, and Eloi of Noyon follow a reference to St Colombanus.[14] The holiness of St Denis is spread by Taurin and Nicaise, who were sent by him as missionaries, though Orderic believed incorrectly that Taurin lived in the third century rather than the

---

[5] *HE*, IV, p. 334.

[6] Ibid.: 'aliique plures episcopi et abbates excellentissimae processere religionis, quorum sanctitas evidentibus miraculis coelitus ostensa est'.

[7] *HE*, III, pp. 304 and 322.

[8] Ibid., p. 304: 'reliquias sanctorum confessorum'.

[9] *HE*, II, p. 4.

[10] Ibid.: 'sanctus ingens monachorum agmen Fontinellae adunavit'.

[11] Ibid.: 'beatus Philibertus fortis signifer insignis aciei apud Gemmeticum emicuit.'

[12] Ibid.; *HE*, III, pp. 76 and 304.

[13] Ibid., p. 304 and, for the quote, pp. 322–4: 'debitaque a suis reverentia cotidie honoratur.' Orderic says nothing concerning the body of Ouen, which was translated after the restoration of the abbey by Abbot Nicholas (*HE*, II, p. 298).

[14] *HE*, IV, p. 334.

fourth.[15] St Taurin appears in the prologue of Book VI, in which Orderic mentions in passing that there were more saints in the past than during his time.[16] As for Nicaise, his name is only included among the list of archbishops of Rouen after 1079.[17] Orderic emphasises the forty-eight-year abbacy of St Leufroy, founder of the abbey of La Croix-Saint-Ouen, which helps make him a 'gloriosus confessor Christi'.[18] With regard to the archbishops of Rouen, he has certain reservations concerning the beginning of the list, citing as first archbishop St Mallonus, followed by around twenty prelates from Avitianus to Hugh of Saint-Denis.[19] Many of these are accorded a distich in Book V.[20]

Numerous historians, including Chibnall, have identified the sources used by Orderic.[21] It should be noted that the two saints of Évreux celebrated in the *Historia ecclesiastica*, namely saints Leufroi and Taurin, are honoured in Usuard's *Martyrology*.[22] Besides these two saints of the diocese of Évreux, Orderic celebrates only saints of the diocese of Rouen. St Laud, the blessed ('beatus') bishop of Coutances, is only praised because he was consecrated by Archbishop Gildard.[23]

This brief survey of the abbots and bishops of the period before the foundation of the duchy of Normandy prompts some important reflections on Orderic's methods. When writing about the body of St Ouen, which was placed with other holy relics in the new cathedral of Rouen completed by the abbot Nicholas, Orderic quickly announces that he does not wish to give a full list of these relics, because, 'There were very many other true fathers of their monks in Normandy whose innumerable spiritual gifts I am compelled to pass over since too long a catalogue might weary the reader.'[24] Finally, in the passage of Book III which deals with saints Wandrille and Philibert, the use of military terminology is striking, functioning as a rhetorical device which clearly has classical roots:

---

[15] The *Vita sancti Taurini* that Ordericus may have read is a forgery (*HE*, III, p. xxvi). For Nicaise, see *HE*, II, pp. 22, 38.

[16] *HE*, III, p. 214.

[17] Ibid., p. 36 n. 4. See also R. Allen, 'The *Acta archiepiscoporum Rotomagensium*: Study and Edition', *Tabularia* «Documents» 9 (18 December 2009), available online through http://www.unicaen.fr/tabularia [accessed 29 May 2014].

[18] *HE*, II, p. 270.

[19] *HE*, III, pp. 48–96.

[20] Ibid., p. 56.

[21] Chibnall, *World*; Nortier, *Les Bibliothèques médiévales*, pp. 219–44.

[22] J. Dubois, *Le Martyrologe d'Usuard* (Brussels, 1965), pp. 251–2 and 282.

[23] *HE*, III, p. 56.

[24] *HE*, II, p. 298: 'Alii quoque plures tunc errant monachorum patres in Neustria; quorum numerosa præterire compellor karismata, ne lectori generet fastidium prolixitas nimia.'

Wandrille is said to have led an army ('agmen') of monks, while Philibert is the standard-bearer ('signifer fortis') of a distinguished legion ('insignis aciei').[25]

Orderic also mentions on numerous occasions the first English bishops to lead the English Church, who were sent initially by Pope Vitalian, and later by Gregory the Great. In Book V, saints Augustine and Laurence, Mellitus of London and Justus of Rochester, as well as Honorius and Deusdedit of Canterbury, are all qualified as 'missionaries of the divine word' ('dispensatores divini seminis').[26] Earlier, in Book IV, Orderic mentions the mission of Augustine and Mellitus, as well as other preachers ('predicatores') of the *verbum Dei* in England: 'Pope Gregory sent to England Augustine and Mellitus and the other missionaries, through whom God brought Ethelbert, king of Kent, Edwin, king of Northumbria [...] into the way of truth.'[27] Later Orderic again mentions the mission of Augustine and Laurent, the 'first missionaries' ('primi praedicatores').[28] Now established as a veritable *leitmotif*, we encounter Augustine again in Book XII: having been appointed the archbishop of Canterbury, he converts King Ethelbert and his successors on the orders of Gregory the Great.[29] Three bishops, Dunstan, Æthelwold and Oswald, are distinguished by their search for holiness and are remarkable for their teachings and miracles. In this connection Orderic wrote that: 'The pursuit of holiness and a good life distinguished these three bishops, inspired their teaching and the miracles they performed.'[30] He groups these three bishops together once again in Book IV.[31] This repetition is surely deliberate, for in Book V Orderic states once again that Dustan of Canterbury, Oswald of York and Æthelwold of Winchester 'were bright stars set over the church of God'.[32] Among the other English saints, Orderic mentions Neot, Botolph (abbot of Icanho (perhaps Iken, Suffolk), 653–4), and Edmund.[33] The contacts maintained by Orderic and

---

[25] Ibid., p. 4.

[26] *HE*, III, p. 62.

[27] *HE*, II, pp. 188–9: 'Gregorius papa Augustinum et Melitum aliosque prædicatores uerbi Dei in Angliam misit.'

[28] Ibid., p. 240.

[29] *HE*, VI, p. 318.

[30] *HE*, II, pp. 242–5: 'Studium sanctitatis et totius honestatis præfatos antistites illuminauit; et dogmatibus eorum ac miraculis per eos exhibitis commode irradiauit.'

[31] Ibid., p. 342.

[32] *HE*, III, p. 82: 'in ecclesiae Dei regimine micuerunt'.

[33] *HE*, II, p. 342; *HE*, VI, pp. 150 and n. 4. Orderic went to Worcester and Crowland, where he spent five weeks writing the *vita* of Guthlac, a copy of which he carried with him on his return to Normandy. Dom Le Michel is known to have found a *vita* of St Botolph at Saint-Évroul, which was

the abbey of Saint-Évroul with English foundations are well known, as is the fact that he visited his native land.[34] However, despite the information collected by Orderic in England, he commits a number of errors when writing of the English saints, and particularly with regard to St Neot.[35]

Of all holy men, Orderic seems to have had a particular interest in warrior saints, which, despite the vocabulary used of them, Philibert and Wandrille were not. The dossier of material to be examined here is at once simple and complex: simple in terms of the information it contains; complex because it is sometimes difficult to put this information in context. Orderic Vitalis mentions warrior saints on four separate occasions within his *Historia ecclesiastica*. In Book VI, begun in around 1130, he describes how the clerk Gerold of Avranches, when preaching sermons to the aristocracy, held up saints Demetrius, George, Theodore, Sebastian, Maurice and Eustace, as well as the Theban Legion, as examples ('exempla') of martyrs.[36] In Book VII, written around the same time, he once again mentions St Sebastian, who was pierced with arrows and hung in chains in a sewer, during the speech allegedly given by Robert Guiscard before his march to Rome in May 1084 to rescue Pope Gregory VII.[37] In Book IX, which describes the fight for Antioch in 1098, the crusaders are said to have gone into battle carrying the banners of saints George, Demetrius and Mercurius, striking great fear into the enemy.[38] Finally, in Book XIII, in the account of the siege of Montferrand in August 1137, during which the besieged where forced into starvation, Orderic recounts the speech given by the patriarch of Jerusalem to four boatloads of men come to the castle's aid, whom he exhorted to fight like saints George, Theodore, Demetrius and Sebastian, and thus earn, if they should die, a similar place in heaven.[39]

Six of the seven saints mentioned by Orderic feature in the work of MacGregor, whose study of knightly piety in the West between 1070 and

---

probably copied into an English manuscript of the twelfth century (Paris, BnF, MS Lat. 13092, fols. 110–113; see Nortier, *Les Bibliothèques médiévales*, pp. 99–123). Saints' lives were also copied in the first half of the twelfth century in a Winchester manuscript which came to Jumièges (Alençon, BM, MS 14, copied on Rouen, BM, MS 1385); see Nortier, *Les Bibliothèques médiévales*, p. 106 n. 52.

[34] See especially, Chibnall, 'General Introduction', pp. 25–7.

[35] *HE*, II, p. 342 n. 2.

[36] *HE*, III, p. 216. Gerold of Avranches also mentions St William, but he will not be discussed in what follows. I am grateful to E. Dehoux for personal communication on the subject of warrior saints; see also E. Dehoux, *Saints guerriers: Georges, Guillaume, Maurice et Michel dans la France médiévale (XIe–XIIIe siècle)* (Rennes, 2014).

[37] *HE*, IV, p. 24.

[38] *HE*, V, p. 114.

[39] *HE*, VI, p. 498.

1200 explains that the cults of these saints began to emerge in the years before the First Crusade. The evidence for this, according to MacGregor, is to be found in the *Laudes regiae* composed at Canterbury in around 1084–95.[40] It can be suggested, however, that these cults were venerated at a much earlier date in the Anglo-Norman world. The remainder of the present discussion explores this hypothesis and argues that, though Orderic composed his *Historia* in the 1130s, and thus well after the start of the First Crusade, the cult of warrior saints had long been established in Normandy.

We start by examining how these cults came to be transmitted to Normandy and, in particular, to the abbey of Saint-Évroul. The warrior saints of the *Historia ecclesiastica* are all martyrs. It is difficult, however, to know how much Orderic, who mentions Roman saints alongside Greek ones, knew about each of the individuals he cites, some of whom had particularly complex hagiographical traditions.

In general Orderic mentions Greek martyrs when dealing with events linked to the Crusades, such as the sieges of Antioch and Montferrand. In the first and fourth examples mentioned, he mixes together Greek and Roman saints. In the second case, the march to Rome, he only mentions those martyrs honoured in the West, in particular Mercurius.

The cult of St George, whose passion is legendary and knightly, was honoured in both the Greek and Latin traditions on 23 April.[41] A sanctuary was established in his honour in the sixth century at Lydda in Cappadocia, from where his cult spread to Constantinople, where nine churches were dedicated to him. The Normans showed particular devotion to St George because of the role he is said to have played in the conquest of Sicily.[42]

St Demetrius, called by the Greeks the 'Great Martyr' ('megalomartyr'), was, after St George, the most famous warrior martyr of the West.[43] His *dies natalis* is 8 October. The first known account of his life is relatively late. It was written in the ninth century by Fozio, who made use of an older account which is now lost. Demetrius is said to have travelled the world preaching the Gospels before establishing himself at Thessalonica. Traditionally believed to have been arrested and killed by the Emperor

---

[40] James B. MacGregor, 'Negotiating Knightly Piety: The Cult of the Warrior-Saints in the West, ca. 1070–ca. 1200', *The American Society of Church History: Studies in Christianity and Culture* 73 (2004), 317–45. The manuscript is Durham, University Library MS Cosin V. V. 6, fols. 19v–21. For an edition, see H. E. J. Cowdrey, 'The Anglo-Norman *laudes regiae*', *Viator* 12 (1981), 37–78, at pp. 72–3.

[41] On the matter of martyrdom, see H. Delehaye, *Les Passions des martyrs et les genres littéraires* (Brussels, 1921).

[42] S. Brodbeck, *Les Saints de la cathédrale de Monreale en Sicile* (Rome, 2010), p. 491, no. 96. Delehaye, *Les Passions des martyr*, p. 401 *et seq*.

[43] Brodbeck, *Les saints de la cathédrale*, p. 440, no. 82.

Maximian, some have suggested he was in fact martyred at Smyrna in Anatolia under Diocletian.[44] A basilica was dedicated in his honour at Thessalonica. His cult was venerated in the East and in Byzantine Italy, and he was also honoured in the Greek tradition in Norman Sicily.[45]

There are two saints of the Greek Church named Theodore, though they were probably actually the same person: the first, also known as Tiron, was martyred in the fourth century close to Amasya as a simple solider, while the second, who is said to have served as a general in the army of the Emperor Licinius, was tortured and then crucified at Heraclea in Thrace during the same period. The date of the feast varies: 9 November, 7 or 17 February, 8 June. In Norman Sicily it was celebrated on 17 February and 8 June, while it also features in the Latin calendars of Cava and Capoue in Campania.[46]

Mercurius was martyred at Kayseri in Cappadocia under the Emperor Decius.[47] The eighth-century *Translatio s. Mercurii Beneventum* tells how the Byzantine Emperor Constans II, when disembarking at Tarento in 663, carried with him the relics of this Greek saint and entrusted them to three monks who deposited them in a church built in a town near Benevento, identified as the ancient town of Aeclanum. A century later, on 26 August 768, Duke Arechis II of Benevento transferred them to his city. There is no reason to doubt this second translation, but the account does confuse St Mercurius of Aeclanum, whose feast is the 26 August, with his namesake of Kayseri, thereby attributing the first translation to Constans II. The cult was observed in the West, in Campania and at Benevento. Mercurius was honoured on 25 November (*dies natalis*) and on 26 August, the date of the translation of his relics. He is celebrated in the *Typicon* of St Saviour of Messina, while the Latin sacramentary of Messina also pays homage to him, though his translation is not commemorated there. A church was established in his honour at Troine in 1131.

These four warrior saints are mentioned in a liturgical composition known as the Exultet 1 of Bari, which was composed during the eleventh century.[48] They constitute what Hippolyte Delehaye called *l'état-major*.

---

[44] Ibid.

[45] This is established from the mention in the *Typicon* of St Saviour of Messina, and the story of his passion in a manuscript dated to before 1126 (Ibid.)

[46] Brodbeck, *Les saints de la cathédrale*, p. 734, no. 166.

[47] Ibid., p. 608, no. 129, and p. 610, n. 2. S. Binon, *Essai sur le culte de saint Mercure* (Paris, 1937).

[48] 'Les Rouleaux d'*Exultet* de Bari et de Salerne', *Comptes rendus des séances de l'Académie des Inscriptions et Belles-Lettres* 41:1 (1897), 97–101, at p. 100; *Exultet: Rotoli liturgici del medioevo meridionale*, ed. G. Cavallo (Rome, 1994) p. 131.

In this regard, Delehaye argues that there is little difference between the passions of saints Theodore, Mercurius and George.[49]

Eustace was a general in the imperial army when he converted to Christianity, along with his wife and two children (his wife is St Theopista). Captured by pirates during a voyage to Egypt, they were sold into slavery. Eustace was forced to become a farm hand, Theopista a servant in a hostel and the two children shop workers. The family was reunited some years later, but having refused to sacrifice to the gods they were roasted to death inside a brass bull. According to tradition, Eustace's conversion came about as the result of an encounter during a hunting expedition, when a stag appeared to him with a crucifix glowing between its antlers. He is commemorated on 20 September in the Roman martyrology, and a church dedicated to him in Rome is mentioned in a letter of Pope Gregory II (715–31).[50]

Sebastian was martyred under Diocletian. A Christian officer, he was ordered to sacrifice to the emperor, but refused to comply. Tied to a tree and shot with arrows, he was rescued and healed by a young widow named Irene. Having returned to full health, he confronted Diocletian in person, criticising his treatment of Christians, for which he was clubbed to death. His body was thrown into the Roman sewers ('cloaca maxima'). Ambrose, bishop of Milan, mentions Sebastian in his commentary on Psalm 118. The story of his martyrdom was written in the 5th century.[51] Finally, Maurice, head of the Theban Legion, was martyred at Agaune at the end of the third century[52].

Having briefly presented the origins of the warrior saints mentioned in the *Historia ecclesiastica*, it is necessary to consider the evidence for their early veneration in Normandy. The Fécamp *Laudes regiae* of the eleventh century, which Orderic must have known, only invokes three saints, namely Maurice, Sebastian and Adrian (whom Orderic never mentions), who are all called upon to help Duke William ('tu illum adjuva').[53] However, it should be noted that the gradual of Saint-Évroul, which dates from the first half of the twelfth century, demonstrates that

---

[49] Delehaye, *Les Passions des martyrs*, pp. 308–12.

[50] *Passio sancti Eustathii*, Bibliotheca Hagiographica Graeca 641–3, and Bibliotheca Hagiographica Latina 276–7. Delehaye thinks that it is a romance of adventure, though the end may be epic: Delehaye, *Les Passions des martyrs*, p. 317.

[51] His passion narrative existed before the sixth century: Delehaye, *Les Passions des martyrs*, pp. 311–12.

[52] O. Wermelinger, P. Bruggisser, B. Naf and J.-M. Roessli, *Mauritius une die Thebaïsche Legion / Saint Maurice et la légion thébaine* (Fribourg, 2005). *Autour de saint Maurice: Politique, société et construction identitaire*, ed. N. Brocard, F. Vannotti and A. Wagner (Besançon-Saint-Maurice, 2012).

[53] Cowdrey, 'The Anglo-Norman *laudes regiae*', p. 68. (The manuscript is Rouen, BM, MS 489 [254], fol. 71.)

the Theban Legion (i.e. *dux* Maurice and his companions ('socii'), as Orderic notes elsewhere), were honoured during Orderic's time at the abbey. Sequences, which are entirely syllabic chants whose melodic theme resides in prolonging the last syllable of the Alleluia, were often composed especially for a particular saint.[54] Unlike Orderic, who cites only Maurice as a saint of the Theban Legion, the sequence in the gradual of Saint-Évroul dedicated to Maurice also mentions Exupère, Candide, Innocent and Victor,[55] who are known thanks to the *passio* of the Theban martyrs written by Eucher de Lyon.[56] Very few other saints are accorded a sequence in the gradual: only Stephen, John, Évroul, John the Baptist, Peter and Paul, Benedict, Laurent, Michael, Denis, Martin and Nicholas. The eleventh-century sacramentary of Saint-Évroul records that the feast of St Maurice was celebrated on the traditional date of 22 September.[57] In the epilogue of Book XIII, Orderic explains that his surname of 'Vitalis' was given to him by the monks of Saint-Évroul because this saint was one of Maurice's companions and because Orderic was tonsured by the abbot Mainer on 21 September 1085, the eve of the feast of St Maurice.[58] It is the *Martyrologium Hieronymianum* that lists Vital among the martyrs of the Theban Legion. The *De officiis* of John of Avranches, which in essence is a redaction of earlier Norman liturgical practices, mentions Maurice among the saints to whom a feast with an octave should be accorded.[59]

It seems, therefore, that the martyrdom of the Theban Legion was the object of a cult in ducal Normandy, or at least at Saint-Évroul. But the precise point at which the abbey, re-founded in 1050, and the duchy begun to honour St Maurice remains unclear. At least four pieces of evidence can be found in support of an early date. For example, the abbey of Saint-Maurice of Agaune held lands in the ninth century in the lower valley of the Canche, near Quentovic, which were close to possessions belonging to the abbey of Fontenelle; the saints of Fontenelle helped heal dependants of the abbey of Saint-Maurice at Bloville, as the Miracles of St Wandrille attest.[60] St Maurice had been venerated in England since

---

[54] A. Dennery, 'Liturgie et musique au XIIe siècle en l'abbaye de Saint-Évroul', in *Cahiers du Léopard d'or*, vol. 3: *Le XIIe siècle: Mutations et renouveau en France dans la première moitié du XIIe siècle*, ed. F. Gasparri (Paris, 1994), pp. 325–51.

[55] Paris, BnF, MS Lat. 10508, fols. 91–92v.

[56] Monumenta Germaniae Historia, Scriptores rerum Merovingicarum, III, pp. 32–41.

[57] Rouen, BM, MS 273 [A 287], fol. 188. L. Delisle, *Mémoire sur d'anciens sacramentaires* (Paris, 1886), no. CXXVII, pp. 306–8.

[58] *HE*, VI, p. 554. The Hieronymian martyrology classifies Vital among the warrior martyrs of the Theban Legion.

[59] *De officiis ecclesiasticis*, ed. R. Delamare (Rouen, 1923), p. lv.

[60] C. Mériaux, *Gallia irradiata: Saints et sanctuaires dans le nord de la Gaule du haut Moyen Âge* (Stuttgart, 2006), pp. 117–18.

the eighth century, and his cult had developed thanks to the intervention of Oswald, bishop of Worcester,[61] and King Athelstan (924–39), who, according to William of Malmesbury, received the banner ('vexillum') of St Maurice in 926.[62] Alcuin's veneration of Maurice is also well known. There were, of course, frequent liturgical exchanges between England and Normandy before the Conquest of 1066. Similar connections existed between Normandy and Germany. In 937, Otto, king of Germany, founded the church of Magdeburg, which became the cathedral dedicated to St Maurice. I have shown elsewhere how German clerks had been travelling to Normandy since the beginning of the eleventh century, carrying with them the relics of St Nicholas, who was particularly venerated by the Ottonians.[63] Might they also have taken the relics of St Maurice? Finally, Maurice was the patron saint, alongside St Benigne, of the Benedictine abbey of Dijon, whose abbot from 990 was William of Volpiano, the restorer of monastic life at Fécamp and Jumièges.[64] It was from Jumièges that monks were despatched to re-found the abbey of Saint-Évroul, whose sacramentary, as we have already noted, celebrated St Maurice. Even if the importance of the dedication to Maurice at Dijon had begun to decline from the year 1000, it is important to note that a manuscript containing a collection of sermons to be used during the feast of Maurice and his companions was composed at Saint-Bénigne in the period 990–1003.[65] It is possible that these sermons, perhaps authored by William of Volpiano, circulated between Dijon, Jumièges and Saint-Évroul.

---

[61] *St Wulfstan and his World*, ed. Julia S. Barrow and N. P. Brooks (Aldershot, 2005), p. v; V. Ortenberg, *The English World and the Continent in the Tenth and Eleventh Centuries: Cultural, Spiritual, and Artistic Exchanges* (Oxford, 1992), pp. 69–70. My thanks to Anne Wagner for her help with these sources.

[62] William of Malmesbury, *Gesta regum Anglorum: The History of the English Kings*, ed. and trans. R. A. B. Mynors, completed by R. M. Thomson and M. Winterbottom, Oxford Medieval Texts, 2 vols. (Oxford, 1998), I, p. 219; L. H. Loomis, 'The Holy Relics of Charlemagne and King Æthelstan: The Lances of Longinus and St Mauricius', *Speculum* 25 (1950), 437–56, at p. 445.

[63] V. Gazeau and J. Le Maho, 'Les Origines du culte de saint Nicolas en Normandie', in *Alle origini dell'Europa: Il culto di San Nicola tra Oriente e Occidente*, vol. I: *Italia–Francia; atti del convegno, Bari, 2–4 dicembre 2010*, ed. G. Cioffari and A. Laghezza, Nicolaus Studi Storici: Rivista del Centro Studi Nicolaiani, Anno XXII, fasc. 1–2 (2011), pp. 153–60.

[64] A. Rauwel, 'Le Culte de saint Maurice en Bourgogne ducale', in *Autour de saint Maurice: Politique, société et construction identitaire*, ed. N. Brocard, F. Vannotti and A. Wagner (Besançon-Saint-Maurice, 2012), pp. 397–404, at p. 403.

[65] F. Dolbeau, 'Trois sermons latins en l'honneur de la Légion Thébaine', in *Mauritius und die Thebaïsche Legion / Saint Maurice et la légion thébaine*, ed.

Numerous churches are dedicated to Maurice throughout Normandy,[66] and it is likely that his was one of the earlier cults to develop, much like that of St George, whose relics are first mentioned by Gregory of Tours in the sixth century.[67] According to the *Gesta abbatum* of Fontenelle, George's relics arrived in the future Normandy via the Cotentin in 747.[68] The *Vita Wandregesili*, on the other hand, has an earlier reference to a chapel dedicated to St George.[69] This is the oldest mention of the cult. Though little is known about this cult's development, it seems to have taken hold in the tenth century – that is to say, shortly after the installation of the Vikings in Normandy. The monks of Fontenelle are known to have possessed a relic of St George, since it is mentioned among the treasures confiscated by the count of Flanders in 944.[70] In 965, Duke Richard I witnessed a charter by which Walter, count of Dreux, approved the donation of the church of Saint-Georges[-Motel], in the diocese of Évreux, to the abbey of Saint-Père de Chartres.[71] Around fifteen churches are named in honour of St George, making it one of the most popular dedications. One of these existed in Bayeux from at least 1032,[72] while a

O. Wermelinger, P. Bruggisser, B. Naf and J.-M. Roessli (Fribourg, 2005), pp. 377–402, at pp. 380, 382, 386–9, 417–18.

[66] Saint-Maurice-en-Cotentin, Manche, cant. Barneville-Carteret; Saint-Maurice-lès-Charencey, Orne, cant. Tourouvre; Saint-Maurice-du-Désert, Orne, cant. La Ferté-Macé; Saint-Maurice-sur-Huisne, Orne, cant. Nocé. In the diocese of Rouen: the church of Argueil, Eure, ch.-l. cant. Marcouville, com. Bosguérard de Marcouville; the church of Petitville, Seine-Maritime, cant. Lillebonne; Saint-Maurice-de-Malaunay, Seine-Maritime, com. Malaunay; Saint-Maurice-en-Bray, Seine-Maritime, cant. Forges-les-Eaux; the church of Vesly, Eure, cant. Gisors; Saint-Maurice-d'Etelan, dép. Seine-Maritime, cant. Lillebonne.

[67] Gregory of Tours, *De gloria martyrum: Glory of the martyrs*, ed. and trans. R. Van Dam (Liverpool, 2004), p. 93. The cult also existed in Italy in the sixth century (Cf. C. Walter, *The Warrior Saints in Byzantine Art and Tradition* (Aldershot, 2003), p. 113).

[68] *Chronique des abbés de Fontenelle (Saint-Wandrille)*, ed. P. Pradié (Paris, 1999), p. 118. There is no mention of St George in the Hieronymian martyrology: J. Laporte, 'Les Recensions de Fontenelle du martyrologe hiéronymien et l'histoire du monastère', *Revue mabillon* 29 (1939), 1–16.

[69] Monumenta Germaniae Historia, Scriptores rerum Merovingicarum, V, pp. 13–24. For the *Vita prima*, see *Acta Sanctorum*, t. II Novembris, 2 a, p. 931 and 1 a, p. 1894.

[70] N. Huyghebaert, *Une translation de reliques à Gand en 944: Le 'Sermo de Adventu Sanctorum Wandregisili, Ansberti et Vulframni in Blandinium'* (Brussels, 1978), par. 31 A, p. 33.

[71] M. Fauroux, *Recueil des actes des ducs de Normandie (911–1066)* (Caen, 1961), no. 2. Saint-Georges[-Motel], Eure, cant. Nonancourt.

[72] Fauroux, *Recueil*, no. 64; Many Norman churches carry a dedication St George in Normandy, see: J. Fournée, 'Le Culte de saint Georges en

charter of Le Bec bears witness to the existence in 1041 of the church of Saint-Georges-du-Vièvre.[73] Among the relics belonging to the nuns of La Trinité de Caen, founded by the Conqueror's wife, Matilda, was an ampoule containing the blood of St George.[74]

As for St Demetrius, there is reason to think that his cult spread alongside that of St George, with whom he was closely affiliated in the Byzantine world. However, there is no mention of his relics in the Fontenelle account of 747. On the other hand, his relics were among those conserved by the nuns of La Trinité de Caen, the most prestigious female house in the duchy, before 1066.[75] The relics included the dust, bones and oil of the saint.[76] This last piece of information is particularly interesting for what it reveals about Demetrius's status as a myroblite, that is, a saint whose relics produced *myron*, or holy oil.[77] Demetrius is mentioned in the calendars of the twelfth century, such as that of Le Bec, where the office for 8 October includes three lessons,[78] and those of Jumièges[79] and Saint-Ouen de Rouen.[80]

With regards to Theodore, his head was conserved from 1120 at the cathedral of Chartres,[81] with which the abbey of Saint-Évroul had strong liturgical links. Under Abbot Robert de Grandmesnil (thus before 27 January 1061, and almost twenty-five years before Orderic's arrival), the office of St Évroul, the monastery's patron, had been composed by Arnulf, precentor of Chartres, a disciple of Bishop Fulbert.[82] The *passiones* of Theodore are also to be found among the manuscripts of the libraries of Fécamp and Jumièges.[83]

It is difficult to know if the cult of St Mercurius was particularly

---

Normandie', *Annuaire des cinq départements de la Normandie* (Caen, 1986), pp. 105–27.

[73] Fauroux, *Recueil*, p. 41.

[74] L. Musset, *Les actes de Guillaume le Conquérant et de la reine Mathilde pour les abbayes caennaises* (Caen, 1967), p. 141, no. 29.

[75] Ibid.

[76] Ibid.

[77] Walter, *The Warrior Saints*, p. 90 et seq.

[78] Paris, BnF, MS Lat. 1105.

[79] Rouen, BM, MS 209–210 [Y 175]; Rouen, BM, MS 211 [A 145]; Rouen, BM, MS 240 [A 253]; Rouen, BM, MS 267 [A 401].

[80] Rouen, BM, MS 233 [Y 21]. But it is not in the eleventh-century sacramentary of Fontenelle.

[81] *Cartulaire de Notre-Dame de Chartres*, ed. E. de Lépinois and L. Merlet (Chartres, 1862), I, p. 60. M.-J. Bulteau, *Monographie de la cathédrale de Chartres* (Chartres, 1850), p. 109.

[82] *HE*, II, p. 108.

[83] Fécamp: Rouen, BM, MS 1388, fol. 156v; Jumièges: Rouen, BM, MS 1391, fol. 156v and MS 1399, fol. 150v.

venerated in Normandy, or whether Orderic's reference is to Mercurius of Kayseri or Mercurius of Aeclanum/Benevento. Given that he is mentioned alongside three other Greek saints, it seems likely that it is Mercurius of Kayseri. On the other hand, the Lombards had established a cult in honour of an Italian St Mercurius in the eighth century, and this had spread throughout Gaul and, by consequence, into Normandy. The Greek *vita* was translated at an early date into Latin, while the calendar of Santa Sofia di Benevento mentions no fewer than five feasts in his honour. Hymns of all sorts are dedicated to him and his cult was vibrant in southern Italy.[84]

Finally, Eustace, whose presence in Orderic's text is hard to explain. The cult seems to have had little following in Normandy, given that only one church is dedicated in his honour.[85] However, the library of Jumièges, whose links with Saint-Évroul have already been noted, conserved a *Passio sancti Eustachi* in the eleventh century and a second example in the twelfth.[86] The vision and conversion of St Eustace also appears among the capitals of the chapter house of the abbey of Saint-Georges de Boscherville, which were carved in the 1160s. He is the only saint to be represented on these capitals, which otherwise depict scenes from the Old Testament.[87] Saint-Georges de Boscherville had been founded as a secular college in the middle of the eleventh century, and was transformed into a Benedictine abbey in 1115. The first six monks to be established there came

---

[84] Binon, *Essai sur le culte de saint Mercure*, pp. 101–2.

[85] There is a single village in Normandy with the name of Eustace: Saint-Eustache-la-Forêt, dép. Seine-Maritime, cant. Bolbec. There is only one further example in the whole of France. Jean Fournée indicates forty-five places of cult asscoaition in the diocese of Rouen but does not give his sources (J. Fournée, 'Les Maladreries et les vocables de leurs chapelles', *Cahiers Léopold Delisle* 46:1–2 (1997), 49–142, at p. 74).

[86] Rouen, BM, MS 1383, fol. 5, and MS 1399, fol. 140v. Paul Meyer thinks that the Latin translation of St Eustache's *passio* was introduced to the West in the tenth century: P. Meyer, 'Fragments d'une vie de saint Eustache' *Romania* 36 (1907), 12–28. Jacques Dubois considers that: 'la présence de l'éloge d'Eustache dans le manuscrit de Fécamp du martyrologe d'Usuard au 20 septembre ne s'explique pas par l'usage de Saint-Bénigne ou de Fécamp qui n'ont jamais eu de fête de saint Eustache au 20 septembre. Dès le XIIe siècle, le saint fut inscrit une seconde fois dans le manuscrit de Fécamp le 2 novembre avec un bref éloge. Sa fête fut introduite à Fécamp seulement au XIIIe siècle et placée au 3 novembre, puisque le 2 était occupé par saint Bénigne' (J. Dubois, 'À la recherche de l'état primitif du martyrologe d'Usuard: Le manuscrit de Fécamp', in his *Martyrologes: d'Usuard au Martyrologe Romain* (Abbeville, 1990), p. 128 and n. 1). This passage is not from Usuard, according to Dubois.

[87] Kathryn A. Morrison, 'The Figural Capitals of the Chapterhouse of Saint-Georges-de-Boscherville', in *Medieval Art, Architecture and Archaeology at Rouen*, ed. J. Stratford, British Archaeological Association Conference Transactions 12 (Leeds, 1993), pp. 46–50.

from Saint-Évroul. Moreover, St Eustace has links with both St George and St Theodore (the latter because both he and Eustace encounter miraculous stags).[88] This is perhaps the reason why Orderic chose to associate Eustace with Theodore, along with two other Greek saints, Demetrius and Mercurius. The means by which the cult of St Eustace was introduced to Normandy is unknown, but the evidence suggests that the community at Saint-Évroul played a role in its diffusion.

St Sebastian, whom Orderic twice associates with saints of the Greek East, did not lend his name to many Norman churches.[89] However, numerous copies of his *passio* were to be found in libraries throughout Normandy, including two at Fécamp (of the eleventh and twelfth centuries),[90] a third at Saint-Évroul (twelfth century),[91] and a fourth at Jumièges (tenth to eleventh centuries).[92] The passions of saints Sebastian,[93] George,[94] Eustace[95] and Theodore[96] are found together in a tenth-century manuscript conserved at the municipal library in Rouen, which once belonged to the Capuchin convent in Mortagne,[97] located in the south of Normandy.

Orderic's treatment of St Nicholas is the final area for analysis, a subject on which he was not entirely accurate. Nicholas was one of the saints venerated at Saint-Évroul, as testified by his numerous mentions in the *Historia ecclesiastica*. Orderic reports at length the translation to Bari, which took place on 9 May 1092, in Book VII.[98] A little later on in the same book, he tells of the arrival in 1092 of a relic of St Nicholas at the priory of Noron, which was taken there by William Pantulf.[99] He repeats this information in Book V.[100] Much earlier in the *Historia*, in Book III, he informs us that Thierry, the first abbot of Saint-Évroul, stopped in Cyprus on the way to Jerusalem and died in the church of St Nicholas.[101]

[88] H. Delehaye, 'La Légende de saint Eustache', in his *Mélanges d'hagiographie grecque et latine* (Brussles, 1966), p. 219. N. Thierry, 'Le Culte du cerf en Anatolie et la vision de saint Eustache', *Monuments et mémoires* 72 (1991), 33–100.

[89] Saint-Sébastien-de-Morsent, dép. Eure, cant. Évreux-Sud.

[90] Rouen, BM, MS 1400, fol. 45, and MS 1388, fol. 11.

[91] Rouen, BM, MS 1389, fol. 9v.

[92] Rouen, BM, MS 1380, fol. 163.

[93] Rouen, BM, MS 1370, fol. 1 et seq.

[94] Ibid., fol. 32 et seq, and fol. 200v et seq.

[95] Ibid., fol. 155 et seq.

[96] Ibid., fol. 210 et seq.

[97] Mortagne-au-Perche, dép. Orne, ch.-l. cant.

[98] *HE*, IV, pp. 54–68.

[99] Ibid., pp. 70–2.

[100] *HE*, III, pp. 162.

[101] *HE*, II, p. 70.

In relating the final days of Arnold of Échauffour (d. 1064), a descendant of Saint-Évroul's co-founder William Giroie, Orderic tells how Arnold, already sick, had a dream in which he saw an old man of good countenance, whom he took to be St Nicholas and with whom he spoke.[102] During the abbacy of Mainer (d. 1089) the monk Roger de Hauterive was sent into the Vexin, where he founded a chapel dedicated to St Nicholas, bishop of Myra, which would later become a priory.[103] St Nicholas appears again when Orderic narrates how William the Conqueror, worried by rumours of an English revolt in December 1067, was prevented from crossing the Channel by rough seas. Fortunately 'the church of God was celebrating the feast of St Nicholas, bishop of Myra, and all over Normandy prayers were offered for the good duke'.[104] The saint interceded on William's behalf, and the seas calmed. When Orderic relates how Avitian, bishop of Rouen, attended the council of Arles in 314, he makes sure to mention that, at around the same time, a council was held in Nicaea, where 318 fathers gathered, among them Nicholas of Myra.[105] In the prologue to Book VI, Orderic pauses to name the ancient fathers ('antique patres'), whom he described as those:

> whose tongues were the keys of heaven, who, filled with spiritual gifts, shone forth as the sun in the Church, and who, by the power of the Almighty, ruled over the elements of the world and powers of the air, [and] have now gained their reward and dwell in bliss with their heavenly king in Paradise.[106]

The list of these fathers, which includes Martial, Taurin, Silvester and Martin, closes with the name of Nicholas.[107] Elsewhere, Orderic took the

---

[102] Ibid., p. 124: 'in somnis vidit'.

[103] Ibid., p. 150. Mainier's successor, Roger du Sap, began to build there a church in stone.

[104] Ibid., p. 208: 'sancti Nicholai Mirreorum præsulis solennitatem Æcclesia Dei celebrabat, et in normannia pro deuoto principe fideliter orabat'. It should be noted that in the mass entitled 'Pro rege' in the sacramentary of Saint-Évroul (BM, MS 273 [A 287], fol. 257), two prayers were to be read that began with these words: 'Quesumus, omnipotens Deus, ut famulus tuus ille rex Anglorum, qui tua miseratione suscepit regni gubernacula [...] Haec, Domine, salutaris sacramenti perceptio famulum totum illum regem Anglorum ab omnibus tueatur adversis.' Like other establishments, Saint-Évroul no doubt prayed for the prince in Rouen.

[105] HE, III, p. 50.

[106] Ibid., pp. 210–11: 'quorum linguæ clauis cœli factæ sunt; qui diuinis karismatibus pleni ut phebus in æcclesia fulserunt, et elementis mundi aerisque potestatibus in uirtute omnipotentis imperantes dominate sunt; iam cum rege suo superna mercede potiti felices in cœlis constitunt'.

[107] Ibid., p. 214.

time to copy part of a life of St Nicholas.[108] In addition, the gradual of Saint-Évroul contains a sequence on Nicholas.[109] Finally, the sacramentary contains a number of masses, among them 'De s. Nicholao'[110] and 'De s. Ebrulfo'.[111] These saints seem equal in importance.

Orderic provides us with a great deal of information about the saint-bishop of Myra, and his accounts of episodes before the translation of 1087, such as the dream of Arnold of Échauffour in 1064 or the fact that prayers were said for Duke William in December 1067, demonstrate that Nicholas's cult was already well established in Normandy. However, it is surprising that Orderic, who is normally so eloquent when speaking of his heroes, says nothing about how the cult of Nicholas was introduced to Normandy. In fact, the cult seems to have been developed at an early date, around the years 1010–20, under the auspices of Robert, archbishop of Rouen, and Isembert, abbot of La Trinité de Rouen, two key figures in the Norman Church at the beginning of the eleventh century whom Orderic was well aware of. Isembert, who was German, was responsible for introducing chants for St Nicholas, and the cult no doubt arrived in Normandy thanks to his support; he may even have arrived with relics procured from Theophanu, wife of Otto II.[112] Orderic's silence here is strange, especially if we consider the fact that his eighth book recounted the foundation of the abbey St Nicholas of Angers in 1020 by Count Fulk Nerra.[113]

In conclusion, what do these case studies show us? First of all, that the use of hagiographical material is an important element of Orderic's *Historia ecclesiastica*, but can be haphazard and is sometimes not particularly informative. Orderic creates lists and often repeats himself. If he happens to note that liturgical texts – antiphons, responses, hymns – were written in his abbey, he does not identify them. And yet he must have known of the existence of the gradual and the sacramentary that still survive today.

On the whole, the models of sanctity which Orderic appears to promote are, for Normandy, those of the Frankish era, and for England those of the Anglo-Saxon period, with a particular focus on martyr saints, missionaries and warrior saints. Orderic can be said to have favoured two saints in particular, namely Maurice and Nicholas. In fact, all of Normandy is said to have prayed to St Nicholas to ask that he might

---

[108] Rouen, BM, MS 1389, fol. 13, noted in appendix 2, below, item 18. See also, Escudier, 'Orderic et le scriptorium', p. 22.

[109] Paris, BnF, MS Lat. 10508, fols. 99–101v.

[110] Rouen, BM, MS 273 [A 287], fol. 254.

[111] Ibid., fol. 254v.

[112] Gazeau and Le Maho, 'Les Origines du culte de saint Nicolas en Normandie'.

[113] *HE*, IV, p. 70.

ensure the duke could cross the Channel safely in the middle of winter. In the *Laudes regiae* St Maurice (along with saints Sebastian and Adrian) is similarly petitioned on William's behalf. However, as has been established, any examination of this particular aspect of the *Historia ecclesiastica* is limited by the fact that only two liturgical texts survive for Saint-Évroul, while Orderic makes lists but offers no further explanation or detail.

One way to further our understanding would be to consider the particular saints to which the churches belonging to Saint-Évroul were dedicated. A significant number of churches in Normandy are dedicated to St Maurice, but was Orderic aware of this? Furthermore, there are numerous toponyms in the vicinity of Saint-Évroul that include the name Nicholas, in particular churches founded by families of German origin, just like the abbot Isembert. Orderic offers us information that is admittedly incomplete, but also perfect for further investigation; therein lies his importance.

With regard to the cults of warrior saints in Normandy, it seems clear that the abbeys of Fontenelle-Saint-Wandrille, Jumièges, Saint-Évroul, Saint-Étienne and La Trinité de Caen, played a central role in their development. The devotion of some of these abbeys to these cults is reflected in the names of their monks. Two Jumièges monks, for example, are known to have had the name Ursus, recalling another companion of St Maurice and a member of the Theban Legion. No other examples of this name are to be found in the abbeys of Normandy, while Eustace, abbot of Jumièges, is likewise the only Norman Benedictine abbot so named.[114] As in the *Laudes regiae*, in which saints Maurice and Sebastian are called upon to help Duke William, Orderic invokes these saints in his accounts in order to aid warriors and princes.

Although Orderic often simply mentions warrior saints in his *Historia ecclesiastica*, this chapter has attempted to show the means by which their cults were transmitted, and how outside influences and cultural exchanges between Italy, England, Burgundy and Germany allowed those cults to develop in Normandy long before the 1070s. Orderic might mention these saints when writing of the Crusades, but their cults are in fact much older. The evidence suggests that the cults of saints George, Theodore and Eustace were well established in England, but those of Demetrius and Mercurius were not, as the Anglo-Saxon calendars make clear.[115] In this respect, it would be interesting to conduct further investigation into the precise role played by Orderic in the process by which these cults spread across the Channel, especially given the strong links he maintained with his native land, where he had been educated between 1075 and 1085.

---

[114] V. Gazeau, *Normannia monastica*, vol. 2: *Prosopographie des abbés bénédictins (X^e–XIIe siècle)* (Caen, 2007), pp. 156–8, 192–3, 159–160.

[115] *English Kalendars before A.D. 1100*, ed. F. Wormald, Henry Bradshaw Society 72 (London, 1934).

Orderic's Secular Rulers and Representations of Personality and Power in the *Historia ecclesiastica*

William M. Aird

AT the beginning of February 1113, King Henry I of England toured the monastery of Saint-Évroul.[1] Orderic Vitalis noted that the visit, coinciding with Candlemas, was a joyous occasion during which Henry 'sat for a while in the monks' cloister, made a thorough examination of their establishment and, after noting the regularity of their monastic life, praised them warmly'.[2] To emphasise the ties between the king and the abbey, and perhaps to prompt further generosity, the king may have been shown the precious liturgical vestments that his mother, Queen Matilda, had presented to Saint-Évroul.[3] The queen had also provided funds for the monastic refectory.[4] The following day, on entering the chapter-house, Henry 'humbly asked to be admitted to their fraternity'. His request was granted and the king ordered a charter listing 'everything that the abbey of Saint-Évroul possessed on that day'.[5]

Later, when the document was brought to Henry at Rouen, he 'willingly confirmed it, making a cross, and handed it to his magnates who were present to be similarly ratified with the sign of the

---

I should like to thank the organisers of the conference at which an earlier version of this chapter was delivered. In addition, I wish to record my regard for Marjorie Chibnall, who, after examining my doctoral thesis, never failed to provide friendship and support.

---

[1] *HE*, VI, pp. 174–7. For the political context, see C. Warren Hollister, *Henry I*, edited and completed by A. Frost (New Haven and London, 2001), p. 231; J. A. Green, *Henry I: King of England and Duke of Normandy* (Cambridge, 2006), pp. 125–6.

[2] *HE*, VI, p. 174: 'In claustro monachorum diu sedit, esse eorum diligenter considerauit, et perspecta religionis moderatio illos laudauit.'

[3] *HE*, II, pp. 148–51.

[4] D. Roach, 'The Material and The Visual: Objects and Memories in the *Historia ecclesiastica* of Orderic Vitalis', *HSJ* 24 (2013), 63–78.

[5] *HE*, VI, p. 174: 'Sequenti uero die in capitulum uenit, societatem eorum humiliter requisiuit et recepit [...] Tunc consilio Rodberti comitis de Mellento rex iussit cartam fieri, ibique omnia quæcumque Vticensis abbatia ipso die possidebat breuiter colligi. Quod et factum est.' For the charter, see *Orderici Vitalis Ecclesiasticae Historiae Libri Tredecim*, ed. A. le Prévost, 5 vols. (Paris, 1838–55), V, pp. 196–9.

cross'.[6] Orderic explained that the charter had been made because the monks faced 'greedy heirs' seeking to recover possessions granted in alms to the abbey by their relatives. To counter these threats the monks had secured the king's confirmation of their lands, hoping that his charter would deter those wishing to challenge possession of the named properties. Those who wanted to make a claim against the monks were prohibited from doing so except in the king's court.[7] Orderic ends his account of the king's visit by noting that Henry looked to strengthen his duchy's weak points against his enemies.

Although he does not explicitly say so, Orderic probably saw, met, and perhaps talked with the king in February 1113. Orderic was 'of Henry's generation', born just seven years after him.[8] It is uncertain whether Orderic had encountered the king's father or his elder brothers, but when he wrote about contemporary rulers, it was probably with Henry I foremost in his mind.[9] The *Historia* presents Henry I demonstrating qualities that medieval monks like Orderic expected in a king. He was pious and respectful of those who had entered the monastic life, and, moreover, such was his knowledge of monasticism that he was able to judge how far the monks of Saint-Évroul adhered to St Benedict's precepts. In the early twelfth century new monastic orders threatened the established Benedictine houses' access to patronage, and in this context the king's approval of Saint-Évroul's constitution was significant.[10] In addition, and as a clear sign of his imprimatur, Henry wished to enter the monks' confraternity, offering in return an advocate's protection against threats to the abbey's endowment. Directly related to this was Henry's concern to defend Normandy against its enemies, and for Orderic, living on the duchy's vulnerable southern frontier, the king's protection was an important consideration.[11]

Henry I's visit to Saint-Évroul was also significant for its role in the genesis of Orderic's *Historia ecclesiastica*.[12] The king's inquiry into the regularity of monastic practices at Saint-Évroul stirred the community's institutional memory, and drafting the charter for Henry's confirmation at

---

[6] *HE*, VI, p. 174: 'Deinde Ernaldus prior et Gislebertus Sartensis Rotomagum regi cartam detulerunt. Ipse uero libenter eam cruce facta firmavit, et optimatibus suis qui aderant crucis signo similiter corroborandam tradidit.'

[7] Ibid., pp. 174–7. Cf. *Orderici Vitalis Ecclesiasticae Historiae*, ed. le Prévost, V, p. 197.

[8] Hollister, *Henry I*, p. 5; Green, *Henry I*, p. 20.

[9] Orderic may have seen King Louis VI of France and Pope Calixtus II at the Council of Rheims in October 1119: *HE*, VI, pp. xx and 252–77.

[10] Orderic's tract on the new monastic orders is rather defensive; see *HE*, IV, pp. xl–xliii and 310–37.

[11] Ibid., pp. 256–7.

[12] Chibnall, 'General Introduction', pp. 32, 65; cf. Green, *Henry I*, p. 3.

Rouen necessitated a careful rehearsal of the monks' proprietorial claims.[13] In return for his support, the king could expect the aid of St Évroul, and the goodwill of his monks and their patrons during his campaign in the region.[14] Regardless of whether the king actually behaved as Orderic recorded, Orderic presented Henry I's visit to Saint-Évroul as an exemplary interaction between a secular ruler and a Benedictine monastic community. Part of Henry's reward for supporting the monks of Saint-Évroul was Orderic's partisan memorialisation of the king; but is this episode typical of Orderic's representation of secular rulers?

In the *Historia*'s prologue, Orderic wrote that: 'I have occasion to touch truthfully on some matters concerning the good or evil leaders of this wretched age.'[15] He was writing in, and about, a period of significant change in Western Europe.[16] By 1200 a more administrative model of kingship had emerged.[17] In addition, since the middle of the eleventh century, long-established ideas about the nature of kingship and its relationship with the Church had been questioned by those who advocated a more distinct separation of the secular and ecclesiastical in society. At issue was the conception of what constituted 'right order' in the world, and whether secular rulers or their ecclesiastical counterparts should take the lead in Latin Christendom. By implementing a programme of ecclesiastical reform and promoting the primacy of the Roman see, an increasingly 'imperial' or monarchical papacy claimed moral superiority for the clergy, thereby challenging, *inter alia*, notions of sacral kingship.[18] In addition, there has been a renewed interest in ritual

---

[13] M. Chibnall, 'Charter and Chronicle: The Use of Archive Sources by Norman Historians', in *Church and Government in the Middle Ages: Essays Presented to C.R. Cheney*, ed. C. N. L. Brooke, D. E. Luscombe, G. H. Martin and D. M. Owen (Cambridge, 1976), pp. 1–17, at pp. 12–14.

[14] *Orderici Vitalis*, ed. le Prévost, V, p. 199: Henry's charter is dated 'anno quo comes Andegavensis mecum pacem fuit et Cenomannum de me, meus homo factus, recepit'.

[15] *HE*, I, pp. 130–1: 'In relatione quam de restauratione Vticensis coenobii, iubente Rogerio abate simpliciter prout possum facere institui; libet ueraciter tangere nonnulla de bonis seu malis primatibus huius nequam seculi.'

[16] For an overview, see R. I. Moore, *The First European Revolution, c. 970–1215* (Oxford and New York, 2000), and John D. Cotts, *Europe's Long Twelfth Century: Order, Anxiety and Adaptation, 1095–1229* (Basingstoke, 2013).

[17] C. W. Hollister and J. W. Baldwin, 'The Rise of Administrative Kingship: Henry I and Philip Augustus', *American Historical Review* 83:4 (1978), 867–905.

[18] F. Oakley, *The Mortgage of the Past: Reshaping the Ancient Political Inheritance (1050–1300)* (New Haven and London, 2012), pp. 15–41, and C. Morris, *The Papal Monarchy: The Western Church from 1050 to 1250* (Oxford, 1991).

communication, political theatre, and the representation of kingship. Attempts have been made to tease out the political ideology that informed the views of the medieval writers.[19] What did Orderic expect from the kings and other secular rulers whose deeds constitute so much of the *Historia ecclesiastica*? By what criteria did Orderic judge these kings and their suitability to occupy their office?[20]

The most dramatic manifestation of these developments was the ideological conflict between the Holy Roman Empire and the papacy; given that Orderic wrote mainly after the settlement at Worms in 1122, we might ask how he represented the confrontation between Pope Gregory VII and Emperor Henry IV.[21] The narrative hook for Orderic's portrait of the emperor was Henry IV's invasion of Italy early in 1084, which drove Pope Gregory from Rome.[22] Orderic wrote that Gregory, who had been an oblate monk, 'was an active promoter of learning and monasticism all his life and unremittingly waged war on sin' ('assiduumque certamen contra peccatum exercuit'). Throughout his career Gregory strove to uphold the *lex Dei* and, driven by this 'zeal for truth and justice', attacked 'every kind of wickedness sparing no offenders through fear or favour'. [23] By contrast, the emperor was 'an incorrigible rebel against the divine law' ('lex divina'), and was duly admonished, corrected and finally excommunicated by Gregory.[24] Clearly Orderic judged the legitimacy of those who held both secular and ecclesiastical power according to their adherence to, and promotion of, God's law.

---

[19] For example, G. Koziol, 'England, France, and the Problem of Sacrality in Twelfth-Century Ritual', in *Cultures of Power: Lordship, Status, and Process in Twelfth-Century Europe*, ed. T. N. Bisson (Philadelphia, PA, 1995), pp. 124–48.

[20] P. Buc, '*Principes gentium dominantur eorum*: Princely Power between Legitimacy and Illegitimacy in Twelfth-Century Exegesis', ibid., pp. 310–28. See also Lucien Musset, 'L'Horizon géographique, moral et intellectuel d'Orderic Vital, historien anglo-normand', in *La chronique et l'histoire au Moyen Age: Colloque des 24 et 25 mai 1982*, ed. Daniel Poirion (Paris, 1984), pp. 101–22. I am grateful to Charlie Rozier for drawing my attention to this article.

[21] H. E. J. Cowdrey, *Pope Gregory VII, 1073–1085* (Oxford, 1998), and I. S. Robinson, *Henry IV of Germany, 1056–1106* (Cambridge, 2003). For an overview, see K. G. Cushing, *Reform and the Papacy in the Eleventh Century: Spirituality and Social Change* (Manchester, 2005).

[22] *HE*, IV, pp. 6–11.

[23] Ibid., pp. 6–7: 'omnique uita sua sapientiae et religioni admodum studuit, assiduumque certamen contra peccatum exercuit [...] Zelo quippe ueritatis et iusticiae inflammatus omne scelus arguebat'.

[24] Ibid.: 'Henricum ergo Teutonicorum regem quia diuinae legis preuaricator erat incorrigibilis sepe admonuit, corripuit, ed postremum excommunicauit.'

Orderic's account is striking in that, like some writing during the Investiture Contest itself, he emphasised Henry's moral failings and, particularly, his lasciviousness.[25] Henry had deserted his wife, Bertha, 'and gave himself up to the sordid pleasures of adultery, like a pig wallowing in the mire [*ut porcus luto gaudens*], obstinately and persistently defying both the laws of God [*Deique legibus*] and the exhortations of good men'. In a chronologically confused passage, Orderic suggested that, as a direct result of his adultery, Henry suffered defeat in battle at the hands of his repudiated wife's brother-in-law.[26] The papacy had first intervened in Henry IV's private life when he had tried to dissolve his marriage to Bertha in 1069.[27] Orderic also gives a garbled account of the problems caused by Henry IV's subsequent marriage to the Russian princess Eupraxia-Adelaide.[28] Perhaps drawing on reports of the accusations made by Empress Eupraxia-Adelaide against her husband at the synod of Constance in April 1094 and the papal council of Piacenza in March 1095, Orderic reported that the German king exploited meetings of his court to procure his mistresses by eliminating his rivals *en route*.[29] Pope Gregory VII's attempts to correct Henry's sinful life were ignored. Finally, Gregory excommunicated and deposed him.[30] Orderic's narrative conflates events that had occurred in the pontificates of Gregory VII and Urban II, but the point to notice, however, is the association of Henry IV's opposition to the papacy with his descent into an a moral mire.[31] Henry's licentious behaviour emphasised his inheritance of original sin, itself emblematic

---

[25] Ibid.: 'Nam princeps prefatus uxorem suam Eustachii Boloniensium egregii comitis filiam reliquit, et sordidis adulterii uoluptatibus ut porcus luto gaudens inhesit, Deique legibus et bonorum exhortationibus omnino infestus obstitit.' Orderic echoes Gregory's letter to Bishop Hermann of Metz, 15 March 1081, justifying his deposition of the emperor: H. E. J. Cowdrey, *The Register of Pope Gregory VII, 1073–1085* (Oxford, 2002), 8.21, pp. 387–95. Cf. M. McLaughlin, '"Disgusting acts of shamelessness": Sexual Misconduct and the Deconstruction of Royal Authority in the Eleventh Century', *Early Medieval Europe* 19:3 (2011), 312–31.

[26] *HE*, IV, pp. 6–9.

[27] Bertha of Turin died on 27 December 1087; Robinson, *Henry IV*, p. 266.

[28] On Bertha, see *HE*, II, pp. 206–7 and n. 4; Robinson, *Henry IV*, pp. 60–1 (Bertha), and 289–91 (Eupraxia-Adelaide, daughter of Vsevolod, grand prince of Kiev). The marriage to Eupraxia-Adelaide was part of Henry's attempt to win allies in Saxony, rather than Kiev. Eupraxia-Adelaide joined a rebellion against Henry in 1094, later appearing at the Council of Piacenza in March 1095 to denounce him.

[29] *HE*, IV, pp. 8–9.

[30] Ibid., p. 8 and n. 1: again, Orderic's narrative is confused.

[31] Orderic's accusations of sexual impropriety against Henry IV are mild compared with those made by papal polemicists writing in the 1080s: see McLaughlin, 'Disgusting acts of shamelessness', pp. 327–31, at p. 329.

of humankind's breach of the *lex divina*. The political significance of the emperor's sexual depravity was that it highlighted the distinction between the imperial office and the man who occupied it. The quality of Henry's *mores* was the criterion by which his fitness for the office of kingship was judged. By extension, it was argued, when the sins of the imperial office-holder became intolerable in the opinion of his fellow Christians, they had an obligation to try to correct his behaviour or, if that failed, to reject his authority.

In describing Henry's war against his son Conrad, Orderic branded the emperor a 'public enemy' ('publicus hostis'), and noted how he defeated and killed his own son. In the aftermath of his victory Henry 'usurped the imperial power', gathered an army and attacked Rome. At this point Orderic speculated that Henry had forgotten the Old Testament:

> It had, I think, totally escaped his memory how Absalom gathered great forces against his father David, waged war by the advice of Achitophel the Gileonite, attacked Jerusalem while his father withdrew his forces, and finally destroyed many thousand warriors; but nevertheless, after he had wrought his evil will on many, he himself died a wretched death. Similarly Henry took up arms against his father and afterwards endured harsh persecution at the hands of his own son.[32]

The Biblical *exemplum* of Absalom's revolt against his father, King David, was employed on several occasions by Orderic, and filial disloyalty may have had a particular resonance for him given the nature of his relationship with his own father, Odelerius.[33]

Orderic viewed Emperor Henry IV as a threat to the peace and unity of the Universal Church, rather than its protector. Although Orderic's account is confused, he clearly, but perhaps unsurprisingly, favoured Pope Gregory VII. Henry IV's failings as a ruler are linked by Orderic with his inability to control his libido; his adultery, like his earlier rebellion against his father, and the corruption at his court, were the outward signs of his

---

[32] *HE*, IV, pp. 8–11: 'Menti eius ut reor penitus exciderat quod Absolon ingentes turmas contra Dauid patrem suum congesserat, consilio Achitophel Gilonitis arma leuauerat, ipsoque patra cum suit discendente Ierusalem inuaserat, ac ad ultimum multa bellatorum milia pessundederat, sed nefaria uoluntate in multis complete miserabiliter perierat. Sic iste contra patrem suum arma sustulit meritoque postra diram a prole sua persecutionem pertulit.' Cf. 2 Samuel, 17–18. King David was a serial adulterer: Steven L. McKenzie, *King David: A Biography* (Oxford, 2000), pp. 141–3.

[33] *HE*, IV, pp. 228–9; William M. Aird, *Robert Curthose, Duke of Normandy (c. 1050–1134)* (Woodbridge, 2008), pp. 79–80. For further discussion on Orderic's relationship with his father, see discussions in the chapter by van Houts in the present volume, 'Orderic and his Father, Odelerius'.

sinful nature. In one so powerful that could lead not only to personal damnation for the emperor, but also to disaster for the community he ruled.[34] In his account of Henry IV's demise in 1106, Orderic reinforced this negative representation of the emperor. At his death Henry was under another sentence of anathema; as a consequence, his body, the instrument of his sinfulness:

> was not received into the bosom of mother earth, but rotted like a beast's deserving neither the burial common to mankind, nor any reverence. He reigned for about fifty years, but reaped only the terrible reward of his enslavement to crime.[35]

When Orderic examined the rulers of France he identified similar ethical failings undermining their royal authority. Philip I of France, a patron of Saint-Évroul's monks at Maule, was associated with the disorders in Normandy during the reign of Duke Robert Curthose.[36] The first extended reference to Philip in the *Historia* concerns his notorious adulterous affair with Bertrade, countess of Anjou.[37] Bertrade initiated the liaison because she feared that her husband, Count Fulk, would abandon her.[38] Fulk was another ruler whose moral turpitude undermined his authority. Around 1089, Robert of Normandy was threatened by a revolt of the men of Maine, but because he was seriously ill at the time and unable to attend to the matter himself, he prudently asked Fulk to deal with the Manceaux and then visit Normandy.[39] When Fulk arrived in the duchy, he offered Robert an alliance. Orderic employs *sermocinatio*

---

[34] R. Meens, 'Politics, Mirrors of Princes and the Bible: Sins, Kings and the Well-Being of the Realm', *Early Medieval Europe* 7:3 (1998), 345–57; for Orderic's period, see B. Weiler, 'William of Malmesbury on Kingship', *History* 90:297 (2005), 3–22.

[35] *HE*, V, pp. 196–7 and n. 3: 'Sed quia pro sceleribus suis apostolico anathemate perculsus occidit, extra matris telluris gremium ut beluinum cadauer computruit, nec communi sepultura mortalium contegi uel honorari meruit. Hic fere quinquaginta annis regnauit, sed dira flagitiosae seruitutis stipendia receipt.' Cf. *HE*, VI, pp. 80–1; and Robinson, *Henry IV*, pp. 343–4. Henry IV's body was buried before the altar in the cathedral at Liège, then exhumed and reburied in an unconsecrated chapel outside the city. It was exhumed once again and, despite resistance from the citizens of Liège, taken to Speier. Five years later it was finally buried in the cathedral.

[36] *HE*, III, pp. 206–7 and n. 1.

[37] *HE*, IV, pp. 260–5. A. Fliche, *Le Règne de Philippe Ier, roi de France (1060–1108)* (Paris, 1912), p. 45. Cf. G. Duby, *The Knight, the Lady and the Priest* (London, 1984), pp. 3–21.

[38] *HE*, IV, pp. 182–93. Kimberley A. LoPrete, 'Gendering Viragos: Medieval Perceptions of Powerful Women', in *Victims or Viragos*, ed. C. Meek and C. Lawless (Dublin, 2005), pp. 16–38, at pp. 32–4.

[39] *HE*, IV, pp. 182–5.

to dramatise the negotiations, and it is unlikely that he had access to verbatim accounts.[40] The *Historia* relates that Fulk told Robert of his love for Bertrade, the daughter of Simon de Montfort. She was being brought up by her aunt Helwise, wife of Count William of Évreux. Fulk asked Robert's permission to marry Bertrade and the duke duly sent messengers to Évreux. However, Count William came to the ducal court and refused to agree to the marriage, claiming that Duke Robert was using his niece as a pawn in his attempt to secure Maine. That said, Count William was prepared to negotiate, demanding the estates of his uncle, Ralph 'donkey-head'.[41] In addition, he sought the restoration of his nephew, William of Breteuil, to his inheritance. Duke Robert took counsel with 'prudent men' and decided to agree to Count William's terms so as not to lose the chance of settling matters in Maine.[42]

Each of the rulers involved in this episode was censured by Orderic. Fulk of Anjou 'was a man with many reprehensible, even scandalous, habits, and gave way to many pestilential vices'.[43] Fulk's inner vices took external form in his unusual shoes. Originally designed to accommodate his bunions, these 'pulley-shoes' became the height of fashion:[44]

> Before then shoes always used to be made round, fitting the foot, and these were adequate to the needs of high and low, both clergy and laity. But now laymen in their pride seize upon a fashion typical of their corrupt morals. What honourable men once thought shameful and utterly rejected as filth, the men of this age consider

---

[40] On *sermocinatio*, or the rhetorical use of invented speeches, see Matthew Kempshall, *Rhetoric and the Writing of History* (Manchester, 2011), pp. 339–40.

[41] *HE*, IV, pp. 184–5: Ralph was so named in jest, 'because of his huge head and shaggy hair' ('qui pro magnitudine capitis et congeries capillorum iocose cognominatus est Caput Asini').

[42] Ibid., pp. 186–7: the duke's chief counsellors were Edgar Atheling, William of Arques, a monk of Molesme, and, perhaps surprisingly, given Orderic's damning comments elsewhere, Robert of Bellême. Orderic's intention might have been to suggest that Duke Robert's regime was flawed because he relied on the counsel of shady characters like Robert of Bellême. Elsewhere Orderic (*HE*, IV, pp. 298–9 and nn. 2, 3) compares the tyrannical behaviour of Robert of Bellême with that of Pharaoh, Ishmael, Phalaris the Sicilian (who roasted his enemies in a bronze bull), Nero, Decius, and Domitian. On the appearance of the *prudentes* and *sapientes* in the sources, see Alexander Murray, *Reason and Society in the Middle Ages* (Oxford, 1978), p. 127.

[43] *HE*, IV, pp. 186–7.

[44] Pulley-shoes were shoes with very long toes, sometimes stuffed with wadding, that curled upwards 'like scorpions' tails' and tied at the knee. See Chibnall's comment in *HE*, IV, p. 187 n. 4, where she refers to a specimen of these 'souliers à la poulaine' in the Musée de Cluny, Paris.

sweet as honey and flaunt abroad as though it were a special grace.⁴⁵

Orderic's association of pride ('superbia') with corrupt morals ('peruersis moribus') is significant, given that pride was considered the root cause of humankind's alienation from God. The fashion spread to the court of King William Rufus, and this provoked Orderic's unrestrained diatribe against the fashions, hairstyles and sexual *mores* of lay society.⁴⁶ Again, this reminded his monastic audience of the explicit link between embodiment and sinfulness. It was also an attack on the behaviour of the young, who had fallen away from the probity of men of the Conqueror and Pope Gregory's generation. Orderic's meditation on the evils of the world was his contribution to a corpus of contemporary writings that he identified as 'long laments about the sins and sorrows of this age'.⁴⁷ He was resigned to the fact that his task was merely to report the sinful world around him, and he felt powerless to change things:

> I would far rather write of holiness and miracles performed by the saints than of the trifles of fools and frivolous extravagances, if only our princes and bishops devoted themselves wholly to lives of spiritual grace and performed miracles that proclaimed their sanctity. But I have no power to force them to live holy lives; and so leaving these matters aside I write a factual account of what they really do.⁴⁸

Philip I's affair with Bertrade of Montfort was emblematic of this moral corruption among the princes of Christendom. On hearing of Bertrade's plan to leave her husband, this 'weak prince [*mollis princeps*] [...] agreed to the crime and received her rapturously'. The king then set aside his own wife, Bertha, and married Bertrada. The outcome of this 'detestable sin of adultery' was that the kingdom of France was exposed to 'terrible threats and preparations for war between the rival lords', but Bertrade's womanly wiles brought Philip and Fulk

---

⁴⁵ Ibid., pp. 187–8: 'Nam antea omni tempore rotundi subtolares ad formam pedum agebantur, eisque summi et mediocres clerici et laici competenter utebantur. At modo seculares peruersis moribus competens scema superbe arripiunt, et quod olim honorabiles uiri turpissimum iudicauerunt, et omnino quasi stercus refutauerunt, hoc moderni dulce quasi mel estimant, et ueluti speciale decus amplectentes gestant.'

⁴⁶ Ibid., pp. 188–9.

⁴⁷ Ibid., pp. 190–1: 'ruinam mundi et miseros mortalium euentus elegiacis modis luculenter denotauit.'

⁴⁸ Ibid., pp. 192–3: 'De sanctitate et miraculis sanctorum mallem scribere multo libentius quam de nugis infrunitorum friuolisque nepotationibus, si principes nostri et antistites sanctis perfecte insisterent carismatibus, et prodigiis pollerent sanctitatem preconantibus. Ast ego uim illis ut sanctificentur inferre nequeo, unde his omissis super rebus quae fiunt ueracem dictatum facio. Nunc autem ad narrationis ordinem redeo.'

together.⁴⁹ She prepared a sumptuous feast and 'on the following night prepared couches for them in the same chamber, while she herself attended to all their wants in a fitting way'.⁵⁰ Orderic's salacious overtones suggest that because both men were unable to control their libidos they were susceptible to the influence of a resourceful woman. The ability of a king to govern his own bodily urges was essential for successful rulership. All these men, led by their lust rather than by the duty to God imposed on them by kingship, surrendered themselves to a woman's cunning. This unnatural subordination inverted the normative hierarchy of gender relationships and compromised their claims to secular authority.

As in the case of Emperor Henry IV, the Church attempted to recall the sinful monarch to the righteous path. Pope Urban II rebuked the king for his marital infidelity, but Philip continued to 'wallow in his shameful adultery until he had got two sons, Philip and Florus, by the adulteress'.⁵¹ Philip was excommunicated and, for a period of fifteen years, the king's public image suffered.⁵² During that time, Philip:

> never wore his crown, nor put on the purple, nor took part in any solemn celebration in royal state. As soon as the clergy heard of the king of France approaching any town or city, all the bells stopped ringing and all sung offices were silenced. So it was a time of public mourning, and all the divine offices were performed only in private as long as the erring prince remained in that diocese.⁵³

Philip and the clergy of the royal domains publicly acknowledged his sinfulness, enacting rituals appropriate for a king's death. The king's public

---

⁴⁹ Ibid., pp. 260–1 and n. 3: 'Denique mollis princeps comperta lasciuae muleris uoluntate flagitio consensit, ipsamque relicto marito Gallias expetentem cum gaudio suscepit […] Abominabile crimen mechiae in solio regni Galliae proh dolor perpetratum est, unde inter opulentos riuales minarum ingens tumultus et preliorum conatus exortus est.' Orderic erroneously asserted that Bishop Odo of Bayeux had performed the ceremony in return for custody of the churches of the town of Mantes.

⁵⁰ Ibid., pp. 260–3: 'nocte sequenti ambobus in uno conclaui strata pararet, et apte prout placuit illis ministraret'. Marjorie Chibnall noted that, although 'details in Orderic's account seem to belong rather to romance than to history', there was some corroboration for his story in Abbot Suger's *Life of Louis VI* (HE, IV, p. 262 n. 1).

⁵¹ HE, IV, pp. 262–3: 'in adulterii fetore diu putridius iacuit, donec filios duos Philippum et Florum ex adultera genuit'.

⁵² Ibid., pp. 262–3 and n. 5.

⁵³ Ibid., pp. 262–3: 'Quo tempore nunquam diadema portauit, nec purpuram induit neque solennitatem aliquam regio more celebrauit. In quodcumque oppidum uel urbem Galliarum rex aduenisset, mox ut a clero auditum fuisset, cessabat omnis clangor campanarum, et generalis cantus clericorum. Luctus itaque publicus agebatur, et dominucus cultus priuatim exercebatur, quamdiu transgressor princeps in eadem diocesi commorabatur.'

sins forced the clergy to celebrate the divine offices behind closed doors. It was another inversion of right order: if the king could not refrain from his adultery, at least it should have remained private. Openly flaunting his liaison meant that liturgical celebrations that should have been open affirmations of faith were instead forced into hiding. There are signs, however, of attempts to mitigate the effects of Philip's excommunication, as the bishops 'on account of his royal dignity' ('pro regali dignitate') conceded that the king and his household were allowed to hear Mass recited by his chaplain. This highlights the difficulty encountered by the papacy in ensuring that its excommunications were effective if local bishops, with an eye to their own relationship with the Crown, failed to enforce the penalty, or, as here, lessened its impact.

In a passage that bears comparison with the undignified treatment of Emperor Henry IV's corpse, Orderic provided a particularly visceral conclusion to his account of Philip I of France's adultery. He prefaced it by pointing out that France was full of 'pious and learned bishops' ('religios eruditis presulibus florebat') who counselled the king, but Philip remained obstinately deaf to their exhortations to amend his life. Indeed, Philip continued to 'rot in his wickedness' ('putidus in malicia perdurauit'). As the king increasingly suffered 'decaying teeth, scabies, and other infirmities and ignominies according to his deserts', he began to disengage from government, passing the administration of the kingdom over to his son Louis, 'still an adolescent in the first flower of youth' ('primo flore iuuentius pubesceret').[54] Elsewhere Orderic had recorded arguments *against* entrusting kingdoms and duchies to callow youths, so it is interesting that in the case of France the young Louis' appointment was condoned.[55] As Philip's body deteriorated, ravaged by his sinfulness, his authority and health both ebbed away, leaving him with no option but to surrender the kingdom to his son.

Orderic's representations of the Norman rulers, with whom he was most familiar, reiterate the themes already encountered, but with a level of detail derived from his familiarity with the historical context. Book VII of the *Historia ecclesiastica*, written between 1130/1 and 1133, provides an extended account of William the Conqueror's death.[56] As ever, Orderic was influenced by the pressing concerns at the time of writing.[57] His narrative of the Conqueror's demise begins by noting how the garrison of Mantes crossed into Normandy and ravaged the diocese of Évreux, stealing cattle, taking prisoners and eventually provoking William's

---

[54] Ibid., 264–5: 'ideoque dolori dentium et scabiei multisque aliis infirmatibus et ignomis merito subiacuit'.

[55] E.g. *HE*, III, pp. 98–101.

[56] On books VII and VIII, see *HE*, IV, pp. xii–xix.

[57] Cf. ibid., pp. xix–xx: Orderic's narrative of the 1087 succession was coloured by the arrangements made by Henry I in 1126–7.

retaliation.⁵⁸ Orderic set out the Conqueror's claims to the Vexin, and how, when Philip I rejected them, the Conqueror attacked Mantes late in the summer of 1087. William's demise was brought about by his bodily weakness: approaching sixty and heavy, he suffered exhaustion brought on by the heat, and collapsed during the attack.⁵⁹ Orderic provides a brief summary of his qualities as a ruler and these may be contrasted with the vices practised by Henry IV and Philip I:

> He indeed, who all his life long had relied on the counsel of wise men, feared God as a faithful servant should, and stood firm as the tireless defender of holy Mother Church, kept his renown untarnished to the end; his death was as noble as his life.⁶⁰

William was taken from Mantes to Rouen and then, because the city was too noisy, carried to the church of Saint-Gervais to be cared for by his physicians. Realising that death was approaching, the Conqueror called his sons William and Henry to his side (Robert was with the king of France after another estrangement from his father).⁶¹ The king made his will and recompensed Mantes for the destruction he had caused. Finally, 'weeping, he uttered this eloquent last speech, which deserves to be remembered for all time'.⁶²

Orderic imagined William reviewing his life and dreading 'the terrible judgement of God', as he had been stained by all the blood he shed over his lifetime. Orderic allowed the Conqueror to deliver his own *epitaphium*, or funeral lament.⁶³ Here is to be found the oft-quoted description of the character of the Normans:

---

⁵⁸ Ibid., pp. 74–9: for the Vexin, see Judith A. Green, 'Lords of the Norman Vexin', in *War and Government in the Middle Ages: Essays in Honour of J. O. Prestwich*, ed. J. Gillingham and J. C. Holt (Woodbridge, 1984), pp. 46–63. Cattle- and slave-raiding have been associated with the practices of England's insular neighbours: see, for example, J. Gillingham, 'Conquering the Barbarians: War and Chivalry in Twelfth-Century Britain', *HSJ* 4 (1993), 57–84.

⁵⁹ *HE*, IV, pp. 78–9: M. Hagger, *William, King and Conqueror* (London, 2012), p. 168.

⁶⁰ *HE*, IV, pp. 78–9: 'Ille uero qui semper in omni uita sue sapientum consilio usus fuerat, Deumque ut fidelis seruus timuerat, sanctaeque matris aecclesiae indefessus defensor extiterat, usque ad mortem laudabili memoria uiguit, et sicut uita sic etiam finis uenerabilis extitit.'

⁶¹ W. M. Aird, 'Frustrated Masculinity: The Relationship between William the Conqueror and his Eldest Son', in *Masculinity in Medieval Europe*, ed. Dawn M. Hadley (London, 1999), pp. 39–55.

⁶² *HE*, IV, p. 80: 'allocutionem perenni memoria dignam admixtis interdum lacrimis eloquenter sic edidit'. The Conqueror's lengthy death-bed oration follows (pp. 80–95).

⁶³ Kempshall, *Rhetoric and the Writing of History*, p. 215 and n. 363.

If the Normans are disciplined under a just and firm rule they are men of great valour, who press invincibly to the fore in arduous undertakings and, proving their strength, fight resolutely to overcome all enemies. But without such rule they tear each other to pieces and destroy themselves, for they hanker after rebellion, cherish sedition, and are ready for any treachery. So they need to be restrained by the severe penalties of law and forced by the curb of discipline to keep to the path of justice. If they are allowed to go wherever they choose, as an untamed ass does, both they and their ruler must expect grave disorder and poverty. I have learnt this by now through repeated experience.[64]

The Conqueror attributed his success to God's support, particularly important after his victory at Hastings.[65] Amid the list of successful campaigns, however, William expressed dread at the recollection of the brutality that he had unleashed in winning his victories. He was a repentant sinner expressing heartfelt contrition as he lay dying, and it was clearly important for Orderic to portray a king whom he considered to be strong and effective in a way that emphasised how much of that ruler's success was owing to God's grace.

The Conqueror's treatment of the Church was exemplary: he 'hated and forbade simony', never sold ecclesiastical offices, and provided men of good character as leaders of the Church. As Orderic puts it, 'These are the men I [William] chose as my constant companions; I learnt truth and wisdom in their society, and so was always happy to follow their good counsels.'[66] Another mark of the Conqueror's exemplary rule was his monastic patronage. He built abbeys that were 'the fortresses by which Normandy is guarded: in these men learn to fight against devils and the sins of the flesh'.[67]

---

[64] HE, IV, pp. 82–3: 'Normanni si bono rigidoque dominatu reguntur strenuissimi sunt, et in arduis rebus inuicti omnes excellunt, et cunctis hostibus fortiores superare contendunt. Alioquin sese uicissim dilaniant atque consumunt, rebelliones enim cupiunt, seditiones appetunt, et ad omne nefas prompti sunt. Rectitudinis igitur forti censura coherceantur, et freno disciplinae per tramitem iusticiae gradi compellantur. Si uero ad libitum suum sine iugo ut indomitus onager ire permittuntur, ipsi et princeps eorum penuria et confusione probrosa operientur. Pluribus hoc experimentis iamdudum edidici.'

[65] Ibid., pp. 84–5: 'auxiliante Deo, qui iustus iudex est'; and pp. 90–1: 'sed custodiente Deo'.

[66] Ibid., pp. 90–1: 'Tales socios ad colloquium elegi, in horum contubernio ueritatem et sapientiam inueni, ideoque semper gaudens optabam eorum consiliis perfrui.' William's counsellors were Lanfranc, archbishop of Canterbury, and abbots Anselm of Bec, Gerbert of Saint-Wandrille and Durand of Troarn.

[67] Ibid., pp. 92–3.

Here, once again, Orderic's text emphasises the Christian's manly struggle against carnality.[68]

The Conqueror's self-delivered funeral oration also provided advice for his sons, and, in effect, this outlined Orderic's expectations of a righteous ruler. William's sons were to keep company with 'good and wise men' and obey their counsel.[69] The teaching of the 'holy philosophers' was:

> to know good from evil, preserve justice [*iusticiam*] in all things, shun evil with determination, be merciful and helpful to the sick and poor and law-abiding, overthrow and punish the proud and wicked [*superbos et iniquos*], refrain from harming the humble, be a devout worshipper in the Church, cherish the service of God above all riches, and obey the divine law [*diuinæ legi*] by night and day, that is in adversity and prosperity.[70]

Similar advice was given by the Conqueror's half-brother, Odo, bishop of Bayeux, to his nephew Duke Robert.[71] Bishop Odo encouraged Robert to conduct ducal government vigorously and to be 'gentle as a lamb to good men and to the obedient and humble, but harsh as a lion to evil men and rebels and law-breakers'.[72] Odo then noted the parlous state of ducal rule in Robert's Normandy:

> Monks and widows cry out to you, and you slumber; you hear of unspeakable outrages again and again and take no notice. This is not how the holy David acted, or Alexander the Great, or Julius Caesar, or Septimius Severus; Hannibal the Carthaginian, or Scipio Africanus, or Cyrus the Persian, or Marius the Roman. But why do I waste time with an obscure recital of foreigners, whose names even mean nothing to you?[73]

---

[68] Jacqueline Murray, 'Masculinizing Religious Life: Sexual Prowess, the Battle for Chastity and Monastic Identity', in *Holiness and Masculinity in the Middle Ages*, ed. P. H. Cullum and K. J. Lewis (Cardiff, 2004), pp. 24–42.

[69] *HE*, IV, pp. 92–3.

[70] Ibid.: 'Piorum sophistarum doctrina est bonum a malo discernere, iusticiam omnimodis tenere, nequitiamque omni molimine cauere, infirmis et pauperibus ac iustis parcere et subuenire, superbos et iniquos comprimere ac debellare, et ab infestatione simplicium refrenare, aecclesiam sanctam deuote frequentare, diuinitatis cultum super omnes diuitias amare, et diuinae legi nocte dieque, id est in aduersis et prosperis infatigabiliter obtemperare.'

[71] Ibid., pp. 150–5. See also D. Bates, 'The Character and Career of Odo, Bishop of Bayeux', *Speculum* 50 (1975), 1–20.

[72] Orderic's view of Bishop Odo was positive (*HE*, IV, pp. 114–17), perhaps due to his son John's interaction with Saint-Évroul (see ibid., p. 116, n. 2).

[73] Ibid., pp. 150–1: 'Clamant ad te monachi et uiduae et dormis inaudita facinora frequenter audis et paruipendis. Non sic egit sanctus Dauid

Next Odo listed Robert's ducal ancestors and urged him to imitate their determination, through which they had 'conquered the kingdoms of the world [...] restrained tyrants, and civilised barbarous peoples'.[74] Orderic's local concerns rise to the surface when he has Odo deliver a diatribe against the 'rebellious sons of Talvas', apparently the chief threat to Robert's rule. Their removal would allow 'the people of God' to flourish and offer prayers for his salvation. Duke Robert was to 'stand up worthily *as a good prince should* for the peace of holy Mother Church and for the defence of the poor and helpless; put down all opponents with resolution'.[75]

Despite occasionally conceding that Duke Robert could rule with determination, more often than not Orderic represents the Conqueror's eldest son as ineffective:

> All men knew that Duke Robert was weak and indolent; therefore trouble-makers despised him and stirred up loathsome factions when and where they chose. For although the duke was bold and daring, praiseworthy for his knightly prowess and eloquent in speech, he exercised no discipline over either himself or his men. He was prodigal in distributing his bounty and lavish in his promises, but so thoughtless and inconstant that they were utterly unreliable. Being merciful to suppliants he was too weak and pliable to pass judgement on wrongdoers; unable to pursue any plan consistently he was far too affable and obliging in all his relationships and so he earned the contempt of corrupt and foolish men.[76]

nec magnus Alexander, non sic Iulius Caesar nec Seuerus Afer, non sic Anniba Cartaginiensis nec Scipio Affricanus, non Cirus Persa nec Marius Romanus. Quid moror in relatione barbarorum obscura, quorum etiam nomina tibi sunt incognita?' See also Kempshall, *Rhetoric and the Writing of History*, pp. 69, 108; and G. Garnett, 'Robert Curthose: The Duke who Lost his Trousers', ANS 35 (2013), 213–43.

[74] HE, IV, pp. 150–1: 'Horum queso rigorem emulare et efficaciam sicut illi predecessorum suorum sectati sunt uigorem et industriam, qui regna mundi per immensos labores optinuerunt, tirranos compresserunt, et seuas gentes edomuerunt.'

[75] Ibid., pp. 152–3: 'ut bonus princeps pro pace sanctae matris aecclesiae, et pro defensione pauperum debiliumque laudabilitier exurge, et resistentes uirtute contere' [emphasis added].

[76] Ibid., pp. 114–15: 'Omnes ducem Robertum mollem esse desidemque cognoscebant, et iccirco facinorosi eum despiciebant, et pro libitu suo dolosas factiones agitabant. Erat quippe idem dux audax et ualidus, militiæque laude dignus; eloquio facundus, sed in regimine sui suorum inconsideratus. In erogando prodigus, in promittendo diffusus, ad mentiendum leuis et incautus. Misericors supplicibus, ac ad iusticiam super iniquos faciendam mollis et mansuetus, in definitione mutabilis, in conuersatione omnibus nimis blandus et tractabilis; ideoque peruersis et

Orderic's characterisation of Curthose is significant not least for its removal of the chivalric ideal from the list of qualities essential to effective rulership: prowess gave way to prudence.[77]

Books VIII, X and XI of the *Historia* deal with the interaction between Robert and his two younger brothers, William Rufus and Henry.[78] Rufus was 'a man of military valour and worldly magnificence, though far too prone to pride, lust, and other vices; but he remained indifferent to God and attendance at church and divine worship'.[79] Here again we find the principal sin of pride ('superbia'), which was particularly associated with chivalry.[80] Its combination with lust ('libido') characterised monastic criticisms of the moral failings of contemporary courtly society. Elsewhere, Orderic elaborated on Rufus's vices and emphasised the consequences for the king's subjects:

> William Rufus, the young king of England, was wanton and lascivious, and droves of his people all too readily imitated his corrupt morals. A masterful, bold and warlike man, he gloried in the display of many knights. He delighted in the honours of knighthood and granted them readily for the sake of worldly show. He failed to protect the peasants against his vassals, whose knights or squires and men-at-arms were allowed to ravage their possessions with impunity. Having a tenacious memory and a determined will, for both good and evil, he terrorized thieves and robbers, and successfully enforced internal peace throughout his realm. He bound some of his subjects to him by generosity, and held the rest in check

> insipientibus despicabilis. Corpore autem breuis et grossus ideoque 'breuis ocrea' est a patre cognominatus. Ipse cunctis placer studebat, cunctisque quod petebant aut dabat aut promittebat uel concedebat. Prodigus dominium patrum suorum cotidie imminuebat insipienter tribuens unicuique quod petebat, et ipse pauperescebat, unde alios contra se roborabat.'

[77] Murray, *Reason and Society*, pp. 124–30. Medieval rulers were still expected to be successful commanders in warfare, and most kings of this period would probably have wanted to be remembered as such: cf. J. Gillingham, 'Conquering Kings: Some Twelfth-Century Reflections on Henry II and Richard I', in *Warriors and Churchmen in the High Middle Ages: Essays Presented to Karl Leyser*, ed. T. Reuter (London, 1992), pp. 163–78.

[78] Book IX (*HE*, V, pp. 4–191) concerns the First Crusade.

[79] Ibid., IV, pp. 110–11: 'Nam militari probitate et seculari dapsilitate uiguit, et superbiæ libinidique aliisque uiciis nimium subiacuit, sed erga Deum et æcclesiæ frequentationem cultumque frigidus extitit.'

[80] L. K. Little, 'Pride Goes before Avarice: Social Change and the Vices in Latin Christendom', *American Historical Review* 76:1 (1971), 16–59 at p. 19; A. Katzenellenbogen, *Allegories of the Virtues and Vices in Medieval Art* (Toronto, 1989).

by force and fear, so that no-one dared to breathe a word against him.[81]

Again, the intimate connection between personal morality and effective government is made clear. Rufus was a forceful king, but indulged the appetites of his knights at the expense of the defenceless. In addition, he was the worst kind of carnal sinner: 'He never had a lawful wife, but gave himself up insatiably to obscene fornications and repeated adulteries. Stained with his sins, he set a culpable example of shameful debauchery to his subjects.'[82] The stability and maturity associated with marriage was seen as a necessary corrective to the debaucheries of medieval youth.[83] Clearly Orderic judged that Rufus was not an *exemplum* to be emulated by his subjects.

Even Henry I, seen by many as Orderic's ideal king, was criticised for his moral failings.[84] Nevertheless, in writing of Henry's seizure of Normandy from Robert in 1106, Orderic emphasised the king's firm government:

> up to the end of his life he always devoted himself to preserving peace, and after he had secured the lasting prosperity he desired he never declined from his early power and strict justice. He shrewdly kept down illustrious counts and castellans and bold tyrants to prevent seditious uprisings, but always cared for and protected men of peace and monks and the humble people.[85]

---

[81] *HE*, IV, pp. 178–9: 'Guillelmus Rufus Albionis rex iuuenis erat proteruus et lasciuus quem nimis inhianter prosequebantur agmina populorum impudicis moribus. Imperiosus et audax atque militaris erat; et multitudine militum pompose tripudiabat. Militiæ titulis applaudebat illisque propter fastum secularem admodum fauebat. Pagenses contra milites defendere neglegebat quorum possessiones a suis tironibus et armigeris impune deuastari permittebat. Tenacis memoriae et ardentis ad bonum seu malum uoluntatis erat, terribilis furibus et latrunculis imminebat; pacem serenam per subiectam regionem seruari ualenter cogebat. Omnes incolas regni sui aut illexit largitate, aut compressit uirtute et terrore; ut nullus contra eum auderet aliquo modo mutire.' Cf. ibid., pp. 278–9.

[82] *HE*, V, pp. 202–3: 'Legitimam coniugem nunquam habuit; sed obscenis fornicationibus et frequentibus mœchiis inexplebiliter inhesit, flagitiisque pollutus exemplum turpis lasciuiæ subiectis damnabiliter exhibuit.' Cf. Ibid., pp. 292–3. On Rufus's sexuality, see F. Barlow, *William Rufus* (London, 1983), pp. 102–10.

[83] G. Duby, 'Youth in Aristocratic Society: Northwestern France in the Twelfth Century', in *The Chivalrous Society: Essays by Georges Duby*, trans. Cynthia Postan (London, 1977), pp. 112–22.

[84] Cf. A. Cooper, '"The feet of those that bark shall be cut off": Timorous Historians and the Personality of Henry I', ANS 23 (2001), 47–67.

[85] *HE*, VI, pp. 98–9: 'et usque ad uitæ suæ finem semper paci studuit, atque iugi felicitate potitus ut uoluit, nunquam a pristino robore iusticiæque seueritate decidit. Egregios comites et oppidanos et audaces tirannos

Whereas Rufus had neglected the defenceless, Henry kept their oppressors in check.

The meeting between Pope Calixtus and Henry at Gisors in November 1118 demonstrated that the king knew how to win over the Church. Henry prostrated himself before the pope and 'showed him respect and reverence, acknowledging him to be the shepherd of the whole Church and his own close kinsman'. Through this public act of humility, Henry demonstrated that he could set aside *superbia* and was worthy of the pope's kiss of peace and joyful embrace.[86] Calixtus asked Henry to emulate Solomon and make peace with his enemies, including those who supported his nephew William Clito.[87] The pope also urged Henry to release his brother Robert, who had been incarcerated since 1106, and restore Normandy to him.[88] Henry then launched into a long defence of his actions, emphasising the deleterious effect of Robert's weak rule. Monasteries and churches had been destroyed and their sanctuaries desecrated. This was a return to the devastation of the Viking attacks.[89] Henry claimed that his offers of help were rejected by Robert, eventually leaving him no choice but to invade Normandy: 'When I saw appalling wickedness triumphant, I did not wish to refuse my service to holy Mother Church, but endeavoured to use the office laid on me by heaven for the general good.'[90] Orderic's justification of Henry's actions probably owed much to the propaganda issued by the king in the wake of his victory over his elder brother. It is doubtful that verbatim accounts of the interview between the pope and the king were available, but Orderic preserved the main thrust of Henry's case.[91]

Given Orderic's favourable opinion of Henry I, it is instructive to examine how he addressed the king's personal failings, among the most severe of which was, again, an inability to control his libido:

> ne rebellarent callide oppressit, placidos uero et religiosos humilemque populum omni tempore clementer fouit atque protexit.'

[86] For *humilitas* as the root of the tree of virtues, see Katzenellenbogen, *Allegories*, p. 67.

[87] Sandy B. Hicks, 'The Impact of William Clito upon the Continental Policies of Henry I of England', *Viator* 10 (1979), 1–21.

[88] *HE*, VI, pp. 284–5.

[89] Cf. *HE*, III, pp. 302–5.

[90] *HE*, VI, pp. 286–7: 'Ego autem tanta uidens scelera preualere, seruitium meum sanctæ matri æcclesiæ nolui subtrahere, sed officium quod michi diuinitus iniunctum est studui multis salubriter exercere.'

[91] Ibid., p. 288 n. 1. At the same meeting Calixtus arranged a treaty between Henry and Louis VI of France: ibid., pp. 290–1. Henry also met Innocent II at Chartres, 13 January 1131: ibid., pp. 420–1. J. Gillingham, 'The Meetings of the Kings of France and England, 1066–1204', in *Normandy and its Neighbours, 900–1250: Essays for David Bates*, ed. D. Crouch and K. Thompson (Turnhout, 2011), pp. 17–42.

Possessing an abundance of wealth and luxuries, he gave way too easily to the sin of lust; from boyhood until old age he was sinfully enslaved by this vice, and had many sons and daughters by his mistresses [...] I confidently assert that no king in the English realm was ever more richly or powerfully equipped than Henry in everything that contributes to worldly glory.[92]

The frank admission that Henry could not control his libido militates against representing Orderic as an uncritical partisan of the king and suggests that, fundamentally, the authority of even the most effective rulers was compromised by their vulnerability to carnal temptation.[93]

Before bringing this selective survey of Orderic's representation of secular rulers to a close, and as a partial antidote for the painful litany of miserable sinners discussed so far, it is worth examining a line of kings who, in Orderic's opinion,'adhered to the catholic faith from ancient times, and have had great regard for the Christian religion'.[94]

After discussing the sinfulness of the king of France, Orderic embarked on a lengthy digression prompted by the notice of a joint expedition against the Scots in 1091 by Rufus and his elder brother, Robert.[95] Again, political events are linked with ethical values, as the death of Archbishop Lanfranc of Canterbury in 1089 heralded a period of moral decline:

At that time great evils appeared and increased rapidly all over the world. Men of knightly rank abandoned the customs of their fathers in style of dress and cut of hair; in a little while townsmen and peasants and all the lower ranks followed their example. Because the divine law was broken everywhere the wrath of Heaven rightly brought down punishment on the heads of the guilty through disasters of many kinds.[96]

---

[92] HE, VI, pp. 98–101: 'Diuitiis deliciisque affluens libidini nimis deditus fuit, et a puericia usque ad senectutem huic uitio culpabiliter subiacuit; et filios ac filias ex pelicibus plures genuit [...] audacter assero, quod nullus regum in regno Anglico, quantum pertinet ad secularem fastum fuit ditior seu potentior Henrico.' Cf. the epitaph provided by Orderic, ibid., pp. 450–3.

[93] William of Malmesbury suggested that throughout his extra-marital affairs Henry remained in control of his fleshly lusts: *Gesta regum Anglorum*, ed. and trans. R. A. B. Mynors, completed by R. M. Thomson and M. Winterbottom, Oxford Medieval Texts, 2 vols. (Oxford, 1998), I, pp. 744–5; K. Thompson, 'Affairs of State: The Illegitimate Children of Henry I', *Journal of Medieval History* 29:2 (2003), 129–51.

[94] HE, IV, pp. 278–9: 'En causa Scottorum qui ab antiquis temporibus adheserunt catholicæ fidei, et christianæ gratanter seruierunt simplicitati.'

[95] Ibid., pp. 268–79.

[96] Ibid.: 'Eo tempore multa malicia in terris orta est; et uehementer augmenta est. Militares uiri mores paternos in uestitu et capillorum tonsura

As noted earlier, Orderic associated abominable fashions with societal crisis and represented the courts of all the Conqueror's sons as particularly dissolute, though Henry I, at least, attempted reforms.[97] So, in the midst of this decline in morals, King Malcolm III of Scotland attacked northern England. In linking the depravity of the royal court to the Scottish invasion, Orderic reinforced the idea that failing to obey the *lex divina* provoked God's righteous anger ('ira'), resulting in punishment.[98]

In 1091 Rufus and his brother Robert confronted Malcolm III, and Orderic provided a lengthy account of the negotiations between Rufus and the Scots king, with Robert acting as intermediary.[99] Using Malcolm's speech, Orderic highlighted a fundamental problem for the many medieval vassals required to acknowledge more than one lord: the question of divided loyalties. Indeed, this was one of his major themes in his account of the division of England and Normandy between Robert and Rufus in 1087, and again in writing of the wars of succession after 1135.

Orderic's account is confused because he collapsed the events of 1091 to 1093 into one continuous narrative.[100] It is clear, however, that he regarded the murder of the Scots king in November 1093 as dishonourable, for he tells us that, at the news of Malcolm's death, 'the king of England and his magnates were grieved beyond measure and felt deep shame [*erubuerunt*] that such a disgraceful and cruel deed should have been perpetrated by Normans'.[101] The event drew comparisons with the Old Testament

---

derelinquerunt; quos paulo post burgenses et rustici et pene totum uulgus imitati sunt. Et quia diuinæ legis preuaricatio nimis exuberauit; cœlestis iræ animaduersio multis uariisque calamitatibus reos merito protriuit.' The notice of Lanfranc's death acts as an introduction to the campaign of 1091.

[97] Similar contemporaneous diatribes are found elsewhere: see K. A. Fenton, 'Men and Masculinities in William of Malmesbury's Presentation of the Anglo-Norman Court', in *HSJ* 23 (2014), 115–24; and especially S. Yarrow, 'Men and Masculinities at the Courts of the Anglo-Norman Kings in the *Ecclesiastical History* of Orderic Vitalis', *HSJ* 23 (2014), 105–14. For Henry I's reforms, see *HE*, VI, pp. 65–7; and P. Stafford, 'The Meanings of Hair in the Anglo-Norman World: Masculinity, Reform, and National Identity', in *Saints, Scholars and Politicians: Gender as a Tool in Medieval Studies*, ed. M. van Dijk and R. Nip (Turnhout, 2005), pp. 153–71.

[98] M. C. McCarthy, S.J., 'Divine Wrath and Human Anger: Embarrassment Ancient and New', *Theological Studies* 70 (2009), 845–74.

[99] *HE*, IV, pp. 270–1: for the context, see J. A. Green, 'Anglo-Scottish Relations, 1066–1174', in *England and her Neighbours, 1066–1453. Essays in Honour of Pierre Chaplais*, ed. M. Jones and M. Vale (London, 1989), pp. 53–72.

[100] *HE*, IV, pp. 270–1 n. 3.

[101] Ibid., pp. 270–1: 'Quod audiens rex Anglorum regnique optimates ualde contristati sunt; et pro tam feda re tamque crudeli a Normannis commissa nimis erubuerunt.'

account of the assassination of Abner son of Ner, killed by Joab and Abishai while returning from the court of King David.[102] The saintly Queen Margaret's reaction to Malcolm's death was to summon the Scots nobles, commend her sons, Edgar, Alexander and David to them, and then make preparations for her own death. After receiving the Eucharist, she died with a prayer on her lips. In writing of Margaret, Orderic also notes her refoundation of the abbey of Iona and her decision to send her daughters Edith and Mary to be educated by her sister Christina at Romsey.[103] The fate of these girls was also of interest to Orderic, given that Edith later married Henry I.[104]

The account of the Scots royal dynasty continues with Edgar's succession with Norman help in 1097, the reign of his brother Alexander (1107–24), and, finally, David I, who received considerable praise from Orderic. In contrast with the king of France and the Holy Roman Emperor, the sons of Malcolm and Margaret lived exemplary lives:

> all these brothers in turn reigned in Scotland, giving abundant evidence of their good character and love of God [*bonis moribus et amore Dei*]; and they led praiseworthy lives in the way appropriate for young laymen.[105]

It is significant that Orderic does not impugn the personal morality of these Scots kings. No mention is made of Edgar's sexuality – not that there seems to have been anything scandalous to report – and it is merely stated that Alexander married a natural daughter of Henry I. However, when it came to David's marriage to Matilda of Senlis, Orderic had a most bizarre tale to tell.

David fled the internal strife Scotland experienced after the death of Malcolm III and grew up in the household of Henry I.[106] David's marriage to Judith, the daughter of Earl Waltheof of Northumbria, gave him the English counties of Northampton and Huntingdon and a place among England's elite. David and his wife had a son, Henry, and two daughters, Clarice and Hodierna, but their first-born son had been 'cruelly murdered

---

[102] 2 Samuel, 3:22–7.

[103] *HE*, IV, pp. 272–3.

[104] C. Keene, *Saint Margaret, Queen of the Scots: A Life in Perspective* (Basingstoke, 2013); and L. L. Huneycutt, *Matilda of Scotland: A Study in Medieval Queenship* (Woodbridge, 2003).

[105] *HE*, IV, pp. 274–5: 'Sic omnes isti fratres uicissim in Scotia regnauerunt, bonisque moribus et amore Dei pollentes uiguerunt, atque pro modulo suo utpote adolescentes uirique seculares laudabiliter uixerunt.' Cf. J. Huntington, 'The Taming of the Laity: Writing Waltheof and Rebellion in the Twelfth Century', *Anglo-Norman Studies* 32 (2010), 79–95.

[106] J. A. Green, 'David I and Henry I', *Scottish Historical Review* 75:1 (1996), 1–19.

by the iron fingers of a certain wretched clerk'.[107] This clerk had been blinded and had his hands and feet cut off for killing a priest celebrating Mass at the altar of his church in Norway. Earl David, 'for the love of God', took pity on the clerk and provided food and clothing for the priest and his young daughter. The man was allowed to caress David's two-year-old son, but, at the prompting of the devil, he stabbed the child with his iron prosthetic fingers and 'tore out the bowels of the suckling in his nurse's arms'.[108] The man's grisly punishment was to be bound to the tails of four wild horses and torn to pieces. This story seems to be unique to Orderic's account and punctuates an otherwise unremarkable account of David's rise to power.[109]

Orderic also provides a selective account of David's reign as king of the Scots, recording the rebellion in the year of David's succession, in favour of Malcolm Macbeth, a bastard son of Alexander.[110] David was victorious because he was 'wiser, more powerful and wealthier' than his opponent.[111] A later revolt by Angus, earl of Moray, and Malcolm Macbeth in 1130 was put down by David and his troops and resulted in the annexation of Moray.[112] 'In this way', Orderic concludes:

> David grew more powerful than his predecessors, and the kingdom of Scotland became famous for its religious zeal and learning. This is why I have somewhat prolonged this digression on the Scots, who have adhered to the catholic faith from ancient times, and have had great regard for the Christian religion.[113]

---

[107] *HE*, IV, pp. 274–5.

[108] Ibid., pp. 276–7: 'Hic postmodum a Dauid comite in Anglia pro amore Dei susceptus, et uictu uestituque cum filia paruula sufficienter sustentatus; digitis ferreis quibus utebatur utpote mancus, bienem filium benefactoris sui quasi mulcere uolens immaniter pupugit; et sic instigante diabolo inter manus nutricis uiscera lactentis ex insperato effudit.'

[109] S. Marritt, 'Crowland Abbey and the Provenance of Orderic Vitalis's Scandinavian and Scottish Material', *Notes & Queries* n. s. 53:3 (2006), 290–2. I am grateful to Professor Judith Green for this reference.

[110] *HE* (IV, pp. 276–7 and nn. 2, 3) erroneously begins David's reign in 1125 (*recte* 1124). Marjorie Chibnall suggested that Malcolm may have been a son of Angus, earl of Moray; cf. R. Oram, *Domination and Lordship: Scotland 1070–1230* (Edinburgh, 2011), p. 66, n. 113.

[111] *HE*, IV, pp. 276–7.

[112] Ibid., pp. 276–7 and n. 5.

[113] Ibid., pp. 276–9: 'Sic Dauid aucta potestate super antecessores suos exaltatus est studioque eius religionis et eruditis personis regio Scottorum decorata est. En causa Scottorum qui ab antiquis temporibus adheserunt catholicæ fidei, et christianæ gratanter seruierunt simplicitati; inceptam epanalempsim aliquantulum protelaui, sed nunc ad propositum nitor opus de nostris regredi.'

Orderic's account of the Scots kings is noteworthy, not least because it serves as a caveat against placing too much emphasis on the negative aspects of Anglo-Norman representations of their insular neighbours. Much of this positive portrayal of David and his family may be connected with Orderic's knowledge of the king's upbringing at Henry I's court and his later support for the Empress Matilda in her struggles with King Stephen. Nonetheless, the Scots kings, and David in particular, are presented as successful, God-fearing rulers. There is no hint of sexual impropriety in their conduct and, as a consequence, their *regnum* provided something of a golden age.

Orderic's *Historia ecclesiastica* provides a wealth of information on the kings and other rulers of Christendom. There is hardly a royal dynasty of the eleventh and early twelfth centuries that he did not mention, though his information was not always accurate. His discursive style allowed him to digress whenever his narrative threads led him into other regions of Europe.[114] However, at the heart of the *Historia* were the deeds of the Norman ruling house, but such were the connections that men from Normandy established throughout Christendom and beyond in this period that their story encompassed many other peoples and their rulers. Despite his claims to be shut off in his cloister, away from the world of the court, Orderic provided a shrewd and plausible assessment of the political consequences of rulers' decisions. For example, in his account of Fulk of Anjou's marriage to the daughter of Baldwin II of Jerusalem, he noted that it was Fulk's decision to remove the leading magnates of the kingdom from his counsels and replace them with 'Angevin strangers' that led to difficulties in Outremer.[115] Although the situation was more complicated than Orderic realised, his analysis is certainly worth considering.

In his *Etymologies*, Isidore of Seville noted that there was an ancient proverb concerning kingship: 'You will be king [*rex*] if you behave rightly [*recte*]; if you do not, you will not.' Isidore identified two royal virtues, justice and mercy, 'but mercy is more praised in kings, because justice itself is harsh'.[116] Orderic expected high moral standards from kings and did not hesitate to expose their failings. His kings and rulers are a varied group reflecting an underlying truth about kingship, namely that its effectiveness is heavily reliant on individual character. There are heroes and villains among the kings in the *Historia ecclesiastica*. Orderic admired Magnus III 'Barelegs', king of Norway, whom he described as 'physically strong and handsome, brave and generous, active and honourable, and

---

[114] For example, his account of Alfonso I, 'the Battler', King of Aragon (1104–34), was prompted by the expedition of Rotrou of Mortagne to Spain: *HE*, VI, pp. 396–9.

[115] Ibid., pp. 390–3.

[116] *The Etymologies of Isidore of Seville*, trans. Stephen A. Barney, W. J. Lewis, J. A. Beach and Oliver Berghof (Cambridge, 2006), IX, iii, 4–5, p. 200.

outstanding for his integrity'.[117] Magnus had two sons by his lawful wife ('de legali conubio'), Eysteinn and Olaf, and another, Sigurd, with a noble English captive. Sigurd became a crusader and married the daughter of the prince of Kiev on the way home, before eventually succeeding to his father's throne.[118] Orderic devotes considerable space to Magnus's attack on the Irish, doubtless because Normans settled on the Anglo-Welsh frontier became embroiled in the campaign.[119] Orderic suggested that the *casus belli* was Magnus's marriage to a daughter of the Irish king, but war broke out after he had sent her home when her father failed to keep his bargain.[120] Later, Magnus himself met an heroic death standing with his back to a tree, defending himself against the onslaught of 'thousands'.[121]

Although not in Magnus's case, many of the kings Orderic discussed were criticised for sexual impropriety. Their inability to resist the temptations of the flesh was related to their failings in governance, in that a king's control of his own body and its urges became a metaphor for his ability to regulate the body politic.[122] Orderic expected kings to rule effectively and recognised that force was needed to ensure that the vulnerable in society were protected from rapacious barons and their *milites*. However, throughout his *Historia*, Orderic's monastic vocation obliged him to comment on the vanity of the world and the ultimate futility of pursuing earthly glory. Towards the end of Book XIII, Orderic wrote:

> How changeable are the fortunes of this present life! Earthly joys soon pass and vanish in a moment from those who pursue them eagerly. Worldly honour, like a bubble, suddenly bursts and vanishes, humiliating and disappointing those who wish to grasp it for themselves. In this fashion lovers of the world pursue corruptible things, are corrupted as they scale the steep heights of vice, and suddenly fall back to be besmirched in the depths. When with difficulty they laboriously achieve the highest honours and utter empty boasts they are hurled down in a moment, leaving to those who still live and breathe nothing but cautionary tales, which

---

[117] *HE*, V, pp. 218–19: 'Rex enim Magnus erat corpore fortis et formosus, audax et largus, agilis et probus, et multa honestate conspicuus.'

[118] Ibid., pp. 218–21 and n. 3.

[119] Ibid., pp. 220–5.

[120] Ibid., p. 222 n. 1. See also Marritt, 'Crowland Abbey and the Provenance', pp. 290–2.

[121] *HE*, VI, pp. 48–9. Cf. *HE*, V, pp. 218–25.

[122] Tilman Struve, 'The Importance of the Organism in the Political Theory of John of Salisbury' in *The World of John of Salisbury*, ed. M. Wilks (Oxford, 1994), pp. 303–17. C. J. Nederman, 'The Physiological Significance of the Organic Metaphor in John of Salisbury's *Policraticus*', *History of Political Thought* 8:2 (1987), 211–23.

eloquent narrators tell about them in many places. The almighty Creator teaches mortals, driving home the lesson in many ways for their good so that they may not anchor their hopes in the sea of this frail world, or set their hearts on its transient delights and rewards for their destruction. Here, as the apostle says, we have no continuing city, but we seek one to come.[123]

Orderic's expression of *contemptus mundi* suffused his portrayal of kings and rulers in the *Historia*, and his narrative became increasingly apocalyptic in tone as he began to deal with contemporary events, especially the upheavals of Stephen's reign and the violent disturbances in the duchy related to repeated Angevin invasions.[124] In May 1136 the brutality and bloodshed reached the threshold of Orderic's own monastery, and brigands plundered the possessions of the men of Saint-Évroul. Retaliation by the locals only succeeded in provoking an attack from the men of Laigle, kinsmen of the brigands, who set fire to the town of Saint-Évroul, destroying eighty-four houses. Orderic describes the abject fear of his fellow monks that the abbey itself might be destroyed, and he makes clear that it was only a change in the direction of the wind, ascribed to God's mercy, that saved Saint-Évroul's church and monastic buildings together with the monks' books and liturgical vessels.[125]

As Orderic approached his sixty-seventh birthday his world seemed to be falling apart. He saw 'the princes [*optimates*] of this world overwhelmed by misfortunes and disastrous setbacks', and consoled himself by putting his trust in the 'Supreme King':

> What more shall I say? Amid such happenings, almighty God, I appeal to thee, and humbly implore thee in your mercy to pity me. I give thanks to you, supreme King, who freely created me and ordained my life according to your gracious will. For you are my King and my God, and I am your servant and the son of your

---

[123] HE, VI, pp. 476–7: 'Vicissitudines presentis uitæ quam mutabiles sunt. Secularia gaudia cito transeunt, eosque a quibus summopere affectantur in puncto deserunt. Mundanus honor instar bullæ subito crepat ac deficit, sibique inhiantibus insultat atque decipit. Amatores mundi sic corruptibilia sequuntur, sic per abruta uiciorum gradientes corrumpuntur, subitoque sordentes in ima labuntur. Et dum sullimes fastus laboriose uix adipiscuntur inde nequicquam tumentes in momento precipitantur, et concinnæ solummodo narrationes inter residuos qui uitalibus auris perfruuntur, ab eloquentibus de illis passim sparguntur. Omnipotens itaque creator terrigenas instruit, et pluribus modis salubriter erudit, ne in hoc fragilis seculi pelago anchoram suæ spei figant, neque transitoriis delectationibus siue lucris letaliter inhereant. Non habemus hic manentem ciuitatem ut dicit apostolus sed futuram inquirimus.'

[124] Ibid., pp. 458–9, 490–5; cf. pp. 528–9.

[125] Ibid., pp. 460–3.

handmaid, one who from the beginning of my life has served you as far as I was able.[126]

In the last few years of his life Orderic witnessed the unedifying spectacle of Normandy's descent into chaos as magnates supporting either King Stephen or his rivals (Geoffrey, count of Anjou, and his wife, Matilda) devastated the countryside, defiled churches and oppressed the defenceless. It would be surprising if these events had not had a significant effect on Orderic's representation of secular rulers and their abilities. As the war between Stephen and the Angevins unfolded, Orderic began to intervene in his own narrative, pointing out what King Stephen *should* have done and the abject folly of what he actually did. This is seen clearly in Orderic's account of the arrival in England of Matilda, countess of Anjou, and her half-brother Robert, Earl of Gloucester, in the autumn of 1139.[127] Stephen allowed Matilda and her retinue to travel peacefully between the castles held by her supporters, and Orderic noted that:

> In granting this licence the king showed himself either very guileless or very foolish, and prudent men must deplore his lack of regard for both his own safety and the security of the kingdom. *He could easily have stamped out* the flames of terrible evil that were being kindled if he had acted with the foresight characteristic of wise men and had immediately driven off the wolf from the entrance to the sheepfold; and if, after saving the sheep, he had nipped the malevolence of trouble-makers in the bud and had struck down with the sword of justice, after the fashion of his ancestors, the pestilential strength of those who desired rapine and slaughter and the devastation of their country, and so brought down destruction on their heads.[128]

---

[126] Ibid., pp. 552–3 and n. 1: 'Quid amplius dicam? Inter haec omnipotens Deus eloquium meum ad te conuerto, et clementiam tuam ut mei miserearis suppliciter exoro. Tibi gratias ago summe rex qui me gratis fecisti, et annos meos secundum beneplacitam uoluntatem tuam disposuisti. Tu es enim rex meus et Deus meus, et ego sum seruus tuus et ancillæ tuæ filius qui pro posse meo a primis tibi uitæ meæ seruiui diebus.' There are echoes of Psalm 116 here. Cf. *HE*, VI, pp. 528–9.

[127] Ibid., pp. 534–5. Orderic also criticises the '*obstinatus princeps*' for turning 'a deaf ear to the advice of prudent men' before the Battle of Lincoln: ibid., pp. 540–3.

[128] Ibid., pp. 534–5 (emphasis added): 'In hac nimirum permissione magna regis simplicitas siue socordia notari potest, et ipse a prudentibus quod suæ salutis regnique sui securitatis immemor fuerit lugendus est. Ingens enim nimiæ malitiæ fomentum facile tunc extinguere potuisset, si calliditatem sapientum imitatus lupum ab introitu ouilis statim expulisset, si saluatis ouibus malignantium nequitiam in ipso initio preoccupasset, et uires letiferas in capitibus eorum qui rapinas et cedes hominum patriæque depopulationem querebant gladio iustitiæ more patrum præsecuisset.' Cf.

Not only does this passage suggest mounting frustration with the king at his inability to act decisively, it also indicates Orderic's growing impatience with political ineptitude and the misery it brought. He had levelled these criticisms and others at Robert Curthose in sections of the *Historia* written during the later years of Henry I's reign, a reign which, in Orderic's opinion, had provided much-missed security for Normandy.[129]

For Orderic, the Normans were responsible for their own misfortunes, but if only they would 'live according to the law of God [*secundum legem Dei*] and be united under a good prince [*sub bono principe*] they would be as invincible as were the Chaldeans under Nebuchadnezzar and the Persians and Medes under Cyrus and Darius and the Macedonians under Alexander'.[130] The real villains of the last book of the *Historia ecclesiastica* were the magnates of Normandy and England. Writing in the aftermath of Stephen's capture at the Battle of Lincoln, Orderic voiced the sorrow of clerks, monks and simple people at the capture of one who 'was humble and kind to men who were good and meek'.[131] He had no doubt that without the villainous machinations of the 'dolosi optimates' ('deceitful nobles'), Stephen 'would have been an open-handed and benevolent protector of his country'.[132]

It was obvious to Orderic that, faced with the turmoil of the late 1130s, earthly kings could not guarantee peace and order. In this context it was entirely appropriate for Orderic to begin his *Historia* with a life of the King of Kings, a reminder to his audience that there was an alternative to the weaknesses of worldly princes.[133] Henry I's death brought widespread civil disturbance in Normandy, and Orderic's verse eulogy for the dead king, the 'peace lover' and 'the Church's guardian' ended with a prayer:

> O Christ, give us a leader who will love peace and justice
> And preserve them, and lead back your people to you.
> Smite the backs of the turbulent with the rod of justice
> That your people might render you service in safety. Amen forever.[134]

M. Chibnall, *The Empress Matilda* (Oxford, 1991), pp. 80–1; E. King, *King Stephen* (New Haven and London, 2010), pp. 115–18 and 325–6.

[129] *HE*, VI, pp. 472–3. Writing after Henry I's death, Orderic characterised his reign as a period of strong government for Normandy: ibid., pp. 98–101. Cf. ibid., pp. 228–9, for Normandy under Robert Curthose.

[130] *HE*, VI, pp. 456–7.

[131] Ibid., pp. 544–5: 'Infortunium regis luctum peperit clericis et monachis populisque simplicibus, quia idem rex humilis et mansuetus erat bonis ac mitibus.'

[132] Ibid., pp. 544–5.

[133] Ibid., I, pp. 134–50.

[134] Ibid., VI, pp. 452–3: 'Christe ducem prebe qui pacem iusticiamque/ Diligat ac teneat, populumque tuum tibi ducat./ Iusticiæ uirga turgentum percute dorsa/ Vt secura tibi tua plebs posit famulari. Semper Amen.'

In essence, for Orderic, a king's duty was to lead his people towards their Creator. That so many kings were morally incapable of doing so is the tragedy at the heart of Orderic's work. At the end of Book VII, after describing the Conqueror's funeral, Orderic expatiated on the vanity of worldly glory. Contemplating the image of the decaying corpse of the Conqueror, Orderic observed:

> Rich and poor are of the same nature; both alike fall victim to death and decay. Therefore 'put not your trust in false princes', O sons of men, but in the true and living God, who is the creator of all things. Meditate on the books of the Old and New Testament, and from them heap up examples to teach you what to shun and what to pursue. Trust not in oppression and become not vain in robbery. If riches increase, set not your heart upon them. For all flesh is grass, and all the goodliness thereof is as the flower of grass. The grass withers and the flower thereof fails, but the word of the Lord shall stand forever.[135]

Orderic's representation of kingship in the *Historia ecclesiastica* was shaped by the moral didacticism of his monastic understanding of the ethical purpose of historiography.[136] Even strong and effective rulers had their faults and, ultimately, his advice echoed that of the Psalmist:

> Do not put your trust in princes, in human beings, who cannot save. When their spirit departs, they return to the ground; on that very day their plans come to nothing.[137]

---

[135] Ibid., IV, pp. 108–9, and nn. 1–3: 'Diuitis et pauperis par est conditio, et similiter ambos inuadit mors et putredo. Nolite ergo confidere in principibus falsis O filii hominum; sed in Deo uiuo et uero qui creator est omnium. Veteris et noui testamenti seriem reuoluite, et exempla inde multiplicia uobis capessite; quid cauere quidue debeatis appetere. Nolite sperare in iniquitate, et rapinas nolite concupiscere. Diuitiæ si affluant; nolite cor apponere. Omnis enim caro ut fœnum; et omnis Gloria eius ut flos fœni. Exaruit fœnum et flos eius decidit; uerbum autem Domini manet in æternum.'

[136] Cf. Sigbjørn Olsen Sønnesyn, *William of Malmesbury and the Ethics of History* (Woodbridge, 2012).

[137] Psalm 146:3–4.

Worldly Woe and Heavenly Joy: The Tone of the *Historia ecclesiastica*

Emily Albu

THE last conversation I had with Marjorie Chibnall left me unsettled. We were talking, of course, about Orderic Vitalis, and she was questioning the conclusions in my book on Norman historians. There I had written that Orderic's 'experiences as a resident in what was essentially a Norman war zone on the duchy's southern frontier, and as an acute student of the Normans' – a treacherous people prone to violence against friends and family – 'left him especially world-weary.'[1] Orderic's *Historia ecclesiastica* seemed to show persistent signs of the author's fatigue, pessimism, and depression. Not that anyone could blame him for that, given the world in which he lived. But Chibnall thought me mistaken. Orderic's faith and the satisfying rhythms of his monastic devotion, she suggested, guided him to a mature and balanced sensibility.

Chibnall knew Orderic and his *Historia ecclesiastica* better than any other reader of our age. Had I misinterpreted his work and done a disservice to its author? The Durham conference and this collection of essays have offered the welcome opportunity to reread the history with a fresh mind and make a fresh judgement, asking finally what difference tone makes in our understanding of the historian and the history he was recording and interpreting.

Orderic's earliest forays into historical writing offer tantalising signs of the direction he would take. Perhaps as early as 1095, when he was barely twenty years old, Orderic began his redaction of William of Jumièges' *Gesta Normannorum ducum*, completing most of the manuscript by 1109 and adding his final interpolation in (or after) 1113.[2] This task, along with compiling the *Annals of Saint-Évroul* and copying Bede's *Historia ecclesiastica*, trained Orderic to write history. By 1114, he was at work on his own *Historia ecclesiastica*.

Even as he copied William of Jumièges' *Gesta*, Orderic altered the tenor of that history by adding details that darkened its tone. Some are quite brief, like the three words asserting that the French king Louis IV died

---

[1] Albu, *Normans in their Histories*, p. 180; and see p. 6.
[2] *GND*, I, p. lxviii. E. M. C. van Houts, 'Quelques remarques sur les interpolations attribués à Orderic Vital dans les *Gesta Normannorum Ducum* de Guillaume de Jumièges', *Revue d'histoire des textes* 8 (1978), 213–22.

'after many sufferings' ('post multos merores').[3] Such a slight insertion might barely register on the reader's consciousness. Yet as these bleak notices accumulate, they make their mark. Consider, for instance, Orderic's new chapters on the turmoil caused by criminals who appropriated the church of St Gervais as a storehouse for their loot. For Orderic, the episode illustrated the omnipresence of evil in the world and the eternal damnation that awaits the wicked.[4] While the benevolent and 'very good humoured' Ivo, bishop of Séez, 'longed for quiet and peaceful times', Orderic wrote, he found his see rocked by the disturbances of robbers and plunderers. 'For the perfidy of the evildoers does not cease to disturb the calm of the good.'[5] The violent deaths of the perpetrators, 'killed by God's just judgement without the blessing of a last confession or the viaticum', inspired Orderic to add a grim warning:

> Behold, how these events fulfil the truth which we are told in the letters of St Paul the Apostle: 'Anyone who destroys God's temple will himself be destroyed by God.' [I Corinthians 3:17] May robbers and desecrators of churches, having thus heard about these deaths, take care that they avoid similar crimes, for else in the end they will suffer similar punishments; and even, if secular prosperity is their part a little longer, they shall not triumph in the security they derive from it. It is good for them to know that worldly pleasure evaporates as quickly as smoke and results in everlasting grief. Or, as one eminent poet declares, attacking the impious:
>
>> You are wrong to rejoice, for in the end
>> The fruit of wickedness will be your part:
>> Darkness, flames and lamentation –
>> God, merciful indulger, as a just avenger
>> Guards what is his and punishes evil.[6]

---

[3] *GND*, I, pp. 118–19.

[4] *GND*, II, pp. 112–15.

[5] Ibid., pp. 112–13: 'Sagax enim idem erat ac decorus, et affabilis multumque iocosus, ac serene pacis cupidus. Sed perfidia malorum non cessat perturbare quietem bonorum.'

[6] Ibid., pp. 116–17: 'Ecce in his uere completum uidimus, quod in epistolis beati Pauli apostoli audiuimus: "Si quis templum Dei uiolauerit, disperdet illum Deus." Raptores ergo et fractores ecclesiarum sui similium interitum comperto caueant, ne, dum, similia perpetrant, simili punitione tandem pereant, et si mundana prosperitas paululum eis comitatur, non inde securi glorientur. Illis nimirum scire conuenit, quod mundi gaudium quasi fumus ad modicum transit, ac permansurum merorem adquirit, ceu quidam egregius in poemate suo impios arguens uersificator ait:

Vos male gaudietis, quia tandem suscipietis/ Nequitie fructum, tenebras, incendia, luctum,/ Nanque pius dultur iustusque tamen Deus ultor/ Que sua sunt munit, que sunt hostilia punit.'

Orderic found evil not only present in human society but also lurking in wild places, like the spot to which Lombards lured Thurstan Scitel, the first Norman mercenary to seek his fortune in Apulia.[7] There Thurstan met an enormous flame-throwing dragon nestled in a den of snakes. Before the dragon fell by the hero's sword, the beast's fiery breath incinerated Thurstan's shield, inflicting damage that ultimately proved deadly.[8] This episode looks ahead to the haunting elements of epic and romance that would lend a sense of foreboding to sections of Orderic's *Historia ecclesiastica*.

Orderic's interpolations into William's history especially reveal a young man turning a critical eye on the Normans and their capacity for creating mayhem. His very first insertion anticipates that tendency, as he emended the rubric found at the conclusion of William's Book I: William's 'Explicit de origine Dacorum et eorum pressuris liber primus', in Orderic's version reads, 'Explicit liber primus de Normannorum crudelitate qua Neustria grauiter oppressa est.' In place of a rather vague summation – 'Here ends the first book, on the origin of the Dacians [Danes] and their afflictions' – Orderic has substituted a bold indictment: 'Here ends the first book on the cruelty of the Northmen [Normans], by which Neustria was violently crushed.'[9] Orderic's substitution of 'Normanni' for 'Daci', furthermore, explicitly links the Normans to their brutal ancestry as Viking marauders. William of Jumièges would not refer to the assailing 'Dani' as 'Normanni' until ii.10(16), with the final attack of Rollo's army against the Franks, immediately preceding Rollo's conversion and the treaty that created the origins of Normandy.[10]

As Orderic's additions become longer and more frequent, they feature the foul deeds of Norman magnates whose penchant for evil passed from one generation to the next. Wherever he could, Orderic found examples of divine retribution for their sins, as when Warin, the eldest son of the 'very cruel and ambitious' William I of Bellême, 'became possessed by a demon and choked to death' after he 'without any reason had cruelly decapitated Gonthier of Bellême, a good and friendly soldier who had not suspected any harm but on the contrary had smiled at him and greeted him in a friendly fashion'.[11] Warin's brother Robert, 'the heir to William of Bellême's power and to his cruelty', likewise wreaked havoc on his neighbours until his capture, imprisonment, and 'miserable death' ('miserabiliter occidunt'),

---

[7] Ibid., pp. 156–7.

[8] Ibid.

[9] My translation. See *GND*, I, p. xxxvi, for the names of these peoples.

[10] Ibid., pp. 62–7.

[11] *GND*, II, pp. 50–1: 'Multum quippe crudelis et cupidus erat [...] postquam Gunherium de Belismo militem bonum et amabilem, qui nil mali suspicabatur, sed potius ei ridens ut amico congratulabatur, sine causa capite crudeliter priuauerat.'

his head shattered with axes at the hands of kinsmen avenging the hanging of their own father and brothers by Robert's men.[12] After Robert's murder, 'his brother William Talvas succeeded him in their father's honour. In everything shameful he was worse than his brothers and the same boundless wickedness has flourished to this day among his heirs.'[13]

In his turn, Arnulf, son of William Talvas, exiled his father.[14] 'Though he took his father's property he did not avoid his father's wickedness and therefore his wretched death was well deserved.'[15] Robbing a nun of her pig, he ignored the nun's tears and pleas for the pig's return, instead ordering the animal to be slaughtered and cooked. Late in the evening, Arnulf ate his fill of pork, 'but not with impunity' ('Sed non impune'). That very night he was strangled in his bed.

Perhaps the worst offender in this troublesome family, in Orderic's additions, was Arnulf's sister Mabel of Bellême, who somehow raised kindly daughters but, more predictably, reared horrendous sons. These men 'were dangerous, greedy and like madmen they harmed the poor'.[16] 'It is not our task', Orderic added here, 'to describe how cunning, warlike, and perfidious they were, how frequently they rebelled against their neighbours and peers and how deeply they sank below them because of their wickedness.'[17] Orderic would save those details for the *Historia ecclesiastica*.[18]

For Orderic, the Bellême kinsmen frighteningly represented the chaotic impulses that he saw as the Norman legacy. Like Mabel's surprisingly pious daughters, even some of the Bellême men could lead holy lives. Albert of Bellême became a monk of Jumièges and eventually served as abbot of Saint-Mesmin-de-Micy. The kindly Ivo, bishop of Séez, who yearned for a just and tranquil world was in fact Ivo III of Bellême, son of William I of Bellême and so the brother of the notorious Robert and William Talvas and the uncle of Arnulf, thief of the nun's pig.[19] Other Norman magnates

---

[12] Ibid., pp. 56–7: 'Rodbertus, Willelmi Belesmensis potestatis heres et crudelitatis.'

[13] Ibid.: 'Quo defuncto Willelmus Talauacius, frater eius, successit in honore paterno. Ipse cunctis fratribus suis in omnibus flagitiis deterior fuit, et in seminis heredibus immoderate nequitia usque hodie uiguit.'

[14] Ibid., pp. 113–14.

[15] Ibid., pp. 112–13: 'Paternam quidem possessionem inuasit, sed nequiciam non deuitauit, unde tristi fine perire meruit.'

[16] Ibid., pp. 118–19: 'Illi uero ferales et cupidi ac inopum rabidi oppressores extiterunt.'

[17] Ibid.: 'Quam callidi uel militares seu perfidi fuerint, aut quantum super uicinos paresque suos excreuerint, iterumque sub eis pro facinoribus suis deciderint, non est nostrum in hoc loco enarrare.'

[18] Ibid., p. 119; *HE*, II, p. 48, III, pp. 134–8.

[19] *GND*, II, p. 113 n. 5.

remained in the secular realm yet still 'loved God and justice' ('Quidam optimatum qui Deum et iustitiam amant') and loyally served their duke.[20] But most, like the rebels who harried the duchy in William the Conqueror's day, were in the mould of Mabel and her brother Arnulf. 'The sons of disorder, who rejoice in dissension and who do their utmost to afflict those who wish to live in peace, saw that they could not harm the ordinary people as much as they would like.' So they meditated on the country's ruin, killing the friends and protectors of the young Duke William and colluding with the French king, 'and scattered his firebrands here and there along the border of Normandy'.[21] Writing later in Duke William's lifetime, William of Jumièges only dared whisper to his intimates that these men still held power, feigning loyalty to the duke.[22] Decades after those events, from the security of his monastery, Orderic could name the culprits.[23]

William of Jumièges' *Gesta* ended with the seventh book, on the reign of Duke William from the troubled years of his minority in Normandy to his conquest of England and suppression of rebellions there. Robert of Torigni would add an eighth book, taking the *Gesta* through the generation after the Conqueror, but Orderic kept the history's original structure while inserting a great deal throughout William of Jumièges' final book, much of it countering the *Gesta*'s generally positive tone. Although the passage of time certainly freed Orderic to offer information too delicate for the Conqueror's contemporaries to record, his additions suggest a further impulse, signified by a notable willingness to supply details embarrassing to Duke William. Arguably the most sensitive of these concern the duke's illegitimacy: he was called the Bastard, since he was the child of Duke Robert's concubine, Herleva, and not the offspring of a sanctified Christian marriage. Orderic first hinted at the irregularity of William's birth by adding 'apud Falesiam' (born 'at Falaise') to his narrative account of Duke Robert's departure on pilgrimage to Jerusalem. William of Jumièges stressed Robert's insistence in presenting his 'only son' as heir to the duchy.[24] Orderic's slight insertion offers the alert reader a curious detail, suggesting a wrinkle suppressed in William's narrative: the child was born at some distance from the ducal residence in Rouen. In the next book, Orderic addressed the matter directly by explaining the pretext for rebellions against the young duke, reporting the protests of

---

[20] Ibid., pp. 98–9.

[21] Ibid.: 'Porro filii discordie, qui dissensionibus gaudent, et innocenter uiuere uolentes affligere student, dum per se tantum nocere simplicibus quantum uellent se non posse uident [...] Henricum igitur regem Francorum adeunt, et ticiones eius per Normannicos limites hac illacque spargunt.'

[22] Ibid.

[23] Ibid., pp. 92–7; p. lxxi notes that Orderic here, 'in a moment of inconsistency', repeats William's unwillingness to provide those names.

[24] Ibid., pp. 80–1: 'Exponens autem eis Wilelmum suum filium.'

his kinsman, Roger of Tosny, who expressed outrage that the child should inherit lands and authority:

> Upon hearing that the young William had succeeded his father in the duchy, he became very indignant and arrogantly refused to serve him, saying that as a bastard William should not rule him and the other Normans. William was the son of Herleva, concubine of Duke Robert and daughter of Fulbert, chamberlain of the duke, and as a bastard was despised by the native nobility and especially by the descendants of the dukes Richard.[25]

Before Orderic wrote this no historian had named Herleva as the mother of Duke Robert's son.[26] Neither William of Jumièges nor his contemporary, William of Poitiers, had even mentioned the child's problematic status as an illegitimate child.

Orderic went further by filling in the blanks to explain a curious episode at the duke's siege of Alençon sometime during the battles that raged in southern Normandy in the years 1047–52, as Duke William fought Count Geoffrey of Anjou.[27] William of Jumièges had discreetly omitted the precise taunts hurled down against Duke William by the men in a fortification defending besieged Alençon, though the duke's brutal punishment of the mockers – he ordered their hands and feet to be cut off – suggests that their ridicule had offended him deeply. Orderic was first to supply the details:

> Thus, without delay, as he had ordered, thirty-two men were maimed. For they had beaten pelts and furs in order to insult the duke and despisingly had called him pelterer because his mother's parents had prepared corpses for burial.[28]

In Orderic's world, where lineage meant a great deal, William's maternal line was a source of humiliation. While other historians of the Normans passed over the duke's illegitimate birth and the resulting charges opposing his authority, Orderic did not shrink from recording that information.

---

[25] Ibid., pp. 94–7: 'Comperiens autem quod Willelmus puer in ducatu patri successerit, uehementer indignatus et tumide despexit illi seruire, dicens quod nothus non deberet sibi aliisque Normannis imperare. Willelmus enim ex concubina Rodberti ducis nomine Herleua, Fulberti cubicularii ducis filia natus, nobilibus indigenis et maxime ex Ricardorum prosapia natis despectui erat utpote nothus'.

[26] GND, I, p. lxxv. For perceptive observations on Orderic's interpolations on William the Conqueror, the Conquest, and the English, see ibid., pp. lxxi–lxxv.

[27] GND, II, pp. 122–3 n. 4.

[28] Ibid., pp. 124–5: 'Nec mora sicut iusserat triginta duo debilitati sunt. Pelles enim et renones ad iniuriam ducis uerberauerant ipsumque pelliciarium despectiue uocitauerant eo quod parentes matris eius pollinctores extiterant.'

Traces of Orderic's ambivalent or even hostile attitude towards William neither begin nor end with commentary on the duke's embarrassing ancestry. As Elisabeth van Houts has noted, as early as Book IV of the *Gesta* Orderic changed William of Jumièges' 'our duke' to an impersonal 'the duke'.²⁹ With Duke William's assault on Orderic's boyhood homeland, Orderic's long and frequent interpolations invite a critique of the victor at Hastings and of the disruptive Normans whom William's conquest thrust upon the English. So, as the battle ended with a rout of the English forces, Orderic introduced the episode in which victorious Normans, armed and mounted as they chased down the fleeing Englishmen, collided with an ancient rampart and 'fell, one on top of the other, thus crushing each other to death'.³⁰ To be sure, Orderic directly followed this with the pronouncement that God had also punished the English that day for their collective sins, for the merciless slaughter of Earl Tostig and King Harold of Norway, and of so many others in the battle just ended, and especially for the murder of the innocent Alfred Aetheling, whose assassination offered a pretext for the Norman invasion. Yet Orderic concluded this chapter with a compelling indictment of the Normans, who were in his view clearly the more grievous offenders in God's eyes:

> The following night the same Judge avenged the English and plunged the fierce Normans into the Abyss of destruction. For they had been guilty of coveting the goods of other men contrary to the precept of the law, and as the Psalmist says: 'Their feet were swift to shed blood' and so they encountered grief and wretchedness in their ways.³¹

Immediately after this passage added by Orderic, the *Gesta*'s original text by William of Jumièges continues its generally pro-Conquest version of events, opening with the words 'Fortissimus igitur dux': 'The most valiant duke returned from the slaughter of his enemy to the battlefield at midnight.' Orderic did not let this language stand, downgrading 'fortissimus' to 'fortis' and omitting subsequent authentication of the Conqueror's royal claim, which included the Londoners' acknowledgment of William as their 'hereditary lord ('hereditario domino').³² Likewise, Orderic reduced the *Gesta*'s celebratory account of the duke's coronation

---

²⁹ GND, I, p. lxx.
³⁰ GND, II, pp. 168–9: 'ac sese, dum unus repente super alterum cadebat, uicissim extinguebant'.
³¹ Ibid., pp. 170–1: 'Idem quoque iudex sequenti nocte Anglos uindicauit et furentes Normannos in cecam uoraginem precipitauit. Ipsi enim contra preceptum legis rem alienam immoderate concupierunt ac ueloces, ut psalmographus dicit, "pedes eorum ad effundendum sanguinem fuerunt". Ideoque contricionem et infelicitatem in uiis suis offenderunt.'
³² Ibid.: 'Fortissimus igitur dux ab inimicorum strage reuersus nocte media ad campum belli est regressus.' See also Elisabeth van Houts's notes at pp. 170–1, and her commentary at GND, I, p. lxxiv.

as king of England to fewer and more sober words, 'removing pro-Norman sentiments'.[33] He revealed his English sympathies with the elimination of the adjective 'treacherous' ('perfidos') in assessing the men who rebelled, unsuccessfully, against Norman control of Dover. Just as Orderic's very first small insertion had implicated the Normans in the predations of their Viking ancestors, so his final interpolation suggests that the apparent calm in England following the Norman Conquest would not last. Accordingly, he inserted a single word, 'parumper' ('for a while'), into a sentence proclaiming the quieting 'storms of wars and rebellions' (bellorum ac seditionum tempestate').[34] Orderic's Gesta would not end with a triumphant promise of peace.

Sympathies with his childhood home in England, where he must have learned about the trauma of conquest and its aftermath, surely informed the attitude of Orderic the young adult and historian apprentice.[35] His experiences living among fractious Normans who disturbed the lands near his Norman monastery would only have darkened his worldview further. Two brief interpolations mirror a specific moment that disrupted Orderic's own boyhood, an event that left an indelible impression and forever shaped the way he experienced his own life and interpreted the lives of others. In those two passages Orderic amplified accounts of boys imperilled because they found themselves alone, without protectors.

The first of these incidents marks Orderic's earliest significant change in the Gesta's text.[36] Up to this point he had faithfully copied the words of William of Jumièges. But here a memory seems to have moved him to supplement the speech of Theobald I, count of Blois, Chartres, and Tours, as Theobald contrived to trick the Viking Hasting into selling him the town of Chartres and fleeing Theobald's lands. William of Jumièges had the count persuade Hasting that the French king would destroy him if he lingered:

> Do you not know that King Charles desired your death on account of the Christian blood you have shed in the past? For he remembers the enormous crimes you then inflicted upon him and has therefore determined to expel you from his country.[37]

In place of '[the crimes] you then inflicted upon him' Orderic has expressly taken the narrative deeper into the mind and imagined memories of King Charles:

[33] GND, II, p. 172 n. 1.

[34] Ibid., pp. 182–3.

[35] On the emotional impact suffered by the English, see Elisabeth van Houts, 'The Trauma of 1066', History Today 46:10 (October 1996), 9–15.

[36] GND, I, pp. 56–7.

[37] Ibid.: 'Ignoras regem Karolum te uelle morte oppetere ob Christianorum sanguinem a te olim fusum iniuste? Reminiscitur enim malorum que illi tunc improbe intulisti et ideo de terra te exterminare decreuit.'

For he remembers the enormous crimes *you and your men inflicted upon him while he was still a boy deprived of a guardian, and his men quarrelled among themselves.*[38]

Orderic has even changed William's 'intulisti' ('you caused' or 'you brought against') to the charged 'intorsisti', with its root in torture and the rack.

These are strong words, not taken from Dudo and not retained by Robert of Torigni.[39] They seem to come, rather, from Orderic's own sense of what the king must have experienced. Unlike Robert, who added many tales from Dudo's *De moribus* into the early books of his own copy of the *Gesta*, Orderic in fact took little from Dudo's imaginative history. Yet he did borrow a slight detail from Dudo's account of the aftermath of William Longsword's assassination, when the French king Louis IV took Longsword's son in his arms to display him before the people of Rouen and to mollify them with promises that he would safeguard and nurture the child, Longsword's heir and the future Duke Richard I.[40] Here Orderic has drawn from Dudo the report that the king was acting 'on the advice of Bernard the Dane' ('consilio Bernardi Dacigene') when he performed that gesture of protection and good will.[41] This rare borrowing shows Orderic paying close attention to the account of an orphaned boy in foreign hands and dangerous circumstances. As we turn now to Orderic's *Historia ecclesiastica*, we will see why the childhood perils of a French king and a Norman duke, both bereft of a father's protection, would have especially moved the young monk.

As he neared the end of his life, while concluding the final book of his masterwork,[42] Orderic paused to remember how his own father cut him off when he was only a ten-year-old boy, sending him from his English homeland across the Channel to Normandy, to live among strangers who spoke an alien language. As I have discussed elsewhere, even when Orderic exonerated his father as promising in God's name 'that if I became a monk I should taste of the joys of Paradise with the Innocent after my death', he coloured this moment with the language of grief and the haunting sense of abandonment:[43]

---

[38] Ibid.: 'Reminiscitur enim malorum, que illi, dum adhuc puer erat et suis inter se dissidentibus adiutore carebat, cum tuis improbe intorsisti.'

[39] GND, I, p. 57 n. 2.

[40] Dudo of Saint-Quentin, *De moribus et actis primorum Normanniae ducum, auctore Dudone Sancti Quintini decano*, ed. Jules Lair (Caen, 1865), p. 225.

[41] GND, I, pp. 100–1.

[42] HE, VI, pp. 552–5.

[43] Albu, *Normans in their Histories*, p. xx. On the relationship between Orderic and his father, Odelerius, see van Houts, above: 'Orderic and his father, Odelerius'.

And so, glorious God, who commanded Abraham to depart from his homeland and kin and father's house, you inspired my father Odelerius to renounce me entirely and to bind me completely to you. So, weeping, he handed me over, a weeping child, to the monk Rainald, and bound me over into exile for love of you, and he did not see me ever again. [...] So I left behind my homeland and parents and every relative and intimates and friends. And they weeping and wishing me well, commended me with kind prayers to you, almighty God.[44]

This fateful moment, I think, led the young Orderic to pay special attention to young men cut adrift without familial protection as he copied and supplemented the *Gesta* of William of Jumièges. When he imagined a deathbed speech for William the Conqueror in the *Historia ecclesiastica*,[45] Orderic wrote an affecting apologia for the old king, whose own father, Duke Robert, had abandoned the eight-year-old boy to go on pilgrimage to the Holy Land, never to return. In words designed to inspire the reader's sympathy – 'I was a tender little boy, only eight years old' ('tenellus eram puer utpote octo annorum') – Orderic lets the old king interpret his many acts of violence as a natural response to a childhood of treachery and terror, during which his kin repeatedly betrayed him and even attempted his murder. Though Orderic's paternal abandonment had a very different context – his father did not ride far away to save his own soul but instead sent his son to the physical security and promised salvation of the monastic life – Orderic connected the two events by writing of both in the first person, with similar language and emotional resonance. Orderic inserted long speeches into his history perhaps more often than any other medieval historian, often using them to 'express ideas and views that Orderic held as his own', as he does in giving the Conqueror the following famous assessment of the Normans (also in his deathbed speech): unless restrained by a strong hand, 'they maul and devour one another, for they long for rebellions, hanker after seditions, and are ready for every abomination'.[46]

---

[44] *HE*, VI, pp. 552–5: 'Iccirco gloriose Deus qui Abraham de terra patrisque domo et cognatione egredi iussisti, Odelerium patrem meum aspirasti ut me sibi penitus abdicaret, et tibi omnimodis subiugaret. Rainaldo igitur monacho plorans plorantem me tradidit, et pro amore tuo in exilium destinauit, nec me unquam postea uidit [...] Gratanter facta inter me et te genitore meo proloquente conuentione huiuscemodi, patriam et parentes omnemque cognationem et notos amicos reliqui, qui lacrimantes et salutantes benignis precibus commendauerunt me tibi O summe Deus Adonai.'

[45] *HE*, IV, pp. 80–95.

[46] Ibid., pp. 82–3: 'Alioquin sese uicissim dilaniant atque consumunt; rebelliones enim cupiunt, seditiones appetunt, et ad omne nefas prompti sunt.' John O. Ward, 'Ordericus Vitalis as Historian in the Europe of the

As we shall soon see, another impulse might also have impelled Orderic to identify with the Conqueror and give him this extraordinary speech. Consider how Orderic casually identified William as the Bastard at the very beginning of Book III, the first book he wrote: Orderic records that his masters had charged him with writing about the Normans, who 'up to the time of William the Bastard devoted themselves to war rather than reading or writing books'.[47] The reminder of the duke's illegitimacy seems jarring in Orderic's *Historia ecclesiastica*, which presents the Bastard with virtues and crimes neatly balanced, a pious patron of the Church who was also a murderer of innocents.[48] In inventing a deathbed speech for the old king, Orderic imagined a sad and desperate apologia that evokes sympathy, and even excused William's cruelties on the grounds that kinsmen had bullied, harassed and threatened him when he was an abandoned child. Specifically, Orderic has William recall the humiliation and danger he suffered as a bastard, whose illegitimate birth left him especially vulnerable. His own cousin Guy, William cries, 'called me a bastard and cursed me as low-born and unfit to rule'.[49] A few years later two of William's uncles, another William and Mauger, archbishop of Rouen, justified rebellion against the boy by levelling a similar charge. 'They belittled me', the king laments again, 'calling me a bastard.'[50]

These accusations may have resonated personally with Orderic, for Chibnall suggested that Orderic might have had reason to question his own legitimacy.[51] In a close reading of Orderic's account of his father's renunciation, she noted that he used the rare word 'abdicare' twice in the passage recalling his father's sending him away to Saint-Évroul. Orderic would have found this word in Bede's *Historia ecclesiastica*, which he had copied, knew intimately, and viewed as a model for his own work. 'In particular', Chibnall noted, 'Bede used it to tell how King Eadbald renounced his unlawful wife after his conversion to Christianity. Odelerius's act of renunciation may have been similarly inspired; the language of his son suggests that he at least linked the two.'[52] Orderic's writings contain no mention of his mother, who was presumably an

Early Twelfth-Century Renaissance', *Parergon* 31:1 (2014), 1–26, at pp. 10 and 13.

[47] *HE*, II, p. 2: 'usque ad Guillelmi nothi, tempora magis bellare quam legere uel dictare laborauerunt'.

[48] See for instance *HE*, II, pp. 231–9, for a reckoning of both extremes.

[49] *HE*, IV, pp. 82–3: 'me nothum degeneremque et principatu indignum detestatus indicauit'.

[50] Ibid., pp. 84–5: 'me uelut nothum contempserunt'.

[51] Chibnall, *World*, pp. 9–10.

[52] Chibnall here cites Bede, *The Ecclesiastical History of the English People*, ed. Bertram Colgrave and R. A. B. Mynors, Oxford Medieval Texts (Oxford, 1969), p. 154.

English woman. Yet his vocabulary of abandonment hints at what Chibnall viewed as Odelerius's 'unease' at his own marriage. Had Odelerius repudiated Orderic's mother as he advanced toward higher spirituality or aspired to higher ecclesiastical honours? If this is so, the son's language implies that, on some level, he tied this act to his father's exiling him from the family fold. If Odelerius was renouncing an unlawful marriage and exiling a son from that union, Orderic's words hint at worries that his own legitimacy was at stake. Did he fret that he himself was in some sense, like the king, a bastard?

Although Orderic never mentioned his English mother in any of his extant writings, another of his long speeches shows how keenly he identified with her people and his boyhood home. When the newly victorious William offers the monk Guitmund promotion over the English monks, Guitmund declines: he tells William he will not accept authority over those whose language and customs he does not understand, and 'whose beloved ancestors and friends you have either put to the sword, driven into bitter exile, or unjustly imprisoned or enslaved'.[53] Chastising the newly crowned king for riding roughshod over the conquered land as if it were 'the spoils of robbery' ('amplissimam praedam'), the monk displays Orderic's historical learning by reciting in some detail the ages of conquerors past – the Babylonians and Persians, Greeks and Romans – who now burn in the depths of Hell. According to Guitmund, this fate awaits William as well, unless he curbs his pride and wages 'the more dangerous battle against the evils of the spirit'.[54] Like their haughty predecessors, the Normans, too, from the Viking Rollo to his descendant William, have enjoyed a moment of worldly glory, challenged by warriors who were their equals in ferocity.

> What shall I say of the Gepids and Vandals, Goths and Turks, Huns and Heruli and other barbarians whose only thought is to plunder and ravage and destroy in despite of peace? They disturb the land, burn houses, harass old and young, destroy prosperity, butcher men, spread ruin and trouble everywhere.[55]

For Orderic's mouthpiece, Guitmund, the millennial implications are clear:

---

[53] *HE*, II, pp. 272–3: 'quorum patres karosque parentes et amicos occidistis gladio uel exhæredatos opprimitis exilio, uel carcere uel indebito intolerabilique seruitio'.

[54] Ibid., pp. 274–5: 'spiritualis nequitiæ grauius ac periculosius certamen cautius agite'.

[55] Ibid., pp. 276–7: 'Quid de Gepidis et Wandalis, Gothis et Turcis, Hunis et Herulis, quid de aliis loquar barbaris quorum conatus ad nichil est aliud nisi furari et rapere, et conculcata pace iugiter furere? Terram turbant, ædes concremant, orbem uexant, opes dissipant, homines iugulant, omnia fœdant et inquietant.'

All these signs portend the end of the world, as we may learn from
the words of truth: 'Nation shall rise against nation and kingdom
against kingdom: and great earthquakes shall be in divers places and
famines and pestilences and fearful sights and great signs shall be
from heaven.'[56]

Guitmund's indictment and his threat of William's eternal damnation
did not move the king to remorse and good behaviour. On the contrary,
the rebellions in England led him to merciless retaliation, the massacre
of a defenceless people and the indiscriminate destruction of foodstuffs,
producing a famine that killed, in Orderic's assessment, 'more than 100,000
Christian folk of both sexes, young and old alike'.[57] Orderic grieved for all
those who died a slow, painful death by starvation and lay that sin directly
on the king, to whom the just Judge would deliver a certain punishment.
This long passage continues with a biting critique of Normans, both
churchmen and lay nobility, whose arrogance toward the defeated and
pandering to the king earned their ultimate doom. Orderic presses the
point repeatedly:

O fools and sinners! why did they not ponder contritely in their
hearts that they had conquered not by their own strength but by
the will of almighty God, and had subdued a people that was greater,
and more wealthy than they were, with a longer history: a people
moreover amongst whom many saints and wise men and mighty
kings had led illustrious lives, and won distinction in many ways at
home and on the battlefield? Instead they should have remembered
with fear, and pondered in the depths of their hearts the true saying
that is written: 'With the same measure that ye mete withal it shall
be measured to you again.' [Luke 6:38][58]

Other elements of Orderic's history reinforce the dark tone that his
powerful speeches convey. The wolf metaphor and treacherous themes
common to Norman histories have also found their way into Orderic's

---

[56] Ibid., pp. 276–7: 'His itaque signis mundi portenditur finis, sicut ipsius
patenter edocemur uoce ueritatis, "Exurget gens contra gentem, et regnum
aduersus regnum, et erunt terræmotus magni per loca, et pestellentiæ et
fames, terroresque de cœla et signa magna erunt."'

[57] Ibid., pp. 232–3: 'christianæ gentis utriusque sexus et omnis ætatis homines
perirent plus quam centum milia'.

[58] Ibid., pp. 268–9: 'Insipientes et maligni cur cum tota contritione cordis non
cogitabant, quod non sua uirtute sed Dei gubernantis omnia nutu hostes
uicerant, et gentem maiorem et ditiorem et antiquiorem sese subegerant,
in qua plures sancti prudentesque uiri regesque potentes micuerant,
multisque modis domi militiæque nobiliter uiguerant? Sententia ueritatis
iugiter eis timenda, et cordi medullitus inserenda esset dicentis, "Eadem
mensura qua mensi fueritis, remetietur uobis."'

narrative, as I have shown elsewhere.[59] I have also treated the elements from the emerging genre of romance that entered Orderic's pages, lending an aura of mystery through eerie, sinister moments that evoke dangers lurking in an uncertain world.[60] Candles with odd markings descend onto an altar at Séez;[61] a Muslim princess rescues an imprisoned Norman Crusader;[62] young men sit in the great hall at Conches and describe their dreams to a noble lady.[63] Orderic was the first Latin historian to interpret the obscure and ominous *Prophecies of Merlin* that he found in Geoffrey of Monmouth's *Historia regum Britanniae*.[64] A similar sense of foreboding haunts Orderic's famous account of 'Herlechin's household', the company of dwarves, Ethiopians, demons and freshly dead sinners marching through the woods on a dark winter's night and stopping to enlighten a terrified priest about the tortures of the damned.[65]

Frequent suspicions of poisoning add to the pervasive sense of danger. Orderic is far from alone among Norman historians in making these accusations. Indeed, so common was the charge that David Douglas added an appendix to his study of William the Conqueror titled, 'On poisoning as a method of political action in eleventh-century Normandy'.[66] Yet in examining Douglas's examples, if we except the deaths of Duke Richard III and his brother Duke Robert I, which are ascribed to poisoning in quite a few texts, we find Orderic at the heart of the allegations. Sometimes he is the first known accuser of a poisoning, sometimes the sole source, and he often dwells on the most curious or compelling details.

Already, when copying William of Jumièges' *Gesta*, Orderic had inserted an accusation of poisoning into the chapter recounting the death of King Henry I of France. Orderic had gathered better information than William found for the king's death, as van Houts has noted. Still she thought that Orderic's story of poisoning 'has to be taken with a pinch of salt'.[67] The young Orderic, however, found it plausible. Later, during the decades when he was writing his *Historia ecclesiastica*, the mature Orderic's view of human behaviour had not improved. Suspicious deaths continued to invite his accusation of poisoning. When William of Montreuil, who had grown wealthy in southern Italy, offered treasures to Saint-Évroul, for instance, Orderic reported that poisoners worked to foil his plan.[68] But

---

[59] Albu, *Normans in their Histories*, pp. 1, 197, 205–10.
[60] Ibid. pp. 211–12.
[61] *HE*, IV, pp. 288–9.
[62] *HE*, VI, pp. 358–79.
[63] *HE*, IV, pp. 216–19.
[64] *HE*, VI, pp. 380–9.
[65] *HE*, IV, pp. 236–51.
[66] D. C. Douglas, *William the Conqueror* (Berkeley, 1964), pp. 408–15.
[67] *GND*, I, p. lxxii.
[68] *HE*, II, pp. 60–1: 'pro cupiditate auri quod ferebat'.

when conniving Romans poisoned one of William's emissaries, 'greedy for the gold that he carried', they murdered this man for nothing, since another emissary, the knight Anquetil, absconded with 'gold and precious vestments, a silver chalice, and many other rich treasures' intended for the monastery.[69]

Another episode of alleged poisoning combines several dark motifs into its narrative. Acting as an agent of 'Satan, who never ceases to molest the human race',[70] Robert son of Giroie allied with the Angevins to stir up rebellion against Duke William. With Angevin aid he fortified his castles of Saint-Céneri and La Roche-Mabille and held them against the duke's assaults. 'But', wrote Orderic, invoking one of his favourite biblical sayings, 'human strength is transient and withers as the flower of grass.'[71] In a tranquil moment with his wife Adelaide by the winter fire, Robert saw that she was holding four apples. Disregarding her protests he ate two of them, not realising that they were poisoned. It took five days for the poison to work through his body and kill him. As apparent evidence of the poisoning, witnesses confirmed that even after three weeks the corpse did not emit a stench, perhaps because the poison had dried up all the body's moisture, essentially mummifying the victim.[72] Along with the cluster of dark motifs here – the persistent work of Satan on earth, the transience of human existence, deadly danger even at the home hearth – Orderic has added the hint of treachery by a trusted spouse, whom Orderic has casually introduced as the duke's kinswoman. Why was Adelaide holding poisoned apples? Did Orderic suspect that she was acting as the duke's agent in poisoning her rebellious husband?[73] Whatever truths lie behind it, this episode of poisoned apples on a wife's lap at the family fireside evokes anxiety.

Accusations of poisoning continue to multiply in Orderic's pages. Sometimes he indicated his reservations, as when reporting that Count Walter, nephew of Edward the Confessor, and his wife Biota 'both died at the same time, poisoned – so the rumour goes ('ut ferunt') – by the evil machinations of their enemies'.[74] In a speech detailing King

---

[69] Ibid., pp. 60–1: 'aurum et pallia preciosa calicemque argenteum aliasque preciosas species protulit'. For more on this episode, see the contribution by Daniel Roach in this volume, 'Saint-Évroul and Southern Italy in Orderic's *Historia ecclesiastica*'.

[70] Ibid., pp. 78–9: 'Sathana qui numquam humano generi nocere desistit'.

[71] Ibid., pp. 80–1: 'Sed quia mortalium robur labile est subitoque ceu flos foeni marcet.'

[72] Ibid., pp. 80–1.

[73] Chibnall footnoted this passage (*HE*, II, p. 79): 'Since Robert's wife, Adelaide, was a kinswoman of Duke William it is possible that she did poison him, though tales of poisoning were widespread and not always true (cf. Douglas, *WC*, Appendix F, pp. 408–15).'

[74] *HE*, II, pp. 118–19: 'Walterus et Biota coniunx eius per inimicorum machinamenta simul ut ferunt, letali ueneno fraudulenter infecti obierunt.'

William's alleged crimes, Orderic had English rebels repeat the rumour that William had poisoned Walter and Biota, as well as Count Conan, 'a man of such valour that his death cast the whole of Brittany into deep mourning'.[75] More often, Orderic wrote about poisoning directly and with authority, sometimes in detail, as with an episode concerning the notorious Mabel of Bellême. When she sent her servants to Arnold of Échauffour, son of William Giroie, pressing him to dine with her, Arnold declined, remembering a friend's warning that she planned to poison him. By chance an unsuspecting Gilbert, brother of Mabel's husband, Roger of Montgomery, drank the wine intended for Arnold and died two days later. Undeterred by the mistaken murder of her husband's only brother, Mabel tried again, this time with success, when she bribed Arnold's chamberlain to serve his lord her poisoned wine.[76] Orderic especially mourns the sorrows of Arnold's bereft children: 'At an early age they were deprived of their father who was still in the flower of manhood; and being forced to dwell in the houses of others, as I have already related, had to endure hardship and want from infancy.'[77] While Douglas doubted the credibility of such episodes of alleged poisoning,[78] the frequency of the charge gives one pause. If 'an apprehension of venom' did haunt the Norman world, as recorded by its chroniclers, Orderic was especially prone to suspect foul play.

Orderic's world throbbed with such troubling energies. For him the trope of the devil at work served as more than a rhetorical device to explain otherwise inexplicable evil. The devil and his demons were ever contriving to disrupt human events and corrupt souls. They worked on the highest plane of secular affairs and even in Orderic's own monastery, plying their mischief to derail the spiritual aspirations of the monks. So a demon tempted Romanus, a monk of Saint-Évroul, to steal 'linen and breeches and things of that kind', tormenting him at night until his shrieks and confessions of guilt brought fellow monks, who offered temporary relief by sprinkling him with holy water.[79] Nothing could save Romanus for long, though, and the abbot finally had to defrock and expel him. Orderic knew of many such wayward monks, led astray by the demons

---

Chibnall noted (ibid. p. 118 n. 2) that 'Orderic is the only authority for this story of poisoning', and some authorities have doubted the rumour, while others found a credible motive in Walter's possible claim to the English throne.

[75] Ibid., pp. 312–13: 'quem mortuum Britannia tota pro ingenti probitate ineffabili luctu defleuit'.

[76] Ibid., pp. 122–5.

[77] Ibid., pp. 124–5: 'Qui patre dum adhuc uiridi iuuenta maxime floreret in teneris annis destituti, et in externis domibus ut supra satis ostendimus constitute, coacti sunt inopias pluresque iniurias ab infantia perpeti.'

[78] Douglas, *William the Conqueror*, p. 415.

[79] *HE*, II, pp. 42–3: 'qui instinctu dæmonis staminia, femoralia, et cætera huiusmodi furabatur'.

that lie in wait for the idle. 'Strive constantly to avoid sloth as deadly poison', wrote Orderic, recalling Benedict's prescription that 'Idleness is the enemy of the soul.'[80]

> Live with this precept, which an experienced doctor has written in the lives of the Fathers, that only one demon tempts the monk who is active in doing good, but a thousand demons assault the slothful monk and prick him with so many temptations that he comes to scorn the monastic cloister and longs to see the pernicious sights of the world and experience its perilous delights [...] Pray, read, chant psalms, write, persevere with such things, and consciously arm yourselves with them against the wiles of the devil.[81]

These teachings are, of course, central to Benedictine monasticism. Osbern, abbot of Saint-Évroul in the time of William the Conqueror, who 'was severe to the idle and disobedient' ('Asper erat ineptis et contumacibus'), so hated sloth that he whipped the novices when they flagged in their lessons.[82] Orderic takes evident pleasure in the stories of men like the abbot, who faithfully battled against the ever-present temptations of the forces of evil – and he assumed that his readers would as well. So he included in the *Historia* an abridged version of Bishop Felix's *Life of St Guthlac*, an English warrior turned monk who worked miracles while tormented by demons.[83] This struggle is the constant battle of the righteous, as Orderic noted concerning the monastery at Bec: 'There many clerks and laymen have lived and still live under the monastic rule, fighting against the devil and working for the glory of God.'[84]

Certainly Orderic also allowed glimmers of hope, with worldly woe assuaged by the joys of monastic fraternity and the expectations of life everlasting in the next world. So he delighted in the famous hospitality of Bec,[85] and the 'innumerable spiritual gifts' ('quorum numerosa praeterire') of Norman monasteries (though he stopped himself from attempting a

---

[80] Ibid., pp. 50–1: 'Ocia uelut letale uirus totis nisibus deuitate, quia sicut sanctus pater Benedictus dicit, "Ociositas inimica est animæ."'

[81] Ibid., pp. 50–3: 'Illud etiam sepe uobiscum reuoluite, quod in uitis Patrum dicitur a quodam probate doctore, quia unus solummodo dæmon temptando uexat laborantem in bonis monachum, mille uero dæmones impugnant ociosum, innumerisque temptationum iaculis undique stimulatum cogunt fastidire monasteriale claustrum, et appetere damnosa sæculi spectacula et noxiarum experientiam uoluptatum [...] Orate, legite, psallite, scribite, aliisque huiusmodi actibus insistite, eisque contra dæmonum temptamenta uos sapienter armate.'

[82] Ibid., pp. 106–7.

[83] Ibid., pp. 325–33.

[84] Ibid., pp. 12–13: 'Ibi usque hodie multi clericorum et laicorum sub monachili scemate uiuunt.'

[85] Ibid., pp. 296–7.

complete accounting, lest this should tire his reader).[86] Miracles gathered from saints' lives like Isembard of Fleury's *Life of St Judoc* pepper the narrative, providing examples of God's presence working to combat evil and bring comfort. Prayers of the blessed Judoc (who died c. 668), for instance, felled an eagle that was carrying off the holy man's hens and rooster,[87] and God sent him boatloads of food as a reward for his charity towards beggars. Judoc's prayers also caused a spring to bubble up, bringing waters that healed the sick and cured blindness. After Judoc died, the duke of Ponthieu opened his tomb, curious to see the uncorrupted body. 'Springing back in terror Duke Drochtric cried, "Ah! Saint Judoc." He was struck deaf and dumb on the spot, and remained enfeebled in body until his death.'[88]

Like this story of an irreverent duke at St Judoc's grave, Orderic's miracle tales frequently come with a dark subtext, a moral and a warning. So, when King William allowed the execution of the saintly Earl Waltheof,[89] miracles occurred at the tomb and the king faced both common opprobrium and the just disapproval of God, bringing uprisings and adversity 'so that he could never again enjoy lasting peace'.[90] Orderic concluded this episode ominously: 'The omnipotent judge orders all things rightly and leaves no sin unpunished, for he never fails to mete out punishment either in this world or in the world to come.'[91]

Miracles like those at Waltheof's tomb in the eleventh century were rarities. The distant past, thought Orderic, produced more wonders, while the fraught Norman age enjoyed far fewer:

> Behold, while sinners carry great burdens that destroy them
> The marvellous works of saints now cease, and that most justly;
> Transgressors who defy the law deserve only
> Punishment from the wrath of heaven, not miracles.[92]

As 'human activities always turned towards evil' ('Humana exercitia quæe semper ad nefas prona sunt'),[93] so Orderic's world had degenerated:

---

[86] Ibid., pp. 298–9.

[87] Ibid., pp. 156–7.

[88] Ibid., pp. 158–9: 'et intus irreuerenter intuitus et mox exterritus ait, "Ah, sancte Iudoce." Statim surdus et mutus factus est, et usque ad mortem omni corpore debilitatus est.'

[89] Ibid., pp. 320–3.

[90] Ibid., pp. 350–1: 'nec umquam postea diuturna pace potitus est'.

[91] Ibid., pp. 350–1: 'Omnipotens arbiter omnia iuste disponit, nullamque facinus impunitum relinquit, quia hic aut in futuro sæculo omnia punit.'

[92] *HE*, VI, pp. 8–9: 'En peccatores letalia pondera gestant,/ Lucida sanctorum iuste magnalia cessant./ Preuaricatores qui legem transgrediuntur./ Irae celestis penas non signa merentur.'

[93] *HE*, II, pp. 246–7.

Just as the sea is never wholly still and safe, but is tossed continually as it ebbs and flows; and although it may seem calm sometimes to those who are safe on shore, nevertheless by its continual movement and tossing it fills sailors with fear: so this present age is continually troubled by change and fluctuates ceaselessly through all the changing moods of joy and sorrow.[94]

As Richard Barton has observed after examining the theme of emotions in the *Historia ecclesiastica*, 'anger and shame are ubiquitous, while love and joy are rare'.[95] Sorrow predominates in this earthly existence, in its transitory nature, as expressed in Orderic's most frequent biblical imagery:[96]

All flesh is grass, and all the goodness thereof is as the flower of the field: The grass withereth, the flower fadeth: because the spirit of the Lord bloweth upon it: Surely the people are grass. The grass withereth, the flower fadeth, but the word of our God shall stand forever.
(Isaiah 40:6; cf. I Peter 1:24–5)

When Orderic uses this image, it is directed more towards the transience of human life than the eternity of the Word or the expectations of life everlasting in the next world. Orderic's base line is worldly woe.

The opening and closing lines of the *Historia*'s individual books highlight this point of view. Book III begins with an introduction to the battle of good and evil within the world:

My first task is to tell of the vine of the Lord of Hosts, which his strong right hand tends and preserves throughout the world against the wiles of Behemoth.[97]

Book III ends with a genuine expression of weariness and the need for a break in writing. When Orderic began the next book, which would be

---

[94] Ibid., pp. 303–4: 'Sicut mare nunquam tutum certa soliditate quiescit, sed inquetudine iugi turbatum more suo defluit, et quamuis aliquando tranquillum obtutibus spectantium appareat, solita tamen fluctuatione et instabilitate nauigantes territat, sic præsens sæculum uolubilitate sua iugiter uexatur, innumerisque modis tristibus seu lætis euidenter uariatur.'

[95] Richard E. Barton, 'Emotions and Power in Orderic Vitalis', ANS 33 (210), 41–59, at p. 43.

[96] See, for instance, Orderic's evocation of the 'Ubi sunt?' motif at 2.319 on the death of the mighty William fitz-Osbern, steward of Normandy and 'the first and greatest oppressor of the English': 'Truly the glory of this world falls and withers like the flower of grass: even as smoke it fades and passes.' ('Vere gloria mundi ut flos foeni decidit et arescit: ac uelut fumus deficit et transit.') Albu, *Normans in their Histories*, pp. 200–1.

[97] HE, II, pp. 4–5: 'Opus in primis arripiam de uinea Domini sabaoth, quam ipse forti dextera colit et protegit in toto mundo contra insidias Behemoth.'

Book IV in the final version, he summarised the grievous state of affairs he found at this point in history:

> In the time of Pope Alexander II [1061–73] many kingdoms far and wide were afflicted with divers catastrophes; and many thousands of men plunged into the pit of destruction. The inhabitants of the western lands endured grave tribulations and dire calamities. For when the virtuous kings, Henry of France and Edward of England, were dead, the French and English long had cause to mourn them, since they received as successors lords little like them in virtue and graciousness. Once the fathers of the country were taken away, tyrants who abused the power of royal dominion took their place. England, desecrated by the cruelty and perfidy of Harold, was on her way to ruin; and once deprived of lawful heirs, fell under the sway of foreign invaders led by the conquering William. So she provided a mournful theme of ruin for the pen of true historians.[98]

Book IV closes with the murder and mayhem of Robert Curthose's first rebellion against his father, William the Conqueror: 'Mortal men are oppressed by many misfortunes, which would fill great volumes if the whole tale of them were written down. But now, numbed by the winter cold, I turn to other pursuits; and weary with toil, resolve to end my present book here.'[99] Orderic will resume in the warmth of spring.

When Orderic set out to write his final three books, he placed seventy-eight lines of verse between the tenth and eleventh books, as a kind of prologue to Book XI and a commentary on the work as a whole.[100] The poem offers a prayer that a merciful God will counteract omnipresent evil:

---

[98] Ibid., pp. 190–1: 'Temporibus Alexandri secundi papæ plurima per orbem regna calamitatibus concussa sunt, et multiplices populorum concursus in sui perniciem debachati sunt. Hæc in occiduis partibus terrigenæ senserunt, et grauia subeuntes detrimenta nimis experti sunt. Defunctis enim optimis regibus Henrico Francorum, et Eduardo Anglorum, Franci et Angli diu luxerunt funus eorum, quia post illos uix adepti sunt dominos illis consimiles uirtutibus et nectare morum. Patribus patriæ de medio ablatis, successere tiranni abutentes freno regiæ dominationis. Anglia tunc Heraldi seuicia periurioque polluta corruit, et genuinis hæredibus orbata externis prædonibus Guillelmo uictori fauentibus subiacuit, unde flebile tema de sua ruina piis historiographis ad dictandum tribuit.'

[99] Ibid., pp. 360–1: 'Multa terrigenis imminent infortunia, quæ si diligenter scriberentur omnia, ingentia replerent uolumina. Nunc hiemali frigore rigens aliis occupationibus uacabo, præsentemque labellum hic terminare fatigatus decerno.'

[100] *HE*, VI, p. xvii.

> Tread down the power of Satan, who forever rages against you,
> As he strives to harass your servants in all places.[101]

This prayer moves into a long lament for the current dearth of miracles and surplus of sin:

> While I hope for renowned deeds and would like to write of wonders,
> in Christ's name filling my parchment with miracles;
> while I love to praise the one who rules the whole world,
> who can free us easily from all woes,
> I am forced to speak of dark deeds I see and suffer.
> I relate the capricious acts of fickle men;
> For love of the world drags mankind to perdition,
> And the file of justice does not smooth away the rust from them.[102]

The few chosen people work diligently for good ('Ad bona feruentes electi sedulo currunt');[103] but the devil (the two-headed snake, Amphisilena, referenced below) is winning the battle between good and evil, as a relentless stream of verses insists:

> Now is the time when the evil beast with ten horns triumphs,
> Leprous sin stains the mad rabble all the world over,
> God pointed out Behemoth to his friend Job figuratively;
> The cunning demon rages abroad in this world of sinfulness.
> Frenzied Erinys is let loose among earth dwellers
> And daily drags down her captives to the abyss of Hades.
> Amphisilena misleads and makes sport of mortals,
> Cheating them by his wiles of the delights of heaven.
> Alas! the deadly serpent infects them with a venom
> That turns them into madmen, and makes them slay each other.
> The foolish endure disease and pestilence; the wicked
> Heap sin on grievous sin to their own undoing.
> We look on human misfortunes and dire disasters,
> With which a zealous writer might cover his parchment;
> If he wishes to pour out empty words on various subjects
> He will find abundant materials in these calamities.[104]

---

[101] Ibid., pp. 8–9, lines 3–4: 'Contere uim Sathanæ qui seuit iugiter in te,/ Dum famulos uexare tuos molitur ubique.'

[102] Ibid., lines 18–25: 'Inclita dum spiro mirandaque scribere uellem,/ Prodigiis implens in Christi nomine pellem./ Eius amo laudes cui totus subiacet orbis,/ Qui potis est cunctis leuiter nos demere morbis./ Cogimur atra loqui quæ cernimus aut toleramus,/ Instabiles actus mutabilium memoramus,/ Nam mundanus amor hominum trahit agmen ad ima,/ Iusticiæ nec eos polit a rubigine lima.'

[103] Ibid., pp. 10–11, line 9.

[104] Ibid., pp. 10–11, lines 18–33: 'Nam lentos stimulant monitis celeresque refrenant./ Cornua dena gerens mala bestia iam dominatur,/ Effera

Orderic is not finished with this dirge, in which Satan claims much more space than God:

> The envious foe of the whole human race is called
> By many names in the Scriptures given from heaven.
> He becomes lion, or wolf, dragon, partridge, and basilisk,
> Hawk, boar, fox, dog, bear, leech, or horned serpent,
> Or deadly snake, when he lays snares for us
> And plans to destroy the foolish by force or deceit.
> A thousand other names will occur to clever readers
> According to the cunning tricks the enemy practises.
> He corrupts thousands with vices and often destroys them.
> Alas, many great legions of men eternally perish!
>
> Holy king, good Jesus, Chief Priest, save us.
> Do not let the old serpent poison us with the damned;
> But draw us up, purged of sins, from the sea of the world,
> And mercifully unite us with the saints in the court of heaven.
>   Amen.[105]

What pessimism Chibnall saw in Orderic's *Historia* she ascribed to his experiences living in 'a time of great upheaval and war in the secular world, and disorder in the church'; his abbey lay on the frontier, perilously close to armies from Maine and Anjou and to the French king, amid warring 'predatory stipendiary knights' and bandits of l'Aigle, and was especially threatened in times of weak ducal rule (Robert Curthose) or in the wake of a duke's death (Henry I in December 1135). This last event, particularly,

---

plebs passim scelerum lepra maculatur./ Iob Dominus tipice Behemoth monstrauit amico/ Dæmon in hoc mundo furit insidiosus iniquo./ Terrigenas furibunda super grassatur Erinis,/ Cotidieque suos Erebi contrudit in imis./ Ludit et illudit mortalibus amphisilena,/ Decipiendo quibus paradisi tollit amena./ Heu male uirus eis infundit letifer anguis,/ Quos facit amentes et mutuo se perimentes./ Morbos et pestes stulti subeunt et iniqui,/ Insuper adiciunt sibi pessima nequiter ipsi./ Cernimus humanos casus miserasque ruinas,/ Vnde sagax pelles implere quit auctor ouinas./ Si uult diversis de rebus inania uerba/ Fundere, thema frequens satis inuenit inter acerba.'

[105] Ibid., pp. 10–13: 'Nominibus multis in scriptis celitus actis/ Humani generis uocitatur liuidus hostis./ Nam leo necne lupus, draco, perdix et basiliscus,/ Miluus, aper, uulpes, canis, ursus, irudo, cerastes/ Et coluber fit atrox, dum nobis insidiatur;/ Exitiumque dolo seu ui stolidis meditatur./ Cætera mille patent lectoribus ingeniosis/ Nomina pro uariis quibus utitur artibus hostis./ Innumeros foedat uiciis et sepe trucidat,/ Proh dolor ingentes pereunt plerunque phalanges. // Rex sacer erue nos, bone Iesu, summe Sacerdos,/ Ne cum damnandis nos inficiat uetus anguis,/ Sed uiciis mundos trahe mundi de pelago nos;/ Et socia sanctis supera clementer in aula. Amen.'

shadowed the final months of Orderic's writing and life, and civil war was raging still at the time of his death.[106] In the summer of 1141, 'when he ended his history for the second time and added the epilogue describing his own life, disaster seemed to have overwhelmed his world.'[107]

Despite the signs of distress in his *Historia*, Chibnall concluded that Orderic held to an idealistic vision of the Norman nobles, who are habitually given heroic epithets signalling generosity, bravery, nobility, and beauty, though their actual deeds often evinced cruelty and barbarism.[108] She judged his less attractive prejudices as merely the conventional assumptions of his age, which he did not question: peasants should not try to avoid their assigned life of hard manual labour; no one should aim to rise above the status inherited at birth; Muslims deserved any pain they suffered at the hands of Christians.[109] Within his own twelfth-century monastic world, Chibnall argued, Orderic lived a satisfying life, cherished by his brother monks, as he himself wrote in reflecting on his many years at Saint-Évroul: 'I have lived as a monk in that abbey by thy favour for fifty-six years, and have been loved and honoured by all of my fellow monks and companions far more than I deserved.' ('In prefato cenobio lvi annis te fauente conuersatus sum, et a cunctis fratribus et contubernalibus multo plus quam merui amatus et honoratus sum.)'[110] So, Chibnall concluded, 'he ended his writing, at the darkest moment of the Anglo-Norman civil wars in 1141, on a note of peace and joy': 'strengthened by the grace of God, [I] enjoy the security of obedience and poverty' ('gratia Dei corroboratus, securitate subiectionis et paupertatis tripudio').[111] At the same time she also urged readers to exercise a certain restraint in their judgement of him: 'we should do well not to attempt too psychological a study, for he has left no analysis of his personal feelings; the impression that emerges from his work is that of an essentially balanced character, sustained by deep faith.'[112] Yet throughout the pages of the *Historia*, Orderic has left hints of childhood trauma and the continuing distress of living in a troubled world – clues that point to the unsettling sorrow at the heart of his work.

---

[106] Chibnall, *World*, pp. 27, 33.

[107] Chibnall, 'General Introduction', p. 41.

[108] Ibid., pp. 40–1.

[109] Ibid., p. 41. He also assumed that women could harbour dangerous passions. So the 'fierce lust' of Norman women compelled their husbands to abandon England and return home, lamenting and asking 'what could honourable men do if their lascivious wives polluted their beds with adultery and brought indelible shame and dishonour on their offspring?' *HE*, II, pp. 218–21.

[110] *HE*, VI, pp. 554–5.

[111] Ibid., pp. 550–1.

[112] Chibnall, 'General Introduction', p. 39.

Orderic injected his own feelings into the *Historia*, overtly in the prefaces and conclusions of books, less directly but rather obviously in the speeches, in the frequent suspicions of poisoning, and in clearly interpretive passages, as when he compared Normandy under Robert Curthose's rule to the time of the Old Testament prophet Joel, who saw the four plagues of the canker-worm, the locust, the grub, and the hopper devouring the lawless people who had overtaken Israel.[113] The insertion of a hand drawn in the margin of Orderic's *Life of Christ* – perhaps drawn by Orderic himself – illustrates how deeply he could identify with the texts he was copying and writing.[114] This text presents the parable of the labourers in the vineyard, pruning the vine of the holy Church, some beginning their work in the morning, some at night, but all equally rewarded. The marginal hand points to 'Mane puericia est.' The morning means, in Orderic's interpretation, from childhood – an interpretation that accords with his own life story, as he explicitly explained in the epilogue to Book XIII of the *Historia ecclesiastica*.[115] Orderic placed himself within Christ's parable, and at the end of his life he was awaiting his reward.

Was the tone of worldly woe, then, just an expression of Orderic's monastic upbringing and life? When contemplating the persistent attacks on Thierry, an abbot whose other-worldliness he admired, for instance, did Orderic automatically think of the devil at work when he wrote: 'The old enemy never ceases to disturb the peace of the Church with every kind of trial, and uses those who are loved by worldly ambition to torment the men who fight single-mindedly for the catholic faith and make a brave stand for the cause of virtue'?[116] Was this simply a truism that any monk would invoke? When Orderic described the debilitating ailments of Reginald, who was raised at Saint-Évroul, he recalled Psalms 33:20 (34:19) with, 'it is truly written: "Many are the afflictions of the righteous"' ('Sed sicut scriptum est, "multæ tribulationes iustorum"'), and asked God to 'have mercy upon him, and when he is purged from all sin free him from this harsh prison of the flesh, granting him eternal rest in the company of thy faithful servants'.[117] When Orderic wrote of King Harold's enjoying

---

[113] Ibid., pp. 52–3, commenting on *HE*, IV, p. 288.

[114] Chibnall thought this might be his own drawing: Chibnall, 'General Introduction', p. 54. See this parable, for instance, at *HE*, II, pp. 4–5.

[115] *HE*, VI, pp. 554–5.

[116] *HE*, II, pp. 64–5: 'Antiquus hostis nunquam cessat æcclesiæ quietem uariarum stimulis temptationum impugnare; et per eos quos potest mundanæ uanitati subiugare, in simplicitate catholicæ fidei prudenter uigilantes et in uirtutum culmine uiriliter stantes atrociter molestare.'

[117] Ibid., pp. 128–9: 'clementer illius miserere ipsumque ab omni expurgans scelere; ereptum de carnis molesto carcere, in æterna requie famulorum tuorum collegio insere'.

only a brief moment of euphoria between the two invasions of 1066,[118] he found nothing surprising, 'since worldly fortune is driven away like smoke before the wind', again recalling biblical passages.[119] After the Battle of Hastings, Orderic offered Harold and others as examples proving the hard truth: 'Changeable fortune often brings a hard and bitter fate to mortal men on earth, for some climb from the dust to the height of power, others are dashed from great prosperity to groan in the depths of despair.'[120] Are these just the expected sentiments of a man of faith, the commonplace expressions of a monastic sensibility?

The frequency of such statements suggests otherwise. Orderic's mind moved easily to melancholy or despair, passions he thought potentially lethal. When the pope imprisoned Pontius, abbot of Cluny, Orderic described Pontius as grieving so deeply that he fell ill and died. But when Peter the Venerable, Pontius's successor as abbot, reported the same events, he wrote that Pontius died of malaria ('the Roman sickness') without noting despair as a contributing factor.[121]

Orderic was writing with a moral purpose that might have encouraged an earnest tone but did not mandate the gloom that so distinguishes his writing from the historical works he knew and drew from. He could imitate the epic mode of William of Poitiers for a brief period, for instance when he followed William's celebration of the Conqueror's prowess at Hastings,[122] but the mood was short-lived, and soon deflated.[123] Similarly, Orderic's ninth book, on the First Crusade, contains heroic episodes

---

[118] Ibid., pp. 170–1.

[119] Ibid.: 'prosperitas mundi ut fumus ante uentum cito deficit'. Chibnall cites Psalms 67[68]:3 and Wisdom 5:15.

[120] *HE*, II, pp. 178–9: 'Vergibili fortuna mortalibus in terris suppeditante ualde aspera et inopinata; quidam de puluere prosiliunt ad magnarum potestatum culmina, aliique de summo apice subito pulsi gemunt in ingenti mesticia.'

[121] *HE*, VI, pp. 314–15: 'Qui non multo post enormi merore affectus aegrotauit'; see also p. 314 n. 3. Peter the Venerable, *De miraculis* i. 6, ii. 13. Giles Constable, *The Letters of Peter the Venerable*, 2 vols. (Cambridge, MA, 1967).

[122] *HE*, II, pp. 174–7.

[123] P. Bouet, 'Orderic Vital, lecteur critique de Guillaume de Poitiers', in *Mediaevalia Christiana, XIe–XIIIe siècles: Homage à Raymonde Foreville de ses amis, ses collègues et ses anciens élèves*, ed. C. E. Viola (Paris, 1989), pp. 25–50. Leah Shopkow has shown how Orderic reshaped William of Poitiers' recounting of the Conqueror's coronation, for instance, recasting a triumphant event 'as the moment when a potentially great alliance began to go wrong.' Shopkow, *History and Community*, pp. 97–8. See especially pp. 96–105, where she concludes: 'Orderic's dark moral view of human history can be read as a delayed response to the optimistic moralism of William of Poitiers.'

derived from his main source, the *Historia Ierosolimitana* of his friend Baldric of Bourgueil. Yet Orderic concluded this section, too, with an explanation that he was stopping to rest for a while, 'weary with writing and investigating events in distant lands of the east'.[124] The final sentence of this book, expressing his reason for hoping eventually to resume the work, in Chibnall's translation reads as follows:

> For I believe there will be some men after me like myself, who will eagerly peruse the events and transitory acts of this generation in the pages of chroniclers, so that they may unfold the past fortunes of the changing world for the edification or delight of their contemporaries.[125]

While the English sounds upbeat, the last four words in Orderic's own Latin betray a different mood: 'labentis seculi casus preteritos'. This is 'the past fortunes of the changing world', but 'labentis' ('changing') has the root sense of 'slipping away' and 'falling into ruin.' In Orderic's Christian world, it could also mean 'falling away from the true faith' (hence the passive form, our 'lapsed'). 'Casus' (here translated 'fortunes') indicates falling, first literally, but also through moral failings. *Casus* are happenstance occurrences – 'fortunes' with the ominous resonance of misfortune and calamity; this word, too, at root means 'a fall.' The book's final word, 'preteritos', is 'past' but also 'lost' or 'perished.' The Christian resonances here are sombre, evoking degeneration, loss and woe.

Compare this mood with the impish fun, layered humour, and bemusement of Dudo of Saint-Quentin, or with the heroic stance of William of Poitiers. Both these men, of course, were clerics living and writing farther from the monastery and closer to the secular world of the courts. For a monastic text, consider William of Jumièges' *Gesta*, which Orderic altered to add dark shadings.

It may be even more revealing to contrast the tone of Orderic's *Historia ecclesiastica* with that of Bede's, a text that Orderic had copied and that 'constantly provided a model for the form and content of different parts of [his *Historia*].'[126] Orderic knew that Bede's monastic, spiritual, and scholarly career resembled his own to a remarkable degree, and Chibnall thought Bede to have been 'the historian most frequently in Orderic's mind as he wrote'.[127] Yet the tone of Bede's *Historia ecclesiastica* differs strikingly

---

[124] *HE*, V, pp. 190–1: 'Hic quia scribendo et res longinquas utpote in Eois climatibus actas indugando fessus requiescere inhelo sextum Æcclesiasticæ Hystoriæ librum finire decerno.'

[125] Ibid., pp. 190–1: 'Mei nimirum similes autumo quosdam esse futuros; qui generationis huius ordines a cronographis auide perscrutabuntur et actus transitorios, ut coessentibus sibi ad ædificationem seu delectationem retexere possint labentis seculi casus preteritos.'

[126] Chibnall, 'General Introduction', p. 56.

[127] Ibid., pp. 56–7.

from Orderic's. Bede reported wars and persecutions; he included many accounts of sin and retribution; he evoked storm-inducing demons.[128] But he did not produce digressions lamenting the incessant battling between good and evil or the devil's constant efforts to damn human affairs. Miracles abound. With Bede as his model, it is easy to see why the paucity of miracles in his own day would have discouraged Orderic. Perhaps most strikingly, Bede – unlike Orderic – saw benign associations and almost universally efficacious effects in the miracles he related. So Augustine restored sight to a blind man, by this miraculous healing persuading the English to abandon their dating of Easter.[129] Bede knew of a man risen from the dead after witnessing the torments of the damned and hearing the sweet singing that signalled 'the joys of the heavenly kingdom' ('gaudia regni caelestis'), and he saw how this knowledge led the man to live the rest of his life as an austere model to others 'in his unwearied longing for heavenly bliss' ('infatigabili caelestium bonorum desiderio').[130] Even the death of a man who repented too late held value as a negative model, driving hearers to salvation.[131]

For Bede, poison served primarily as a metaphor for heresy, the topic that exercised him most deeply, matched only by his distress at incorrect computations for the dating of Easter.[132] When he noted that 'almost everything that the island [Ireland] produces is efficacious against poison', he was referring to snake bites rather than attempted murder by humans.[133] He did report an attack on King Edwin by a man with a poison-smeared sword, yet the king's eventual acceptance of Christianity led to his complete recovery.[134] Bede wrote about years when the plague brought sudden death, causing some survivors to 'forget the sacred mysteries of the faith into which they had been initiated and take to the false remedies of idolatry, as though they could ward off a blow inflicted by God the Creator by means of incantations or amulets or any other

---

[128] Bede, HE, 1.17, pp. 54–7. Latin and English translations of Bede are from Bede's Ecclesiastical History of the English People, ed. Bertram Colgrave and R. A. B. Mynors (Oxford, 1969). Text henceforth noted as Bede, HE.

[129] Ibid., 2.2, pp. 134–41.

[130] Ibid., 5.12, pp. 488–99.

[131] Ibid. 5.13–14, pp. 498–505.

[132] Ibid., 1.8, pp. 34–7 on Arianism and 'the poison of its error'; and ibid., 1.10, pp. 38–9, on Pelagianism as a 'treacherous poison.' For Bede's impassioned interest in the proper method of computing Easter, see especially 3.25, pp. 294–309.

[133] Ibid., 1.1, pp. 18–21: 'omnia pene quae de eadem insula sunt contra uenenum ualent'.

[134] Ibid., 2.9, pp. 162–7. See also the poisoning of Hereric, father of the abbess Hild, casually noted in an episode focusing on a dream foretelling Hild's exemplary life and joyful approach to death (4.23, pp. 410–11).

mysteries of devilish art',[135] but he most often ended such episodes with miraculous healing or inspirational preaching.

While Bede believed that slothfulness ('segnitia') afflicted the Church in his lifetime, he did not dwell on its base effects, nor did he interject morose commentary on the current state of the world.[136] On the contrary, he approached his subject with a sense of wonder. When describing Pope Gregory's lamentation at his required immersion in worldly affairs, for instance, Bede marvelled:

> He used to think nothing but thoughts of heaven, so that, even though still imprisoned in the body, he was able to pass in contemplation beyond the barriers of the flesh. He loved death, which in the eyes of almost everybody is a punishment, because he held it to be the entrance to life and the reward of his labours.[137]

Bede's *Historia ecclesiastica* is full of joy, earthly pleasure in anticipating 'the joys of heaven'.[138] Many of his miracle stories describe a joyful death, the 'beautiful ending' of a life lived in that happy anticipation.[139] The 'heavenly joy' of my chapter's title in fact appears sparingly in Orderic, but often in Bede.[140] Bede understood that demons and evil-doers could wreak

---

[135] Ibid., 4.27 (25), pp. 432–3: 'multi fidem quam habebant iniquis profanabant operibus, et aliqui etiam tempore mortalitatis, neglectis fidei sacramentis quibus erant inbuti, ad erratica idolatriae medicamina concurrebant, quasi missam a Deo Conditore plagam per incantationes uel fylacteria uel alia quaelibet daemonicae artis arcana cohibere ualerent'.

[136] For instance, when describing the life of Aidan, bishop of Northumbria, which was 'in great contrast to our modern slothfulness' ('In tantum autem uita illius a nostri temporis segnitia distabat'), Bede stressed Aidan's own devotion to study and his positive influence on everyone around him (3.5), pp. 226–7.

[137] Ibid., 2.1, pp. 124–5: 'ut nulla nisi caelestia cogitare soleret, ut etiam retentus corpore ipsa iam carnis claustra contemplatione transiret, ut mortem quoque quae pene cunctis poena est, uidelicet ut ingressum uitae et laboris sui praemium amaret'.

[138] So, for instance, the monk Owine 'heard the sound of sweet and joyful singing descend from the sky to the earth', and angels summoning a holy bishop to 'the joys of heaven' ('uocem suauissimam cantantium atque laetantium de caelo ad terras usque discendere', 'aeterna gaudia'; 4.3, pp. 340–3).

[139] See 4.24, pp. 414–21, with the 'beautiful ending' ('pulchro uitam suam fine conclusit') of Caedmon's life spent making 'songs about the terrors of future judgement, the horrors of the pains of hell, and the joys of the heavenly kingdom' ('de terrore futuri iudicii et horrore poenae gehennalis ac dulcedine regni caelestis multa carmina faciebat').

[140] See, for instance, Bede, *HE*, 4.27 (25), pp. 432–3, as Cuthbert 'sought to convert the neighbouring people far and wide from a life of foolish customs to a love of heavenly joys' ('uulgus circumpositum longe lateque

havoc, but his *Historia ecclesiastica* did not dwell on evil, or its prevailing power, or the devil's overwhelming strength. Before summarising the events he had described, Bede ended his work proper on a positive note.[141] Though the Britons remained hostile to the English 'through their inbred hatred' and opposed the catholic Church 'by their incorrect Easter and their evil customs', yet the English and the Church were gaining ground.[142] Monastic communities were growing 'in these favourable times of peace and prosperity' ('adridente pace ac serenitate temporum'). Echoing psalms of praise, he concluded: 'Let the earth rejoice in His perpetual kingdom and let Britain rejoice in His faith and let the multitude of isles be glad and give thanks at the remembrance of His holiness.'[143]

In the end, does tone matter? Why pay attention to the emotional colouring of Orderic's work? The answer is quite simple: because the tone conveys strong emotional meaning, it affects our reading of the *Historia ecclesiastica*. It shades our interpretation of the world that Orderic inhabited and presented. Its darkness may well give us a true impression of a tumultuous time and place. Historians would do well to stay attuned to the persuasive effect of tone on our reading of the *Historia* and our appraisal of Orderic's world.

Finally, the tone of Orderic's work may have contributed to its relative obscurity in the centuries after 1141, the year when the *Historia ecclesiastica* ended. A quarter of a century after Orderic's death, monks at St Stephen's, Caen, copied most of Books VII and VIII into a manuscript that Wace used as source material for his *Roman de Rou*. Robert of Torigni also had some knowledge of the *Historia*, and small sections, excerpted, continued to circulate. Monks glossed and annotated Orderic's manuscript, but his work remained little read outside the monastery. Chibnall blamed its length for this 'restricted' use: 'Too cumbrous to be widely circulated, it appears never to have been cited by name before the sixteenth century.'[144]

While size was certainly a deterrent, did the *Historia*'s dark tone also limit its reading, copying, and influence? More focused works on the Norman conquest of England, the *Gesta Guillelmi* of William of Poitiers and the poem called the *Carmen de Hastingae Proelio*, also had slight

---

a uita stultae consuetudinis ad caelestium gaudiorum conuertere curabat amorem').

[141] Ibid., 5.23, pp. 556–61.

[142] Ibid., 5.23, pp. 560–1: 'Brettones, quamuis et maxima ex parte domestico sibi odio gentem Anglorum, et totius catholicae ecclesiae statum pascha minus recto moribusque inprobis inpungent'.

[143] Ibid., 5.23, pp. 560–1: 'In cuius regno perpetuo exultet terra, et congratulante in fide eius Brittania, laetentur insulae multae et confiteantur memoriae sanctitatis eius.'

[144] Chibnall, 'General Introduction', pp. 112–15.

readership in the Middle Ages.[145] But the histories with broader scope, which Orderic was continuing, survived in greater abundance. We still have about thirteen manuscripts of Dudo's *De moribus* and forty-seven of the *Gesta Normannorum ducum*.[146] Dudo wrote an imaginative tale in alternating prose and verse, laced with classical allusions and witticisms to amuse French clerics, and posing as an epic celebrating the Normans' rise from Viking marauders to civilised lords of western Christendom. William of Jumièges continued Dudo's *De moribus* with a simpler account of the Normans and their dukes, written from the monastery but still essentially positive in its view of secular rulers and affairs. Dudo's work and, especially, William's had broad appeal, to the court and a larger readership. Where was the audience for Orderic's *Historia*? It is not a celebratory study designed to enthral or inspire. We may well admire Orderic's broad vision, in both time and space,[147] but we should not be surprised that the work's dark tone won him few readers before modern historians came to find the *Historia ecclesiastica* so valuable.[148]

---

[145] The two manuscripts of the *Gesta Guillelmi* known in the Middle Ages are both presumed lost. On the textual tradition, see William of Poitiers, *Gesta Guillelmi*, ed. R. H. C. Davis and Marjorie Chibnall, Oxford Medieval Texts (Oxford, 1998), pp. xliii–xlv. The *Carmen* survives in a single twelfth-century manuscript and another 66-line fragment. For the Latin text with interlinear English translation, see *Carmen de Triumpho Normannico; The Song of the Norman Conquest*, trans. Kathleen Tyson (London, 2014); see also *The Carmen de Hastingae proelio*, ed. Frank Barlow (Oxford, 1999).

[146] GND, I, p .xxi.

[147] On the theme of place in the *Historia ecclesiastica*, see Hingst, *Written World*.

[148] On Orderic's importance for historians of the Norman world, see, for example, the droll opening of Thomas Bisson's C. Warren Hollister Memorial Lecture at the 2004 Haskins conference: 'Orderic Vitalis, without whom, I suspect, the Charles Homer Haskins Society would not exist, wrote the following words …'; address published as Thomas Bisson, 'Hallucination of Power: Climates of Fright in the Early Twelfth Century', *HSJ* 16 (2005), 1–11, at p. 1.

Orderic Vitalis, Historical Writing and a Theology of Reckoning

Giles E. M. Gasper

ORDERIC Vitalis does not present his *Historia ecclesiastica*, or for that matter his additions to William of Jumièges, as works of theology or of obvious theological interest. Indeed he indicates on occasion that he saw his work in a very different light, though he did so perhaps more as a reflection on his times than by his own inclination. Towards the beginning of Book V, written about 1128, Orderic recounts the appetite of his fellow monks for the history of their own house and their reluctance to set any of it down in writing:

> They were only too willing to read the deeds of their abbots and of the brethren of their house, and to learn of the building of its modest property, first given by its poor but pious founders and patiently augmented by the continual care of its father abbots; but they shrank from bending their minds to the task of composing or writing down their traditions.[1]

This record Orderic set himself to complete, as far as he was able. A significant disappointment in this process, if not an impediment, was the deterioration he observed in the behaviour of his contemporary society:

> The altercations of prelates and bloody wars of princes provide more material for the historian's pen than the treatises of theologians or the fasts and prophecies of ascetics.[2]

In these prefatory remarks Orderic contrasts the abundance of miracles

---

[1] *HE*, III, pp. 6–7: 'Libenter quippe legissent actus abbatum fratrumque suorum, et paruarum collectionem rerum suarum quae ab egenis sed deuotis fundatoribus tenuiter auctae sunt ingenti sollicitudine partum, sed ad dictani seu scribendi sedimen suum renuerunt incuruare ingenium.'

[2] Ibid., pp. 8–9: 'Historiographis ad scribendum uberius tema dant praesulum litigia, et cruenta principum proelia quam theologorum sintagmata, vel xerofagorum parsimonia siue prodigia.' Chibnall notes on p. 8 n. 3 that Alençon 2, a twelfth-century codex from Saint-Évroul contemporary with Orderic, includes a glossary of Hebrew and Greek words and an entry 'sintagmata: doctrina' on fol. 109; *Catalogue des manuscrits en écriture Latine portant des indications de date, de lieu ou de copiste*, ed. Charles Samaran and Robert Marichal, 7 vols. (Paris, 1959–84), VII, p. 3. I am very grateful to Charles Rozier for details on the manuscript and its current bibliography.

performed through God's will by the Fathers of older times, and the plentiful record of these miracles in books, with the spiritual decadence and poverty of his own time. Miracles have dried up, and been replaced by 'a growing frenzy of vices in those who give themselves up to fleshly lusts', which was taken to indicate the proximity of the time of Antichrist.[3] Theological treatises might be better and more useful material for a writer to set down for posterity, but Orderic is confined to what he has at his disposal: history will have to suffice.

The theological revolution of the later eleventh and twelfth centuries was well underway during the course of Orderic's writing career.[4] However, its appearance within Orderic's narrative is patchy. Unsurprisingly, he reserves his attention in this context for monastic theologians, and principally those within Normandy in the second half of the eleventh century. Lanfranc and Guitmond of Aversa receive due notice for their role in the debates against Berengar of Tours and the Eucharistic controversy, though the contribution to this polemic of figures such Durand of Troarn is not mentioned.[5] The intellectual developments of the schools occupy no space in Orderic's narrative: there is no Abelard, no Hugh of Saint-Victor, no Bernard of Clairvaux, no Anselm of Laon, no *Glossa ordinaria*. Monastic writers closer to Orderic's adult lifetime and experience (for example those of the new orders, especially the Cistercians, towards whom he was mostly antipathetic) feature much less frequently, if at all.[6] Absences can be explained by geographical focus, and by authorial background, taste and narrative strategy, but, nevertheless, the absences should be noted.

---

[3] *HE*, III, pp. 8–9: 'in his qui carnaliter amant se ipsos grassabitur rabies uiciorum'.

[4] See among recent literature the work of C. Mews, 'William of Champeaux, Abelard and Hugh of Saint-Victor: Platonism, Theology and Scripture in Early Twelfth-Century France', in *Bibel und Exegese in der Abtei Saint-Victor zu Paris: Form und Funktion eines Grundtextes im europäischen Raum herausgegeben von Rainer Berndt SJ*, ed. Rainer Berndt SJ (Munster, 2009), pp. 131–63. Alexander Andrée on the school of Laon, 'Laon Revisited: Master Anselm and the Creation of a Theological School in the Twelfth Century,' *Journal of Medieval Latin*, 22 (2012), 257–81, and his edition of Anselmi Laudunensis, *Glosae super Iohannem*, Corpus Christianorum Continuatio Mediaevalis, 267 (Turnhout, 2014). L. Smith, *The Glossa Ordinaria: The Making of a Medieval Bible Commentary* (Leiden, 2009), treats the creation of the gloss in the context of wider theological change. Among older literature, J. de Ghellinck, *Le Mouvement théologique du XIIe siècle* (Paris, 1914) retains its place as a foundational narrative, as do the influential studies of A. Wilmart, *Auteurs spirituels et textes dévots du Moyen Âge latin* (Paris, 1932; repr. Études Augustiniennes, 1971).

[5] *HE*, II, pp. 250–3 (Lanfranc), pp. 270–1 (Guitmond), pp. 298–9 (Durand, remembered for his musical composition).

[6] *HE*, VI, pp. 426–7, on the novelties of the Cistercians.

Orderic's most detailed commentary on monastic theology is devoted to Anselm of Bec, in the description of that monastery after the death of Abbot Herluin. It is an instructive example of Orderic's literary, historical and monastic priorities. Anselm, according to Orderic, 'pondered deeply on the obscure statements in the Scriptures, illuminating them in his teaching and writing, and explained the dark sayings of the prophets for men's spiritual good'.[7] Where Lanfranc assembled a great store of learning in the liberal arts and theology ('liberales artes' and 'sacra lectio') at Bec, Anselm magnificently increased it. The diligence of the Bec community in keeping copies of Anselm's works is matched by Orderic in mentioning some by title: *De trinitate* [On the Trinity], *De veritate* [On Truth], *De libertate arbitrii* [On Free Will], *De casu diaboli* [On the Fall of the Devil] and *Cur Deus homo* [Why the God-man]. (The first title probably refers to the *Monologion* and possibly the *Proslogion*.) Finally, the aptitude of the Bec monks in theological problem-solving is noted and held up as the crown of monastic living.

Orderic's *Historia ecclesiastica* is in no way a history of intellectual developments, or speculative theology, whether or not these were areas which held his personal interest. It contains, for all of that, a great deal of material that can be used to gain a theological insight on Orderic and his world. The commitment to ecclesiastical history holds the church and church communities very tightly to the centre of Orderic's narrative. The commitment to monastic life creates an equally powerful theme within his wider ecclesiological concerns. Moreover, the moral judgment which underpins Orderic's decisions on what and how to write anchors the *Historia ecclesiastica* to a series of Christian ethical positions. Although he makes no claims as to the broadly philosophical nature of his enterprise, it is clear that in all of the areas above, and throughout his writings, Orderic's mode of thought is premised on the faithful exposition of Christian life and teachings, especially as mediated through the monastic life. In light of this a consideration of Orderic's writing from an historical-theological perspective is both appropriate and useful in bringing to the fore these aspects of his conceptual world.

Historical theology, as a modern investigative tool, is focused fundamentally on the historical, social and cultural landscapes in which theological ideas and systems take shape.[8] In some cases this interest can

---

[7] HE, II, pp. 294–7: 'Obscuras sacrae Scripturae sententias sollerter indagauit, strenue uerbis aut scriptis dilucidauit et perplexa prophetarum dicta salubriter enodauit.'

[8] Historical theology as a disciplinary focus takes form especially in the eighteenth and nineteenth centuries, and the development of the history of dogma, exemplified by A. von Harnack, *Lehrbuch der Dogmengeschichte* (Frieburg im Breisgau, 1886–9) – *History of Dogma*, trans. N. Buchanan, E. B. Speirs, W. M. Gilchrist and A. B. Bruce (London, 1894–9). An excellent modern summary is provided by A. E. McGrath, *Historical*

be directed primarily at major figures within the period and the theological influences they represent and transmit. In terms of the historical evolution of theological thought this is perfectly justifiable, related as it is to systematic theology. However, as distinct from systematics, a different kind of historical theology lays emphasis on the context, and valorises the contextual in the analysis of theological development. As expressed by McGrath: 'Theology has a history, and the impact of the local, the circumstantial, on the universal is vitally important in that context. The universality of Christianity is complemented, rather than contradicted, by its particular application.'[9] Such analysis applies both to thinkers identified as canonical through processes in themselves important in historical-theological terms, and also, crucially, to any expression of theological thought.[10]

Historical theology overlaps not only with systematic theology but also with church or ecclesiastical history. The latter may be defined briefly as the history of Christianity with emphasis laid on the institutional development of the churches. The overlapping interests with the theological are clear, but the two disciplines remain differently focused. There are many aspects of the institutional life of the churches, and of the history of their changes and evolutions, which have no particular relevance for theological reflection. Again as observed by McGrath, for the church historian: 'Christianity is set within the flux of history, and church history aims to explore the particular place of Christian ideas, individuals and institutions within that flux. That influence is two-way: Christianity both influences and is influenced by culture.'[11]

These definitions are schematic, and emerge, broadly speaking, within modern theology as a consequence of the sixteenth-century reformations. The parsing of theology and the ideological significance of historical

---

Theology: An Introduction to Christian Thought, 2nd edn (Oxford, 1998; repr. 2011).

[9] McGrath, *Historical Theology*, p. 9.

[10] For the eminent Swiss theologian Karl Barth, one of the dominant voices of twentieth-century theology, the relationship between Scripture, the Christian faith and what he terms the *Weltanschauung*, was central to an understanding of Christianity. 'The Christian faith is bound neither to an old nor to a modern world-picture. The Christian Confession has in the course of the centuries passed through more than one world-picture. And its representatives were always ill-advised when they believed that this or that world-picture was an adequate expression for what the Church, apart from creation, has to think.' Karl Barth, *Dogmatics in Outline*, trans. G. T. Thomson (London, 1949), p. 59. Original publication: Karl Barth, *Dogmatik im Grundriss* (Zollikon-Zürich, 1947). That which provides unity is the incarnated Christ, a position familiar to high-medieval theology, and to Orderic's monastic meditations.

[11] McGrath, *Historical Theology*, p. 8.

interpretation took different shape within Protestant and Roman Catholic definitions of theological authority. The extent to which these definitions would have been recognised by Orderic and his contemporaries is far more questionable. Orderic's lifetime coincided with a shift in the expression of Christian thinking in the West, with the beginnings of a distinction between biblical exegesis and the systematic examination of theological problems. A growing interest in historical writing can also be identified, in which ecclesiastical history as inherited from the early church and earlier medieval period enjoyed a resurgence.[12] It would be difficult, however, and distorting, to seek to identify practitioners of historical theology in the medieval period.

To make such an identification is not the purpose of this investigation; but there is more to be said in terms of the working definition of historical theology and its usefulness as a heuristic tool. Historical theology enshrines the temporal as a mode of analysis, and this applies as much to the circumstances of an individual life as it does to the relationship between the local and the universal in terms of theological development. The location of the author of theological reflection, not merely in relation to their sources and context but also to themselves, that is to say, within their own life cycle, has an important effect on the nature of their thought. Historical-theological analysis, or sensitivity at least, brings the chronological and situational into sharper focus. The Augustine of *Retractiones* is not the Augustine of *Confessiones*, self-evidently; but to put the two in dialogue, the older and the younger, is to see part of a historical-theological analysis at work. Historical theology need not, of course, be chronologically constrained; comparison across time is as legitimate backwards as forwards. For example, the question of whether anything in Augustine could be considered 'Calvinist' is not illegitimate in an investigation seeking to increase our understanding of the particular contexts of theological questions.

Historical theology is about the present as much as the past, and can be as much about the individual as the institution, if not more so. To trace an individual history of theological reflection provides a microcosm for larger and longer interpretative arcs. For this to be possible, knowledge of the individual, and an extended stay in his or her company, are requisite.

---

[12] Twelfth-century historical writing has generated a significant amount of scholarship for the past thirty years. For a recent discussion of the philosophical and theological dimensions of high-medieval history, see S. O. Sønnesyn, *William of Malmesbury and the Ethics of History* (Woodbridge, 2012). Ecclesiastical history and its place within monastic communities is the subject of an unpublished Durham PhD thesis by Charles C. Rozier, 'The Importance of Writing Institutional History in the Anglo-Norman Realm, c. 1060–c. 1142, with Special Reference to Eadmer's *Historia Novorum*, Symeon of Durham's *Libellus de exordio*, and the *Historia Ecclesiastica* of Orderic Vitalis' (University of Durham, 2014).

Orderic provides a very interesting example of both. The rest of this chapter examines how Orderic's observations on his own life, especially in his older years, together with the reconstruction of the *Historia ecclesiastica*, might be seen in the context of monastic community and monastic theological reflection, and how those concerns have more than temporal, historical interest. What this cannot be is a consideration of age *per se* in the *Historia ecclesiastica*, though that would be an excellent theme to follow through Orderic's writing in his attitudes towards, and descriptions of, the young and the old, especially in the context of community.[13] Nor will this chapter trace a sustained theological treatment of any one particular theme within Orderic's work. He wrote, as he states, history, and a history of the church and its patrons, protectors, and pillagers, not a history of doctrine. Nevertheless, the framing of a theology of reckoning, of the hope and desire for salvation, of living, therefore, in right fashion, and of obedience to the rule, can be identified and commented upon.

Orderic famously summed up his own life at the end of Book XIII of the *Historia ecclesiastica*:

> Now indeed, worn out with age and infirmity, I long to bring this book to an end, and it is plain that many good reasons urge me to do so. For I am now in the sixty-seventh year of my life and service to my Lord Jesus Christ ...[14]

While such statements are conventional among medieval authors, there is no particular reason to doubt Orderic's words or sentiment here. A comparison might be made with Eadmer of Canterbury, who finished his collection of miracles attributed to, or associated with, Anselm probably not long after the death of Ralph d'Escures, at the end of 1122:

> I have written these things as best I could, O reverend father Anselm, to show the quality of your life, and I have purposefully omitted many things which might well with loud acclaim be ascribed to the greatness of God's working in you. But I have had regard to the unbelief of certain men who to this day with jaundiced minds are your detractors and assert that I have written too much. Now my white hairs and trembling fingers constrain me to lay down my pen, both persuading and compelling me to turn myself wholly to prayer

---

[13] See *HE*, II, pp. 18–19, for the insistence that the (re-)foundation of Saint-Évroul included men of all ages and ranks.

[14] *HE*, VI, pp. 550–1: 'Ecce senior et infirmitate fatigatus librum hunc finire cupio, et hoc ut fiat pluribus ex causis manifesta exposcit ratio. Nam sexagesimum septimum aetatis meae annum in cultu Domini mei Iesu Christi perago ...'

so that I may be found worthy to obtain some share in your merits in eternal life.[15]

Eadmer is more elaborate here than Orderic, and certainly more defensive (Orderic, after all, noted that he had enjoyed a good standing with all of his community, and the same cannot be said of Eadmer), but Eadmer was also making a statement of fact – he was sixty-two when he wrote, and died only about five years later. For both men these were the last things they wrote. Perhaps Orderic had in mind the final years of William of Poitiers, whom he had described earlier as follows: 'In his old age he gave himself up to silence and prayer, and spent more time in composing narratives and verse than in discourse.'[16]

Orderic moves to contrast the fate of secular rulers, rulers of the world, with his own security in a life of monastic obedience and poverty.

> I give thanks to thee, supreme King, who didst freely create me and ordain my life according to thy gracious will. For thou art my King and my God, and I am thy servant and the son of thine handmaid, one who from the beginning of my life has served thee as far as I was able.[17]

The more straightforward narrative of his life is given exegetical depth in the quotation from Psalm 115:16: 'the son of thine handmaid [ancillae tuus filius]'. The quotation is apt, coming as it does from a psalm of reckoning, account and satisfaction. The verses surrounding the quotation move through a sequence of humility, the means to salvation through God, and the powerful notion of death as something seen differently from the perspective of the Lord. The voice of the individual is most prominent, but spoken before the whole community of God's creation.

---

[15] Eadmer, 'A Brief Description of the Miracles of the Glorious Father Anselm of Canterbury', in *The Life of St Anselm, Archbishop of Canterbury, by Eadmer*, ed. and trans. R. W. Southern (Oxford, 1972), pp. 170–1: 'Haec pro designanda qualitate vitae tuae reverende pater Anselme qualicunque stilo digessi, ex industria multa preteriens quae magnitudini gratiae Dei quae tecum operabatur sullimi preconio possent ascribi. Peperci enim incredulitati quorundam qui usque hodie tibi non sincero animo detrahunt, et quae scipsi nimia esse contendunt. Iam cani capitis digitique trementes me a scribendo compescunt, et ut meritorum tuorum aliquam partem in vita perenni merear adipisci continua prece insistam, suadent atque compellunt.'

[16] *HE*, II, pp. 258–9: 'In senectute sua taciturnitati et orationi studuit, et plus in dictando seu uersificando quam sermocinando ualuit.'

[17] *HE*, VI, pp. 552–3: 'Tibi gratias ago summe rex qui me gratis fecisti, et annos meos secundum beneplacitam uoluntatem tuam disposuisti. Tu es enim rex meus et Deus meus, et ego sum seruus tuus et ancillae tuae filius qui pro posse meo a primis tibi uitae meae seruiui diebus.'

I have believed, therefore have I spoken; but I have been humbled exceedingly.
I said in my excess: Every man is a liar.
What shall I render to the Lord, for all the things that he hath rendered to me?
I will take the chalice of salvation; and I will call upon the name of the Lord.
I will pay my vows to the Lord before all his people:
Precious in the sight of the Lord is the death of his saints.[18]

Then comes the passage quoted by Orderic, followed by verses of praise, with the community once again supporting the speaker's anguished yet hopeful activity:

Thou hast broken my bonds:
I will sacrifice to thee the sacrifice of praise, and I will call upon the name of the Lord.
I will pay my vows to the Lord in the sight of all his people:
In the courts of the house of the Lord, in the midst of thee, O Jerusalem.[19]

The use and resonance of Psalm 115 sets up Orderic's presentation of his life, and the closing of his historical writing.

The life story that follows may owe something also to the conventions of Bede, who concluded his own *Historia ecclesiastica* with a summary of his life and a list of his works. Bede records the place of his birth, the age at which he was given to abbots Benedict and Ceolfrid (seven), and the years in which he was made deacon and priest (his nineteenth and thirtieth).[20] These details are mirrored in Orderic's account, though Orderic's is more detailed yet omits any mention of his other intellectual achievements.

For the present purpose, it is the exegetical grounding of Orderic's description of his life that is worth noting. Beginning with his baptism, which underlines the Christocentric mode, Orderic recalls his teacher Siward and then the climatic moment of his life: being given and sent to Saint-Évroul by his father at the age of ten. The old man calls to mind his younger self at the moment of parting, and the weeping with which

---

[18] Psalm 115:10–15: 'credidi propter quod locutus sum ego adflictus sum nimis/ ego dixi in stupore meo omnis homo mendacium/ quid reddam Domino pro omnibus quae tribuit mihi/ calicem salutis accipiam et nomen Domini invocabo/ vota mea Domino reddam coram omni populo eius/ gloriosa in conspectu Domini mors sanctorum eius.'

[19] Psalm 115:16–19: 'dirupisti vincula mea: tibi immolabo hostiam laudis et in nomine Domini invocabo/ vota mea Domino reddam in conspectu omnis populi eius/ in atriis domus Domini in medio tui Hierusalem.'

[20] Bede, *Ecclesiastical History of the English People*, ed. and trans. B. Colgrave and R. A. B. Mynors (Oxford, 1969; repr. 1992), pp. 566–7.

that moment was accompanied. Genesis 12:1, the instruction to Abraham to leave his homeland, is highlighted, perhaps also recalling to Orderic's readers the next verse, in which God promises to make of Abraham a great nation.[21] In remembering the ten-year-old boy, Orderic, fifty-six or fifty-seven years later, records that his obedience to his father's wishes was helped by the latter's promise that 'if I became a monk I should taste of the joys of paradise with the Innocents after my death'.[22]

The importance of proper living for the new exile, who compares himself to Joseph in Egypt, stresses the importance of his community. Like Joseph, Orderic states, he heard a language he did not understand.[23] He invokes the parable of the vineyard in Matthew 20:1–16, in which the virtues of patience and humility are stressed. Orderic's use of the parable also elides the earthly and heavenly kingdoms. The parable begins by likening heaven to a household: 'The kingdom of heaven is like to an householder, who went out early in the morning to hire labourers into his vineyard.'[24] Recalling his own early oblation, Orderic views himself as one of those who worked in the vineyard from morning, mapping, in this way, his own monastic experience back onto the description of heaven. He speaks expectantly, 'and I have waited knowing that I shall receive the penny that thou hast promised, for thou dost keep faith'.[25] The record of monastic life is accompanied with a record of ordination, before Orderic ends with a touching and beautiful prayer: 'Sic, sic, Domine Deus plasmator et uiuificator meus' ('Thus, thus, O Lord God, my creator and life-giver').[26] God is thanked for his mercies and his forgiveness invoked:

---

[21] Genesis 12:1–2: 'And the Lord said to Abram: Go forth out of thy country, and from thy kindred, and out of thy father's house, and come into the land which I shall shew thee. And I will make of thee a great nation, and I will bless thee, and magnify thy name, and thou shalt be blessed.' ('dixit autem Dominus ad Abram: egredere de terra tua et de cognatione tua et de domo patris tui et veni in terram quam monstrabo tibi. faciamque te in gentem magnam et benedicam tibi et magnificabo nomen tuum erisque benedictus.')

[22] *HE*, VI, pp. 552–3: 'si monachus fierem, quod post mortem meam paradisum cum Innocentibus possiderem'.

[23] Ibid., pp. 554–5: 'Linguam ut Ioseph in Aegipto quam non noueram audiui.' When Joseph's brothers enter Egypt in the time of famine they are overheard and understood by their as yet unrecognised brother, 'And they knew not that Joseph understood, because he spoke to them by an interpreter.' ('Nesciebant autem quod intelligeret Ioseph, eo quod per interpretem loqueretur ad eos.') Genesis 42:23.

[24] Matthew 20.1: 'simile est enim regnum caelorum homini patrifamilias qui exiit primo mane conducere operarios in vineam suam'.

[25] *HE*, VI, pp. 554–5: 'et denarium quem pollicitus es securus quia fidelis ex expectaui'.

[26] Ibid., pp. 556–7. 'Plasmator meus' is also used in the Fécamp *First Chronicle*, and may have liturgical origins in prayers after the mass. See M. Arnoux,

'Spare me, O Lord, and do not let me be destroyed; look compassionately according to thine inexhaustible goodness on the work of thy hands, and pardon and wash away all my sins.'[27] The same is sought for Orderic's friends and benefactors, before a final appeal to the intercession of the Virgin Mary, and an orthodox doxology, 'O Lord God, Father omnipotent, creator and ruler of the angels, true hope and eternal beatitude of the just ...'.[28]

The character Orderic creates for himself within this section of his work emerges as steadfast, and is articulated through a mode of expression permeated with biblical resonance.[29] A comparison to the *Rule of St Benedict* is helpful here, to contextualise how Orderic conceptualises a life well – that is, virtuously – lived. The *Rule*'s Chapter 4, on the tools of the spiritual craft, contains a set of maxims which offer a fairly uncompromising version of Augustinian pessimism on post-lapsarian humanity and its inclination towards sin. The monk is enjoined to: 'Fear Judgment Day. Have a healthy fear of hell. Long for eternal life with the desire of the Spirit. Keep your eye on death every day. Maintain a strict control over your actions at every moment.'[30] Orderic's self-assessment is in keeping with these injunctions. Chapter 49, on the observance of Lent, is more explicit:

> At all times the lifestyle of a monk ought to have a Lenten quality. However, because few have that kind of strength, we urge them to guard their lives with all purity during these Lenten days. All should work together at effacing during this holy season the negligences of other time. The proper way to do this is to restrain ourselves from all evil habits and to devote ourselves to tearful prayer, reading, compunction of heart and asceticism [...] Let him deny his body

---

'Before the *Gesta Normannorum* and Beyond Dudo: Some Evidence on Early Norman Historiography', *ANS* 22 (1999), 29–48, in Appendix 2, p. 45.

[27] *HE*, VI, pp. 556–7: 'Parce michi Domine, et ne confundas me [sed secundum] infatigabilem bonitatem tuam pie plasma tuum respice, et omnia peccata mea dimitte et absterge.'

[28] Ibid.: 'O Domine Deus omnipotens Pater conditor et rector angelorum, uera spes et aeterna beatitude iustorum ...'.

[29] Chibnall's description of the passage as a 'declaration of faith' rather flattens the effect that Orderic achieves; see her introduction to *HE*, VI, p. xvii.

[30] T. Kardong, *Benedict's Rule: A Translation and Commentary* (Collegeville, MN, 1996), p. 81; Latin at p. 79: 'Diem iudicii timere, gehennam expavescere, vitam aeternam omni concupiscentia spirituali desiderare, mortem cotidie ante oculos suspectam habere. Actus vitae suae omni hora custodire'. The Latin text used by Kardong is from *RB 1980: The Rule of St Benedict in Latin and English with Notes* (Collegeville, MN, 1981). Notes and commentary on Chapter 4 are to be found at pp. 83–102.

some food, some drink, some sleep, some chatter, some joking, and let him await Holy Easter with the joy of spiritual desire.[31]

The tone of Chapter 49 matches Orderic's expression in the summation and cessation of his history.[32] The end of his Lenten vigil approaches, but he has acted as he should have in order to enjoy the Easter which will follow and the completion of the punishment of sin in life. In a similar manner to this chapter of the *Rule*, in which although the individual monk takes centre-stage the community is never far away, Orderic recalls his own life as experienced personally and in the community. The chapter's insistence that joy should be part of the Lenten experience, as well as that of Eastertide, and the fact that this joy is grounded in the action of the Holy Spirit, is not absent from Orderic's reflections either.[33]

Orderic died sometime after 1141. The final section of his work can be seen to emphasise Benedictine values, as well as biblical sensitivity in constructing the presentation of his life. A little earlier he had undertaken the reshaping of the *Historia ecclesiastica*, an action that might suggest an instinct to submit the 'altercations of prelates and bloody wars of princes' to a similar process of accounting, reckoning and cessation. By 1136–7 he

---

[31] Kardong, *Benedict's Rule*, p. 402; Latin at p. 401: 'Licet omni tempore vita monachi quadragesimae debet observationem habere, tamen, quia paucorum est ista virtus, ideo suademus istis diebus quadragesimae omni puritate vitam suam custodire omnes partiter, et neglegentias aliorum temporum his diebus sanctis diluere. Quod tunc digne fit si ab omnibus vitiis temperamus, orationi cum fletibus, lectioni et compunctioni cordis atque abstinentiae operam damus [...] id est subtrahat corpori suo de cibo, de potu, de somno, de loquacitate, de scurrilitate, et cum spiritalis desiderii gaudio sanctum Pascha exspectet.' Notes and commentary on Chapter 49 are to be found at pp. 402–10.

[32] Orderic's decision to stop writing is connected explicitly to old age: 'Now indeed, worn out with age and infirmity, I long to bring this book to an end ('Ecce senior et infirmitate fatigatus librum hunc finire cupio'); *HE*, VI, pp. 550–1. Henri Nouwen writes movingly about the point in aging where the past is no longer a prime concern: 'Once in a while we meet an old man or woman looking far beyond the boundaries of their human existence into a light that seems to embrace him or her with gentleness and kindness [...] The vision which grows in aging can lead us beyond the limitations of our human self. It is a vision that makes us not only detach ourselves from preoccupation with the past but also from the importance of the present. It is a vision that invites us to a total, fearless surrender in which the distinction between life and death slowly loses its pain.' Henri J. M. Nouwen and Walter J. Gaffney, *Aging, The Fulfillment of Life* (New York, 1976), p. 79. Whether Orderic had reached a similar stage is a matter for speculation, but it serves to underline the importance of age in assessing his authorial career at all stages.

[33] Kardong, *Benedict's Rule*, pp. 408–10, for Benedict's emphasis on community and pneumatologically grounded joy.

had completed Books I and II, and added them to the history as a whole.[34] Book I moves through the life of Christ, the Roman emperors and the history of Western Christendom, offering a chronological sketch running up to Orderic's own time of writing; Book II moves through the lives of the Apostles, and then church leaders, including popes to his own day. Orderic in Book II does not employ the strategy of a near-contemporary at Bec, the anonymous author of 'The Profession of Monks', who asserts that monasticism stretched right back to the apostles and the events of Pentecost.[35] Orderic's aim is to produce something larger than a history of monasticism alone. Books I and II connect the individual and temporal with the cosmic and eternal. They also grant a properly historical-theological context to the rest of Orderic's work, bound as they are to the Incarnation and a Christocentric playing out of human life and existence.

It is perhaps here that we find another context for Orderic's regular concern with the preservation of memory. In the book with which he started his work (Book III), he states concerning the record of Saint-Évroul's development that: 'It would be impossible for me to catalogue everything which each man bestowed on his house, but I hope with God's aid to leave a true record of some things, as occasion offers, for the benefit of future generations.'[36] A little later, and in a slightly wider context, he remarks:

> I consider it a worthy task to preserve for later generations the memory of those fathers who governed the monasteries of Normandy so wisely in the time of King William, and strove all their lives to serve the eternal King whose reign is immutable. I believe their followers have left long accounts of their lives for future generations, but nevertheless it is a pleasing task for me at least to name here with my own masters a few whom I love above the rest, not for any worldly profit, but simply for love of the wisdom and piety with which heaven endowed them.[37]

---

[34] See 'Composition of the *Historia ecclesiastica*' (p. xiv above).

[35] *Three treatises from Bec on the Nature of Monastic Life*, ed. and trans. G. Constable and B. S. Smith (Toronto, 2008), pp. 30/31 ff.

[36] *HE*, II, pp. 150–1: 'Singillatim omnia quae domui suae singuli contulerunt omnino describere nequeo sed tamen aliqua prout competentem referenda facultatem uidero, iuuante Deo ueraciter intimare pro communi commodo posteritati cupio.'

[37] Ibid., pp. 292–3: 'Operae precium esse reor patrum memoriam posteris intimare qui Normanniae monasteria sub rege Guillelmo prudenter rexere, et aeterno regi qui incommutabiliter regnat studuerunt usque ad mortem digniter obsecundare. Sequaces eorum multa de eis ut reor scripta posteritati dimisere sed tamen quosdam quos prae caeteris amo non pro temporali mercede, sed pro solo amore sapientiae et religionis sibi coelitus inditae dulce michi est cum magistris meis in hac saltem pagina nominare.'

When Orderic came to write the preface to Book III, after the *Historia* was restructured, he began with yet another reformulation of the context for memorialisation. Through an invocation of the Creator, the authority of Scripture, and knowledge of the love of Christ, Orderic's task – to record the deeds of the Normans – is placed in a broader context still, of emulation of the saints and the redemptive act of Incarnation.[38]

Orderic's reflection on reckoning and the passing of life appears in the very structure of his *Historia*, and as part of the gathering of his experience of monastic and Christian living. There are also other contexts in which Orderic's theological vision, in a broad sense, can be explored. It would be quite possible to read Orderic's history through the senses of scripture, for literal and moral reading, and occasionally allegorical and spiritual reading, are all part of the multi-dimensional way in which he writes.[39] How far this is liturgically grounded would be another fruitful avenue to pursue. As for Orderic's sense of age and death, and the context for his theological ruminations, a helpful parallel is offered in Aers's discussion of *Piers Plowman* as a meditation on the subject.[40] Aers offers a sensible reminder of the recognisable Augustinian tenet that death, no matter how stoically endured, is still a punishment for sin: 'And is there anything about the world at the beginning of the twenty-first century that should make us find Augustine's vision unimaginably alien? I do not think so.'[41] If this is the case for Langland, it is so for Orderic as well. Aers notes particularly the inseparability of Langland's meditations on growing old and his meditations on the church; this no less so for Orderic. His emphasis on his house and the wider monastic community, including the epitaphs of which he was so devoted a collector, compiler and composer, speak of this most powerfully. It is in the relation of the record of local, temporal, transient human existence to the cosmic landscape of salvation that Orderic's theological reflections are to be placed. Through this, the extent to which his understanding of both underpinned his *Historia ecclesiastica* as it evolved to its final articulation may be better appreciated.

---

[38] Ibid., pp. 2–3.

[39] For example, Orderic makes striking use of the Heptateuch and Kings in this regard, which have an interesting commentary in Chapter 42 of the Rule, where reading them after supper is prohibited: 'because it will not be good for weak minds to hear those parts of Scripture at that time of day; let those books be read at other times'.

[40] D. Aers, 'The Christian Practice of Growing Old in the Middle Ages', in *Growing Old in Christ*, ed. S. Haeurwas, C. B. Stoneking, K. G. Meador and D. Cloutier (Grand Rapids, MI, 2003), pp. 38–59, at pp. 56–9.

[41] Ibid., p. 46.

Jesus Christ, a Protagonist of Anglo-Norman History? History and Theology in Orderic Vitalis's *Historia ecclesiastica*

Elisabeth Mégier

As is well known, Orderic began his *Historia ecclesiastica* as a history of his own monastery, Saint-Évroul in Normandy, but progressively expanded it to what is almost a comprehensive history of contemporary Christianity, embracing a geographical area from Spain to the Holy Land, from England to Sicily, with, however, a strong focus on the Anglo-Norman world. At a certain stage of the composition, Orderic decided to place two additional books ahead of this Norman history (the original Book I became Book III, and so on) dedicated to apparently quite different themes. Most of Book I consists of a kind of Gospel harmony, an extensive life of Christ, followed by the history of the apostles up to the descent of the Holy Spirit; a brief world chronicle ordered by the reigns of the Roman emperors fills the chronological gap between Pentecost and Orderic's present time. Book II contains the (also very extensive) lives of the apostles and evangelists and a second chronicle, arranged chronologically by the pontificates of the Roman popes.

Modern scholarship has made little attempt to understand and explain the relationship between these two books and the rest of the work,[1] and the fact that in Marjorie Chibnall's edition they appear only in the form of summaries and extracts has not helped to clarify their role in Orderic's

---

[1] The addition of the subjects contained in Books I and II of the *Historia ecclesiastica* has been seen as a rather unsuccessful attempt to conform to the genre of universal chronicles: see Hans Wolter, *Ordericus Vitalis: Ein Beitrag zur Kluniazensischen Geschichtsschreibung* (Wiesbaden, 1955), p. 69; Anna-Dorothee von den Brincken, *Studien zur lateinischen Weltchronistik bis in das Zeitalter Ottos von Freising* (Düsseldorf, 1957), p. 203. A more favourable view is expressed by Orderic's editor, Marjorie Chibnall (see below), and by Roger D. Ray, 'Orderic Vitalis and his Readers', *Studia monastica* 14 (1972), 17–33, at p. 28. Hingst, *Written World*, p. 112, suggests that 'Orderic's liturgical meditations on the life and body of Christ [...] influenced his decision to begin his *Ecclesiastical history* with the temporal life of Jesus.'

general project.² This chapter will stress the coherence of Orderic's work as a whole, and, by summing up and developing in greater detail some points of a previous study,³ I will show that by introducing Christ and some of the major figures of early Christendom as distinctive subjects, Orderic clarifies a meaning present in his narration from the beginning. I will suggest further that this meaning is not simply a question of moral judgement, but implies a fully coherent theology of history, which has been mostly neglected or misunderstood by modern observers because it was uncommon at Orderic's time, and does not correspond to our current conceptions concerning this matter.⁴

In Chibnall's view the *Historia ecclesiastica* is made of two heterogeneous components which, however, 'were loosely but persuasively joined by the metaphor of the vine'.⁵ By this she alludes to the representation of the Church as God's vineyard, which appears at several crucial points of the composition: in the opening sentence of Book III, which introduces Orderic's report on the first monastic foundations – the 'first shoots of the vine' – in Normandy; in the epilogue of the whole work at the end of Book XIII, where Orderic presents himself, in his capacity as the author, as one of the labourers in the vineyard; and again at the beginning of Book I, as an introduction to the life of Christ. This shows, Chibnall explains, that Orderic saw the Church as a whole, comprising all of Christian life,

---

² *HE*. For the complete text of Books I and II one must refer to *Orderici Vitalis Ecclesiasticae historiae libri tredecim*, ed. Auguste Le Prévost, 5 vols. (Paris, 1838), I, cited here as *HE* LeP.

³ Elisabeth Mégier, '*Cotidie operatur*: Christus und die Geschichte in der *Historia ecclesiastica* des Ordericus Vitalis', *Revue Mabillon* n. s. 10 (1999), 169–204, reprinted in Elisabeth Mégier, *Christliche Weltgeschichte im 12. Jahrhundert: Themen, Variationen und Kontraste: Untersuchungen zu Hugo von Fleury, Ordericus Vitalis und Otto von Freising*, Beihefte zur Mediaevistik 13 (Frankfurt am Main etc., 2010), pp. 243–82.

⁴ Johannes Spörl calls Orderic's theology of history 'konservativ', 'unoriginell': Johannes Spörl, *Grundformen hochmittelalterlicher Geschichtsanschauung: Studien zum Weltbild der Geschichtsschreiber des 12. Jahrhunderts* (Munich, 1935), pp. 61 ff. Beryl Smalley gives a similar judgement in her *Historians in the Middle Ages* (New York, 1974), p. 87. The recent attempt made by Hans-Werner Goetz to fit Orderic's life of Christ into what he sees as the standard scheme of salvation history is in my opinion misleading, and tends to rule out Orderic's originality: Hans-Werner Goetz, *Gott und die Welt: Religiöse Vorstellungen des frühen und hohen Mittelalters* (Berlin, 2011) I/2, p. 232. More pertinent is Nico Lettinck, *Geschiedsbeschouwing en Beleving van de eigen Tijd in de eerste Helft von de twaalfde Eeuw* (Amsterdam, 1983), esp. pp. 102–6 and p. 212; see also Ray C. Petry, 'Three Medieval Chroniclers: Monastic Historiography and Biblical Eschatology in Hugh of St Victor, Otto of Freising, and Ordericus Vitalis', *Church History* 34 (1965), 282–93, at pp. 284 ff. and p. 291.

⁵ Chibnall, *World*, pp. 177 ff.

so a history of the Church, a *Historia ecclesiastica*, could certainly cover all kinds of subjects. It is arguable that there is more to be found in the metaphor of the vine than Chibnall has inferred. When Orderic says, at the beginning of Book III, the original first book: 'My first task is to tell of the vine of the Lord of Hosts which his strong right hand tends and preserves throughout the world against the wiles of Behemoth',[6] he refers not only to the Church as the vineyard of the Lord of Hosts but also to the Lord of Hosts as the cultivator of the vineyard. The epilogue where Orderic remembers his life and his toils in the *vinea Sorech* is a prayer addressed to God 'who has ordained the years of his servant according to his gracious will', and whom Orderic wants to thank for his gifts and mercies.[7] The same double theme, the Church and God, appears again in Book I, when Orderic presents Jesus Christ not only as 'the true vine', but also as the 'highest patron of the household, who has planted the vine, and takes care of it from morning until the eleventh hour, by the labourers he sends'.[8]

In other words, Orderic not only creates a formal unity by the repeated reference to a certain metaphorical image of the Church, but also a unity of meaning by the equally repeated reference to the corresponding representation of God. The divine Lord, the promoter and protector of his vine, the Church, is Orderic's reference in his original contemporary Norman history, and then becomes, in the person of Jesus Christ, a character within the narration. The divine presence which Orderic sees at work in his own time and surroundings is the same as that embodied in the earthly life and action of Jesus Christ. So the subject matter of the additional books, as announced by Orderic at the beginning of Book I, is none other than that of Orderic's original project, as announced at the beginning of Book III, and alluded to in the conclusion of the work; that is, the mutual relationship between the Church and God.

The characteristics of this relationship, which are also the same in the history of Christ and of his first followers as told in Books I and II, and in Norman history as told in Books III to XIII, are, in fact, quite specific. Orderic's God, who takes care of his vine and listens to the prayers of his servants, must be a benevolent God, close to humankind. Orderic does not, like many of his colleagues, associate God's design in history with a succession of events or stages concerning certain privileged protagonists,

---

[6] *HE*, II, p. 4: 'Opus in primis arripiam de uinea Domini sabaoth, quam ipse forti dextera colit et protegit in toto mundo contra insidias Behemoth.'

[7] *HE*, VI, p. 554.

[8] *HE*, I, p. 134: 'Omnipotens uerbum per quod Deus pater omnia condidit, uitis uera summusque paterfamilias qui uineam plantauit, et a mane usque ad undecimam horam intromissis operariis excolit, ut uberem fructum ex eadem colligere possit, eandem uineam id est sanctam aecclesiam nullo tempore desistit colere, eiusque palmites per omnia mundi climata nobiliter propagare.'

such as the rise and fall of empires, or the growth of the universal dominion of the Church, but with the moral betterment of individual persons.[9] The events of history are God's means of educating his creatures, as we read for instance in the epilogue of Book VI:

> For the omnipotent Creator, who first made the world, likewise wonderfully guides its course, and by teaching those men who are willing to hear restrains them from the deadly lust for evil things and encourages them to a better life by revealing marvellous deeds. For the human race is continually instructed by the putting down of the proud and the exaltation of the lowly, the damnation of sinners and the salvation of the just, so that it may not be made blasphemous by the terrible enemy of God, but may always fear the judgement and love the rule of God, avoiding the sin of disobedience and constantly offering faithful service to Father, Son and Holy Spirit, one God, King of the saints, Lord of all things, who lives and reigns throughout all ages. Amen.[10]

Orderic expresses the same idea on several other occasions.[11]

---

[9] The best-known example is Otto of Freising as the author of the *Chronica sive Historia de duabus civitatibus*. On this author see Hans-Werner Goetz, *Das Geschichtsbild Ottos von Freising: Ein Beitrag zur historischen Vorstellungswelt und zur Geschichte des 12. Jahrhunderts* (Köln-Wien, 1984). For a comparison between Otto and Orderic, see Mégier, *Christliche Weltgeschichte im 12. Jahrhundert*, pp. 169–88, 243–63.

[10] *HE*, III, p. 360: 'Cunctipotens creator ut ab inicio cepit sic mire disponit cursus saeculorum, et dociles instruens animos terrigenarum, a noxio reuocat appetitu infimorum, ac prouocat ad meliora mirabilium exhibitione gestorum. Nam deiectione sullimium, et exaltatione humilium, damnatione reproborum, et saluatione iustorum, incessanter eruditur genus humanum, ne per execrabilem theomachiam fiat prophanum, sed ut diuinum semper metuat iudicium et diligat imperium, inoboedientiae deuitet reatum, et fidelem iugiter offerat famulatum Patri et Filio Spirituique Sancto uni Deo regi sanctorum, Dominoque uniuersorum, qui uiuit et regnat per infinita secula seculorum, Amen.' Cf. ibid., p. xv. Chibnall's translation, which I adopt, is not always quite faithful to Orderic's intention, the *infima* are base or vile rather than evil things, which suggests an opposition not so much between good and evil but between wordly and monastic values. However, in other cases the problem is effectively wickedness, *nequitia*, for example in *HE*, VI, p. 226: 'Inter haec omnipotens Deus mirifica in orbe magnalia monstrauit quibus intuentium corda ut castigarentur a nequitia commonuit.'

[11] See the text quoted in the preceding note, and *HE*, III, pp. 12 ff.; *HE*, VI, p. 476. On history as divine pedagogy, see Peter v. Moos, *Geschichte als Topik: Das rhetorische Exemplum von der Antike zur Neuzeit und die 'historiae' im 'Policraticus' Johanns von Salisbury*, Ordo: Studien zur Literatur und Gesellschaft des Mittelalters und der frühen Neuzeit 2 (Hildesheim, 1988), esp. pp. 8–10.

This pedagogical design of Orderic's historical writing includes both salvation of the just and damnation of sinners, but its general tone is of trust and confidence. God does punish to lead men to do good, but he also relieves and rewards. Orderic lets his readers observe the chain that leads from sin to divine punishment, from punishment to conversion, from conversion to divine pardon and assistance, and it is this last aspect that is most emphasised. An episode regarding the fate of Saint-Évroul is emblematic. In the troubled period at the end of the Carolingian reign the monastery had been robbed of its principal relics and other treasures by the attendants of Hugh the Great, and Orderic inserts into his report an imaginary speech made by the prior:

> Divine chastisement has fallen upon us for our sins and the sins of our fathers […] we see that the omnipotent judge who destroyed Jerusalem and the temple of Solomon by the hands of Nebuchadnezzar and the Chaldaeans has in the same way justly brought this holy place to the ground by the hands of Hugh and the Franks and has punished it with various afflictions.[12]

While pursuing the robbers, the monks, helped by a miracle, gain the favour of Hugh the Great, who takes care of their sustenance; they are also well received in Orléans, where they find a new home. In this Orderic (who now speaks in his own name) sees a sign of God's mercy to those who turn back from their errors:

> But the kind Lord, who chastises sinners to bring them back to the right path, rewards with fatherly love those who turn to him and shows mercy in wonderful ways to those in need.[13]

Similarly, commenting on the escape of a group of imprisoned crusaders, Orderic writes:

> Merciful God, who created all things and knows how to chastise his servants for their sins, likewise miraculously helps suppliants and those who humbly call upon him, and, working even through

---

[12] This is one of Oderic's frequent allusions to biblical episodes which provide analogies to present events, cf. Elisabeth Mégier, 'Diuina pagina and the Narration of History in Orderic Vitalis' *Historia ecclesiastica*', *Revue bénédictine* 110 (2000), 106–23, reprinted in Mégier, *Christliche Weltgeschichte im 12. Jahrhundert*, pp. 283–99.

[13] *HE*, III, pp. 316–18: 'Pro peccatis nostris et patrum nostrorum diuina percussio super nos descendit […] Ecce iudex omnipotens sicut per manus Nabuchodonosor et Chaldaeorum Ierusalem et templum Salomonis destruxit, sanctuariumque suum iuste humiliauit, sic per manus Hugonis atque Francorum hunc locum pluribus modis affligendo puniit […] Benignus autem Dominus qui erroneos uerberat, ut rectum ad callem reducat, conuersos paterno affectu demulcet, mirisque modis indigentibus suffragium exhibet.'

their enemies, encourages them with a hope of better things. This
Abraham and Joseph proved under Pharaoh among the Egyptians,
this Tobias and Raguel [...].

Orderic continues with a long list of Old and New Testament examples,
and concludes:

> Mortals are chastised with the whips of oppression because of the
> sins to which human frailty is prone, and as they suffer under the
> whip are forced to appeal tearfully to the mercy of the heavenly
> Creator. But God our King, who saves those who put their trust in
> him, is powerful to hear the pleas of his spouse, the Church.[14]

So, in general terms, it is a kind, merciful, loving God who appears
in the *Historia ecclesiastica*.[15] Orderic's favourite term to qualify him is
'benignus' and its derivatives, together with 'misericors', 'clemens', 'pius'.
This God is ready to pardon and to help the Church, in the first place
those of its exponents who are particularly dear to Orderic, like the monks
and the crusaders, but also all other kinds of person, like a young peasant
woman from Flanders saved from a flood 'by the pity of the merciful God',
along with her baby, her hen and her chickens.[16]

This merciful God cannot be better represented than by Jesus Christ.
In fact, already in the original part of the *Historia ecclesiastica* Orderic
tends to emphasise Christ's presence as a person; for instance, to the
generally biblical image of God cultivating his vineyard he adds the more
specifically evangelical image of God rescuing his ship from a storm. This
is how Orderic comments on the designation of a new abbot of Saint-
Évroul in a critical situation:

> The eternal ruler of all things skilfully sails his ship among the
> storms of the world, steering it wisely. He bountifully [*benigniter*]

---

[14] HE, V, p. 358: 'Benignus autem Deus qui omnia creauit, sicut seruos suos pro peccatis tribulationibus castigare nouit, sic supplicibus et humiliter inuocantibus eum mirabiliter succurrit, et per ipsos etiam inimicos illis spe melius subuenit. Hoc experti sunt sub Pharaone Abraham et Ioseph inter Aegiptios, hoc Tobias et Raguhel [...] hoc etiam apostoli aliique sancti predicatores feliciter senserunt [...] Flagellis quippe oppressionis terrigenae pro sceleribus humanae fragilitatis uerberantur, et clementiam conditoris coelesti uerbere afflicti lacrimabiliter exorare coguntur. Deus autem rex noster qui saluos facit sperantes in se potenter suae sponsae preces exaudiuit ecclesiae, et auxiliatus est uincto duci et eius collegis.'

[15] One can observe that Orderic also uses such terms, in particular 'benignus', 'benigniter', 'benignitas', to describe the relationship between human beings, especially where monks are concerned.

[16] HE, VI, p. 440: 'Miseratione uero misericordis Dei mulier saluata est, et in tanta uicinitate mortis cum paruulis rebus quas secum habebat morti coelitus erepta est.'

helps the labourers toiling daily in his vineyard and, imbuing them with divine grace, strengthens them to face toils and perils. Consider how he directs his church amidst the tumults of war and the clash of arms, and preserving and enlarging it in many ways leads it on to safety! The monastery of Saint-Évroul has truly proved this [...] striving with the help of God's mercy it has been preserved against the threats of wicked men.[17]

Here the intervention of Jesus Christ is only suggested; Orderic is more explicit elsewhere, when again writing about the problems faced by Saint-Évroul from its unruly neighbours:

But bountiful [benignus] Jesus, who is the true spouse of the Church, miraculously stretched forth his hand over the raging waves that threatened to engulf the ship of the church, and bade them be still.[18]

The second image added here, Jesus as spouse of the Church, appears also on several other occasions. For instance, we read on behalf of the persecution of the Church in Gaul at the time of Diocletian:

However, he who promised that he could never forsake his followers miraculously strengthened his spouse in the fierce tempests of tribulation and freed, protected, and raised her up again [...] So he did not suffer her whom he so deeply loved to be deprived of good teachers for long during the storms of persecution.[19]

Christ's promise to be near his Church at all times is made more explicit by Orderic's quoting his words in John 5:17 (here regarding the deliverance of the imprisoned crusaders already mentioned):

---

[17] *HE*, III, pp. 116–18: 'Aeternus dispositor rerum nauem suam inter procellas seculi potenter uehit et sapienter gubernat, et in uinea sua colonos cotidie laborantes benigniter adiuuat, atque infusione celestis gratiae contra labores et pericula corroborat. En ecclesiam suam inter bellicosos tumultus et militares strepitus prouide dirigit [...] Hoc Vticense monasterium plausabiliter expertum est, quod in sterili rure et inter pessimos affines consitum est sed ope supernae pietatis contra perfidorum minaces conatus defensatum est. Mainerius abbas mense iulio huius aecclesiae curam suscepit.'

[18] *HE*, II, p. 54: 'Sed benignus Iesus qui est uerus aecclesiae sponsus, quamuis saeuirent ad deprimendam aecclesiae nauem maris fluctus, ipse mirabiliter emicuit in ereptione suorum comprimendo contrarios conatus.'

[19] *HE*, III, pp. 46–8: 'Ceterum ille qui suis semper se affuturum esse promisit, in immensis tribulationum procellis sponsam suam mirabiliter confortauit, ac liberauit, protexit et exaltauit, et honorabilibus triumphis palam magnificauit, insuper aeterno diademate coram patre suo in coelesti Ierusalem remunerabit. Ergo quam tantum diligit inter furias persequentium pedagogis illustribus destitui diu non desiit.'

So indeed he who said, 'My Father works hitherto, and I work', in recent times has visited in their prison those champions of his of whom I discourse in writing for the information of generations to come, out of wonder at the divine works, and he has brought them great joy with the sweet nectar of kindness [*benignitas*].[20]

So, by the evocation of God's benevolence, combined with its personification, Jesus Christ obtains an eminent place in the *Historia ecclesiastica* even before becoming a subject in his own right in Book I. Not only does Orderic, like other medieval historians, emphasise the role of divine guidance and operation, but (and this is not so common) he also tends to present this divine guidance and operation distinctly as the action of the Son.

It is not unreasonable to suppose Orderic was aware that the kind of relationship between God and men which he wanted his historical narrative to show might not always be evident in contemporary experience. This means that the addition of the life of Christ and the lives of his first followers to the contemporary history of the Normans can be seen as an attempt to increase the visibility of God's benevolence. This might have seemed more and more necessary as Orderic's historical horizon widened from the monastic world of Saint-Évroul to its secular surroundings. In this secular world the contradiction between divine benevolence and the weight of human sin and suffering needed, in Orderic's eyes, to be resolved by the personal intervention of Christ as the Saviour.

We can see, in any case, that the whole life of Christ, as narrated by Orderic in concord with the Gospels, bears witness to his benign and merciful disposition. We find here vocabulary and formulations similar to those we have met in the original books. Christ is the 'clemens dominus' ('mild Lord'), 'benignus doctor' ('gentle teacher'), 'benignus opifex' ('benevolent creator'), and 'fons pietatis' ('fountain of mercy'); he acts 'misericordia motus' ('moved by compassion'), so as to further human salvation ('consulens humanae saluti').[21] The episode of the storm at sea is explicitly related to Christ's action in the present:

> This is how the same Emmanuel operates daily in the sea of this world, when the ship of his church is tossed about by the waves of adversity, and is almost overcome by the enormity of danger. But as He is tearfully implored, with faith, by those who belong to Him, He is speedily present, and assists them wonderfully by the power

---

[20] *HE*, V, p. 358: 'Sic nimirum ille qui dixit, Pater meus usque modo operatur et ego operor, athletas suos de quibus futurorum noticiae pro diuinorum admiratione operum scribendo loquor, nuper in ergastulo uisitauit, et mellifluo nectare benignitatis suae ubertim laetificauit.'

[21] *HE* LeP, I, pp. 22, 23, 58, 26, 51.

of His divinity, and sustains them forcefully, having calmed down without delay the perilous assaults.[22]

There are also some specific themes expressing divine benevolence which connect Books I and II with the rest of Orderic's work. One of them is the theme of miracles, combined with the theme of sanctity. In the original books this appears in a largely negative way. Orderic deplores the scarcity of saints and miracles in his own time,[23] and one could think that his inserting a number of lives of former saints, including the life of St Évroul, and the lives of the saints Judoc, Guthlac, and William of Gellone, into Books III to VI was an attempt to compensate for this deficiency; one can also suppose that he did not consider this compensation sufficient. To present the lives of the apostles and evangelists, saints *par excellence*, would certainly help to reinforce the idea. Here, miracles and admirable examples of virtue abound, and the same can be said, *a fortiori*, of the life of Jesus Christ, which Orderic sums up as 'the continuation of the miracles of our Lord Jesus Christ, which are written in the four Gospels'.[24] In his narration he does not fail to report a single miracle mentioned in the Gospels. Christ and the saints also provide models for saintly Christian behaviour, which Orderic found so cruelly

---

[22] Ibid., p. 20: 'Sic idem in salo huius saeculi Emmanuel quotidie operatur, dum navis Ecclesiae suae diuersarum procellis tribulationum iactatur, et pene discriminum enormitate periclitatur. Sed quia cum fide flebiliter a suis invocatur, presto adest, et virtute deitatis suae mirabiliter eis suffragatur, et continuo sedatis tentationibus fortiter opitulatur.' (Following Hrabanus Maurus; cf. ibid., I, p. 140)

[23] *HE*, III, p. 8: 'Si pontifices nostri aliique rectores orbis tantae sanctitatis essent ut pro illis ac per illos miracula diuinitus fierent, sicut olim ab antiquis patribus crebro facta sunt [...] excusso torpore memetipsum exercerem, et digna relatu noticiae posterorum auidae scripto transmitterem. Verum quia nunc est illa tempestas, qua multorum refrigescit karitas, et abundat iniquitas, sanctitatis indicia cessant miracula, et multiplicantur facinora, ac luctuosa in mundi querimonia. Historiographis ad scribendum uberius tema dant praesulum litigia, et cruenta principum proelia, quam teologorum sintagmata, uel xerofagorum parsimonia siue prodigia. Antichristi tempus appropinquat, ante cuius faciem ut dominus beato Iob insinuat, praecedet egestas miraculorum, nimiumque in his qui carnaliter amant se ipsos grassabitur rabies uiciorum.' Similar *HE*, III, p. 214, or IV, p. 192.

[24] Ibid., I, p. 137: 'Continuatio miraculorum domini nostri Iesu Christi, quae in iiii euangeliorum libris scripta sunt'; similar to p. 150: 'Ecce iuuante Deo simpliciter prosecutus sum continuationem quandam a natiuitate Christi usque ad aduentum spiritus paracliti, et singula saluatoris miracula ex euangelicis codicibus seriatim breuiterque congessi [...] dum dominica miracula per quattuor libros diffusa compaginaui.'

lacking in the present,[25] in particular for humility, as a lesson for the modern prelates who are 'addicted to worldly pomp and wealth'.[26]

The most important specific theme which unites the entire *Historia ecclesiastica* is, however, that of sin and salvation, or more precisely of God's offer of salvation, in this world or in the next, for repentant and/ or penitent sinners. This is expressed in Orderic's Latin by the theme of *poenitentia*, a word which comprises, without distinction, the notions of repentance, penitence and penance. The second term, the most general of the three, seems to me the best in the majority of cases (Chibnall's varying translations will not be challenged here). We can note that it is this theme in particular which gives Orderic the opportunity of bringing God's benevolence to terms with his justice, and/or confers a positive meaning to the darker sides of the events with which Orderic, by the widening of his perspective, is more and more frequently confronted.

For Orderic, the idea of improving one's life is inseparable from the idea of *poenitentia* in all its meanings. We see that this theme appears already at the start of Book III, the original first book. Orderic has to explain why the first foundation of Saint-Évroul, and of other monasteries 'in the region once called Neustria, and now Normandy', at the time of the Merovingian kings, did not last. This gives him the opportunity, right at the beginning, not only to present a model case of disaster caused by sin and of restoration by divine mercy, but also to remind the reader of the vital importance of *poenitentia*. As the power of the Frankish kingdom increased, he tells us:

> the sins of greed, pride and lust filled the hearts of all men from the highest to the lowest. They fell headlong into the snares of vice [...] Divine grace long spared the sinners and urged them to repentance in divers ways. Those who withdrew from the snares of evil gained the forgiveness of God; but all who hardened their hearts in their wickedness felt the scourge of his wrath.[27]

[25] See the quotation in n. 23, above. Christ teaches by his example, *exemplo docuit*, when he resists temptation: *HE* LeP, I, p. 14. Avoiding his enemies for some time, he gives an 'exemplum vitandi temeritatem tradentium' (ibid., p. 32), but he also recommends following the example of his passion (ibid., p. 41): 'Postquam Dominus mysterium suae passionis et resurrectionis ostendit, hortatur eos una cum turba ad sequendum suae passionis exemplum, promittens quod perpessos comitetur praemium.'

[26] *HE*, III, p. 214. Christ's baptism is an 'exemplum humilitatis': *HE* LeP, I, p. 10; he teaches humility by words and examples: 'Sed coelestis doctor ad humilitatem eos exemplis omnino provocavit et dictis': ibid., p. 70; cf. p. 46: 'Ille vero ad patientiam et humilitatem eos invitavit, et seipsum totius exemplum justitiae sequendum ostendit.'

[27] *HE*, II, pp. 4–6: 'Postquam regnum Francorum fauente Deo ualde super uicinas gentes sublimatum est [...] nimia cupiditas et superbia atque libido proceres et mediocres infimosque inuaserunt, et in nequitiarum laqueos

So Neustria fell victim to the Norman invaders because it resisted *poenitentia*; finally, however, divine mercy granted 'consolation' by the same Normans, who, having become Christians, reconstruct what they had destroyed. From here on, the theme of repentance, penitence, and penance accompanies Orderic's entire narrative, as a sort of *leitmotiv*.

God has in many ways promoted penitence, so that sinners may obtain mercy. Orderic affirms the pedagogical function of natural calamities such as bad weather, epidemics, famine:

> In the year of our Lord 1109, the second indiction, divine vengeance caused a number of scourges to punish the sins of men and, as always, made use of terror with fatherly solicitude, thereby calling sinners to repentance and showing forgiveness and salvation to the penitent.[28]

Certain spectacular events can be understood as divine warnings: the collapse of the roof of the abbey church in Cluny, for instance, in the aftermath of a riot there. By this disaster, in which nobody was hurt:

> our compassionate Lord terrified everyone because of the presumptuous attack, but nevertheless through his limitless mercy preserved them safely [...] Thanks to the divine hand they [...] were miraculously preserved in order to have time for repentance.[29]

The miraculous inscription that appeared on the altar candles of St Peter's in Coutances had a similar function.[30] It can also be the mischance of

---

praecipitantes contra salutis suae auctorem ne fideliter ei oboedirent erexerunt [...] Diuina autem pietas peccantibus diu pepercit, multisque modis ad poenitentiam inuitauit. Resipiscentibus autem a maliciae laqueis ueniam clementer contulit, sed perseuerantibus in nequitiis iracundiae suae flagellum intulit [...] Sed dispensante diuinae pietatis arbitrio, ex eadem gente unde uenit Neustriae desolatio, inde nimirum non multo post processit consolatio.'

[28] *HE*, V, p. 166: 'Anno ab inc. Domini 1109 indictione secunda, ultio diuina hominum scelera pluribus flagellis puniit, et mortales solito terrore cum pietate terruit, ut peccatores ad poenitentiam inuitaret, et poenitentibus ueniam et salutem clementer exhiberet.' See also *HE*, III, p. 348, for the admonition Orderic places in the mouth of the abbot Geoffrey of Crowland.

[29] *HE*, VI, pp. 312–14: 'Ipsa die terribile prodigium illic contigit. Ingens basilicae nauis quae nuper edita fuerit corruit, sed protegente Deo neminem lesit. Sic pius Dominus omnes pro temeraria inuasione insperata ruina terruit, sua tamen omnes immensa benignitate saluauit [...] Porro (populus) diuina manu ab immanis casus contritione illesus euasit, miroque modo reseruatus penitere postmodum potuit.'

[30] *HE*, IV, p. 266: 'Sic nimirum uisum est illis [to those who try to understand the inscription], ut diuinitus diceretur Petro qui caput est orbis, iudex seculi et clauiger regni coelestis: manda Petre iram de coelo ut effundatur

others that leads to penitence, like in the case of the men of Laigle who plundered the possessions of Saint-Évroul: 'Many of them received hard blows and died, so that some were brought to repentance by the downfall of others.'[31]

Orderic affirms that the penitent sinners are spared, but those who are impenitent ('impoenitentes') receive their punishment. This is what happened to a particularly wicked enemy of Saint-Évroul, Mabel of Bellême, who was murdered by a knight she had wronged:

> but in the end the just judge, who mercifully spares penitent sinners and sternly smites the impenitent, allowed that cruel woman who had shed the blood of many and had forcibly disinherited many lords and compelled them to beg their bread in foreign lands, to perish herself by the sword of Hugh, whom she had unjustly deprived of his paternal inheritance.[32]

However, Orderic insists on the positive outcome of the affair: after her death, her similarly depraved widower repents of his misdeeds and amends his life.[33]

The worst fate that can befall somebody is death without repentance, and this is why the disorder anticipated for the reign of Robert Curthose could be so disastrous. It threatens souls as well as bodies, as announced in a prophecy addressed to Queen Matilda:

> many thousands of men will be destroyed by fire and sword, amongst whom many will perish without penance or the last sacrament, and be dragged down to the raging fires of Hell for their sins.[34]

On the other hand, this is more a danger to be avoided than something that really happens. The only specific case reported by Orderic concerns

---

super populum tarisum, id est totum aridum peccato. Misererem pro misererer ei, si lacrimas dignae poenitentiae michi offerret.'

[31] *HE*, VI, p. 462: 'Plures eorum duros ictus perpessi corruerunt, unde nonnulli ad poenitentiam aliorum deiectione lacessiti sunt.'

[32] *HE*, III, pp. 134–6: 'Denique iustus arbiter qui peccatoribus pie parcit, et impoenitentes districte percutit, crudelem feminam quae multo sanguine madebat, multosque nobiles uiolenter exhaeredatos per externa mendicare coegerat, permisit perire gladio Hugonis cui castrum quod in rupe Ialgei situm est abstulerat.' On these events see also the chapter by Vincent Debiais and Estelle Ingrand-Varenne, above.

[33] Ibid., pp. 138–46: 'Praefatus igitur heros mala quae plerunque fecerat Vticensibus recoluit, pristinosque reatus sequentis uitae emendatione sagaciter abolere studuit.'

[34] Ibid., p. 106: 'Cetus fidelium utriusque sexus dispergentur, hominumque multa milia ferro uel flamma perimentur, ex quibus multi sine poenitentia et uiatico labentur, et pro reatibus suis ad tartara seua trahentur.'

a particularly condemnable person, a certain Robert who had usurped the charge of abbot of Saint-Pierre-sur-Dives, and had not only acted as a traitor against King Henry I, but had also abandoned his monastic status. He is slain by a peasant with whom he was quarrelling, 'and so the wretch perished unshriven as he deserved for his sins'.[35] To others, on the contrary, God gives time for penitence, as we have seen in the case of the citizens of Cluny and Coutances.

Orderic is happy, moreover, to report an episode where enemies choose not to fight a battle because of the risk for their souls, and repent of their sins instead:

> Whilst both forces were preparing for the uncertain verdict of battle, and many were enduring the pangs of fear at the thought of death and the woes that come to sinners after death [a negotiation is conducted successfully]. So by the grace of God who softens the hearts of princes the sins of the repentant in both armies were forgiven.[36]

When Orderic reports stories of battles and death his consolation is to mention the last-minute penitence performed by the dying heroes. For instance, Richard, son of William the Conqueror, dies after a hunting accident, 'penitent and absolved and fortified with the last sacrament'.[37] William Clito, wounded in battle, even confirms his penitence by asking to become a monk.[38] On the other hand, for the accidental killer of Richard, son of Robert Curthose, penitence as a monk enables him to avoid vengeance.[39]

The *Historia ecclesiastica* also includes, without such dramatic circumstances, a long series of protagonists who perform penance at the end of their lives by entering a monastery, and giving alms or donations to the Church. Orderic relates in detail the pious end of Ansold of Maule, a great benefactor of Saint-Évroul, who after a life in arms prepares for death by confession and penitence ('confessione et poenitentia') over seven

---

[35] HE, V, p. 82: 'Et ita exigentibus culpis sine poenitentia miser trucidatus est'.

[36] HE, II, pp. 308–10: 'Dum utraque acies ad ambiguum certamen pararentur, horribilesque pro morte et miseriis quae mortem reproborum sequuntur, timores mentibus multorum ingererentur [...] Deo tamen uincente legati pacis utrinque suscipiuntur [...] Sic gratia Dei mitigante corda principum reatus poenitentium utrobique indulti sunt, et beniuolae plebes serena pace tempestuosam nigredinem tumultuum procul pellente palam laetatae sunt.'

[37] HE, III, p. 114: 'Poenitens et absolutus atque sacro uiatico communitus'. See also HE, IV, p. 50; HE, VI, p. 376.

[38] HE, VI, p. 376: 'scelerumque poenitens monachatum petiit, et dominici corporis perceptione cum confessione munitus obiit.'

[39] HE, V, p. 282: 'Reatum enim homicidii per poenitentiam contemptor mundi expiauit, et maliuolum rancorem parentum et amicorum preclari tironis declinauit.'

weeks, and is accepted as a monk in the priory of Maule for his last days. Orderic quotes at length the speeches Ansold is supposed to have made to his son and his wife, as well as his last words: 'Into thy hands, Lord God, I, once a sinner but now repentant, commend my spirit as a servant ought to commit himself to his lord.'[40] Before being executed, Orderic's particular hero, Count Waltheof, spends a whole year in penitence, regretting his sins and reciting the psalms in prison.[41] Orderic is even ready to praise a woman, Isabel, wife of Ralph of Tosny, who 'repenting the mortal sin of luxury in which she had indulged in her youth, left the world' and, entering a nunnery, 'worthily reformed her life'.[42] There are also those who have wronged the monks of Saint-Évroul but finally, repenting, make amends and join the monastic community, such as the young man who has stolen a horse from them and who, having fallen ill, and 'repenting of his misdeeds, sought forgiveness from the monks and resigned himself and all his possessions to Saint-Évroul'.[43] Arnold of Echauffour, who had attacked the abbey and its possessions by fire and sword, is led to penitence and compensation for the injury done, and finally also became a monk there.[44]

It is especially meritorious to end one's life as a 'penitent pilgrim' on the way of God', that is, on the way to Jerusalem: this is the fate of Walter Tirel, who was responsible for the death of King William Rufus.[45] Fulk of Anjou is particularly to be praised; as penitence for his crimes, he not only

---

[40] *HE*, III, pp. 192–1: 'Aeger fere VII septimanis ad tribunal Summi iturus sese confessione et poenitentia preparauit. [...] Vnde memor aeternae salutis ex toto ad Dominum se conuertit [...] tertia denique die [...] Christo qui in cruce pependit sic se quodam sophista preloquente commendauit: "In manus tuas domine Deus licet olim peccator, nunc uero poenitens commendo sicut seruus se debet committere domino suo spiritum meum."' (The 'sophista' has yet to be identified.)

[41] *HE*, II, p. 320: 'Multoties peccata sua deflebat [...] Spacio itaque unius anni iuxta sacerdotum consilium poenituit, et cotidie centum quinquaginta psalmos Dauid quos in infantia didicerat in oratione Deo cecinit.' For other examples, see *HE*, III, pp. 258 and 84.

[42] *HE*, III, p. 128: 'Isabel uero postquam in uiduitate diu permansit, laetalis lasciuiae cui nimis in iuuentute seruierat poenitens seculum reliquit [...] (et) uitam suam laudabiliter in timore Dei perseuerans salubriter correxit.'

[43] Ibid., p. 244: 'Factique sui poenitens ab Vticensibus ueniam petiit se et omnia sua sancto Ebrulfo deuouit'.

[44] *HE*, II, p. 92: 'Memorque paternae pietatis pro malefactis contra coenobium Sancti Ebrulfi plorauit, poenitensque congruam emendationem promisit', and ibid., p. 124.

[45] *HE*, V, p. 294: 'Denique post multos annos Ierusalem expetiit, et in uia Dei poenitens Gualterius obiit'. Another example is *HE*, III, p. 318. Orderic does not seem to distinguish between pilgrimage and crusade.

undertakes a pilgrimage to Jerusalem, but also provides a yearly income for the Templars.[46]

According to Orderic, kings themselves set the example. On his deathbed William the Conqueror remembers his sinful life, and begging for the prayers of the priests and clerics in order to obtain salvation, he orders his treasures to be distributed among churches and the poor.[47] More explicitly, Henry I, seeing his end near, not only pronounces an amnesty and 'implored all to devote themselves to the preservation of peace and protection of the poor', but also, 'after making confession, received penance and absolution from the priests'.[48]

Penance not completed in this life has to be undergone in purgatory, as we learn from the vision experienced by the priest Walchelin, narrated by Orderic in Book VIII.[49] What Orderic reports most gladly, however, is the restoration of penitent sinners to God's favour after their chastisement. What we have seen in the paradigmatic case of the monasteries in Normandy can happen also to individual clerics, and even to lay people. For instance, Robert Giroie (who belongs to the family of the founders of Saint-Évroul) suffers a long series of calamities, loses his possessions and his wife, but finally regains his former position:

> Just as calm returns after great storms and gladdens the hearts of men, so divine justice often chastises sinners, and merciful goodness tempers their punishments, pardons the penitent, and gently rewards them when they have been purified. So Giroie, schooled by much suffering, gave thanks to God, by whose aid he had recovered his former honour after many struggles.[50]

It can be argued that Orderic wanted to make God's call for penitence and his offer of mercy more convincing by showing them directly in action in the earthly life and deeds of Jesus Christ. The narration of the life of

---

[46] HE, VI, p. 310: 'Scelerum ergo quae fecerat penitentiam agere studuit'.

[47] HE, IV, pp. 80–95.

[48] HE, VI, p. 448: 'Deinde katholicus rex de seruanda pace et tutela pauperum omnes obsecrauit, et post confessionem poenitentiam et absolutionem a sacerdotibus accepit.'

[49] HE, IV, pp. 236–50. In particular, the slayer of a priest who had died 'tanti non peracta poenitentia piaculi' is cruelly tormented by demons (p. 238). See Elisabeth Mégier, 'Deux exemples de "prépurgatoire" chez les historiens: A propos de *La naissance du Purgatoire* de Jacques Le Goff', Cahiers de civilisation médiévale 28 (1985), pp. 45–62, reprinted in idem, *Christliche Weltgeschichte im 12. Jahrhundert*, pp. 11–38.

[50] HE, IV, pp. 294–6: 'Sicut post nimiam tempestatem serenitas redit, hominesque laetificat, sic diuina iustitia reos plerumque uerberat et clemens bonitas afflictos mitigat et penitentes iustificat, purgatosque pie remunerat. Geroianus itaque multis calamitatibus eruditus Deo gratias egit, cuius ope post multos agones pristinum honorem recuperauit.'

Christ insists upon these same themes and emphasises them even more than the Gospels. In Orderic's presentation, the incarnation of the Son of God is not the beginning of a new era in history,[51] but the divine act of pardon by which man is delivered from damnation. This is how Orderic comments on the birth of Christ:

> May the entire multitude of the faithful rejoice in the Holy Spirit, and adore relentlessly the eternal Creator, offering him the sacrifice of praise with all its might, by whose decree his only Son, who with him and the Holy Spirit is coeternal and consubstantial, became man, and who has absolved his servant from deadly guilt by the unmerited death of his Son. Indeed the mild Creator, who grieved the fall of his creature which he had made in his image and resemblance, decreed by the inestimable counsel of his inexhaustible profundity that his coequal Son should visit the condemned servant in his prison, and carry man pitifully back to the flock from captivity on his own shoulders, perfectly delighting the nine orders of the angels by the restoration of their number.[52]

On Christ's passion, Orderic writes:

> Subsequently in his thirtieth year he mildly suffered his passion on the cross as a remedy for men; destroying death by which humankind had been held imprisoned in the fetters of a just damnation for five thousand years, he despoiled Hell, and having

---

[51] Here I contradict Goetz, *Gott und die Welt*, p. 232.

[52] *HE*, I, p. 135: 'Omnis credentium multitudo in spiritu sancto exultet, aeternumque creatorem indesinenter adoret, eique tota uirtute sacrificium laudis immolet, qui unicum filium suum sibi sanctoque spiritui coaeternum et consubstantialem incarnari constituit, et a reatu mortis seruum indebita morte filii absoluit. Clemens enim conditor qui plasma suum quod ad imaginem et similitudinem sui fecerat lapsum esse condoluit, inestimabilique consilio inexhaustae profunditatis suae decreuit, ut coaequalis sibi damnatum in ergastulo filius seruum uisitaret, hominemque de captiuitate propriis ad gregem humeris pie reportaret, nouemque ordines angelorum sui restauratione numeri perfecte letificaret.' Like Chibnall, I have been unable to trace these formulations back to a particular source. Orderic uses a vocabulary that is quite common in patristic and medieval texts, but combines the themes it refers to in an original way, for instance by relating the theme of the good shepherd to the release from hell. For comparison, see the texts (including Latin and Anglo-Saxon poetry) quoted by Jaroslav Pelikan, *The Christian Tradition: A History of the Development of Doctrine* (Chicago, 1971), esp. pp. 143–52; and by Celia Chazelle, *The Crucified God in the Carolingian Era: Theology and Art of Christ's Passion* (Cambridge, 2001), esp. pp. 51–8 and 25–8. I give my own translation for this and the two following passages not translated by Chibnall.

vanquished Satan the old serpent, he rose, victorious, from the dead on the third day.[53]

We can see that Orderic is not at all interested in a question which troubles many of his colleagues, namely, why the Saviour came so late in the course of time, and thereby abandoned a great part of humanity to damnation. For him it is clear that Christ saves humankind as a whole, from the beginning of the world.

Christ has come to earth to save sinners, and the remission of sins is not only announced as the theme, but forms the essential content, of the life of Christ in the *Historia ecclesiastica*. It is the central point in most of the episodes Orderic focuses on: the meal in the house of the publican (Matthew 9:10–13), Jesus and the sinner (Luke 7:36–50), the encounters with the adulteress (John 8:1–14) and with Zachaeus (Luke 19:1–9), the parable of the prodigal son (Luke 15:11–32).[54] Two of Orderic's favourite, and quite evangelical, appellations for Christ are 'verus archiater' and 'coelestis medicus' ('the true/divine physician')[55] – Christ heals humankind from both illness and from sin.[56]

This is, according to Orderic, exactly what happens in the present, too; the mute and the deaf, the blind and the lame healed by Christ signify different categories of sinner saved by the Church:

> In a similar way, the Lord achieves this spiritually in the Holy Church, by whose operation the multitude of sinners is saved every day [...] All their like are healed daily by divine intervention, and guided along the path of salvation [...] Now also the faithful rejoice

---

[53] *HE*, I, p. 164: 'Deinde xxx tercio aetatis suae anno passionem in cruce hominum pro remedio clementer pertulit, et destructa morte qua genus humanum uinculo iustae damnationis irretitum quinque milibus annorum tenuerat infernum spoliauit, deuictoque Satana serpente antiquo uictor a mortuis tercio die resurrexit.' Here Orderic combines, among others, the theme of the harrowing of hell with the theme of the six ages, or *millennia*.

[54] *HE* LeP, I, pp. 22, 9, 30, 36, 52, and 55.

[55] Ibid., pp. 16, 19, 20. According to Hubert Lutterbach, the theme of Christ as a physician occurs only rarely in the Middle Ages: Hubert Lutterbach, 'Der *Christus medicus* und die *sancti medici*: Das wechselvolle Verhältnis zweier Grundmotive christlicher Frömmigkeit zwischen Spätantike und früher Neuzeit', *Speculum* 47 (1996), pp. 239–8. See also Arnold Angenendt, *Geschichte der Religiosität im Mittelalter*, 4th edn (Darmstadt, 2009), p. 131.

[56] *HE* LeP, I, p. 20: 'Verus archiater singulis manus imposuit, verbo spiritus iecit, et omnes male habentes curauit [...]; gentiles, quos daemon possidebat, per fidem liberantur, et aegroti a morbis peccatorum emendatioris vitae remedio sanantur.'

for the conversion of sinners, and magnify the God of Israel who has made all things good.[57]

Again in accordance with the Gospels, even with a stronger emphasis, Orderic presents the twin themes of penitence and the remission of sins. Like the synoptists, he places the call for conversion and penitence at the beginning of Jesus's public life,[58] and not content to repeat every mention of *poenitentia* he finds in the Gospels,[59] he also adds some of his own, or takes them from other sources. When Christ commands the leper he has healed to present himself to the priest and offer a sacrifice, Orderic follows Hrabanus Maurus by suggesting that this implies an invitation to confession and penance.[60] He is particularly happy to repeat, on the subject of Luke 7:36–50, the comment made by Bede, who explains that Christ turns to those who repent and are penitent, and shames the false justice of those who believe themselves to be righteous.[61] Or, again following Bede, he adds a definition of 'true penitence' to Christ's praise of penitent sinners.[62] It is the 'penitent brother' who has to be forgiven

---

[57] *HE*, I, p. 142: 'Haec similiter in sancta aecclesia Dominus spiritualiter operatur, cuius ope turba peccatorum cotidie saluatur [...] Tales cotidie diuinitus sanantur, ac per uiam salutis perducuntur [...] Nunc quoque pro conuersione reorum fideles exultant: et Deum Israel qui bona cuncta facit pie magnificant.'

[58] *HE* LeP, I, p. 17.

[59] Ibid., p. 27: 'Tunc coepit Jesus exprobrare civitatibus, in quibus factae sunt plurimae virtutes ejus, quia non egissent poenitentiam in praedicatione ejus' (Matthew 11:20 ff.); ibid., p. 28: 'Poenitentes Ninivitas meriti comparatione praeposuit' (Matthew 12:41 and Luke 11:32); ibid., p. 50: 'Nuntiatis quibusdam a Pilato occisis, ait omnes, nisi poenitentiam agant, similiter perituros' (Luke 13:3).

[60] Ibid., p. 59: 'Quo iussu confessionem et poenitentiam peccatorum insinuavit'.

[61] Ibid., p. 30: 'Omnia quibus illicite usa prius ad peccatum fuerat, Deo poenitens devota immolat [...] Falsa tumens iustitia pharisaeus aegram reprehendit de aegritudine et medicum de subventione, a quo duorum parabola redarguitur debitorum [...] Peccatricis bona poenitentis enumerantur, et mala falsi justi corriguntur a Judice, cujus oculis intima quaeque nuda panduntur. Tandem Jesus Mariae peccata remisit.' (cf. *HE*, I, p. 141).

[62] Ibid., p. 52: 'Murmurantibus de peccatorum convivio parabolam ovis et dragmae ponit, quarum sicut perditio possessorem contristavit, sic inventio laetificavit. Gaudium itaque de poenitentis salute futurum angelis commendatur. Poenitentia vera est perpetrata mala plangere et deflenda non iterare. Debet etiam qui commisit prohibita, sibimetipsi abscidere concessa, ut voluntati satisfaciat divinae.' (Luke 15:1–7)

seven times seventy,[63] and, like Bede, Orderic makes it clear that St Peter repented of his denial.[64] The references to penitence continue in the rest of Book I and in Book II, in the chronicles as well as in the saints' lives.

So it can be concluded that by his various additions, and in particular by his life of Christ, where we meet the Saviour directly as a person, Orderic exemplifies and brings nearer to his readers the very aspects of God's relationship with his Church, or with man in general, that he intends to show in the *Historia ecclesiastica* as a whole. This means that there is effectively a connection between the life of Christ and contemporary Norman history in Orderic's historiographical concept. It is the same Jesus who heals and pardons in his earthly life, and who acts in the present as the protector of his Church and as the resort for sinners. He is a person clearly referred to already in Orderic's narration of contemporary events from Book III onwards, before he becomes a specific subject in Book I through Orderic's narration of his life and action on earth. Therefore, it is perhaps not absurd to call him a protagonist of Norman history (or of history in general, into which Norman history is included).

On the other hand, Christ is a protagonist of a very special kind. He acts in history as a person, but, and here we come to the properly theological aspect, as a divine person, he does not really belong to it. One of the particularities of Orderic's presentation is, in fact, his insistence on Jesus's being God. Introducing his life of Christ, Orderic's first thought goes not to Christ as a historical person, but to Christ as the eternal principle of being. Concluding his general prologue, Orderic declares:

> First of all I will tell of the Beginning that has no beginning, by whose aid I aspire to come to the End that has no ending, where I may sing devout praises with those above for ever and ever, to him who is alpha and omega.[65]

---

[63] Ibid., p. 53: 'Poenitenti vero fratri etiam septuagies septies praecipit remittendum.'

[64] Ibid., p. 72: 'Quod timet, naturae est, quod sequitur, devotionis, quod negat, obreptionis, quod poenitet, fidei.'

[65] *HE*, I, p. 132: 'In primis ordior de principio sine principio, cuius ope ad finem sine fine peruenire desidero, deuotas laudes cum superis in aeternum caniturus alfa et omega.' This formulation resembles Saint Anselm's *Monologion*, whose Chapter XVIII is entitled 'quod sit sine principio et sine fine'. See *Sancti Anselmi Cantuariensis archiepiscopi opera omnia*, ed. Franciscus Salesius Schmitt (Seckau, 1938), I, pp. 32 and 38. However, Orderic's words could also be a reference to Revelation 1:8. On Saint Anselm's works and his influence, see R. W. Southern, *Anselm and his Biographer: A Study of Monastic Life and Thought, 1059–c. 1130* (Cambridge, 1963); R. W. Southern, *Saint Anselm: A Portrait in a Landscape* (Cambridge, 1990); and G. E. M. Gasper, *Anselm of Canterbury and his Theological Inheritance* (Aldershot, 2004). On the other hand, it is possible that

Christ's first appellation in the prologue of Book I is 'the almighty Word by whom God created all things'.[66] This means that he is placed, primarily, not in the context of a historical situation, but in the context of divine creation. Orderic follows the exegetical tradition that sees in Christ the *principium*, the beginning, in which according to Genesis 1:1 the world was made. He could rely in this respect on the Church history of Eusebius of Caesarea,[67] one of his two great models, together with Bede. This tradition is not usually taken up by medieval historians, whose presentation of Christ, as we have noted before, has much more to do with historical change at a certain moment than with first and/or eternal beginnings. Orderic, on the contrary, accentuates in Christ not what is historically new but what is divinely permanent. So if Jesus takes care of his vine, the Church, it is in his divine quality as the creative Word of God, who operates always and everywhere, independently of the limits of historical times, places and situations: 'from morning to the eleventh hour by the workmen he sends', 'through every climate of the world', in order to collect from it plenty of 'fruit'.[68]

In fact, in Orderic's comments on Christ's birth (quoted above)[69] it was in his quality as the Son of God, God himself, coeternal, consubstantial and coequal to the Father and the Holy Spirit, that Christ could accomplish his work of redemption. This is why Orderic insists on these three qualifications, repeating them again at the beginning of Book II,[70] and this is why at the beginning of Book I he specifies that in becoming a man, Christ:

> remained what he had been, and took on what he was not, without mixture or division, governing all things with the Father and the

---

Orderic was aware of the distinction made by Abelard, following Saint Augustine, between the Father, *principium sine principio*, and the Son, *principium de principio*: see *Theologia Christiana* in *Opera theologica II (Petrus Abaelardus)*, ed. Eligius M. Buytaert, CCCM 12 (Turnhout 1969), p. 310; and *Sancti Aurelii Augustini de genesi ad litteram imperfectus liber*, ed. Iosephus Zycha, CSEL 28/1 (Prague-Vienna 1894), p. 462.

[66] *HE*, I, p. 134: 'Omnipotens uerbum per quod Deus pater omnia condidit'.

[67] Eusebius Caesariensis, *Historia ecclesiastica*, I.2, 1–4, in *Eusebius Werke II, Die Kirchengeschichte*, ed. F. Winkelmann, GCS NF 6 (Berlin; 1999), pp. 11–13.

[68] *HE*, I, p. 134: 'Omnipotens uerbum per quod Deus pater omnia condidit, uitis uera summusque paterfamilias qui uineam plantauit, et a mane usque ad undecimam horam intromissis operariis excolit, ut uberem fructum ex eadem colligere possit, eandem uineam id est sanctam aecclesiam nullo tempore desistit colere, eiusque palmites per omnia mundi climata nobiliter propagare.'

[69] Above, n. 52.

[70] *HE*, I, p. 164.

holy Spirit by his divinity, but enduring the infirmities of our flesh by the humanity he had assumed.[71]

Here, Orderic clearly acknowledges Christ's humanity, with its limitations and its misery, as also shown by his extensive report on Jesus's conception and birth.[72] However, throughout his narration of Christ's life Orderic takes advantage of every possible opportunity to affirm his divinity. The new star that appeared in the sky at the birth of Jesus proves his being the sublime God, and the magi adore him as such;[73] 'shining by the blaze of his divinity' he chases the merchants from the temple;[74] he is the 'wisdom of the Father' who 'lays open the secrets of his divinity'.[75] He assists his Church in the stormy sea of this world 'virtute deitatis suae',[76] the rising of Lazarus is a 'deitatis mirabile miraculum', and the Jews who want to kill the resuscitated Christ cannot oppose his omnipotence.[77] Christ teaches not like the scribes and pharisees, but 'having everything in his power like God';[78] he is the Lord of the earth and of the sea, he is God and man; in his prayer for us, he demands much greater things than human frailty could ask for.[79] The saints can also heal the sick or even raise the

---

[71] Ibid., p. 135: 'Filius itaque Deo homo factus id quod fuit permansit, et quod non erat assumpsit non commixtionem passus nec diuisionem, cum patre sanctoque spiritu regens omnia per diuinitatem, infirma uero nostrae carnis tolerans per assumptam humanitatem.' Chibnall notes the resemblance between this text and Augustine, *De consensu euangelistarum* I, 35, 53, where we read: 'manens id quod erat, factus quod non erat.' There are also similarities with other mainly Carolingian texts: see for instance *Paschasii Radberti De assumptione sanctae Mariae uirginis*, ed. Albert Ripberger, CCCM 56C (Turnhout, 1985), XII, 75, p. 142, but here again Orderic's formulations seem to be essentially his own. On this theme in general, see H.-M. Diepen OSB, 'L'"Assumptus Homo" patristique', *Revue Thomiste* 63 (1963), 32–52.

[72] HE I, p. 134.

[73] Ibid., p. 135: 'Sed quamvis virgo mater divae prolis alligaret membra pannis involuta, et pedes manusque stricta cingeret fascia, tenerque infans inter arta conditus praesepia vagiret pro humana, quam Patris velle susceperat, miseria, sublimis tamen Deus, orto in aethere novo sidere, monstratus est, et a Magis orientalibus divinitus illustratis in Bethleem requisitus, ibique in cunabulis inventus, ac ut Deus adoratus est.'

[74] HE LeP, I, p. 14.

[75] Ibid., p. 31: 'Murmurantibus [...] Judaeis et blasphemantibus, sophia Patris respondit, arcana divinitatis suae, ut teologus Joannes refert, multipliciter manifestavit.'

[76] Ibid., p. 20, see the quotation above, n. 22.

[77] Ibid., pp. 60 ff.

[78] Ibid., p. 19: 'Erat enim eos docens, sicut Deus omnium potestatem habens, non sicut scribae et pharisaei.'

[79] Ibid., pp. 19, 29, 36 and 70.

dead,[80] however, only Christ is, as we saw, the 'coelestis medicus', 'verus archiater', whose salvific action not only restores health, but includes also the remission of sins.[81]

There is another, if indirect, indication that Orderic wishes to emphasise Christ's divinity. Being God does not prevent Christ, in Orderic's presentation, from being a person acting in history, but it does prevent him from being fully integrated into the course of time. Orderic repeatedly calls his work *chronographia*, and he does not hesitate to apply this term to the whole *Historia ecclesiastica*.[82] However, he uses it mostly for the parts of his work which by their form correspond to the historiographical genre of *chronica* inaugurated by Eusebius and St Jerome, namely the 'chronicles', to use their customary title, of the emperors and popes in Books I and II, to which can be added the 'chronicle' of the bishops of Rouen in Book V.[83] But when we come to the life of Christ several indications show that Orderic did not see it, and did not want it to be seen, as a part like any other of a *chronographia*, a narration concerned with time.

As Orderic starts his whole historical narration with Jesus Christ, and goes on to his own time, he might have used the years of incarnation to establish a line of succession from Christ to the present. But this is not what he does. In the emperors' and popes' chronicles that connect Christ, or the apostles and evangelists, with the contemporary Normans, the order of time is given by the duration of reigns and pontificates. In the later parts of the rulers' chronicle, where the succession of the Roman emperors no longer provides the leading division, the French and English kings having become equally important, the years of incarnation are used now and again to determine a date, but they do not provide the structure of the narrative. In the 'Norman' part of the *Historia ecclesiastica* the years of incarnation are mentioned more and more often, and they do become a structuring device towards the end of the work, where Orderic follows the events from the beginning to the end of each year. But no continuous time-line has been drawn from Christ to the present. Besides, though Orderic does not forget to indicate, in agreement with Bede's *Chronica maiora*, the date of Christ's birth by Roman and biblical reckoning, chronology is only a secondary theme in his presentation of this event. More important is the narration

---

[80] For instance *HE*, III, pp. 291 and 294.

[81] *HE* LeP, I, pp. 19–20.

[82] *HE*, I, p. 138.

[83] Ibid., pp. 150, 191; *HE*, III, p. 96. Orderic does not use, for his own work, the term *chronica*, reserving it instead for the specific genre of world chronicles: see *HE*, II, pp. 186–8, where it designates the works of Marianus Scotus and John of Worcester; or ibid., p. 282, where it refers to some non-specified sources for when St Évroul lived.

of the Annunciation and of the Nativity according to the Gospels, and the connection with biblical prophecy.[84]

Historical time receives more attention when Orderic arrives at the beginning of Christ's public activity. Here he declares himself obliged to offer secure dates, on account of his having decided to compose a *chronographia*,[85] and here he assembles, with the aid of Bede and Eusebius, all kinds of chronological information that can be drawn from the comparison of the Gospels with other historical sources, especially Josephus, concerning, *a posteriori*, Christ's birth, and also, in advance, his passion. This gives the impression that Orderic wants to avoid interrupting the ensuing narration of the life of Christ with topics that do not really belong to it: in other words, it suggests that he intends to distinguish between chronological information and the life of Christ. He then concludes:

> This I have made known to the learned reader about the series of times [...] Now I will commence the intended work about my Lord, in whose almighty benignity I trust, and whose aid I invoke faithfully in order to execute worthily to his praise the work I have begun.[86]

This implies effectively — and the invocation added here contributes to this effect — that the following report about Christ as a subject is different from *chronographia*, which is concerned with the succession of time. Similarly, Orderic's way of expressing himself when passing from the life of Christ to the history of the Christian rulers makes *chronographia* appear as a new topic beginning at this point:

> With the help of God I have, artlessly, pursued a certain continuous report from the birth of Christ until the coming of the Holy Spirit, and I have compiled orderly and shortly the different miracles of the Saviour from the Gospel books [...] Now, as I intend to write a *chronographia* so that the order of times may become clearer for the reader, I wish to insert some information that the ancient fathers have published in their works about this subject.[87]

---

[84] *HE*, I, p. 134; cf. Bede, *De temporum ratione*, LXVI, ed. C. W. Jones, CCSL 123B (Turnhout, 1977), p. 495.

[85] *HE*, I, p. 138: 'Quia chronographiam decreui contexere iustum est ut in primis certitudinem temporum diligenti designem conamine.'

[86] Ibid., p. 139: 'Haec de temporum serie studioso lectori rimatus intimaui [...] Amodo propositum opus de meo aggrediar domino, cuius in omnipotenti benignitate confido, et opem ut inceptum digne peragam ad laudem ipsius fideliter inuoco.'

[87] Ibid., p. 150: 'Ecce iuuante Deo simpliciter prosecutus sum continuationem quandam a natiuitate Christi usque ad aduentum spiritus paracliti, et singula saluatoris miracula ex euangelicis codicibus seriatim breuiterque

Being the *principium sine principio*, the timeless principle of being, Christ cannot belong to the ordinary human time-series. If he acts in history, he does so at all times, every day, *cotidie*, and not at a certain period succeeding other periods, or at a certain moment: God cannot be assimilated to history. However, he has to be searched for in history – so history on the one hand has eminent dignity as the site of God's presence, and on the other hand remains radically different from God. This kind of theology of history did not have much success in the Middle Ages, but it is quite remarkable that it could exist at all.

congessi [...] Nunc quia certam proposui cronographiam scripto protelare, ut lectori clarius pateat ordo temporum, quaedam libet inserere, quae antiqui patres in opusculis suis ediderunt de eadem re. Eusebius enim Cesariensis'.

'Studiosi abdita investigant':
Orderic Vitalis and the
Mystical Morals of History

Sigbjørn Olsen Sønnesyn

THE time has long since passed when Bishop Stubbs could say that William of Malmesbury 'aspired to the art of history', implying a failure on William's part to attain the lofty standards of the august art.[1] But while the realisation that medieval monks did not try (and fail) to attain modern standards of historiography is becoming universally accepted, the standards, methods, and aims of medieval monastic historiography are still a matter of discussion.[2] In what follows I would like to make two closely interrelated points about Orderic Vitalis as a historian addressing and guiding his audience: first, that Orderic provided an accurate and substantial description of his ideal reader, that is, the sort of reader likely to derive benefit from reading his works; and second, that grasping the characteristics of Orderic's ideal reader will illuminate Orderic's own aims and methods in writing.

---

[1] *Willelmi Malmesbiriensis Monachi de Gestis Regum Anglorum*, ed. W. Stubbs, 2 vols. (London, 1887–9), I, p. x.

[2] Notable contributions to this debate include: J. Gillingham, 'Civilizing the English? The English Histories of William of Malmesbury and David Hume', *Historical Research* 74 (2001), 17–43, cf. his 'The Context and Purposes of Geoffrey of Monmouth's *History of the Kings of Britain*', ANS 13 (1990), 99–118; P. A. Hayward, 'The Importance of Being Ambiguous: Innuendo and Legerdemain in William of Malmesbury's *Gesta Regum* and *Gesta Pontificum Anglorum*', ANS 33 (2011), 72–102; J. Tahkokallio, 'Monks, Clerks, and King Arthur: Reading Geoffrey of Monmouth in the Twelfth and Thirteenth Centuries' (unpublished doctoral dissertation, University of Helsinki, 2013); B. Weiler, 'William of Malmesbury, Henry I, and the *Gesta Regum Anglorum*', ANS 31 (2009), 157–76; J. O. Ward, 'Orderic Vitalis as Historian in the Europe of the Early Twelfth-Century Renaissance', *Parergon* 31 (2014), 1–26; Hingst, *Written World*; C. C. Rozier, 'The Importance of Writing Institutional History in the Anglo-Norman Realm, c. 1060–c. 1142, with special reference to Eadmer's *Historia Novorum*, Symeon of Durham's *Libellus de exordio*, and the *Historia Ecclesiastica* of Orderic Vitalis' (unpublished doctoral thesis, Durham University, 2014); S. O. Sønnesyn, *William of Malmesbury and the Ethics of History* (Woodbridge, 2012).

Let us begin by revisiting the following, perhaps deceptively familiar, passage from Book VIII of the *Historia ecclesiastica*:

> I find many things in the pages of Scripture which, if they are subtly interpreted, seem to resemble the happenings of our own time. But I leave the allegorical implications and explanations appropriate to human customs to be interpreted by scholars, and propose now to relate a little further the simple history of Norman affairs.[3]

Now, I use the term 'deceptively familiar' here because this passage has been noted and discussed by most students of Orderic's methods and aims as a historian, but with a great variety of translations and interpretations. Chibnall, whose translation is quoted above, appears to indicate that Orderic surrendered questions of morals and spiritual exegesis to scholars – her translation of Orderic's *studiosi* – while Orderic himself remained content with transmitting simple and unadulterated facts. Ray, however, gives a very different rendering of this same passage in his article on Orderic and his readers:

> The point [of this passage] certainly is not that Orderic has here gotten demur about 'allegoricae allegations' [...] On the contrary, he simply wants it known that his major business is to provide 'simplex historia'. For those who want stronger meat he enters encouragement to press on – which, by the way, is pretty good medieval pedagogy, since in raising the question of higher meanings and leaving it open on the firm footing of 'simplex historia', he permitted the reader to make his own discovery of the text's moral possibilities.[4]

In what follows I would like to use Ray's remark about good medieval pedagogy as my point of departure for a study of the moral epistemology behind Orderic's historical texts. Most of us accept as sincere Orderic's repeated insistence that he wrote primarily for the edification of his readers, but it may be useful, I would suggest, to investigate in somewhat greater detail exactly how he envisioned his text could contribute to this edification. It is clearly evident from the passage just quoted that any moral message contained in Orderic's text is not to be found on the surface, as the logical conclusion of the narrative itself. On the contrary, it is only attainable for the persistent, ardent, assiduous reader – the *studiosi* to whom Orderic relinquished the task of finding the allegorical and

---

[3] *HE*, VIII, p. 16, and IV, p. 228: 'Multa intueor in diuina pagina, quæ subtiliter coaptata nostri temporis euentui uidentur similia. Ceterum allegoricas allegationes et idoneas humanis moribus interpretationes studiosis rimandas relinquam, simplicemque Normannicarum historiam rerum adhuc aliquantulum protelare satagam.'

[4] R. D. Ray, 'Orderic Vitalis and his Readers', *Studia Monastica* 14 (1972), 17–33, at pp. 20–3.

moral significance of his history.[5] If we want to acquire a clearer picture of Orderic's moral epistemology, that is, what moral knowledge was and how it could be attained, the *studiosi* could offer an approach through which we may attain such a picture. The presuppositions, practices, and methods distinguishing the *studiosi* from other readers constitute the epistemological framework within which Orderic expected and desired his work to be read, and according to which he shaped his text. My purpose in what follows, therefore, is to attempt at least a sketch of a definition of the *lector studiosus* as Orderic envisioned him.

There are good reasons for being sceptical of the extent to which analyses of a single term may provide understanding of the conceptual basis that governs its use, but treated with caution the study of individual uses of a term may point us in the right direction. Orderic frequently used the term *studiosus* and cognates in the *Historia ecclesiastica*. He often talked of the *studium boni* or the *studium religionis* as distinct marks of excellence in the historical characters he portrayed in a good light;[6] and in general *studium* seems to denote not any sort of eager application but specifically a desire to do good. A highly illuminating instance of the term for our present purposes is found in the preface to Book VI of the *Historia*. Orderic begins:

> The sharpness of the human mind always needs to be suitably exercised in useful learning, and, by remembering the past and studying the present, happily to acquire virtues for the future. Every man should daily learn how he ought to live, and appropriate the powerful examples of heroes of the past for his own benefit.[7]

Ignorance of the past, Orderic goes on, brings a certain form of blindness to the present and the future; it is only from studying the past that one may acquire the trained eye that brings understanding of present and future events.[8] Then, the crux of the matter:

---

[5] For a somewhat different take on this, see Emily Albu's observation that Orderic's vocabulary occasionally seems to subvert the surface text – see Albu, *Normans in their Histories*, pp. 180–213.

[6] See, for example, *HE*, III, p. 164, for a representative example.

[7] Ibid., p. 212: 'Humani acumen ingenii semper indiget utili sedimine competenter exerceri, et preterita recolendo, presentiaque rimando ad futura feliciter uirtutibus instrui. Quisque debet quemadmodum uiuat cotidie discere, et fortia translatorum exempla heroum ad commoditatem sui capessere.'

[8] Ibid.: 'Plerumque multa quæ uelut inaudita putantur rudium auribus insonant, et noua modernis in repentinis casibus frequenter emanant; in quibus intellectuales inexpertorum oculi nisi per reuolutionem transactorum caligant.'

The assiduous therefore investigate what has been hidden [*studiosi ergo abdita investigant*] – and, kindly holding on to whatever they consider helpful for a favourable mind, they hold such knowledge in high regard. They labour out of benevolence, and show the past to those to come without ill will.[9]

Although this preface is replete with the stock *topoi* of historical prefaces of the classical and medieval periods,[10] it also offers, I would argue, illustrations of the modes of thought that constitute Orderic's historiographical practice, and particularly his moral epistemology. I would in particular draw attention to four aspects of the remarks just quoted that all serve to position Orderic within what amounts to a definitive moral and epistemological framework – not, however, as proof demonstrating Orderic's appropriation of this framework, but as illustrations of pervasive tendencies.

First, we find the vestiges of the dominant moral paradigm of classical and medieval ethics – and in the absence of a systematic treatise on ethics from Orderic's pen, vestiges are all we have to go on. Of course, it would have been remarkable, to say the least, to find that Orderic rejected the moral paradigm universally propounded elsewhere. Moral development and progress, on Orderic's account, take the form of virtues that enable man to live as he ought, and in the acquisition of which the imitation of examples plays a major part. While never discussing this in any detail, Orderic always conforms to the basic structure of moral thought transmitted from classical Greece through Cicero and the neo-Platonists to patristic thought and beyond.[11] The goal and purpose of moral development, and indeed of human life in general, is to attain happiness,

---

[9] Ibid.: 'Studiosi ergo abdita inuestigant, et quicquid benignæ menti profuturum autumant, pie amplexantes magni existimant. Ex beneuolentia laborant, et preterita posteris sine inuidia manifestant.'

[10] See for instance T. Janson, *Latin Prose Prefaces: Studies in Literary Conventions* (Stockholm, 1964); A. Gransden, 'Prologues in the Historiography of Twelfth-Century England', in *England in the Twelfth Century*, ed. Daniel Williams (Woodbridge, 1990), pp. 55–82.

[11] The best single treatment of this process of transmission of an ethical paradigm is T. H. Irwin, *The Development of Ethics*, 3 vols. (Oxford, 2007–8), here vol. I, treating the earliest Greeks up to the late medieval West. For the hugely influential Augustinian synthesis of classical and Christian thought on this topic, see for example, E. Morgan, *The Incarnation of the Word* (London 2010); and R. N. S. Topping, *Happiness and Wisdom: Augustine's Early Theology of Education* (Washington, DC, 2012), esp. p. 155. See also A. MacIntyre, *Dependent Rational Animals: Why Human Beings Need the Virtues* (London 1999). See also Sønnesyn, *William of Malmesbury and the Ethics of History*, pp. 33–41.

beatitudo.[12] *Beatitudo* consisted in a life in which the full capabilities and potential of human beings were realised. The virtues were defined as stable habits of character that disposed those who embodied them to live such a life. In the classical world this equated to the life of a citizen of a political community, embodying the virtues that constituted excellence in this context. Christian revelation, with the emphasis on the necessity of Grace and the utter transcendence of God, transposed the ideal life of the classical world to a life lived in enjoyment of God, a mode of thought we also find deeply embedded in Orderic's writings.[13] Attainment of the true goal of human existence, the beatific vision of God, was thus moved beyond the ability of humanity unaided by the free gift of grace, and beyond earthly existence. In the monastic ethics on which Orderic would have been nurtured, then, the moral life on earth consisted in developing the virtues that opened human beings for the workings of grace, preparing them for the beatific vision only attainable in the afterlife. I will have to let this brief sketch suffice when it comes to the basic structure of the moral paradigm to which Orderic adhered, and move on to the ways in which he attempted to contribute to a way of life conducive to the true goal of human existence.

For that purpose, let us move on to the three remaining aspects of the passage quoted from the preface to Book VI. I will first present them briefly as they appear in Orderic's text, before I sketch out their role in the traditions of moral thought he inherited. First, we need to repeat that moral knowledge, the ultimate reward for the assiduous reader of history, is not found on the surface, not transmitted propositionally, not, as it were, automatically evident to any reader whatever. What distinguishes the *studiosi* from other readers is precisely the ability of the former to reach what the text conceals, the *abdita*, and not just what it lays open. Orderic frequently employs the verb *rimari* [e.g. *studiosis rimandas relinquam*] to denote the process of learning from the past, a verb that

---

[12] See, among a host of equally enlightening alternatives, R. Holte, *Béatitude et sagesse: Saint Augustin et le problème de la fin de l'homme dans la philosophie ancienne* (Paris, 1962); É. Gilson, *Introduction à l'étude de saint Augustin* (Paris, 1969), pp. 1–10; J. Marenbon, *Boethius* (Oxford, 2003), pp. 102–12; S. O. Sønnesyn, '"Ut sine fine amet Summam Essentiam": The Eudaemonist Ethics of St Anselm', *Mediaeval Studies* 70 (2008), 1–29; B. Goebel, '"Beatitudo cum iustitia": Anselm von Canterbury über Gerechtigkeit, Freiheit und das Verhältnis von Gerechtigkeit und Glück', in *Gott und die Frage nach dem Glück: Anthropologische und ethische Perspektiven*, ed. Jörg Disse and Bernd Goebel (Frankfurt am Main, 2010), pp. 60–120; L. E. Goodman, 'Happiness', in *The Cambridge History of Medieval Philosophy*, ed. R. Pasnau, 2 vols. (Cambridge, 2010), I, pp. 457–71.

[13] In addition to the works referred to above, see also S. O. Sønnesyn, '"In vinea Sorech laborare": The Cultivation of Unity in Twelfth-Century Monastic Historiography', *ANS* 36 (2013), 167–87.

originally meant to rip open or rip apart to find what is hidden within.¹⁴ The *studiosi*, then, are precisely those who manage to penetrate beneath the surface to find the *abdita*. This may, if read in isolation, seem like so much muddled esotericism, but in fact it taps into a vigorous tradition of moral teaching stretching back as far as Plato's depiction of Socrates, at least. The Socratic mode of teaching recognised as fatally flawed the model of teaching in which knowledge is transmitted from an active teacher to a passively receiving pupil.¹⁵ Instead, a dialectical, self-reflective process through which the inquiring agent was led to discover moral truths for himself was presented as the only viable mode of teaching ethics. The Delphic injunction to know your 'self' – *gnothi seauton*, Latinised as *nosce teipsum* – was not a surrender to subjectivism, but, on the contrary, an invitation to reflect on one's own experience to arrive at understanding that could not be attained in any other way.¹⁶ Aristotle's claim that the good man is the measure of all things forms a necessary complement to this notion; the good man, virtue incarnate, is the measure of ethics, and an organic whole cannot be summed up propositionally, only experienced.¹⁷ Within the Socratic tradition, then, which constituted the framework within which Plato, Aristotle, and also later Roman and neo-Platonic moral philosophers worked out their ethical thought, moral development and perfection is thus a process of acquiring knowledge, an inquiry. In a Christian context, where the alpha and omega of all moral knowledge, that is, God, is considered radically beyond human comprehension, this tendency is only amplified. There is an irreducible element of mysticism in these moral epistemologies; but they are saved from vacuous, relativistic subjectivism by the objective nature of moral truth, and the strongly held notion that this objective truth is available to individual experience.

Second, and following closely from the mystical nature of moral knowledge, this process relies on activity and effort on the part of the reader; it is not a matter of passive reception of the text, not a matter of straightforward transmission of information, but of the reader making his

---

¹⁴ See, for example, A. Blaise, *Dictionnaire Latin–Francais des auteurs Chrétiens* (Turnhout, 1954), p. 724.

¹⁵ See, for example, M. F. Burnyeat, 'Wittgenstein and Augustine *De magistro*', *Proceedings of the Aristotelian Society, Supplementary Volumes* 61 (1987), 1–24; and C. T. Mathewes, 'Augustinian Anthropology: *Interior intimo meo*', *Journal of Religious Ethics* 27 (1999), 195–221.

¹⁶ The literature here is formidable; I would particularly like to mention P. Courcelle, *Connais-toi toi-même de Socrate à saint Bernard*, 3 vols. (Paris, 1974–5); E. Booth, *St Augustine's 'notitia sui' Related to Aristotle and the Neo-Platonists* (Louvain, 1980).

¹⁷ See above all T. Chappell, '"The good man as measure of all things": Objectivity without World-Centredness in Aristotle's Moral Epistelomogy', in *Virtue, Norms, and Objectivity: Issues in Ancient and Modern Ethics*, ed. C. Gill (Oxford, 2005), pp. 233–55.

own discoveries guided where necessary by the author. This is also borne out by Orderic's statements on the moral function of history. Every man, he said, ought to seize for his own use and benefit what the examples of past heroes show; this is something every *homo studiosus*, *scriptor* or *lector* needs to do. The human mind needs to be exercised – *exerceri* – in order to gain the experience that can be developed into moral knowledge. Such experience was acquired through engaging in communal practices, and learned through habituation and imitation. These provided a sort of apprenticeship, and understanding could subsequently be attained through meditating on the experience of imitating models of excellence.[18] Active participation was a prerequisite for, and not a consequence of, understanding; this was as true for Aristotelian and Ciceronian civic virtue as it was for the monastic ethics of twelfth-century Latin Christendom.[19]

Third, we should also note that the *studiosi* already comprise a moral category. The knowledge they uncover through their labours is put to use for the good of others – *ex benevolentia laborant; pie amplexantes* – as they kindly embrace what they find to be useful, and do their best to pass it on. It is in this communal sharing that moral knowledge reaches its fulfilment. The *studiosus* is already, at least to some extent, leading a moral life. The ability to grasp moral truth requires a moral agent; epistemology and ethics form one organic whole. Again, this notion is found in classical as well as Christian moral epistemologies, from Plato to Cistercian mysticism.[20]

At this point one could with some justification object that so far I have only presented the moral thinking one might associate with Orderic's more generic remarks, and that there is a risk of over-interpretation inherent in such a procedure. Such an objection would have to be conceded in principle; but there are some strong indications that the elements discernible in the preface to Book VI have informed Orderic's approach to his writing in a profound way. Initially this may seem unlikely, however; in order to accept that even the secular course of history, which occupies so much of the *Historia ecclesiastica*, concealed a mystery that could bring about moral reform and progress in the reader, we would need to see how such historical lessons could be appropriated even in monastic seclusion. In the classical tradition of historical writing, moral teaching could be conveyed through presenting as models for imitation examples of outstanding civic virtue, and how those who embodied

---

[18] Mathewes, 'Augustinian Anthropology'; Chappell, 'Good man as measure'; Topping, *Happiness and Wisdom*; Morgan, *Incarnation of the Word*; A. MacIntyre, *Three Rival Versions of Moral Enquiry: Encyclopaedia, Genealogy, and Tradition* (Notre Dame, IN, 1990).

[19] In addition to references given above, see in particular P. Hadot, *Philosophy as a Way of Life* (Malden, MA, and Oxford, 1995).

[20] See, for example, Chappell, 'Good man as measure', cf. É. Gilson, *The Mystical Theology of Saint Bernard* (London, 1940).

that virtue had contributed significantly to the common good of the community.[21] Readers could then try to introduce such virtue in their own lives, and through reflecting on how this affected both themselves and their surroundings they could slowly arrive at an understanding of moral truth.[22] It is not immediately evident how such a procedure could translate to a monastic context; after all, it is hardly practical for monks to imitate secular dukes and kings in their conquering neighbouring kingdoms, subduing rivals, or donating endowments to the Church. Yet Orderic seems to suggest that everything he wrote could offer something of value to the *studiosus*. How are we to take this? Through what sort of practice could the narration of secular history be ripped open to reveal the mysterious truth within?

This question has largely been settled by the perceptive studies published by Ray in the 1970s. He showed, to my mind utterly convincingly, that the main contexts within which Orderic intended his text to be read were the liturgical cycle and the *lectio divina*, which combined to form the backbone of monastic practice. But this poses the question of how, precisely, the liturgy and the *lectio* could empower the *studiosus* to penetrate the underlying mystery of history.

Orderic emphasised the need for active and assiduous application on the part of the devout monk. Sloth, *inertia*, was severely censured; the moral life required effort, *studium*. The main practices where such efforts should be spent were the liturgy, reading, and writing: *orate, legite, psallite, scribite*, was the injunction delivered to the monks of Saint-Évroul by the quondam teacher there, Thierry. The liturgy, centred on the cyclical repetition of the full Psalter every week, was crucial to the monastic vision of a good way of life, that is, a life in fulfilment of human nature. Gregory the Great provided a striking formulation of the doctrine that the chanting of the Psalter made the soul open and receptive to the workings of grace in man:

> When the voice of the psalms is expressed from the intention of the heart, through this act a path is made for God to the heart, so that He may fill the attentive mind with the mysteries of prophecy or compunction. Thus it is written: *The sacrifice of praise shall glorify*

---

[21] I have discussed this in greater detail in Sønnesyn, *Ethics of History*.
[22] See in particular B. Stock, *Augustine the Reader: Meditation, Self-Knowledge and the Ethics of Interpretation* (Cambridge, MA, and London, 1996). See also D. Robertson, *Lectio Divina: The Medieval Experience of Reading* (Collegeville, MI, 2011); cf. E. Morgan, *The Incarnation of the Word: The Theology of Language of Augustine of Hippo* (London, 2010); J. Leclercq, *The Love of Learning and the Desire for God: A Study of Monastic Culture* (New York, 1961), esp. pp. 15–22; and H. de Lubac, *Medieval Exegesis: The Four Senses of Scripture*, multiple vols. (Grand Rapids, MI, and Cambridge, 1998–), here e.g. vol. I, pp. 230–67.

me, and there is the way by which I will shew him the salvation of God. In the sacrifice of praise, then, a path or way of showing is made for Jesus; for while compunction is poured out through the psalmody, a way is made through our hearts by which we may ultimately reach Jesus.[23]

In patristic theology prayer was never regarded as capable of bringing about a change in the unchangeable God; rather, prayer brought about a change in the praying subject.[24] As the quotation from Gregory the Great illustrates, this was as true for public, communal prayer through the liturgy as it was for private devotion. The Divine Office, all through the patristic period into the Middle Ages, was a channel of divine grace, profoundly transforming those who participated in its celebration. As such, a life devoted to the Divine Office was thus both the supreme life of moral progress, and also the realisation of the goal of this progress as attainable in this immanent, temporal existence.[25]

The effect of the Divine Office was not limited to the strictly moral sphere. The great twentieth-century theologian Yves Congar has called the liturgy of the Church 'a means other than writing of transmitting everything, in a way that is profoundly educative'.[26] There is clear continuity here with the patristic view propagated in the early and high Middle Ages. The liturgy constituted a matrix of meaning, a multi-layered expression of the Word of God fulfilled in the Word Incarnate, which was made incarnate anew in every valid celebration of the Eucharist. I would dare to venture that it seemed no coincidence to Eadmer of Canterbury that his master, Saint Anselm, caught the whole argument of his *Proslogion* in a flash when lost in meditation during Matins; the workings of grace

---

[23] Gregory the Great, *Homeliae in Hiezechihelem propheta*, 1.1.15, ed. M. Adriaen, CCSL 142 (Turnhout, 1971), p. 12: 'Vox enim psalmodiae cum per intentionem cordis agitur, per hanc omnipotenti Domino ad cor iter paratur, ut intentae menti uel prophetiae mysteria uel compunctionis gratiam infundat. Vnde scriptum est: Sacrificium laudis honorificabit me, et illic iter est quo ostendam illi salutare Dei [...] In sacrificio igitur laudis fit Iesu iter ostensionis, quia dum per psalmodiam compunctio effunditur, uia nobis in corde fit per quam ad Iesum in fine peruenitur.'

[24] See R. Fulton, 'Praying with Anselm at Admont: A Meditation on Practice', *Speculum* 81 (2006), 700–33; M. A. Edsall, 'Learning from the Exemplar: Anselm's Prayers and Meditations and the Charismatic Text', *Mediaeval Studies* 72 (2010), 161–96; S. Boynton, 'Prayer as Liturgical Performance in Eleventh- and Twelfth-Century Monastic Psalters', *Speculum* 82 (2007), 896–931.

[25] Among an enormous number of relevant passages, cf. Augustine, *Enarrationes in Psalmos* XLIX.21, ed. D. E. Dekkers and J. Fraipont, 2 vols. (Turnhout, 1990), I, pp. 590–1; and Augustine, *Enarrationes in Psalmos* CXXXIV, ed. Dekker and Fraipont, II, pp. 1937–57.

[26] Y. Congar, *The Meaning of Tradition* (New York, 1964), p. 125.

through liturgy combined illumination with edification.[27] In the liturgical celebration and commemoration of saints and other temporal persons, institutions, and events, a path was formed through the temporal into the eternal, and the presence of the eternal in the temporal was revealed through the reception of the temporal into the infinite cycle of the liturgy. Past and present are united in being embodied in the voice and mind of the participant of the liturgy, and this embodiment is a *sine qua non* for genuine moral progress within the monastic tradition of ethics. The pivotal point of the liturgy, the Eucharist, allows for the physical and concrete reception of the incarnated Word of God; but this sacrifice is echoed by the sacrifice of praise, the sacrifice of the Word as word, that frames the celebration of the Eucharist in the liturgical cycle.

I would argue that it is crucial to place Orderic within such a scheme. I do not need to rehearse here Ray's copious documentation of the way liturgical elements saturate the *Historia ecclesiastica*;[28] but I will mention one example to illustrate how Orderic is at his most liturgical when he offers his most detailed and profound justifications for his historical endeavours. Let us again, then, return to the crucial preface to Book VI. Having praised the assiduous students of history for their benevolent work, and criticised the nay-sayers for their lethargy, Orderic admits that recent history offers few models of sanctity for imitation, being dominated instead with signs of the decline of mankind. But this does not mean it is unworthy of record: 'We should nevertheless write truly about the course of the world and of human affairs; and accounts of the time [*chronographia*] should be sung to the praise of the Creator and just governor of all things.'[29] It is, then, only in being sung to the praise of the creator that historical narratives truly reach the fullness of their meaning. There is substantial evidence to suggest that Orderic's history was in fact used liturgically, and the text itself is laced with liturgical references. Statements such as the one just quoted suggest that this was integral to the function and meaning of the text; it was only as embodied in songs of praise that its full meaning was laid bare, *diuinitus inspiratum*.

In the same manner, and with ultimately the same purpose and effect, the practice of *lectio divina* may also be regarded as aiming at the embodiment of the Word of God in the reader. As Leclercq and McGinn have explained, the monastic practice of *lectio divina*, slow reading and

---

[27] Eadmer of Canterbury, *The Life of St Anselm, Archbishop of Canterbury*, ed. R. W. Southern (Oxford, 1962), p. 30.

[28] For the importance of reading Orderic in a monastic context, see also Chibnall, *World*, pp. 58–114, and the contribution to this present volume by T. O'Donnell: 'Meanders, Loops, and Dead Ends: Literary Form and the Common Life in Orderic's *Historia Ecclesiastica*'.

[29] *HE*, III, p. 214: 'De cursu tamen seculi et rebus humanis ueraciter scribendum est, atque ad laudem creatoris et omnium rerum iusti gubernatoris cronographya pangenda est.'

meditation on shorter passages of Scripture, was recognised as a way of making the Word of God once more incarnate in the world, allowing it to mould and transform the seeking mind.[30] The monk would read the passage slowly, over and over again, to internalise the words and fix them in his memory. The various layers of meaning of the text were brought into focus each in their turn. To the four senses usually attributed to Holy Scripture – the historical, allegorical, tropological and anagogical – there corresponded four stages of *lectio divina*: *lectio* itself, where the literal or historical sense of the text was made clear; *mediatio* where the allegorical or spiritual significance was, as it were, released; *oratio* in which the reader would use the text as a basis for prayer concerning his or her own life in the light of the text; and *contemplatio*, the grace-infused contemplation of the Glory of God. The end of all this, moreover, was not the attainment of abstract knowledge, but the transformation and reform of life itself. *Operatio* was the terminus of the whole procedure, as Leclercq has emphasised.[31]

McGinn has highlighted the very close affinity between, and mutually complementing roles of, liturgy and *lectio divina* in early and high medieval monasticism:

> *Lectio divina* for the medieval monk and nun was always meant to be in harmony with the communal prayer of the whole Church, the Body of Christ. It was not a higher form, or substitute for, liturgical observance; rather, it was the opportunity for the individual to implement in his or her life a personal consciousness of the inner (i.e. 'mystical' in the medieval sense) meaning of the corporate prayer of the Christ's bride, the church, performed seven times each day in the *opus Dei*.[32]

If liturgy provided the framework, *lectio divina* allowed for the application of this framework in the innermost self of the *monachus*.

There is space here for just one example to place Orderic in relation to the monastic tradition of *lectio*. A particularly illuminating instance for our present purposes is found at the very beginning of Book II, which chronicles the birth and early development of the Church. Orderic mentions that Saint Luke addressed his Acts of the Apostles to Theophilus, before making sure that the reader gets the full significance of this name:

> Theophilus indeed means one who loves God, by which [name] is designated every[one who is] assiduous [*studiosus*] and comprehending, and fervent in the continual meditation of divine

---

[30] Leclercq, *Love of Learning*, esp. pp. 15–17; B. McGinn, *The Growth of Mysticism* (London, 1994), e.g. pp. 132–46.

[31] Cf. Leclercq, *Love of Learning*, p. 16.

[32] McGinn, *Growth*, p. 132–3.

law [i.e. Scripture], to whom God's word is rightly addressed, and by whom this word is vigorously perceived, and tenaciously retained in the cement of true love.[33]

The *studiosus* is here one who makes God's Word his own in love, who meditates and through meditation allows the Word to live in him. In the context of the reader of Scripture, then, Orderic's *studiosus* is not the learned and analytical scholar, but the devout disciple.

Another frequently overlooked but arguably essential affinity between liturgy and *lectio divina* is found in the use of concrete historical circumstances, past and present alike, as points of departure for the ascent of the mind towards the transient and eternal. In his classic study of medieval exegesis, de Lubac gave a wealth of evidence supporting his claim that the historical sense of Scripture had always carried crucial importance in theory, but that the twelfth century saw a renewed emphasis on the importance of basing spiritual ascent on a firm, literal grounding.[34] In sum, then, the two pillars of medieval monastic practice, the liturgy and *lectio divina*, provided their practitioners with a framework, a matrix of meaning, within which particular, temporal events could find their place in the timeless order of God; simultaneously, they offered a mode of reading through which the individual life was transformed in the image of the incarnate Word of God as revealed in history. This, then, I would like to argue, is the sole context within which Orderic's corpus as a whole can be seen to contribute to moral edification.

Again we find examples of this in Orderic's own text, though, as before, this example allows for a number of interpretations and is therefore not conclusive on its own. In mentioning St William at the start of Book VI, Orderic finds occasion to insert a brief life of this saint recently come into his hands. He claims he had, until then, found it hard to come by a trustworthy and dignified account: 'Jongleurs sing a popular song about him, but a reliable account, carefully written by pious scholars and reverently read aloud by assiduous readers [*studiosi lectores*] for all the brothers to hear [*communi fratrum audientia*] is certainly to be preferred to that.'[35] Here, the liturgical setting for which this text was composed offers validation and adds rich layers of meaning to the narrative. I would argue,

---

[33] HE, I, p. 164–5: 'Theophilus quippe interpretatur Deum diligens, quo designatur omnis studiosus et intelligens, et in diuinæ legis meditatione iugi feruens, ad quem sermo Dei iure dirigitur et a quo idem uiuaciter percipitur, glutinoque dilectionis ueræ tenaciter retinetur.'

[34] See in particular vol. I of de Lubac, *Medieval Exegesis*.

[35] HE, III, p. 218: 'Vulgo canitur a ioculatoribus de illo cantilena, sed iure preferenda est relatio authentica, quæ a religiosis doctoribus solerter est edita, et a studiosis lectoribus reuerenter lecta est in communi fratrum audientia.'

as Ray has argued before, that Orderic offers his own work to be appraised by this same standard and within this same framework.

In fact, I would like to conclude by suggesting that the depiction Orderic offers of his teacher John of Rheims amounts to a portrayal of Orderic's model reader within precisely this sort of scheme. John is described as sharp of mind and persistent in study, ('ingenio acer studioque pertinax'), and one who 'worked avidly at tracing the mysteries concealed in books'.[36] The knowledge he thus acquired he strove to pass on to his brethren through word and example.[37] Crucially for our present concerns, John was particularly renowned for his exegetical ability and his constant devotion to the liturgical cycle, even rising from his bed for night prayers during his final illness.[38] It was within this framework that John was able to penetrate into the concealed mysteries, and it was within this same framework, he laboured all his life to guide others into the same life of meditative study. As such, I would argue, he was a prime example of the *lector studiosus*.[39]

History contained hidden mystery because the eternal Verbum had become incarnate, thus imbuing history with divine significance. The Church, Christ's body on earth, was thus the continued embodiment of this mystery within time, and a *Historia ecclesiastica*, a history of the Word Incarnate as manifest in every and any region or period, could reveal the concealed mysteries to the assiduous reader. It is no coincidence, I would argue, that Orderic chose to frame his Norman narrative with the life of Christ and the growth of the Church as his body in what we know as Books I and II.[40] In this, he was merely making explicit the implicit principle that had informed his historiography all along: the incarnation of the Word was the foundation for a spiritualisation of history that, in becoming a subject for meditation, could transform and reform the lives

---

[36] Ibid., pp. 166–70: 'Hic ingenio acer studioque pertinax fuit, et in habitu monachico fere xlviii annis uixit, et in indagandis librorum abditis mysteriis uehementer laborauit.'

[37] Ibid.: 'aliosque uiriliter dimicare uerbis et exemplis docuit'.

[38] Ibid.: 'Subprioris curam diutius gessit, uicesque abbatis in diuinæ legis prolatione sepius explevit [...] In senectute plus quam vii annis calculi molestia languit, diutinoque morbo emens lecto non decubuit, sed cotidie ad diuinum opus surgens Deo gratias egit.'

[39] Ibid.: 'Ingenio subtilis erat, cito carmen agebat,/ Metro seu prosa pangens quæcumque uolebat./ Otia uitabat, maiorum scripta legebat,/ Commoda priscorum carpens documenta uirorum./ In cultu Christi laudabiliter uigilauit,/ Nocte dieque Deo sua reddere uota sategit/ Actibus et uerbis exemplar erat pietatis/ Divinæ legis frequenter opaca reuoluit,/ Mistica discipulis grato sermone retexit.'

[40] Cf. the contribution by Mégier within the present volume: 'Jesus Christ, A Protagonist of Anglo-Norman History? History and Theology in Orderic Vitalis's *Historia ecclesiastica*'.

of *lectores studiosi*. Orderic never set out to present a self-enclosed moral system; the true moral content of history is brought out in monastic practices and in devout monks and nuns. It is only in an interpretive, praying community that the *abdita* may be brought to light, painstakingly, and not once for all, but continuously repeated in the perpetual drive to interior and communal reform that formed the heart of early twelfth-century monasticism. The *studiosi* were not scholars in ivory towers, elevated beyond mere mortals on account of their knowledge; they wore coarse black wool, and this exterior habit was merely the extension of the interior monastic habits that rendered them able to penetrate into the mystery of the Word incarnate.

Meanders, Loops, and Dead Ends: Literary Form and the Common Life in Orderic's *Historia ecclesiastica*

Thomas O'Donnell

THIS chapter considers the literary forms of Orderic Vitalis's *Historia ecclesiastica* as a way to think about the relationship between identity, history-writing and the practice of the monastic common life during the early twelfth century. Anne L. Clark has characterised medieval monastic practice in general as the process of 'dismantling of the autonomous person' and 'the reconstruction of that being into a member [...] [of] the monastic community itself'.[1] Without denying the *Historia*'s place within political discourse or its powerful administrative and economic motivations, I will situate the text's form within eleventh- and twelfth-century discussions of this transition from a secular individual to a member of a monastic community. In doing so, I wish to suggest not only the sensitive artistry of Orderic's style but also its foundations in the rhetoric and practices of the monastic common life.

Orderic has usually been overlooked as an artist. Some of this neglect stems from the *Historia*'s Norman provenance and its Latin language, both of which place the work in an odd relation to the literary histories of both Britain and France. The *Historia*'s breadth and shape can be dismaying as well, for Orderic frequently challenges the reader's expectations about how rhetorical history should sound and what it should be about.[2] He is given

---

Versions of this chapter were read at the Columbia University Medieval Guild in New York, at the 'Orderic Vitalis: New Perspectives on the Historian and his World' conference in Durham and at the 2014 Medieval Academy of America Conference in Los Angeles. I am grateful for the comments I received on each occasion but would especially like to thank Susan Boynton, Emma O'Loughlin Bérat, Elizabeth Tyler and John Diehl for their corrections and advice. This volume's editors, especially Daniel Roach and Charlie Rozier, deserve special thanks for both their patience and their many improving suggestions. A fellowship at the Stanford Humanities Center made the final revisions of this chapter possible.

---

[1] 'Medieval Latin Spirituality: Seeking Divine Presence', in *The Oxford Handbook of Medieval Latin Literature*, ed. R. Hexter and D. Townsend (Oxford, 2012), pp. 465–84, at p. 467.

[2] For negative assessments of Orderic's literary style, see e.g. Delisle, 'Notice', pp. xli–xliv; and Antonia Gransden, *Historical Writing in England*, vol. 1: *c. 500 to c. 1307* (London, 1974), p. 161.

to digressions, and he frequently interrupts himself by inserting into the *Historia* verse epitaphs, occasional poems, saints' lives, charters, miracles, local histories, genealogies, misogynist gossip, a whole history of the First Crusade lifted from Baldric of Bourgueil, and (seemingly) whatever has come into his head at any given moment. For example, in Book III, where Orderic discusses the foundation of Saint-Évroul in 1050, he begins with a potted history of Normandy from the Merovingian age, moves on to discuss the foundation of Le Bec, then makes a feint at the foundation of Saint-Évroul but gets distracted by a genealogy of the Giroie family from the tenth century onwards, and then by extended stories of supernatural punishments visited upon unworthy clerics. Orderic finally returns to the foundation of the community itself by copying out a pancarte from the monastery's archive, but in order to make sense of this he must launch into a dynastic history of the Norman dukes, and so gets swept away describing the conquest of England in 1066. Multiply the digressive, multivocal structure of this one book by thirteen and the difficulties of the rest of the *Historia* become clear. Meanwhile, scattered here and there within Orderic's normally smooth, chiming prose are several passages where clear Latin expression slips from his grasp. Between the centrifugal narrative structure and these linguistic obscurities, fastidious critics might be forgiven for finding Orderic as barbarous as he sometimes likes to call himself.

In this essay, however, such critics will not be forgiven. Here I will justify Orderic's unusual form by looking at the *Historia* from two different, yet complementary, perspectives. First, I consider the *Historia*'s overall structure and suggest that its swirling narrative reflects its character as a community history of Saint-Évroul. Its complexities aim to represent, at a basic diegetic level, one version of the monastic 'common life' that twelfth-century religious reforms had turned into a *cause célèbre*. Orderic presents the diverse individual histories of Saint-Évroul's myriad inhabitants, patrons, enemies and possessions as the history of the house as a whole in a manner that stresses the need for monks, in the words of contemporary reformers, to leave behind personal differences and achieve 'one heart and one soul' (Acts 4:32).[3] The tortuous, principled inclusivity of Orderic's text can be compared to other literary attempts at unifying heterogeneous communities at contemporary monastic houses, but Orderic's convoluted manner brings a new subtlety to the endeavour to represent the common life. Second, I look at individual passages in the text with a very tight focus, especially Orderic's famous autobiographical remarks. I highlight Orderic's use of specific compositional techniques borrowed from the liturgy, and show how he subordinates his individual experience to a pedagogical, communal end. Throughout I wish to emphasise the degree to which the

---

[3] For the 'reformation of the twelfth century', see Giles Constable, *The Reformation of the Twelfth Century* (Cambridge, 1998), and nn. 12–14, below.

Historia was a tool for spiritual renewal as well as for moral instruction and political gamesmanship, and that the *Historia*'s formal qualities added to its utility.

Marjorie Chibnall observed that the foundation for Orderic's writing was a method of interpolation and compilation that evoked several models and authorities simultaneously.[4] By contrast, Orderic's Norman predecessors William of Jumièges and William of Poitiers worked more narrowly, drawing inspiration from single *auctores* like Dudo of Saint-Quentin or Suetonius. As antecedents, Orderic looked to Bede's own *Historia ecclesiastica* and *Historia abbatum*, and also to the *Historia ecclesiastica* of Eusebius, as translated by Rufinus; to the *Gesta Normannorum ducum* and the *Gesta Guillelmi*; and to the individual biographies, saints' lives, documents, oral tales and miracle collections that inform various sections of the work. This gallimaufry of sources is held by the *Historia* within a loose, almost improvisational structure, generally subordinated to Orderic's own style but never masking its own diversity. Certainly, digressions and heterogeneity were not uncommon in medieval histories. Bede himself presented official correspondence and verse in his work, and institutional histories and biographies frequently included epitaphs, hymns and occasional poetry. Nevertheless, Orderic carried this tendency to polymorphism further than most other rhetorically minded historians of his age.

The complex sequence of the *Historia ecclesiastica*'s composition, through phases that are variously Norman, Anglo-Norman, and universal, also creates problems for the reader. Books III through VI, on the history of Saint-Évroul, its patrons, and William the Conqueror's *regnum*, were composed first. They probably respond, in a developing way, to a commission Orderic received from his abbot.[5] Books VII through XIII were likely already underway before Book VI was finished, and include his accounts of the Crusades, the new monasticism and the careers of William the Conqueror's successors in Normandy and England. Finally, a gospel harmony and universal chronicle were added to the beginning as Books I and II. All the same, the *Historia*'s humility *topoi* point to omissions rather than wordiness as the work's major flaws: Orderic excuses himself for not including enough marvels or for sticking to earthly events and eschewing subtle theological analysis, explaining that the world's evils have stopped up the flow of miracles, while theology remains beyond his powers.[6]

---

[4] Chibnall, 'General Introduction' pp. 48–63. See also Shopkow, *History and Community*, pp. 160–3.

[5] *HE*, I, pp. 29–35.

[6] For example, see *HE*, III, pp. 8–9, 214–15; *HE*, VI, pp. 8–13, 436–7. Chibnall, *World*, pp. 179–80; Roger D. Ray, 'Orderic Vitalis and his Readers', *Studia Monastica* 14 (1972), 15–33.

The *Historia* thus balances broad inclusivity and Orderic's awareness of the epistemological limits and historical contingency of his work (and, one might say, of the work of any historian). As Roach has argued, stories appear in the *Historia* not because they are simply noteworthy or marvellous, but because they are associated with patrons, friends, enemies, or relics of the monastery.[7] For example, a description of relics of St Nicholas at Saint-Évroul's priory at Noron required a digression on the history of those relics, an account of the relic's donors, and further details about Saint-Évroul's links to southern Italy.[8] The many other histories pieced together in the *Historia* similarly establish Saint-Évroul's social connections to neighbouring clergy, to a local robber, or to the community's various lords and patrons, so that the *Historia*'s contents complement and enlarge upon the information contained within the list of Saint-Évroul's confraternity agreements.[9] Yet, as Roach makes clear, these social connections constitute narrative threads with ends inside Saint-Évroul as well as outside of it. Within Saint-Évroul they were attached to the relics, inscriptions, donations and people who represented, in material terms, the social bonds recorded textually in the confraternity agreements. It is therefore not enough to think of the *Historia*'s diegetic bubbles and oxbows as reactions to the world 'around' Saint-Évroul; rather, as the histories of individual monks and gifts within the monastery, they correspond to the inner world of Saint-Évroul as well. It is in this way that the loopiness of Orderic's back-and-forth, expansive narrative offers a compelling representation of the experience of living within a community.[10]

This manner of representing community gains significance in light of the anxious attention given to community life by twelfth-century religious reformers. While many scholars of the twelfth century still dwell on the period's expressions of religious and secular individualism, Caroline Walker Bynum pointed out long ago that the period also saw renewed interest in the concepts of group and community, which coincided with the challenges to traditional monasticism raised by the new monastic

---

[7] See D. Roach, 'The Material and the Visual: Objects and Memories in the *Historia ecclesiastica* of Orderic Vitalis', *HSJ* 24 (2013), 63–78, at pp. 77–8.

[8] *HE*, IV, pp. 54–75. For St Nicholas's relics, see Roach's contribution to this volume.

[9] For Saint-Évroul's confraternity agreements with individuals and other communities, see Chibnall, *World*, pp. 67–70. On the affective dimensions of confraternity agreements, see Benjamin A. Saltzman, 'Writing Friendship, Mourning the Friend in Late Anglo-Saxon *Rules of Confraternity*', *Journal of Medieval and Early Modern Studies* 41 (2011), 251–91.

[10] For more on the back-and-forth nature of the *Historia*, see Daniel Roach, 'Narrative Strategy in the *Historia ecclesiastica* of Orderic Vitalis' (unpublished PhD thesis, University of Exeter, 2014).

orders.[11] As a result, the requirements of clergy's communal life gained greater specificity during Orderic's lifetime. Not all observers agreed on what should constitute the proper 'common life' of the clergy, but, despite their differences, most commentators defined 'vita communis' and related collocations like 'communiter vivere' with reference to Acts 4:32, where it is said that the 'multitude of believers had but one heart and soul [...] but they held everything in common'.[12] Exponents of the twelfth-century reforms argued that this passage, as well as Matthew 19:21 ('If you wish to be perfect, go, sell what you have, and give it to the poor, and you will have treasure in heaven'), required all clergy to renounce private property.[13] As is well known, attempts to define the limits of this renunciation fed into larger controversies over the respective virtues of the lives led by monks, nuns, canons, hermits, and others.[14] Since comments made in the heat of these debates emphasised the practical steps necessary to institute the reforms these reformers envisaged, it can sometimes appear as though the common life primarily consisted of the abolition of private clerical property.[15]

---

[11] Caroline Walker Bynum, 'Did the Twelfth Century Discover the Individual?', in her *Jesus as Mother: Studies in the Spirituality of the High Middle Ages* (Berkeley, 1982), pp. 82–109.

[12] Usually the term 'vita communis' referred to the lives of monks, nuns and canons; the status of secular clergy was more ambiguous. See *Mittellateinisches Wörterbuch bis zum ausgehenden 13. Jahrhundert*, ed. Otto Prinz *et al.* (Munich, 1999), II, s.v. 'communis', IA2b, where 'vita communis' refers specifically to monks and canons. The related term *coenobita* (from the Greek word κοινός, meaning 'common') could sometimes be employed to refer narrowly to monks and nuns living in community, but *monachi*, *religiosi*, and their derivatives were the normal terms for men and women in the religious life. See Giles Constable, *The Reformation of the Twelfth Century* (Cambridge, 1998), pp. 7–13; and Julia Barrow, *The Clergy in the Medieval World: Secular Clerics, their Families and Careers in North-Western Europe, c. 800–c. 1200* (Cambridge, 2015), pp. 98–100.

[13] Constable, *Reformation*, esp. pp. 156–7.

[14] The literature on the debates among twelfth-century reformers is enormous. For useful guides, see Constable, *Reformation*; Lester K. Little, *Religious Poverty and the Profit Economy in Medieval Europe* (Ithaca, NY, 1978); and John Van Engen, 'The "Crisis of Cenobitism" Reconsidered: Benedictine Monasticism in the Years 1050–1150', *Speculum* 61 (1986), 269–304.

[15] See Little, *Religious Poverty*, pp. 70–83, 99–112. Cf. Constable, *Reformation*, pp. 125–67, which emphasises the diversity of reform rhetoric. For hermits, see Tom Licence, *Hermits and Recluses in English Society, 950–1200* (Oxford, 2011), pp. 27–41. For a hermit's critique of the cenobitic life, see G. Morin, 'Rainaud l'Ermite et Ives de Chartres: Un épisode de la crise du cénobitisme au XIe–XIIe siècle', *Revue bénédictine* 40 (1928), 99–115.

Yet eleventh- and twelfth-century authors of all stripes, from hermits and monks to cathedral canons, also insisted on what they saw as the community-building effects of dispossession, such as increased charity and spiritual unity.[16] In *Contra clericos regulares proprietarios*, for example, Peter Damian cites Acts 4:32 and declares:

> See, where there is no diversity of goods, there flourishes a unity of wills. Surely where there is no division of wealth, the desires of many minds are kindled into a union of charity. For mind is divided from mind in that place where fellowship of possession is not maintained, and where the ownership of possessions is individual, there the mind of the possessors is not one [...] Therefore any cleric who ventures to have private property cannot be following in the footsteps of the apostles, for he will not share one heart and one soul with his brothers.[17]

Traditionalists shared these same values but objected to the reformers' idea that canons and secular clerks could achieve such unity, believing that monks and nuns fulfilled the apostolic ideal best of all. Had not St Augustine referred to Acts 4:32 when he derived the word 'monachus' from Greek 'μόνος' ('one'), because monks 'live in unity in order to make up one man'?[18] Advocates for the eremitic life could counter that men living in community were hardly living 'singly', and as authorities they could cite St Jerome and St Isidore of Seville, for whom the oneness of the monk lay in literal solitude, not in spiritual unity.[19] But the Augustinian vision of monasticism bolstered the arguments of twelfth-century apologists for traditional cenobitism, including Ivo of Chartres, Hamelin of St Albans, Honorius Augustodunensis, Geoffrey of Auxerre, Alan of Lille, and the anonymous chronicler of Petershausen. The latter adds to Augustine's idea of social unity the idea of 'singularity of heart', and to some extent he combines both Augustinian and Hieronymian traditions by insisting that the monks' purity of heart depends on separation from the

---

[16] Jean Leclercq catalogues the wide variety of spiritual meanings attached to common property during the Middle Ages in *La Vie parfaite: Points de vue sur l'essence de l'état religieux* (Turnhout, 1948), pp. 82–103.

[17] 'Ecce ubi non erat diversitas rerum, vigebat unitas voluntatum. Nimirum ubi non est divisio census, in unionem charitatis plurimarum mentium conflatur affectus. Illic enim mens a mente dividitur, ubi facultatum communio non tenetur: et ubi possessionum diversa proprietas, ubi mens possidentium non est una. [...] Quisquis ergo clericus proprietatis conatur habere peculium, non valet apostolorum tenere vestigia: quia non erit illi cum fratribus cor unum et anima una.' *PL* 145, 479B–490B (486A). All translations from Latin are my own.

[18] J. Leclercq, 'Études sur le vocabulaire monastique du Moyen Age', *Studia Anselmiana* 48 (1961), 7–38 (quotation at p. 9 n. 10); cf. p. 28 n. 76.

[19] Leclercq, 'Études', pp. 10–18.

world.[20] Meanwhile the author of the *Libellus de diversis ordinibus et professionibus qui sunt in aecclesia* wrote in support of traditional monasticism that:

> he is rightly called 'one' and 'alone' [*unus et solus*], who has the one and only intention of living with his brothers [*unum et solum cum fratribus uiuendi habet affectum*] and [keeps that intention] totally cut off from the pleasure of worldly things [...] The brother does not lose the privilege of the name if he sets aside worldly things with brothers 'dwelling in unity', whose company is 'good and pleasant' [...] Then the monk is truly one and alone if he feels as one with his brothers; he worships the one and only God; and, in the words of Solomon, 'as a brother helped by his brother' he establishes 'one strong city' in his heart, that is, love of God and of his neighbour.[21]

Other writers described this process of unity concretely as the displacement of the monks' own will by that of another, as though giving up personal agency were just one further, perfecting step in the renunciation of worldly goods. In the words of one treatise that circulated in England during the twelfth century, the good monk advances from being one who 'subjects his own will to another, as if made into a beast of burden that is driven this way and that with the bridle of obedience' into one who, 'inasmuch as he has nothing more to offer, longs for the commands of a stranger's will [*alienę uoluntatis*], willing nothing on his own, so to speak, and knowing nothing but Jesus Christ and him, crucified'.[22]

---

[20] For Ivo, see *PL* 162, 261B–261C. For the others, see Leclercq, 'Études', pp. 17–26, 38, 155.

[21] *Libellus de diversis ordinibus et professionibus qui sunt in aecclesia*, ed. and trans. G. Constable and B. Smith (Oxford, 1972), pp. 18–19: 'ille unus et solus recte dicitur, qui unum et solum cum fratribus uiuendi habet affectum, et a uoluptate secularium omnino seggregatum [*sic*] [...] non perdit prerogatiuam nominis, si frater cum fratribus quorum "bona et iocunda in unum habitantium" societas est secularia postponat [...] Tunc enim monachus uere unus et solus est, si cum fratribus unum sentiat, unum et solum Deum colat, et secundum Salomonem "frater adiutus a fratre unam ciuitatem fortem" dilectionem Dei scilicet et proximi in corde suo constituat.' The *Libellus* borrows language from Psalm 132:1 and Proverbs 18:19.

[22] 'propriam uoluntatem [...] alteri subiecerit, ut iumentum factus quod freno obedientię circumferatur [...] et tamquam non habens ultra quid offerat, alienę uoluntatis expectat imperia, nichil se tamquam per se uolens, nichil sciens nisi ihesum christum et hunc crucifixum.' Jean Leclercq, 'Nouvelle Réponse de l'ancien monachisme aux critiques des cisterciens', *Revue bénédictine* 67 (1957), 11–93 (91.376–82). The conception of obedience as a sacrifice of the will pre-dated even Benedict and is found in collections of the sayings of the desert fathers. See Adalbert de Vogüé, 'Obéissance

Twelfth-century conceptions of traditional monasticism thus insisted more than ever on a definition of the common life as a social and spiritual unity made possible through personal renunciation (including the abrogation of individual property), obedience, and charity. The desire for unity found practical expression in typical monastic customs like subjection to an abbot, group prayer, and shared eating and sleeping quarters. When Orderic himself had occasion to defend traditional monastic observance against 'new rites' inspired by the eremitical and Cistercian movements, it was precisely these customs that he held up as the surest foundations for holiness. For example, against the charge that black monks no longer worked with their hands, he claimed that this was to free monks to devote their time to the choir, 'to sacred reading and prayers for all their benefactors and to the mysteries of heaven'.[23] Likewise, he portrays adaptations of the *Regula sancti Benedicti* to northern climates as sanctioned by the earliest authorities and as a matter best left to the judgment of abbots, not to be questioned by over-scrupulous renegades. According to Orderic, monks deviate from the letter of the *Regula* not because they lack zeal, but because they are obedient. His choice of form for the arguments just cited reinforces our sense of the wisdom of common action over personal initiative. He puts these words in the mouths of the monks of Molesme in a reply to their abbot, Robert, and thus pits the corporate voice of a group of observant, anonymous monks against the innovations of an anxious, impractical individual. The awkwardness of this situation, in which principles based on the collective authority of abbots and founders and on the practices of Tours and Cluny are used to resist the spiritual authority of the monks' actual abbot, should be obvious, but in Orderic's narrative it is Robert himself who has driven the monks to such audacity.[24] Orderic refrains here, as elsewhere, from expressing his views in the plainly theological language used by an Ivo or a Peter Damian, but by means of form and example he nevertheless communicates the practical meaning of theoretical debates over the common life.

The praise of the monastic order pronounced by Orderic's father, Odelerius, in Book V of the *Historia* likewise emphasises the monks'

et autorité dans le monachisme ancien jusqu'à saint Benoît', in *'Imaginer la théologie catholique': Permanence et transformations de la foi en attendant Jésus-Christ; Mélanges offerts à Ghislain Lafont*, ed. J. Driscoll (Rome, 2000), pp. 565–600, at p. 571. For a discussion of obedience in eleventh-century English monasteries, see Katherine O'Brien O'Keeffe, *Stealing Obedience: Narratives of Agency and Identity in Later Anglo-Saxon England* (Toronto, 2012), esp. pp. 6–8, 33–4.

[23] *HE*, IV, pp. 310–11, 318–21: 'lectionibus et sacris orationibus pro cunctis benefactoribus suis et coelestibus misteriis'. For monks as intercessors, see Van Engen, 'Crisis', pp. 292–7.

[24] *HE*, IV, pp. 316–21.

obedience and shared enterprise. Coming as a digression in the midst of a section detailing Saint-Évroul's patrimony and patrons, the speech justifies lay generosity to monks. In the context of Orderic's narrative, Odelerius's speech is delivered to Roger of Montgomery in recommendation of founding a monastery at Shrewsbury. 'When I consider the customs of all the mortal men in the world and carefully look into the lives of hermits and canons', Odelerius says, 'I see that all of these are inferior to the life of monks who live according to canons and the *Rule*':[25]

> Pains are what they possess – and wretched clothing, bland and scanty food, and the forfeiture of their own wills for the love of the Lord Jesus. What shall I say of their chastity and of their every kind of temperance, what of the silence of monks and their shamefastness, and what finally of their obedience? The scale of their so many virtues overwhelms my mind, and I confess that I am unable adequately to put them into words. True cenobites are shut up inside royal cloisters like the daughters of a king, so that they will not be wickedly defiled by Shechem the son of Hamon the Hivite, to the dishonour of a stern father and to the disgrace of their warlike brothers, if they wander abroad without shame like Dinah the daughter of Leah. Within their own walls, they are their own guardians, lest they should fall, and if inside their sanctuaries they do fall away from the right path, they are their own accusers. And in every way they busily work to refine themselves, like gold in the furnace, from all dross of sin.[26]

Odelerius's speech champions the observances of traditional cenobitism as the best method for the perfection of poverty and singleness of heart. In a familiar progression, the monks' renunciation of material wealth leads in

---

[25] *HE*, III, pp. 144–5: 'dum omnium qui in terra sunt mortalium ritus discutio, et heremitarum atque canonicorum uitas diligenter perspicio; omnes monachorum qui canonice uiuunt et ordinate reguntur uita inferiores uideo.' For more on this section of the *Historia*, see the contribution by van Houts in this volume, 'Orderic and his Father, Odelerius'.

[26] *HE*, III, pp. 144–5: 'Asperitas illis inest et uilitas in uestitu, siccitas et parcitas in uictu; et propriarum resecatio uoluntatum propter amorem Domini Ihesu. Quid de castitate et omni continentia, quid de silentio monachorum et modestia, quid denique dicam de oboedientia? Tantarum copia uirtutum magnitudine sui meum obtundit ingenium; fateorque me non posse sufficienter illam exprimere per oris officium. In regalibus claustris ueri coenobitae ueluti filiae regis clauduntur, ne si per exteriora tanquam Dina Liae filia impudenter [Chibnall: impudentur] euagantur; a Sichem filio Emor Euei ad iniuriam rigidi patris ferociumque dedecus fratrum turpiter corrumpantur. Ipsi tutores ne labantur in septis suis sibi fiunt, et lapsi per excessum in penetralibus suis accusatores sui sunt; seseque ut aurum in fornace ab omni scoria uitiorum omnimodis excoquere satagunt.'

turn to 'the forfeiture of their own wills'. Obedience and personal restraint are both the expression of this sacrifice and the means of its support. Orderic also presses the idea of the monks' physical separation from the world. The need for strict stability and enclosure inspires a particularly high-flown passage that strings together references to the royal daughter of Psalms 44:14 (45:13) and to the unfortunate Dinah of Genesis 34, whose rape by Shechem was brutally avenged by her brothers. Despite the apparent incompatibility between female exempla and the male monastic life, these two scriptural references were well established in the literature of enclosure. Orderic's immediate inspiration for bringing them together probably lay with Jerome's *Epistula* 22,[27] but Marbod of Rennes had also recently addressed both male and female religious with a poem warning them against Dinah's example.[28] Understanding Odelerius's words, which I have translated literally, requires knowing that Shechem represents Satan (as he does for Marbod and Jerome) and that the crime against Dinah had by now been interpreted as her own fault, though Orderic does not explain this. This is just one place in the *Historia* where Orderic's pen appears to get ahead of him. The somewhat off-centre superimposition of biblical figures upon historical events is not atypical of Orderic, and we shall see in his epilogue how he exploits the elasticity of scriptural references.

The reference to Dinah also offers Orderic a transition to the passage about monastic 'guardianship' and 'accusation' with which this section ends. Fault-finding inside the monastery distressed some hermits, who saw it as a failure of charity,[29] but in the highly controlled form described here it was at the heart of the disciplinary regime established in Benedict's *Regula*.[30] The sudden thickening of reflexive pronouns in the final sentence of the passage ('ipsi tutores [...] in septis suis sibi fiunt', 'in penetralibus suis accusatores sui sunt', 'seseque [...] ab omni scoria [...] excoquere satagunt') drives home Orderic's equation of personal introspection and

---

[27] *Epistulae* 22.1 and 22.25. Orderic also compares monks living in cloisters to the 'daughters of a king' in the speech he gives to the monks of Molesme in Book VIII, for which see *HE*, IV, pp. 320–1.

[28] Marbod, 'De Raptu Dinae', *PL* 171, 1682D–1684C (1684B): 'Nemo tamen solis putet haec recitanda puellis;/ Scripsimus haec per quae sexus doceatur uterque./ Ne velut effundi mens nostra per avia mundi,/ Sed legem matris teneat, mandataque patris.' For further monastic interpretations of the Dinah legend, see Joy A. Schroeder, *Dinah's Lament: The Biblical Legacy of Sexual Violence in Christian Interpretation* (Minneapolis, MN, 2007), pp. 18–19; and Gilbert Dahan, 'La Matière biblique dans le *Planctus* de Dina de Pierre Abélard', in *Hortus troporum: Florilegium in honorem Gunillae Iversen*, ed. A. Andrée and E. Kihlmann, Acta Universitatis Stockholmensis: Studia Latina Stockholmensia 54 (Stockholm, 2008), pp. 255–67, at pp. 264–7.

[29] E.g. Rainaud's criticisms in Morin, 'Rainaud l'Ermite', p. 104.

[30] E.g. chapters 23, 27, 46, 70.

communal surveillance. This is not simply a twelfth-century panopticon; Orderic's picture of mutual accusation and of the shifting tides of personal opposition within the monastery illustrates the difference between the common life and uniformity. The monastic community includes and overrides individual voices, but it does not stifle them totally.

This observation brings us back to the sprawling, inclusive form of the *Historia*. In filling his history of Saint-Évroul with the stories of other people, particularly of fellow-monks and patrons, Orderic suggests that the history of a monastic community should be the history of the community it contains. As evinced by Odelerius's speech, the common life of monks consists in the charitable accommodation of the monastic individual to the will of others – both superiors and brothers. Despite the language of loss and forfeiture commonly associated with monastic renunciation, the charitable accommodation of Orderic's monks to one another amounts to a process of addition and superimposition, not subtraction. Orderic's multiplying narrative reflects this process of accumulation and convergence, representing the community of Saint-Évroul not as a seamless whole but as a group of different pieces fitted together. The disorder of the work, meanwhile, with its interruptions, digressions, and unexpected asides, presents the process of achieving the ideal of unity in a touchingly unidealised way. Orderic does not keep to a straight line, partly because people do not relate to one another in straight lines. Personal relationships are instead a series of loops, meanders, and – often – dead-ends. The content of the *Historia* offered Orderic and his fellow monks the chance to think through their own connections to church, world and family, but the work's complex form suggests that these connections were not concentric; rather, they cut across and branched off one another.

Orderic's style is ill-suited to the representation of homogeneous identities. Certainly, the *Historia* does explore a kind of identity for Normandy and Saint-Évroul,[31] but its digressions and commentary demonstrate that identitarian narratives are themselves composed of individual histories irreducible to 'Norman' or 'English' identity, for example the histories of a particular relic or tomb inscription, of the eschatological history culminating in the history of the First Crusade, or of people like Orderic himself. The same resistance to coherent narratives of national triumph informs Orderic's engagement with William of Jumièges' *Gesta Normannorum ducum* and William of Poitiers' *Gesta Guillelmi* across his career. In his version of the *Gesta Normannorum ducum*, Orderic generally simplifies William of Jumièges' turgid style and tones down the older monk's patriotic support of William the Conqueror's family, but towards the end of his version he actually introduces new material on the deeds of Norman aristocratic families

---

[31] Albu, *Normans in their Histories*, pp. 180–213.

who had special connections to Saint-Évroul.³² In this way he widens the *Gesta*'s perspective to take in more than ducal politics, and makes the text a repository for local knowledge of use to his monastery. Orderic's insertions are not handled gracefully. More often than not, they interrupt William's more chronologically and geographically unified narrative. Yet the copiousness of Orderic's information here draws attention to the complexity of events that William of Jumièges' praise for 'our duke' had somewhat flattened,³³ and his interpolations foreshadow the social proliferation of the *Historia*. Likewise, Orderic's adaptation of William of Poitiers' text in the *Historia* reduces the verbal complexity of his source but complicates the treatment of the events themselves, usually by neutralising William's partiality for the Conqueror. While Chibnall thought Orderic toned down William of Poitiers' adulation because of his experiences as an Englishman,³⁴ I would like to suggest that Orderic's even-handedness was also informed by his monastic practice. Indeed, as shall be seen in the following section, Orderic's remembrance of England cannot be severed from his cultivation of monastic renunciation.

In adapting the form of his historical writing to a renewed emphasis on the common life, Orderic was not alone. Other historians and scribes produced identifiably 'communal' works in response to calls for reform. Two well-studied examples are the eleventh-century collection of saints' lives known as Douai MS BM 849, written for the monks of Marchiennes, and John of Worcester's twelfth-century *Chronica chronicarum*. Each in its own way demonstrates discursive commitments to plurality and inclusion. Three main scribes produced the copy of *Chronica* in Oxford MS Corpus Christi College 157, beginning their work as early as the 1090s and bringing it to an end as late as the 1140s.³⁵ The *Chronica* scribes added new material, particularly from Bede, Asser and a version of the *Anglo-Saxon Chronicle* to Marianus Scotus's universal chronicle from Mainz. Richard Southern and Antonia Gransden emphasised the way these additions represented an English antiquarianism, but Martin Brett demonstrated that the *Chronica* developed over time to include not just 'old' material, but also the newest research, as it were, from Symeon of Durham, Eadmer, and William

---

³² GND, I, pp. lxix–lxxvii.

³³ Ibid., p. lxx. In Orderic's phrasing, 'our duke' is simply 'the duke'.

³⁴ *Gesta Gvillelmi of William of Poitiers*, ed. M. Chibnall (Oxford, 1998), p. xxxv. Cf. Albu, *Normans in their Histories*, pp. 182–8, who sees Orderic as openly critical of William the Conqueror in his copy of the *Gesta*; and Shopkow, *History and Community*, pp. 97–105, who remarks on Orderic's nuanced judgement of the Norman dukes.

³⁵ *The Chronicle of John of Worcester*, vol. 2: *Annals from 450 to 1066*, ed. R. R. Darlington and P. McGurk, trans. J. Bray and P. McGurk (Oxford, 1995), pp. xxi–lxxxi.

of Malmesbury.[36] Moreover, the scribes 'internationalised' Marianus's original text, which had focused on papal and imperial 'universal' history, with information from Flemish saints' lives, Norman annals, Frankish regnal lists, new papal annals from Germany, and Hugh of Fleury's history from the Loire Valley. This variety no doubt reflected the diversity of personnel at Worcester, which included Anglo-Danes, Normans, Irishmen, Welshmen, and Franks.[37] The dependence on non-English sources increased as the work went on, and many times the scribes would go back over their work to cram new information into the margins or in tiny lettering over erasures. Rather than forge a univocal 'English' identity for an 'English' public (such as William of Malmesbury or Henry of Huntingdon might have done), the *Chronica* coordinated the different textual experiences of a diverse readership in a form that broadcasts the work's collaborative foundations and suggests a deliberate avoidance of creating one single historical master-narrative.[38]

The same resistance to monolithic history can be seen in Douai MS

---

[36] R. W. Southern, 'Aspects of the European Tradition of Historical Writing: 4. The Sense of the Past', *Transactions of the Royal Historical Society*, 5th series 23 (1973), 243–63; A. Gransden, 'Cultural Transition at Worcester in the Anglo-Norman Period', in *Medieval Art and Architecture at Worcester Cathedral: The British Archaeological Association Conference Proceedings for the Year 1975* (Leeds, 1978), pp. 1–14; M. Brett, 'John of Worcester and his Contemporaries', in *The Writing of History in the Middle Ages: Essays Presented to Richard William Southern*, ed. R. H. C. Davis et al. (Oxford, 1981), pp. 101–26.

[37] A list of professed monks of Worcester written into the Durham *Liber Vitae* between 1099 and 1109 includes names with associations that are variously English ('Godricus', 'Leouricus', 'Goduuinus', 'Ordricus', etc.), Norman ('Willelmus', 'Warinus'), Anglo-Danish ('Hem(m)ingus', 'Vlf', 'Vhtredus'), Frankish ('Karolus', 'Henricus', 'Gilebertus', 'Arnulfus', 'Martinus'), and Irish ('Colu(m)banus', 'Patricius'), as well as biblical and Latin names without ethnic affiliations (although 'Thomas' is clearly the Norman prior of that name). Onomastic evidence can only pushed so far, but at least this shows that the monks of Worcester did not derive their self-identifications solely from Norman and Anglo-Saxon name-stocks. See *Durham Liber Vitae*, ed. D. Rollason et al., 3 vols. (London, 2007), III, pp. 25, 127. Meanwhile, the Welshman Bishop Urban of Llandaff was ordained at Worcester and was probably educated there. See D. Walker, 'Urban (d. 1134)', *Oxford Dictionary of National Biography* (Oxford, 2004); online edition at <http://www.oxforddnb.com/view/article/48565> [accessed 25 November 2014].

[38] For the 'Englishness' of William of Malmesbury and Henry of Huntingdon, see J. Gillingham, 'Henry of Huntingdon and the Twelfth-Century Revival of the English Nation', in his *The English in the Twelfth Century: Imperialism, National Identity, and Political Values* (Woodbridge, 2000), pp. 123–44.

BM 849. According to Snijders, this book was made for the monks of Marchiennes between 1024 and 1033, after Bishop Gerard I of Cambrai and Baldwin IV of Flanders had refounded the ancient female monastery as a male house.[39] The new establishment was probably composed of men taken from three very different communities: elite members of the reformed community of St. Vaast, led by Abbot Leduin; members of the less prestigious house of Denain, which Gerard I had dissolved; and one or more canons of Cambrai. Snijders has suggested that the diverse origins of new monks of Marchiennes would have brought marked differences in their levels of literacy and their attitudes towards the house's history. The lives of the seventh-century foundress Rictrude, her daughter Eusebia and their male colleague Jonatus collected in Douai MS BM 849 respond to these differences by telling, in different forms, 'blatantly contradictory stories about the early history of Marchiennes and life choices of its patron saints' (p. 898). Basically, the simpler prose lives addressed to the less sophisticated monks minimise Rictrude's early leadership, and the more complex metrical lives addressed to a more learned group within the monastery stress Rictrude's responsibility for guiding a mixed group of men and women. In using this manuscript, the monks of Marchiennes would have been confronted with a 'complex and multilayered' identity for their house, 'which was unfit to be streamlined into a ready-made interpretation that would be acceptable for the entire community' as a whole (p. 898). The manuscript faithfully reflects presumably real divisions among the monks, rather than papering them over or splitting the difference between them. All the same, the modes of presentation, distinguishing between simple prose and ornate verse, would have guaranteed that at least some of the monks were spared a version of history not to their taste.

Aside from offering parallels, these two books also suggest what might be unique about the *Historia ecclesiastica*. Much more explicitly than the monks of Worcester or Marchiennes, Orderic involves non-monastic family and friends within the monastic community. And whereas the collaboration among Worcester monks is made plain by the number of easily identifiable scribal hands in Oxford MS Corpus Christi College 157, and while elements of style and language within the Marchiennes lives presuppose different audiences for each version of the monastery's history, Orderic's history conveys its sense of spiritual unity through the voice of one individual historian directed at a single Saint-Évroul audience. In other words, if the *Historia* does imagine its narrative as a kind of image of the monastery's network of family and friends, then it does so

[39] For the following details on the refoundation and the composition of Douai MS BM 849, see T. Snijders, 'Textual Diversity and Textual Community in a Monastic Context: The Case of Eleventh-Century Marchiennes', *Revue d'histoire ecclésiastique* 107 (2012), 897–930, at pp. 899–907.

through Orderic's own self-conscious adoption of a particular narrative persona who does not push any single agenda and humbly accepts his own limitations. The second section of this chapter therefore turns to the formal elements of Orderic's self-presentation in the autobiographical sections of Book V and the Epilogue in Book XIII, considering them not as straightforward self-revelation, but rather as conscious fictions that only partially transmit Orderic's 'real' personality. In shifting our focus from the overall structure of the *Historia* to Orderic's crafting of his authorial voice, we also turn from thinking about the way Orderic's text *represents* the common life as a collection of different narratives to thinking about the way his voice attempts to *perform* a unified, monastic subjectivity while addressing a diverse audience.

The 'autobiographical' passages of the *Historia ecclesiastica* are generally considered three. First, in the prologue to Book V, Orderic gives a brief account of his origins in 'the furthest regions of the Mercians'.[40] Then, the speech of his father, Odelerius of Orléans, in praise of the monastic life concludes with Odelerius's announcement that he will be sending his eldest son Orderic to Normandy as a monk. Finally the story of Orderic's oblation and the family's painful separation is fully told in the *Historia*'s epilogue at the end of Book XIII.[41] Together, these passages form the basis for our knowledge about Orderic's early life and offer the clearest evidence that Orderic thought of himself as an Englishman. Yet these self-revelations do more than offer a national frame for Orderic's writing. First, they display Orderic's assimilation of biblical, liturgical, and earlier historiographical modes into the *Historia*. All three elements bolster his personal and textual authority. Second, they are occasions for Orderic to broadcast his own textual performance of some of the monastic virtues cited by Odelerius in Book V: namely, the forfeiture of his own will, shamefastness, and obedience. In this connection, it is less important to know whether Orderic truly practised these virtues than to reflect on his possibly fictive performance of them within the *Historia* as a means either to acquire them or to communicate their importance to his fellow monks. Third, Orderic's self-writing shapes his own experience into an object of meditation for other monks. For even as the *Historia*'s autobiographical moments situate Orderic in a very specific life narrative, they also exemplify one path for moving from a personal life formed out of familial, ethnic and linguistic identities towards a common life of spiritual unity and obedience.

It is convenient to begin with the epilogue, which richly illuminates the relation between Orderic's personal subjectivity and the forms of community adopted elsewhere in the *Historia*. As Chibnall has suggested, Orderic's account of himself in the epilogue is modelled on Bede's

---

[40] *HE*, III, pp. 6–7: 'extremis Merciorum finibus'.
[41] See van Houts, 'Orderic and his Father, Odelerius'.

autobiographical notice at the end of his own *Historia ecclesiastica*.[42] First, Orderic explains that he is bringing his book to a close not only because of his advancing age but also because the evils of the time have grown so great that he can no longer describe them. He then declares his gratitude for God's favour, and especially for his separation from his father, which he justifies as having been for his own good, because it freed him from any 'fleshly love of kin' that might have shaken his commitment to cenobitism.[43]

> And so, glorious God, who commanded Abraham to depart from the land and the house of his father, and from his kindred, you inspired Odelerius my father to renounce me utterly and to subdue me to you in every way. Weeping, therefore, he gave me, weeping [*plorans plorantem me tradidit*], to Reginald the monk and sent me away into exile for your love, and he never saw me again.[44]

This ostensibly 'personal' passage conflates biblical typology and Augustinian confession in confusing ways. In particular the figure of Abraham stands in an odd relation to both Orderic and his father. Strictly speaking it is Orderic who is analogous to the patriarch, leaving his homeland for a land of monastic promise. But quite obviously Odelerius is also an exile and he is also bound for the monastery, so in some sense the Abrahamic role suits him just as well.[45] Certainly Abraham's sacrifice of Isaac must also be recalled here, too. What to make of all this ambiguity? On one level the typological confusion supports the idea that Orderic's emotion robs him of the kind of authorial control over language possessed by someone like William of Malmesbury or Eadmer of Canterbury. On another level, however, ambiguity seems to be precisely the point, since the referentially unstable figure of Abraham allows Orderic to credit a grief to his father that corresponds to his own and thus to imagine a

---

[42] Chibnall, 'General Introduction', pp. 5–7.

[43] *HE*, VI, pp. 552–3: 'parentum carnalem affectum'.

[44] Ibid.: 'Iccirco gloriose Deus qui Abraham de terra patrisque domo et cognatione egredi iussisti, Odelerium patrem meum aspirasti ut me sibi penitus abdicaret, et tibi omnimodis subiugaret. Rainaldo igitur monacho plorans plorantem me tradidit, et pro amore tuo in exilium destinauit, nec me unquam postea uidit.'

[45] Abraham frequently served as a model of exile for solitaries (because he was exiled) and cenobites (because he was obedient), but, as the object of sacrifice himself, Isaac was also available for typological games. For instance Peter of Celle cannot decide, when he went on retreat to Mont-Dieu, whether he was more like Abraham or Isaac: 'Cum Isaac uel Abraham ad Montem Dei ascendi, sed asinus cum pueris carnalium sensuum in conuallibus me expectat. Cum hostiam iubilationis immolauero, iterum rediturus sum. Sed ubi est uictima holocausti?' Jean Leclercq, 'Nouvelles Lettres de Pierre de Celle', *Studia Anselmiana* 43 (1958), 160–79, at p. 167.

moment of shared feeling between the two of them. For one instant, they are both Abrahams. Ambiguity also seems to motivate Orderic's climactic polyptoton 'plorans plorantem'. The divisions among subjects are muddled and contact between the father and son is extended – syntactically, at least – at the very moment of separation.

Such subjective muddling is analogous to Orderic's eager appropriation of the histories of friends, patrons, and enemies in the body of the work itself. Whereas in his prologues Orderic uses *topoi* of modesty and obedience to integrate his writing within monastic practice, here he combines learned rhetorical figures and the polysemy of *lectio divina* to expand his individual subjectivity into something more inclusive and communal. Through the figure of Abraham he first appropriates his father's subjectivity, and then appropriates other exiled (that is, monastic) Christians.

Elsewhere in the epilogue Orderic exploits biblical precedent to render his personal experience more communal. After the passage referring to Abraham, Orderic continues, 'Thus at ten years old I crossed the Channel, arrived in Normandy like an exile, and unknown to all I knew no one. Like Joseph in Egypt, I heard a language I did not understand.'[46] Here the biblical reference offers a concrete detail that captures the panic of his younger self, sold off, as it were, into slavery abroad. Yet this reference comes not, as might be expected, from the story of Joseph's enslavement in Genesis. Rather, it comes from the Psalms, specifically Psalm 80, verse 6 (81:5). In full the verse reads 'testimonium in Ioseph posuit illud, cum exiret de terra Aegypti: linguam, quam non noverat, audiuit.' ('[The Lord] ordained it for a testimony to Joseph, when he came out of Egypt: he heard a language that he did not know.') According to the complex analysis that Augustine offers of this psalm in the *Enarrationes in Psalmos*, by 'Joseph' is meant 'God's chosen people', and the passage out of Egypt indicates 'baptism'. Augustine explains that the unknown language therefore signifies the Christian mysteries, which bewilder those who have not been washed in the blood of Christ.[47] By sending Joseph back into Egypt, Orderic's reference flips the patristic interpretation on its head. Just as he stretches out the figure of Abraham until the patriarch could prefigure both Orderic and his father, so here too he distorts Joseph in order to offer a powerfully ambiguous message about the experience of monastic renunciation (which indeed was sometimes referred to as 'Egypt', after the monastic order's origins in the Thebaid). As signs of the monastic life, Joseph's new language and the land of Egypt indicate both 'salvation' and self-denying 'servitude'.

[46] *HE*, VI, pp. 554–5: 'Decennis itaque Britannicum mare transfretaui, exul in Normanniam ueni, cunctis ignotus neminem cognoui. Linguam ut Ioseph in Ægipto quam non noueram audiui.'

[47] *Enarrationes in Psalmos LI-C*, ed. E. Dekkers and J. Fraipont, Corpus Christianorum Series Latina 39 (Turnhout, 1959), LXXX.8, p. 1124.

In order to understand the ambiguities of this passage, and how they might relate to the meaning of the *Historia* in general, more should be said about the monastic origins of Orderic's style here. The closest parallel to Orderic's creative reappropriation of the figures of Joseph and Abraham comes from the field of liturgical composition. Within the monastic Divine Office, psalms and readings would be punctuated by musical phrases sung by the choir or parts of the choir. These sung pieces, called responsories or antiphons depending on the type of text they accompanied and on the manner of their performance, were generally composed out of language adapted from Scripture. Sometimes biblical expressions are quoted outright or rearranged minimally to suit the melody; sometimes they are borrowed to elevate the language of non-biblical texts such as a saint's life or patristic sermon; and often scraps of biblical language are pieced together to present an original idea, even if the words meant something rather different in their original scriptural context.[48] In the passage concerning Joseph, Orderic assumes the style of a responsory by 'misquoting' a biblical text in order to suit his narrative. Indeed, a ready parallel to Orderic's formulation can be found in a responsory widely attested from the tenth century until the end of the Middle Ages and used during the third week of Lent. Here too the language that Joseph did not understand was the speech of his Egyptian taskmasters: 'When Joseph entered into the land of Egypt he heard a language that he did not know; his hands laboured in bondage and his tongue spoke wisdom among princes.'[49]

Recognising the liturgical foundations of Orderic's language makes it

---

[48] For a detailed analysis of the different ways that authors drew on biblical and patristic language to compose responsories and other original liturgical pieces, see R. Jacobsson, 'The Antiphoner of Compiègne: Paris, BNF MS Lat. 17436', in *The Divine Office in the Latin Middle Ages: Methodology and Source Studies, Regional Developments, Hagiography*, edited by M. E. Fassler and R. A. Baltzer (Oxford, 2000), pp. 123–78, esp. pp. 158–63. Similar protocols informed the composition of sequences, another genre of liturgical performance. See G. Iversen, *Chanter avec les anges: Poésie dans la messe médiéval: Interprétations et commentaires* (Paris, 2001).

[49] 'Joseph dum intraret in terram Aegypti linguam quam non novit audivit manus ejus in laboribus servierunt et lingua ejus inter principes loquebatur sapientiam.' CANTUS: A Database for Latin Ecclesiastical Chant <http://cantusdatabase.org/id/007037> [accessed 6 October 2014]. Rupert of Deutz also quotes Psalm 80 (81) when reflecting on his difficult transition from (francophone) Liège to (German-speaking) Deutz and on his appointment as abbot there in preference to native monks, in his work *De incendio*. Unlike Orderic, however, Rupert justifies the comparison with a scrupulous interpretation of the whole Psalm. See H. Grundmann, 'Der Brand von Deutz 1128 in der Darstellung Abt Ruperts von Deutz: Interpretation und Text-Ausgabe', *Deutsches Archiv* 22 (1966), 385–471, at pp. 418–20, 458.

easier to see the role of his own story as part of the community of stories inside the *Historia*. Monastic prayer was the dominant lens through which medieval monks and nuns sought to understand themselves and their world. When medieval religious performed psalms and prayers, shared biblical and patristic words and images became the basis for personal meditations and, from there, for spiritual regeneration.[50] Responsories and antiphons played an important role in monastic prayer (and thus monastic self-understanding and self-transformation), because they underlined the meaning of their associated readings within the Divine Office, often by adducing further Scriptural parallels.[51]

Just as responsories contextualise and interpret service readings, so Orderic's comparison of himself to Joseph fashions a meaning out of his harrowing experience of oblation, which might be shared with other monastic readers. It does so by bringing together two biblical uses of the figure of Joseph. One, drawn from the Psalms, is inherently spiritual, because 'Joseph [...] leaving the land of Egypt' must always be either the Hebrews or, for Augustine, the Christian community he believed that the Hebrews prefigured. The second, drawn from Genesis, is basically historical and refers to the suffering that Joseph experienced as a slave. By aligning his own experience with that of this reconfigured Joseph, Orderic insists simultaneously on his historical experience, which is prefigured in Joseph's exile but is essentially individual, and on its spiritual meaning as a type of the exile from the world experienced by all monks. In the practical terms used elsewhere in this chapter, Orderic's liturgical and psalmodic rewriting of his life makes his 'personal' history 'common' and makes the spiritual unity of the cloister possible.[52] The somewhat awkward coordination of biblical figures thus accomplishes the same work, in miniature, that the idiosyncratic, 'jumbled' arrangement of material in the *Historia ecclesiastica* performs on a large scale. It fuses a new wholeness out of disparate, competing parts.[53]

---

[50] For prayer as a tool for self-transformation based on recalled words and images, see especially R. Fulton, 'Praying with Anselm at Admont: A Meditation on Practice', *Speculum* 81 (2006), 700–33.

[51] Jacobsson, 'The Antiphoner of Compiègne', p. 170. For antiphons, see M. E. Fassler, 'Hildegard and the Dawn Song of Lauds: An Introduction to Benedictine Psalmody', in *Psalms in Community: Jewish and Christian Textual, Liturgical, and Artistic Traditions*, ed. H. W. Attridge and M. E. Fassler, Symposium Series 25 (Atlanta, 2003), pp. 215–39, at pp. 222–3.

[52] Monika Otter has suggested that Goscelin's use of psalmodic language in his letter to Eve had a similar goal of creating an elastic textual persona that both he and his addressee might share. See her 'Entrances and Exits: Performing the Psalms in Goscelin's *Liber Confortatorius*', *Speculum* 83 (2008), 283–302.

[53] This is not the only place in the *Historia* where Orderic splices together material from 'history' and the psalms in the manner of liturgical

The compositional protocols of the liturgy were particularly appropriate to the production and performance of 'common' monastic subjectivities. The musical performance of prayer frequently struck observers as the epitome of monks' corporate existence and the principal expression of their personal sacrifice.[54] In Book V, Orderic has Odelerius exclaim, 'Who can recount the vigils of monks, their hymns and their psalms, their prayers and their alms, and their daily offerings of mass with showers of tears? The followers of Christ devote themselves wholly to this so that by crucifying themselves they might please God in all things.'[55] Later Orderic has the monks of Molesme define the virtue of cenobitic life in nearly identical terms. In response to Robert's call for less singing and more manual labour, the monks reel off a list of the appropriate activities for monks that includes their reading, meditations, and silence and culminates in the 'Davidic hymns and other mystical chants [that] they sing together day and night unto the Creator'.[56] In seeking a somewhat musical answer to the challenge of how to square personal and group experience, Orderic was thus relying on an established connection between communal singing and the common life. Later in Orderic's autobiographical epilogue he returns to the idea that the common life can be understood as a kind of group musical performance. When he first arrived at Saint-Évroul the monks gave him a new name, 'Vitalis'. He explains that this was because 'Orderic' sounded to them 'absonum', literally 'out of tune'. Whereas the name 'Orderic' embedded the young monk within a specific English setting and a single moment of time – his baptism on the river Severn by a priest named Orderic – the name 'Vitalis' brought him into harmony with his new community and folded his identity into the liturgical cycle. A moment of likely ethnic chauvinism thus becomes a gesture of communal welcoming through the language of liturgy and music.

To what extent does Orderic's coordination of different narratives through writing, and especially through quasi-liturgical writing, relate to his probable role as a cantor or precentor at Saint-Évroul?[57] Fassler and others have drawn attention to the fundamental affinity between

composition. Odelerius's combined allusion to Dinah and the 'daughters of a king' brings together history (from Genesis) and allegorical language (from the Psalms). See above pp. 306–7.

[54] Clark, 'Medieval Latin', pp. 468–9.

[55] HE, III, pp. 144–5: 'Quis referre potest monachorum uigilias, ymnos et psalmodias, orationes et elemosinas, et cum lacrimarum imbribus missarum oblationes cotidianas? Christi sequaces ad hoc omnino uacant; ut sese crucifigentes Deo per omnia placeant.' Cf. Colossians 1:10.

[56] HE, IV, pp. 320–1: 'dauiticos ymnos aliasque misticas modulationes nocte dieque creatori concinant'.

[57] See Charles C. Rozier in this volume 'Orderic Vitalis as Librarian and Cantor of Saint-Évroul'.

medieval liturgy and medieval history-writing. Both cultural forms strove to fashion images of the past that were of use to the present. But despite our modern preference for using chronicles and discursive history in reconstructing past events, during the Middle Ages historical narrative was more frequently encountered in worship, at least for the men and women of the church. Liturgical routines included saints' lives, miracle stories and distinctive musical arrangements, and they profoundly shaped participants' understanding of the local past in relation to the history of the church and the world. The composition of new readings and hymns could be used as a vital forum for presenting new views of the past.[58] Certainly, the high Middle Ages witnessed a remarkable number of cantors or precentors who also composed historical works: Osbern of Canterbury, Eadmer of Canterbury, William of Malmesbury, Hugh the Chanter, Symeon of Durham, and Lawrence of Durham definitely served as precentors at some point in their careers, while Sigebert of Gembloux, Rupert of Deutz and John of Worcester combined historical and liturgical interests in their writing without being explicitly labelled precentors or cantors. Fassler is no doubt right that there appears to be 'a profound relationship between these two ways of expressing the past'.[59]

Just what this relationship was remains to be seen. Most likely, it was expressed diversely by different writers. The texts produced by the aforementioned historians differ from one another hugely in their aims, their sources, their geographic and chronological scope and their style. To my mind, the liturgical training of these men cannot explain their historiography any more than their histories should determine our understanding of their musical work. In the case of Orderic, liturgical and musical styles of composition offered powerful tools for achieving the pedagogical and spiritual ends of his work, while the intensity of music and the liturgy could support Orderic's remarkable feeling for his subjects and his occasional bursts of emotion. By contrast, a cold wind blows through the classical arcades of William of Malmesbury's large-scale histories, and Eadmer's hagiographic apologetics seem small-minded in comparison. The hapless, passionate Osbern probably presents the best analogue for Orderic, though he cannot manage either Orderic's rigour or his creative depth.

It seems therefore that the importance of Orderic's probable role

---

[58] M. E. Fassler, 'The Liturgical Framework of Time and the Representation of History', *Representing History, 900–1300: Art, Music, History*, ed. R. A. Maxwell (University Park, PA, 2010), pp. 149–71; M. E. Fassler, *The Virgin of Chartres: Making History through Liturgy and the Arts* (New Haven and London, 2010), pp. vii–x, 79–129. Cf. Snijders, 'Textual Diversity', pp. 911–14, where the liturgical readings on the life of St Rictrude seem carefully chosen to avoid controversy within a potentially fractured community.

[59] Fassler, 'The Liturgical Framework', p. 168.

of cantor lies most of all in the authority that such an office would have conferred on him and in the access it would have opened to the people, books and objects that lie behind the stories he tells in the *Historia*. Additionally, if Orderic were personally involved in coordinating the day-to-day singing of the Saint-Évroul monks, then we might speculate about the connections between gathering the monks together in song and the coordination of individual stories within the *Historia*. Both the choir and the pages of the *Historia* provided images of Saint-Évroul as a more or less harmonious whole.

In any case, it is clear that Orderic's use of liturgy in the epilogue transforms his personal experience into an object of meditation for himself and his readers. Earlier in the *Historia*, Orderic puts this personal transformation at the centre of his compositional practice, and he relates it explicitly to the *Historia*'s use as a tool for educating young monks about 'their own affairs'. In the lengthy speech in Book V on the advantages of the monastic life, Odelerius presents himself as an exemplary patron who gives not only his worldly goods but also himself and his sons to support the monastic life:

> Behold, I have a house on the banks of the river Meole, which you [Roger of Montgomery] gave me recently, next to which I have begun to build a stone church, just as I vowed to do a year ago before the altar of Peter, prince of the Apostles in Rome. I gladly offer to the Almighty the church, which, as I have said, I have recently established to fulfil a vow freely made, as well as my house and its furnishings [...] Finally I will give myself and my son Benedict, now five years old, and all my goods to the monastery [of Shrewsbury] [...] Furthermore I have already given over [*mancipaui*] my first-born son [Orderic] to a teacher of the liberal arts, to be instructed in letters, and I have sought out for him a place of safe refuge among the servants [*uernulas*] of God at Saint-Évroul in Normandy [...] Thus for the love of the Redeemer I am renouncing my first-born son and sending him across the sea into exile, so that he can fight [*militet*] for the heavenly king of his own free will [*ultroneus*] as an exile among strangers, and so that there, free [*liber*] from every tie of kinship and fatal affection, he might be truly strong in the monastic observance and the worship of the Lord.[60]

---

[60] HE, III, pp. 146–7: 'Ecce super Molam fluuium michi domus est quam nuper dedisti iuxta quam sicut anno transacto ante aram sancti Petri principis apostolorum Romæ uotum feci, lapideam ædificare basilicam cepi. Basilicam itaque quam ut dixi. sponte uoto constrictus facere nuper institui; domumque meam cum omni apparatu meo gaudens offero cunctipotenti [...] Deinde meipsum et Benedictum filium meum iam quinquennem et omnia mea tradam monasterio [...] Porro primogenitum meum iamdudum litteris imbuendum liberali didascalo mancipaui, eique locum tutæ mansionis inter uernulas Dei apud Vticum in Neustria

Orderic confesses, however, that he betrays the 'fatal affection' he claims his father meant to spare him, by returning to his father's memory often:

> I beg your pardon and do not take it ill if I pass on some memorial in writing of my father, whom I did not see after he drove me into exile like a reviled stepson for the love of his creator. Forty-two years have passed since then, in which many changes of affairs have taken place all over the world, while I think often of these things, and insert certain of them into these pages. Warily fighting sloth, thus in composition I occupy myself.[61]

As in the epilogue, Orderic paints a painfully ambiguous picture of his father and of his father's choice to offer him as a monk. The language of social and psychological freedom found in words like 'milito',[62] 'liber', and 'ultroneus' contrasts with words having to do with slavery and rejection, like 'mancipo', 'uernula', 'exosus', and 'priuignus'. But in offering an excuse for the intrusion of his father into Saint-Évroul's history, Orderic does more than show his hand. He deliberately makes the literary transformation of his memory into an engine for continued, meaningful composition, which provides his brothers with material for meditation: 'Now I will return to the matter I had begun, and I shall expound to my juniors native to this land, as a foreigner, about their affairs, of which they are ignorant, and in this way with God's help, I shall profitably serve them.'

Orderic's service here includes both educating the monks about their past and encouraging them to think and feel about it in the right ways. The 'matter' in Book V to which Orderic returns is an account of the monastery's possessions, recorded as a series of family histories of Saint-Évroul's patrons and directed at the novices of the monastery, 'so that when they make use of them [the monastery's possessions] they might know

---

procuraui [...] Sic pro redemptoris amore primogenitum michi filium abdico et trans pontum in exilium destino, ut ultroneus exul inter externos regi militet æthereo, ubi liber ab omni parentum cura et affectu lætifero, eximie uigeat in obseruantie monastica et cultu dominico.'

[61] Ibid., pp. 150–1: 'Parce queso bone lector, nec molestum tibi sit precor; si de patre meo aliquid memoriæ tradiderim litterarum, quem non uidi ex quo me uelut exosum sibi priuignum, et pro amore creatoris pepulit in exilium. Iam xlii anni sunt; in quibus multæ mutationes rerum late per orbem factæ sunt. Dum sepe de his cogito, et quædem cartis insero; caute resistens ocio, sic dictans me exerceo.'

[62] While 'milito' can mean 'to be a soldier' or simply 'to fight', in the *Historia ecclesiastica*, Orderic typically uses the related words 'miles' and 'militaris' to refer to free knights. See the *Dictionary of Medieval Latin from British Sources*, ed. R. E. Latham *et al.* (London, 1975–), s.v. *miles*, 6, and *militaris*, 2. Meanwhile, the monks of Molesme refer to the noble origins of monks (and thus their freedom from servile labour) by calling them 'egregii [...] milites'. *HE*, IV, pp. 320–1.

by whom and when they were given or sold at a price'.⁶³ The monks must know about these things to counter the venality of their lay neighbours, who would cheat them of their true deserts. 'For the greedy possessors of earthly goods gasp after what is fleeting, thinking little about what is highest and eternal, and so many do scarcely anything at all for hope of heaven unless they see that it will benefit them on earth.'⁶⁴ By implication, a very different habit of thought must accompany the monks' use of their acquisitions. Orderic therefore uses this section to make clear the moral purpose and social meaning of the monks' patrimony. He relates the monks' success in acquiring property to the recognition of their monastic discipline, and in each notice of donation he comments on the donor's penitent or charitable intentions and the monks' undertaking to pray for them or their relatives. While it is often observed by modern scholars that recording property transactions and the lives of donors facilitated liturgical commemoration and aided temporal administration, cultivating the memory of exemplary patrons might also serve a more inward purpose. Above all, the memorialisation of the monks' friends and possessions could be a means to keep the monks who were 'making use of them' from 'gasping after what is fleeting' and to have them reflect on 'what is highest and eternal' instead. Simply because they have so much of it, the monks' own wealth must inspire a spirit of detachment and sustain their purity of heart. Wealth transforms them, in the words Orderic gives to Odelerius, into 'God's true poor'.⁶⁵

This context suggests that Orderic's digression on his father and his own feelings is not so much about the preservation of personal identity as it is about the pursuit of the common life. Within the highly determined narrative of property and family descendance in Book V, both Odelerius and Orderic function as exempla of renunciation comparable to the donations made by revered patrons. The writings of the common life analysed above suggested that cenobites' material destitution must proceed to the renunciation of personal will (called 'uoluntas' but also 'affectus') and the acceptance of a servant's role. Orderic echoes this language and performs these gestures, at least textually, when he transforms his 'fatal affection' ('affectus lætifer') into something of service to his fellow monks.

The pious wish to serve in fact resumes the language of Orderic's first autobiographical passage in the prologue of Book V. This prologue explains that Orderic will begin Book V with the year of his own birth.

---

[63] HE, III, pp. 122–3: 'ut utentes eis sciant a quibus uel quo tempore datæ sint uel precio comparatæ.'

[64] Ibid., pp. 122–5.

[65] Ibid., pp. 144–5. Orderic's identification of the truly poor with wealthy monks reflects twelfth-century interpretations of the beatitudes. See Constable, *Reformation*, pp. 146–8. For a more general appreciation of Orderic's rendering of the 'space' of Saint-Évroul, see Hingst, *Written World*, pp. 1–18, 92–109.

Beginning historical work within one's own lifetime was a historiographic commonplace, because it implied that henceforward the historian would be more or less an eyewitness to the events described. In the course of staking out this familiar rhetorical terrain, Orderic describes his baptism, his early education, and his arrival in Normandy as a young boy. He boasts, 'I, who came here from the furthest regions of the Mercians as a ten-year-old English boy, a barbarous and ignorant foreigner thrown amongst clever men native to this land, have endeavoured with God's grace to commit to writing the deeds and experiences of the Normans for the Normans to read.'[66]

As in the other autobiographical moments already considered, the prologue to Book V stresses Orderic's role as a 'foreigner' ('aduena', 'exul', 'Ioseph') eagerly serving the Normans. What distinguishes Orderic's pretended service from other examples of monastic obedience is that it depends always on his status as a foreigner. This never-omitted fact ought to alert us to the pedagogical use of Orderic's self-presentation. It parallels Hugh of Saint-Victor's reflection in the *Didascalicon* on the benefits of exile to the student, who wishes that his mind might 'learn, bit by bit, first to change about in visible and transitory things, so that afterwards it may be able to leave them behind altogether'.[67] Orderic follows this principle to its logical conclusions. He can teach because he has come from so far, from the 'furthest regions of the Mercians'. In this respect, Orderic's later comparison of himself to Joseph in Egypt, when 'his hands laboured in bondage and his tongue spoke wisdom among princes', becomes even more salient.[68] Orderic's lesson consists in asking 'clever men' to learn from the 'barbarous and ignorant' and in inviting 'native' readers to adopt his own 'foreign' experience as their own. They might thus achieve the spiritual unity required by the high medieval common life, just as his book adopts seemingly external matters as the history of Saint-Évroul itself.[69]

---

[66] *HE*, III, pp. 6–7: 'ego de extremis Merciorum finibus decennis Angligena huc aduectus, barbarusque et ignotus aduena callentibus indigenis admixtus; inspirante Deo Normannorum gesta et euentus Normannis promere scripto sum conatus.'

[67] Translation from J. Taylor, *The Didascalicon of Hugh of Saint Victor: A Medieval Guide to the Arts* (New York, 1991), p. 101. Like Orderic, Hugh implies that his own teaching authority comes from a long, painful absence from home, but, unlike Orderic, his references derive ultimately from classical *auctores* like Ovid, Vergil, Cicero, and Horace (see p. 216 nn. 83–8).

[68] Augustine also connected hearing the new language of Psalm 80 to 'bearing witness and possessing knowledge' ('testantes et scientes'). See *Enarrationes*, LXXX.8, p. 1124.

[69] Cf. Shopkow's insight that Orderic's approach to the past was basically 'exegetical', *History and Community*, pp. 201–9; and Elisabeth Mégier, '*Divina pagina* and the Narration of History in Orderic Vitalis' *Historia ecclesiastica*', *Revue bénédictine* 110 (2000), 106–23.

In conclusion, this chapter has argued that the difficult form and sometimes obscure language of Orderic's *Historia ecclesiastica* served specific purposes in representing and facilitating the common life of the Saint-Évroul monks. First, the knotty form of the *Historia* as a whole offers a picture of the complex, multiple history of a community where individual monks must relinquish their own, private pasts and accept the pasts of their fellows as their own. Second, Orderic's autobiographical notices, despite their evident grounding in his actual experience, are transformed by him into objects of meditation for his readers, specifically keyed to themes of exile, renunciation, and service. Third, Orderic's use of liturgical forms makes it possible for his monastic readers not simply to imitate his example but to inhabit his experience, through the shared space of biblical types like Joseph and Abraham. The fact that Orderic emerges from his work as someone not simply preoccupied but also somehow over-occupied by the stories he tells points to the insufficiency of the notion that history was first and foremost about recording events or about providing fodder for the creation of 'community identity'. Rather, for Orderic, ecclesiastical history, especially in the expansive, multivalent way he wrote it, offered the chance to come to terms with community as a lived experience and as a spiritual ideal. The form of the *Historia ecclesiastica* thus suggests that by participating imaginatively in the disparate narratives contained within the precincts of Saint-Évroul, the monks might forge the social unity they desired and the singleness of heart the common life demanded.

Orderic and the Tironensians

Kathleen Thompson

THE section of Orderic's *Historia ecclesiastica* that has become known as his 'Treatise on the New Orders' is a valuable insight into the great wave of change that had swept through Western monasticism in his lifetime.[1] At the time he was writing the Cistercians were emerging as the strongest voice in what Marjorie Chibnall described as the 'great debate on the interpretation of the Rule'. While Orderic begins his consideration with the Cistercians, he has important things to say about other monastic initiatives too.[2] He provides, for example, an account of the foundation made at Tiron in the forests of the Perche in the first decade of the twelfth century. Little has been written about the monks of Tiron, although they were during Orderic's lifetime one of the most successful of the new approaches to monasticism, if success is to be measured by the settlement of Tironensian monks all over northern France, Normandy, Anjou, Poitou, Burgundy, Scotland, England and Wales.[3] Orderic's is an early and independent account of the rise of the Tironensian congregation, and it is important because the history of the Tironensians has always been dominated by the life of the founder, Abbot Bernard, the *Vita beati Bernardi Tironensis* (Bibliotheca Hagiographica Latina no. 1251). Orderic captures the stories that had gathered around the founding figure some twenty years after Bernard's death and, as such, is a witness to what can be described as the 'Bernard of Tiron narrative', before that narrative reached its fullest expression in the *Vita*. In considering Orderic's treatment of events at Tiron, then, our understanding of one of the more obscure of the so-called new monastic orders will be increased. Another look at the treatise in a Tironensian context will also be helpful in providing a new perspective on the sources Orderic used in the composition of the *Historia ecclesiastica*.

Orderic's record of the events that led up to the foundation of Tiron starts with the departure from Poitou of the abbot of Quinçay, Bernard, who left his house because he was unwilling to accept that it should be

---

[1] *HE*, IV, p. 310.

[2] Ibid., p. xl.

[3] Kathleen Thompson, *The Monks of Tiron: A Monastic Community and Religious Reform in the Twelfth Century* (Cambridge, 2014), and, 'The Arrival of the Tironensians: Twelfth Century Monastic Foundations in the British Isles', *Nottingham Medieval Studies* 55 (2011), pp. 87–110.

subject to Cluny.⁴ Orderic tells us that Bernard fought an action in defence of his community before Pope Paschal II in Rome, but he was unsuccessful in his appeal. Nonetheless, according to Orderic, Bernard won the respect of the pope for his courage in pursuing the case, and Orderic quotes Proverbs 28:1: 'the righteous man is bold as a lion'. Bernard then declined the pope's request that he should remain in Rome, and took up a wandering lifestyle accompanied by a few monks.

During the course of these wanderings Abbot Bernard visited Bishop Ivo at Chartres and it was with the bishop's encouragement that Bernard settled in the diocese of Chartres in a wooded spot called Tiron. A monastery in honour of the Saviour was built and great numbers flocked to it. Orderic recounts how all potential recruits were received by Bernard and encouraged to practise, for the benefit of the community, the skills they had acquired in the world. A list of joiners and blacksmiths, sculptors and goldsmiths, painters and masons, vine-dressers and husbandmen and skilled artificers of many kinds follows. The outcome was that a new monastery was quickly established in a place where robbery and murder had been common. The account concludes by mentioning the support that Bernard received from important lay figures such as Count Theobald of Blois and his mother, William the Conqueror's daughter Adela, and from Count Rotrou of the Perche and his mother, Countess Beatrix.

To summarise, Orderic presents a picture of a principled and compelling monastic leader who experienced some institutional difficulties at his first house and moved on to found a new and popular community elsewhere. The association between Tiron and the cathedral at Chartres is an important element of Orderic's story; it is effectively the driver for the settlement at Tiron, because it was in response to the bishop's welcome and invitation that Bernard gave up his wandering and built his new house. Orderic's viewfinder is essentially an ecclesiastical one; the action is carefully set in the diocese of Chartres and Bishop Ivo has an important role in his narrative.⁵ The involvement of the bishop may seem slightly surprising at first sight. Ivo was a well-respected canon lawyer, who had risen to prominence as the leader of a community of reformed Augustinian canons, but he is known to have had reservations about some of the ascetic excesses of the new approaches to monasticism. He counselled against them in his famous letter to Rainaud the hermit and encouraged the monks of Coulombs away from them in another letter.⁶

---

⁴ *HE*, IV, pp. 328–30.

⁵ R. Sprandel, *Ivo von Chartres und seine Stellung in der Kirchengeschichte*, Pariser historische Studien 1 (Stuttgart, 1962); Christof Rolker, *Canon Law and the Letters of Ivo of Chartres* (Cambridge, 2010).

⁶ Ivo of Chartres, 'Epistolae', no. 256, ed. J. P. Migne, PL 162 (Paris, 1844–64), pp. 260–2; D. G. Morin, 'Rainaud l'ermite et Ives de Chartres: Une épisode de la crise du cénobitisme au XIᵉ–XIIᵉ siècle', *Revue bénédictine* 40 (1928) 99–115.

Orderic's focus in his profile of the Tironensians is, however, practical rather than intensely spiritual. He describes the settlement on a woodland site and Bernard's response to the pressure of what might have been overwhelming numbers. He tells us that Bernard received all these recruits, whatever their background, and encouraged them to practise their craft for the benefit of the community. There is a sense in Orderic's narrative that the abundant manpower that became available to Bernard was put to good use in speedily erecting a new monastic settlement in a troubled and underdeveloped area, and colourful detail is given:

> So in the place where, shortly before, robbers had normally lain hidden in the grim wood, waiting to fall on unwary travellers and murder them, a noble monastery rose by God's aid in a short space of time.[7]

Orderic's sketch, therefore, can and has been used to contribute to the paradigm of the new orders at work, opening up the landscape, clearing the forest and generally furthering social progress. David Knowles, for example, indicates that Bernard's monks 'practised all the arts and crafts', and others have been even more emphatic: 'A key feature of the Tironensian order was that the monks themselves should be skilled craftsmen, such as carvers, joiners, smiths and painters.'[8]

Where, then, did Orderic get his information and how does it compare to other accounts of Abbot Bernard's foundation? Two potential sources spring to mind: either Orderic received his information directly from the new community at Tiron (which is only some 65 kilometres from Tiron) or he got it from Chartres, which his account indicates had a particularly close relationship with Bernard of Tiron and his monks. Although Orderic was living at Saint-Évroul during the years when Tiron was being founded, his 'Treatise on the New Orders' remains, overall, broadly sympathetic to traditional Benedictine practice, and suggests that he may have had little direct personal contact with the monks at Tiron. It is significant, too, that his account is at odds in one important respect with traditions preserved at Tiron itself. The *Vita Bernardi Tironensis*, produced, judging by all the clues carefully embedded within it, in the monastic scriptorium at Tiron between 1137 and 1143, together with other independent sources, reports that Bernard was abbot of Saint-Cyprien, but Orderic is the only source to describe him as abbot of Quinçay. Both were well-established

---

[7] *HE*, IV, pp. 330: 'Sic ergo ubi paulo ante in horribili saltu latrunculi solebant latitare et incautos uiatores repentino incursu trucidare adiuuante Deo in breui consurrexit monasterium nobile.'

[8] David Knowles, *The Monastic Order in England: A History of its Developmment from the Times of St Dunstan to the Fourth Lateran Council, 940–1216*, 2nd edn (Cambridge, 1966), p. 201; John B. Hilling, *Cilgarran Castle, St Dogmaels Abbey, Pentre Ifan Burial Chamber, Carreg Coetan Burial Chamber* (Cardiff, 1992), p. 31.

monastic foundations. Quinçay, which dated from the seventh century, was situated a short distance south of Poitiers in the modern commune of Saint-Benoît-de-Quinçay, while Saint-Cyprien lies just outside the walls of Poitiers on the banks of the River Clain.[9] Orderic has clearly been told that Bernard's first house was located outside Poitiers, but he has not been told its name, or exactly how far outside Poitiers it lay.

This information is interesting because it is almost correct, but not quite, which suggests a misunderstanding or misremembering. When this is coupled with the key role that Orderic assigns to Bishop Ivo of Chartres, it can be inferred that Orderic derived his information from ecclesiastical circles at Chartres in the 1130s. This is not a surprising conclusion, for there is evidence of links between Saint-Évroul and Chartres which stretched back into the eleventh century. Abbot Robert of Saint-Évroul, for example, had asked Arnulf, the precentor of Chartres and a pupil of Bishop Fulbert, to compose a new office and sent monks there to learn it.[10] There were also historic links between Saint-Évroul's home diocese of Lisieux and the cathedral at Chartres, and spiritual associations are expressed in obituaries.[11] Perhaps Orderic's informant was Pain Bolotin, whose poem *De falsis heremitis* he mentions shortly before he embarks on his description of the new monastic approaches.[12] Bolotin was a career churchman of the old school; he was the son of a local landed family, a canon of the cathedral at Chartres, and no admirer of the new orders. His poem is a masterpiece of invective, full of pious antipathy and what would today be described as class bias:

> Every peasant demands to be considered a monk
> By wearing a white robe that can save him.[13]

---

[9] J. J. van Moolenbroek, *Vitalis van Savigny (+1122): Bronnen en vroege cultus mit editie van diplomatische teksten* (Amsterdam, 1982), translated as *Vital l'ermite: Prédicateur itinerant, fondateur de l'abbaye normande de Savigny*, trans. Anne-Marie Nambot (Assen and Maastricht, 1990), pp. 38–48.

[10] *HE*, II, p. 108.

[11] *Cartulaire de Notre-Dame de Chartres*, ed. E. de Lépinois and L. Merlet (Chartres, 1865), vol. I, no. 51; J. Laporte, 'Tableau des services obituaires assurés par les abbayes de Saint-Évroult et de Jumièges', *Revue mabillon* 46 (1956), pp. 141–55; J. Laporte, 'Les Associations spirituelles entre monastères: L'Exemple de trois abbayes bénédictines normandes', *Cahiers Léopold Delisle* 12:3 (1963), pp. 29–38. I am grateful to Véronique Gazeau for discussing these connections with me.

[12] *HE*, IV, p. 312; for the text of Pain Bolotin's poem, see Jean Leclercq, 'Le Poème de Payen Bolotin contre les faux ermites', *Revue bénédictine* 68 (1958), pp. 52–86.

[13] Ibid., lines 113–14: 'Rusticus omnis, quo sua possit salua tueri,/ Ueste sub alba religiosus querit haberi.'

In passing on what they knew about the early years at Tiron, Bolotin and men like him must have emphasised the bishop's role in the new foundation, stressing that the monks of Tiron would have been nowhere without the support and encouragement of the bishop, not to mention the land conceded to them by the chapter. Of course Abbot Bernard also received land from the laity, and the fair-minded Orderic includes in his account, as we have seen, lay patrons, such as Count Theobald and Count Rotrou. In general, however, the laity is something of an after-thought; the emphasis of Orderic's account is that these events took place in the diocese of Chartres and that the bishop had a significant part to play. In contrast, the *Vita Bernardi Tironensis*, composed at Tiron, clearly takes place in the Perche and contains a myriad of local place names. So we might therefore characterise Orderic's treatment of the foundation of Tiron as the Chartres tradition.

If Orderic had had a chance to compare notes with William of Malmesbury, as William's modern editor suggests he may have done, they would have agreed on many points.[14] William had written about Bernard in the 1120s, and says that he was:

> a famous devotee of poverty; leaving a monastery that had great possessions, he retired with a few companions into a deserted place in the woods and there, when many came flocking to him, for his light could not be hid under a bushel, he erected a monastery more famous for the piety and number of its monks than for the quantity and brilliance of its riches.[15]

Here we have the departure from the original house, the settlement in the woods, the crowds of recruits and the building of a new monastery. There is, however, no reference to Bernard's heroics at the papal court and no starring role for Bishop Ivo. William's account, moreover, homes in on a factor which is surprisingly missing from Orderic's: Bernard was a 'lover of poverty' ('paupertatis amator'). So important is this observation that William begins his remarks with the phrase and points out that Abbot Bernard took his departure from a very rich house.

In contrast to William of Malmesbury, Orderic omitted this key component of Bernard's spiritual insight. He concentrated, instead, on the practicalities of dealing with large numbers at Tiron, and he gives very little idea about why those recruits should have been interested in Abbot

---

[14] William of Malmesbury, *Gesta regum Anglorum: The History of the English Kings*, ed. and trans. R. A. B. Mynors, completed by R. M. Thomson and M. Winterbottom, Oxford Medieval Texts (Oxford, 1998–9), II, p. 255.

[15] Ibid., I, pp. 786–8 cp. 443: 'famosus paupertatis amator, in saltuosum et desertum locum, relicto amplissimarum diuitiarum cenobio, cum paucis concessit, ibique, quia lucerna sub modio latere non potuit, undatim multis confluentibus monasterium fecit, magis insigne religion monachorum et numero quam fulgore pecuniarum et cumulo.'

Bernard in the first place. Of course, if his information was coming from the ecclesiastical establishment in Chartres, then this is not surprising, for those embedded in the liturgical round of cathedral life and the financial arrangements that supported it would have had little sympathy with, or understanding of, the attraction of Christ's gospel of selling existing property to secure a future reward.

There are, then, two early witnesses to the Bernard narrative: William of Malmesbury's account dating from the 1120s and Orderic's dating from the 1130s. Although far shorter, William's is perhaps the more rounded picture and he may have taken his information from a now lost mortuary roll commemorating the founder of Tiron.[16] Orderic's, on the other hand, is a witness to the stories that had become associated with Bernard at Chartres twenty years after Bernard's death. William makes no reference to Bernard's appeal to Rome; his treatment mentions only Bernard's departure from his first house and, if anything, implies that it was the wealth of that house that caused him to leave. There is no indication of conflict precipitating the departure. Orderic's account, on the other hand, describes tensions with the Cluniacs as having caused Bernard's departure. This sets the scene in Orderic's version of events for Bernard to make a high-profile, if unsuccessful, appeal in Rome before the pope, in which his parting riposte seems to have been to accuse the pope of partiality.[17]

From this contrasting treatment we can infer that stories of Bernard's appeal at Rome and his upbraiding the pope for failure to do justice were circulating at Chartres in ecclesiastical circles in the 1130s, but were not widely available elsewhere. We might therefore conclude that the source of these stories was Abbot Bernard. There is, however, a self-promoting quality about this description of Bernard's role in the Roman episode that sits uneasily with Bernard's situation. Bernard had lost his appeal to Rome; he had left Saint-Cyprien and had been forced for some years to resort to a wandering lifestyle, when, according to Orderic's account, he appeared in the diocese of Chartres, and introduced himself to Bishop Ivo. In those circumstances Bernard is unlikely to have regaled audiences at Chartres, where he presumably hoped to settle, with stories of his past failures. An alternative source for the stories, however, can be glimpsed

---

[16] This was first suggested as an underlying source for the *Vita Bernardi* by J. von Walter, *Die ersten Wanderprediger Frankreichs: Studien zur Geschichte des Mönachtums* (Leipzig, 1903/6). There is a French translation of the section on Bernard of Tiron, overseen by von Walter by J. Cahour, 'Bernard de Thiron', *Bulletin de la Commission Historique et Archéologique de la Mayenne* 2nd series 24 (1908), 385–410, at p. 404.

[17] *HE*, IV, p. 328: 'ipsumque quia plenarium sibi rectum non fecerat ad diuinum examen prouocauit'. Bernard appears here to be hinting that the pope had found against him and in favour of the Cluniacs because Paschal had himself been a Cluniac monk.

elsewhere in the pages of Orderic's *Historia ecclesiastica*, where Orderic describes in some detail the visit of Pope Paschal II to Chartres in 1107.[18] In that year the pope made a long tour through France to secure support in his struggles with the emperor. Bishop Ivo and the countess Adela of Blois invited him to celebrate Easter at Chartres, and he was later to have the first of several helpful meetings with the French king, Philip I.

At that Easter gathering in Chartres the pope might well have come face to face with Abbot Bernard, whose appeal the pope had dismissed in Rome some years before. This situation of potential papal embarrassment is not narrated by Orderic, of course, and we would not have known about it but for the chance survival of a damaged piece of parchment in the Tiron archive at Chartres. It describes a grant to Abbot Bernard and his monks made in the presence of the pope, Bishop Ivo and the countess Adela.[19] This act never found its way into the Tiron cartulary, probably because it was in such poor condition, but enough of the text has survived for the nineteenth-century editor of the Tiron cartulary to include it in his printed edition.

How, then, might Pope Paschal have dealt with this situation? A very effective approach would have been to shower Bernard with praise, suggesting how well Bernard had performed in a hearing at the papal court in Rome some years before, when he had presented his case against Cluniac interference in the election of the abbot of Saint-Cyprien. Pope Paschal could have indicated to everyone that he, the pope, had recognised Bernard's sterling characteristics that had been manifested during the hearing. He could praise Bernard's rhetorical skills, which would have been familiar to a Chartrain audience to whom Bernard had probably been preaching. He could also stress how in the early days of his pontificate he, Pope Paschal, had noticed Bernard's potential and thought that he might have been useful in the curia. Finally, Pope Paschal could commend Bernard for his single-minded pursuit of his vocation in the wilderness. The result would have been satisfaction for everyone. Papal embarrassment was avoided and Abbot Bernard's reputation enhanced by the pope's praise, while the nobility and ecclesiastical authorities of Chartres would have enjoyed papal endorsement of the holy man who was proposing to settle in their midst. It was a good story that the pope told, and one that was remembered for many years in Chartres. At some point during the course of his visit, the pope came up with a scriptural allusion, reminding his audience of Proverbs 28:1, 'the righteous man is bold as a lion', and likening Bernard the litigant to that lion. Orderic recorded that quotation some thirty years later, and may even have acquired it from someone who had

---

[18] *HE*, VI, p. 42.

[19] ADEL H 1538, *Cartulaire de l'abbaye de la Sainte-Trinité de Tiron*, ed. L. Merlet (Chartres 1883), I, pp. 14–16 (III and IV).

heard it from the pope's own lips. Here we are again put in mind of Pain Bolotin.

The study of Orderic and the Tironensians, then, puts a new perspective on Orderic's sources. It is well known that the central position of Saint-Évroul on the southern Norman marches meant that Orderic was well placed to secure information from those who were passing, and Marjorie Chibnall comments on his access to 'political gossip at the highest possible level'.[20] In describing the sources for the 'Treatise on the New Orders', however, she concentrates on the written sources. Her appreciation is that of one historian for another: 'he was in his element; he could write with penetration and understanding of the historical changes behind the new movements [...] There was some research behind his treatise.'[21] She contrasts Orderic the historian, 'explaining and interpreting the growth of monasticism from its origins in the deserts of Egypt', with Pain Bolotin, the satirist and pamphleteer, whom Orderic directly cites in the 'Treatise on the New Orders'. Although Chibnall mentions Orderic's reliance on oral sources and his own memory in her commentary on the sources for Books VII and VIII, she does not consider the possibility of personal contact between these two men.[22] Yet what is known of Bolotin's life history suggests that they could easily have met regularly and thus that Bolotin could have shared more than his written texts with the historian at Saint-Évroul. In the 1130s, when work on Book VIII of the *Historia ecclesiastica* was underway, little had been written about Bernard, yet Orderic was able to provide a different perspective from that of William of Malmesbury and an oral source therefore seems likely. The links between Saint-Évroul and Chartres are well known and such networks would have given Orderic access to ecclesiastical gossip at the highest level on this particular subject, and to witnesses who remembered the arrival of Abbot Bernard in Chartres and the foundation of Tiron.

Orderic's narrative thus makes us aware that stories about Abbot Bernard were circulating at Chartres in the generation after Bernard's death, and this observation is important for the perspective that it provides on the composition of the highly developed and artful piece of writing that is the *Vita beati Bernardi Tironensis*. The *Vita* is about Bernard, but it is also about his foundation. It stresses Bernard's devotion to the wilderness and his desire to found his community there, and it is firmly rooted in the locality where the foundation was made. For example, it includes information about the local elite, who supported and protected the community, as well as sketches of named individuals such as Pagan of Le Theil and Robert of La Motte, and, above all, an account of the role of Count Rotrou, alongside some recollections of his life. As such it is a clear

---

[20] *HE*, II, p. xxx.
[21] Chibnall, *World*, p. 194.
[22] *HE*, IV, p. xxiii.

example of the way that a narrative has been manipulated and enhanced in the interests of a monastic community.[23]

In writing a life of their founding father for these purposes the monks of Tiron were faced with something of a problem in accounting for Bernard's withdrawal from his first abbey at Poitiers. They might revere him as the saintly founding father with an innovative approach to monasticism, but he was open to the same criticisms as Robert of Molesme, who had abandoned his charge first as abbot of Tonnerre and then as abbot of Molesme, and had had to be ordered back from Cîteaux by Pope Urban.[24] Indeed, the fact that Bernard had not been ordered back by Pope Paschal was in itself a problem, for it might well imply that he had been irregularly elected in the first place. To address these problems, the author of the *Vita Bernardi* seizes upon Abbot Bernard's appeal to Rome.

The pivotal part of the *Vita* is that between Bernard's departure from Poitiers, the scene of his monastic formation, and his arrival in the Perche, ready for the foundation of the abbey of Tiron. At its end Bernard has reached the scene of his greatest triumph, and during the course of this key section the appeal in Rome, although unsuccessful, is presented as a triumph of its own kind. The *Vita Bernardi* describes the appeal in great detail and a highly developed piece of rhetoric is placed in Bernard's mouth, outlining his case against the arch-abbot of Cluny and all his works. Bernard's denunciation of papal partisanship rings through the central portion of the *Vita Bernardi*, and by the time it was written Pope Paschal was long dead, so the story that he had told at Easter 1107 in Chartres could be further adapted for the glorification of the founder of Tiron.

In the *Vita* the monks of Tiron use all the material at their disposal to eulogise their founder, emphasising his personal asceticism and his commitment to poverty (and doing so at great length), while defining the self-image of the community. They drew on stories associated with Bernard that had been preserved in ecclesiastical circles and they made great use of the memories of the appeal to Rome – or at least of the veneer that Pope Paschal had placed on it. Orderic's account is helpful in Tironensian studies because it preserves an earlier (and less partisan) version of that crucial episode in the *Vita* and it enables us to see how the monks of Tiron used that episode to their advantage. Orderic's capture of the Bernard narrative well before it became the Bernard of Tiron narrative therefore enables us to understand how the oral legacy of Chartres became part of the literary tradition of Tiron.[25]

---

[23] For a study on these themes, see Amy Remensnyder, *Remembering Kings Past: Monastic Foundation Legends in Medieval Southern France* (Ithaca, NY 1995).

[24] *HE*, IV, pp. 312–22.

[25] These ideas are developed in Thompson, *Monks of Tiron*, pp. 8–33.

'One single letter remained in excess of all his sins ...': Orderic Vitalis and Cultural Memory

Benjamin Pohl

DURING the last two decades, the study of 'cultural memory' has become something of a trend in the arts and humanities – a development (or 'turn') which, however, has not always met with sufficient terminological and methodological transparency.[1] More recent research conducted in the field which has come to be known as Cultural Memory Studies has addressed these insufficiencies, seeking to establish a wider interdisciplinary framework and methodological repertoire for studying the past and its preservation in different socio-cultural contexts, while encouraging academic dialogue.[2] Rather than promoting one particular approach, Cultural Memory Studies today offer a platform for scholars to exchange their interests in cultures of memory by drawing on a common vocabulary.[3] Medieval Studies, too, have made their contribution to this development, with scholars exploring the relationships between different forms of memory in the Middle

---

[1] For a critical perspective, see A. Confino, 'Collective Memory and Cultural History: Problems of Method', *The American Historical Review* 102 (1997), 1386–1403; N. Gedi and N. Elam, 'Collective Memory – What Is It?', *History and Memory* 8 (1996), pp. 30–50; H. Grabes, 'Constructing a Usable Literary Past: Literary History and Cultural Memory', in *Literature, Literary History, and Cultural Memory*, ed. H. Grabes, REAL 21 (Tübingen, 2005), pp. 129–43.

[2] *Cultural Memory Studies: An International and Interdisciplinary Handbook*, ed. A. Erll, A. Nünning and S. B. Young, Media and Cultural Memory 8 (Berlin, 2008); *Gedächtniskonzepte der Literaturwissenschaft: Theoretische Grundlegung und Anwendungsperspektiven*, ed. A. Erll and A. Nünning, Media and Cultural Memory 2 (Berlin, 2005).

[3] A. Erll, 'Cultural Memory Studies: An Introduction', in *Cultural Memory Studies: An International and Interdisciplinary Handbook*, ed. A. Erll, A. Nünning and S. B. Young, Media and Cultural Memory 8 (Berlin, 2008), pp. 1–15. As Erll points out, 'it is not the infinite multitude of possible *topics* which characterises cultural memory studies, but instead its *concepts*: the specific ways of conceiving of themes and of approaching objects' (p. 2). For a recent review of the scholarly *status quo*, see M. Tamm, 'Beyond History and Memory: New Perspectives in Memory Studies', *History Compass* 11 (2013), pp. 458–73, at pp. 461–2.

Ages,[4] as well as the discourses on memory established by writers and thinkers of the period.[5] On a broader scale, however, medieval historians have often been wary of applying this framework, and in particular the terminologies offered by Cultural Memory Studies. Their reservation is perhaps partially due to the fact that the terms and concepts used with great confidence by scholars of modernity when reflecting on the tradition of the past are sometimes felt to be misrepresentative of medieval thought (and thus potentially misleading). This is a perfectly legitimate concern, especially when talking about terms such as 'media' or 'mediality', which, at

---

[4] Important work has been done, for example, on the cognitive processes which allowed medieval individuals to memorise the past, such as: M. J. Carruthers, *The Book of Memory: A Study of Memory in Medieval Culture*, Cambridge Studies in Medieval Literature 10 (Cambridge, 2001); M. J. Carruthers, *The Medieval Craft of Memory: An Anthology of Texts and Pictures*, Material Texts (Philadelphia, 2002); and F. A. Yates, *The Art of Memory* (Chicago, 2002). Both Carruthers and Yates are concerned primarily with memory as an art form (*ars*), rather than as a dynamic cultural phenomenon or force (*vis*), which is the focus of the present study. On this important distinction between memory as *ars* and *vis*, see particularly A. Assmann, *Erinnerungsräume: Formen und Wandlungen des kulturellen Gedächtnisses*, 3rd edn (Munich, 2006), p. 28. Other influential studies on memory in the Middle Ages include, for example, M. T. Clanchy, *From Memory to Written Record: England, 1066–1307*, 3rd edn (Oxford, 2012); J. Coleman, *Ancient and Medieval Memories: Studies in the Reconstruction of the Past* (Cambridge, 1992); R. McKitterick, *History and Memory in the Carolingian World* (Cambridge, 2004).

[5] Particularly notable contributions, in this context, include P. J. Geary, *Phantoms of Remembrance: Memory and Oblivion at the End of the First Millennium* (Princeton, 1994); and Elisabeth van Houts, *Memory and Gender in Medieval Europe, 900–1200* (Toronto, 1999). Geary's seminal work was among the first to try to overcome the traditional dichotomies between, on the one hand, individual and collective memory and, on the other, collective memory and history (a distinction famously drawn by Maurice Halbwachs). He also argued for a closer functional relationship between oral and written forms of remembering, thus focusing on the different communicative systems in which memory was retained, received and transformed around the turn of the first millennium. A similar approach was also chosen by van Houts, whose study places great emphasis on the importance of orality, taking into account the predominantly oral culture of the Middle Ages. With a particular focus on family and kinship, as well as on the importance of women as agents of memory, she investigates memory in the shape of material objects, such as heirlooms, tapestries, jewellery, vessels, relics, etc. Along with Geary's book, hers was one of the first studies to focus on the period c. 900–1200 systematically, whereas previous treatises had left a gap between the Carolingian period and the later Middle Ages. Both these studies have greatly informed the approach chosen in the present chapter.

first glance, might seem to represent concepts alien to the Middle Ages.[6] It is one of the aims of the present study to help overcome such barriers and argue for the more confident participation of Medieval Studies within the field of Cultural Memory Studies.

In this discussion, I will investigate how Orderic Vitalis, while writing his *Historia ecclesiastica*, conceived of his own role as a historian in terms of being someone actively engaged in, as well as responsible for, the preservation of the past for future generations. Of course, such a focus on Orderic's historical consciousness (*Geschichtsbewusstsein*) is by no means a novelty, as scholars have published extensively on this topic.[7] What I would like offer here, therefore, is a new close reading and textual analysis of the *Historia* which will argue that one of Orderic's most pressing concerns as a historian was to ensure the long-term preservation of memory for posterity – a task which saw him make an active contribution to the cultural memory canon at Saint-Évroul and beyond. In addition, I will show that this task enjoyed a considerable reputation in the monastic environment at Saint-Évroul, even constituting part of the divine service practised by the monks as part of their daily routine. In doing so, my aim is also to locate Orderic's own historical and scribal outlook not so much in the context of specific socio-political groups, collectives or institutions, but within the wider tradition of medieval historical and religious thought, thereby providing a new window into the unique memory culture which characterised the Anglo-Norman world of the eleventh and twelfth centuries. As mentioned above, the main basis for my analysis will be what Orderic tells us in the pages of his *Historia*. I hope that focusing, first and foremost, on the individual writer and his voice will help to develop our understanding of medieval memory as a socio-cultural phenomenon which, despite its wider socio-cultural application, fundamentally depended on the agency of individuals who were willing, and able, to devote their own labour to literary production.

For the purposes of the present study, cultural memory can be defined as a form of socio-cultural discourse dependent on the more durable

---

[6] This view has since been relativised, for example, by H. Haferland, *Mündlichkeit, Gedächtnis und Medialität: Heldendichtung im deutschen Mittelalter* (Göttingen, 2004).

[7] Chibnall, *World*; Hingst, *Written World*; Shopkow, *History and Community*; J. Blacker, *The Faces of Time: Portrayal of the Past in Old French and Latin Historical Narrative of the Anglo-Norman Regnum* (Austin, TX, 1994). In a wider context, see also H.-W. Goetz, 'Die Gegenwart der Vergangenheit im früh- und hochmittelalterlichen Geschichtsbewusstsein', *Historische Zeitschrift* 255 (1992), 61–97; H.-W. Goetz, 'Historical Consciousness and Institutional Concern in European Medieval Historiography (11th and 12th Centuries)', in *Making Sense of Global History: The 19th International Congress of the Historical Sciences, Oslo, 2000*, ed. S. Sogner (Oslo, 2001), pp. 349–65.

material or – in the wider sense of the term – textual media by means of which individuals and communities constitute and negotiate their notions of the past, and through which they express a collective sense of belonging within both time and space.[8] More generally, this means embracing the working definition proposed by Astrid Erll, who defines cultural memory as 'the interplay of present and past in socio-cultural contexts'.[9] More specifically, cultural memory, in a narrower sense, can be distinguished from oral tradition and everyday communication, the two primary constituents of what is usually referred to as 'communicative' or 'social memory'.[10] Unlike communicative memory, cultural memory is distinguishable by its teleological focus on the *longue durée*, as well as by its ability to link multiple generations within a continuous chain of historical tradition preserved in writing (or other material forms).[11] Cultural memory, therefore, relies fundamentally on the awareness that the past,

---

[8] I base this definition primarily on the seminal works of Jan and Aleida Assmann. See particularly J. Assmann, *Das kulturelle Gedächtnis: Schrift, Erinnerung und politische Identität in frühen Hochkulturen* (München, 1999); A. Assmann, 'Funktionsgedächtnis und Speichergedächtnis: Zwei Modi der Erinnerung', in *Generation und Gedächtnis: Erinnerungen und kollektive Identitäten*, ed. K. Platt and M. Dabag (Opladen, 1995), pp. 169–85. The usefulness of the Assmanns's work for studies of medieval Europe has been demonstrated by *Memoria als Kultur*, ed. O. G. Oexle, Veröffentlichungen des Max-Planck Instituts 121 (Göttingen, 1995); and M. Borgolte, '"Memoria": Bilan intermédiaire d'un projet de recherche sur le Moyen Âge', in *Les Tendances actuelles de l'histoire du Moyen Âge en France et en Allemagne: Actes des colloques de Sèvres (1997) et Göttingen (1998)*, ed. J.-C. Schmitt and O. G. Oexle, Publications de la Sorbonne: Série Histoire ancienne et médiévale 66 (Paris, 2002). Also see J.-C. Schmitt, 'Das Gedächtnis im Mittelalter', in *Kulturelles Gedächtnis und interkulturelle Rezeption im europäischen Kontext*, ed. E. Dewes and S. Duhem, Vice Versa 1 (Berlin, 2008), pp. 33–45.

[9] Erll, 'Cultural Memory Studies', p. 2.

[10] J. Assmann, 'Communicative and Cultural Memory', in *Cultural Memory Studies: An International and Interdisciplinary Handbook*, ed. A. Erll, A. Nünning and S. B. Young, Media and Cultural Memory 8 (Berlin, 2008), pp. 109–18; A. Assmann, 'Memory, Individual and Collective', in *The Oxford Handbook of Contextual Political Analysis*, ed. R. E. Goodin and C. Tilly (Oxford, 2006), pp. 210–24, at p. 213.

[11] A. Assmann, 'Four Formats of Memory: From Individual to Collective Constructions of the Past', in *Cultural Memory and Historical Consciousness in the German-Speaking World since 1500: Papers from the Conference 'The Fragile Tradition'*, Cambridge 2002, ed. C. Emden and D. R. Midgley, Cultural History and Literary Imagination 1 (Oxford, 2004), pp. 19–38; A. Assmann, 'Canon and Archive', in *Cultural Memory Studies: An International and Interdisciplinary Handbook*, ed. A. Erll, A. Nünning and S. B. Young, Media and Cultural Memory 8 (Berlin, 2008), pp. 97–108.

unless codified in more durable media (such as, for example, books), will eventually perish from the memory of present and future generations.

Such awareness can be encountered, for example, in the writings of Isidore of Seville, who in his *Etymologiae* states that 'the use of letters was invented for the memory of things. For lest they fly into oblivion, they are bound by letters. Indeed, in so great a variety of affairs, everything could not be learned by hearing nor held in memory'.[12] For Isidore, then, writing was more than just a simple means of communication: it was a means of enshrining knowledge about the present, which before long would become the past, thus ensuring that the things and events worthy of memory (*memoria*) would remain accessible to those who did not experience them first-hand. Writing, in other words, made memory durable. Orderic was certainly no stranger to the works of Isidore, and he is known to have read the *Etymologiae* and used it, for example, to clarify the etymology of personal names that he included in the *Historia*.[13] Part of this study will be dedicated to exploring how Orderic defined memory and its relationship with the written word, and how his definition compares to (and differs from) that of Isidore. To be clear, I will not be concerned with medieval discourses on *memoria* as a mental faculty and cognitive or rhetorical exercise (such as the *ars memoranda*), which were, of course, popular topics among medieval authors including, for example, Hugh of Saint-Victor and Bartholomeus Anglicus.[14] Neither will I be preoccupied with theological treatises on *memoria* as constituting the gathering of fundamental knowledge about man himself and, ultimately, about God (as was explored in great depth by Augustine and, later on, Thomas Aquinas),[15] or with *memoria* as a spiritual and ritual means of commemorating the dead – again a crucial part of medieval life, especially in a monastic context. Instead, I would like to focus specifically on contexts in which *memoria* was defined by Orderic, and by his contemporaries, as intrinsically linked to literary production and, especially, to the prevailing power of books.

In Book III of the *Historia*, Orderic relates a selection of anecdotes from the life of Thierry de Mathonville, the venerated first abbot of Saint-Évroul during the refoundation and revival of the abbey in the mid-eleventh century.[16] Before coming to Saint-Évroul, Thierry had spent

---

[12] Isidore, *Etymologiae*, I.iii.2: 'Usus litterarum repertus propter memoriam rerum. Nam ne oblivione fugiant, litteris alligantur. In tanta enim rerum varietate nec disci audiendo poterant omnia, nec memoria contineri'; also cf. McKitterick, *History and Memory*, p. 162; Carruthers, *Book of Memory*, pp. 139–40.

[13] *HE*, I, p. 169: 'Simon etenim oboediens, Petrus vero agnoscens, Cephas autem caput interpretatur.' Also cf. Chibnall, *World*, pp. 169–74.

[14] Carruthers, *Book of Memory*, pp. 9–11.

[15] Geary, *Phantoms of Remembrance*, pp. 16–19.

[16] On Thierry, see V. Gazeau, *Normannia monastica (X^e–XIIe siècle)*, 2 vols. (Caen, 2007), II, pp. 273–5.

most of his life as a monk at Jumièges. Like Orderic, he had first been received by his community as a child oblate.[17] His name was bestowed upon him by his godfather, Abbot Thierry (or Theodoricus) of Jumièges and Mont-Saint-Michel, who in turn had been a pupil of William of Volpiano, one of the leading figures in Normandy's monastic reform.[18] According to Orderic, Thierry during the period of his abbacy (1050–7) delegated most of the administrative duties attached to his office to other members of the monastic community, so that he himself could focus more or less exclusively on the fulfilment of the divine service.[19] What precisely this divine service (*cultus divinus*) entailed is also specified by Orderic. For example, intimate contemplation ('intima contemplatio') or prayer ('oratio') gave Thierry a chance to escape the company of his brethren and spend time by himself.[20] At the same time, however, Orderic notes that Thierry also frequently took part in manual labour ('opus manuum'), namely through the production and care of books for Saint-Évroul's library and scriptorium. During the eight years of his abbacy Thierry played a proactive role in bringing the monastery's book collection up to scratch, securing 'all the books of the Old and New Testament as well as the complete works of the eloquent Pope Gregory [the Great] for the library of Saint-Évroul' ('omnes libros Veteris et Novi Testamenti, omnesque libros facundissimi papae Gregorii Uticensium bibliothecae').[21] In addition to overseeing a team of scribes and copyists personally – some of whom had come from Jumièges to Saint-Évroul in his company, including a certain Hugh, Roger and his own nephew, named Ralph – Thierry also frequently put his own pen to parchment. He is credited by Orderic as a distinguished scribe ('scriptor egregius'), to whose pen the library of Saint-Évroul owed a number of liturgical manuscripts, including a book of Collects, a Gradual and an Antiphonary, all of which Thierry himself copied ('propria manu in ipso coenobio conscripsit').[22] Last but not least, he even appears to have been involved in the training and education of

---

[17] Chibnall, 'General Introduction', pp. 16–17. Also cf. Delisle, 'Notice', pp. iii–iv.

[18] On William and his role within Normandy's monastic and ecclesiastical revival, see C. Potts, *Monastic Revival and Regional Identity in Early Normandy* (Woodbridge, 1997), pp. 28–31. Also cf. the special dossier 'Guillaume de Volpiano: Fécamp et l'histoire normande (Actes du colloque tenu à Fécamp les 15 et 16 juin 2001)' = *Tabularia, Études*, 2 (2002), available through <www.unicaen.fr/tabularia> [accessed 2 July 2014].

[19] *HE*, II, p. 48.

[20] Ibid.: 'Exteriores enim curas in quantum poterat, pro dulcedine intimae contemplationis devitabat; seseque divino cultui ferventi sedulitate mancipabat. Assiduus nempe in orationibus erat et in opere manuum quod sibi competebat.'

[21] Ibid., p. 50.

[22] Ibid., p. 48.

novice scribes, some of whom achieved great fame later in their careers.[23] According to the *Historia*, therefore, the production of manuscripts as encouraged and even practised by Abbot Thierry formed an integral part of the divine service at Saint-Évroul. Nowhere does this become more apparent than in Orderic's account of a moral anecdote which, according to Orderic, Abbot Thierry used to recite in front of his monastic pupils.

The protagonist of this story is an unnamed monk (whether of Saint-Évroul or somewhere else we are not told), who 'had committed almost every possible sin against the monastic rule' ('de multis transgressionibus monasticae institutionis reprehensibilis exstitit').[24] When the same monk dies and is presented before the final judge, demons and evil spirits list every single one of his transgressions, hoping to secure the sinner's soul for eternal Hell. Rushing to his defence, the angels plead for mercy on the basis that the monk was, after all, a scribe ('sed scriptor erat') who, despite his many sins, produced a huge book ('enormus librum') within the walls of his monastery, which is presented as material evidence in his defence. Carefully counting each letter in this book and weighing them one-by-one against the number of sins he committed, the angels and demons fighting for the monk's soul eventually find that 'one single letter remained in excess of all his sins', so he is saved from damnation despite the demons' robust protestations. In Orderic's anecdote (or rather Thierry's anecdote as related by Orderic), it is the written book which serves as the ultimate guarantor of the sinful monk's salvation. The significance of books as presented in the *Historia* lies in their inherent dual function both as physical and material objects, consisting of pages, lines and individual

---

[23] Besides Bishop Berengar of Venosa, Orderic also lists a certain Goscelin, Ralph, Bernard, Thurkill and Richard; cf. ibid., p. 50.

[24] Ibid.: 'Quidam frater in monasterio quodam de multis transgressionibus monasticae institutionis reprehensibilis exstitit; sed scriptor erat, et ad scribendum deditus, quoddam ingens volumen divinae legis sponte conscripsit. Qui postquam defunctus est, anima ejus ante tribunal iusti Iudicis ad examen adducta est. Cumque maligni spiritus eam acriter accusarent, et innumera ejus peccata proferrent, sancti angeli e contra librum, quem idem frater in domo Dei scripserat, ostentabant; et singillatim litteras enormis libri contra singula, peccata computabant. Ad postremum una sola littera numerum peccatorum excessit, contra quam daemonum conatus nullum objicere peccatum praevaluit. Clementia itaque Iudicis fratri pepercit, animamque ad proprium corpus reverti praecepit, spatiumque corrigendi vitam suam benigniter concessit.' On this episode, see Delisle, 'Notice', pp. iii–iv; M. Gullick 'How Fast did Scribes Write? Evidence from Romanesque Manuscripts', in *Making the Medieval Book: Techniques of Production; Proceedings of the Fourth Conference of The Seminar in the History of the Book to 1500, Oxford, July 1992*, ed. L. L. Brownrigg (Los Altos Hills, CA, 1995), pp. 39–58, at p. 41.

letters, and, perhaps even more importantly, as media of cultural memory.[25] This can be seen again later in the narrative when, during the *Historia*'s sixth book, Orderic turns to the life and deeds of his monastery's patron, St Évroul (d. 706).

Having related the political struggles of Chlothar II (c. 584–629) against his Frankish rivals, which Orderic seems to have gathered primarily from Gregory of Tours' *Historia Francorum*, he admits to having 'sought out and taken [these events] from [other] chronicles, briefly noting them for the information of my readers, so that they may know in what times the blessed father Évroul passed the eighty-year span of his glorious life on earth'.[26] While explicitly indebting himself to previous chronicles ('chronica'), Orderic also stresses the importance of his own literary achievement in preserving for posterity the memory of Saint-Évroul and its venerated patron saint. The *Historia*, therefore, claims a place among other established works which, at the time when Orderic was writing, constituted the canon of Saint-Évroul's historiographical and hagiographical tradition. According to Orderic, the *Historia*'s composition relied on both written texts and, in their absence, testimony which he had acquired 'not from written sources, but from the oral traditions of old men' ('quae non scripto, sed seniorum relatione didici').[27] With oral testimony thus playing an important supplementary role in the *Historia*'s composition, the main focus and general preference of Orderic's work as a historian nevertheless remain the consultation of written records. As seen in the example of Abbot Thierry's scribal activity and the cautionary tale attributed to him in the *Historia*'s third book, Orderic regarded the writing of manuscripts as a means of fulfilling one's divine service that was both laudable and, as the story of the sinful monk shows, highly efficient with regard to the salvation of one's eternal soul. With producing records of the past being deemed a praiseworthy field of activity, commendable enough indeed to constitute an element of the *cultus divinus*, then it surely follows that failing to produce such records would have been perceived as constituting an act of shame and even sin?

Sure enough, what we find in the *Historia* is precisely this notion of a dichotomy between, on the one hand, salvation gained by preserving the past in the pages of written books and, on the other, sin caused by shameful neglect of the past and failure to produce durable media of cultural memory. While lamenting the often fragmentary nature of the record and the loss of previous writings, Orderic can be seen as pointing

---

[25] For further discussion on Orderic's use of material objects, see D. Roach, 'The Material and the Visual: Objects and Memories in the *Historia ecclesiastica* of Orderic Vitalis', *HSJ* 24 (2013), 63–78.

[26] *HE*, III, p. 282: 'Haec de chronicis rimatus hausi, lectorique meo satisfacere volens, breviter annotavi, ut satis eluceat quibus leraporibus octogenaria floruerit in mundo vita sancti patris Ebrulfi.'

[27] Ibid.

fingers at those whose carelessness and lack of scribal diligence he believes are to be held responsible for the fact that certain events escaped the memory of subsequent generations. Orderic presents such negligence as resulting in irretrievable loss of knowledge in his account of the period following the Viking attacks of the ninth and tenth centuries, which had caused the destruction of Francia's monastic landscape along with many of its precious book collections:

> For during the terrible disturbances that accompanied the ravages of the Danes the records of former times perished in the flames, along with churches and other buildings; and all the ardent labour and desire of later men has been unavailing to restore them. Some things indeed, which were saved from the hands of the barbarians by the care of our forebears, have since perished (shameful to relate) by the abominable neglect of their descendants, who took no pains to preserve the profound spiritual wisdom recorded in the writings of their fathers. With the loss of books the deeds of men of old pass into oblivion, and can in no wise be recovered by those of our generation, for the admonitions of the ancients pass away from the memory of modern men with the changing world, as hail or snow melt in the waters of a swift river, swept away by the current never to return.[28]

Embedded in Orderic's heartfelt complaint regarding the shortcomings of some of his predecessors is a true wealth of information concerning his perception of the relationship between written records of the past and the long-term preservation of cultural memory. It is worth discussing and contextualising these pieces of information in turn, as each of them has something unique to contribute towards a more nuanced understanding of how Orderic and other writers of the period situated their own task as historians within the wider cultural traditions and discourses of the Anglo-Norman world.

Perhaps the most fundamental piece of information which can be extracted from Orderic's statement concerns his notion of the place of books in general, and historical writings in particular, within the daily

---

[28] Ibid., pp. 282–4: 'In nimiis enim procellis, quae tempore Danorum enormiter furuerunt, antiquorum scripta cum basilicis et aedibus incendio deperierunt; quae fervida iuniorum studia, quamvis insatiabiliter sitiant, recuperare nequeunt. Nonnulla vero quae per diligentiam priscorum manibus barbarorum solerter surrepta sunt, damnabiii subsequentium negligentia proh pudor interierunt, qui sagacem spiritualium profunditatem patrum libris insertam servare neglexerunt. Codicibus autem perditis, antiquorum res gestae oblivioni traditae sunt; quae a modernis qualibet arte recuperari non possunt, quia veterum monumenta cum mundo praetereunte a memoria praesentium deficiunt, quasi grando vel nix in undis cum rapido flumine irremeabiliter fluente defluunt.'

routine of monastic life at Saint-Évroul. Scholars have long been aware of the mutual relationship between historical writing and liturgical observance in medieval monastic contexts. Just how routinely these two areas interacted with each other on a daily basis has been observed particularly in relation to the monastic office of the *cantor* (or *precentor*), even though it should perhaps be noted that this strong focus on medieval cantors (including those acting in a cantor-like capacity without holding the actual office) sometimes risks an oversimplification in the face of comparatively little concrete source evidence. Take, for example, Fassler's much-cited statement that the cantor 'supervised all aspects of music-making, he was in charge of the library and the scriptorium, and he oversaw and directed the celebration of the liturgy'.[29] Whether this was always and necessarily the case throughout the period under consideration here is debatable. Fassler's description of the cantor and his responsibilities is essentially based on the evidence of customaries that paint a normative picture, with various separate tasks being customarily united within a single office and fulfilled by a single person holding that office (*Personalunion*). Customaries, however, are prescriptive (rather than descriptive) sources, and as such they often provide an ideal(ised) vision that does not necessarily reflect the practical challenges and administrative realities of monastic day-to-day life accurately. In reality, therefore, the cantor's tasks as defined in the customaries were often divided and delegated between several members of a given monastic community – a scenario which probably occurred more frequently than is sometimes suggested.[30] There is, in fact, concrete evidence that maintaining the monastic scriptorium and looking after the local book collection were tasks which, during the eleventh and twelfth centuries, involved a variety of personnel. People involved in these tasks seem to have ranked from the simple monk or scribe to the abbot himself, who, of course, had to prioritise carefully between the time spent in the scriptorium and the administrative duties of running a monastic community. Examples include the twelfth-century abbot-historian of Mont-Saint-Michel, Robert of Torigni (1154–86), as well as Suger of Saint-Denis, Guibert of Nogent and, not least, Saint-Évroul's own former abbot, Thierry, whose multiple activities in the scriptorium we saw mentioned by Orderic.[31]

---

[29] M. E. Fassler, 'The Office of the Cantor in Early Western Monastic Rules and Customaries: A Preliminary Investigation', *Early Music History* 5 (1985), pp. 29–51, at p. 29. Fassler's pioneering study remains the standard account on cantors in the Middle Ages. For further discussion on the links between this office and historical writing, see contributions in *Medieval Cantors and their Craft: Music, Liturgy and the Shaping of History, 800–1500*, ed. K. A.-M. Bugyis, A. B. Kraebel and M. E. Fassler (York, forthcoming).

[30] The possibility of such a situation is actually recognised by Fassler, 'Office of the Cantor', p. 39.

[31] See, for example, B. Pohl, '*Abbas qui et scriptor*? The Handwriting of Robert of Torigni and his Scribal Activity as Abbot of Mont-Saint-Michel

In the present volume, Rozier has proposed that Orderic may have fulfilled at least some of the tasks which, theoretically, could fall within the cantor's area of responsibility, even though there is no concrete evidence that Orderic was ever appointed into that office.[32] While there can be little doubt that Orderic was involved, in one way or another, in the production of liturgical (or liturgically relevant) books at Saint-Évroul (including Paris, BnF, MS Lat. 10062, listed in Appendix 2 as item 9), the precise nature and extent of his contributions are still a subject of debate.[33] Nevertheless, seeing part of Orderic's literary and scribal activity at Saint-Évroul in the light of what might best be termed a 'cantor-like capacity' certainly remains a plausible suggestion.[34] Scrutinising Orderic's involvement in liturgical matters in addition to, as well as alongside, his activity as a monastic historian has provided important groundwork for this study, namely by generating knowledge which allows us to contextualise some of the statements made in the *Historia* concerning the role of books in monastic life. Returning to Orderic's story of the sinful monk attributed to Abbot Thierry, the terminology used in order to describe the product of the scribe's labour is rather ambivalent. As we have seen, Orderic talks of a 'huge book' ('enormus librum'), as well as of a 'vast volume of divine law' ('ingens volumen divinae legis').[35] In the past, the use of the term *divina lex* has been taken as evidence that Orderic, in his little anecdote, was concerned with the preservation not of any kind

(1154–1186)', *Traditio* 69 (2014), 45–86. I am currently preparing a more comprehensive and comparative study on abbot-historians in central medieval Europe.

[32] See Rozier's contribution to this volume, 'Orderic Vitalis as Librarian and Cantor of Saint-Évroul'.

[33] Traditionally, one of the more controversially discussed aspects of Orderic's involvement in the production of this manuscript is the extent of his contribution to Saint-Évroul's twelfth-century booklist (fol. 80v). My own palaeographical examination of the manuscript led me to conclude that Orderic wrote only small parts of the booklist, most notably its opening lines. This notion, according to which Orderic was merely one of several scribes subsequently contributing to the book list (but probably the first), is now confirmed by the more extensive work of Charles Rozier and Jenny Weston in the present volume (see also Appendix 2, item 9). For previous discussions, see *HE*, I, p. 201; Delisle, 'Matériaux', p. 493; Delisle, 'Notice', pp. vii–xxvii.

[34] More recently, scholars have taken to referring to Orderic and other twelfth-century monastic writers of history as so-called 'cantor-historians' – a term which I choose not to adopt in this chapter for the reasons outlined above. For discussion, see M. E. Fassler, 'The Liturgical Framework of Time and the Representation of History', in *Representing History, 900–1300: Art, Music, History*, ed. R. A. Maxwell (University Park, PA, 2010), pp. 149–71, at p. 168; and *Medieval Cantors and their Craft*, ed. Bugyis et al.

[35] *HE*, II, p. 50.

of book (let alone history), but of Scripture. In a similar vein, Orderic's complaint about the loss of the profound spiritual wisdom recorded in the writings of the fathers ('sagacem spiritualium profunditatem patrum libris insertam') is commonly translated as '... of the Fathers' (specifically with a capital 'F'), thus identifying these texts with the patristic writings of the early Church.[36] While these are, of course, perfectly valid translations, one does wonder whether it might have been a somewhat broader concept of writing that Orderic had in mind.

Orderic's definition of monastic literary culture was perhaps less constrained by questions of genre than it was informed by the notion of historical writing as part of the *cultus divinus* identified earlier in this chapter. If this was indeed the case, recording the events of the past and acknowledging their significance within the broader concept of salvation history (*Heilsgeschichte*) could in itself have qualified as constituting part of the *divina lex*. Orderic's role model, the Venerable Bede, had famously described the recording of past events in accordance with the divine plan as the one 'true law of history' ('vera lex historiae').[37] It was Bede who, probably more than any other writer, informed Orderic's training as a monastic historian, and it was Bede's *Historia ecclesiastica gentis Anglorum* that provided Orderic with a direct template for the composition of the *Historia*.[38] When re-reading Orderic's statements in the context of this Bedean notion of history, it becomes obvious that it was not merely the wisdom of the Church Fathers that Orderic deemed worth recording,

---

[36] *HE*, III, p. 283.

[37] *Bede's Ecclesiastical History of the English People*, ed. B. Colgrave and R. A. B. Mynors, Oxford Medieval Texts (Oxford, 1998), p. 6.

[38] See A. Gransden, 'Bede's Reputation as an Historian in Medieval England', in *Legends, Tradition and History in Medieval England*, ed. A. Gransden (London, 1992), pp. 1–30; R. H. C. Davis, 'Bede after Bede', in *Studies in Medieval History: Presented to R. Allen Brown*, ed. C. Harper-Bill, C. J. Holdsworth and J. L. Nelson (Woodbridge, 1989), pp. 103–16. Orderic was not, of course, the only twelfth-century historian thus indebted to Bede. In the preface to his *Historia Anglorum*, Henry of Huntingdon also explicitly admits to having 'followed the Venerable Bede's *Ecclesiastical History* wherever I could'; see *Historia Anglorum: The History of the English People*, ed. D. E. Greenway, Oxford Medieval Texts (Oxford, 1996), pp. 5–7: 'Haec ergo considerans, hujus regni gesta et nostra gentis origines jussu tuo, praesul Alexander, qui flos et cacumen regni et gentis esse videris, decurrenda suscepi: tuo quidem consilio Bedae Venerabilis ecclesiasticam, qua potui, secutus Historiam, nonnulla etiam ex aliis excerpens auctoribus, inde chronica in antiquis reservata librariis compilans, usque nostrum ad auditum et visum praeterita repraesentavi.' Also cf. D. E. Greenway, 'Henry of Huntingdon and Bede', in *L'Historiographie médiévale en Europe: Actes du colloque org. par la Fondation Européenne de la Science au Centre de Recherches Historiques et Juridiques de l'Université Paris I du 29 mars au 1er avril 1989*, ed. J.-P. Genet (Paris, 1991), pp. 43–50.

but also that of one's own fathers (and forefathers), handed down across several generations and enshrined in the pages of books. Once these books were lost or destroyed, the deeds of the ancestors were forever committed to oblivion ('Codicibus autem perditis, antiquorum res gestae oblivioni traditae sunt'), irretrievable for the memory of subsequent generations ('quae a modernis qualibet arte recuperari non possunt'). In the prologue of the *Historia*, Orderic writes that:

> since new events take place every day in this world, these should be systematically committed to writing for the glory of God, so that – just as past deeds have been handed down by our forebears – present happenings should be recorded now and passed on by the men of today to future generations.[39]

Once again, it is the terminology employed by Orderic which betrays his concern for what modern scholars have called the 'mediality' of cultural memory.[40] Orderic evidently distinguishes carefully between the deeds of the ancestors ('res gestae antiquorum'), which he situates in the distant past, and their reflection in the memory of present generations ('memoria praesentium'). In fact, he speaks of a restoration or recuperation ('recuperatio') of past monuments ('monumenta') in present contexts.

Chibnall translated the Latin word *monumenta* as 'admonitions'.[41] However, Latin authors of the Middle Ages regularly referred to *monumenta* in the sense of 'reminders', not least, of course, in contexts such as the commemoration of the dead and the creation of *monumenta nominis* in the shape of sepulchres, statues and epitaphs.[42] Consulting the standard dictionaries of Medieval Latin also supports such a translation.[43] However, 'reminders' is not the only possible translation of the word *monumentum* provided in the dictionaries. There are also more

---

[39] *HE*, I, pp. 130–1: 'Decet utique ut, sicut novae res mundo quotidie accidunt, sic ad laudem Dei assidue scripto tradantur; ut et, sicut ab anterioribus praeterita gesta usque ad nos transmissa sunt, sic etiam praesentia nunc a praesentibus futurae posteritati litterarum notamine transmittantur.'

[40] A. Erll, 'Literatur als Medium des kollektiven Gedächtnisses', in *Gedächtniskonzepte der Literaturwissenschaft: Theoretische Grundlegung und Anwendungsperspektiven*, ed. A. Erll and A. Nünning, Media and Cultural Memory 2 (Berlin, 2005), pp. 249–76; A. Erll, 'Literature, Film, and the Mediality of Cultural Memory', in *Cultural Memory Studies: An International and Interdisciplinary Handbook*, ed. A. Erll, A. Nünning and S. B. Young, Media and Cultural Memory 8 (Berlin, 2008), pp. 389–98.

[41] *HE*, III, p. 286.

[42] See the entry 'MONUMENTUM NOMINIS' in *Glossarium ad scriptores mediae et infimae Latinitatis*, ed. C. d. F. Du Cange, 2nd edn, 10 vols. (Niort, 1883–7), V, p. 514.

[43] *A Latin Dictionary*, ed. C. T. Lewis and C. Short (Oxford, 1879), n.p: '[T]hat which preserves the remembrance of any thing'; *An Elementary Latin*

specific renderings, such as that given by Lewis and Short, who refer to *monumenta* as 'written works, monuments, or records' of the past.[44] Such a notion of *monumentum* as referring to 'a tradition, chronicle, [or] story',[45] as well as – in the plural – to 'books of history, [or] chronicles',[46] is by no means a modern invention, even though the most well-known use of this expression is perhaps that adumbrated by the *Monumenta Germaniae Historica*. In fact, the usage of the term *monumentum/monumenta* in this sense can be traced as early as the Roman period. It occurs, for example, as *veterum monumenta virorum* or *monumenta rerum gestarum* in the works of Virgil, Horace and Cicero,[47] all of whom are shown by Chibnall to have exercised an influence on Orderic's writing and, arguably, also on his outlook on history.[48] The Vulgate Bible, too, knows of a similar usage of *monumentum*, as is evident in the Prophecy of Malachi, which tells of a 'book of memories' ('liber monumenti') written by God for the fearful to read.[49]

Consequently, Orderic's use of the term *monumenta* in the sixth book of the *Historia*, where it occurs in close proximity to expressions such as 'res gestae', 'memoria' and, not least, 'codici',[50] might perhaps be better understood, not so much in the sense of admonition, but as emphasising the importance of written texts (or books) for the preservation of the past in the media of cultural memory. At the end of his prologue Orderic expresses his wish that, according to Chibnall's translation, 'present happenings should be recorded and passed on [...] to future generations'.[51] Turning to the original Latin wording, we can see that this statement includes important additional information. According to Orderic, the present happenings ('[res] praesentia') shall be preserved and handed down to posterity specifically 'by use of books (or letters)' ('futurae posteritati litterarum notamine transmittantur'). The subject matter of which Orderic talks, in this context, cannot be confined to either Scripture

---

Dictionary, ed. C. T. Lewis (New York, 1890), n.p.: '[T]hat which brings to mind'.

[44] Lewis and Short, *Dictionary*, n.p.

[45] Lewis, *Dictionary*, n.p.

[46] Lewis and Short, *Dictionary*, n.p.

[47] Cicero, *De Oratore ad Quintum fratrem libri tres*, I, 201: 'Iam illa non longam orationem desiderant, quam ob rem existimem publica quoque iura, quae sunt propria civitatis atque imperi, tum monumenta rerum gestarum et vetustatis exempla oratori nota esse debere.'

[48] *HE*, I, p. 63.

[49] Malachi 3:16: 'Tunc locuti sunt timentes Dominum, unusquisque cum proximo suo: et attendit Dominus, et audivit, et scriptus est liber monumenti coram eo timentibus Dominum, et cogitantibus nomen ejus.'

[50] *HE*, III, p. 285.

[51] *HE*, I, pp. 131.

or patristic literature. Indeed, what he is concerned with, in the first instance, is the production and preservation of historical records. In fact, Orderic informs his readers that, despite his original intention of writing ecclesiastical history, he was soon commissioned by his superiors to record Norman events ('de Normannicis eventibus materia').[52] In his fifth book Orderic explicitly refers to his own work as relating 'Norman deeds and events' ('gesta et eventus Normannis').[53] Ultimately, therefore, the *Historia* became essentially what Orderic described as 'an account of the deeds of the Normans for Normans to read'.[54] Orderic thus places himself in the tradition not only of Orosius, Eusebius, Bede and Paul the Deacon – all of whom he names explicitly in the *Historia*'s prologue – but also of previous Norman chroniclers such as Dudo of Saint-Quentin and William of Jumièges. It is, of course, hardly surprising to find William included in the list of historians whom the *Historia* mentions by name, given that Orderic had revised William's *Gesta Normannorum ducum* between c. 1095 and 1109 (about a generation before the subsequent redaction written by Robert of Torigni).[55] Similarly, it is no coincidence that some of the *Gesta Normannorum*'s content resurfaces in the pages of the *Historia*.

The key function of written records in the preservation of historical tradition and cultural memory is made explicit at various points throughout the *Historia*. Producing historical writings within the walls of the monastic scriptorium, both at Saint-Évroul and elsewhere, was regarded as constituting an integral part of the divine service, whereas negligence or failure in accomplishing these scribal tasks was deemed shameful and even constituted sin. Just how tangible this dichotomy must have been in the minds of Orderic and his fellow brethren at Saint-Évroul can be exemplified through another passage from the third book of the *Historia*. Following the tale of the sinful scribe as told by Abbot Thierry, Orderic pledges that on Judgement Day he himself 'shall not be condemned along with the idle servant who hid his talent in the earth'.[56] Instead, Orderic promises to apply his own talent inside the abbey's scriptorium, thereby outdoing his fellow brethren, who 'shrank from bending their minds to the task of composing or writing down their

---

[52] *HE*, II, pp. 2–4.

[53] *HE*, III, p. 6.

[54] Ibid., pp. 6–7: 'Tandem ego de extremis Merciorum finibus decennis Angligena huc advectus, barbarusque et ignotus advena callentibus indigenis admistus, inspirante Deo, Normannorum gesta et eventus Normannis promere scripto sum conatus.'

[55] *GND*, I, p. lxviii.

[56] *HE*, II, pp. 2–4: 'Haec et alia hujusmodi diligenter perpendens, pater Guarine, aliquid quod aliquibus in domo Dei fidelibus prosit seu placeat, decrevi simpliciter edere, arreptum vero sedimen vigilanter tenere, ne cum servo torpente pro absconso in terra talento damner, Domino ad judicium veniente.'

traditions'.[57] Clearly, what informed this promise was to a large extent the experience gained from historical precedent. As shown above, Orderic was very much aware of the terrible damage which the Viking invasions had inflicted on Frankish libraries during previous centuries, when 'the records of former times perished in the flames, along with churches and other buildings' ('antiquorum scripta cum basilicis et aedibus incendio deperierunt').[58] Also, Orderic recognised that history could easily repeat itself if precautions were not taken by himself and his fellow scribes. This threat must have seemed all the more real to Orderic given his awareness of the Normans' Scandinavian heritage, to which he repeatedly draws attention.[59] According to Orderic, the Normans were traditionally, and remained inherently, a warlike people, whose members until recently 'were more addicted to the pursuit of arms than of learning, and up to the time of William the Bastard devoted themselves to war rather than reading or writing'.[60]

In the face of such threats, whether imminent or informed by historical precedent, it should not surprise us to find that Orderic shows little sympathy for those who neglect their duties as scribes and historians. That Orderic was not the only one to express these concerns, not alone in censuring those who failed to record past events for posterity, is made evident in the writings of other twelfth-century historians, including, for example, those of William of Malmesbury. In his *Gesta regum Anglorum*, William expresses severe dissatisfaction with the work of his close

[57] Ibid., pp. 2–4: 'Libenter quippe legissent actus abbatum, fratrumque suorum, et parvarum collectionem rerum suarum, quae ab egenis sed devotis fundatoribus tenuiter auctae sunt ingenti sollicitudine Patrum; sed ad dictandi seu scribendi sedimen suum renuerunt curvare ingenium.'

[58] *HE*, III, p. 282.

[59] On this topic, see B. Pohl, 'Keeping it in the Family: Re-reading Anglo-Norman Historiography in the Face of Cultural Memory, Tradition and Heritage', in *Norman Tradition and Transcultural Heritage: Exchange of Cultures in the 'Norman' Peripheries of Medieval Europe*, ed. S. Burkhardt and T. Foerster (Aldershot, 2013), pp. 219–52; Elisabeth van Houts, 'Scandinavian Influence in Norman Literature of the Eleventh Century', *ANS* 6 (1984), 107–21; L. Musset, 'L'Image de la Scandinavie dans les oeuvres normandes de la période ducale (911–1204)', in *Nordica et Normannica: Recueil d'études sur la Scandinavie ancienne et médiévale, les expéditions des Vikings et la fondation de la Normandie*, ed. L. Musset, Studia Nordica (Paris, 1997), pp. 213–32; C. Carozzi, 'Des Daces aux Normands: Le Mythe et l'identification d'un peuple chez Dudon de Saint-Quentin', in *Peuples du Moyen Age: Problèmes d'identification; séminaire Sociétés, idéologies et croyances au Moyen Age*, ed. C. Carozzi and H. Taviani-Carozzi (Aix-en-Provence, 1996), pp. 7–26.

[60] *HE*, II, pp. 2–3: 'Quoniam ipsi de Dacia prodeuntes, non litteris sed armis studuerunt, et usque ad Guillelmi Nothi tempora magis bellare quam legere vel dictare laboraverunt.'

contemporary, Eadmer of Canterbury. What appears to displease William the most is the fact that Eadmer 'omits two hundred and twenty-three years after Bede which he thought unworthy of remark, and in that interval history is defective without the protection of letters [or books]' ('absque litterarum patrocinio claudicat cursus temporum in medio').[61] According to William, written letters (or books) evidently constitute the only efficient defence ('patrocinium') against oblivion, which is why in writing the *Gesta* he set out to 'to mend the broken chain of history' ('voluntati fuit interruptam temporum seriem sarcire'). This conception of history as a chain linking generations by means of written records is strikingly reminiscent of Walter Benjamin's notion concerning 'the chain of tradition which passes a happening on from generation to generation'.[62] What further unites Benjamin's 'chain of tradition' with the notions of history and memory expressed by Orderic and William during the mid-twelfth century is that they both essentially rely on mechanisms of selection.

Just how essential Orderic considered these processes of selection to be with regard to the preservation of memory is evidenced in the fifth book of the *Historia*. Here, Orderic informs his readers that:

> [i]f our bishops and other rulers were so holy in their lives that miracles might be performed by God's will for them and through them – as they so often were by the fathers of old – and spread abroad in books [*diffusa per codices*] to warm the hearts of their readers, reminding men of this age of the glory and wondrous works of their first masters, then I would shake off sloth and exert myself to write down [*scripto transmitterem*] things worthy to be told [*digna relatu*] for the eager eyes of future readers.[63]

---

[61] *Gesta regum Anglorum: The History of the English Kings*, ed. R. A. B. Mynors, completed by R. M. Thomson and M. Winterbottom, 2 vols. (Oxford, 1998–9), I, pp. 14–15: 'Ita praetermissis a tempore Bedae ducentis et viginti et tribus annis, quos iste nulla memoria dignatus est, absque litterarum patrocinio claudicat cursus temporum in medio; unde mihi, tum propter patriae charitatem, tum propter adhortantium auctoritatem, voluntati fuit interruptam temporum seriem sarcire, et exarata barbarice Romano sale condire.'

[62] W. Benjamin, 'From "The Storyteller" and "Theses on the Philosophy of History"', in *The Collective Memory Reader*, ed. J. K. Olick, V. Vinitzky-Seroussi and D. Levy (New York, 2011), pp. 99–103, at p. 102.

[63] *HE*, III, pp. 9–10: 'Si pontifices nostri aliique rectores orbis tantae sanctitatis essent ut pro illis et per illos miracula divinitus fierent, sicut olim ab antiquis patribus crebro facta sunt, atque sparsim diffusa per codices, lectorum corda suaviter imbuunt, et gloriam priorum miranda magistrorum signa praesentibus recolunt, excusso torpore, memetipsum exercerem, et digna relatu notitiae posterorum avidae scripto transmitterem.'

This statement provides a further example of how the production of writings ('scripta') and books ('codices') constitute a means of overcoming sinful idleness and paralysis ('torpor') – an admonition which might well have been aimed at Orderic's less productive brethren at Saint-Évroul, whom he criticised elsewhere in the *Historia*, as we saw above. In addition, Orderic's words are informed by a fundamental distinction between, on the one hand, memorable events (events which could be remembered) and, on the other, events worth remembering (events which should be remembered).

Similar distinctions in favour of events deemed worthy of remembrance ('memoria digna videbantur') can also be encountered in Bede,[64] as well as in William's *Gesta regum Anglorum*. As was seen earlier, William's critique of Eadmer's historical method was based on the fact that Eadmer had failed to record what happened during the 200 years or so following Bede's account. According to William, this was not simply a case of idleness or sloth, but in fact reflected a serious misjudgement on Eadmer's part, given that he is said to have omitted these events from his record because he deemed them 'unworthy of memory' ('quos iste nulla memoria dignatus est').[65] In the light of such harsh criticism, it is, perhaps, a little hypocritical to find William arguing that, with regard to the composition of his own *Gesta*, 'it will be easier if I leave to the end the kingdoms of the East Angles and East Saxons, which I consider unworthy of my own labours, and of the memory of posterity [*memoria putamus indigna*]'.[66] Writing about a generation after William and Orderic, Gervase of Canterbury produced what might be the most straightforward and to-the-point expression of this principle. Gervase readily informs his readers that he had 'no desire to note down all those things which are memorable, but only those things which ought to be remembered, that is, those things which are clearly worthy of remembrance'.[67] In a similar, yet somewhat more tentative, vein, Bede had previously admitted to having 'diligently sought to put on record [...] those events which I believe to be worthy of remembrance [*memoratu digna*] and likely to be welcome to the inhabitants [of the English provinces]'.[68] Orderic seems to have adopted

---

[64] *Bede's Ecclesiastical History*, pp. 2–4.

[65] William of Malmesbury, *Gesta regum Anglorum*, I, p. 14.

[66] Ibid., pp. 16–17: 'Quod profecto fiet expeditius, si regna Orientalium Anglorum et Orientalium Saxonum post aliorum tergum posuero, quae et nostra cura et posterorum memoria putamus indigna.'

[67] *The Historical Works of Gervase of Canterbury*, ed. W. Stubbs, Rolls Series, 2 vols. (London, 1880), I, p. 89: 'Non tamen omnia memorabilia notare cupio, sed memoranda tantum, ea scilicet quae digna memoriae esse videntur'; the translation is taken from C. Given-Wilson, *Chronicles: The Writing of History in Medieval England* (London, 2004), p. 61.

[68] *Bede's Ecclesiastical History*, pp. 6–7: 'Ut qui de singulis provinciis sive locis sublimioribus quae memoratu digna atque incolis grata credideram

Bede's model and, in writing his *Historia*, singled out precisely those events which he believed were worthy of memory and would be looked upon favourably by his readers. In this way, he also perpetuated the notion of memory as dependent on writing, which had been established by Isidore in his *Etymologiae*.[69]

I would like to end this chapter with a number of observations – rather than finalised conclusions – as to how the close textual analysis of Orderic's *Historia* can help us to understand better the dynamic relationship between cultural memory and the production of historical writings at Saint-Évroul (and perhaps beyond). First of all, it must be emphasised that recording the past in written records (including, of course, the *Historia* itself) represents a proactive step towards establishing what might be called a 'cultural memory canon'. Orderic reveals a heightened awareness that these records are indispensable to the preservation of memory for the sake of future generations, which is why their production came to be considered one of the most important and valued tasks of everyday monastic life. This discussion has argued that, at Saint-Évroul, writing history was considered an integral part of the *cultus divinus*, encouraging scribes to work towards the salvation of their souls by producing manuscripts. By generating these *monumenta*, writers such as Orderic played their part in ensuring that the events of the past (and knowledge thereof) remained accessible to posterity. That this task was not taken light-heartedly is evidenced further by the fact that negligence or failure in complying with one's scribal duties was considered a sin, criticised not only by Orderic, but also by his contemporaries, including the English historian William of Malmesbury.

The fact that Anglo-Norman writers during the twelfth century generally showed little sympathy for such negligence in producing historical records is perhaps not entirely surprising, given the previous disruption of literary culture caused by the prolonged series of Viking attacks on both sides of the Channel, which continued to serve as a historical precedent. There was evidently no doubt among Orderic and his contemporaries that the preservation of the past through cultural memory was essentially dependent on the production and transmission of stable memory media. Without the help of books, these memories risked being lost forever, just 'as hail or snow melt in the waters of a swift river, swept away by the current never to return',[70] or, in Isidore's words, 'flying into oblivion' ('oblivione fugiant').[71]

---

diligenter adnotare curavi, apud omnes fructum piae intercessionis inveniam.'

[69] Isidore, *Etymologiae*, I.iii.2.
[70] *HE*, III, p. 284.
[71] Isidore, *Etymologiae*, I.iii.2.

The Reception of Orderic Vitalis in the Later Middle Ages

James G. Clark

CAEN, 14 August 1417: three hundred and thirty years since, as Orderic Vitalis memorably described, the presence of a king of England (or, rather, of his mortal remains) had endangered the abbey of Saint-Étienne. Now the convent had reason to fear the proximity of another monarch from across the Channel, this time very much alive.[1] The thirty-year-old invader Henry of Monmouth (Henry V) was approaching the town, and its defending garrison was undertaking the desperate work of laying waste its environs. Meanwhile, the vanguard, under the king's second brother, Thomas, duke of Clarence, set camp and weighed the prospects for the siege-battle to come.[2] Long after nightfall – perhaps only shortly before matins, given the season – a hooded figure stole from the precinct wall (whose fortifications had only recently been renewed), heading for the tents of the attackers. A monk of Saint-Étienne, whose name is remembered as Gérard, entered the tent of the young prince (which would have been clearly marked), rousing him with valuable intelligence and a heartfelt plea. The defenders had determined to destroy the abbey rather than to see it serve as a portal for the invasion force, and Brother Gérard had taken it upon himself to give up Saint-Étienne to the English if in turn the church might be saved:

> humbly and tearfully [he] pleaded [...] It has fallen especially to you to save our monastery, to you who [are] descended from the line of kings who founded, built and endowed this place of ours.[3]

---

[1] Orderic's account of the chain of calamities that accompanied the Conqueror's funerary rights – riotous panic at Rouen, a flash fire at Caen, public protest over the Duke's land-grabbing at the graveside and, finally, the ghastly bursting of his body – held the attention of the readers who consulted his history at first hand and, through them, found a wider audience: *HE*, IV, pp. 104–9. See also L. V. Hicks, *Religious Life in Normandy, 1050–1300: Space, Gender and Social Pressure*, Studies in the History of Medieval Religion 33 (Woodbridge, 2007), p. 150.

[2] For a narrative outline of the Lancastrian assault on Caen, see J. H. Wylie, *The Reign of Henry the Fifth*, 3 vols. (Cambridge, 1914), III, pp. 57–60.

[3] *The St Albans Chronicle: The 'Chronica maiora' of Thomas Walsingham*, ed. W. Childs and L. Watkiss, Oxford Medieval Texts, 2 vols. (Oxford, 2010), II, pp. 716–17: 'Cui confestim flexis genibus flebiliter supplicauit ut loci sue ruine succurreret, qui iam diruendus erat nisi maturius subueniret.

Clarence, a commander who matched Orderic's image of a knight of 'great enterprise' and 'quick wits' in the field and (like his elder brother) was as well schooled in his forbears' histories as were those Norman archetypes, recognised the opportunity perhaps as much for its propaganda as its tactical potential.⁴ His troops entered the abbey and turned it into their campaign headquarters. King Henry was welcomed there four days later. And from its towers, the English artillery was trained on the town.

Gérard's great hope for Saint-Étienne was not quite realised. The church was damaged by the blasting of the English bombards.⁵ When Caen fell, on 4 September, the abbey was taken into military custody and its movables sequestered. How much was then lost is unclear. The same authority that reported Gérard's desperate scheme alleged that the defending garrison had already 'robbed the place of both its provisions and its other treasures [...] gaining ill repute for their manifest sacrilege'.⁶ He also claimed that Clarence added lustre to his reputation by executing a person found thieving various valuables from the monks (whether a

---

"Vobis", inquit, "specialius conuenit nostrum seruare monasterium, qui de regum linea discendistis qui locum nostrum fundauerunt, extruxerunt atque dotauerunt. Quapropter incunctanter utamini me duce preuio et ego uos inducam et gaudere faciam loco nostro."' While Walsingham's tale of Brother Gérard is unique, the historical resonance of the Lancastrian entry into Saint-Étienne ran through the English accounts of Henry V's campaigns – a measure of the renewed taste for early history which can be traced in English manuscripts in the half century between Brétigny and Agincourt: '[Normandy] belongs to him entirely by right dating from the time of William I, the conquerer': *Gesta Henrici Quinti: The Deeds of Henry V*, ed. J. Roskell and F. Taylor, Oxford Medieval Texts (Oxford, 1975), p. 17. Cf. '[his] trew titull of conquest and right heritage': *The Brut, or the Chonicles of England*, ed. F. W. D. Brie, 2 vols., Early English Texts Society o.s. 131, 136 (London, 1906, 1908), II, p. 374.

⁴ These were, in Orderic's view, the martial attributes of Robert of Bellême: *HE*, IV, pp. 297–8: 'Miles quidem magnus erat in armis et acerrimus, ingenio et eloquentia cum fortitudine pollebat'. Clarence's taste for books seems to have reached beyond conventional connoisseurship, as there is a copy of John Gower's *Confessio amantis* among his surviving volumes: A. I Doyle, 'Books In and Out of Court', in *English Court Culture in the Later Middle Ages*, ed. J. W. Sherborne and V. J. Scattergood (London, 1983), pp. 168–70. See also J. E. Krochalis, 'The Books and Reading of Henry V and his Circle', *Chaucer Review* 23:1 (1988), 50–77, at p. 57.

⁵ '[the] vyolence of there incredible noyse or sound brake the windows of the temple of St Stephens': *The First English Life of King Henry the Fifth, Written in 1513 by an Anonymous Author Known Commonly as the Translator of Livius*, ed. C. L. Kingsford (Oxford, 1911), p. 86.

⁶ *The St Albans Chronicle*, I, pp. 716–17: 'diripientibus tam uictualia quam alia loci iocalia latenter in uillam commigrauerunt, notabiles sacrilegio manifesto'.

member of the garrison or a townsman is unclear).[7] Other accounts indicate that the invaders also helped themselves. Certainly, plate and other treasures were inventorised, together with all of the abbey's temporal and spiritual properties, and in due course some passed into the possession of the conquering king.[8] A prize from the abbey known to have reached Henry's hands was a book that he would have recognised as a token of the rare quality of the convent's library (it is now BL, MS Cotton Vespasian A XIX). Although the book's post-medieval readers believed it to be authentic booty from the battlefield (their imagination fired by Walsingham's chronicle), it would appear instead to have been commissioned by Abbot William [IV] Cavé (1416–28) for presentation to the new conqueror. After twelve months in the king's custody, the convent received a royal pardon in September 1418 and was awarded the protection of King Henry.[9] It may have been this action, or perhaps that which was codified in the Treaty of Troyes of May 1421, which gave rise to the gift.[10] Certainly, the book bears the professional limning of a presentation volume, and if not finished at the abbey, it was certainly copied from a Saint-Étienne exemplar. It contains a narrative of the deeds and the death of Duke William, founder and foremost patron of the abbey, extracted from the *Historia ecclesiastica* of Orderic Vitalis.[11] Here, the French monks

---

[7] Ibid.

[8] *The Reign of King Henry the Fifth*, vol. 3, ed. J. H. Wylie, part ed. W. T. Waugh (Cambridge, 1929), p. 446; C. Hippeau, *L'Abbaye de Saint-Étienne de Caen, 1066–1790* (Caen, 1855), pp. 129–30.

[9] Ibid., p. 129.

[10] It was almost certainly not the 'goodly French book' which a later authority reported was King Henry's only booty from the siege: *First English Life*, ed. Kingsford, p. 92.

[11] BL, MS Cotton Vespasian A XIX, fols. 104–21, are a direct copy of Saint-Étienne's incomplete shelf-set of Orderic's history, the surviving example of which is now Vatican City, Biblioteca Apostolica Vaticana, MS Reg. Lat. 703B. The Vespasian manuscript is a composite, in which the two quires containing Orderic's history accompany six other items, three of them related by content to Ely Cathedral Priory. The first leaf of the *Historia* is preceded by one of three leaves of a book of hours bearing decorations attributed to the Harvard Hannibal Master, an artist known to have been active at Paris and Rouen in the years of the Lancastrian occupation and a contributor to presentation volumes prepared for English recipients, including Henry VI. This would seem to strengthen the suggested context for the preparation of the Saint-Étienne piece. For a discussion of its origin, see also Elisabeth van Houts, 'Camden, Cotton and the Chronicles of the Norman Conquest of England', *British Library Journal* 18 (1992), 148–62, at pp. 153–4 (plate at p. 154). The first leaf of the *Historia* bears a decorative border closely comparable to the *membra disiecta* of the book of hours. Such matching was typical of Cotton's *modus compilandi*, but Iain Milne has proposed an alternative explanation: that

mobilised Normandy's history to reinstate their old, embattled *Eigenklöster* for a new incumbent.¹²

Rarely can the public reception of a monastic chronicle be captured quite so vividly. Of course, it was not only the siege and submission of Caen that had so charged Norman history at this high-water mark of the Anglo-French war, nor, indeed, was Orderic's text that history's main, or even its primary, source. Both Henry V's campaigns – the invasion of 1417 and the Agincourt adventure two years earlier – had been raised on a historical argument, and in his uneasy exchanges with a fiscally prudent Commons the king had made much of his claim to 'true title' and 'heritage' across the Channel. In fact, the narrative legacy of the Anglo-Norman chroniclers had been pressed into the service of the Crown repeatedly over the course of the previous century, and with an increasing intensity as successive monarchs came to regard the textual and archival riches of the clergy as a potent weapon in the struggle for royal dominion. Such support had first been sought in England as early as 1291, when Edward I caused clerical archives to be scoured for authorities to validate his claim; they responded with excerpts which advanced such cases as 'quomodo Scocie subiectum extiterat'. The Dunfermline compilation suggests that the Scottish Crown had similar recourse to Anglo-Norman history as much as a generation earlier.¹³

The present value of past narrative in these years of dynastic rivalry might seem to favour the old assumption about the chronicle, perhaps especially the monastic chronicle, which still seems to underlie our treatment of these narratives: the belief that the chronicle was, by its very nature, and self-consciously in its execution, a public document and the responsibility of a compiler who occupied, in some sense or other, an official position. While a network of informants in high office, and access to a good many records from princely, pontifical and seigniorial

---

these two elements of the manuscript originated together and were both perhaps the commission of Louis de Luxembourg, some of whose library did pass to Ely Cathedral Priory. See I. R. J. Milne,'"Dum furerent in orbe tempestates": Power in Fifteenth-Century Normandy, the Re-Writing of History and Cotton MS Vespasian A XIX' (unpublished MA dissertation, University of York, 2012), pp. 34–6. I am grateful to Mr Milne for allowing me to read his dissertation.

¹² Hippeau, *L'Abbaye de Saint-Étienne*, p. 130. For Saint-Étienne's rapprochement with the English conqueror see also Milne, 'Dum furerent in orbe', pp. 26–31, at p. 28.

¹³ Edward's request is recorded at Glastonbury and Winchcombe abbeys and also at Wells Cathedral: R. A. Griffiths, 'Edward I, Scotland and the Chronicles of English Religious Houses', *Journal of the Society of Archivists* (1979), 191–9. For the Dunfermline compilation, see A. Taylor, 'Historical Writing in Twelfth- and Thirteenth-Century Scotland: The Dunfermline Compilation', *Historical Research* 83 (2010), 228–52.

chanceries, gave these narratives something of a public voice, it was rare for the custody of a chronicle to be formally constituted. Even where compiler, master and subject were in close proximity, the status and reach of the narrative still proved unpredictable, as the contrasting manuscript traditions of Dudo of Saint-Quentin (ducal and episcopal clerk) and William of Poitiers (chaplain) readily attest. In a monastic setting even the presence of a prolific annalist of proven authority – Matthew Paris, for example – did not preclude others from keeping independent annals of their own.[14] Here the view has also been distorted by a tendency to misrepresent the scriptorium, even where there is a record of professional scribes, as the sole locus for the compilation and copying of texts.[15] In fact, recent investigations have revealed that some chronicles have been wrongly pressed into the mould of one conventual *auctor*, and should stand rather for the multi-vocal character of narrative that prevailed in many monasteries.[16] The majority of surviving manuscripts and fragments are compilations of this kind, and it may be that in time the *auctores*, who were fixed into an almost apostolic succession by their first post-medieval editors, will be recognised as the exception to a historical enterprise that was more typically a tale of variant recensions and rival purposes.

It does seem that the status ascribed to those whom we still tend to think of as the 'major' chroniclers of their day – those whose narratives were most authoritative and fullest – was highly contingent and almost always short lived. In the first place, the authority of their narratives, and certainly any sense of priority that might be attached to them, drew much of its force from the presence and profile of the author's own person. These works was consulted and celebrated most frequently by the brethren in the author's own immediate circle, and those clerks and laymen in its ambit. The author's name could be entirely forgotten after death – witness the more-or-less immediate fate of William of Jumièges (whom Orderic was

---

[14] For this environment see A. Gransden, *Historical Writing in England*, vol. 1: *c. 550 to c. 1307* (London, 1973), pp. 356–79.

[15] The tendency to conceive of scribal activity in quite strictly institutionalised contexts is implicit, sometimes explicit, in many classic accounts of British and mainland European monasteries and their manuscript production, from Claude Jenkins to V. H. Galbraith, and E. A. Lowe to Bernhard Bischoff.

[16] See, for examples, the re-evaluation of the formation and transmission of twelfth-century continuations to John of Worcester's narrative: *The Winchcombe and Coventry Chronicles: Hitherto Unnoticed Witnesses to the Work of John of Worcester*, ed. and trans. P. Hayward, Arizona Center for Medieval & Renaissance Studies: Texts & Studies 373, 2 vols. (Tempe, AZ, 2010); see also the evolution of the narrative that is best known as 'Ralph of Coggeshall's *Chronicon Anglicanum*: H. Webster, 'A Critical Analysis and Edition of Ralph of Coggeshall's *Chronicon Anglicanum*' (unpublished PhD dissertation, University of Bristol, 2015).

almost alone in recalling by name) – or remembered fitfully at best. It was not uncommon for their narratives not to be reproduced at all. The larger part of Matthew Paris's great histories were known to late medieval monks of St Albans only through his own, venerable autographs, some of which had to be restored to the abbey by a dedicated reader, an earlier generation having given them away.[17]

The particular dynamics of monastic life, perhaps especially the monastic life that prevailed before the reforms that followed Lateran IV in 1215, also did much to shape the special status ascribed to these living *auctores*. Before the canons of the Council compelled the Benedictines to organise themselves into chapters under a central, presiding authority, the culture of their cloisters was by no means corporate.[18] It drew much of its character from connections that did not even follow the filial lines of parent and offspring foundations, but were markedly more eclectic (Chibnall's word) or even contingent, arising from the very particular personal, social and regional affiliations of a given generation.[19] Before the reformers steered them towards the universities and a clerical syllabus of education and formation, the rotation of brethren around their network – what the mendicants came to call the *mutationes fratrum* – was markedly more vigorous as a means of refreshing leadership, spiritual and intellectual life. The standing of the chroniclers of the monastic golden age – active in narrative say between the pontificates of Gregory VII (1073–85) and Innocent III (1198–1215) – was secured in this way. They became known within their networks, and it seems their textual exemplars often travelled with them. In the wake of the thirteenth-century reforms, by contrast, beyond the house of his profession the monk most likely would know, or have been known at, his university *studium*; as we might expect, it was from there that the bulk of textual exemplars then flowed.[20]

---

[17] For example, the historical anthology annotated by Matthew which 'per quorundam negligenciam fuerat deperditus', only to be recovered after 1420: BL, MS Royal 13 D V, fol. 37v. Another manuscript, wholly written by Matthew, was permanently lost to the abbey in the second quarter of the fifteenth century; it passed through the collections of secular bibliophiles before entering the royal collection: BL, MS Royal 14 C VII.

[18] For the creation of central, captiular governance after 1215, see J. G. Clark, *The Benedictines in the Middle Ages* (Woodbridge, 2011), pp. 289–98.

[19] For Chibnall's characterisation of Orderic's network, see Chibnall, *World*, p. 62. For these environmental dynamics elsewhere in the Anglo-Norman milieu, see, *inter alia*, A. Lawrence-Mathers, *Manuscripts in Northumbria in the Eleventh and Twelfth Centuries* (Cambridge, 2002), pp. 252–61; J. Burton, *The monastic Order in Yorkshire, 1069–1215* (Cambridge, 1999), pp. 287–92; *Winchcombe and Coventry Chronicles*, I, pp. 96–8, 144–6, 166–8, 181.

[20] For the exchange of texts between universities and later medieval monasteries, see, for example, J. I. Catto, J. Ziolkowski and M. Twomey, 'University and Monastic Texts', in *The Cambridge History of the Book in*

On the face of it, the standing of Orderic Vitalis and his work would seem to follow this pattern. Chibnall herself did not linger long on the matter of reception, at least in the posthumous sense, observing that, on the balance of evidence, the great ecclesiastical history was 'not well thumbed'.[21] More recent critical studies have revealed that Orderic actually left a considerable legacy to his younger contemporaries, most of them a generation and a half younger, but all writers whose careers were undoubtedly underway before Orderic died: fellow Benedictine Robert of Torigni (d. 1184), who was a monk of Bec (1128) and then abbot of Mont Saint-Michel (1154); and two secular clerks, Wace (d. after 1174), a canon of Bayeux, and (perhaps) Master Eustace of Boulogne (fl. 1148–59), who may be identified as the compiler of the Warenne chronicle.[22] Even so, the testimony of their texts has strengthened Chibnall's general implication that as a textual authority Orderic was best known to those he encountered directly, or at least those whose careers developed in the same circles scarcely two decades after his death. Yet though this was a somewhat circumscribed period of sustained readership, reaching perhaps no further than the death of Renouf (d. c. 1159), the last abbot of Saint-Évroul who would have known Orderic as a monk, it was nonetheless intense.[23]

There was a modest anchor-hold for Orderic's memory at his mother house. His obit was recorded, and the holograph manuscripts of his great history were marked with his name, as 'partes Vitalis'.[24] The convent's copy of William of Jumièges' *Gesta Normannorum* from which he had drawn his own redaction was also retained, though without conspicuous recognition of his own contribution to the text;[25] examples of his scribal stints were also retained in ten manuscripts, though readers led to them by the abbey's early (c. 1136) library catalogue would have found no explicit reference to

Britain, vol. 2: *1100–1400*, ed. N. Morgan and R. M. Thomson (Cambridge, 2008), pp. 219–49.

[21] Ibid., p. 218.

[22] For Robert of Torigni's monastic career, see V. Gazeau, *Normannia monastica*, vol. 2: *Prosopographie des abbés bénédictins (Xe–XIIe siècle)* (Caen, 2007), pp. 220–5. For the chronology of Wace's clerical service, see *The History of the Norman People: Wace's Roman de Rou*, ed. and trans. G. S. Burgess and Elisabeth van Houts (Woodbridge, 2004), pp. xiii–xvi. For Master Eustace's active career in the service of Count William of Warenne, see *The Warenne (Hyde) Chronicle*, ed. Elisabeth van Houts & R. C. Love, Oxford Medieval Texts (Oxford, 2013), pp. xxvii–xxviii, xviii.

[23] V. Gazeau, *Normannia monastica: Prosopographie*, p. 287.

[24] Three-quarters of the shelf-set now survives: BNF, MSS Lat. 5506 A, B, and Lat. 10913. The conventual *ex libris* inscription cemented the personal identification of the narrative: 'Iste liber est de armariolo sancti Ebrulfi. Quarta pars Vitalis': BnF, MS Lat. 5506B.

[25] Now, Rouen, BM, MS 1174 (Y14). See also *GND*, I, p. cxii.

the copyist, and when the last of his contemporaries had gone, would have been unaware that he still instructed them from a sequence of marginal observations.[26] Among these manuscripts were the conventual annals to which he had contributed, which were continued, intermittently, even into the years of the *commendam* abbey in the fifteenth century; again, however, there was no apparent recognition of the particular contribution of Brother Orderic.[27]

It seems contemporary regard was stronger and more sustained at a distance. There was a copy of the *Historia ecclesiastica*– originally, it must be assumed, a complete shelf-set – in the (perhaps larger) library at Saint-Étienne de Caen.[28] This was the copy seen by Robert of Torigni and almost certainly by Wace, the greater part of whose working life was passed in that town. While it may have been this witness to the history that was used by the compiler of the Warenne chronicle, it is just possible that he had met the text at another house, perhaps even a dependent priory, in the same Norman network.[29] Orderic's 'treatise' on the new monastic orders was also known elsewhere; the unique, thirteenth-century copy surviving in a manuscript from Saint-Taurin d'Évreux may imply a discrete circulation, but if so, given that its subject-matter was of undoubted appeal in Benedictine circles, the absence of any other witness is surprising.[30] The exceptionally close integration of the Norman convents of Black Monks, perhaps especially in the first half of the twelfth century, when the internal migration of brethren and internal recruitment of superiors was especially marked, may in fact have militated against the creation of multiple copies of the *Historia*, as the houses appear routinely to have consulted each others' written materials. The existence of at least one shelf-set beyond the house in which it was created thus sets Orderic somewhat apart from the typical monastic chronicler; the text's reproduction implies that it enjoyed a certain level of congregational authority among Normandy's Benedictines, an authority which would have spread in some degree to the duchy's wider constituency of (regular and secular) clergy, at least as their affairs unfolded in a shared and (relatively speaking) settled institutional environment.

Orderic's writing did reach beyond his own immediate horizons, but the routes it followed confirm that in these generations it was always contingency, not corporate authority, even in its most limited form of the

---

[26] *HE*, I, pp. 201–3. See also Nortier, *Les Bibliothèques médiévales*, pp. 99–123, at pp. 103–6, 119–23. See also below, Appendix 2.

[27] Now, BnF, MS Lat. 10062.

[28] Now, Vatican City, Biblioteca Apostolica Vaticana, MS Vat. Reg. Lat. 703B. See also Chibnall, 'General Introduction', p. 121.

[29] *Warenne (Hyde) Chronicle*, pp. xlvi–xlvii.

[30] Now, BnF, MS Lat. 4861, fols. 124r–128r. See also Chibnall, 'General Introduction', pp. 121–2.

filial network of foundations, that shaped transmission and reception. While the *Historia* itself did not reach France or England, it was known – albeit unidentified – indirectly through Robert's redaction of the *Gesta Normannorum ducum* and Wace's *Roman de Rou*. The French manuscript tradition of both texts suggests a wide and sustained readership.[31] The productive, semi-professional scriptoria of England's best-endowed Benedictine houses readily received Robert's *Gesta*, and judging by its script the surviving copy from Reading Abbey must have entered the library when Orderic's last abbot, Ralph, was still in office at Saint-Évroul.[32] While the unique copy of the Warenne chronicle cannot be fixed in England or the European mainland, its English preoccupations are suggestive. There can be little doubt that one or more earlier exemplars lay behind it, and one might speculate that it was known at other monasteries in the Warenne interest, such as Lewes, Castle Acre and Thetford.[33] Wace's *Roman de Rou*, which conveyed Orderic's narrative of Normandy after 1066, may have found readers in England only a generation later, as the French vernacular became a more familiar language of independent study in the cloister. The earliest extant copy, which bears the *ex libris* of the Conqueror's monastery at Battle, was written after 1200.[34]

Orderic's own contribution to the continuation of the *Gesta Normannorum* (Recension E), again concealed under a better-known title, achieved the furthest reach of any of his writings. The number of manuscript witnesses eclipses that of William's own recension (C) and is second only to that of Robert of Torigni (F). Dissemination seems to have been concentrated within the historical compass of the clergy of Normandy, Flanders and the Ile de France; given his own researches in the region, his work may have been more widely known in the Flanders borderland than the manuscript survivors indicate.[35] There were copies of 'his' *Gesta* made in Orderic's lifetime at Liège, Saint-Denis and his own Saint-Évroul; a twelfth-century epitome of the text certainly close to Orderic's own lifetime may be connected with Fleury; three further late twelfth-century copies that lack a provenance are almost certainly from the same northern French region; Saint-Taurin d'Évreux's copy, which dates from the end of the first quarter of the thirteenth century, may have been

---

[31] For these manuscript traditions see *GND*, I, pp. cix–cxix; and *Wace's Roman de Rou*, pp. xxii–xxiii.

[32] Now, BL, MS Cotton Vitellius A VIII, fols. 5–100. For the manuscript tradition of Robert's recension see also *GND*, I, pp. cix–cxix.

[33] The manuscript is now BL, MS Cotton Domitian A XIV, fols. 4r–21v. See also *Warenne (Hyde) Chronicle*, pp. xiv–xviii.

[34] BL, MS Royal 4 C XI, fols. 249r–278r. See also *Wace's Roman de Rou*, pp. xxii–xxiii.

[35] For Orderic's inspection of manuscripts at Saint-Sepulchre's Abbey, Cambrai (*HE*, III), see *HE*, II, pp. 188–9.

made directly from a Saint-Évroul exemplar since it also contains Orderic's treatise on the new monastic orders.[36]

In England, however, Orderic's *Gesta* seems to have been crowded out by five of the other six recensions. Here too we may see the effects of the diverse affiliations and, indeed, the intellectual dynamics, of the English monastic network, and perhaps in particular the disproportionate output and outreach of a handful of Benedictine scriptoria in the south-east of the kingdom – Canterbury, St Albans, perhaps St Edmundsbury – none of which seem to have had strong links with the network of Saint-Évroul. Another Norman 'edition' of the annals had a much wider reach: the so-called 'common root' text originated at, or in the vicinity of, Rouen in the early twelfth-century, then circulated among the major Benedictine houses of the duchy – Jumièges, Mont Saint-Michel, Saint-Évroul – and from there passed across the Channel.[37] This contrast is a further indication that the limits of Orderic's reception at this date were not necessarily typical of writing from his milieu.

Yet Orderic could lay claim to the creation of a certain (modest) textual community connecting the chain of English convents with which his abbey did cultivate contact. Just as in the abbey's Norman network, it was an affinity formed from internal recruitment that led Orderic to the Lincolnshire abbey of St Guthlac at Crowland. The epitome of the lengthy, eighth-century life of Guthlac by the monk Felix that he was commissioned to complete by Abbot Geoffrey, together with a discrete life of the prospective saint Earl Waltheof of Northumbria, and a short *narratio* of the abbey's origin, informed, and gave narrative form to, a communal memory which shaped a series of literary projects in the generations that followed.[38] The mid-twelfth-century Guthlac Roll, which visualised the legendary founders and benefactors of the abbey perhaps to guide a scheme of stained glass, at the very least shared with Orderic a common conception of these figures, and his writing may have been a direct point of reference; a thirteenth-century witness to the epitome of Felix, of an unspecified provenance, points to some tangible transmission.[39] The anonymous narrative *Vita et passio Waldevis comitis*, which was compiled to mark the translation of the 'relics' of Waltheof in

---

[36] The Évreux copy is now BnF, MS Lat. 4861. See also *GND*, I, pp. ciii–cviii, at p. cvi.

[37] For the origin and reception of the Norman annals, see *Winchcombe and Coventry Chronicles*, I, pp. 13–14.

[38] For the connection and the commissions see *HE*, II, pp. xxv–xxvii; Chibnall, *World*, pp. 36, 107–8.

[39] The Guthlac Roll survives as BL, MS Harley Rolls Y 4. See also *Felix's Life of Saint Guthlac: Texts, Translations and Notes*, ed. B. Colgrave (Cambridge, 1956), pp. 12–14, 179, 181. The thirteenth-century copy of the epitome is now Douai Bibliothèque, MS 852. See also *HE*, II, pp. xxvi–xxvii.

1219, also absorbed Orderic's work.[40] The abbey's composite narratives that unfolded in the centuries that followed, a *Vitae abbatum* and the *Historia Croylandensis*, conveyed traces of Orderic's original as far as fifteenth-century readers. Here Orderic's commissions remained in hand, or continued to be remembered, and seem to have been woven into a complex fabric of 'false' history which was used to cover the wide gaps in the abbey's narrative and archival records.[41] It might be said that for a time Orderic himself formed a material part of the Crowland tradition, and that a communal memory remained of his presence in its ambit. Certainly, it was his personal authority that drew William of Malmesbury to Crowland before 1125, as part of a circuit of monasteries he visited modelling (perhaps self-consciously) Orderic's own journeys.[42]

In fact, Orderic's *abbreviatio* of Felix's *Vita Guthlaci* continued to attract attention in England after the hagiographical industry of these generations had slowed. The life of the Crowland saint that occupies three chapters (XVII, 195–7) of the copy of John of Tynemouth's *Historia aurea* made at the Benedictine abbey of Bury St Edmunds in 1377 draws directly from Felix, but carries verbal echoes from Orderic at three critical moments in the narrative: the wonders that attended Guthlac's birth (Felix, chapter 5); his entry into a religious life at Repton (Felix, chapters 19–20); and his death, and its date (Felix, chapter 50).[43] John does not identify his sources,

---

[40] The text survives in Douai Bibliothèque, MS 801. For the preparation and purpose of this narrative see H. Birkett, *The Saints Lives of Jocelin of Furness: Hagiography, Patronage* (York, 2010), pp. 119–120.

[41] A. Hiatt, *The Making of Medieval Forgeries: False Documents in Fifteenth-Century England*, British Library Studies in Medieval Culture (London, Toronto and New York, 2004), pp. 38–48, at p. 42.

[42] William followed Orderic not only to Crowland but also Thorney and Worcester: R. M. Thomson, *William of Malmesbury* (Woodbridge, 1987), pp. 73–4.

[43] The Bury copy of the *Historia aurea* is now Oxford, Bodleian Library, MS Bodley 240, fols. 277a–278b. The first of these echoes is in the description of the heavenly portent as 'prodigium caelestis', where John uses the same formulation as Orderic. The second is in Guthlac's renunciation of 'worldly ways' ('seculi pompis') at the age of twenty-four to take the habit, for which John gives 'habitum monachalem sucepit' and Orderic 'tonsuram habitumque clericalem suscepit'; for Guthlac's abbess, Ælfdrida, John gives 'Elfrida' and Orderic 'Eldrid'. The third echo is is Guthlac's last moments, when he raised his eyes heavenward and stretched out his hands: John gives 'et oriente sole elevatis oculis ad celum extensisque in altum manibus', and Orderic 'oriente vero sole vir Dei sublevatis paulisper membris velut exsurgens et manus ad altare extendens corporis et sanguinis Christi communione se munivit et elevatis oculis ad celum et extensis in altum manibus'. Finally, for Guthlac's giving up his spirit to eternal joy in the year of our Lord 715, John has 'animam ad gaudiam perpetue exultacionis emisit anno domini 715', and Orderic 'anno ab incarnacione domini DCCXV

and though the Bury compilers named some in the margins they made no comment here. Throughout his history, John followed Ranulf Higden's *Polychronicon* very closely, but while Ranulf's account of Guthlac's entry into the religious life itself echoes Orderic's formulation, his note of the saint's death is different.[44]

John of Tynemouth was almost certainly a secular clerk, who perhaps held the Yorkshire living of Wheatley and may have received the patronage of Thomas de la Mare, prior of Tynemouth and subsequently abbot of St Albans (1340–9; 1349–96).[45] It is apparent from his great hagiographical compendium, *Sanctilogium*, that he had visited churches in the east and south-west of England and gained access to hagiographical and liturgical texts. Among these was the text of an antiphon for Guthlac which is not known from other sources and which may point to his having visited Crowland, where he would also have found Orderic's *abbreviatio* in the manuscript compilation that is now Douai, Public Library, MS 852.[46] The *Historia aurea* was well received in the Benedictine network between c. 1375 and c. 1400, with copies, epitomes and interpolated revisions found at several of the principal abbeys and priories such as Durham Priory and St Albans, apparently conveying a trace of Orderic, albeit anonymously, to another generation of English monks.[47]

The very close integration of a monastic network formed of social and spiritual affinities and the frequent traffic of men and manuscripts shaped Orderic as a historian (as much as it did William) and sustained the early reception of his work. This was a very particular network, which was not, in fact, coterminous with the upper reaches of the monastic hierarchy. Certainly in England, Orderic was unknown, directly or

---

animam ad perenne gaudium emisit'. While the act of raising his eyes and hands is derived from Felix's *Vita*, chapter 50, the date clause would seem to connect John's version of this scene with Orderic.

[44] *Polychronicon Ranulfi Higden monachi Cestrensis*, ed. C. Babington and J. R. Lumby, Rolls Series 41, 9 vols. (1865–86), VI, p. 166.

[45] Richard Sharpe, *A Handlist of the Latin Writers of Great Britain and Ireland before 1540* (Turnhout, 1997), pp. 333–4; John Taylor, 'Tynemouth, John (fl. c. 1350)', *Oxford Dictionary of National Biography Online* (Oxford, 2004) [http://www.oxforddnb.com/view/article/27466].

[46] For John's research for his *Sanctilogium*, see S. Harper, 'Traces of Lost Late Medieval Offices? The *Sanctilogium Angliae, Walliae, Scotiae et Hiberniae* of John of Tynemouth (fl. 1350)', in *Essays on the History of English Music in Honour of John Caldwell: Sources, Style, Performance, Historiography*, ed. E. Hornby and D. Maw (Woodbridge, 2010), pp. 1–21, at pp. 9, 13. For the Douai manuscript, see *Felix's Life*, pp. 31–41, where it is presented as the tenth in Colgrave's list of manuscripts.

[47] The Durham copy is now Lambeth Palace Library, MSS 10–12. The St Albans copy is now Cambridge, Corpus Christi College, MSS 5–6. See also Sharpe, *Latin Writers*, p. 334.

indirectly through his writings, to any of the energetic convents in the vanguard of the Lanfrancian reform. Rather, this was a network of houses that had come to be linked by a pattern of internal migration which may have run for only two generations (say between the second and third quarters of the twelfth century), and bore some resemblance to the briefly flourishing textual communities formed in an earlier monastic age, of Bede and Aldhelm, Aelfric and Abbo of Fleury. It was an environment already changing by the time of Orderic's death around 1142. The last dispatches of William of Malmesbury himself were of the burning of churches, among them those of Hyde (Winchester) where the Warenne witness to Orderic was, eventually, received.[48] The continual disturbance of routine conventual life during England's anarchy was not experienced in the Norman network, but there were moments of crisis – the devastation of Saint-Évroul by a flash fire in 1136 is one example.[49] There was also a certain institutional instability, signalled in some cases by a succession of superiors of brief tenure in the middle years of the century.[50] There were protracted wrangles over rights, too, played out against the background of Henry II's growing conflict with Alexander III (1159–81): Saint-Étienne de Caen's exempt status was not secured until 1172.[51] The steady advance of the new orders into the region only heightened the tension.[52] That Orderic's 'treatise' on this subject gave voice to an anxiety growing in the network is evident from its audience beyond Saint-Évroul. It might be suggested that the uncertainty – in England, the downright

---

[48] *William of Malmesbury: Historia Novella; The Contemporary History*, ed. E. King, trans. K. Potter, Oxford Medieval Texts (Oxford, 1998), pp. 104–5. In 1146 Crowland was also lost to a fire, which may have consumed much of the material known to Orderic: Hiatt, *Making of Medieval Forgeries*, p. 42.

[49] Nortier, *Les Bibliothèques médiévales*, p. 106.

[50] Saint-Évroul itself had experienced some discontinuities in administration towards the mid-century under an expatriate, peripatetic superior, Richard of Leicester. Generally, the disadvantages of the vigorous exchange of personnel within a close-knit network seem to have been absenteeism on the one hand, or rejection on the other: Abbot Richard was at Thorney, in England, when he died; Abbot Alain of Saint-Wandrille was forced to retreat to Saint-Étienne: Gazeau, *Normannia monastica: Prosopographie*, pp. 49, 285–6.

[51] Hippeau, *L'Abbaye de Saint-Étienne*, pp. 47–52, at pp. 51–2; Gazeau, *Normannia monastica: Prosopographie*, p. 52.

[52] Savigny, whose founder, Vital de Mortain, was a canon of Saint-Évroul, was affiliated to Cîteaux by the middle years of the century; meanwhile, at the time of Orderic's death, the Norbertines (Premonstratensians) were extending their northern French network, not only through *ab ignitio* foundations but also through the conversion of formerly secular chapters. For a brief survey see L. Grant, *Architecture and Society in Normandy, 1120–1270* (New Haven and London, 2005), pp. 22–4.

insecurity – of the monasteries' institutional status encouraged a change in their historical outlook, as a result of which the narration of *res gestae* over the *longue durée* became a secondary priority, while attention shifted to providing proof of rights and origins. For foundations of long standing there was now a greater impulse to pinpoint the principal properties and privileges on which their institution was raised; for recent settlements, amid a cacophony of claim and counter-claim over proprietary rights, it was imperative to secure a single, unequivocal account of their beginnings.

New intellectual currents also encouraged change. In the monasteries of the Anglo-Norman or Angevin heartland the last quarter of the twelfth century has been characterised as a time of 'the coming of the masters', as the tastes, teaching and trained men of the secular schools passed into the principal monasteries in ever greater numbers.[53] As might be expected given the geographical concentration of the schools, there were early signs of an intellectual affinity with the northern French cloisters. Richard of Préaux anticipated the direction of travel early in the century, and in the second quarter, at Bec and then Mont Saint-Michel, Robert of Torigni won the kind of acclaim increasingly associated with schoolmen: 'virum tam divinorum quam secularium librorum inquisitorem'.[54] A new direction for the monks of the mount became unequivocal with the entry of early witnesses to Master Abelard's fresh approach to old authority.[55] Bec itself experienced a sudden cultural shift with the end-of-life profession (in 1164) of Bishop Philippe de Harcourt of Bayeux, who entered with a personal library of 140 books, among them new staples of the emerging school syllabus, such as Gratian's *Decretum*.[56] At Jumièges the intellectual enterprise of the brethren was steadily transformed by Master Alexandre, who entered in 1171 and was raised to the abbacy in 1198. He carried with him the glossed Scriptures and new commentaries – such as those by Peter Lombard and Petrus Comestor – of the school curriculum; as abbot he directed the in-house production of further modish textbooks.[57] Alexandre's abbacy coincided with the

---

[53] R. M. Thomson, *Manuscripts from St Albans Abbey, 1066–1235*, vol. I: *St Albans Abbey* (Cambridge, 1982), p. 44.

[54] W. L. North, 'St Anselm's Forgotten Student: Richard of Préaux and the Interpretation of Scripture in Early Twelfth-Century Normandy', in *Teaching and Learning in Northern Europe, 1000–1200*, ed. S. N. Vaughn and J. Rubenstein (Turnhout, 2006), pp. 171–26; Nortier, *Les Bibliothèques médiévales*, p. 39.

[55] From Mont Saint-Michel, the manuscript Avranches, BM, MS 135 contains a twelfth-century copy of the *Expositio hexameron*; Avranches, BM, MS 12 is an early thirteenth-century witness to *Sic et non*.

[56] Nortier, *Les Bibliothèques médiévales*, pp. 42–4.

[57] Ibid., pp. 149–51. See also G. Nortier-Marchand, 'La Bibliothèque de Jumièges au Moyen Âge', in *Jumièges: Congrès scientifique du XIIIe centenaire, Rouen, 10–12 juin 1954*, 2 vols. (Rouen, 1955), II, pp. 599–614.

great age of monastic masters in England – John de Cella of St Albans (1195–1214) and Alexander Nequam of Colchester (1213–17), among others – and as it ended Lateran IV prescribed a scholastic syllabus as a means of claustral reform. By the second decade of the thirteenth century, a scholastic turn had begun at Orderic's Saint-Évroul, too. Under Abbot Roger de Salmonville (1218–33) there arrived examples of glossed Scriptures and the almost obligatory copy of Comestor's scholastic history; as if in recognition of the convent's shift of emphasis, two of the its benefactors – Master Jean of Saint-Évroul and Master Guillaume de Bucheio – presented the monks with, respectively, a copy of 'totum corpus bibliae glossatum' and the increasingly popular schoolroom companion, the *Catholicon*.[58] The new syllabus, and the new schemes of copying that supplied it, seem to have stifled some of the earlier patterns of compilation; it might also be suggested that the new emphasis on the study of sacred page encouraged a new preference in historiography, with the late antique model of *historia ecclesiastica* being replaced by universal histories founded on biblical history.

While the teaching of the schools increasingly separated these communities from their older traditions of narrative, any residual ties came close to being severed by the close of the thirteenth century. In part this was pure contingency. There were disastrous fires at Bec and Saint-Ouen in 1248 and 1260, respectively, which ravaged their book-collections, among other treasures.[59] The library at Norwich Cathedral Priory was entirely destroyed by fire in 1272.[60] St Albans Abbey sold some of its earliest and most valuable manuscript books, chronicles among them, to settle the debts of two maladroit abbots between 1307 and 1334.[61] While not every house suffered such severe trauma many seem progressively to have loosened their hold over their early narratives and archives: the subsequent re-creation of foundation collections in the later fourteenth and fifteenth century was, at one level at least, a necessary, pragmatic response to a great void which had opened in the institutional record.[62]

For the religious of Orderic's old Norman network the rent in the

---

[58] Nortier, *Les Bibliothèques médiévales*, pp. 109–10.

[59] Ibid., pp. 46, 185.

[60] For the Norwich fire see N. R. Ker, 'Medieval Manuscripts from Norwich Cathedral Priory, *Transactions of the Cambridge Bibliographical Society* 1 (1949–53), 1–28.

[61] The St Albans losses are lamented by Thomas Walsingham in his continuation of the abbey's *Gesta abbatum*: see *Gesta abbatum monasterii sancti Albani*, ed. H. T. Riley, Rolls Series 28, 3 vols. (1864–6), II, p. 200.

[62] Alfred Hiatt has highlighted the impulse of later medieval monastic communities to 'reconnect' with their early, pre- and post-Conquest history not only at Crowland but also at Winchester, Bury St Edmunds and St Augustine's, Canterbury: Hyatt, *Making of Medieval Forgeries*, pp. 42, 51–61.

textual tradition was deepened by the renewal of the Anglo-French war. For eighty years of on-off warfare Saint-Étienne itself escaped serious damage, but conventual life was disrupted by a determined effort to recast the abbey as a military redoubt. Between the disaster of Poitiers (1356) and submission of Normandy (1419), her sister houses were under constant attack. Jumièges was abandoned four times, in 1358, 1370, 1382–3 and 1417.[63] Saint-Évroul was damaged – and conventual life perhaps stalled – in 1361, when a costly rebuild was required; further assaults caused it to be abandoned in 1366 and 1370.[64] Fécamp was pillaged in 1363, and in 1410 English privateers put it to the flame.[65] Even Saint-Étienne did not entirely escape disturbance before 1417, particularly in the decade after the Treaty of Brétigny (1360), under Abbot Guillaume de Harcourt.[66]

This experience did not merely disrupt the monastic life of these places and deprive them of much of the fabric of their past; it would not be an exaggeration to suggest that it projected them into something of an existential crisis. The causes of the war itself, the rival claims to territory and lordship, exposed tensions surrounding the monasteries' seigniorial status which had been largely dormant since the struggles of the Angevins. The coincidence of the papal schism (1378–1417) transposed any particular enquiry over rights into a general question of the relationship between temporal and spiritual jurisdiction; practically it also made either the challenge to, or the defence of, rights very difficult to resolve. The sense of the wider canvas over which the monks' cause necessarily was to be pursued seemed to align their fortunes with those of their royal authority, whose inherited status as founder of monasteries (if not always of their monastery) they remained dimly aware.[67] It has been suggested that interest – among the compilers of chronicle manuscripts – in the piety

---

[63] Hippeau, *L'Abbaye de Saint-Étienne*, p. 108; M. de Frondeville, 'Jumièges et la guerre de cent ans', in *Jumièges: Congrès scientifique du XIIIe centenaire* (Rouen, 1955), pp. 89–94, at pp. 91–3.

[64] '[l'abbaye] a este arse et gastee et detruicte en telle maniere que la dite abbaye inhabitale et lesdits abbe et religieux fuissent dispersees': Jacques Thirion, *Abbaye de Saint-Evroult en Ouche*, Abbeyes et prieures de Normandie 25 (Rouen, 1979), pp. 10–11.

[65] M. de Frondeville, 'L'Abbaye et le port de Fécamp pendant la guerre de cent ans', in *L'Abbaye bénédictine de Fécamp: L'Ouvrage scientifique de XIIIe centenaire, 658–1958*, 3 vols. (Fécamp, 1959–61), pp. 143–9, at pp. 145, 147; Nortier, *Les Bibliothèques médiévales*, pp. 13, 17.

[66] Hippeau, *L'Abbaye de Saint-Étienne*, pp. 112–17.

[67] For the difficult dynamics facing the institutional church in the course of the war see, for example, J. B. Henneman, 'Financing the Hundred Years' War: Royal Taxation in France in 1340', *Speculum* 42:2 (1967), 275–98, at pp. 291–2; C. T. Allmand, 'The English and the Church in Lancastrian Normandy', in *England and Normandy in the Middle Ages*, ed. D. Bates and A. Curry (London, 1994), pp. 287–98, at pp. 293–5.

of the Norman dukes 'faded in [...] late medieval England'.[68] While it may be true that templates of lordship now tended to be fashioned from early English magnates and princes, the ecclesiastical patronage of the Normans remained very much in focus. The identification of monastic readers with the hereditary rights of their monarch was only strengthened, of course, when royal writs required archives to be searched. Although the English houses only rarely suffered direct attack during the war, these lines of thought can be traced through the English monastic network in the fourteenth and fifteenth centuries just as clearly as in Normandy and northern France.[69] Here there was a further contextual influence: the clamour over a new heterodoxy – Lollardy – that was perceived to be spreading widely, and appeared to be fiercely anti-monastic. Such was the concern, that the question of systematic secularisation was raised in the Commons at the very moment that the Crown contemplated an offensive war in 1385 (against Scotland) and again in 1410 (against the French).[70]

The response in both constituencies was to rebuild their historical records. In the first instance, and for most houses for the first time since at least the last quarter of the twelfth century, there was a determined effort to elaborate clearly the basis for their own foundation and their fundamental claim to rights. Perhaps it was at Mont Saint-Michel itself that the early vernacular history of the mount, *Li Romanz du Mont Saint Michel*, was made c. 1340; interestingly, this codex later appears to have passed into English circles, perhaps at the moment that the records of Normandy were capturing the interest of the incomers.[71] Certainly under Abbot Pierre Le Roy (1386–1410), the archival and historical enterprise at Mont Saint-Michel was especially productive: two early fifteenth-century volumes were devoted to the early history of the foundation and its environs; a purchased *Chroniques de Saint-Denys* extended the historical diet.[72] The rare preservation of a sequence of catalogues or inventories from Fécamp makes it possible to trace both the fall and

---

[68] I. Afanasyev, 'An Unrealised Cult? Hagiography and Norman Ducal Genealogy in Twelfth-Century England', *Historical Research* 88 (2015), 193–212, at p. 212 n. 103.

[69] The one notable attack in 1377 was suffered by the Francophone priory at Lewes, whose manor of Rottingdean was burned while the (French) prior was taken hostage. See J. G. Clark, "Cariloco, John de (d. 1396)', *Oxford Dictionary of National Biography Online* (Oxford, 2014) [http://www.oxforddnb.com/view/article/104409].

[70] M. Aston, *Faith and Fire: Popular and Unpopular Religion in England, 1350–1600* (London, 1993), p. 112; G. L. Harriss, *Shaping the Nation: England, 1360–1461*, The New Oxford History of England (Oxford, 2005), pp. 337, 393.

[71] BL, Add. MS 26876.

[72] Avranches, BM, MSS 211, 213. The *Chroniques* is now BnF, MS Fr. 73. See also Nortier, *Les Bibliothèques médiévales*, pp. 76, 87.

rise of the book collection during these years of disturbance: in 1362 the disorder of books – and break-up of a multi-volume manuscript of Vincent of Beauvais' great historical compendium – but in 1400 and 1425 a progressive reorganisation which included, interestingly, the custody of certain volumes in the treasury, presumably to guard against further losses. Among the new accessions of these years was a volume devoted to narratives of Norman history.[73] At Jumièges there was a refreshing of domestic texts in respect of liturgy, but the main focus of new book provisions under the persistent absentee Simon du Bosc (1390–1418) and his successor Nicolas le Roux (1418–31) was to stimulate academic study.[74] Abbot Michel Philippe de Saint-Martin of Saint-Évroul (1408–38) may have hoped for similarly weighty contributions to the convent's recovery, but what he did achieve was again cast into confusion with the late sacking of the house in 1440.[75]

In the English network it seems there was a special effort to recover what had been lost. The broken chain of charters was repaired, and missing cartularies replaced. At Crowland Abbey it would appear that these critical documentary defences were rebuilt from the narrative abstract which had been provided by Orderic two centuries before.[76] It seems to have been this same impulse at Winchester (Hyde) that caused the Warenne narrative to be combined with a later cartulary.[77] The early foundation histories were recovered, recopied and continued: a general return to a common ground of pre- and post-Conquest history is striking in surviving manuscripts from a cross-section of houses. At the same time there was a wider exploration of the origins of monastic foundations, even of the monastic order itself. This is especially marked in the English manuscripts, and it might be seen as the intellectual foundations of a renewed institutional interest in ties to the monastic order across the Channel that was increasingly apparent as the English offensive continued. Several houses seem to have taken the opportunity of occupation to renew

---

[73] Ibid., pp. 14–16, 30. The volume, dating from the fourteenth century, is now Rouen, BM, MS 1233.

[74] Nortier, *Les Bibliothèques médiévales*, pp. 156–7.

[75] The manuscripts surviving from this period point to an effort to reinvigorate mainstream monastic study, such as preparations for academic study in Scripture and theology: Nortier, *Les Bibliothèques médiévales*, p. 111.

[76] Orderic's representation of early charters was reproduced in the late (after 1486) narrative account known as the 'pseudo-Ingulf', preserved in BL, MS Cotton Otho B XIII. Two generations earlier there was also a restatement of foundation history in a continuation of the *Vitae abbatum* which survives in BL, MS Cotton Vespasian B XI. See also Hiatt, *Making of Medieval Forgeries*, pp. 41, 49, 63.

[77] BL, MS Cotton Domitian A XIV, fols. 4r–21r (Warenne); 22r–237r (cartulary). See also *Warenne (Hyde) chronicle*, p. xiv.

both regular communications and the old movements of personnel which had been so much a feature of their twelfth-century connections.[78]

The recovery of the early monastic records was accompanied by the retrieval and renewal of those documents and narratives which outlined the 'heritage' and 'title' of the Crown, to which task, in England at least, the monks were now regularly called by the king's writ. A 'breuis relacio de Guillelmo comiti Normannorum' – perhaps to be identified as the narrative attributed to a monk of Battle – was among the rich holdings of the monks of St Augustine's Canterbury; a genealogy of Norman dukes was acquired by, if not made at, St Mary's Abbey, York.[79] The conjunction of the two is sometimes conspicuous in the compilations that survive, such as the compendium made by Andrew Aston of St Edmundsbury in the closing years of the French war, early in the reign of Henry VI, which contains much important material on his own church together with a self-contained treatise on the origins of the monastic order, a copy of Dudo of Saint-Quentin's *Historia* and a digest of the descent of the English royal claim to the duchies of Aquitaine and Normandy ('Declaratio quomodo ducatus Acquitaniae et Normanniae est ad reges Angliae devolutus').[80] From the inherited rights of their present monarch, it was natural for these monastic readers to reach for their greater narrative heritage. At Durham Priory, Robert Brakenbury took up the convent's precious early copy of William of Jumièges' *Gesta*.[81] A volume catalogued as 'hystoria Normannorum et Anglorum' was among books provided for conventual use at Ramsey Abbey in the middle years of the fourteenth century.[82] At Worcester a new compilation outlining the history of the see and

---

[78] See, for example, the trail of correspondence between Christ Church Cathedral Priory at Canterbury and its contacts in northern France: *Literae Cantuarienses: The Letter Books of the Monastery of Christ Church, Canterbury*, ed. J. B. Sheppard, Rolls Series 85, 3 vols. (1887–9), III, pp. 140–2, 281.

[79] *St Augustine's Abbey, Canterbury*, ed. B. Barker-Benfield, Corpus of British Medieval Library Catalogues 13, 3 vols. (London, 2008), BA1. 1494g, p. 1416. For the Battle narrative see Elisabeth van Houts, 'Brevis relatio de Guillelmo nobilissimo comite Normannorum, written by a monk of Battle Abbey', in *Chronology, Conquest and Conflict in Medieval England*, Camden Society 5th series 10 / Camden Miscellany 34 (1997), pp. 1–48. The York genealogy is now Oxford, Bodleian Library, MS Lyell 17, fol. 52vb.

[80] Now BL, MS Cotton Claudius A XII, fols. 5r–78v (Dudo of Saint-Quentin); fols. 84r–199r (register and miscellany of Andrew Aston). See also *Memorials of St Edmund's Abbey at Bury*, ed. T. Arnold, Rolls Series 96, 3 vols. (1890–6), III, pp. 77–174, at pp. 156–8.

[81] Now BL, MS Harley 491.

[82] *English Benedictine Libraries: The Shorter Catalogues*, ed. R. Sharpe, K. Friis-Jensen, J. P. Carley and A. G. Watson, Corpus of British Medieval Library Catalogues 4 (London, 1996), B68. 21, p. 353.

cathedral priory opened with a 'brevis annotatio regum tam Anglorum quam Normannorum'.[83] It was as another expression of what was clearly a widespread mood in the monastic network that Thomas Walsingham of St Albans made his faux-antique compilation of 'Neustrian' history (down to 1419), *Ypodigma*; there was nothing new in his history, but he was the only one of these readers to see reasons for present caution in the record of the past.[84]

The return to the narrative record of the Anglo-Norman era was not confined to monastic readers. In the early years of renewed conflict the Crown's principal concern was to mobilise the records so as to underpin diplomacy and the repeated efforts to secure a territorially advantageous peace. By the end of the fourteenth century, there were signs in the royal circle of a more focused interest in narrative history. During the Ricardian peace (beginning 1389) the king's uncle Thomas of Gloucester devoted a space in his remarkable library to Norman history.[85] His nephew, Henry of Monmouth, and Henry's brothers were cultivating the same bookish tendency even before the occupation of their old patrimony was assured.[86] King Henry, certainly, did not merely appropriate the materials presented to him but appears to have attached a priority of his own to the Norman past. A copy of Robert's recension of the *Gesta* (F) was among the books he gifted to his Birgittine foundation at Syon; perhaps the 'goodly French book of [...] historie' that was reportedly his only booty from Caen was in fact the *Roman de Rou*.[87] The monks of Caen did not introduce their new master to the narratives of the Anglo-Norman past, but perhaps

---

[83] Now BL, MS Cotton Caligula A X, fols. 197r–200r.

[84] 'Dumque memor fui dierum antiquorum recolens fraudis, facinora factions et sclera commissa per hostes, anxiatas est in me spiritus meus': *Ypodigma Neustriae*, ed. H. T. Riley, Rolls Series 28/7 (1876), p. 4.

[85] Among the 'livres de diverses rymances et destoire' was 'item i livre appellez Neustria sub clipeo ove claspes de laton pris (xx d)': Viscount Dillon and W. H. St John Hope, 'Inventory of the goods and chattels belonging to Thomas, duke of Gloucester, and seized at his castle at Pleshy, co. Essex, 21 Richard II (1397); with their values as shown in the escheator's accounts', *Archaeological Journal* 54 (1897), 285–308, at pp. 300–3 (p. 302). The inventory survives as TNA E136/77/44.

[86] 'libros saepe legens', as one contemporary represented it: Krochalis, 'Books and Reading of Henry V', pp. 50–77, at p. 61. For the conspicuous consumption of books in the Lancastrian circle see also J. J. G. Alexander, 'Painting and Manuscript Illumination for Royal Patrons in the Later Middle Ages,' in *English Court Culture in the Later Middle Ages*, ed. J. W. Sherborne &andV. J. Scattergood (London, 1983), pp. 141–62, at pp. 149–51.

[87] The Syon book is now, Oxford, Bodleain Library, MS Bodley 212. See also *Syon Abbey*, ed. V. Gillespie and A. I. Doyle, Corpus of British Medieval Library Catalogues 9 (London, 2001), p. xxxvi. For the French book, see *First English Life*, ed. Kingsford, p. 92.

their manuscript did persuade him to make a place in them for their own history.[88]

The continuing transmission of Anglo-Norman prose chronicles in these years was not itself a result of this turn, but it was marked by these preoccupations. The so-called 'Mohun chronicle', a family history which traced the descent of the Mohuns from the Conquest and offered a summary of the French royal line, was recopied c. 1340, around the beginning of the war; a copy of the mid-fourteenth-century north of England *Anonimalle* chronicle carried a royal genealogy; a late cartulary of Newenham Abbey (Devon) incorporated a vernacular genealogy of the kings of France.[89] The recovery or renewal of what would have been, for the well-informed monastic and mendicant readers of the later fourteenth and fifteenth centuries, somewhat venerable, or 'classic' narratives in an 'old' vernacular might also be seen as propelled by a sense of their present resonance. Wace's *Roman de Rou* was written out by or for a Carmelite of the London convent; fresh copies of the *Roman de Brut* entered conventual collections, one with the conspicuous relevance of a continuation covering the *gesta* of Edward III.[90]

By the reign of Henry V these narrative interests were also passing into secular clerical and lay reading circles. These were, of course, the same constituencies that staffed the defence and administration of the English domain across the Channel and, after 1435, managed the negotiated withdrawal. That the narratives of Anglo-Norman history had become a staple in the formation of the graduate clerk in fifteenth-century England is signalled by the making of John Norfolk's historical anthology, which combines Dudo of Saint-Quentin and William of Jumièges, at Oxford in 1445; appropriately enough, Norfolk was inaugural subwarden of All Souls College, a new foundation for training a fresh cadre of government servants, and dedicated to the memory of the fallen in the French wars.[91]

---

[88] King Henry also sacked Bec in 1421 and may well have added manuscripts to his growing haul, though nothing as resonant as the Vespasian manuscript is known: Wylie, *Reign of King Henry V*, III, p. 315; Nortier, *Les Bibliothèques médiévales*, p. 49.

[89] J. Spence, *Reimagining History in Anglo-Norman Prose Chronicles* (Woodbridge, 2013), p. 19. See also J. Spence, 'The Mohun Chronicle: An Introduction, Edition and Translation', *Nottingham Medieval Studies* 55 (2011), 149–215. The Mohun chronicle is BL, Add. MS 62929. The *Anonimalle* is now BL, MS Royal 20 A XIII, fol. 150v. The Newenham cartulary is now Oxford, Bodleian Library, MS Top. Devon d. 5, the genealogy at fols. 98v–99r.

[90] The Wace text survives in BL, MS Royal 13 A XVIII, fols. 77r–173r. The *Roman de Brut* is in BL, MS Harley 636 (from Christ Church, Canterbury), and BL, MS Egerton 3028 (with continuation).

[91] The manuscript is now BL, MS Harley 3742, fols. 1r–57v (Dudo); 57v–69r (William of Jumièges), with Norfolk's name at fol. 240v. For Norfolk's

Although the shade of Orderic might seem never to have been very far from the narrative records recovered and renewed in this period, his own writing occupied only a limited space in this enterprise. The Vespasian manuscript presented to Henry V had been prepared for a place in the Lancastrian collection of deluxe books. If it is permissible to reason backward from its apparent presence in Henry VIII's library at Richmond Palace in 1535, then it would seem that not only its material value but also its narrative were sufficiently prized for it to remain at the core of the royal collection for more than a century.[92] It remained in the royal collection when the greater part of that collection was housed at Westminster Palace in 1542, and was among several authorities of early Norman history – a valuable corrective to the view that it was the second generation of post-Reformation antiquarians that recovered the Anglo-Norman era for English readers.[93] It has long been recognised that Henry Tudor's historical imagination self-consciously referenced the Lancastrian conqueror of the previous century, and the Vespasian manuscript affirms the intellectual continuity.[94] It is perhaps most likely that it was at Westminster Palace that an anonymous copyist made a fair copy of the Vespasian manuscript, and was apparently interested enough in its origin (and exemplar) at Saint-Étienne to reproduce the memorable rubric, 'de quodam libro antique monasterii sancti Stephani de Cadomo, cuius monasterii fundator quondam extitit', from its first leaf.[95]

---

career see A. B. Emden, *A Biographical Register of the University of Oxford to AD 1500*, 3 vols. (Oxford, 1957–9), II, p. 1363. Norfolk bequeathed books to All Souls but the Harley manuscript was not among them: N. R. Ker, *Records of All Souls College Library*, Oxford Bibliographical Society new series 16 (1971), pp. 215–16.

[92] The manuscript is inventorised as 'vita et gesta ducum Normannorum': *The Libraries of Henry VIII*, ed. J. P. Carley, Corpus of British Medieval Library Catalogues 7 (London, 2000), H1. 113, p. 27.

[93] For this view see van Houts, 'Camden, Cotton and the Chronicles of the Norman Conquest', pp. 149–50. The other Norman narratives in the royal collection at Westminster in 1542 were Robert of Torigni's *Chronica* (a twelfth-century manuscript, now BL, MS Royal 13 C XI, acquired from the hospital of St Thomas, London) and one, perhaps two, copies of Dudo of Saint-Quentin: *Libraries of Henry VIII*, ed. Carley, H2. 1033; H2. 226; H2. 720, pp. 64, 184.

[94] For an account of this imaginative attachment, and direct imitation, of the conqueror of Normandy, see L. Wooding, *Henry VIII*, 2nd edn (London, 2015), pp. 22–3, 28–9; S. J. Gunn, 'The French Wars of Henry VIII', in *The Origins of War in Early Modern Europe*, ed. J. Black (Edinburgh, 1987), pp. 28–51; C. S. L. Davies, 'Henry VIII and Henry V: The Wars in France', in *The End of the Middle Ages? England in the Fifteenth and Sixteenth Centuries*, ed. J. L. Watts (Stroud, 1998), pp. 235–62.

[95] The manuscript is formed of two quires, of which only one contains the 'Caen' copy. It is now London, College of Arms, MS 38. See also W. H.

This reproduction points to a renewed demand for this narrative history, perhaps stimulated by the reopening of the war in 1541.

The signs of continuing interest in the narrative record are stronger here than in the monastic context. The recovery of the French houses after the restoration of the monarchy was institutional not intellectual. The advancing influence of the reformed Benedictine unions in the second half of the fifteenth century was felt in the old Norman network, but not deeply enough to reinvigorate conventual life. The preparation of a fresh copy of the 'partes Vitalis' at Saint-Évroul was perhaps not the symbol of intellectual reformation that it might first appear, since it seems to have been one of a number of actions required of the convent by its episcopal visitor – among them the rebuilding of the library precisely because a proper pattern of education and formation had not been able to prosper under the commendatory abbot Felix de Brie.[96] Yet this was wholly typical of the reception of Orderic's work in the four centuries since his death. In a mutable environment for monastic religion, his great *opus* continued to be recognised as a potent statement of the place and purpose of monastic society in the wider realm.

Black, *Catalogue of the Arundel Manuscripts in the College of Arms* (London, 1829), p. 65.

[96] Nortier, *Les Bibliothèques médiévales*, pp. 112–13. See also Chibnall, 'General Introduction', pp. 115, 122.

Appendix 1

Archaeological Investigations at the Abbey of Saint-Évroult-Notre-Dame-des-Bois

Anne-Sophie Vigot

IN recent decades, much scholarly interest has been devoted to the abbey of Saint-Évroult-Notre-Dame-du-Bois, rescuing from oblivion its ruins which seemed to have been lost in the Pays d'Ouche. Before being subject to archaeological excavations carried out between 1998 and 1999, essentially, the majority of studies focused on the history of the abbey and its foundation. Much of this was concerned to record the accomplishments of its founding saint, Évroul. Chibnall's translation of Orderic's *Historia ecclesiastica* provides most of our knowledge on the history of the monastery.[1] No detailed architectural survey was carried out until the mid-twentieth century, when the complex was recorded as a 'Monument Historique'.[2] Nevertheless, this research remained imprecise, since it concentrated only on the buildings still standing. The insight that V. Hincker brought to the analysis of the conventual buildings, which have long-since disappeared, is essential to our understanding of the organisation of the abbey and the life of its monks.[3] The items found in the survey that he made of the chapter-house allow us not only to place the architecture of this building within a movement of Norman Gothic reconstruction, but also to understand the function of the room itself, which seems to have enjoyed a privileged role in the life of the community.

By the end of Hincker's research in 1999, two thirds of the chapter-house remained unexamined. New excavations carried out in 2013 and 2014 have allowed us to answer some of the outstanding questions concerning the plan of this room. In order to better understand the interest and objectives of such an investigation, it is appropriate to revisit the origins of, and various modifications made to, the abbey. It will be

---

Translated from the original French by Charles C. Rozier and Giles E. M. Gasper.

---

[1] HE.

[2] Ministère de l'éducation nationale: Beaux-arts, Inventaire supplémentaire des Monuments Historiques, 27 July 1927.

[3] V. Hincker, 'Saint-Évroult-Notre-Dame-du-Bois "Abbaye d'Ouche" (Orne), Document final de synthèse: Histoire de l'abbaye et étude analytique des vestiges, I, II, sites no. 61386001 A. H.; Rapport des fouilles du 15/07 au 15/11/1999' (Caen, 1999).

necessary to evaluate existing research, before exploring the issues of the project and presenting the archaeological investigation itself.

The abbey of Saint-Évroul is found in the département of Orne in the municipality of Saint-Évroult-Notre-Dame-du-Bois, midway between towns of L'Aigle and Gacé. At the heart of the Ouche forest and an important river network, the geographical environment was suitable for the foundation of a community. Orderic Vitalis is the principal historian of this abbey, and with just title, since he spent the greater part of his life there between the end of the eleventh century and beginning of the twelfth. He tells us that in the seventh century A.D., Évroul, a monk of Bessin, established a small community in the forest of Ouche and introducing Christianity there. This community installed and developed itself in such a way as to endure and eventually become one of the most important abbeys in the medieval world.[4]

Little is known of the community's development following the death of its founder in 706, until the ninth century. The charter of confirmation signed by Charles the Simple in 900 firmly attests its continued existence.[5] In the ninth and tenth centuries the monks were replaced by a group of canons, which enabled the survival of the community. In the tenth century the abbey suffered from the territorial disputes involving the duchy of Normandy and royal power.

At the beginning of the eleventh century the lords of the region began to restore the building.[6] This sudden attraction to the abbey is part of a revival of ecclesiastical politics in the duchy of Normandy during the tenth and eleventh centuries.[7] The political situation of the duchy stabilised, and Duke William took advantage of the existing religious harmony to ensure equilibrium.[8] The prosperity of the monastery between the eleventh and fourteenth centuries was due, essentially, to its financial and intellectual wealth; monetary wealth came from the donations made in honour of the return of the relics of St Évroul and other saints, and cultural wealth as a result of the abbey's important scriptorium. It was just after this first restoration that Orderic Vitalis was sent to Saint-Évroul. He then participated actively in the intellectual life of the monastery. During this

---

[4] Orderic's account of the early community appears in *HE*, III, pp. 264–343.

[5] Alençon, BM, MS 14, fols. 38r–v, discussed in *HE*, III, p. 322 n. 2. For a French translation, see: 'Traduction de la charte de Charles le Simple', in *Vies des saints dans le diocèse de Sées et histoire de leur culte* (L'Aigle, 1873), I, p. 522–616, at p. 557.

[6] *HE*, II, pp. 12–21; J. Thiron, *Abbayes et prieurés de Normandie: Abbaye de Saint-Évroult-en-Ouche (Orne)*, Année des Abbayes Normandes 25 (Rouen, 1980), pp. 5–6.

[7] V. Gazeau, 'Recherches sur l'histoire de la principauté normande (911–1204)', Habilitation à diriger les recherches, vol. I, présenté devant l'université Paris I-Panthéon-Sorbonne (2002), p. 264.

[8] Ibid.

Appendix 1: Archaeological Investigations at Saint-Évroul

Fig. 1 Aerial view of the monastic church of Saint-Évroul, showing the excavations from 2014 on the site of the chapter-house

period of growth the abbey changed and followed the architectural fashion of the time. In this way large-scale rebuilding was instigated over the course of the thirteenth century.

The influence of the monastery decreased with the Hundred Years War, after which the monks had to adapt to and adopt reform from Cluny, and then in the early modern period the Maurist reforms.[9] The fifteenth century saw the start of the harmful era of commendatory abbots. The abbey, which fell victim to a fire in the sixteenth century, found its rescue in the arrival of monks from Saint-Maur in the seventeenth century.[10] The Revolution marked the final point in the foundation's already precarious existence. After having experienced four phases of restoration (in the eleventh century, the thirteenth century, after the Hundred Years War and

---

[9] L. de la Sicotière and A. Poulet-Malassis, *Le Département de l'orne archéologique et pittoresque, par une société d'antiquaires et d'archéologues*, ed. J.-F Beuzelin (Alençon, 1845), p. 93.

[10] Ibid., pp. 93–4.

before the Revolution), of which three were phases of total reconstruction, the buildings of the community in Ouche disappeared almost entirely.

Already from the beginning of the nineteenth century scholars were interested in Saint-Évroul. They published reports of their visits in journals published for local audiences.[11] At the same time public awareness was gradually growing. At Saint-Évroul there was a desire to preserve the monument and to conduct archaeological excavations.[12] The first archaeological explorations were carried out by Mr Metayer-Masselin, who completed research on the chapter-house on 27 October 1879.[13]

The excavation methods were far removed from current methods. The surveys proved, for the most part, to confuse the information. The north–south trenches made in the chapter-house are a case in point. These trenches totally disrupted the stratigraphy of the location to the depth of more than a metre. These primitive archaeological investigations continued at the beginning of the twentieth century, but they did not provide precise reports, which limits their usefulness.

The abbey was classified as a 'Monument Historique' on 17 January 1967. This ensured that the clearing operations, and any subsequent investigations among the ruins, would be better supervised. The only existing study which allows for a reproduction of the complete plan of the abbey was undertaken by V. Hincker between 1998 and 1999. The three objectives of these investigations were: to clear the remaining ruins of the abbey, to compile an inventory of stone blocks from the ruins, and to establish seven surveys to allow the organisation of the conventual buildings to be reconstructed. In 2003–5, my own MA dissertation focused on the chapter-house of the abbey.[14] This research made it possible to synthesise all the historiographical information pertaining to the abbey of Saint-Évroul, to use the results obtained in previous excavations, and to highlight the architectural reconstruction of the chapter-house. Anthropological methods have developed a different aspect from that of architecture, in casting the space as a place of burial. It is necessary to understand the occupation of the ground, and to know who was buried there.

A number of questions have featured prominently in previous discussions of the Saint-Évroul chapter-house. Notable among these

---

[11] See, for example, F. Galeron, 'Promenade aux ruines du monastère de Saint-Évroult (Orne)', *Révue normande* 1:2 (1831), 172–86; E. A. Freeman, *Sketches of Travel in Normandy and Maine*, ed. W. H. Hutton (London, 1897), pp. 154–67.

[12] A-L. Letacq 'Les Souvenirs de l'abbaye de Saint-Évroult', *Bulletin des Amis des monuments ornais* 3(1903), p. 85.

[13] Hincker, 'Saint-Évroult-Notre-Dame-du-Bois "Abbaye d'Ouche"', p. 100.

[14] A.-S. Vigot, *La Salle capitulaire de l'abbaye de Saint-Évroult-Notre-Dame-du-Bois: L'Apport de l'archéologie*, Mémoire de maîtrise d'histoire, sous la direction de C. Hanusse, 2 vols. (2005).

is whether the original structure was a model of particularly Norman building styles. The architectural elements uncovered during different archaeological operations date from the thirteenth and fourteenth centuries, and are contemporaneous with the abbey church. The room was constructed in the gothic style, and whether from its position (situated against the south transept of the abbey church), or quite simply by its rectangular shape, which follows a west–east orientation, it appears to adhere to the model of construction followed in Normandy at that time. A comparison with other Norman abbeys in which the chapter-house would have been reconstructed in the same period allows the chapter-house at Saint-Évroul to be associated with the model followed by Fontaine-Guérard, Jumièges, Plessis-Grimoult, Saint-Georges-de-Boscherville and Hambye. Above all, there are strong similarities with the chapter-house at the abbey of Saint-Pierre-sur-Dives, principally concerning the layout: in both locations the chapter-house had two separate naves of three central pillars, dividing the chapter into six bays.

The 2013–14 excavations paid particular attention to the construction of the room, which inscribes the importance of this space within the monastery. According to the *Rule of St Benedict*, the chapter-house was the place where the monks spent most of their time together. Two functions seem intended for it: it was a privileged meeting-place, and an important living space. It must be noted as well that the leading figures who came to stay in the abbey were received there, for the chapter-house was one of the few parts of the monastery which such guests could enter. The chapter-house had to do honour to the monks, since it reflected the abbey as a whole.

A privileged meeting place among the living, the chapter-house seems to have had a similar function after death. Funerary and anthropological analysis suggests that the chapter-house was commonly used as a place of burial for at least two centuries (thirteenth and fourteenth), and undoubtedly in other periods too. The number of graves found in the small area excavated indicates clearly that a very large part of the underground space must have been occupied by burials. Other places in the monastery were also used as burial space, but the materials exhumed in the trenches excavated in 1999 have shown that particular attention was given to the graves of the chapter-house. The consistency of funerary practices, namely burial in wooden nailed coffins, suggests that these burials were subject to very particular rituals. These practices are sober but deeply devout. Burials with grave goods are found in just two places: the chapter-house itself, and the eastern gallery of the cloister, that is to say, close to the chapter-house entrance.

Initial anthropological study of a small sample of the chapter-house burials indicated that the individuals were relatively elderly, and all men. That might reflect a traditional monastic population, but more advanced anthropological and paleopathological analysis revealed the probability that lay men, women and children were also buried among the monks and abbots. Evidence indicating the health of these individuals is an important element in establishing the privileged status of those buried in the chapter-house of Saint-Évroul.

It seems, therefore, that the notions of a privileged burial place and of a privileged population are connected in this context. It can be presumed that, for the most part, burial in the chapter-house was reserved for individuals of a certain rank who had made significant donations. This study, made on the basis of a limited sample-size merits in-depth investigation of the issue after a more exhaustive survey of the room.

The investigations begun in 2013 had several objectives. The first was to interpret the nature of the remains from before the foundation of the thirteenth-century building. The structures in counter-relief along with the graves could be assessed. It does not seem that the excavated structures from the trench made in 1999 in the chapter-house could correspond to a previous chapter. It would be helpful to confirm or deny this, and to establish with what else the layout might correspond. An earlier funerary space is certainly present, and could be part of the monks' cemetery of the eleventh and twelfth centuries.

It was important to identify potential models for the chapter-house building at Saint-Évroul. In 1969 Beck carried out a study listing the architectural characteristics of the known Norman chapter-houses, classifying them into two categories: French or Norman.[15] On the basis of an engraving of the abbey from the *Monasticon Gallicanum*, Beck suggested that the chapter-house at Saint-Évroul belonged to the French model.[16] Nevertheless, the first reconstruction of the plan of the chapter-house, made in 2005, leaves the suggestion that this is a misinterpretation of the engraving.

A brief overview of research concerning the chapter-houses of existing abbeys shows that that very few of them have been excavated comprehensively. More than 180 monasteries are listed (and the list is

---

[15] Bernard Beck, 'Recherches sur les salles capitulaires en Normandie, notamment dans les diocèses d'Avranche, Bayeux et Coutances', *Bulletin de la société des Antiquaires de Normandie* 58 (1965–66), Société des Antiquaires de Normandie, Archives du Calvados, Route de Lion-sur-Mer (Caen, 1969), 7–126. Beck drew on Dom M. Germain (bénédictin de la Congrégation de Saint-Maur 1645–1694), *Le monasticon Gallicanum: collection de 168 planches de vues topographiques des monastères bénédictins de la Congrégation de Saint-Maur; avec deux cartes des établissements de l'Ordre de Saint-Benoit*, overseen by M. Peigné-Delacourt, preface by Léopold Delisle (Paris, 1882), [168 engravings].

[16] Dom M. Germain, *Monasticon gallicanum: Collection de 168 planches de vues topographiques, représentant les Monastères de l'Ordre de Saint-Bénoit, Congrégation de Saint Maur; avec deux Cartes des Établissements Bénédictins en F.*, overseen by M. Peigné-Delacourt, preface by M. L. Delisle (Paris, 1871).

not exhaustive), in Basse- and Haute-Normandie and neighbouring departments of Orne, Sarthe, Mayenne and Eure-et-Loir.[17] Of these, around thirty have received partial excavations or straightforward surveys, of which nine have seen a partial or comprehensive exploration of the chapter-house. The most recent detailed excavation of a chapter-house is that of the abbey Saint-Germain-la-Blanche-Herbe (Ardenne) made in the 1980s. Few of the 180 monasteries belonged to the same monastic order as Saint-Évroul. As such, it was deemed sensible to compare the surviving practices from one congregation to another.

The principal objective of the anthropological study conducted following the work of 1998–9 concerning the people buried in the chapter-house of Saint-Évroul was to try to identify the status or the social origin of those persons who lay beneath the ruins. The conclusions resulting from the study of a third of the people indicated that it was a mixed population of individuals who had known above-average living standards. The chapter-house was, without doubt, for this period the burial place of a privileged group, both lay and ecclesiastical. A comprehensive excavation of the whole group might support these observations.

The conference 'Pots in the Grave, Ninth to Eighteenth Centuries: Different Perspectives on a Funerary Practice in Western Europe', organised by CRAHAM for 30–1 May 2012, made it possible to compile a national inventory of discoveries in the discipline. The first graves in the chapter-house of Saint-Évroul contained at least ninety-four individual ceramic pieces, according to a minimum count of individual pieces. These elements came from fourteen graves and a jumbled ossuary, showing evidence of funerary deposits accompanying the deceased. Comprehensive excavation of the chapter-house would allow the completion of the catalogue, so as to glimpse more clearly their distribution.

Although the site has been classed as a historical monument since 17 January 1967, over the years the ruins have continued to degrade and suffer from lack of care. It was hoped that by developing a programme of new research on this abbey, interest among the different local and national stakeholders would be rekindled, in order to emphasise the value this monastery that was one of the most flourishing centres of monastic life in Normandy during the Middle Ages.

The area excavated in 2013 was approximately 200 m², already partially explored in its central third by a trench dug from east to west in 1999. In order to conduct a comprehensive excavation of the room a project of about four years' duration was planned. The first year was given over to the restoration of this part of the site (clearing the undergrowth, removing the architectural blocks stored since the last archaeological activity on the site of the chapter-house, etc.), then to a comprehensive excavation on

---

[17] Vigot A.-S., *La Salle capitulaire de l'abbaye de Saint-Évroult-Notre-Dame-du-Bois (61)*, Rapport final d'opération: fouille programmée, Service régional d'archéologie de Basse-Normandie (2014), p. 38.

the plan of the ground levels and the walls surrounding the building, and finally a topographical summary of the site. At the end of this activity, a preliminary assessment on the state of conservation of the remains could be made. It was also possible to respond to the issue concerning the architectural plan of the room.

Significant disruptions have changed the landscape of the abbey site since its abandonment after the Revolution. Through punitive excavation, exploration or re-use of the abandoned space, the sub-soil of the vanished chapter-house has been disturbed. An important trench made during the excavations of 1999 penetrates the room from east to west. This trench came to re-cut four parallel sections in a perpendicular fashion, very probably from the 'excavations' carried out in the nineteenth century. These piercings have disrupted almost all soil levels, medieval and modern. In addition, a consequent distortion of the walls, and even of their foundation levels, can be noted. It seems, nevertheless, that the major part of the funerary levels were conserved.

At the end of the 1999 activities it was possible to produce a proposal for architectural reconstruction. The 1999 discovery *in situ* of the essentials of the walls and masonry structures (for example, wall columns and central piers) confirmed the reconstruction initially proposed. The chapter-house at Saint-Évroul was, then, a rectangular room oriented west–east, adjoining the south transept of the church, consisting of two aisles divided into four bays each. The internal dimensions are 9m in width by 14.6m in length. The foundations are thick, between 2.6m wide for the eastern and western walls, and 2.3m for the south wall. The foundations reached 1.45m in depth on the south wall. Three central piers separate the two aisles. Their foundation, unevenly preserved, is rectangular in shape with dimensions of approximately 1.5 to 1.75m by 2m. These piers should have supported round arches, which then rested on wall columns, placed opposite. The wall columns still in place against the elevation of the north wall, find their counterparts in the foundation trench of the south wall.

This ceiling must have supported the dormitory located above. The discovery in 2013–14 of two walls extending perpendicular to the room towards the south, one beginning from the centre of the south wall of the chapter-house, indicates that another building was joined to it, and, in particular, that the floor cannot have covered the entirety of the space. Indeed, it seems that the eastern part of the chapter-house was freestanding to the east and articulated towards the exterior of the abbey. Two buttresses were identified on the eastern façade of the chapter-house. One is located in the centre of the wall and must have functioned as a support; the second is a double buttress, reinforcing the south-east corner of the room.

Although they have greatly disturbed the site, the numerous recovery trenches have produced a large number of pieces of stonework, elements of architectural terracotta, and even stained glass. The layers of paint from the stonework suggest the room was painted with stripes of white, yellow and red. The numerous floor tiles recovered indicate an interesting variety of decoration, ranging from floral motifs to geometric shapes, as well as mythological and animal figures. This heterogeneous collection, together with fragments of a flat grave, indicate that this ground must have been put together from the stoneware of numerous re-openings, linked to funerary practices. These artefacts also give clues to the different periods of reconstruction in the chapter-house. Taking into account those elements still in place, and the historiographical information, it seems that the walls date from the thirteenth century. The dormitory, however, appears to have collapsed, and was rebuilt at different times. In this way, the elements of the vaults confirm a restoration of the chapter-house ceiling towards the end of the Middle Ages. Similarly, the typology of stained glass suggests a restoration of the windows during the Maurist period.

The excavation of 2014 confirmed these first observations and allowed the chapter-house to be contextualised in relation to the neighbouring buildings. In addition, these subsequent investigations provided an enhanced picture of the funerary space.

Two openings made to the west and south of the chapter-house situated the room within the context of the abbey and the monastic life carried out within these buildings. The western opening revealed the presence of the cloister gallery. Although the soil was disturbed and the tiles are no longer in place, the construction levels of this soil and the funeral levels are intact. It was possible to excavate a tomb dating from the thirteenth century, which held the body of an adult male subject, in primary position, interred in a coffin, accompanied by incense pots. The west of the gallery is bordered by the foundation of the low wall supporting columns opening onto the cloister. This foundation is 1.7m in width. A gutter of stone construction runs along the wall. It is 0.3m wide. To the south, a room is attached to the chapter-house; its western wall is a continuation of that from the chapter-house. This building, oriented north–south, is approximately 8.5m wide in its internal dimensions. An opening in the eastern wall of this building seems discernable; would this overlook a furnished exterior space?

As far as the chapter-house is concerned, further investigations provide new information on the chronology of construction. It would seem that the foundations of the walls could in fact date from the eleventh century, as the contemporary graves are radio-carbon dated to this period. This information completes the phasing identified in 2013. An earlier wall of the chapter-house, oriented from south-west to north-east, was identified in the north-eastern corner of the room. It is likely that this was a construction linked to the earlier abbey of the eleventh century.

The excavation conducted in 1999 revealed the presence of sixteen medieval tombs in the equivalent of one third of the chapter-house, which indicates a significant density of occupation. Though the trenches dug in the nineteenth-century greatly disrupted the soil levels of the chapter-house, the discovery of several graves at the bottom of these recovery trenches indicates that funeral levels have not been completely affected. The excavation of a third of the remaining space revealed at least three phases of occupation for the sepulchral space. The first occupation dates from the eighth century, being from the foundation of the monastery by the monk Évroul; a second complex could be contemporaneous with the first permanent construction of the chapter-house during the eleventh century; and, finally, the most recent graves could date from the thirteenth to the fourteenth centuries. It is difficult to know the context of the first group, but, nevertheless, their presence suggests that the original monastic foundation, which until this point had been very difficult to localise, must have occupied the same location as the current ruins. The campaigns to come will enable excavation of the rest of the funerary complex and perhaps further knowledge of the earlier occupation

The remains of the chapter-house that are visible today could be contemporary to the time of Orderic Vitalis, who described so fully the life within its walls. The earlier funerary occupation allows the suggestion that the earliest abbey must be located in the same place. The results of these excavations indicated that further archaeological investigations are necessary in order to respond to the unresolved issues. This gave rise to a successful application for authorisation to excavate, in Autumn 2014, for three years (2015–17).

The task for the 2015–16 campaigns is to excavate the whole funerary space present in the chapter-house and in the adjoining cloister-gallery. The lower level of the chapter-house has been divided into three sections, stretching from west to east. At the time of writing, the east and west sections are still to be explored. It is expected that there will be around fifty identifiable graves, and the remains of around eighty identifiable individuals (given that graves often contain the bodies of more than one person, or the remains of other, more ancient, burials). Having removed the levels on which people used to walk, the earliest levels are now partially visible, and seem to correspond to a funerary occupation contemporary to the period of Évroul. These levels will be explored at the same time as the burials. Finally, the last year, 2017, could give rise to a geophysical survey allowing the identification of the existing abbey buildings. Following from these last campaigns, a complete analysis of grave furnishings will remain important; even though context-less, the majority of artefacts discovered on the site provide valuable information on its evolution, the decoration of the room and its modifications.

Appendix 2

Descriptive Catalogue of Manuscripts Featuring the Hand of Orderic Vitalis

Jenny Weston and Charles C. Rozier

THE principal discussions of manuscripts featuring Orderic's hand to date are those listed in works by Léopold Delisle, Marjorie Chibnall and Denis Escudier.[1] The following appendix aims to provide a more detailed picture of the precise nature and locations of Orderic's contributions within the surviving manuscript corpus, including the addition of Rouen, Bibliothèque municipale, MS 540, as discussed by Weston, above. The manuscripts are listed according to institution. Each entry contains the shelfmark, approximate date of production, dimensions, total number of folia, textual contents, as well as a brief description of Orderic's contribution with precise folia numbers.

1 Alençon, Bibliothèque municipale, MS 1

(1100–1200; 300×192 mm; 148 fols.; Old Testament book of *Prophets*, with prologue of St Jerome)

Fols. 30v–32v: Orderic added three poems or hymns; one on the transient nature of worldly glory, one penitential piece, and one litany.

All three pieces are presented in a uniform format, with the text in two columns and with green and red capitals at the beginning of each line. Indications of pitch were added to the first three lines of the text beginning '*Mundi forma*' on fol. 30v, though it is almost impossible to know whether Orderic was responsible for these.[2]

Either Orderic or another scribe with a very similar hand revised or corrected the first poem at a later date. This is shown by the erasure of previous text and the addition of new lines in a much darker ink on fol. 30v, at: col. 1, lines 26–7; col. 2, lines 15 and 17; col. 2, lines 19–20.

---

[1] Delisle, 'Matériaux'; M. Chibnall, 'Manuscripts copied or annotated by Orderic', in *HE*, I, pp. 201–3; D. Escudier, 'L'œuvre entre les lignes d'Orderic Vital', in *Le livre au Moyen Age*, ed. Jean Glenisson (Turnhout, 1988), pp. 193–5; Escudier,'Orderic Vital et le scriptorium'.

[2] On this possibility, see Escudier, 'L'œuvre entre les lignes'.

The third poem may be incomplete. While the main text ends a quarter of the way down the page, coloured capitals were added to the remaining space but with no additional text. These coloured capitals have been either much damaged or partly erased.

References

Delisle, 'Matériaux', pp. 497–500
HE, I, p. 202
Escudier, 'L'œuvre entre les lignes'
Escudier, 'Orderic et le scriptorium', pp. 24, 26–7

(C. Rozier)

2 Alençon, Bibliothèque municipale, MS 6

(1100–1200; 325×235 mm; 161 fols.; compendium of Gregory's *Homilies on Ezechiel*; numerous saints' *Lives* and miracle-stories)

Fols. 134r–140v: Orderic copied the whole of the prose narrative *Life* of St Launomar.

Fol. 143v: Orderic began the accompanying verse *Life* of Launomar, before temporarily handing over to other scribes on fols. 144v–145r, and again at 145v (at which point another scribe finishes the remainder of the text).

Fols. 150r–151v: Orderic also copied sections of the *Passion* of SS Nereus and Achilles. He began the text, adding the title and *incipit*, and completed the whole of the first page. A different scribe copied the text on fols. 151v–162, with Orderic adding rubrics (for examples, see fols. 152v–153r, 154r), *incipits* (see the opening of the *Passion* of St Peregrine, fol. 155v), *explicits* (fol. 156v), as well as one marginal correction (fol. 156r).

References

Delisle, 'Matériaux', pp. 500–2
HE, I, p. 202
Escudier, 'Orderic et le scriptorium', p. 27

(C. Rozier)

3 Alençon, Bibliothèque municipale, MS 14

(900–1200; 290×200 mm; 156 fols.; miscellany of various saints' *Lives* and miracle-stories)

Fols. 12r–19r: Orderic copied the whole of the *Life* of St Willibrord.

Fols. 19r–23r: Orderic copied a sermon and a verse *Life* of Willibrord by Alcuin.

Fols. 23r–43v: Orderic copied the main text of Wolstan's prose *Life* of St Æthelwold, including a chapter list at the beginning and chapter-headings throughout.

Fols. 34v–36r: Orderic copied a hymn and office of St Æthelwold.

Fols. 36r–37r: Orderic copied a hymn of St Birin.

Fol. 37r–v: Orderic copied a hymn on St Swithun.

Fol. 38r–v: Orderic copied Charles the Simple's diploma for the first monastery at Saint-Évroul.

Orderic also made marginal annotations to Amalarius's *De officiis* and rubricated the main text (for examples, see fols. 51v, 56v, 58v, 61r, 72r, 80r).

Fol. 85r: Orderic copied the first section of the *Passion* of St Christina (of Bolsena?). He also added the *explicit* on fol. 89v, as well as the *incipit* for the following text.

Fols. 109r–110v: Orderic copied the *incipit* and the first section of a text on the judicial ordeal, titled 'Ordo ad iudicium faciendum', and then completed the end section on fol. 115r–v.

Orderic copied sections of a *Life* of St Germain, including fols. 116r and 116v (lines 1–5, 24–5 and 34–7), and rubricated the whole text (fols. 116r–131r). He also added a marginal note highlighting the revelation of Germain's holiness on fol. 131r.

Fol. 138r: Orderic copied the first part of an account of the translation of St Martin, copied the majority of fol. 140r, wrote lines 1–18 on fol. 140v, and added the end of the text on the passions of SS Sergius and Bacchus from fols. 150r–156r. He also rubricated and corrected this text (see, for example, fols. 142r, 143r–v, 145v).

References

HE, I, p. 202
Delisle, 'Matériaux', pp. 502–3
Wulfstan of Winchester, *The Life of St Æthelwold*, ed. and trans. M. Lapidge and M. Winterbottom (Oxford, 1991), pp. cxiii–cxviii

(C. Rozier)

4 Alençon, Bibliothèque municipale, MS 26

(1100–1200; 355×265 mm; 190 fols.; miscellany of Bible commentaries)

Fols. 36v–91r: Orderic's handwriting can be found in various places throughout Bede's commentary on Ezra. He copied portions of the main text (last five lines of fol. 37r, column 2, the last three lines of fol. 59v, and fols. 68v–70r). He was responsible for marginal notes on fols. 65v and 88r. Orderic also added various rubrics and *incipit/explicit* headings (see fols. 36v, 48v, 62r, 78r). On fol. 82v he copied the first part of the text around the initial. Marginal and in-text corrections can also be found on fols. 39r, 45r, 65v, 68r, 82r, 88r and 90v.

Fols. 91r–190r: Orderic copied, corrected, and added sections to Anselm of Laon's commentary on St Matthew's Gospel ('*Expositio ex diversis auctoribus a domino Ansello laudunensis philosopho exquisitissimo collecta*').[3]

Orderic was responsible for copying the main text on fols. 110v–118r and 135r–190v. He added corrections and marginal notes to the following: fols. 99v, 100r–102r, 122r, 127r, 130r, 132v, 133r, 134r.

References

HE, I, p. 202
Delisle, 'Matériaux', pp. 503–4

(C. Rozier)

5 Oxford, St John's College, MS 17

(1100–10; 340×250 mm; 177 fols.; miscellany of computistical treatises, diagrams and tables from Thorney Abbey)

Fol. 21v: Orderic made a single note within a calendar. He recorded the feast of St Évroul in the space for 4 Kalends January with the note: 'Hic sup(er) astra pius conscendit pastor ebrulfus'.

References

HE, I, p. 203
The Calendar and the Cloister: Oxford, St John's College MS17 (2007), McGill University Library Digital Collections Program <http://digital.library.mcgill.ca/ms-17> [accessed August 2014]

(C. Rozier)

---

[3] B. Smalley raises some issue with the attribution of this text to Anselm of Laon, citing this manuscript. See Beryl Smalley, *The Gospels in the Schools, c. 1000–c. 1280* (London, 1985), p. 15.

6 Paris, Bibliothèque nationale de France, MS Latin 5506, I

(1123–41; 234×140 mm; 195 fols.; Orderic Vitalis, *Historia ecclesiastica*, Prologue and Books I and II)

This is Orderic's autograph copy of the *Historia ecclesiastica*, containing the Prologue and Books I and II. Orderic copied the main text for the entire volume, supplied the rubrication and initials (some of which are decorated with penwork motifs), and added various corrections in the margins.

Unlike other examples of his work, Orderic used a larger minuscule script for the *incipit* headings of each section (as opposed to capitals or uncials). For instance, see the opening of Book I (fol. 7r).

Orderic's rather unusual paragraph mark is present throughout the volume (for examples, see fols. 8v, 138r and 141r).

References

HE, I, pp. 118–21 and 201
Escudier, 'Orderic Vital et le scriptorium', pp. 19–21 and 27
Delisle, 'Notice', pp. xciii–xciv
Delisle 'Matériaux', pp. 486–9

(J. Weston)

7 Paris, Bibliothèque nationale de France, MS Latin 5506, II

(1123–41; 235×145 mm; 200 fols.; Orderic Vitalis, *Historia ecclesiastica*, Books III–VI)

This is Orderic's autograph copy of the *Historia ecclesiastica*, Books III–VI. It is likely that the vast majority of the book was copied by Orderic himself, though some sections may have been added by a scribe with remarkably similar handwriting. Chibnall, for example, suggests that fols. 1r–20r were written in a hand similar to Orderic's, but probably not his own. (See Chibnall, *HE*, I, pp. xxxix–xl and p. 118 n. 2.) Orderic provided the rubrication and initials throughout.

For examples of Orderic's paragraph mark, see fols. 30r, 35r, 36r and 91v.

References

HE, I, pp. 118–21 and 201
Escudier, 'Orderic et le scriptorium', pp. 19–21 and 27
Delisle, 'Notice', p. xciv
Delisle, 'Matériaux', pp. 486–9

(J. Weston)

8 Paris, Bibliothèque national de France, MS Latin 10913

(1100–41; 240×155 mm; 502 pp.; Orderic Vitalis, *Historia ecclesiastica*, Books IX–XIII)[4]

Note: The folia for this volume have been numbered incorrectly. This present entry refers to the modern page numbers.

This is Orderic's autograph copy of the *Historia ecclesiastica*, Books IX–XIII. He copied the vast majority of the primary text (pages 9–502), with only very brief sections added by a different hand (for example, the lower part of p. 40).

References

Delisle, 'Matériaux', pp. 486–9
Escudier, 'Orderic et le scriptorium', p. 19
HE, I, pp. 118–21

(J. Weston)

9 Paris, Bibliothèque nationale de France, MS Latin 10062

(1100–1200; 260×180 mm; 163 fols.; chapter-book of Saint-Èvroul with various books bound together, including a *Liber memorialis* and necrology, calendar, Saint-Èvroul book-list, Gospel lectionary, *Rule of St Benedict*, excerpts from Bede's *De temporum ratione*, and annals)

Fols. 1r–36v: Orderic did not add to the *Liber memorialis* text, which appears to have been written in several later hands throughout. Orderic's obit features on fol. 19v.

Fols. 37r–77v: The hand that copied the main text of the martyrology looks similar to that of Orderic, but it is not close enough to confirm as his work. Chibnall's suggestion that Orderic added details on St Lawrence on fol. 71r remains plausible, though several features, including the pronounced forks on ascenders in lines three and five of the addition and the supralineal contraction marks, are not consistent with Orderic's usual style.[5] Overall, the main scribe of the martyrology wrote in a style similar to Orderic's, particularly in the execution of characteristic letter-forms for **r**, **t** (and its ligature), **x** and the abbreviations for 'et'; the scribe also uses a similar form to Orderic's 'general abbreviation' contraction-mark. However,

---

[4] As Escudier notes, no autograph copies of Books VII and VIII exist: Escudier, 'Orderic et le scriptorium', p. 19.

[5] Chibnall suggests that Orderic added details about SS Eusebius and Lawrence on fols. 71r and 90v, but we disagree with this identification. See, *HE*, I, p. 201.

the text uses a different abbreviation for '-orum', and lacks Orderic's characteristic 'horizontal-descender g', the 'sharp-feet m', and the 'tangle effect' noted by Weston, leaving larger gaps between letters and lines than are commonly found in Orderic's work. It is possible that the martyrology was copied by a close associate of Orderic, perhaps a teacher, a pupil, or another contemporary who was trained in the same location. Orderic may have made small corrections to the text, such as at fols. 37r (col. 2, lines 7–9).

Fols. 78r–81v: Confraternity agreements, copied in a hand almost identical to the scribe of the martyrology. Numerous hands of varying dates made additions to these lists over time, including possibly Orderic, who appears to have added an agreement with the monastery of Saint-Trinity in Venosa: 'P(ro) def(uncto) mo(nacho) cenobii s(an)ct(e) trinitatis venusie', which forms the last line of main body text on fol. 78r. This single agreement displays Orderic's characteristic contraction-mark, his ampersand, 'flag-kicked r', his 'horizontal-descender g', and is larger than the majority of the other entries, in line with the general aspect of Orderic's writing.

Fol. 80v: Orderic copied the first three lines of the St-Évroul book-list, including the *incipit*, and may also have recorded possession of a book containing the miracles of St Stephen mid-way through line 23 ('Miracula S. Stephani').

Fols. 82r–97v: Orderic corrected parts of the lectionary, such as at fols. 90v and 95v. He also supplied a brief section of the main text on fol. 95r.

Fols. 98r–122r: Orderic corrected parts of the *Rule of St Benedict*. For examples, see fols. 100v (col. 2, 'redditur ...'); 105r (col. 2, 'scamnis ...'); 106v (col. 2, 'Vespertina ...'); and 110v (col. 2, 'ut sciat ...'). He also supplied brief sections of the main text, such as at fol. 99r.

Fol. 123r: Orderic added a small note about the events of the year 1099 AD, commemorating the dedication of the abbey church at Saint-Évroul, the succession of Pope Paschal, and the capture of Jerusalem (col. 2, 'Prefate [...] reddita est').

Fols. 130r–132r: It is possible that Orderic copied the extracts from Bede's *De temporum ratione*. There are some differences in the execution of certain letter-forms and abbreviations, however, which may suggest that it was actually copied by a scribe trained by Orderic, or one of Orderic's teachers.

Fols. 132r–137v: It is possible that Orderic copied various parts of the computational texts and tables (see fols. 132v–135v, 136v and 137v). However, the artistic and compressed nature of the text makes this difficult to confirm.

Fols. 138r–161v: Orderic added the names of various popes and made other corrections and additions to the annals (for examples, see fols. 148r, 149r,

150r and 152r). He began making additions from fol. 145v onwards. These earlier entries are initially sporadic, and seem intended to supplement the main outline of papal, regnal, and imperial succession. For example, on fol. 148r, Orderic noted the death of King Cædwalla of Wessex in Rome (689), the death of Archbishop Theodore of Canterbury (690), Pope Sergius's ordination of St Willebrord as Bishop of the Frisians (695), and Theodosius succeeding Anastasius as Byzantine Emperor (715). These supplementary additions continue until fol. 152r, at which point Orderic made a lengthy addition recording the struggle for Byzantine imperial succession between Constantine VII, his guardian Romanus, and Stephen son of Romanus, which he records for the year 954. Orderic then added most of the annals from 1084 (fol. 153v, col. 2) down to the end of the 1130s (fol. 154v). His last entry in the annals records the Second Lateran Council of 1139. This entry is much larger and slightly less regular in form than the bulk of Orderic's entries within the annals.

162r–164v: Calendar, with no evidence of Orderic's hand.

References

Delisle, 'Matériaux', pp. 493–6
Escudier, 'Orderic et le scriptorium', p. 24
HE, I, p. 201

(C. Rozier and J. Weston)

10 Paris, Bibliothèque nataionale de France, MS Latin 10508

(1100–1200; 205×120 mm; 159 fols.; gradual of Saint-Évroul; Gui d'Arezzo's *Micrologus sive de arte musica*)

Fols. 6r–129v: Orderic may have been responsible for rubricating the gradual, including the *incipits* (written in a combination of capitals and uncial letters), coloured initials, and coloured lines for the musical notation. The initials, in particular, bear a striking resemblance to those added to BnF, MS Lat. 10913.

References

Escudier, 'Orderic et le scriptorium', p. 24 and n. 32
B. Bischoff, *Latin Palaeography: Antiquity and the Middle Ages*, trans. D. Ó Cróinin and D. Ganz (Cambridge, 1990), p. 174 (for Guido d'Arezzo's text)

(J. Weston)

11 Paris, Bibliothèque nationale de France, MS Latin 12131

(1100–1200; 290×195 mm; 82 fols.; collection of works on the Trinity by Vigilis Tapensis, Potamius, Athanasius, and Jerome)

Fols. 1r–82v: Orderic rubricated the entire volume. For the *incipit* headings he used capitals, written in bright red/orange ink and occasionally highlighted with green (for examples, see fols. 1r, 8r, 22r, 64r and 78v). In certain places, Orderic also added a sub-*incipit* written in brown capitals (for example, fols. 1r, 8r, 25v, 64r, 68r and 78v).

On some occasions Orderic added the first few words of the main text after the *incipit* (for examples, see fols. 25v, 64r and 75v).

Orderic also made some corrections to the text (see fols. 21r–v and 64r), and added various notes to the margins (see fols. 14r, 18r and 43v).

On fol. 80v Orderic supplied a small marginal note next to a letter from Guitmund (abbot of La Croix-Saint-Leufroi) to Herfast.

References
HE, I, pp. 201–2, and II, p. 270 (for Guitmund)

(J. Weston)

12 Paris, Bibliothèque nationale de France, MS Latin 6503

(1100–1200; dimensions unknown; 70 fols.; composite collection of works including Latin–Greek vocabulary, Latin homilies, *Lives* and *Passions* of saints, and the 'Tale of the Sacrilegious Carollers')

Fols. 59r–60v: Orderic copied the *Passion* of SS Donatianus and Rogatianus, including the *incipit*. (Note: a different hand copied the lower part of fol. 60v.)

Fols. 61r–62r: Orderic copied 'The Legend of the Dancers' (also known as the 'Tale of the Sacrilegious Carollers'). An abridged version of this tale is told in William of Malmesbury, *Gesta regum Anglorum*, ii. 174.[6]

Fols. 62v–68v: Orderic copied a selection of unidentified homilies.

Fols. 69r–70r: Orderic copied a Latin homily titled *Sermo ad populum de dedicatione ecclesie*. According to Mark Atherton, this sermon is preserved in only a few surviving manuscripts.

---

[6] For a printed Latin edition of the 'Tale of the Sacrilegious Carollers', see *Roberd of Brunnè's Handlyng Synne [...] With the French treatise on which it is founded, 'Le Manuel des Pechiez' of William of Wadington*, ed. F. J. Furnivall (London, 1862), p. xxviii.

References

William of Malmesbury, *Gesta regum Anglorum: The History of the English Kings*, ed. and trans. R. A. B. Mynors, completed by R. M. Thomson and M. Winterbottom, Oxford Medieval Texts, 2 vols. (Oxford, 1998–9), I, pp. 294–7

Mark Atherton, 'The Image of the Temple in the *Psychomachia* and Late Anglo-Saxon Literature', *Bulletin of the John Rylands University Library of Manchester* 79:3 (1997), 263–85, at fol. 91, p. 283

HE, I, p. 201

Delisle, 'Matériaux', p. 496

(J. Weston)

13 Rouen, Bibliothèque municipale, MS 31 (A. 024)

(1100–1200; 320×200 mm; 183 fols.; *Liber pontificalis*; Ambrose's *Expositio de psalmo*; Letter from Jerome to Pope Damasus I; Gospels)

Fols. 9r–15v: Orderic copied the opening pages of the *Liber pontificalis*. Fol. 9r features a large historiated initial, typical of manuscripts copied by Orderic. This section also features Orderic's unique paragraph mark (see fols. 10r, 11r, 13r). On fol. 15v Orderic stopped copying mid-sentence, at which point another scribe took over.

Fol. 41r–v: Orderic copied the opening pages of Ambrose's *Expositio de psalmo*. There is a large space where the initial was meant to be added, but was not. Like other examples, Orderic only copied the first part of the text, ending mid-sentence on fol. 41v, at which point another scribe took over. Orderic returned as primary scribe at the bottom of fol. 44r, continued to copy until the top of fol. 45r, then stopped mid-line, and let another finish the text.

Orderic added various marginal notes and corrections throughout (see fol. 42r, for example, where his additions are surrounded by a small border).

It is possible that Orderic supplied the *incipit* headings for the Gospel section (see for example fol. 88r).

References

Escudier, 'Orderic et le scriptorium', p. 23

F. Avril, *Manuscrits normands, XIe–XIIe siècles* (Rouen, 1975), pp. 70–1

(J. Weston)

14 Rouen, Bibliothèque municipale, MS 540 (U. 148)[7]

(1100–42; 165×110 mm; 67 fols.; Anselm of Canterbury's *De libero arbitrio* and *De casu diaboli*; *Vitae sanctae Oportunae virginis*)

Fols. 15r–54r: Orderic corrected Anselm's *De casu diaboli*. On fol. 26r, for example, Orderic may have added a correction over an erasure (the words 'alitate' and then one line lower 'sed'). This correction is suggested by the larger script and the change in ink-colour over the erasure. On fol. 46v Orderic supplied a portion of missing text in the margin.

Fol. 54r: Orderic copied the top line in the last section of Anselm's *De casu diaboli*. He stopped mid-sentence, at which point another scribe finished the remainder of the text.

Fol. 54r–v: Orderic copied the large initial **G**, the *incipit* in uncial capitals, and the opening twelve lines of the *Vita sanctae Oportunae virginis*. He carried over to the verso (fol. 54v) and copied one and a half lines, ending mid-line, at which point another scribe took over.

Fol. 55v: Orderic added the *excplicit* for the prologue of the *Vita* in rubricated uncial capitals.

Fol. 65r: It is possible that Orderic added a few words of text ('sca' in'cessione').

Fol. 67v: Orderic may have added the marginal abbreviated word 'templum'.

(J. Weston)

15 Rouen, Bibliothèque municipale, MS 1174 (Y. 14)

(1100–1200; 298×210 mm; 139 fols.; composite MS including Angelomus's commentary on the book of Kings, a fragmentary treatise on marriage, Gilbert Crispin's, *Disputatio Judaei et Christiani*, a mystical treatise on the 'Wings of the Cherubin', and Orderic's interpolated but incomplete edition of William of Jumièges' *Gesta Normannorum ducum*)

Fols. 1r–100v: Orderic copied short sections and provided corrections in Angelomus's commentary on the biblical book of Kings. In most cases Orderic copied only a line or two of the primary text (often beginning directly after the addition of a large initial). The contrast between Orderic's handwriting and that of the second scribe is very noticeable in most cases (see for example fols. 3r–v, 4r, 8r–9v). Orderic occasionally

---

[7] A more detailed description and discussion of Orderic's additions within this manuscript is offered in J. Weston above, 'Following the Master's Lead: The Script of Orderic Vitalis and the Discovery of a New Manuscript (Rouen, BM, 540)'.

copied longer sections of text, sometimes beginning and ending mid-sentence (see for example fols. 11r–12v, 14r and 19r–20r).

Orderic also provided corrections for Angelomus's text. Specific examples can be found at fols. 1r, 2v, 17v, 36r, 45r, 56r, 73v, 82v and 98r. On both fols. 94v and 96r Orderic added a large marginal correction surrounded by a decorative border. Orderic also added *incipit* and *explicit* headings in various places (see fols. 16v and 32r).

Fols. 101–105v: Orderic corrected a fragmented treaty on marriage (for examples, see fols. 103v and 105r). The text is unknown, though it includes a passage borrowed from 1 Corinthians 7: 'mulier sui corporis potestate non habet …'.

Fols. 116r–139v: Orderic copied the text of William of Jumièges' *Gesta Normannorum ducum* (now incomplete), including headings and initials, making substantial additions to William's base-text. Orderic's unique paragraph mark can be found throughout this text (see fols. 125v, 126v and 127v).

References

Escudier, 'Orderic et le scriptorium', pp. 23, 25
Avril, *Manuscrits normands*, p. 72
Delisle, 'Matériaux', pp. 490–2
The Gesta Normannorum ducum of William of Jumièges, Orderic Vitalis, and Robert of Torigni, ed. and trans. Elisabeth van Houts, 2 vols. (Oxford, 1992), I, pp. lxvi–lxxvii and ciii–civ

(J. Weston)

16 Rouen, Bibliothèque municipale, MS 1343 (U. 43)

(1113–37; 315×215 mm; 186 fols.; *Sermo de dedicatione ecclesiae*; Remigius of Auxerre, *Expositio missae*; *Gesta salutatoris*; *Distinctiones theologicae*; Bede's *Historia ecclesiastica gentis Anglorum*; works of Severus Sulpicius and Gregory of Tours; a collection of *Passions*)

Fols. 1r–33v: Orderic corrected the *Sermo de dedicatione ecclesiae*, Remigius of Auxerre's *Expositio missae* and the *Gesta saluatoris*, with most of his additions appearing in the margins (for examples, see fols. 8v, 9r, 10r, 18r, 25v, 27r, 29v, 32v). Orderic also provided some of the *incipit* and *explicit* headings in uncial capitals (see fols. 1r, 10r–v, 33v).

Fols. 33v–186v: Orderic served as principal scribe for the remainder of the volume. The texts include: *Distinctiones theologicae* (fol. 33v); Bede's *Historia ecclesiastica gentis Anglorum* (fols. 34r–129v); a poem written about the state of the Church (fols. 121v–122r); works of Severus Sulpicius including letters (fols. 130r–130v and 139v–144r), the *Life of St Martin* (fols. 130v–139v), and *Dialogi* (fols. 144r– 162r); *De vita et virtutibus sancti Martini* (fols. 162r–163v); Gregory of Tours, *De miracula sancti Martini* (fols. 163v–176r); and a collection of *Passions* (fols. 177r–186v).

References

Avril, *Manuscrits normands*, pp. 72–3
Delisle, 'Matériaux', pp. 504–6

(J. Weston)

17 Rouen, Bibliothèque municipale, MS 1376 (A. 449)

(1100–1200; 228×170 mm; 59 fols.; Gregory of Tours, *De gloria martyrum, Vita S. Gregorii Lingonensis*; Boethius, *In libro de consolatione*; hymns; *Passio S. Luciani*; *Passio SS Saviniani, Potentiani, et Altini*)

Fols. 30v–43v: Orderic began copying mid-word ('pretereuntes') in Gregory of Tours' *Vita S. Gregorii Lingonensis*. He was also responsible for the *incipit* headings.

Fol. 43v: At the bottom of this folio, Orderic copied a hymn, including small musical notation above the words and possible indications of pitch.

It is possible that Orderic corrected parts of the *Passio SS Saviniani, Potentiani, et Altini* (see the word 'hystoria', fol. 53v, col. 2, 9 lines from the top).

References

Avril, *Manuscrits normands*, p. 73
Omont, *Catalogue général des manuscrits des bibliothèques publiques de France, départements Tome Premièr*, Rouen (Paris, 1886), pp. 342–3

(J. Weston)

18 Rouen, Bibliothèque municipale, MS 1389 (U. 35)

(1075–1100; 316×220 mm; 154 fols.; miscellany of saints' *Lives*, passions and miracles)

Although Denis Escudier identifies this manuscript as one copied by Orderic, subtle differences in certain letter-forms and abbreviations cast some doubt on this arribution.

Fols. 11v–12v: Orderic may have been responsible for completing the *Life* of St Silvester.

Fols. 12v–20r: Orderic may have copied the whole of the *Life* of St Nicholas.

Fol. 99v: Orderic may have also added five marginal notations to another hagiographical work. The subject of this is unknown, obscured by the deterioration of the *incipit* and *explicit*, which were originally written in a blue ink, but have now faded. He may also have copied sections of the main text (see fols. 99v–100r).

References

Escudier, 'Orderic et le scriptorium', p. 22

(C. Rozier)

Select Bibliography

Aird, William M., *Robert Curthose, Duke of Normandy (c. 1050–1134)* (Woodbridge, 2008)

Albu, Emily, *The Normans in their Histories: Propaganda, Myth and Subversion* (Woodbridge, 2001)

Alexander, Alison, 'Annalistic Writing in Normandy, c. 1050–1225' (unpublished PhD thesis, University of Cambridge, 2011)

Angold, Michael, 'Knowledge of Byzantine History in the West: The Norman Historians (Eleventh and Twelfth Centuries)', ANS 25 (2003), 19–33

Barton, Richard E., 'Emotions and Power in Orderic Vitalis', ANS 33 (2011), 41–59

Bates, David, *Normandy before 1066* (London and New York, 1982)

—— 'The Conqueror's Earliest Historians and the Writing of his Biography', in *Writing Medieval Biography: Essays in Honour of Professor Frank Barlow*, ed. David Bates, Julia Crick and Sarah Hamilton (Woodbridge, 2006), pp. 129–41

Bauduin, Pierre, 'Une famille châtelaine sur les confins normanno-manceaux: Les Géré (X^e–XIIIe s.)', *Archéologie médiévale* 22 (1992), 309–56

Bickford Smith, James, 'Orderic Vitalis and Norman Society, c. 1035–1087' (unpublished DPhil thesis, University of Oxford, 2006)

Bisson, Thomas N., 'Hallucinations of Power: Climates of Fright in the Early Twelfth Century', HSJ 16 (2006), 1–11

Blacker, Jean, *The Faces of Time: Portrayal of the Past in Old French and Latin Historical Narrative of the Anglo-Norman Regnum* (Austin, TX, 1994)

—— 'Women, Power, and Violence in Orderic Vitalis's *Historia Ecclesiastica*', in *Violence Against Women in Medieval Texts*, ed. Anna Roberts (Gainesville, FL, 1998), pp. 44–55

Bouet, Pierre, 'Orderic Vital, lecteur critique de Guillaume de Poitiers', in *Mediaevalia Christiana XIe–XIIIe siècles: Hommage à Raymonde Foreville*, ed. C. E. Viola (Paris, 1989), pp. 25–50

—— 'L'Image des évêques normands dans l'œuvre d'Orderic Vital', in *Les Évêques Normands du XIe siècle*, ed. Pierre Bouet and François Neveux (Caen, 1995), pp. 253–75

Chibnall, Marjorie, 'Ecclesiastical Patronage and the Growth of Feudal Estates at the Time of the Norman Conquest', *Annales de Normandie* 8 (1958), 103–18

—— 'Orderic Vitalis and Robert of Torigni', *Millénaire monastique du Mont Saint-Michel* 2 (1966), 133–9

—— 'The Merovingian Monastery of St Evroul in the Light of Conflicting Traditions', *Studies in Church History* 8 (1971), 31–40

—— 'Charter and Chronicle: The Use of Archive Sources by Norman Historians', in *Church and Government in the Middle Ages: Essays Presented to C. R. Cheney on his 70th Birthday*, ed. C. N. L. Brooke, D. E. Luscombe et al. (Cambridge, 1976), pp. 1–17

—— 'Le Privilège de libre élection dans les chartes de Saint-Évroult', *Annales de Normandie* 28 (1978), 341–2

—— 'The Translation of the Relics of St Nicholas and Norman Historical Tradition', in *Le relazioni religiose e chiesastico-giurisdizionali. Atti del IIo Congresso Internazionale sulle Relazioni fra le due Sponde Adriatiche* (Rome, 1979), pp. 33–41

—— *The World of Orderic Vitalis* (Woodbridge, 1984)

—— 'Anglo-French Relations in the Work of Orderic Vitalis', in *Essays in Medieval History Presented to G. P. Cuttino*, ed. J. S. Hamilton and Patricia J. Bradley (Woodbridge, 1989), pp. 5–19

—— 'Women in Orderic Vitalis', *HSJ* 2 (1990), 105–21

—— 'Les Moines et les patrons de Saint-Évroult dans l'Italie du Sud au XIe siècle', in *Les Normands en Méditerranée: Dans le sillage des Tancrède*, ed. Pierre Bouet and François Neveux (Caen, 1994), pp. 161–70

—— *Piety, Power and History in Medieval England and Normandy*, Variorum Collected Studies (Aldershot, 2000)

—— 'Canon Law as Reflected in the *Ecclesiastical History* of Orderic Vitalis', in *Law as Profession and Practice in Medieval Europe: Essays in Honor of James A. Brundage*, ed. Kenneth Pennington and Melodie Harris Eichbauer (Farnham, 2011), pp. 219–30

Classen, Peter, '*Res Gestae*, Universal History, Apocalypse: Visions of Past and Future', in *Renaissance and Renewal in the Twelfth Century*, ed. R. L. Benson and G. Constable (Oxford, 1982), pp. 387–417

Cooper, Alan, '"The feet of those that bark shall be cut off": Timorous Historians and the Personality of Henry I', *ANS* 23 (2001), 47–67

Decaëns, Joseph, 'Le Patrimoine des Grentemesnil en Normandie, en Italie et en Angleterre aux XIe et XIIe siècles', in *Les Normands en Méditerranée: dans le sillage des Tancrède*, ed. Pierre Bouet and François Neveux (Caen, 1994), pp. 123–40

Delisle, Léopold, 'Notice sur Orderic Vital', in *Orderici Vitalis ecclesiasticae historiae libri tredecim*, ed. and trans. A. Le Prévost, 5 vols. (Paris, 1838–5), V, pp. i–cvi

—— 'Vers et écriture d'Orderic Vital', *Journal des savants* n.s. 1 (1903), 428–40

—— 'Notes sur les manuscrits autographes d'Orderic Vital', part 1 of 'Matériaux pour l'édition de Guillaume de Jumièges, préparée par Jules Lair, avec une préface et des notes par Léopold Delisle', *Bibliothèque de l'école des chartes* 71 (1910), 481–526

Escudier, Denis, 'L'œuvre entre les lignes d'Orderic Vital', in *Le Livre au Moyen Âge*, ed. Jean Glenisson (Turnhout, 1988), pp. 193–5

—— 'Orderic Vital et le scriptorium de Saint-Évroult', in *Manuscrits et enluminures dans le monde normand (X^e–XVe siècles)*, ed. Pierre Bouet and Monique Dosdat, 2nd edn (Caen, 2005), pp. 17–28

Fournée, Jean, 'Le Prieuré de Maule et les moines de Saint-Evroult', *Nos ancêtres les Maulois: Chroniques du pays de Mauldre* 23 (1990), 7–18

Gazeau, Véronique, 'La Mort des moines: Sources textuelles et méthodologie (XIe–XIIe siècles), in *Inhumations et édifices religieux au Moyen Âge entre Loire et Seine*, ed. Armelle Alduc-Le Bagousse (Caen, 2004), pp. 13–21

—— *Normannia monastica*, 2 vols. (Caen, 2007)

Gazeau, Véronique, and J. Le Maho, 'Les Origines du culte de Saint Nicolas en Normandie', in *Alle origini dell'Europa: Il culto di San Nicola tra Oriente e Occidente I. Italia-Francia; atti del convegno, Bari, 2–4 décembre 2010*, ed. G. Cioffari and A. Laghezza, Nicolaus. Studi Storici: Rivista del Centro Studi Nicolaiani, anno XXII, fasc. 1–2 (2011), pp. 153–60

Gransden, Antonia, 'Prologues in the Historiography of Twelfth-Century England', in *England in the Twelfth Century: Proceedings of the 1988 Harlaxton Symposium*, ed. Daniel Williams (Woodbridge, 1990), pp. 55–81

Hagger, Mark, 'Kinship and Identity in Eleventh-Century Normandy: The Case of Hugh de Grandmesnil, c. 1040–1098', *JMH* 32 (2006), 212–30

Hicks, Leonie V., 'Coming and Going: The Use of Outdoor Space in Norman and Anglo-Norman Chronicles', *Anglo-Norman Studies* 32 (2009), 40–56

—— 'Monastic Authority and the Landscape in the *Ecclesiastical History* of Orderic Vitalis', in *Authority and Gender in Medieval and Renaissance Chronicles*, ed. Julian Dresvina and Nicholas Sparks (Cambridge, 2012), pp. 102–20

Hingst, Amanda Jane, *The Written World: Past and Place in the Work of Orderic Vitalis* (Notre Dame, IN, 2009)

van Houts, Elisabeth, *Local and Regional Chronicles*, Typologie des sources du Moyen Âge 74 (Turnhout, 1995)

—— 'Camden, Cotton and the Chronicles of the Norman Conquest of England', in *Sir Robert Cotton as Collector: Essays on an Early Stuart Courtier and his Legacy*, ed. C. J. Wright (London, 1997), pp. 238–52

—— *Memory and Gender in Medieval Europe, 900–1200* (Basingstoke, 1999)

Krappe, Alexander Haggerty, 'The Legend of the Death of William Rufus in the *Historia Ecclesiastica* of Ordericus Vitalis', *Neophilologus* 12:1 (1927), 46–8

Loud, Graham A., 'Monastic Chronicles in the Twelfth-Century Abruzzi', *ANS* 27 (2005), 101–31

—— *The Latin Church in Norman Italy* (Cambridge, 2007)

—— 'Varieties of Monastic Discipline in Southern Italy during the Eleventh and Twelfth Centuries', *SCH* 43 (2007), 144–58

Marritt, Stephen, 'Crowland Abbey and the Provenance of Orderic Vitalis's Scandinavian and Scottish Material', *Notes & Queries* 53:3 (2006), 290–2

Mégier, Elisabeth, '*Cotidie operatur*. Christus und die Geschichte in der Historia ecclesiastica des Ordericus Vitalis', *Revue Mabillon* 71 (1999), 169–204

—— '*Divina pagina* and the Narration of History in Orderic Vitalis' Historia Ecclesiastica', *Revue bénédictine* 110:1–2 (2000), 106–23

Mouktafi, Sabrine, 'Textes épigraphiques et manuscrits: La Place des inscriptions dans l'*Histoire ecclésiastique* d'Orderic Vital (1114–1141). Mémoire et biographie' (unpublished Master's thesis, University of Poitiers, 2003)

Musset, Lucien, 'L'Horizon géographique, moral et intellectuel d'Orderic Vital, historien anglo-normand', in *La Chronique et l'histoire au Moyen Âge: Colloque des 24 et 25 Mai 1982*, ed. Daniel Poirion (Paris, 1984), pp. 101–22

Nortier, Geneviève, *Les Bibliothèques médiévales des abbayes bénédictines de Normandie: Fécamp. Le Bec. Le Mont Saint-Michel. Saint-Évroul. Lyre. Jumièges. Saint-Wandrille. Saint-Ouen* (Paris, 1971)

Otter, Monika, *Inventiones: Fiction and Referentiality in Twelfth-Century English Historical Writing* (Chapel Hill, NC, and London, 1996)

—— 'Functions of Fiction in Historical Writing', in *Writing Medieval History*, ed. Nancy Partner (London, 2005), pp. 109–30

Partner, Nancy F., 'The New Cornificius: Medieval History and the Artifice of Words', in *Classical Rhetoric and Medieval Historiography*, ed. Ernst Breisach (Kalamazoo, MI, 1985), pp. 5–59

Petry, Ray C., 'Three Medieval Chroniclers: Monastic Historiography and Biblical Eschatology in Hugh of St. Victor, Otto of Freising, and Ordericus Vitalis', *Church History* 34 (1965), 282–93

Pontieri, Ernesto, 'L'abbazia benedettina di Sant'Eufemia in Calabria e l'abate Roberto di Grantmesnil', *Archivio storico per la Sicilia orientale* 22 (1926), 92–115

Ray, Roger, 'The Monastic Historiography of Ordericus Vitalis' (unpublished PhD thesis, Duke University, 1967)

—— 'Orderic Vitalis and his Readers', *Studia Monastica* 14 (1972), 17–33

—— 'Orderic Vitalis and William of Poitiers: A Monastic Reinterpretation of William the Conqueror', *Revue belge de philologie et d'histoire* 50 (1972), 1116–27

—— 'Orderic Vitalis on Henry I: Theocratic Ideology and Didactic Narrative', in *Contemporary Reflections on the Medieval Christian Tradition: Essays in Honor of Ray C. Petry*, ed. George H. Shriver (Durham, NC, 1974), pp. 119–34

Roach, Daniel, 'The Material and the Visual: Objects and Memories in the Historia ecclesiastica of Orderic Vitalis', *HSJ* 24 (2013), 63–78

—— 'Orderic Vitalis and the First Crusade', *Journal of Medieval History* 42:2 (2016), 177–201

Roche, Thomas, 'The Way Vengeance Comes: Rancorous Deeds and Words in the World of Orderic Vitalis', in *Vengeance in the Middle Ages: Emotion, Religion and Feud*, ed. Susanna A. Throop and Paul R. Hyams (Aldershot, 2010), pp. 115–36

Shopkow, Leah, *History and Community: Norman Historical Writing in the Eleventh and Twelfth Centuries* (Washington, DC, 1997)

Spiegel, Gabrielle M., *The Past as Text: The Theory and Practice of Medieval Historiography* (Baltimore, MD, 1999)

Stafford, Pauline, 'The Meanings of Hair in the Anglo-Norman World: Masculinity, Reform, and National Identity', in *Saints, Scholars, and Politicians: Gender as a Tool in Medieval Studies. Festschrift in Honour of Anneke Mulder-Bakker on the Occasion of her Sixty-Fifth Birthday*, ed. Mathilde van Dijk and Renée Nip (Turnhout, 2005), pp. 153–71

Thompson, Kathleen, 'Family and Influence to the South of Normandy in the Eleventh Century: The Lordship of Bellême', *Journal of Medieval History* 11:3 (1985), 215–26

—— 'Robert of Bellême Reconsidered', *ANS* 13 (1991), 263–86

—— 'Orderic Vitalis and Robert of Bellême', *Journal of Medieval History* 20:2 (1992), 133–41

—— 'The Lords of Laigle: Ambition and Insecurity on the Borders of Normandy', *ANS* 18 (1996), 177–99

Thorpe, Lewis, 'Orderic Vitalis and the *Prophetiae Merlini* of Geoffrey of Monmouth', *Bibliographical Bulletin of the International Arthurian Society* 29 (1977), 191–208

Truax, Jean A., 'From Bede to Orderic Vitalis: Changing Perspectives on the Role of Women in the Anglo-Saxon and Anglo-Norman Churches', *HSJ* 3 (1991), 35–52

Walker, Barbara MacDonald, 'The Grandmesnils: A Study in Norman Baronial Enterprise' (unpublished PhD thesis, University of California Santa Barbara, 1968)

Ward, John O., 'Ordericus Vitalis as Historian in the Europe of the Early Twelfth-Century Renaissance', *Parergon* 31:1 (2014), 1–26

Watkins, Carl, 'The Cult of Earl Waltheof at Crowland', *Hagiographica* 3 (1996), 95–111

—— 'Memories of the Marvellous in the Anglo-Norman Realm', in *Medieval Memories: Men, Women and the Past, 700–1300*, ed. Elisabeth van Houts (Harlow, 2001), pp. 92–112

—— 'Sin, Penance and Purgatory in the Anglo-Norman Realm: The Evidence of Visions and Ghost-Stories', *Past & Present* 175 (2002), 3–33

White, Geoffrey H., 'Orderic and the Lords of Bellême', *Notes & Queries* 156:10 (1929), 165–8

Wolter, Hans, *Ordericus Vitalis: Ein Beitrag zur kluniazensischen Geschichtsschreibung* (Wiesbaden, 1955)

Yarrow, Simon, 'Prince Bohemond, Princess Melaz, and the Gendering of Religious Difference in the *Ecclesiastical History* of Orderic Vitalis', in *Intersections of Gender, Religion and Ethnicity in the Middle Ages*, ed. Cordelia Beattie and Kirsten A. Fenton (Basingstoke, 2010), pp. 140–57

Manuscripts Cited

Alençon, Bibliothèque municipale

MS 1
MS 6

MS 14
MS 26

Avranches, Bibliothèque municipale

MS 12
MS 135

MS 211
MS 213

Douai Bibliothèque

MS 801

MS 852

London, British Library

Add. MS 26876
Add. MS 62929
MS Cotton Caligula A X
MS Cotton Claudius A XII
MS Cotton Domitian A XIV
MS Cotton Otho B XIII
MS Cotton Vespasian A XIX
MS Cotton Vespasian B XI
MS Cotton Vitellius A VIII
MS Egerton 3028

MS Harley 491
MS Harley 636
MS Harley 3742
MS Harley Rolls Y 4
MS Royal 4 C XI
MS Royal 13 A XVIII
MS Royal 13 C XI
MS Royal 13 D V
MS Royal 14 C VII
MS Royal 20 A XIII

London, College of Arms

MS 38

Oxford, Bodleian Library

MS Bodley 212
MS Junius 121
MS Hatton 113
MS Hatton 114

MS Lyell 17
MS Laud. Misc. 725
MS Top. Devon d. 5

Oxford, Library of St John's College

MS 17

Paris, Bibliothèque nationale de France

MS Français 73	MS Latin 10062
MS Latin 1105	MS Latin 10508
MS Latin 4861	MS Latin 10913
MS Latin 5506 I	MS Latin 12131
MS Latin 5506 II	MS Latin 13092
MS Latin 6503	

Rouen, Bibliothèque municipale

MS 31 (A. 024)	MS 1343 (U. 43)
MS 209-210 (Y. 175)	MS 1370
MS 211 (A. 145)	MS 1376 (A. 449)
MS 233 (Y. 21)	MS 1380
MS 240 (A. 253)	MS 1383
MS 267 (A. 401)	MS 1385
MS 273 (A. 287)	MS 1388
MS 456	MS 1389 (U. 35)
MS 461	MS 1391
MS 540 (U. 148)	MS 1399
MS 1174 (Y. 14)	MS 1400
MS 1233	

Vatican City, Biblioteca Apostolica Vaticana

MS Reginensis Latina 703B
(formerly 703A)

General Index

Abelard, Peter, 16, 248, 279n65, 365
Achard (St), 173
Adela, daughter of William I, King of England and Duke of Normandy, 325
Adela, wife of Stephen, and countess of Blois and daughter of William I, king of England, 330
Adelaide of Le Puiset, ii, 27n44, 29n57, 36, 138, 231
Agilus, abbot of Rebais, 173
Alexius Comnenus, Emperor of Byzantium, 86, 88, 90
Amatus of Montecassino, 78, 80, 82n22, 93n65
Ambrose (St) of Milan, 54, 57, 179, 394
Angers, abbey of Saint Nicholas, 187
Anjou, counts of, 214, 222
Annals of Saint-Évroul, *see under* Saint-Évroul, abbey of
Anquetil of Noyer, 83–4, 231
Anselm (St)
　as abbot of Bec, 201n66, 249, 252
　as archbishop of Canterbury, 18, 38, 292
　works of, 40–2, 58, 147n17, 148n20, 170, 278n65, 395
Ansold of Maule, 92, 129, 130, 132–4, 142, 165, 272–3
Apulia, 80, 81, 82, 84, 90, 92, 96, 98, 219
Aquitaine, duchy of, 370
Arnold of Échauffour, son of William, son of Giroie, 84, 186, 187, 232, 273
Arnold of Grandmesnil, son of Robert, 89
Arnold of Tilleul, monk at Saint-Évroul, 89, 98, 99n92, 165
Atcham, Shropshire, birthplace of Orderic Vitalis, 7, 20, 27n44, 33, 100, 110, 111n38

Auffay, lords of, 141, 142n59, 164; canons of, 108
Augustine (St) of Canterbury, 175
Augustine (St) of Hippo, 17, 251, 256, 259, 303, 313–14, 316, 337
Avitian, archbishop of Rouen, 186

Baldric, abbot of Bourgueil, later Bishop of Dol, 127, 128, 143
　his *Historia Ierosolimitana*, 9, 241–2, 299
Baldwin IV, count of Flanders, 311
Bayeux, town of, 182
Bec-Hellouin, abbey of, 93, 183, 233, 258, 299, 358, 365, 366, 372n88
Bede
　his *Chronica maiora*, 281
　his commentary on *Ezra*, 388
　his *De temporum ratione*, 71, 282, 390, 391
　his *Historia abbatum*, 300
　his *Historia ecclesiastica gentis Anglorum*, 11, 19, 103, 118, 217, 227, 242–5, 254, 277–9, 300, 312–13, 342–4, 347, 349, 350, 351, 364, 396
Benedict, son of Odelerius of Orléans and brother of Orderic Vitalis, xii, 20, 23–5, 27n44, 29n57, 32, 319
Berengar, monk of Saint-Évroul and Abbot of Venosa, 68, 85, 87–8, 92, 98, 339n23
Bernard (St) of Clairvaux, 248
Bernard, abbot of Tiron, 324–32
Bernard, son of Geoffrey of Neufmarché, 108
Bohemond I (Mark), son of Robert Guiscard, 90
Bolotin, Pain, 327–8, 331
Brittany, 232

Caen, town of, 352–3, 355, 371
  abbey of Holy Trinity, 153, 183, 188
  abbey of Saint-Étienne and St Stephen, 9, 11, 12, 153, 245, 188, 352–5, 359, 364, 367, 372–3
Calabria, 70n43, 78, 84, 85, 86, 92
Cambrai, visited by Orderic Vitalis, 11, 311, 360n35
Carmen de Hastingae Proelio, 245–6
Chartres
  bishops of, 303, 325, 327, 328
  cathedral of, 183, 325, 327, 329
  abbey of St Peter, 182
Chibnall, Marjorie
  her influence on Orderic Vitalis studies, ix-x, 4–6
  her perspectives on the *Historia ecclesiastica* of Orderic Vitalis, 3, 5, 7–9, 12, 18n6, 28, 73–4, 94, 99, 143–4, 145–6, 156–7, 165–6, 174, 217, 238–9, 242, 245, 261–2, 285, 300, 309, 331, 346, 357–8
  her edition of the *Historia ecclesiastica* of Orderic Vitalis, 4, 5, 6, 13, 105–6, 146, 172, 260, 375
  her translations in the *Historia ecclesiastica* of Orderic Vitalis, 23n34, 27n45, 68n30, 73–4, 100, 242, 263n10, 269, 275n52, 285, 345–6
  her *World of Orderic Vitalis*, 172
  on the life and family of Orderic Vitalis, 7, 22, 27–8, 33, 34n80, 36, 102n8, 116, 227–8, 238–9
  on the manuscripts copied or annotated by Orderic Vitalis, 43–4, 47, 55n37, 58n40, 65, 71, 385, 389, 390
  on Orderic's wider career, 30n59, 61–2, 70–1
Cluny, abbey of, 35, 149, 241, 270, 272, 305, 324–5, 328–30, 332, 377
  Orderic's visit to, 43
Constantius, father of Odelerius of Orléans, xii, 20, 22

Coutances, town of, 272
  bishops of, 174
  church of Saint-Peter, 270–1
Crowland, 103n12, 111n38, 112, 366
  abbey of, 36, 102, 364n48, 369
  Orderic's visit to, 11, 43, 102, 175
  Orderic's history of, 11–12, 102, 157, 175, 210n109, 270, 361–3, 369
  cult of Earl Waltheof at, 11–12, 123; see also Waltheof II, Earl of Northumbria
Crusades, 4, 8, 9, 89, 91n60, 139, 176, 177, 188, 204n78, 212, 230, 241, 264, 265, 266, 273n45, 299, 300, 308

Damian, Peter, 303, 305
David I, king of Scotland and earl of Northumbria, 209–11
Delisle, Léopold, 3, 4–5, 9, 13, 30, 37, 43–7, 50n40, 145, 154, 385
Demetrius (St) of Thessaloniki, 176–7, 183, 185, 188
Dudo of Saint-Quentin, his *De moribus Normannorum ducum*, 18–19, 225, 242, 246, 300, 347, 356, 370, 372, 373n93
Durazzo, siege of, 88, 90, 91–3, 96

Eadmer of Canterbury, 2, 72, 106, 109–11, 118–19, 123, 147n17, 148, 170, 252–3, 292, 309–10, 313, 318, 349–50
Erembert, monk of Holy Trinity, Venosa, 95–6
Eusebius of Caesarea
  his *Historia ecclesiastica*, 2, 11, 279, 300, 347
  his *Chronicle*, 281–2
Eustace (St), 176, 179, 184–5, 188
Eustace, abbot of Luxeuil, 173
Everard, son of Odelerius of Orleans and brother of Orderic Vitalis, xii, 20, 23–5, 29
Everard, son of Roger of Montgomery, 36

Évreux, bishops of, 147, 174, 182, 199
  abbey of Saint-Taurin, 359–60
Évroul (St), *see also* Saint-Évroul,
    abbey of
  his cult, 180, 183, 375
  office of, 68, 183
  in the *Historia ecclesiastica* of Orderic
    Vitalis, xiv, 68, 172, 268, 340

Faron, abbot of Meaux, 173
Fécamp, abbey of Holy Trinity, 35*n*81,
    42–4, 60, 153, 179, 181, 183–5,
    255*n*26, 367–9
Fontenelle, abbey of, 173, 180, 182–3, 188
Fredesenda, mother of Robert
    Guiscard, 86
Fulcher of Chartres, his *Historia
    Hierosolymitana*, 148
Foulcoius of Beauvais, 127–8, 143

Geoffrey of Malaterra, his *De rebus
    gestis Rogerii et Roberti*, 78, 80, 89
Geoffrey of Monmouth, his *Historia
    regum Britanniae*, 230
Geoffrey, prior of Saint-Évroul and
    Abbot of Crowland, 36, 270*n*28,
    361
George (St), 176–7, 179, 182–5, 188
Gervase of Canterbury, 72, 350
Gilbert, bishop of Lisieux, 7, 136
Giroie, family of, 3, 35, 79–84, 98, 137,
    160–1, 167, 186, 231–2, 274, 299
Godebald, clerk of Roger of
    Montgomery, xiii, 20, 32–3
Grandmesnil, family of, 3, 21*n*18, 35,
    78–9, 81, 35, 36*n*88, 78–9, 81–2,
    84–93, 98–99, 142*n*59, 147, 160–1,
    183, 327
Guibert of Nogent, 17, 342
Guitmund, abbot of La Croix-Saint-
    Leufroi, 393
Guitmund, monk of Saint-Évroul,
    67–8
Guitmond of Aversa, 248
Gunfrid, monk of Saint-Évroul, 82

Guthlac (St), 10, 103, 112, 116, 175*n*33,
    233, 268, 361–3; *see also* Crowland,
    abbey of

Harold, king of England, 223, 236,
    240–1
Henry I, king of England, 27*n*43, 32*n*65,
    100, 125, 147, 155, 157*n*63, 158, 162,
    189–91, 200, 204–9, 211, 215, 238,
    272, 274
  his visit to Saint-Évroul in 1113, 8, 19,
    162, 157*n*63, 162, 189–91
Henry I, king of France, 230, 236
Henry II, king of England, 32*n*65, 156,
    364
Henry IV, king of Germany/Holy
    Roman Empire, 34–5, 192–5,
    198–200
Henry V, king of England, 352–5,
    371–3
Henry VI, king of England, 370
Henry VIII, king of England, 373
Henry, archdeacon of Huntingdon, 2,
    310, 344*n*38
Henry of Sully, abbot of Fécamp, 43
Herbert of Lavardin, clerk of Roger of
    Montgomery, xiii, 20
Herbert of Montreuil, monk of Saint-
    Évroul, 85
Hildebert of Lavardin, 127
Hubert of Montreuil, monk of Saint-
    Évroul, 85
Hugh IV, archbishop of Rouen, 159*n*76,
    174
Hugh 'the Great', duke of the Franks
    and count of Paris, 264, 271
Hugh Fresnel, 148
Hugh, monk and cantor of Saint-
    Évroul, 73–4, 338
Hugh of Bayeux, 163
Hugh of Eu, 129, 131, 136, 141
Hugh of Fleury, 310
Hugh of Grandmesnil, 36*n*88, 84, 88–9,
    142*n*59
Hugh of Saint-Victor, 248, 322, 337

Hugh Pain, 148
Hugh Payen, 159
Hugo Cantor, 318
Hugo Falcandus, 12

Isembert, abbot of La Trinité, Rouen, 187
Isidore of Seville, his *Etymologiae*, 211, 303, 337, 351
Ivo, bishop of Chartres, 303, 305, 325, 327–30
Ivo, bishop of Séez, 218, 220

John, bishop of Cremona, 149
John of Avranches, archbishop of Rouen, 129, 132, 134, 136, 139, 141, 180
John of Bari, his *Translatio* of St Nicholas, 93–4
John of Ravenna, abbot of Fécamp, 35n81, 43
John of Rheims, monk of Saint-Évroul
  his writings, 7, 31n61, 74, 130–2, 133–4, 142–3, 148
  as tutor to Orderic Vitalis, 7, 74, 129, 147, 296
  epitaph of, by Orderic Vitalis, 74, 129–30, 132, 142–3, 296
John of Tynemouth, his *Historia aurea*, 362–3
John of Worcester, his *Chronica chronicarum*, 2, 281n83, 309, 318
Josephus, Flavius, his historical writings, 2, 282
Judoc (St), in the *Historia ecclesiastica* of Orderic Vitalis, 10, 172, 234, 268
Jumièges, abbey of, 35, 73, 93, 154, 156, 173, 176n33, 181, 183–5, 188, 220, 338, 361, 365, 367, 369, 379

Lanfranc, prior of Bec, abbot of St Etienne at Caen and archbishop of Canterbury, 62–3, 67, 70, 75, 207–8, 248–9, 364
Liber pontificalis, 11, 54–5, 394; *see also* under Orderic Vitalis

Louis IV, king of France, 217–18, 225
Louis, VI, king of France, 147, 190n9, 198n50, 199, 206n91

Mabel of Bellême, xii, 36, 129, 130, 136–8, 141–2, 165, 220–1, 232, 271
Magnus III, king of Norway, 211–12
Mainer, abbot of Saint-Évroul, 18n8, 24, 35, 36, 180, 186
Malcolm III, king of Scotland, 208–9
Marbodius of Rennes, 127
Matilda, of Flanders, queen of England, 183, 189, 271
'Empress' Matilda, daughter of Henry I of England, 211, 214
Matilda of Senlis, 209
Mauger, archbishop of Rouen, 227
Maurice (St) of then Theban Legion, 176, 179–82, 187–8
Maurilius, archbishop of Rouen, 130
Maule, priory of Saint-Évroul, 92–3, 129, 130, 143, 165, 195, 273
Mercurius (St), 176–9, 183–5, 188
Meaux, abbey of, 173
Michel-Philippe de Saint-Martin, abbot of Saint-Évroul, 369
Mont Saint-Michel, abbey of, 153, 155, 358, 361, 365, 368
Much Wenlock, priory of, 35

Nicholas II, pope, 84
Nicholas (St) of Myra
  in *Historia Ecclesiastica* of Orderic Vitalis, 10, 79, 90–1, 93–6, 99, 172, 185–8
  Orderic Vitalis copies his *Life*, 397
  translation of relics from Myra to Bari, 10, 79, 90–1, 93–4, 96, 98
  his cult in Normandy, 10, 79, 94, 98, 99, 181, 186–8, 397
  later theft of relics, 94–5
  relics at Noron, priory of Saint-Évroul, 94, 96–7, 185, 301
  relics at abbey of Holy Trinity, Venosa, 90, 94–6, 98

Normans, depiction of in writings of Orderic Vitalis, 1, 7–9, 15, 26, 28, 78–9, 81–2, 91–2, 125–6, 173–4, 177, 187, 199–204, 208, 214–16, 217–46, 259, 261, 269–70, 299, 308, 314, 322, 347–8

Noron, priory of Saint-Évroul, 94, 96–7, 165, 185, 301

Odelerius of Orléans
  early life, 19–22
  education, 21–2
  his role in the foundation of St Peter's abbey, Shrewsbury
  his relationship with unknown mother of Orderic Vitalis, 20, 27–30, 33
  arrangements for the oblation of Orderic Vitalis, 320–1
  journey to Rome in 1082, 20, 23, 30, 33–5
  his death, 26

Odo, bishop of Bayeux, 32n67, 116, 198n49, 202

Omer, abbot of Boulogne, 173

Orderic, priest at Atcham, 20, 27n44, 33

Orderic Vitalis
  arrival at Saint-Évroul, xii, 7, 20, 22, 23–6, 35–6, 101, 180, 226, 254–5, 312–17, 376
  autobiography in his *Historia Ecclesiastica*, xiii, 7–9, 19–27, 36, 72, 212, 240, 252, 261, 312–16, 322
  death, xiii, 9, 36, 257, 364
  early education, xii, 7, 20–2, 23, 25, 28–30, 46, 112–16, 125, 254–5
  early life and family, xii, 7, 14, 17–36, 101–2, 107–12, 116–17, 125, 180, 224–6, 254–5, 312, 320; *see also* Benedict, son of Odelerius of Orléans *and* Everard, son of Odelerius of Orléans *and* Odelerius of Orléans
  epitaphs written by, 10, 15, 127, 129–32, 142–4, 300

Orderic Vitalis, *continued*
  handwriting of, 7–8, 37–60
  historical writings
    Historia ecclesiastica: audiences of, 1–2, 75–7, 85, 88, 92, 99, 135, 172, 241–2, 284, 311, 335, 350, 355–6; chronology of composition, xiv, 8–9, 26, 28, 36, 83, 119–20, 135, 176, 177, 190–1, 199, 225–6, 227, 247, 257–8, 300, 329, 331; editions of, 3–6, 13, 43, 146, 172; manuscripts of, 5, 8–9, 11–12, 13, 45, 68–9, 105, 119, 139, 245, 359, 373–4, 389–90; purposes of, 1–2, 8–9, 11, 67, 75–7, 78–99, 100, 143–4, 154–5, 165–6, 169, 190–1, 241, 252, 258, 260, 282–3, 284–97, 300, 308–9, 319–23, 335, 345–8, 350; reception of, 3–5, 9, 10, 11–12, 13–14, 15, 245–7, 298–9, 321, 345, 352–74; sources and models used in, 83–6, 87, 89, 93–7, 99, 102, 106, 110, 112, 114–15, 123, 127, 130–44, 145–71, 172, 174, 179, 184–5, 233, 219, 227, 230, 253–9, 265–6, 276–9, 281, 292, 294–5, 299–300, 305–9, 312–14, 325–32, 337, 340, 344–7, 350–1; structure of, xiv, 4–5, 8–9, 80–1, 87–8, 90–3, 98–9, 139–40, 145, 165, 175–6, 259, 260, 281, 296, 298–32
    additions to annals at Saint-Évroul, 7–8, 44, 71, 98, 217, 391–2
    additions to *Gesta Normannorum ducum*, 1, 3–4, 7–8, 18–19, 45, 54, 78–9, 84, 155, 217–26, 230, 242, 247, 308–9, 347, 360–1, 396
    additions to historical writings at Crowland, 12, 361–3, 369
    additions to the *Liber pontificalis*, 11, 54–5, 394
    his knowledge of other historians, 8, 9, 11, 89, 110, 114–15, 123, 146, 340–1, 344–7, 350–1, 356–7
    use of charters in, 8–9, 15, 36, 87, 108, 114, 130, 138, 145–71, 189–90

Orderic Vitalis, *continued*
  historical writings, *continued*
    physical objects in, 4, 6, 79, 83–4, 90–7, 99, 131, 136, 153, 157, 161–4, 166–8, 301, 339–40
    knowledge of English, 15, 100–26
    knowledge of hagiography, 10, 15, 40–1, 54–5, 59, 66, 93–7, 112, 116, 146, 172–88, 233, 361–3, 386–7, 390, 393, 397–8
    knowledge of music, 6, 10, 59, 67–70, 72, 317–19, 392, 397
    knowledge and use of poetry, 6, 10, 14, 30–1, 127–44, 236–8, 300, 385
    knowledge of theology and exegesis, 6, 10, 15, 39–42, 54, 57, 58, 172, 247–59, 260–83, 284–97, 386, 388, 393–6
    Latin style of, 6, 14, 15, 18, 140–4, 217–46, 299, 308
    as librarian/cantor, 14, 61–77, 317–19, 343, 391
    manuscripts copied by, 6, 7–8, 9–10, 14, 15, 16, 30–1, 37–60, 61, 65–6, 68–72, 75, 155, 187, 217, 240, 343, 385–98
    mother of, xii, 7, 14, 20, 27–30, 33–4, 101, 227–8
    travels away from Saint-Évroul, 6, 10–11, 36, 42–3, 101–2, 176
    tutor to junior scribes, 38, 47, 54–60, 61, 65–6, 75
    vocabulary of, 100–26, 149, 174–6, 193, 195, 199, 219, 227–8, 242, 269, 286, 288–9, 291, 320, 343, 345–6
Orléans, xii, 20–2, 35, 36, 264
Orosius, Paulus, 11, 347
Osbern, abbot of Saint-Évroul, 85, 98, 149–50, 169, 233
Osbern of Canterbury, 318
Oswald, bishop of Worcester, 181
Ouen (St) 173–4; *see also* Rouen, abbey of Saint-Ouen

Paul the Deacon, 11, 347
Peter of Maule, 129, 130, 132–4, 142, 165, 170
Philibert (St), 173–6
Philip I, king of France, 147, 195–200, 330
Philippe of Harcourt, bishop of Bayeux, 365
Pontius, abbot of Cluny, 241

Ralph, abbot of Sées, 96–7
Ralph d'Escures, 252
Ralph, monk of Saint-Évroul and nephew of abbot Thierry, 338
Ralph of Cravent, 165
Ralph of Montpinçon, 165
Ralph of Tosny, 161, 273
Reginald 'the Great', monk of Saint-Évroul, 85
Reginald Chamois, monk of Saint-Évroul, 85
Reims, city of, 28
  council of (1119), 43, 149 158*n*66
  Orderic's attendance at, 43
Richard, I, duke of Normandy, 182, 222, 225
Richard III, duke of Normandy, 230
Richard of Leicester, abbot of Saint-Évroul, 149, 364*n*50
Richard of Préaux, 365
Richard, son of Robert Curthose, 272
Richard, son of William I, King of England, 272
Robert I 'the Magnificent', duke of Normandy, 18, 20, 152*n*41, 221–2, 226, 230
Robert I of Grandmesnil, 21*n*18, 78, 79, 81, 84, 85, 86, 87, 88, 89, 90, 93, 98, 160, 161, 183
Robert II, archbishop of Rouen, 187
Robert II 'Curthose', duke of Normandy, 195–6, 200, 202–8, 215, 236, 238, 240, 271, 272

Robert II of Grandmesnil, patron and Abbot of Saint-Évroul, 21n18, 78–9, 81, 84–93, 98, 147, 160, 161, 183, 327

Robert, abbot of Molesme, 305–6, 332

Robert Brakenbury, monk of Durham, 370

Robert, earl of Gloucester, 214

Robert Gamaliel, monk of Saint-Évroul, 85

Robert Guiscard, 79, 81, 84–92, 176

Robert of Bellême, 100, 125, 196n42, 219–20, 353n4

Robert of Cricklade, 72

Robert of Rhuddlan, 142n59, 143, 155, 164–5

Robert of Torigni, abbot of Mont-saint-Michel, 2, 12, 18–19, 221, 225, 245, 342, 347, 358–60, 365, 371

Robert, son of Giroie, 231, 274

Robert, son of Guitmund de Maisnil, 98

Roger I, count of Sicily, 87, 93n65

Roger Borsa, duke of Apulia and Calabria, 89

Roger de Hauterive, 186

Roger of Argences, abbot of Fécamp, 43

Roger of Le Sap, abbot of Saint-Évroul, 68, 70n43, 96–7, 161–2, 186n103, 191n15, 338

Roger of Montgomery, earl of Shrewsbury, xii, 7, 19–20, 22, 24, 28–9, 31n62, 32–3, 35, 36, 114, 136–8, 142n59, 157n63, 158–9, 232, 306, 319

Roger of Salmonville, abbot of Saint-Évroul, 366

Roger of Tosny, 222

Roger of Warenne, 147n11

Roger de Witot, 159

Rollo, first duke of Normandy, 28, 129–31, 141, 144, 219, 228

Romanus, monk of Saint-Évroul, 232

Rouen, city of, 134–5, 136, 189, 190–1, 200, 221, 225, 352n1, 354n11, 361

abbey of La Trinité, 187

Rouen, city of, *continued*
  abbey of Saint-Ouen, 149, 156, 183
  archbishops of, 7, 130, 134, 140, 159n76, 173, 174, 186, 227, 281
  cathedral of, 131, 135, 174
  diocese of, 174, 182, 184n85

Rule of St Benedict, 66, 70, 149, 256, 305, 379, 390–1

Saint-Euphemia, abbey of, 78, 84–9, 93, 96, 98–9

Saint-Évroul, abbey of, xii, 1, 6, 7, 8–9, 15, 20, 23, 35–6, 42–3, 60, 68, 69–70, 72, 73, 75–7, 78–99, 100, 101–2, 129n8, 133, 138, 143, 145, 148, 149, 153, 154, 156, 158, 159, 163–4, 177, 181, 185, 188, 189, 213, 227, 239, 240, 254, 260, 266, 308, 317, 331, 347, 375–84
  abbey church and monastic buildings, 70, 161–2, 189, 213, 364, 366–7, 375–84
  abbots of, 24, 84–6, 86–7, 89, 98, 102n10, 142n59, 148, 149–50, 154, 183, 185, 233, 265–6, 327, 337, 342–3, 358, 360, 366–7, 369, 377, 378–9; *see also* Mainer, abbot of Saint-Évroul *and* Michel-Philippe de Saint-Martin, abbot of Saint-Évroul *and* Osbern, abbot of Saint-Évroul *and* Robert of Grandmesnil, abbot of Saint-Évroul *and* Roger of Le Sap, abbot of Saint-Évroul *and* Roger of Salmonville, abbot of Saint-Évroul *and* Richard of Leicester, abbot of Saint-Évroul *and* Thierry of Mathonville, abbot of Saint-Évroul *and* Warin of Les Essarts, abbot of Saint-Évroul
  annals written at, 7–8, 44, 71–2, 98, 160n62, 217, 391–2
  archaeological excavations at, 15, 375–84
  'chapter-book' of (now Paris, BnF M 10062), 8, 65–6, 69–72, 97–8, 155, 163, 343, 390–2, 343, 390–2

Saint-Évroul, abbey of, *continued*
  charters of, 98, 106, 111, 112*n*39, 114, 122, 145–71
  early (pre-1050) history of, 5*n*24, 149, 264, 269, 340, 376, 384
  later medieval history after death of Orderic Vitalis, 364, 366–7, 369, 374, 376–9
  library of, 14, 15, 61–2, 65–6, 72, 74, 75, 146, 184–5, 338, 343, 366
  manuscripts of, 8, 9, 12, 14, 30, 37–60, 61–2, 65, 66, 74, 75, 98–9, 129*n*8, 146–7, 163, 179–80, 186*n*104, 187, 188, 247*n*2, 360–1, 374, 385–98
  music and liturgy of, 67–8, 72, 73, 74, 75–6, 83, 88, 98, 163, 167–8, 181, 183, 185, 186*n*104, 187, 188, 189, 291, 317–19, 341–3, 385–7, 390–2
  necrology of, 9, 83, 97–8, 390
  patrons and possessions of, xiv, 3, 28, 36, 76, 77, 78–99, 106, 110*n*32, 111, 133–4, 138, 142*n*59, 145, 147*n*16, 148–9, 155, 156, 158, 161–4, 167–8, 170, 186, 188, 189–91, 230–1, 247, 252, 258, 267, 272–4, 299–300, 306, 308–9, 319–20, 366, 376, 379–80
  priories and dependencies of, 79, 87–8, 92–3, 97, 185, 188, 195, 301, 319; *see also* Maule, priory of Saint-Évroul *and* Noron, priory of Saint-Évroul
  relations with other religious foundations, 42–3, 60, 68, 69–70, 72, 75, 78–99, 174–5, 183, 184, 301, 327, 331, 361, 391
  restoration of in 1050, xiv, 8, 70, 73, 78, 80, 83, 87, 88–90, 145, 181, 252*n*13, 299, 376
  school of, 14, 36, 37–60, 61, 65, 72, 75, 291, 338–9, 366, 376
  tombs and burials at, 10, 127–44, 165, 379–84
  visit of King Henry I in 1113, *see* Henry I, King of England and Duke of Normandy, his visit to Saint-Évroul

St Peter's abbey, Shrewsbury, *see* Shrewsbury, St Peter's abbey
Saint-Taurin, abbey of, 359–60
Saint-Wandrille, abbey of, 188, 201*n*66, 364*n*50
Sebastian (St), 176, 179, 185, 188
Serlo, bishop of Séez, 7, 18*n*8
Shrewsbury, town of, xii, 7, 20, 22, 30, 32–3, 100, 108, 109*n*28, 112–14, 122, 125
  St Peter's abbey, xii, 19–21, 21*n*20, 23–5, 28, 31, 33–4, 306, 319
Siward, priest of Shrewsbury and tutor to Orderic Vitalis, xii, 7, 20, 22, 25, 28–30, 33, 112–13, 116, 125, 254
Siward, son of Æthelgar, 29, 31, 33
Stephen, king of England, 211, 213–15
Stephen, cantor of St Nicholas' in Anger and cleric at Bari, 95
Symeon of Durham, 72, 75, 309, 318

Taurin (St), 173–4, 186; *see also* Saint-Taurin, abbey of
Theodelin of Tanaisie, 83
Theodore (St), 176, 178–9, 183, 185, 188
Thierry of Mathonville, abbot of Saint-Évroul, 35*n*65, 73, 83, 92, 98, 142*n*59, 147, 185, 240, 291, 337–40, 342–3, 347
Thomas, archbishop of York, 142, 147*n*17
Thomas de la Mare, prior of Tynemouth and abbot of St Albans, 363
Thomas, first duke of Clarence, 352–3
Thomas of Anjou, monk of Saint-Évroul, 85
Thomas of Gloucester, 371
Thomas Walsingham, 371
Thorney, abbey of, 103*n*12, 362*n*42, 364*n*50, 388
Thurstan, monk of Saint-Évroul, 85
Thurstan Scitel, 219
Tiron, monastery of, 15, 324–32

Venosa, abbey of Holy Trinity, 69–70, 85–8, 90–6, 98, 391

Vita beati Bernardi Tironensis, 324, 326, 328, 331–2

Wace, *Roman de Rou*, 11–12, 245, 358–60, 372

Walter 'the small', monk of Saint-Évroul, 85

Waltheof II, earl of Northumbria, 12, 123, 172, 209, 234, 361–2, 273; see also Crowland Abbey

Wandrille (St), 173–46, 180

Warenne, family of, 147

Warenne Chronicle, 12, 358–60, 364, 369

Warin of Les Essarts, abbot of Saint-Évroul, 102n10, 147n14, 158

Warin, son of Osmund, 163

Warin, son of William I of Bellême, 219

William I 'Bonne-Âme', archbishop of Rouen, 7, 147n14

William I 'Longsword', duke of Normandy, 129–31, 141, 144, 225

William I of Bellême, 219–20

William I 'the Conqueror', king of England and duke of Normandy, 18–19, 21n18, 24, 31n62, 84, 106, 108, 110, 112, 142, 149, 155, 158, 160–2, 166–7, 168, 179, 186–8, 199–202, 221–3, 226–36, 241, 258, 272, 274, 300, 309, 325, 328, 348, 353n3, 354, 376

William II 'Rufus', king of England, 115, 159, 197, 200, 204–6, 273

William, abbot of St Euphemia, 98–9

William, abbot of Saint-Michael's, Mileto, 88

William, abbot of Saint-Stephen's Caen, 139

William Clito, 147n16, 206, 272

William, count of Évreux, 196

William Giroie, 79–84, 98, 160, 186, 232

William Gregory, cantor of Saint-Évroul, 73–5

William of Apulia, 78, 80, 86–7n43, 92n63

William of Arques, monk of Molesme, 196

William of Breteuil, 145, 147n11, 159, 161, 163, 196

William of Corbeil, 116

William, (St) of Gellone, *Life* of, 10, 176n36, 268, 295

William of Grandmesnil, 88–90, 92, 99

William of Jumièges, 1, 8, 12, 18–19, 78, 102n8, 145n4, 217, 221–6, 230, 241, 246, 247, 300, 308–9, 347, 356–7, 358, 360, 363, 370, 372, 396

his *Gesta Normannorum ducum*, 1, 8, 12, 18–19, 78, 217–19, 221–6, 230, 241, 246, 247, 308–9, 347, 358, 360, 370, 372, 396

interpolations by Orderic Vitalis, 1, 8, 12, 18–19, 78, 217–19, 221–6, 230, 241, 246, 247, 308–9, 347, 360, 396

interpolations by Robert of Torigni, 225, 360

William of Malmesbury, 1–2, 72–3, 92n63, 101n7, 101n12, 106, 108, 110, 111n38, 116, 118–19, 123, 148, 154, 170, 181, 207n93, 284, 309–10, 313, 318, 328–9, 331, 348–51, 362, 364, 393

William of Montreuil, 81–2, 230–1

William of Moulins, 165

William of Poitiers, 11, 102n8, 102–3n11, 156, 241–2, 245, 252n13, 253, 300, 308–9, 356

his *Gesta Guillelmi II ducis Normannorum*, 11, 21n18, 31n62, 110, 112, 114–15, 123, 222, 241–2, 245, 252n13, 308–9

William of Roumare, 148, 159, 167

William of Volpiano, 181, 338

William Pantulf, 90, 96–7, 98, 165, 185

William, son of Hugh of Grandmesnil, 88, 89, 90, 92, 99

William, son of Ingran, 87

William, son of Osbern, 235n96

William, son of Osmund, 163

William Talvas, 220
William Vallin, monk of Saint-Évroul, 13
Worcester, town of, 113, 310, 311
   historical writing at, 2, 11, 309, 370–1
   Orderic Vitalis' visit to, 11, 175n32

Printed in the USA
CPSIA information can be obtained
at www.ICGtesting.com
JSHW051517010823
45777JS00003B/133